MITCHELL'S BUILDING CONSTRUCTION

Components
and Finishes

Harold King   *ARIBA*

Alan Everett   *ARIBA*

B. T. Batsford Limited

© *Chapters 1 to 11 and 18 Harold King 1971*
© *Chapters 12 to 17 Alan Everett 1971*
7134 0518 X (hard cover) 7134 0519 8 (paperback)

Printed in Great Britain by
William Clowes and Sons Limited
London, Beccles and Colchester
for the publishers
B. T. Batsford Limited
4 Fitzhardinge Street, London W 1

Contents

Contents of other volumes

The reader is referred to the four other volumes of *Mitchell's Building Construction* for the following:

Environment and Services   Peter Burberry

ENVIRONMENT

1 General significance
2 Moisture
3 Air movement
4 Daylighting
5 Heat
6 Sound

ENVIRONMENTAL SERVICES

7 Thermal installations
8 Electric lighting

UTILITY SERVICES

9 Water supply
10 Sanitary appliances
11 Drainage installations
12 Sewage disposal
13 Refuse disposal
14 Electricity
15 Mechanical conveyors
16 Firefighting equipment
17 Ducted distribution of services

Materials   Alan Everett

1 Properties generally
2 Timber
3 Boards and slabs
4 Stones
5 Ceramics
6 Bricks and blocks

7 Limes and cements
8 Concretes
9 Metals
10 Asbestos products
11 Bituminous products
12 Glass
13 Plastics and rubbers
14 Adhesives
15 Mortars for jointing
16 Mastics and gaskets

Structure and Fabric   Jack Stroud Foster
Part 1

1 The nature of buildings and building
2 The production of buildings
3 Structural behaviour
4 Foundations
5 Walls
6 Framed structures
7 Roof structures
8 Floor structures
9 Fireplaces, flues and chimneys
10 Stairs
11 Building operations and site preparation

Structure and Fabric   Jack Stroud Foster
Part 2

1 Contract planning and site organization
2 Contractors' mechanical plant
3 Foundations
4 Walls and piers
5 Multi-storey structures
6 Floor structures
7 Flues and chimney shafts
8 Stairs, ramps and ladders
9 Roof structures
10 Fire protection
11 Site preparation and temporary works

British Standards and Codes of Practice
are obtainable from
The British Standards Institution
Sales Department
101 Pentonville Road
London N1 9ND

Acknowledgment

The authors and publishers thank the many individuals and firms who have given help and advice in the preparation of this book and those who have given permission to quote from technical literature and other material.

The author of *Components* chapters 1 to 11 and *Roofings* chapter 18 thanks the following for the use of drawings on which various figures are based:

Abbey Hanson Rowe and Partners for figure 76
D. Anderson and Son Limited for figures 268, 269 and part of 255
Boulton and Paul (Joinery) Limited for figure 111
The British Woodwork Manufacturers Association (EMJA Certification Trademark) for figures 45, 107, 110 and 119
Cape Universal for corrugated asbestos cement sheet roofing pages 401 to 410
Copper Development Association for copper roofing figures 280 and 281
Crittall Hope Limited for figures 121, 122, 164 and 167
Crosby and Company Limited for figures 10 and 56
Dixon Components (Building) Limited for figure 223
Expamet Contracts Limited for figures 228, 229 and 230
Fulbora Limited for figure 258
Gardiner Architectural Engineering Limited for figures 94, 135, 136 and 138
Grahams (Seacroft) Limited for figure 102
Aldam Coburn Limited for figures 86, 87, 88 and 92
Hill Brothers Glass Company Limited for figure 166
F. Hills and Sons Limited for figure 75
Louvre (Windows) Limited for figure 140
Lead Development Association for figures 120, 305 and 307
The Marley Tile Company Limited for figures 274, 275, 276, 277, 306 and 308
Mandor Engineering Limited for figure 80
The Nuralite Company Limited for page 393
Paramount Asphalte Limited for figure 256
Permanite Limited for figure 255
Robin Architectural Products for figure 169
The Ruberoid Company Limited for figures 261, 263, 264, 265, 266, 267, 271, 272 and 273
Stramit Limited for figure 225
Tenon Contracts Limited for figures 137, 222 and 224
CIP Tentest Limited for figure 233
Venesta International Construction Materials Limited for figure 226
The author is also indebted to the following:
Arnold Ashton for practical advice regarding joinery manufacture and timber jointing
R. Baker of F. and E. V. Linford Limited for advice on joiners' shop production in chapter 2
R. H. Burford of Crosby and Company Limited for advice in chapter 3 on doors
R. E. Hale of Crittall-Hope Limited for help and advice on the metal windows section in chapter 4 and the SCOLA window-walling in chapter 11
Geoffrey Hamlyn Dip Arch FRIBA for making available the material relevant to the SCOLA system of Industrialized Building in chapter 11 and figures 234 to 247 inclusive
Peter Martin ARICS for reading and commenting on Component Design, chapter 1
A. Morris and T. Temple of Boulton and Paul (Joinery) Limited for information on the factory production of joinery components in chapter 2
Tenon Contracts Limited for information and advice on demountable partitions, chapter 9
G. E. Till and H. A. Bolton of The Ruberoid Company Limited for advice on built-up bitumen felt roofing in chapter 18
Mr Turley of MAC Engineering for advice on Ironmongery, chapter 7

Grateful thanks are due, in addition, to Robert Humphreys for his invaluable work in drawing diagrams and to G. W. Dilks for assisting. To E. M. Thomas for ably translating tape to typescript and to Thelma M. Nye for her most helpful and patient editorial advice.

Shrewsbury 1971   H. K.

The author of chapters 12 to 17 inclusive and the publishers acknowledge with thanks the Controller of Her Majesty's Stationery Office for permission to quote from the Building Regulations 1965, and the Directors of the Building Research Station, the British Standards Institution, and research and development associations for permission to quote from their publications.

I am particularly grateful to the undernamed experts who in many cases expended a considerable amount of their valuable time in correcting and improving my typescript and proofs:

12 Floorings

A. J. Beere MICorrT, AIMF of Tretol Protective Coatings Limited   (*Resin-based floorings*)
J. Bick of the Hardwood Flooring Manufacturers Association
R. T. Gratwick BEM, AIOB of the Polytechnic of North London   (*Maintenance*)
R. H. Harrison of Stuarts Granolithic Company Limited
V. Marriott of Marriott and Price Limited (*Terrazzo floorings*)
J. E. Moore FRIBA of the Polytechnic of North London   (*Sound control*)
J. W. Murray ARIBA, AIArb of the Mastic Asphalt Council and Employers Federation
S. L. Scarlett-Smith MA(Cantab) of Armstrong Cork and Company Limited   (*Sheet floorings*)
E. J. Sigall MInst Marketing of Langley (London) Limited
F. Vaughan BSc, FICeram FGS of the British Ceramic Tile Council
W. J. Warlow of the Building Research Station (*Introduction*)
R. P. Woods BAFor(Cantab), FIWSc of the Timber Research and Development Association

13 Plastering

T. F. Harvey
T. McEwan of British Gypsum Limited
J. F. Ryder BSc of the Building Research Station

14 Renderings

J. F. Ryder BSc of the Building Research Station

15 Wall tiling and mosiacs

F. Vaughan BSc, FICeram FGS of the British Ceramic Tile Council
E. J. Sigall MInst Marketing of Langley (London) Limited

16 Integral finishes on concrete

B. W. Shacklock MSc, FICE, MIStructE, MInstHE of the Cement and Concrete Association

17 Thin surface-finishes

R. S. Hullcoop of ICI Limited
J. E. Todman CGLI, Full Technical Certificate, of the Polytechnic of North London
T. Whiteley BSc, ARIC of the Building Research Station

My thanks are also due to R. E. Sowden BSc (Hons) for metrication and to Margaret Bird for her skilled typewritten transcriptions from my manuscript.

I am extremely grateful to Thelma M. Nye for her patience, encouragement and expert editorial advice.

Infinite thanks are again extended to my wife.

I should be grateful to anyone who is kind enough to draw my attention to any errors and to suggest ways in which the above chapters may be improved.

London 1971   A. E.

SI UNITS

SI Units

Quantities in this volume are given in SI units which have been adopted by the construction industry in the United Kingdom. Twenty-five other countries (not including the USA or Canada) have also adopted the SI system although several of them retain the old metric system as an alternative. There are six SI basic units. Other units derived from these basic units are rationally related to them and to each other. The international adoption of the SI will remove the present necessity for conversions between national systems. The introduction of metric units gives an opportunity for the adoption of modular sizes.

Most quantities in this volume are rounded off conversions of imperial values. Where great accuracy is necessary, exact metric equivalents must be used. In the case of statutory requirements reference should be made to Building Regulations 1965 *Metric Equivalents of Dimensions* (HMSO) and to the equivalents contained in the Constructional Bylaws (London Building Acts 1930–39) published by the GLC.

British Standards, Codes of Practice and other documents are being progressively issued in metric units, although at the time of going to press many of those concerned with Building Construction have yet to be metricated.

Multiples and sub-multiples of SI units likely to be used in the construction industry are as follows:

Multiplication factor	Prefix		Symbol
1 000 000	10^6	mega	M
1 000	10^3	kilo	k
100	10^2	hecto	h
10	10^1	deca	da
0·1	10^{-1}	deci	d
0·01	10^{-2}	centi	c
0·001	10^{-3}	milli	m
0·000 001	10^{-6}	micro	μ

Further information concerning metrication is contained in BS PD 6031 *A Guide for the use of the Metric System in the Construction Industry.*

Quantity	Unit	Symbol	Imperial unit × Conversion factor = SI value		
LENGTH	kilometre	km	1 mile	=	1·609 km
	metre	m	1 yard	=	0·914 m
	millimetre	mm	1 foot	=	0·305 m
			1 inch	=	25·4 mm
AREA	square kilometre	km²	1 mile²	=	2·590 km²
	hectare	ha	1 acre	=	0·405 ha
			1 yard²	=	0·836 m²
	square metre	m²	1 foot²	=	0·093 m²
	square millimetre	mm²	1 inch²	=	645·16 mm²
VOLUME	cubic metre	m³	1 yard³	=	0·765 m³
	cubic millimetre	mm³	1 foot³	=	0·028 m³
			1 inch³	=	1 638·7 mm³
CAPACITY	litre	l	1 UKgallon	=	4·546 litres

Quantity	Unit	Symbol	Imperial unit × Conversion factor = SI value		
MASS	kilogramme	kg	1 lb	=	0·454 kg
	gramme	g	1 oz	=	28·350 g
			1 lb/ft (run)	=	1·488 kg/m
			1 lb/ft²	=	4·882 kg/m²
DENSITY	kilogramme per cubic metre	kg/m³	1 lb/ft³	=	16·019 kg/m³
FORCE	newton	N	1 lbf	=	4·448 N
			1 tonf	=	9 964·02 N
				=	9·964 kN
PRESSURE, STRESS	newton per square metre	N/m²	1 lbf/in²	=	6 894·8 N/m²
	meganewton per square metre	MN/m²† or N/mm²	1 tonf/ft²	=	107·3 kN/m²
			1 tonf/in²	=	15·444 MN/m²
			1 lb/ft run	=	14·593 N/m
			1 lbf/ft²	=	47·880 N/m²
			1 ton/ft run	=	32 682 kN/m
	*bar (0·1 MN/m²)	bar			
	*hectobar (10 MN/m²)	hbar			
	*millibar (100 MN/m²)	m bar			
VELOCITY	metre per second	m/s	1 mile/h	=	0·447 m/s
FREQUENCY	cycle per second	Hz	1 cycle/sec	=	1 Hz
ENERGY, HEAT	joule	J	1 Btu	=	1 055·06 J
POWER, HEAT FLOW RATE	watts	W	1 Btu/h	=	0·293 W
	newtons metres per second	Nm/s	1 hp	=	746 W
	joules per second	J/s	1 ft/lbf	=	1·356 J
THERMAL CONDUCTIVITY (k)	watts per metre degree Celsius	W/m deg C	1 Btu in/ft²h	=	0·144 W/m deg C
THERMAL TRANSMITTANCE (U)	watts per square metre degree Celsius	W/m² deg C	1 Btu/ft²h deg F	=	5·678 W/m² deg C
TEMPERATURE	degree Celsius (difference)	deg C	1 deg F		$\frac{5}{9}$ deg C
	degree Celsius (level)	°C	°F	=	$\frac{9}{5}$ °C+32

* Alternative units, allied to the SI, which will be encountered in certain industries

† BSI preferred symbol

A guide to the SI metric system

COMPONENTS

1 Component design

In order that the form of a component may be properly devised, its function must be carefully defined. Up-to-date manufacturing techniques, user requirements, anthropometric data, and the properties and behaviour of materials, together with appropriate cost analysis data, must be considered in order to reach conclusions which will lead to the design of a satisfactory component. Anthropometric data relates to the measurement of the human form, and this information, in particular the body and reach characteristics, has a direct influence on design of specific components such as fittings, and doors and windows. The study of anthropometrics is also particularly important when considering design in respect of disabled people, and users of wheel chairs.

Components such as windows, ceiling panels and wall and partition units are commonly used in multiples or in combination with each other, and frequently in long runs, thus requiring interrelated preferred dimensions, based on a universally acceptable system of dimensional co-ordination. Sizes should be determined initially from the results of user requirement studies. Following from this, the controlling factors arising out of the appropriate manufacturing techniques must be determined in consultation with manufacturers at an early stage in the development work. These factors include the degree of standardization which is capable of being attained, the method of assembly, the costs of tooling up, the methods of handling stock and problems associated with site and factory transportation and storage.

A component is a composite manufactured product whose design is appropriate to factory production methods, and which has been developed so that minimum site labour is required. The design team will develop the component to give a satisfactory performance against a concise specification, based on research and careful assessment of information received from the client or potential user.

FACTORY PRODUCTION

It is necessary for the designer of a component to understand the discipline of factory production so that collaboration with the manufacturer at design stage will be more useful. Two methods of factory production are appropriate to the manufacture of building components namely, *flow line production* and *batch production*.

Flow line production

Where *flow line production* is in operation, a stream of component parts in various stages of completion travel by conveyor belt through a number of work positions to completion. At each work position, one or more operations are carried out until at the final work position, at the end of the assembly line, the component is complete. The operations are standardized at each work position and careful organization is required so that the necessary materials are always available. Flow line production methods can be highly automated which means a high level capital investment in automatic machinery but using a minimum of labour. With this type of manufacturing process it is not easy for alternative operations to be carried out at a particular work position, but provided that the alternative work can be done in the same space of time as the standard operation, then the system can be modified to this extent. An example would be the fitting of different types of opening light in a standard frame surround. A flow line system is most efficient however when uninterrupted by alternative operations. This presupposes complete standardization, which in its turn requires the development of a co-ordinated system of sizes and dimensions. Flush doors are normally produced by a flow line system, and it is obvious from this example that where a large number of components is involved and the quality of the raw material can be carefully controlled, then factory production and factory applied finishes produce an article of better quality and value, than traditional methods.

19

Batch production

Batch production, is the setting up of machinery to manufacture a batch of components. An example of this would be the moulding of jambs and rails for a timber window, followed by the manufacture of a batch of sill sections, after the machines have been reset. Batch production is not only adopted for machinery operations but is also used for the assembly of parts where quantities, in mass production terms, are comparatively small, or where there is too much variety to allow the efficient use of flow line techniques. Batch production is also the appropriate method where the cost of processing is low in comparison to the cost of setting up the process. In connection with the production of timber components woodworking machines have a high rate of production in relation to the time taken to set the machine up. The relationship of the cost of production to the cost of setting up can however be made more economical if the variety of sections and mouldings can be reduced, for a particular component. Thus where the same moulded cross section of timber can be used for the various parts of say a glazed window wall, then the cost of one machine setting will be spread over the cost of the total length of the moulded sections for the job.

In practice, combinations of both flow line and batch methods are used, for example, in the factory production of timber components the machining will probably be done by batch production, and the assembly of the timber sections into the completed component will be carried out by flow line techniques. It must always be remembered however, that production techniques are continuously being examined, modified, and improved in an effort to overcome difficulties and disadvantages, and it is essential that consultation at design stage be fully developed to facilitate this process.

A simple production line would be a single and continuous operation with the input of raw materials at one end and with the output of finished goods at the other. At the start of the production line there will be a store of raw materials which will allow certain fluctuations in delivery. Where one operation takes longer to perform than the others the line will have to be split or additional machines or men introduced at this point. Storage will also have to be provided at the end of the production line to absorb fluctuations in demand. The theoretical layout of a production line will almost certainly be inhibited by physical limitations of factory space. The proportion of overheads is not so high with mass production as against short runs of a component produced on a small scale. The percentage of the working year during which the factory is operating to full capacity is also a significant element in the cost per unit of the component. Machinery should be capable of being modified so that improvements in the design of a component can be incorporated without undue capital expenditure. In order to produce components economically there is an optimum output in terms of the number of components produced relative to the nature of the component and the type of plant used. However standardized a production system is, it is inevitable that some components will be required to be non-standard or may be required in such small numbers as to make them uneconomic to produce on the standard production line. The higher the degree of automation the more difficult it is to produce non-standard items, and it must be expected that non-standard products will be more expensive and with an extended delivery period. It follows from this that manufacturing techniques which can produce related components economically over the widest possible range, will be more acceptable in the long term.

To allow a manufacturer greater control over the production and detailing, it is a good system to invite quotations for components on the basis of performance specification which indicates the parameters within which the product must perform. The successful contractor, at this stage, can then be consulted in respect of detail and development work.

The various processes in the factory production of a range of standard timber windows are detailed in chapter 4, pages 129–132.

PERFORMANCE SPECIFICATION

Every component will have to fulfil a number of requirements in respect of a minimum standard of performance which will be expected from the component when it is installed. All the relevant factors which will influence the design, appearance and performance of a component must first be set down, and from these considerations the performance specification can be devised. A performance specification is a description of the required performance or function of a component. The specification should, wherever possible, be in measurable terms, and include information as to the required life of the component. This type of specification is of course different from the traditional 'product specification' which describes the materials, standards of workmanship and method of manufacture of a component. A product specification relies on description in terms of current trade practice and thus the performance of a component is pre-determined by the writer and the manufacturer's advice is not normally sought. A performance specification on the other hand does not specify materials or methods of production but by stating the performance standard required allows the manufacturer to select suitable materials and production methods. Thus the incentive to develop economic methods of production lies with the manufacturer.

The success of the performance specification as a descriptive method depends on an agreed list of terms or headings upon which a description of the performance of a component may be based. This will then form the basis of a common means of communication between the architects, structural engineers, services engineers and quantity surveyors who are concerned with description of components. Reference should be made to *Performance Specification Writing for Building Components* DC 9 published by HMSO, which provides guidance notes on the content of performance specifications.

The performance specification should first describe the component and its use in general terms giving information sufficient to allow an intending manufacturer to decide whether he is able to submit a tender. The SfB Revised Classification Symbol should be used. The manufacturer should be invited to state the type and quality of components already manufactured by him which will, in his opinion, satisfy the specification. Reference should be made to any British Standard Specification or Code of Practice which applies to the component and further reference should be made to the Building Regulations or other Acts which may be relevant. The Specification should state the required maximum and minimum life of the component. Manufacturers should be required to give the planned life of the component and their recommended method of maintenance. Any guarantees required to be provided by the manufacturer and the nature of any insurance cover should be specified.

The following check list based on DC 9 is a summary of the main properties relative to a selected list of components as a guide to the contents of a Performance Specification. It is important to note that the numbering system is based on the Marster List of Properties (CIB Report No. 3 1964) published by the International Council for Building Research Studies and Documentation, thus providing a direct link between component and material properties.

This is a check list and it will depend upon particular requirements to be met whether a property should be specified or not. In certain cases the performance specification writer will be unable to set quantified values for the properties but may request the component manufacturer to furnish details in respect of a component offered in response to a performance specification.

Heading	CIB No.	Window	Roof finish	Partition	Internal door set	Ceiling	Floor finish
GENERAL INFORMATION	1.1						
Description of component	1.1.01	×	×	×	×	×	×
Type and quality		×	×	×	×	×	×
Identification of standards,	1.1.02						
quality mark	1.1.03	×	×	×	×	×	×
Purpose and use	1.1.04	×	×	×	×	×	×
Accessories	1.1.05	×	×	×	×	×	×

Component properties to be considered when preparing a performance specification with reference to a selected list of components

Heading	CIB No.	Window	Roof finish	Partition	Internal door set	Ceiling	Floor finish
COMPOSITION and MANUFACTURE	1.2						
Composition	1.2.01	×	×	×	×	×	×
Manufacture and assembly	1.2.02	×	×	×	×	×	×
SHAPE, DIMENSION, WEIGHT	1.3						
Shape	1.3.01	×	×	×	×	×	×
Dimension	1.3.02	×	×	×	×	×	×
Geometric properties	1.3.03	×	×	×	×	×	×
Volume	1.3.04	—	—	—	—	—	—
Weight	1.3.05	×	×	×	×	×	×
GENERAL APPEARANCE	1.4						
Character of visible face	1.4.01						
Evenness	1.4.01.1	×	×	×	×	×	×
Appearance	1.4.01.2	×	×	×	×	×	×
Transparency, translucency	1.4.02	×	—	×	×	×	—
PHYSICAL, CHEMICAL AND BIOLOGICAL PROPERTIES	1.5						
Specific weight	1.5.01	×	×	×	—	×	×
Internal structure	1.5.02	×	×	×	×	×	×
Chemical formulation and material specification	1.5.03	×	×	×	×	×	×
Penetration of air and gases	1.5.04	×	×	×	×	×	×
Properties relating to the presence of water	1.5.05						
Moisture content	1.5.05.1	×	×	×	×	×	×
Solubility in water	1.5.05.2	×	×	×	×	×	×
Capillarity	1.5.05.3	×	×	×	×	×	×
Water absorption	1.5.05.4	×	×	×	×	×	×
Water penetration	1.5.05.5	×	×	×	×	×	×
Water vapour penetration	1.5.05.6	×	×	×	×	×	×
Drying and evaporation	1.5.05.7	×	×	×	×	×	×
Moisture movement	1.5.05.8	×	×	×	×	×	×
Thermal properties	1.5.06						
Thermal movement	1.5.06.1	×	×	×	×	×	×
Specific heat	1.5.06.2	—	×	×	—	×	×
Freezing and melting point	1.5.06.3	—	—	—	—	—	—
Radiation coefficient	1.5.06.4	×	×	×	—	×	×
Thermal conductance	1.5.06.5	×	×	×	×	×	×
Warmth to touch	1.5.06.6	—	—	×	×	—	×
High and low temperatures	1.5.06.7	×	×	×	×	×	×
Thermal shock	1.5.06.8	×	×	×	×	—	×

Component properties to be considered when preparing a performance specification with reference to a selected list of components – continued

Heading	CIB No.	Window	Roof finish	Partition	Internal door set	Ceiling	Floor finish
Strength properties	1.5.07						
Tension	1.5.07.1	×	×	×	×	×	×
Compression	1.5.07.2	×	×	×	×	×	×
Shear	1.5.07.3	×	×	×	×	×	×
Bending	1.5.07.4	×	×	×	×	×	×
Torsion	1.5.07.5	×	×	×	×	×	×
Impact	1.5.07.6	×	×	×	×	×	×
Hardness	1.5.07.7	×	×	×	×	×	×
Resistance to fatigue	1.5.07.8	×	×	×	×	×	×
Mechanical properties	1.5.08						
Resistance to mechanical wear	1.5.08.1	×	×	×	×	×	×
Resistance to the insertion and extraction of nails and screws	1.5.08.2	×	×	×	×	×	×
Resistance to splitting	1.5.08.3	−	×	×	×	−	×
Resistance to tearing	1.5.08.4	−	−	×	−	−	×
Resistance to bursting	1.5.08.5	−	−	−	−	−	−
Rheological properties (flow and deformation)	1.5.09	×	×	×	×	×	×
Frictional resistance	1.5.10						
Coefficient of friction	1.5.10.1	−	×	−	−	−	×
Degree of slipperiness in use	1.5.10.2	−	×	−	−	−	×
Adhesion	1.5.11	−	×	−	−	−	×
Acoustic properties	1.5.12						
Sound absorption, sound reflection	1.5.12.1	×	−	×	×	×	×
Sound transmission	1.5.12.2	×	−	×	×	×	×
Optical properties	1.5.13						
Light absorption, light reflection	1.5.13.1	×	×	×	×	×	×
Light transmission	1.5.13.2	×	−	×	×	×	−
Light refraction and dispersion	1.5.13.3	×	−	×	×	×	−
Optical distortion	1.5.13.4	×	−	×	×	×	−
Electrical properties	1.5.14						
Electrical conductivity (electrical resistance)	1.5.14.1	×	×	×	×	×	×
Dielectric constant	1.5.14.2	−	−	−	−	−	−
Liability to develop and shed electro-static charges	1.5.14.3	×	×	×	×	×	×
Effect of sunlight	1.5.15	×	×	×	×	×	×
Effect of electro-magnetic and particle radiation	1.5.16	−	−	×	×	×	×
Effect of freezing conditions	1.5.17	×	×	×	×	×	×

Component properties to be considered when preparing a performance specification with reference to a selected list of components – continued

Heading	CIB No.	Window	Roof finish	Partition	Internal door set	Ceiling	Floor finish
Effect of fire	1.5.18						
Combustibility	1.5.18.1	×	×	×	×	×	×
Fire resistance	1.5.18.2	×	×	×	×	×	—
Surface spread of flame	1.5.18.3	×	×	×	×	×	—
Effect of chemicals	1.5.19	×	×	×	×	×	×
Effect of impurities	1.5.20	×	×	×	×	×	×
Effect of fungi, micro-organisms and insects	1.5.21	×	×	×	×	×	×
Effect of other building materials	1.5.22	×	×	×	×	×	×
Changes of behaviour during use	1.5.23	×	×	×	×	×	×
Setting time	1.5.23.1	—	×	—	—	×	×
Heat evolution in preparation and application	1.5.23.2	—	×	—	—	×	×
Change in volume	1.5.23.3	×	×	×	×	×	×
Properties important from the point of view of hygiene	1.5.24						
Toxicity	1.5.24.1	×	×	×	×	×	×
Odour	1.5.24.2	×	×	×	×	×	×
Taintability	1.5.24.3	×	×	×	×	×	×
Tendency to deposit dust	1.5.24.4	—	×	×	—	×	×
Injury to skin	1.5.24.5	×	×	×	×	×	×
Liability to vermin infestation	1.5.24.6	×	×	×	×	×	×
Liability to become dirty, ease of cleaning	1.5.24.7	×	×	×	×	×	×
Safety	1.5.24.8	×	×	×	×	×	×
DURABILITY	1.6						
Durability of the component or assembly	1.6.01	×	×	×	×	×	×
Durability of specified component parts	1.6.02	×	×	×	×	×	×
Guarantee of durability	1.6.03	×	×	×	×	×	×
PROPERTIES OF THE WORKING PARTS, CONTROLS, ETC.	1.7						
Method of operation	1.7.01	×	—	×	×	—	—
Connection data	1.7.02						
Mechanical connection	1.7.02.1	×	—	×	×	—	—
Connection to power supply	1.7.02.2	×	—	×	×	—	—
Performance data	1.7.03						
Mechanical data	1.7.03.1	×	—	×	×	—	—
Capacity	1.7.03.2	—	—	—	—	—	—
Other performance data	1.7.03.3	×	—	×	×	—	—

Component properties to be considered when preparing a performance specification with reference to a selected list of components – continued

Heading	CIB No.	Window	Roof finish	Partition	Internal door set	Ceiling	Floor finish
Consumption of energy and ancillary materials	1.7.04						
Supplied energy	1.7.04.1	×	–	×	×	–	–
Ancillary materials	1.7.04.2	×	–	×	×	–	–
Efficiency	1.7.05	–	–	–	–	–	–
Manoeuvrability and control	1.7.06	×	–	×	×	–	–
Other technical data	1.7.07						
Mechanical	1.7.07.1	–	–	–	–	–	–
Thermal	1.7.07.2	–	–	–	–	–	–
Electrical	1.7.07.3	–	–	–	–	–	–
Secondary effects and disturbances during operation	1.7.08	×	–	×	×	–	–
WORKING CHARACTERISTICS	1.8						
Ease of handling	1.8.01	×	×	×	×	×	×
Consistence, workability, working time	1.8.02	–	–	–	–	–	–
Ease of cutting, sawing, bending, etc.	1.8.03	–	×	×	×	×	×
Capability of being jointed to other components	1.8.04	–	×	×	×	×	×
Fixing	1.8.05	×	×	×	×	×	×
Surface treatments	1.8.06	×	×	×	×	×	×
Capability of withstanding rough handling	1.8.07	×	×	×	×	×	×
Capability of withstanding storage	1.8.08	×	×	×	×	×	×

Component properties to be considered when preparing a performance specification with reference to a selected list of components – continued

DIMENSIONAL CO-ORDINATION

Dimensional co-ordination is a system of arranging the dimensional framework of a building so that components can be used within the framework in an inter-related pattern of sizes. It is necessary to establish a rectangular three-dimensional grid of basic modules into which the component will fit. This principle is illustrated in figure 1. It is very important to remember that the modular grid does not give the size of the component, but allots space for it, and so in order to fit correctly, the component will always be slightly smaller than the space allowed for it as shown in figure 2. The first step in producing a rational system of dimensional co-ordination is to agree on the basic dimensions of the enclosing fabric of the building. This building fabric is also known as the *environmental envelope*. The principle of relating components to a planning grid, in this case a module of 100 mm, is shown in figure 3. There are a number of British Standards which give recommendations for the controlling limits of the dimensions and sizes for the structure and components in building, see page 35. It is thus recognized that the rationalization of the building process and the use of industrialized methods will involve the use of an increasing range of factory produced components and, in order to obtain the maximum economy of production and to avoid the waste involved in cutting on site, it is

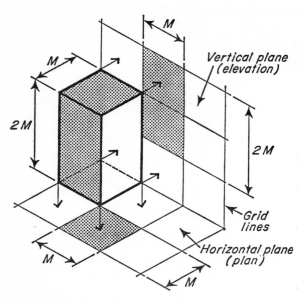

1   Three-dimensional grid of basic modules

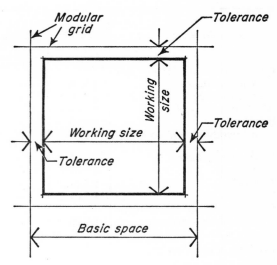

2   Space relationship component to grid

essential that the dimensions of building components are co-ordinated by reference to an agreed range of sizes.

Terms used

An understanding of the various terms used in connection with dimensional co-ordination in building is necessary, since descriptions which previously have been loosely used have now specific meaning.

The following definitions are taken from BS 2900 1970 *Glossary of Terms: Recommendations for the Co-ordination of Dimensions in Building – Metric Units.*

Dimensional co-ordination   The application of a range of related dimensions to the sizing of building components and assemblies and the buildings incorporating them.

Modular co-ordination   Dimension co-ordination using the international basic module (of 100 mm), multimodules, sub-modules and a modular reference system.

The multimodule of 300 mm, the international basic module of 100 mm, and sub-modules of 50 mm and 25 mm are equivalent to the respective

units of size recommended in BS 4011 for the derivation of co-ordinating sizes for building components and assemblies, generally subject to a maximum co-ordinating size of 300 mm based on the 50 mm and 25 mm sizes. See page 28.

Multimodules of 300 mm, 600 mm, 1200 mm, 3000 mm, and 6000 mm, are under consideration internationally for certain categories of buildings.

Module   A convenient unit of size which is used as an increment or coefficient in dimensional co-ordination.

Basic space   A space bounded by reference planes, assigned to receive a building component or assembly including, where appropriate, allowance for joints and tolerances.

Modular grid   A reference grid in which the distance between consecutive parallel lines is the international basic module or a multiple thereof.

Building component   Building material formed as a distinct unit.

Modular building component   A building component whose co-ordinating sizes are in accordance with BS 4011.

Assembly   An aggregate of building components used together.

Co-ordinating space   A space bounded by co-

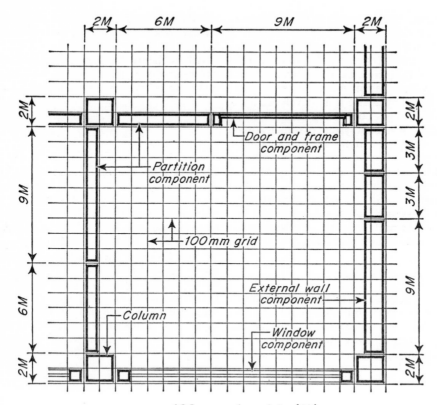

3   Modular co-ordination of components   (*part of building: store room*)

ordinating planes, allocated to a building component or assembly, including allowance for joints and tolerances.

Dimensional co-ordination thus relates industrial techniques to the building process by co-ordinating the size of components within a basic framework, establishing a reference system to enable components to be located, and specifying a system of tolerances. The co-ordination of dimensions is closely connected with the overall development of building technology and the evolution of new building processes.

The traditional pattern of trade following trade with materials cut and fitted on site, made it possible for the later trades to make good any inaccuracies in earlier work. With industrialized processes, completed components arrive on site and there is little opportunity for correcting any errors which may have occurred previously, say

during the coding of the working drawings with reference to the choice of a particular component. Thus, industrialized building presupposes a complete and careful appraisal of requirements at planning stage, and decisions cannot be left until the time the building is being erected.

Simplification of constructional detail at the design stage will assist the mechanization of the manufacturing process and, in order to achieve this, it is necessary to reach agreement on the range of sizes to which particular components are made, so that a manufacturer can arrange production in large enough batches to make large scale investment viable.

The present 'closed' systems of building (see page 236) each have their own dimensional disciplines, eg placing of stanchions, range of floor to ceiling heights, and component sizes. Thus, the components are dimensionally co-ordinated within the particular system, but not within the construction industry generally.

Rationalization has, however, occurred in that a number of different systems have adopted the same range of components, as for instance in the use of standard fenestration units. In order that industrialized building can be fully developed and its economic advantages completely realized, it is necessary to adopt an agreed system of dimensional co-ordination, both on a national and an international scale, and metrication gives the opportunity to do this. Dimensional co-ordination is essential if ranges of components are to be developed towards an 'open' system of standardization (see page 236) in which components can be used throughout the industry without reference to a particular system of construction.

PREFERRED MEASUREMENTS

The increment, or pattern of change of dimension, within a system is important since it determines the norm to which a group of components can be produced in a range of sizes appropriate to the particular component. In each case the designer should use the largest increment available, compatible with function in use and economy in manufacture.

All the theoretical sizes and basic sizes are stated before any deduction is made for fixing or manufacturing tolerances and jointing.

BASIC SIZE

BS 4011 makes recommendations as to the basic sizes to be adopted for the co-ordination of dimensions of building components for all types of building and all forms of construction. The basic sizes are selected as follows (in descending order of preference): 300 mm, 100 mm (basic module), 50 mm, 25 mm. These are the recommended dimensions to which designers should adhere, and which are adopted by Government departments concerned with building. The relative functional requirement of a component will determine which preference is taken as a basis for design. It is important that within each category such as windows, wall panels, floor slabs and similar

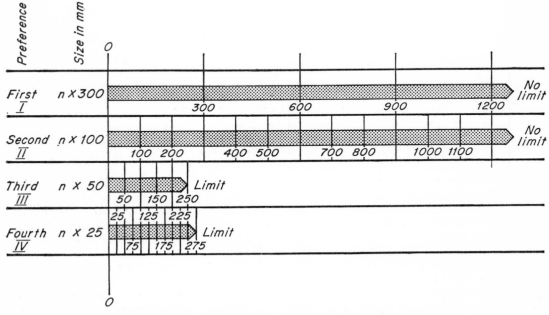

4   Preferences for sizing building components and assemblies (BS 4011: 1966)

components, which may be made from different materials, the preferred sizes should be the same whatever material is used for fabrication.

Where a number of small components is necessary to build up an assembly, as in the case of a metal window, the various parts must be made to fit together so that the overall size of the assembly will fit the basic opening size. The basic size of a

ponents using the preferences set down in BS 4011.

Figure 6, illustrates the situation of a modular component within the planning grid and shows the manufacturing and jointing tolerances which must be accommodated. It will be seen that the basic space must take into account the difference between the expected maximum and minimum

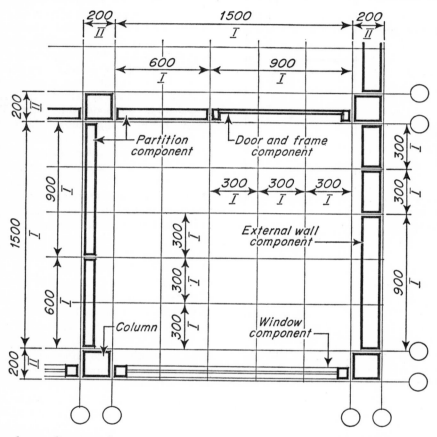

5   Dimensional co-ordination of components   (*part of building: store room only*)

component is the fundamental dimension of the component bounded by the plane of a modular grid. The space on the modular grid designed to receive the component, must include an allowance for joints and tolerances. This space, into which the component will fit, is known as the *basic* or *modular space*. The preferred sizes are shown in graphical form in figure 4, and figure 5 gives an example of the dimensional co-ordination of com-

component size, with an allowance for minimum joint thickness against maximum component size, or alternatively, maximum joint thickness against minimum component size. Figure 7 shows the basic spaces for standard steel windows. See also figure 126, page 153, for the basic spaces for purpose-made steel windows. Increased flexibility in respect of modular spacings can be obtained in several ways. For example, in the case of the basic

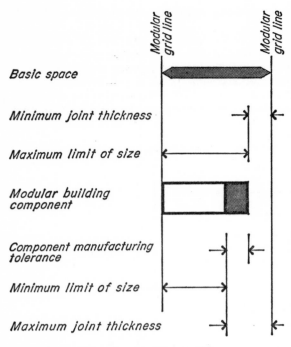

Basic space

Minimum joint thickness

Maximum limit of size

Modular building component

Component manufacturing tolerance

Minimum limit of size

Maximum joint thickness

6 Relationship of a modular building component to a planning grid

spaces for standard steel windows, the lengths of the basic spaces conform to BS 4011 first preference in increments of 300 mm. In order to increase flexibility to fill modular spacings to the second preference increment of 100 mm, it is possible by using one or more pressed steel box mullions, or partition covers in the assembly, to add 100 mm to the length of the assemblies, alternatively by using a wood surround, which will add 100 mm both to the length and height of the assembly. The heights of the basic spaces are derived from the controlling dimensions set out in BS 4330 (see page 35). It is possible to use a combination of basic units of standard frames to fill intermediate heights, and by this means all modular lengths and heights from 900 mm upwards can be achieved in increments of 100 mm.

TOLERANCES

Any system of tolerances is intended to enable components to fit together without, on the one hand, the need for cutting down to size on site, or

on the other hand, excessively wide joints or the ubiquitous cover strip to make up undersized units. Thus it is necessary for components to be manufactured so that the maximum and minimum sizes do not fall outside known limits. Assembly of components on site has increased the importance of tolerances and factory manufacture of components has taken the matter of cutting and fitting on site out of the hands of the craftsman. This means that the problems of tolerance and fit must be solved at the design and manufacturing stage of the work. Assumptions which must be made in respect of fitting a component into a building are derived from the traditional operations of craftsmen, in that components must be made to fit within a space already defined, and that variations in size are accommodated by joints. Thus by stating a system of tolerances which can be used during design and manufacture, the size of a component can be controlled to come within the space allocated to it on site. In order to avoid the cumulative errors which may arise by locating components by reference to those already in position, it is necessary to use grid lines or modular planes to define the spaces assigned to each component. The grid or modular lines thus provide a common system of reference from the design stage through the manufacturing process to the placing and fixing of the item in position. The method in respect of tolerances is that the basic space of the component is the same as the basic size dimensions which it is to occupy. Its actual size must of course be less than its basic size so that it can be fitted in position. The difference is determined by the nature of the component and the method of jointing. Thus, from the actual size a manufacturing size is obtained. This system is applicable to all types of components and will ensure that they will always fit the space allocated to them. The phenomenon of one component infringing on the space which should be occupied by its neighbour, and this effect becoming accumulative, is known as *creep* and is avoided by the use of the grid lines.

Tolerance limits must take into account the general factors of manufacture, the problems of site erection and the disciplines imposed by the design of the joint between components. The characteristics of the materials from which the component is made must be considered in respect

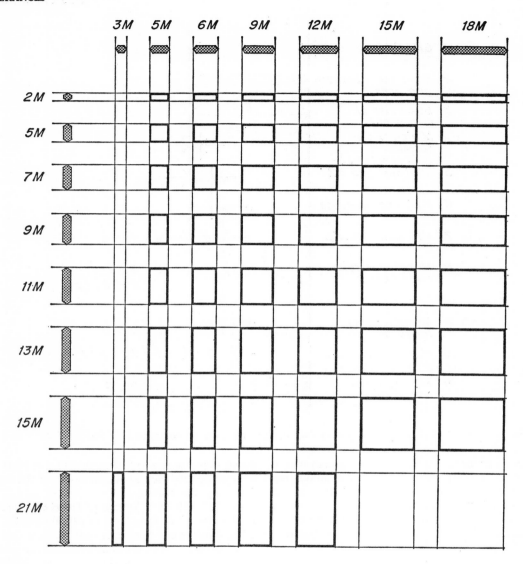

M = 1 module of 100 mm and refers to the size of opening into which the window fits

7   *Basic spaces for standard steel windows (domestic type)*

of the problems of twisting, warping and bending. Tolerance should be expressed as an addition or subtraction from the given 'average' or work size of a component. Thus a component of work size 890 mm with a manufacturing tolerance of 5 mm would be expressed as 890 mm ± 5 mm. The maximum permitted size of this component would be 895 mm and the minimum size 895 mm. The actual measurement of the component delivered to site would be somewhere between the maximum and

31

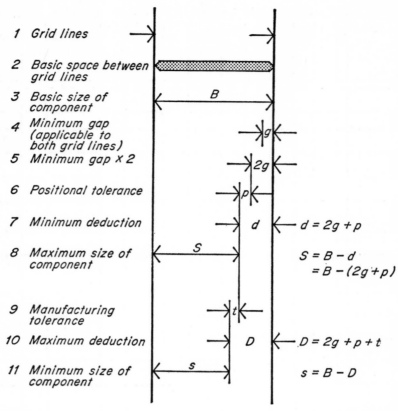

1	Grid lines
2	Basic space between grid lines
3	Basic size of component
4	Minimum gap (applicable to both grid lines)
5	Minimum gap X 2
6	Positional tolerance
7	Minimum deduction
8	Maximum size of component
9	Manufacturing tolerance
10	Maximum deduction
11	Minimum size of component

$d = 2g + p$

$S = B - d$
$\ \ = B - (2g + p)$

$D = 2g + p + t$

$s = B - D$

8 *The size of a jointed component and setting out by reference to one edge (BS 3626: 1963)*

minimum permitted size. The joint design would take into account these deviations in allocating the space allowed for the component. In order to calculate the maximum and minimum sizes for a modular component from a given size based on the design module, the following information must be known:

1 The size of the minimum gap which is to be allowed between the component and the module line or plane of reference in respect of the jointing technique.
2 An allowance to take into account the inaccuracy in the positioning of a component on site. This position tolerance is determined from a knowledge of site assembly procedures.
3 Information on the tolerance to be expected in manufacture which must be obtained from the makers.

From these three allowed variations it is then possible to specify the upper and lower of the manufacturing dimensions.

BS 3626 (1963) *A System of Tolerances and Fits in Building* gives a method of calculating the size of a component which is set out on site by relating one edge of the component to the grid (or module) line. The method is shown graphically in figure 8.

The difference between the basic size B and the maximum size S is known as the minimum deduction d, which comprises two quantities. The first is the minimum gap g, or the permissible distance between the component and the grid line (thus the least distance between two components when assembled will be the sum of their respective minimum gaps, and this distance must be related to the least practicable width of joint). The second quantity in the minimum deduction is the positional tolerance p; the degree of accuracy to which the component is to be assembled. Minimum gap is applied to each side of the component, thus: $S = B - d = B - (2g + p)$.

The minimum size s of the component is derived from the maximum size S, taking account of the manufacturing tolerance t, the value of which is determined by practical consideration of, on the one hand, the cost of obtaining any desired degree of accuracy in the fabrication of the component, whether in a factory or on site and, on the other, the maximum permissible width of joint, $t = S - s$.

Figure 9, again from the BS, shows the method of calculation of the size of a component where it is to be set out by reference to a centre line. By relating the component to the centre line, the variation in the size of the joint is reduced, since the manufacturing tolerance is distributed on each side of the component.

The acceptance of an agreed standard of tolerances also presupposes the acceptance of a system of factory inspection to guarantee that the manufacturing tolerances are maintained. If the designer demands a greater degree of accuracy than the site circumstances or joint detail warrant, then the cost of production will be unnecessarily high. Thus the tolerances should be as generous as the circumstances permit.

To establish tolerance allowances the following procedure is usual. The nominal dimension of a component is fixed and this dimension indicates the zone into which the component must at all times fit. This nominal dimension will be measured between the controlling grid lines and should normally be a simple number since it is by this dimension that the component's size will be identified. The component must fit into this nominal zone in such a way that inaccuracies in manufacture or assembly do not cause overlap or creep over the boundary. Thus the actual size of the component will be less than its normal size. The actual size is the dimension specified to the manufacturer and is then subject to manufacturing tolerances. The upper and lower limits of manufacturing tolerances will be determined by consideration of the nature of the materials of the component, the manufacturing processes and the method of control. When the manufacturing tolerances are known, the assembly position must be examined. The tolerance allowed for placing the component

in position should allow enough room for manoeuvre. This will depend upon the detail of the

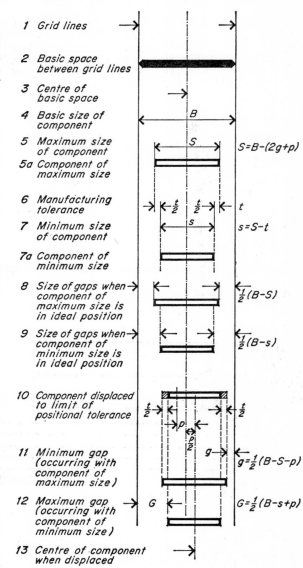

1 Grid lines

2 Basic space between grid lines

3 Centre of basic space

4 Basic size of component — B

5 Maximum size of component — S — $S = B - (2g + p)$

5a Component of maximum size

6 Manufacturing tolerance — $\frac{t}{2}$ $\frac{t}{2}$ — t

7 Minimum size of component — s — $s = S - t$

7a Component of minimum size

8 Size of gaps when component of maximum size is in ideal position — $\frac{1}{2}(B - S)$

9 Size of gaps when component of minimum size is in ideal position — $\frac{1}{2}(B - s)$

10 Component displaced to limit of positional tolerance — $\frac{t}{2}$ $\frac{t}{2}$ p $\frac{p}{2}$

11 Minimum gap (occurring with component of maximum size) — g — $g = \frac{1}{2}(B - S - p)$

12 Maximum gap (occurring with component of minimum size) — G — $G = \frac{1}{2}(B - s + p)$

13 Centre of component when displaced

9 *The size of a jointed component and setting out by reference to the centre line (BS 3626 : 1963)*

component and particularly in respect of its profile and on the assembly techniques to be adopted. Account must now be taken of the form of joint,

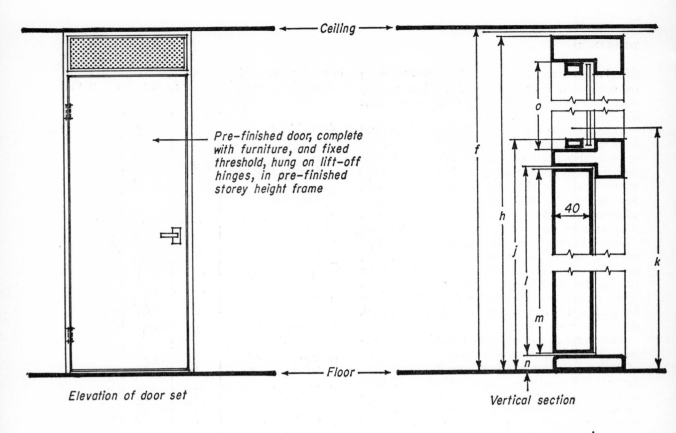

Pre-finished door, complete with furniture, and fixed threshold, hung on lift-off hinges, in pre-finished storey height frame

Elevation of door set

Vertical section

40

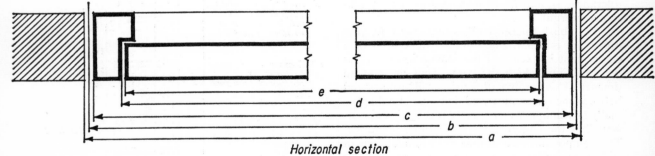

Horizontal section

	All dimensions in mm		All dimensions in mm
a Actual opening— tolerances: −zero; +10 overall		*h* Floor to ceiling set frame overall	*f* −15
b Nominal opening co-ordinating plane	900	*j* Door height set frame overall	2090
c Frame overall	890	*k* Door height set opening	2100
d Width between rebates	830	*l* Door and clearances	2045
e Door width fitted	826	*m* Door height fitted	2040
f Floor to nominal ceiling	for housing: 2300, 2350, 2400	*n* Threshold thickness	15
		o Over panel rebate	for housing: 177, 227, 277

Dimension *f* and *b* are grid line (or basic space) dimensions

10   *Standard door set*

the jointing material to be used, the method of application and the necessity of subsequent maintenance. The maximum and minimum joint widths therefore determine the actual limits of positional tolerance. If the maximum gap is too wide for the jointing technique proposed or the minimum gap is too small, then the actual sizes must be adjusted, and it may be necessary to insist on more accurate manufacturing tolerances. Any extra cost involved will have to be set against the advantages of the chosen jointing method.

In the design of a component, the designer must first select the basic size B or modular space within which the component is to fit. Then the manufacturing tolerance must be agreed t. The designer must then determine the minimum gap g that is practicable between the component and the grid line in respect of the jointing technique to be used. This joint may be a butt joint in the case of built-in furniture components placed next to each other, or it may be a mastic joint between a window and the structural frame. The minimum practical positional tolerance must next be decided p, that is to say the amount of space for manoeuvring into position that can be allowed. Then the three fundamental sizes can be calculated as follows with reference to setting out to one edge:

Minimum size $= s = B - (2g + p + t)$
Maximum size $= S = B - (2g + p)$

Where B = basic size of component
g = minimum gap between component and grid line
p = positional tolerance
t = total manufacturing tolerance.

It follows that if the components are factory made, the manufacturer should state in the catalogue the basic size of the component and the minimum and maximum manufacturing sizes. Where information on these is available, they have been included in the appropriate text in this volume.

Grid lines required for positioning the component should always be shown on the drawing, together with the basic size and minimum gap. The builder should always set out profile on site in accordance with the grid lines, and then set out the component position within this framework.

Figure 10 shows the dimensions of a standard door set designed to fit a basic space of 900 mm wide × 2300, 2350 or 2400 mm high. These are the BS 4330 floor to nominal ceiling controlling dimensions for housing. The figure illustrates the large number of standard dimensions which follow from the choice of overall controlling dimensions. Because of the complete standardization of these dimensions the door would be manufactured complete on 'lift off' hinges, and both door and frame could be prefinished, and fitted with standard lock, latches and threshold. The door set is standardized also in respect of width of frame to 57 mm, 70 mm and 95 mm width of unit, to take various widths of partitions, and all falling within the 100 mm preferred dimension zone. Work on the standardization of joints and a relevant Code of Practice is proceeding in separate British Standards Institution committees. This guidance on practical tolerances and on joint details when available will assist in the derivation of work sizes over a wide range of components.

CONTROLLING DIMENSIONS

The use of grids for the setting out of spaces to be occupied by components is described in BS 4330. The BS makes the following recommendations in respect of vertical dimensions: 'The selection of

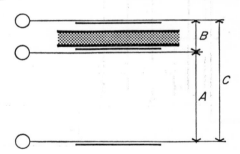

11   *Floor to ceiling heights*

sizes between controlling lines is made for floor to ceiling heights, heights of zones for floors and roofs and floor to floor or floor to roof heights'. Also recommendations are made in respect of changes in level. Figure 11 shows the zones 'A', 'B' and 'C' which are relevant to the controlling dimensions.

Vertical controlling dimension

'A' a floor to ceiling height in mm determined by user requirements to be selected from the following

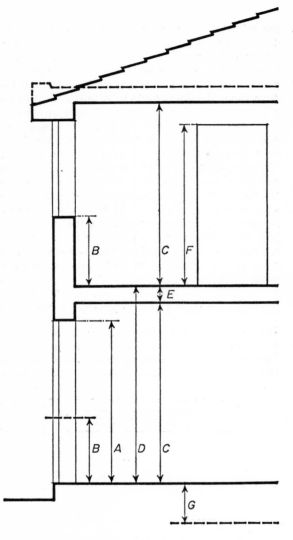

A Window head height
2300 I
2100 II

B Window sill height

0	1000
200	1100
600	1200
700	1400
800	1800
900	2100

C Floor to ceiling height
2500
2400
2350
2300
2100 – garages only

D Floor to floor height
2600 – mandatory height for public sector housing
2700

E Floor thickness
200
250
300

F Door set height
2100

G Change of level

300	1700
600	1800
900	2000
1200	2100
1300	2300
1400	2400
1500	

12   Vertical controlling dimensions for housing

range (2100) 2300, (2350) 2400, 2500, 2600, 2700, 2800, 2900, 3000 mm. The 2100 mm increment applies only to domestic garages, multi-storey car parks and farm buildings, and the 2350 mm height is an additional option for housing only.

'B' the space required within the zone in mm for the structure, services and suspended ceilings to be selected from the following range: 100, 200, (250), 300, 400, 500, 600, 900, 1200, 1500, 1800, 2100 mm, with greater heights in multiples of 300. The 250 mm increment applies only to housing.

'C' floor to floor and floor to roof heights given in mm can be selected from the following range: (2600), 2700 mm with greater heights in multiples of 300 mm from 2700 to 8400 mm and thereafter in multiples of 600 mm. The 2600 mm increment applies only to housing. In order to make the best use of dimensions in co-ordinated components the dimensions 'A' and 'B' should add up to the dimension 'C'. As an example, the vertical controlling dimensions for housing are illustrated in figure 12.

Horizontal controlling dimensions

There are two methods of locating controlling lines in relation to load bearing walls and columns as shown in figures 13 and 14;

1 on the axial lines of the load bearing walls or columns (figure 13) or
2 the boundaries of the zones (figure 14).

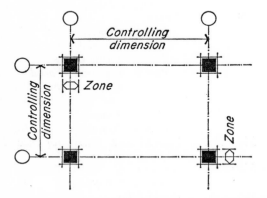

13   *Horizontal controlling dimensions: axial lines*

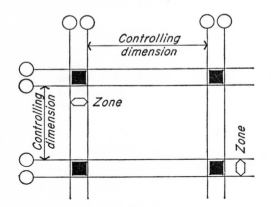

14   *Horizontal controlling dimensions: zone boundaries*

The controlling dimensions should be selected from the following range in respect of the widths of the zone to be allowed for columns and load bearing walls: 100, 200, 300, 400, 500 and 600 mm. If greater widths are required they should be in multiples of 300 mm as a first preference, or 100 mm as a second preference, in accordance with BS 4011. The choice of controlling dimension for the spacing of zones (whichever method is used) should be made from the following: 900 mm in multiples of 300 mm, except that 800 mm may be used for housing. In respect of the intermediate controlling dimensions where joints are most likely to occur within the building between components and assemblies, the following points are made: *Window sill heights.* The height of the controlling line for a window sill should be selected from multiples of 300 mm as a first preference, and 100 mm as a second preference. In respect of *window head heights*, the height of the controlling line for the window head should be selected in accordance with a multiple of 300 mm as a first preference, and 100 mm as a second preference.

The controlling dimensions provide the framework within which buildings may be designed and to which building components and assemblies should be related. Intermediate controlling dimensions are subdivisions of the main framework. The controlling line represents the key reference plane and controlling lines for vertical dimensions represent boundaries for zones, floors and roofs. Controlling lines for horizontal dimensions indicate the axes of load bearing walls and columns or alternatively the boundaries of zones, within which the wall or column lies. A controlling line is shown in respect of the British Standard by a chain dotted line or unbroken line with a circle at the end of the line, as in figure 15. A zone is defined

15   *Controlling dimension lines*

as a space between vertical or horizontal reference planes which is provided for a building component. For instance, zones for floors and roofs contain the structure which will include the finishes, the services, the suspended ceilings and where appropriate allowances for camber and deflection. Zones for load bearing walls contained in the structure will include an allowance for finishes. The British Standard is based on information derived by comparison of building types as follows: Education, health, housing, offices, industrial, hotels, shops and farm buildings. A building designed as part of a local authority building programme, financed by the Department of Education and Science, the Ministry of Health, and the Department of Environment, must be designed in metric units in accordance with the various recommendations put forward by these official bodies. There will be a transitional period when some British Standard components are not available in metric units. Thus the change to metric will not be complete until components are available to the metric British Standards which will be published in accordance with the BSI programme. Modular co-ordination in practice is illustrated in the many industrialized systems of building now in use. Client-controlled systems on the one hand, and the proprietary commercial systems are making a major contribution at the present time to increased productivity in the building industry. However, although the sizes of components are related within a given system and are dimensionally co-ordinated with each other they are not necessarily co-ordinated with components in other systems although the client-sponsored systems are developing towards this, and when the change to metric is complete, all the client-sponsored systems of industrialized building (see chapter 11) will use the same dimensional basis. It is thus possible by means of modular co-ordination that the many closed or separate systems now in use may lead to a more open or general form of industrialized building in which factory made components are widely interchangeable.

Further references

BS 2900 : 1970   *Glossary of Terms (metric units).*
BS 3626 : 1963   *Recommendations for a System of Tolerances and Fits for Building.*
BS 4011 : 1966   *Basic Sizes for Building Components and Assemblies.*
BS 4330 : 1968   *Recommendations for the Co-ordination of Dimensions in Building: Controlling Dimensions.*
PD 6432 : 1969   *Arrangements of Building Components and Assemblies within Functional Groups.*

For further information on modular co-ordination see *Modular Primer* by Eric Corker, ARIBA and A. Diprose, ARIBA, also the *Co-ordination of Dimensions for Building* published by the RIBA, and *the Metric Handbook* published by the Architectural Press.

The principal British Standards relating to components in building construction.

BS 455 : 1957   *Schedule of Sizes for Locks and Latches for Doors in Building.*
BS 459   *Doors*
    Part 1   *Panelled and Glazed Wood Doors*
    Part 2   *Flush Doors*
    Part 3   *Plywood Faced Fire Check Flush Doors, and Wood and Metal Frames*
    Part 4   *Matchboarded Doors*
BS 544 : 1969   *Linseed Oil Putty for use in Wooden Frames*
BS 565 : 1963   *Glossary of Terms Relating to Timber and Woodwork*
BS 584 : 1967   *Wood Trim*
BS 644   *Wood Window*
    Part 1 : 1951   *Wood Casement Windows*
    Part 2 : 1958   *Wood Double Hung Sash Windows*
    Part 3 : 1951   *Wood Double Hung Sash and Case Windows (Scottish type)*
BS 990 : 1967   *Steel Windows for Domestic and Similar Buildings*
BS 1202   *Nails*
    Part 1 : 1966   *Steel Nails*
    Part 2 : 1966   *Copper Nails*
    Part 3 : 1962   *Aluminium Nails*
BS 1210 : 1963   *Wood Screws*
BS 1227   *Hinges Part 1(a) 1967 Hinges for General Building Purposes*
BS 1245 : 1951   *Metal Door Frames—Steel*
BS 1246 : 1959   *Metal Skirtings, Picture Rails and Beads*
BS 1285 : 1963   *Wood Surrounds for Steel Windows and Doors*
BS 1422 : 1956   *Steel Sub-Frames, Sills and Window Boards for Metal Windows*
BS 1567 : 1953   *Wood Door Frames and Linings*

BS 1186	*Quality of Workmanship in Joinery*		
BS 2911	*Letter Plates*		
	Part 1 : 1957	*Manufacture*	
	Part 2 : 1960	*Standard Height and Fixing Recommendations*	
BS 3589	*Glossary of Terms used in Building*		
BS 3621 : 1963	*Thief Resistant Locks for Hinged Doors*		

British Standard Codes of Practice Relevant to Components or Component Design

CP 3 Part 1 : 1964	*Daylighting*
CP 145 : 1969	*Patent Glazing*
CP 151	*Doors and Windows including Frames and Hinges*
CP 151 Part 1 : 1957	*Wooden Doors*
CP 152 : 1966	*Glazing and Fixing of Glass for Buildings*
Supplement No. 1 : 1963	*Recommendations on Safety Aspects of Glass, Glazed or Fixed in Buildings*

2 Joinery

The technique of making timber components is known as *joinery* and is concerned with the craft and machine work involved in joining together fully finished timber, both in softwood and in hardwood. The timber is also used in conjunction with block-board, plywood, chipboard, hardboard and decorative building boards. An important problem to be solved in connection with the use of natural timber is concerned with accommodating moisture movement in order to prevent deformation.

To obtain true surfaces in the finished product the timber is planed and sanded. In connection with this, it is usual to specify that all 'arrises' or edges in joinery work are to be slightly rounded, since perfectly sharp square right angles along the edge of timber are difficult to obtain in practice or maintain in use.

TIMBER FOR JOINERY

Properties of timbers are dealt with in chapter 2 of *Mitchell's Building Construction: Materials*, by Alan Everett, and varieties are described in table 14 of the same volume. Boards are described in *MBC: Materials*, chapter 3.

Softwood

Most softwood used for joinery grows in Scandinavia, Russia or North America. BS 1186: Part I: 1952 *Quality of Timber and Workmanship in Joinery*, gives a list of softwood suitable for joinery under the general headings of Redwood and Whitewood from Scandinavia or Russia, and Douglas Fir and Hemlock from North America. In addition to these broad classifications there is Parana Pine, a commonly used, but in many respects special timber imported from South America.

Logs of timber are sawn into square or rectangular sections before shipment, the ends of the timber being stencilled with the shipper's mark. There are many hundreds of such marks which indicate to the purchaser, the grade of timber and the district in which the timber has been grown,

as well as the name of the importer. Figure 16 (taken from BS 4471 : 1969 *Dimensions for Softwood*), shows the basic sizes for sawn softwood that are imported. These sizes represent a substantial reduction on the previously imported range of imperial sizes. Rationalization with a view to achieving greater economy is the reason for this reduction in available sizes, and the change to metric has provided the opportunity of achieving this objective.

mm	75	100	125	150	175	200	225	250	300
16	×	×	×	×					
19	×	×	×	×					
22	×	×	×	×					
25	×	×	× ·	×	×	×	×	×	×
32	×	×	×	×	×	×	×	×	×
36	×	×	×	×					
38	×	×	×	×	×	×	×		
40	×	×	×	×	×	×	×		
44	×	×	×	×	×	×	×	×	×
50	×	×	×	×	×	×	×	×	×
63		×	×	×	×	×	×		
75		×	×	×	×	×	×		×
100		×		×		×		×	×
150				×		×			×
200						×			
250								×	
300									×

16 Basic cross-sectional sizes of sawn softwood (BS 4471 : 1969)

The sizes have been formulated following a series of International Conferences in agreement between all the major softwood producing countries and the principal European importing countries. The thicknesses from 16 mm to 75 mm inclusive represent the usual range of European production. Similarly the basic European widths shown in the range 75 mm to 225 mm. The larger sizes are normally those of North or South America. Timber is imported in lengths beginning at 1·800 m rising by increments of 300 mm to 6·300 m.

The actual size of any piece of timber will vary up to ±2 per cent according to its moisture content. The sizes shown are those for timber with a moisture content of 20 per cent, which is the percentage at which the timber would, under normal conditions, be converted. Further variation in the basic size would be expected since the sawn timber will not be an exactly uniform size throughout its length. The deviation in respect of thickness and width should not be greater than −1 mm and +3 mm for the smaller sections up to 100 mm. For the larger sections, a deviation up to −2 mm and +6 mm may be expected. Timber is usually specified to 'nominal' sizes and these would be the basic sizes given in figure 16. The nominal dimensions are the size of the unwrought timber converted from the log and 'left from the saw' before undergoing the finishing processes. Processing to the accurate 'finished' sizes involves a reduction in the size of the timber. The amount of reduction would depend upon the use to which the finished timber is to be put. Timber for joinery work would require more work in planing and finishing for example, than semi-finished timber for rough framing. BS 4471 gives details of the average figures to be expected for the reduction of size for various timber uses. (see *MBC: Materials*, table 20). The allowance varies from 3 mm (1·5 mm each face) to 13 mm (6·5 mm each face) depending on the eventual use and size of section.

In respect of conversion of sawn sizes to wrought or 'finished' sizes with regard to joinery work, the metric edition of the *Standard Method of Measurement* advises that: 'Timber shall be deemed to be wrought on all faces and edges and 3·2 mm shall be allowed from the nominal size for each wrought face or edge'. In practical terms 3 mm would be the figure to be borne in mind when designing sections. Thus a section of timber, planed all round, of 50 × 100 mm nominal size will be a minimum wrought or finished size of 44 × 94 mm. If timber is specified on a working detail to the finished size the designer must ensure that the size specified can be economically obtained from the basic sawn sizes available.

Certain timber is required from the timber merchant for factory assembly in jigs, for use in the production of components. In these circumstances uniform size is essential and the absence of tolerance and shrinkage is a valuable economy. In these cases the timber can be specified as *precision timber* in accordance with BS 4471. This is timber which is converted at a specified moisture content (average 18 per cent) and is supplied regularized on one face and one edge to the specified size.

Hardwood

BS 1186 lists several commonly available species of hardwood and their uses in joinery, with special reference to housing. There is a large range of sizes of section available according to species. BS 881 and 589 *Nomenclature of Commercial Timbers*, standardize the terms of reference. See *MBC: Materials*, chapter 2.

Building boards

Plywood, blockboard, hardboard, chipboard and other building boards which may be used in the manufacture of components are also subject to British Standards. These materials are discussed fully in *MBC: Materials*, chapter 3.

Quality of timber

The minimum standards in respect of quality of timber, suitable for use in joinery components, are given in BS 1186. This Standard is written primarily for timber used in housing and similar structures and from this the standard required in other classes of work can be devised.

The Standard covers the moisture content, rate of growth, straightness of grain, and the limitation of defects such as boxed heart, sapwood, checks, splits, shakes and knots.

Where the quality of timber specified cannot be obtained economically, the techniques of laminating, finger jointing and edge jointing may be used, provided that the joints are not conspicuous after painting. Where the component is to be stained or finished clear, these techniques may be excluded by the specification.

One of the most important considerations with regard to the satisfactory performance of a component manufactured from timber, is the moisture content of the timber when the joinery work is delivered from the factory. The acceptable limits are given in table 14.

A typical specification in a Bill of Quantities making reference to BS 1186 would ask for the softwood for joinery work to be 'approved better unsorted Swedish redwood or select merchantable

| | Moisture content | |
	Minimum per cent	Maximum per cent
(a) Internal joinery, including doors, when specially ordered for buildings with central heating	10	12
(b) All other internal doors	12	15
(c) All other internal joinery	14	17
(d) All external doors	12	18
(e) All other external joinery	17	20
From BS 1186 : Part I : 1952		

Table 14

Douglas Fir. The timber to have a moisture content of between 10 and 20 per cent at the time of fixing according to use, being well-seasoned, well cut, sound, bright and square edged, free from warp or other deformation and from signs of rot or decay, worm and beetle, and contain no large, loose or dead knots, checks, splits or other defects. Hardwoods to be prime grade, straight grained, well-seasoned by kiln, to 15 per cent moisture content, free from beetle, or fungus attack, shakes, and wane.' Note that softwood (because it often contains a high proportion of 'non-durable' or 'perishable' sapwood) used in external doors and windows, must be treated with preservative. (See BRS Digest 73.)

FIXINGS

Joinery items will normally be framed, glued and pinned or screwed together. Nails will be used in associated carpentry work. Nails are described in BS 1202 : Part I : 1966 : *Steel Nails*; Part II : 1966 : *Copper Nails*, and Part III : 1962 : *Aluminium Nails*. Wood screws are covered by BS 1210 : 1963.

Adhesives are described in *MBC: Materials*, chapter 13.

The more common nails and screws used in joinery are illustrated in figures 17 and 18 with a guide to the metric sizes in which they will be available.

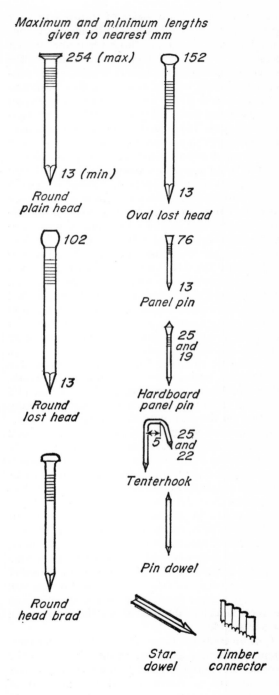

Maximum and minimum lengths given to nearest mm

254 (max) — Round plain head — 13 (min)

152 — Oval lost head — 13

102 — Round lost head — 13

76 — Panel pin — 13

25 and 19 — Hardboard panel pin

25 and 22 — Tenterhook — 5

Pin dowel

Round head brad

Star dowel

Timber connector

17 Nails

Nail heads and their fixings, in timber which is to be painted or receive clear treatment, are usually punched and filled with proprietory filler or plastic wood. Where timber is to receive clear treatment, the filler should be of matching colour. The use of adhesives with a comparatively short setting time of say two hours enables components to be handled within a reasonable time. The production time in respect of gluing techniques can be reduced by the use of radio frequency heating (RFH). The principle of RF is to use synthetic resin adhesives which set faster as the temperature of the glue line is raised. RFH voltage is applied across the timber in the area of the glue line so that the glue, which is a better conductor than the surrounding timber, develops a higher temperature resulting in quicker setting. RFH in woodworking is applicable to long runs of specific components, eg flush doors, and furniture rather than fabrication of specific items in a joiner's shop.

Panel pins are used in the initial fixing of sheet materials to secure the material until the adhesive sets.

Screws are most often used where panels may have to be regularly removed for inspection and maintenance. The best specification requires the use of brass cups, so that the screw can be removed and re-driven without damaging the wood. Where removal is not a consideration, screws can be driven into a counter sinking, so that the head is below the surface, the hole being filled by a small pellet of similar wood glued in afterwards. This technique is known as *screwed and pelleted*. Holes of a diameter slightly less than the screw should always be drilled in preparation.

JOINERY DETAILING

Joinery detailing should take into account the development of new woodworking techniques, bearing in mind the decline of old skills and the rise of new ones. The details should be suited to new materials and the techniques and economic considerations of factory production. They should thus be economical of timber and make the maximum use of machinery and power tools in the joiners' shop.

FRAMING

The contractor is usually required to frame up the

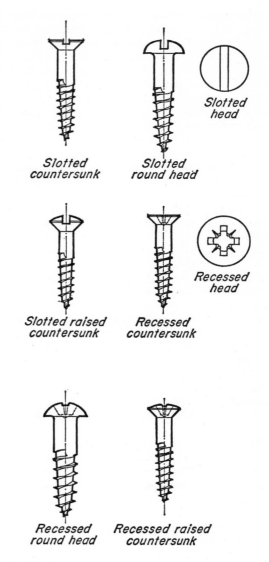

Slotted
head

Slotted
countersunk

Slotted
round head

Recessed
head

Slotted raised
countersunk

Recessed
countersunk

Recessed
round head

Recessed raised
countersunk

18   *Wood screws*

joinery work as soon as possible after the contract is signed. Note that this section of the book is concerned with the manufacture of components and fittings, such as windows, doors and built in fittings, which items do not usually form part of the supporting structure of the building. The use of timber for the structural parts of a building is a technique requiring knowledge of timber engineering, since the nature of timber requires special care to be taken where joints must withstand heavy loads. The structural use of timber in building is more fully discussed in *Mitchell's Building Construction: Structure and Fabric*, Parts 1 and 2, by J. Stroud Foster. Manufactured work should be stored in a dry place, under cover and so arranged that a current of air can freely circulate round it. The components should also be adequately protected from exposure and damage during transport, and storage on site. It is the contractor's responsibility that all the joinery be protected during the course of the work to prevent damage to nosings, arrises and mouldings. This is usually done by the use of strips of hardboard, covering by polythene sheet, or in the case of very special work, by 'boxing in' behind a plywood or hardboard covered frame. The contractor should also, in good quality work, ensure that the heat and humidity conditions in the building are suitable for the joinery to be delivered and fixed, so that the conditions are commensurate with the required moisture content of the timber.

Clear seals are available which can be applied to joinery work at the time of manufacture, and which prevent moisture penetration and so protect the work from moisture movement before the final finish is applied.

When timber is framed up the faces of all the members joined should be perfectly fitted together with true and flush surfaces in alignment throughout the joint.

When the joints are glued, the surfaces to receive the glue must be free from oil, grease or dust, and the glue film must be evenly applied. The manufacturer's particular recommendations should be followed and the following points should be remembered. The moisture content of the timber and the temperature of the room and of the glue are of paramount importance. To attempt to joint wet timber in a cold damp workshop is to invite failure. The correct application of the glue and mixing in respect of the catalyst glues are also vital, as is the observation of the correct procedure in bringing the pieces into contact and cramping up where required.

JOINTS

Methods of framing timber together are the most traditional joints developed and proved by hand-craftsmen over many years and now modified in respect of machine techniques. The most commonly used joints are given below in alphabetical order and classified for the purpose of illustration according to the form of interlock or connection between the members as follows: *butt; combed; dovetailed; dowelled; finger; grooved; housed; handrail; lapped; mitred; mortice and tenon.* BS 1186 : 1955 : *Quality of Timber and Workmanship in Joinery*: Part 2 : *Quality of Workmanship*, gives recommendations regarding the minimum requirements as to fit, tolerances and general workmanship for the most common joints used in joinery manufacture.

Butt

(a) *Square.* In this joint the square ends of timber are placed in juxtaposition, or *butted* together. The joint is also known as a *square edge* joint, or *rubbed* joint. The timbers require careful alignment and the joint relies entirely on the glue for its strength and requires cramping up until the glue has set. The area of gluing is known as the *glue line*. The square butt joint is used principally where boards are joined longitudinally as in the manufacture of counter tops. As the term *square edge* implies, the edges must be perfectly true and square to each other to avoid overall distortion of the finished surface.

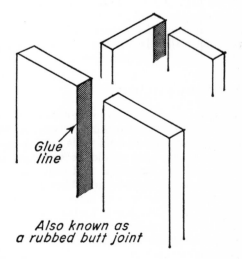

Glue line

Also known as a rubbed butt joint

(*a*)   Square
19   Butt

(b) *Dowelled*. The use of hardwood dowels spaced at say 150 mm along the length help to locate the two parts of the joint but make the joint more difficult to assemble since the dowels must sit perfectly square in the timber. The dowels should project about 25 mm, and be a push fit into the holes, which are drilled very slightly larger than the dowels to ensure a tight joint after gluing. To assist in fitting the joint, the ends of the dowels could be chamfered for an easy lead in, but this increases the amount of hand labour and makes the joint expensive.

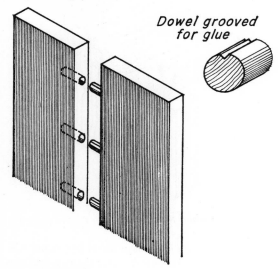

Dowel grooved for glue

(*b*)   *Dowelled*

Button

This type of joint is used in the construction of tables and benches. It is really a *turn-button* joint and has the added advantage that the top can be removed should a replacement be required. The joint is illustrated in figure 42, page 70. This method of connection is similar to the *slotted angle* joint, shown in figure 44, page 73, and allows movement to the table or bench top to take place without deforming the framing.

Combed

This is a commonly used joint which has been developed for machine production. The machining of both members is identical, one member being reversed in the course of assembly. This joint,

which should have an initial push fit, will be glued and dowelled. The dowelling shown is by a metal dowel of star shaped cross section which is driven through the joint after gluing. The joint relies mainly on the glue for its strength and so the surface area of the parts to be jointed by gluing is more extensive than in traditional joints of similar form. Three glue surfaces are most common as shown, but more can be accommodated if the section is big enough for each tongue of the timber to be of workable thickness. The combed joint is used for the corners of window opening lights in mass production components.

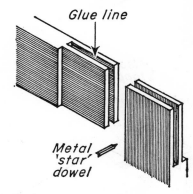

Glue line

Metal 'star' dowel

20   *Combed*

Dovetail

(a) *Hand-cut*   The joint illustrated would be hand made and so is expensive to produce. It would, however, be appropriate in hardwood joinery of special quality and finish; in particular in drawer construction.

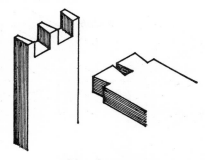

Also known as a common dovetail

(*a*)   *Hand-cut*
21   *Dovetail*

45

(b to e) *Lapped dovetail* This illustrates the difference in form of machine made (21b) and hand made (21c) versions of the same joint. The hand made joint would be appropriate only for high class specialist work in hardwood, but the

machine made version is commonly used between the front and side members in drawer construction. This version is made in a special machine which cuts tail and corresponding notch together as shown in figure 21d. An average machine will form the correct number of tails and notches in timber of up to say 225 mm wide, as shown in figure 21e. This type of dovetail is also known as *stopped dovetail*.

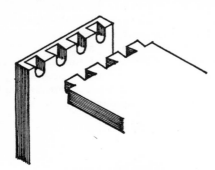

Also known as a 'stopped' dovetail

(*b*) *Lapped – machine made*

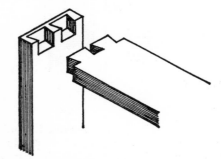

(*c*) *Lapped – handwrot*

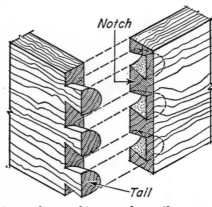

(*d*) *Lapped – machine cut dovetail*

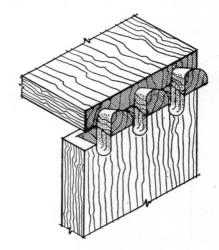

(*e*) *Position when machining*

(f) *Mitred* This is a *secret mitre* and cannot be made by machine. It is used where the two surfaces of the joint are seen and gives the outward appearance of a mitre with the 'secret' strength of a dovetail.

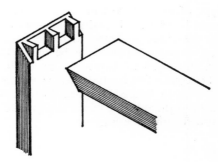

(*f*) *Mitred*

(g) *Corner locking joint* This is a machine made joint but is not a true dovetail in that the parts of the joint do not have the characteristic wedge or 'tail' shape. It is commonly used in shop-fitting and, like the combed joint, relies for its strength on the quality of the glue used.

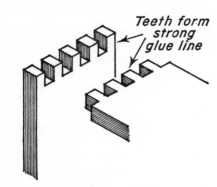

Teeth form strong glue line

(g)   *Corner locking joint*

Dowelled

(a) *Simple dowelled*   The drilling out of holes in timber does not weaken the section so much as a groove or mortice (described later) and thus, this technique when used in conjunction with hardwood dowels gives a satisfactory connection provided

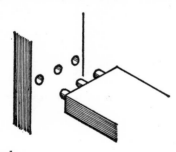

(a)   *Simple*
22   *Dowelled*

that care is taken to ensure that the joint is properly glued. This is a simple joint but not recommended to be carried out by hand, since the holes are difficult to drill in true alignment, unless done by machine on a *jig*. The joint is stronger if made with two rows of dowels where the thickness of the timber members permits this. The dowel in every case will have a shallow V groove cut into it to allow the surplus glue to escape and form a 'key' of adhesive. It is usual to make the

dowel slightly shorter than the hole (say 4 mm) so that the shoulders of the joint fit tight and square when assembled. The shoulder surfaces must also be adequately glued.

(b) *Loose tongue*   A more sophisticated form of dowelled joint in which the loose tongue helps to prevent the opening of the joint should the timber shrink. The tongue can be more easily inserted after the joint is assembled, and should be of plywood.

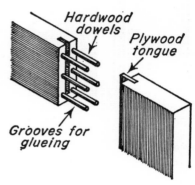

Hardwood dowels

Plywood tongue

Grooves for glueing

(b)   *With loose tongue*

Finger

This is a joint which has been developed to connect two pieces of timber longitudinally, so that the ends of the timbers interlock in the form of wedge shaped fingers of specific proportion. The proportion varies according to the amount of stress the joint must withstand. Dimensions are given in BS 1186: Part 2.

l = Finger length
t = Distance between fingers
b = Width of the finger tip

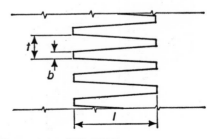

23   *Finger joint (BS 1186)*

Grooved

(a) *Lindermann* This joint is made on a special machine and takes the form of an offset dovetail. It was much used for forming deep strings in staircase construction and is included for reference.

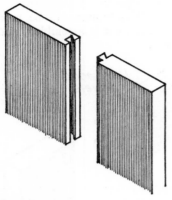

(*a*) *Lindermann*
24 *Grooved*

(b) *Loose tongued* Both pieces of timber forming the joint are grooved and a hardwood or preferably a plywood slip of timber is glued in place on one side of the joint to act as a tongue to strengthen the connection. The whole of the joint is then glued and 'cramped up' until the glue is set. The loose tongues can be in comparatively short lengths. All surfaces in contact must be true, otherwise distortion occurs. This joint is commonly used when connecting pieces of timber longitudinally as in table and bench tops.

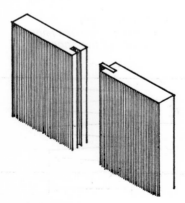

(*b*) *Loose tongued*

(c, d and e). *Tongued and grooved* One board is grooved along its length, with the corresponding board cut to form the profile of the tongue. It is used in the connection of narrow widths of timbers in panelling and the formation of working tops.

The square edge tongue is associated with hand craftsmanship whilst the splayed or rounded tongue is more common in machine work. The profile of the tongue is significant in relation to the gluing area, and gives alignment to the boards. The term *tongued and grooved* is often abbreviated to T & G.

The groove is often cut slightly deeper than the tongue, to ensure a tight joint against the shoulder and further to this, provided that the joint is only to be seen on the face side, the back shoulder can be cut to remain slightly open as shown.

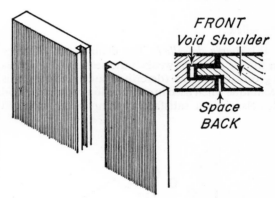

(*c*) *Tongued and grooved* (*i*) *square edge tongue*

(*d*) *Tongued and grooved* (*ii*) *splayed tongue*

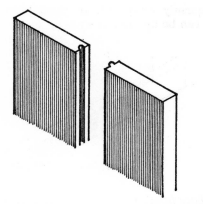

(e)   Tongued and grooved (iii) rounded tongue

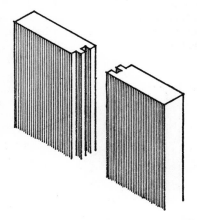

(f)   Double tongued and grooved (iv) square tongue

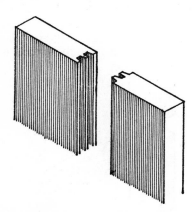

(g)   Double tongued and grooved (v) splayed tongue

(f and g) *Double tongued and grooved*   These are developments of the traditional joint, and are machine made joints used for boards of 40 mm and over in thickness.

Handrail

This joint, as its name implies, was developed to secure the ends of timber used to make up a continuous handrail. It is assembled by means of a bolt threaded at both ends and when tightened produces a very strong and secure joint which is difficult to detect in use. The slots on the underside of the timber are filled with matching timber and cleaned off smooth.

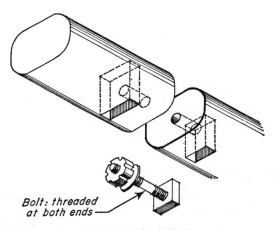

Bolt: threaded at both ends

HANDRAIL JOINT

25   Handrail joint

Housed

(a) *Square housing*   A straightforward method of locating two pieces of timber being jointed at right angles as in shelving. The joint requires careful machining and gluing, and where possible screwing from the back of the housing.

(b) *Dovetail housing – single*   This is a method of joining timbers forming a T shape as in shelving. The groove is cut square on one side and given an upward chamfer to form a single dovetail on the other. The key profile so formed helps to prevent the joint pulling out. Note that this joint can only be assembled by sliding the two parts together, and so the joint is not suitable where the

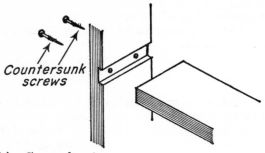

(a) *Square housing*
26   *Housed*

pieces to be connected together are wider than say
300 mm.

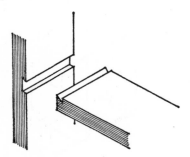

(b) *Dovetail housing – single*

(c) *Dovetail housing – double* The groove is
fully dovetailed with a corresponding increase in
strength as against the single dovetail housing.
There is, of course, a corresponding increase in
cost and difficulty of assembly. Additional fixing
by screwing or pinning is not so essential.

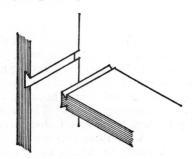

(c) *Dovetail housing – double*

(d) *Face housing* This joint is easily made, and
is used in skeleton framing where the work is

subsequently concealed. In these positions the
fixing can be by nails or screws.

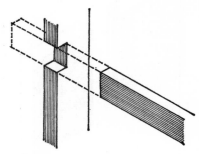

(d) *Face housing*

(e) *Shouldered housing* The groove here is less
than the thickness of the horizontal member; and
will require additional fixing through the face of
the vertical member.

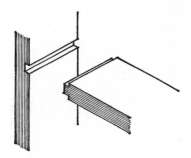

(e) *Shouldered housing*

(f) *Shouldered face housing* An elaboration of
the simple-faced housed joint which provides additional area of contact whilst reducing the amount
of timber to be cut away from the vertical member.

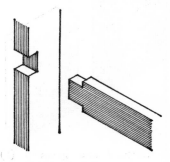

(f) *Shouldered face housing*

(g) *Dovetailed face housing* An interlocking housed joint incorporating the traditional strength of the dovetail profile.

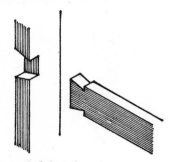

(g)   *Dovetailed face housing*

(h) *Stopped housing* The groove is stopped back from the face of the upright giving a neater appearance on the face. Any joint incorporating a groove is said to be *stopped* if the groove is not carried through to the face of the timber. This is done where the improvement in appearance is considered to outweigh the increase in cost.

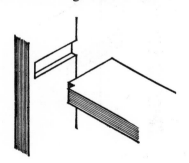

(h)   *Stopped housing*

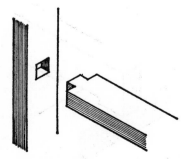

(i)   *Double stopped housing*

(i) *Double stopped housing* Used in skeleton framing where a neat appearance is required; this joint is principally a *locating* joint and does not have the strength of the other types of housing.

(j) *Rail housing* A form of stopped housing used in framing between rails and end pieces as in cabinet construction, where the rail is not so wide as the end piece.

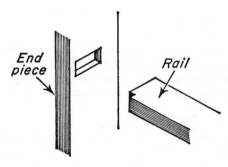

(j)   *Rail housing*

Lapped

(a) *Cogged*, *single* and (b) *double*. These joints are simple interlocking joints, and would be glued in joinery work but probably nailed in carcassing work.

The double cogged is suitable where the timbers overlap and continue.

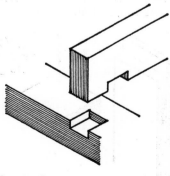

(a)   *Cogged – single*
27   *Lapped*

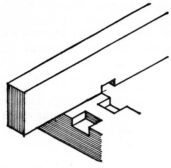

(b)   Cogged – double

(c) *Half lapped* This is the most usual way of extending the lengths of members as in rails or sills where the joint can be fully supported.
The overlap should be screwed and glued.

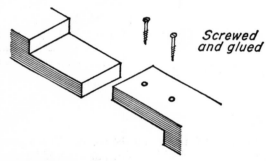

Screwed and glued

(c)   Half lapped

(d) *Rebated* A joint which allows the joining of two pieces of timber at right angles and at the same time conceals the end grain on one face. As with all lapped conditions the joint is secured by pinning or screwing and gluing.

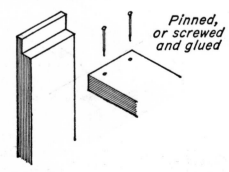

Pinned, or screwed and glued

(d)   Rebated

(e) *Tongued* A joint commonly used between head and jamb of a door lining, it is a stronger version of the rebated joint but does not conceal the end grain. The joint should be strengthened by the use of nails or screws.

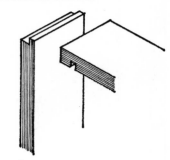

(e)   Tongued

(f) *Tongued and lapped* A joint not much used which combines the features of the tongued lapped and the rebated lapped joints in an obvious manner.

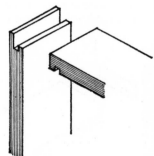

(f)   Tongued and lapped

(g) *Notched – single* and (h) *double* A form of

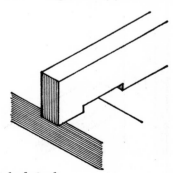

(g)   Notched single

joint similar to the cogged joints, and used in the same circumstances.

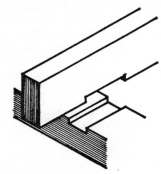

(h)   *Notched double*

Mitred

(a) *Plain*   The grain runs continuously around the joint in this case and, because of the cut in the timber, end grain is glued to end grain.

The quality of the glue is of prime importance and glue that requires no pressure or heat makes assembly easier. Joints which require end grain being glued to side grain should be avoided, as the side grain will split as soon as the joint is stressed. The cut forming a mitred joint is carried out in a mitre machine. The joint is shown reinforced on the internal angle by a perfectly square block – either temporary or permanent. The block can be screwed to both members forming the joint.

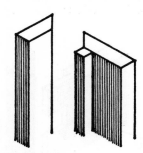

(a)   *Plain (with block)*
28   *Mitred*

(b) *Loose tongued*   This is a development of the plain mitre in that the loose tongue locates the timber to form the joint. To maintain the strength of the timber, the direction of the grain in the hardwood tongue should be at 45° to its edge, or

preferably to be of plywood. The groove can be stopped so that the tongue is hidden on the finished joint. This, however, creates the necessity for hand labours in addition to machine work on the joint. The tongue should be slightly smaller than the depth of the groove to ensure a tight fit on the mitre.

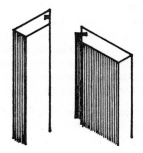

(b) *Loose tongued*

(c) *Lapped*   A more sophisticated form of mitred joint which gives a greater gluing area for increased strength. The shoulders ensure a 90° angle.

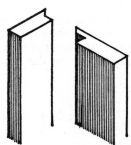

(c)   *Lapped*

Mortice and tenon

The most common joint in use for the connection of flat rectangular sections of timber at right angles, is the mortice and tenon joint. The mortice is the slot cut out of the vertical piece of timber, ready to receive the tenon which is formed on the horizontal member of the joint. The tenon is inserted into the mortice, glued, the wedges driven and the whole joint cramped up until the glue is set. The tenon and wedges are always fitted so that they project when the joint is initially fitted. After the glue has set the surplus timber is cut away, ensuring a perfectly flush and tight face to the work.

Where the joint is prepared for mass production, as in the manufacture of standard windows, the wedges would not be used, but the joint would be secured by a non-ferrous metal star-shaped dowel driven through to engage each part of the joint. A further alternative is the use of a glued hardwood dowel as a 'pin' through the joint. The thickness of the tenon is traditionally one third of the width of the section with a maximum depth of 5 times its thickness. The purpose of the tenon is to resist the stresses produced in the joint and to counteract any tendency for the frame to distort.

(a) *Through tenon* The simplest form of this joint. Usually associated with the junction of middle rail and stile in a door. The top and bottom edge of the mortice should be cut so that the slot is slightly dovetailed, thus increasing the strength of the joint. This dovetailing effect is reasonably easy to obtain with a machine cut joint by moving the timber slightly from side to side during the cutting process.

Where the joint is made in heavy or large sections of timber the joint may be additionally secured by the use of a hardwood or metal star-shaped dowel. Note that the use of a dowel made from metal restricts the amount of finishing work that can be carried out on the timber after the joint has been made.

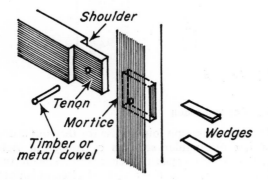

(*a*) *Through tenon*
29   *Mortice and tenon*

(b) *Haunched tenon* This joint is used to connect the side and top rail of a door, since in order to wedge the joint it is necessary to retain a thickness of timber above the tenon. The cutting away of the

front part of the tenon accomplishes this whilst the retention of the haunch minimizes any loss of strength. During the making of the joint the stile is cut longer than required in the finished work so that a 'horn' projects beyond the top rail, this timber resists the pressure from the wedges when the joint is first made. The 'horn' is then cut off to the top of the door and the wedges trimmed to size.

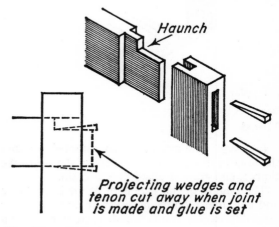

(*b*)   *Haunched*

(c) *Twin tenon* Where the mortice and tenon joint is to be made in a deep rail, say 230 mm and over, there would be a tendency for a deep tenon to shrink. To avoid this, two tenons are cut one above the other out of the depth of the rail. The joint would be dowelled as well as wedged in good class work.

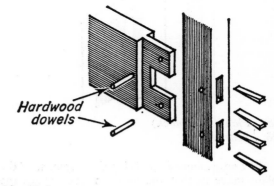

(*c*)   *Twin*

(d) *Twin tenon – double haunched* This is a

locating joint used in framing. It would not be wedged.

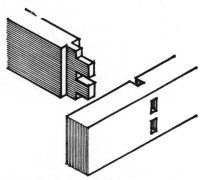

(*d*) *Twin – double haunched*

(e) *Double tenon*   Where the joint is to be made in a thick rail, say 65 mm or more, two tenons are cut, side by side.

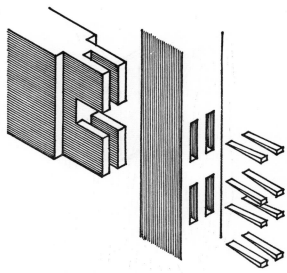

(*f*) *Twin double*

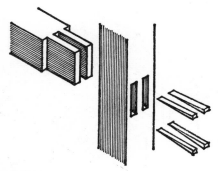

(*e*) *Double*

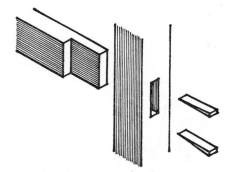

(*g*) *Bare faced*

(f) *Twin double*   A combination of types c and d, used where the rail is wide, and deep. The double tenon and the twin tenon can be haunched by leaving a shoulder of timber at top and bottom of the tenon, this joint allows a mortice lock to be fitted with less possibility of weakening the framework.

(g) *Barefaced tenon*   This variation is used when the two members to be connected are of different thickness and allows one face of the work to be flush.

(h) *Open or slot mortice*   This joint is easily made but cannot be wedged; it is used where the framing is concealed, and is secured by gluing and dowelling.

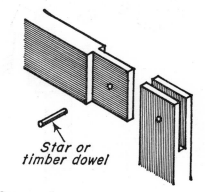

Star or timber dowel

(*h*) *Open or slot*

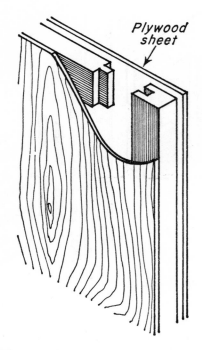

Plywood
sheet

(*i*)   *Stub*

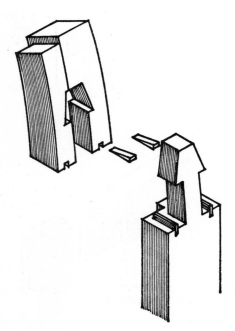

(*j*)   *Hammer head key*

(i) *Stub tenon*   This joint is not a true mortice and tenon joint, since the tenon does not strengthen the connection. It is used to rebate rails in framing, particularly where the frame is covered and therefore strengthened on both sides with a sheet material such as hardboard or plywood.

(j) *Hammer head, key*   This is a very strong joint used at the head of a semi-circular opening, as a connection between the straight and curved members.

Slot-screwing

This is a technique for joining two pieces of wood which relies on a keyhole shape cut out of a metal plate. The plate locates behind the head of a screw which is then slid into position to secure the timber. It is used to connect boards (or battens) forming say a table top. This type of fixing is also often used in locating and hanging fitted cupboards or wall units.

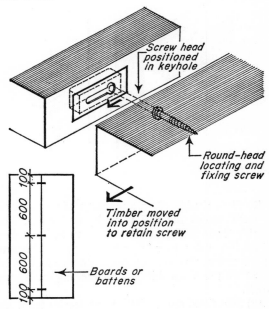

Screw head
positioned
in keyhole

Round-head
locating and
fixing screw

Timber moved
into position
to retain screw

Boards or
battens

30   *Keyhole joint*

JOINER'S SHOP PRODUCTION

The pattern of organization of the building industry at the present time is tending towards more specialization and thus in respect of the fabrication of joinery components, the general contractor will have a separate joinery manufacturing department or section at the works. Alternatively he will employ a specialist joinery sub-contractor who will have the potential in manpower and machinery to do the work. The specialist joiner will maintain his own timber stocks and in some cases kilning facilities. Specialist firms develop a reputation for very high class work for particular applications such as churches, hotels and interior fittings. In joiner's shop production the timber will be thicknessed, planed, moulded, sanded and the joints cut by machine. The parts will then be fitted together, wedged, glued, cramped and finished by hand.

A typical sequence of operations in the manufacture of timber components in a well-equipped joiner's shop will be as follows: The shop foreman 'takes off' the quantities of timber required for the component, from the architect's large scale working details or from the workshop setting out rod, and from these quantities prepares a cutting list. The information contained in the cutting list forms part of the job record which is kept for each project, and is used as a direct reference when choosing the timber required from the storage racks. The amount of timber used will be set down on a *cost/value sheet*, so that eventually the contractor can check the final cost against the estimate.

MACHINING

The basic processes are illustrated in figure 31a–f.

(a) The timber is first cut to length by means of a *circular cross cut saw*. Then a *circular rip saw* is used to cut the timber to size by determining its width and thickness. The timber is cut 'oversize', allowance being made at this stage for planing the finished timber, say 3 mm on each face. The *Standard Method of Measurement* allows a maximum of 3·2 mm. The timber then passes to the *surface planer* to provide a true *face* and *edge*. At this stage any twist or irregularity in the sawn timber is removed. The timber then passes to a *thicknesser* which reduces the timber to the right size.

(b) The *surface planer* and a *thicknesser* is often combined as one piece of machinery as illustrated.

At this stage the timber goes either to the site

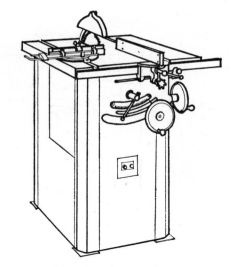

Circular saw bench

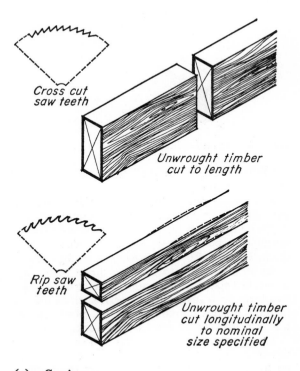

Cross cut saw teeth

Unwrought timber cut to length

Rip saw teeth

Unwrought timber cut longitudinally to nominal size specified

(*a*)   *Sawing*

31   *Machining*

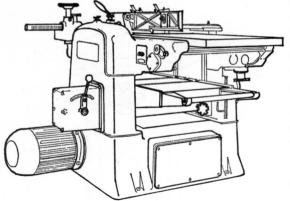

Combined planer and thicknesser

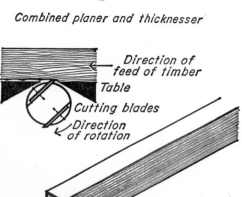

Direction of feed of timber
Table
Cutting blades
Direction of rotation

Timber wrought to finished size specified

(b)   Planing and thicknessing

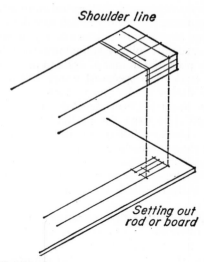

Shoulder line

Setting out rod or board

(c)   Setting-out

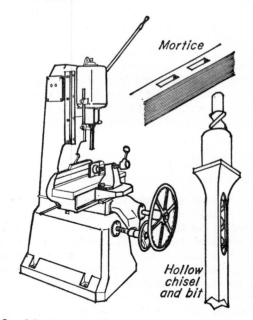

Mortice

Hollow chisel and bit

(d)   Mortising machine

for fabrication, or to the setting-out bench for further machining.

The setting out is done by the shop foreman, who draws the vertical and horizontal sections of the components full size on a plywood sheet or setting-out board, say 225 mm wide × 12 mm thick. This board is also known as a *setting-out rod.*

As an alternative to drawing direct on to plywood, full size drawings can be prepared in negative form on transparent material such as tracing paper. This has the advantage that prints can be taken to provide a record of the work.

The setting-out rods, being full-size working drawings conventionalized by the shop foreman, go to the marker out, who transfers the relevant lines on to the timber. The dimensions from the

setting-out rod can also be used by the shop foreman to produce the cutting list.

Lines of joints and cuts are marked on the timber from the setting-out rod. An accepted convention is used to indicate depth and type of cut required. Since proportions and types of joints

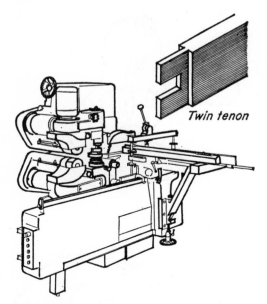

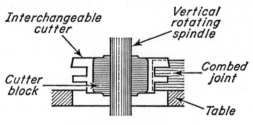

Section through cutter

(e) Tenoning

should be accepted standards, it is not always necessary to specify on a working drawing the setting out details of joints since the joinery contractor must fulfil the general clause in the Specification in respect of 'framing up'.

From the *setting-out bench* (c) the timber travels to the *morticer* (d) or the *tenoner* (e), then to the *spindle moulder* (f).

The timber can be rebated, moulded, grooved or chamfered on the spindle moulder. Standard profiles are usual, but a cutter can be specially made to any reasonable profile and circular work can be carried out.

Surface planer, thicknesser and spindle moulding operations can be combined on one machine, known as a *planer and moulder*. If this machine is used, the mortice and tenon operations are carried out later.

The following machines are ancillary to the main production line machinery.

Router for recessing to any profile as shown in figure 32.

Boring machine for drilling holes in series.

Dovetail machine for fabrication of dovetail joints, mainly used for drawer construction. The dovetail machine cuts front and sides together for a

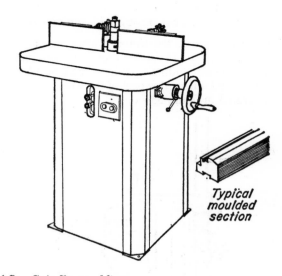

(f) Spindle moulding

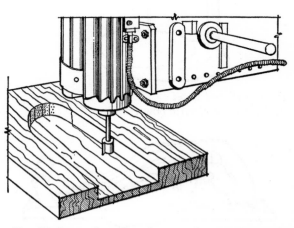

32 *High speed overhead router for cutting square or curved housings*

given number of dovetails for a specified width of timber.

Panel saw (or dimension saw) for cutting sheet materials, such as hardboard, plywood, etc, to size. *Band saw* for cutting circular work.

Sanding machines

(a) *Belt sander*, which consists of a revolving belt of abrasive sheet over which the timber is passed.

(b) *Drum sander*, which consists of a number of drums lined with abrasive sheet over (or under) which the timber passes, on a moving bed.

After machining, the timber passes forward for fabrication. Portable power tools, such as a planer, drill and hand sanding machines – disc or orbital – will be used during this part of the work. These are illustrated in figure 33a–e.

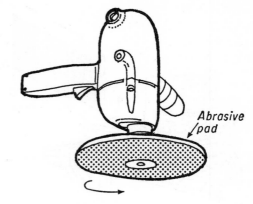

(*c*)   *Disc sander*

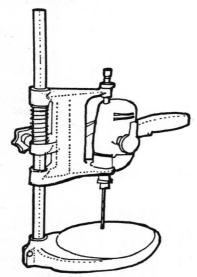

(*a*)   *Drill and stand*
33   *Portable electric power tools*

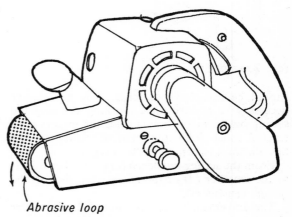

(*d*)   *Orbital*

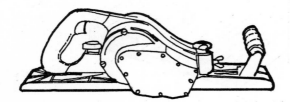

(*b*)   *Planer*

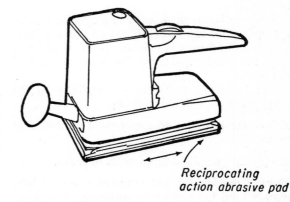

(*e*)   *Reciprocal sander*

FACTORY PRODUCTION

There are several large firms which specialize in, and are organized for, the production of standard joinery components for building such as windows, doors, cupboard fittings, staircases. These firms also manufacture 'standard sections' for skirtings, door linings and frames, and architraves. The sequence of operations is as described for the joiner's shop production except that mass production techniques are more fully exploited and the machine techniques displace the hand work in assembly and finishing. The machinery used in factory production is similar to that used in the joiner's shop except that it is on a bigger scale with a consequently quicker out-put of items.

With the development of industrialized techniques, there will be a steadily increasing demand for components to be delivered fully finished, including decoration, and where applicable in 'working order' with locks, hinges and fastenings in place.

The timber for the manufacture, on a large scale, of standard joinery components such as windows, doors and kitchen fittings as are used in housing, will be bought up to 12 months in advance of production and will require a large area to be set aside for storage.

The following description gives an indication of the processes through which the timber will pass in the conversion from the raw material to the finished product in a well equipped factory.

The timber is first stacked in the open air, and then taken by fork lift truck to an automatic machine which sorts the timber into scantlings of the same length. The timber may require further sorting if the shippers range of quality differs from the manufacturer's requirements.

After being sorted to length the timber is made up into *sets*. Each set contains a given quantity of timber, to produce a standard package for handling. The sets of imported timber are then carefully stacked under cover for a period of up to a year for further air drying. A typical set would be, say, 160 pieces of 100 × 50 mm of the same length of scantling. The majority of the timber for eventual use in external joinery will be air dried from the stacks. Timber for use in stairs and internal fittings, will be kiln dried to a moisture content of, say, 18 per cent. Kilning will take from 2 to 18 days depending on the species and samples will be regularly checked during the kilning process. It is important to remember that the timber is conditioned in the kiln and not just 'dried out'. The kilns are set automatically, and both temperature and humidity are carefully controlled, steam being injected in order to produce the correct artificial atmosphere to reduce the time scale for the process of seasoning.

From the kilns or the covered stacking sheds as appropriate, the timber is fed into the factory for processing into the separate parts which will then be assembled into the finished component ready for delivery to the site.

Figure 34 shows the machine processes involved in producing the sill and jamb sections of a standard window as follows:

(a) The seasoned, unwrought timber of the appropriate section size is first cut to length.
(b) The cut lengths are then passed forward on a conveyor to be planed to size and the initial cuts to form the section profile are made. The sill and jamb sections illustrated, will pass through the machine shop on separate production lines.
(c) The cutting process for the formation of the joints is now carried out. The mortice slots being formed in the sill section and the tenon tongue cut into the ends of the jamb.
(d) The sections now pass through the moulder, which completes the cutting of the profile, forming grooves, throat and chamfers as appropriate.

The maintenance and repair of the woodworking machinery and the sharpening of the cutters is an important facet of the production and will require a special workshop to be set up within the factory. Wherever possible the sharpening process is done by automatic control.

Matters concerning the progress or flow of the various sections of timber through the factory, ie *flowline*, are of vital importance to the successful production of the component, as are the problems associated with *batching* the items in respect of cross sectional profile (see chapter 1). The modular units of length of each section, ie sill, or jamb, must be arranged so as to make the most economic use of the scantling lengths available and, at the same time, give the opportunity to cut out and discard the parts of the scantling which are not up to specification. The manufacturer of components

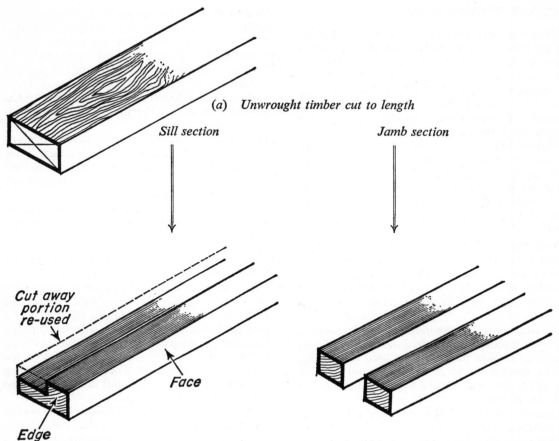

(a)   *Unwrought timber cut to length*

Sill section

Jamb section

Cut away
portion
re-used

Face

Edge

(b)   *Planer and moulder to face and edge*

(b)   *Scantling, cut into section size and passed through planer and moulder to face and edge*

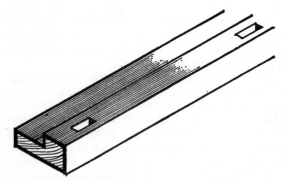

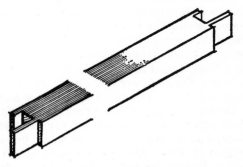

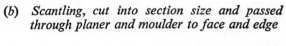

(c)   *Morticer – cuts mortice slots as required*

(c)   *Double end tenon cutter shapes tenons at each end of section*

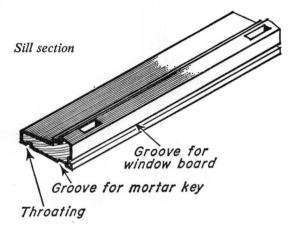

Sill section

Groove for
window board

Groove for mortar key

Throating

(*d*) *Moulder – forms sill profile and completes profile*

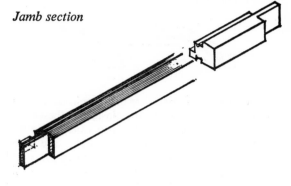

Jamb section

(*d*) *Moulder completes profile with plaster keyway, capillary grooves, etc*

34   Machine fabrication of sill and jamb section

within a modular range allows this cutting to length to be rationalized with a minimum of wastage.

Component parts with similar cross sectional profile will be batched for machining after the overall production target has been agreed. Then the manufacture of a particular cross section can be commenced in accordance with a planned cycle of known duration. Thus sills and jambs may be batched together in order to ensure that production could continue for several weeks in response to the pre-arranged target. This will reduce the *setting up* time for the machines to a minimum number of changes of cutters.

There is careful control during the whole process of manufacture, the parts being inspected at the following stages:

1 Length sorting
2 Cross cutting
3 Cleaning off
4 Finishing moulder

In addition there will be random checks that the profile is correct to size; the accurate machining ensuring that there is not significant variation in overall measurement.

In order to provide the opportunity for the fabrication of non-standard components from standard sections, it is reasonably easy for the manufacturer to cut for stock random lengths of moulded section. These can then be cut to non-standard lengths as required, separately morticed and assembled into frames of non-standard size. This takes the fabrication process out of the main production line and thus the non-standard component is more expensive, though not so costly as to be prohibitive, providing that standard sections (component parts) are used to make up the non-standard frame.

The National House Builders Registration Council require that timber used in the manufacture of components for housing must be treated with preservative. For standard components, similar sections of timber can be bundled together and vacuum impregnated before assembly. It is good practice that structural timber be factory treated with preservative in all types of buildings since the sapwood formed in some imported timbers is particularly susceptible to decay. See also *MBC: Materials*, chapter 2.

The *production* of the various parts of the finished article, ie jamb, sill or transome of a window, can be considered quite separately from the *assembly* of these parts into a finished product. Where production is on a sufficient scale a computer will be used for providing information on stock control, sales analysis, order bookings and invoicing and accounts. Figure 35a–l illustrates the various stages of the assembly of a casement and frame for a standard window.

The opening portions or lights of the window known also as the sashes, or casements, are fabricated separately.

(a) The timber sections are first machined to form the rebate to receive the glass, and then cut to length. The ends of the top rails, stiles and bottom rails of the casement are then machined in the form of a combed joint and loosely fitted together by hand. The loosely assembled casement is placed in a jig with a cramping device which squares and lines up the joints, glues them into position and automatically drives a pin or star dowel at the corners. A synthetic resin glue is used with a two hour drying period.

At this stage the section is *square ended*, ie, the glazing rebate has been formed but the outer profile has not been cut.

(b) The assembled casement is passed forward through a *drum sander* and then through a *moulder* which profiles the outer edges.

(c) The recesses of the hinges are now machine cut. The hinge which is cadmium plated, is in three parts, two interlocking cranked portions, and a separate pin. The single knuckle part of the hinge is dropped in place in the recess and machine screwed into position by zinc plated star screws.

The casement is dipped in preservative after assembly. The vacuum process cannot, in this instance, be used since the face profile is cut after assembly.

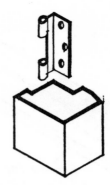

(d) The double knuckle part of the hinge is screwed into position on the jambs of the frame.

(e) The transomes are fitted into the jambs to form H frames, and then assembled and glued.

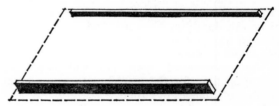

(f) The head and sill are now placed in position on an automatic cramp bed.

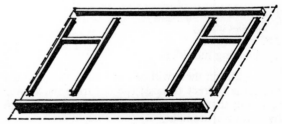

(g) The H frame is set down, on the cramp bed, the joints between the H frame and the head and sill being open and spaced slightly apart.

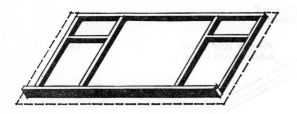

(h) The tenons are glued from a hand dispenser and the frame cramped up tight.

(i) The component is now passed through a drum sander.

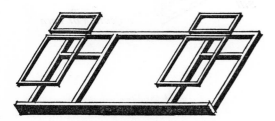

(j) The pre-assembled casements are placed in position on the window frame.

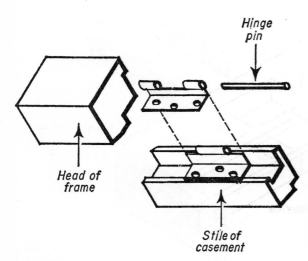

Hinge pin

Head of frame

Stile of casement

(k) The hinge pins are placed on the frame and driven home by a vibrating hammer.

(l) Following this the knots are sealed and the casements wedged open by metal dogs. The whole frame is then immersed in primer and transported through a draught tunnel, so that the surface is touch dry. The opening casements are then temporarily secured by plywood battens and the window frames stacked until required for delivery.

35 *Typical sequence of operations in the factory assembly of a standard timber window frame*

Figure 36 shows a typical standard timber window with all parts named, together with a list of the joints used.

DESIGN OF JOINTS

The possibilities and limitations of the various methods of jointing and assembly thus depend very much on a knowledge of the means of preparation of the timber. The designer, with a basic knowledge of the machines available and the various types of joint which are suitable, can make a choice, having due regard to strength, appearance and cost. The quality of joinery work depends upon three things; good materials, good design and good workmanship. The designer should thus be careful to specify exactly the type and quality of timber and sheet materials to be used and should have in mind, when producing working details, the type of joiner's shop in which the components will be manufactured. The design of the joint is affected by the rebates and mouldings which give character to the profile. Where mortice and tenon joints are used and the tenon is located in the middle third as is traditional, the moulding and the rebate should be positioned to suit this.

A scribed moulding is shown in figure 37. The moulding on one member is continuous, the shoulder of the other member being scribed to the

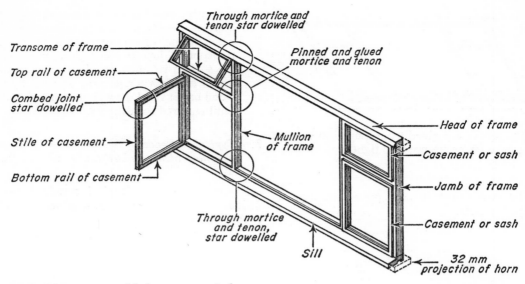

Through mortice and tenon star dowelled

Transome of frame

Pinned and glued mortice and tenon

Top rail of casement

Combed joint star dowelled

Head of frame

Stile of casement

Mullion of frame

Casement or sash

Bottom rail of casement

Jamb of frame

Casement or sash

Through mortice and tenon, star dowelled

Sill

32 mm projection of horn

36   *Typical factory-assembled casement window*

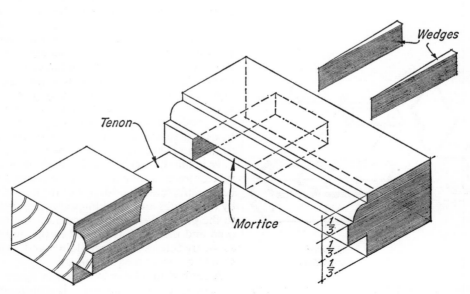

Wedges

Tenon

Mortice

$\frac{1}{3}$

$\frac{1}{3}$

$\frac{1}{3}$

37   *Scribed moulding*

reverse profile to fit onto it. It is essential to make the outer edge of the moulding at or near to a right angle to the main surface, otherwise the

39 and 40. Figure 39 shows a splayed moulding scribed to fit, whilst figure 40 shows the splay cut with a router. This latter technique forms a

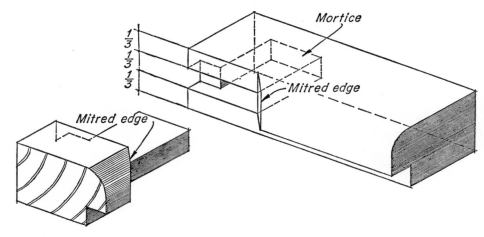

38   *Mitred moulding*

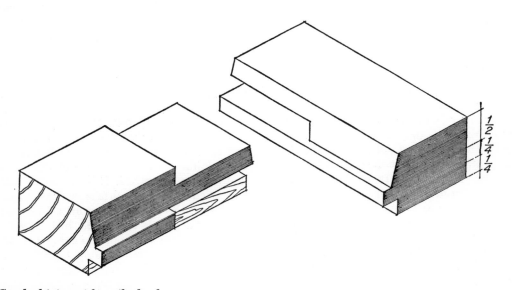

39   *Combed joint with scribed splay*

scribed end would have a feather edge which is not practicable. The mitred moulding, figure 38, avoids this, although this profile is more difficult to join neatly. In the case of the combed joint, the rebate is made to suit the moulding as shown in figures

rounded angle, leaving the full thickness of the member to form the shoulder of the joint. Part of the rounded angle will show end grain which is not entirely satisfactory but this is an easier joint to machine cut.

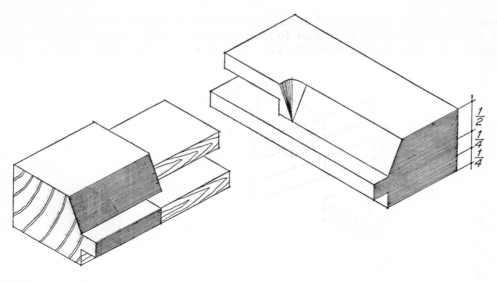

40   Combed joint with splay formed with a router

The high speed router mentioned above can be used for cutting all manner of housings and is illustrated in figure 32, page 59.

WOOD PANELLING

Designs for wood linings take advantage of the opportunity to use veneers of decorative woods such as Sycamore, which is used for its light colour, or Bird's Eye Maple or Walnut which is used for its highly decorative and patterned grain. There are many others which are currently much used, notably Rosewood and Teak. The choice of veneer will depend on the character of the room that the designer has in mind, and certain hardwoods retain popularity over many years whilst others are affected by changes in fashion. A hardwood veneer is usually available on plywood or blockboard and the use of a sheet material gives a large decorative area of panelling provided that a satisfactory method of fixing has been detailed. The problem is to make up panels of a large size which will be quite rigid when in position, and to devise a 'secret' method of fixing so that the joint is not seen. Generally 6 mm or 9 mm plywood is used and this is glued to a light framework to form units which can easily be prepared for jointing, transported to the site and fixed. Normally a length of 3·600 m is the maximum but smaller units are more easily handled and more convenient, providing that the increased number of site joints are acceptable.

Figure 41 shows a typical panel of 9 mm ply on a framing of 19 mm softwood. The framing projects beyond the ply to form a recess and skirting. There is also a recessed band below the capping and at the vertical joints. The frame members will be jointed up, so that the plywood can be glued and secured to the framing from behind. In this example the ply is on the face of the framing so that its edge is exposed. This can be sanded down and when the whole surface is polished or clear finished will give a neat appearance. In the example shown each unit is completed, including the capping, in the joiner's shop. Site fixing is to 50 × 25 mm grounds plugged or shot fired to the wall. Screws are driven in along the top edge, down the free side and along the bottom. Those along the top edge are covered with a hardwood strip, those down the free sides are hidden by the next section and those on the base will not show if set in and covered with a plug. Another good method of fixing is to have rebated grounds screwed to the back and interlocking with similar recessed grounds plugged to the walls.

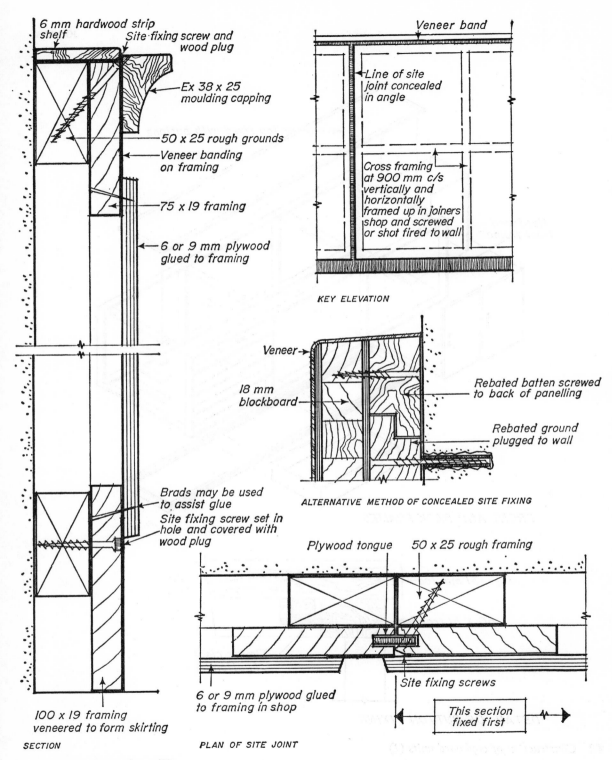

6 mm hardwood strip shelf

Site fixing screw and wood plug

Ex 38 x 25 moulding capping

50 x 25 rough grounds

Veneer banding on framing

75 x 19 framing

6 or 9 mm plywood glued to framing

Brads may be used to assist glue

Site fixing screw set in hole and covered with wood plug

100 x 19 framing veneered to form skirting

SECTION

Veneer band

Line of site joint concealed in angle

Cross framing at 900 mm c/s vertically and horizontally framed up in joiners shop and screwed or shot fired to wall

KEY ELEVATION

Veneer

18 mm blockboard

Rebated batten screwed to back of panelling

Rebated ground plugged to wall

ALTERNATIVE METHOD OF CONCEALED SITE FIXING

Plywood tongue   50 x 25 rough framing

Site fixing screws

6 or 9 mm plywood glued to framing in shop

This section fixed first

PLAN OF SITE JOINT

41   Flush plywood panelling

69

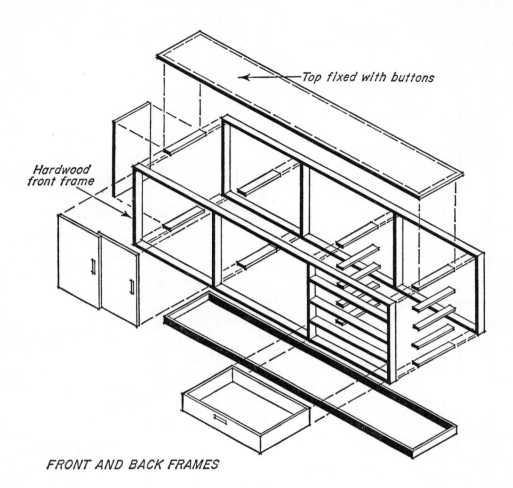

Top fixed with buttons

Hardwood
front frame

FRONT AND BACK FRAMES

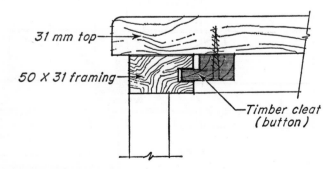

31 mm top

50 X 31 framing

Timber cleat
(button)

DETAIL OF BUTTON FIXING

42   *Construction of cupboard units (1)*

JOINERY FITTINGS

Fittings such as benches and cupboards involve framing members together in three directions. The implications of this are not always sufficiently well considered by designers who work on drawings which are two dimensional. The production of an isometric or axonometric drawing should be normal practice in detailing and would prevent many of the difficulties which arise in practice.

Cupboard units

It is best to consider the design of a fitting as a series of panels in one direction with members in the other direction joining them together. The panels themselves may be framed to the sheet covering and the members in the other direction may be panelled. When constructed in this way it will be seen that a bench could be made of a front frame and a back frame jointed with cross members as in figure 42.

These frames stand on a base which would be filled in to make the bottom of the cupboard. A slab top of cross-tongued boards or veneered blockboard would be fixed with 'buttons' (see diagram) or screws in slotted angles. These methods of fixing allow differential movement. The button fixing which is detailed on the diagram is a method of securing the top to the framing which will allow differential movement during the life of the fitting. The buttons also permit easy removal and replacement as the top becomes worn, say in the case of a bench top. Ends and vertical divisions are formed by panels, each with styles and rails and 'filled in' with plywood or by covering with plywood for a flush finish. Figure 43 shows another way of making the same fitting. Here cross members are made panelled and prepared in the joiner's shop to receive the longitudinal rails and the drawer sides. The aim in designing the fittings should be such that as much fabrication as possible can be carried out in the joiner's shop so that site labour and time in fitting is reduced. A further alternative shown in figure 44 is to make the fittings with solid ends and panels, out of 19 mm or 25 mm nominal blockboard sides, with a thin plywood back for bracing. A light framework is made for the front and back. The edges of blockboard should be lipped by machine or veneers applied. The cupboard to be fitted com-

plete and all furniture fixed in the shop. The top will be fixed as previously described or alternatively by *slot-screwing* as shown in figure 30, page 56.

Standard kitchen unit

Many joinery manufacturers make a standard range of cupboards and fittings which can be supplied from stock for kitchen units. The British Woodwork Manufacturers issue standards for this type of fitting which is manufactured under licence from the BWMA by approved firms, under the trade mark EJMA. Details of a typical fitting are shown in figure 45.

Cupboard fitting

The cupboard and drawer fitting shown in figure 46 is a single item of joinery for fixing *in situ* after fabrication in the joiner's shop. It is built up of slabs of blockboard with all exposed edges lipped and cupboards and door faces of a veneered blockboard. The blockboard horizontal members would be housed and glued to the side panels.

Counter fitting

The detail of a counter with glass screen shown in figure 47 is an example of a basic framework built out of 75×50 mm softwood and covered with 18 mm ply. The top is also of 18 mm ply veneered in plastic sheets. The framing of small members under the counter will give support to the hardwood nosing which itself helps to stiffen the construction.

Shop front details

The shop front details in figures 48 to 52 incorporate a great variety of different materials to produce a comprehensive selection of details. The fascia is framed out of 50×50 mm softwood and finished with 100×25 mm tongued and grooved and splayed hardwood boarding. The frame to the shop windows is of 100×50 mm hardwood, the glazing being secured with external hardwood beads fixed with brass counter sunk cups and screws. The showcases have a frame formed from a small steel angle screwed on a hardwood surround. The glass being retained by another angle finished

71

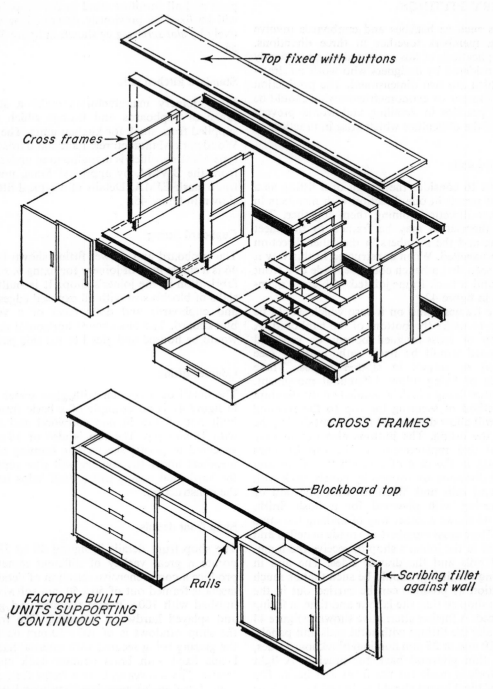

Top fixed with buttons

Cross frames

CROSS FRAMES

Blockboard top

Scribing fillet
against wall

Rails

FACTORY BUILT
UNITS SUPPORTING
CONTINUOUS TOP

43   Construction of cupboard units (2)

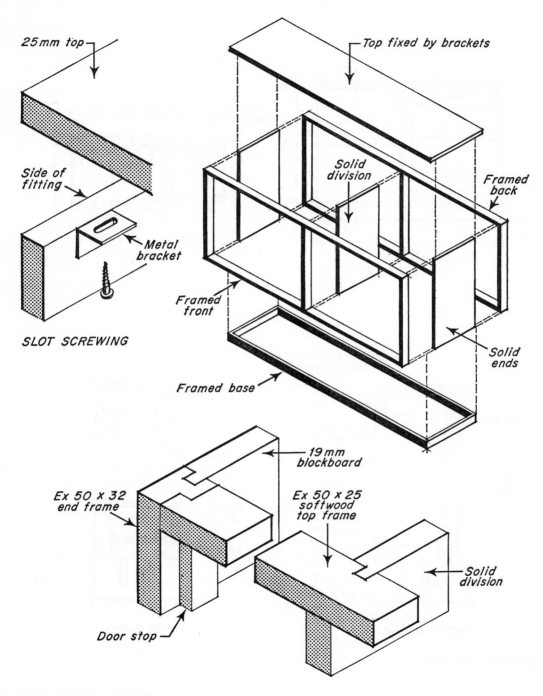

25mm top

Top fixed by brackets

Side of fitting

Solid division

Framed back

Metal bracket

SLOT SCREWING

Framed front

Solid ends

Framed base

19 mm blockboard

Ex 50 x 32 end frame

Ex 50 x 25 softwood top frame

Solid division

Door stop

44   Construction of cupboard units (3)

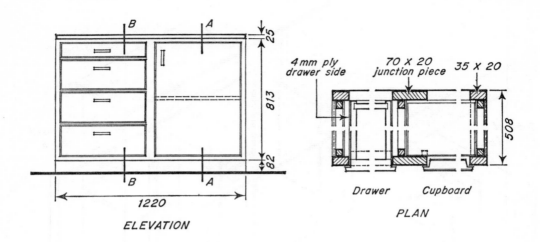

ELEVATION

PLAN

4mm ply drawer side

70 X 20 junction piece

35 X 20

Drawer   Cupboard

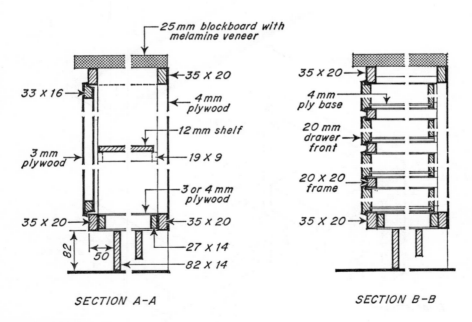

25 mm blockboard with melamine veneer

35 X 20

33 X 16

4 mm plywood

12 mm shelf

3 mm plywood

19 X 9

3 or 4 mm plywood

35 X 20

35 X 20

27 X 14

82 X 14

SECTION A-A

35 X 20

4 mm ply base

20 mm drawer front

20 X 20 frame

35 X 20

SECTION B-B

45   Standard kitchen unit

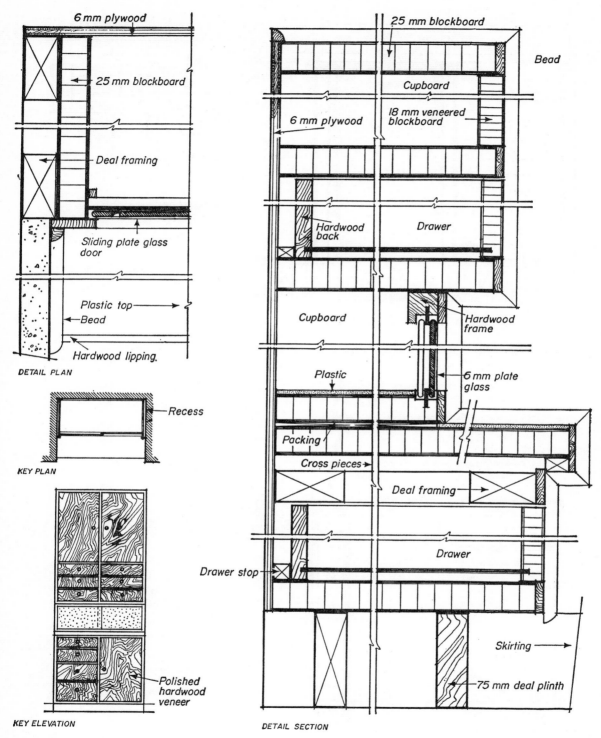

6 mm plywood

25 mm blockboard

Deal framing

Sliding plate glass door

Plastic top

Bead

Hardwood lipping

DETAIL PLAN

Recess

KEY PLAN

Polished hardwood veneer

KEY ELEVATION

25 mm blockboard

Bead

Cupboard

18 mm veneered blockboard

6 mm plywood

Hardwood back

Drawer

Cupboard

Hardwood frame

Plastic

6 mm plate glass

Packing

Cross pieces

Deal framing

Drawer stop

Drawer

Skirting

75 mm deal plinth

DETAIL SECTION

46 Cupboard fitting

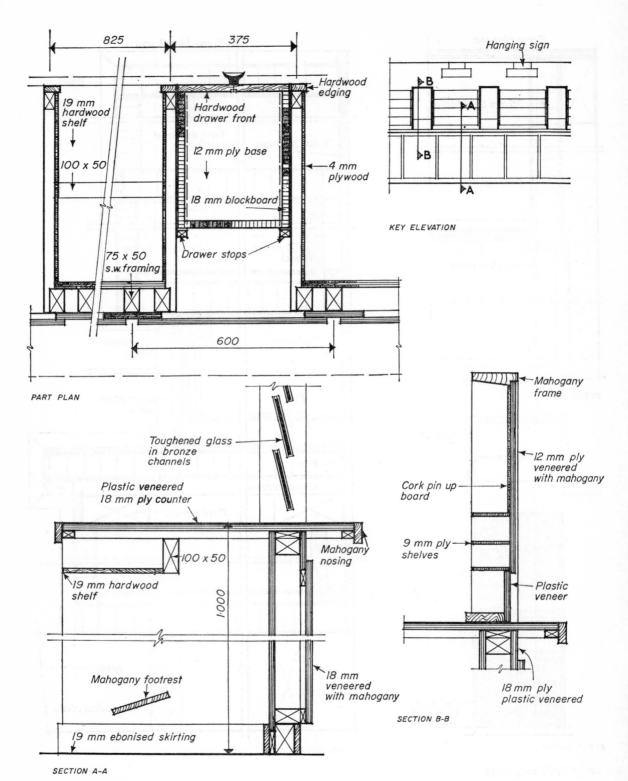

825

375

19 mm
hardwood
shelf

100 x 50

75 x 50
s.w. framing

Hardwood
edging

Hardwood
drawer front

12 mm ply base

4 mm
plywood

18 mm blockboard

Drawer stops

600

PART PLAN

Hanging sign

B

A

B

A

KEY ELEVATION

Toughened glass
in bronze
channels

Plastic veneered
18 mm ply counter

100 x 50

19 mm hardwood
shelf

Mahogany
nosing

1·000

18 mm
veneered
with mahogany

Mahogany footrest

19 mm ebonised skirting

SECTION A-A

Mahogany
frame

12 mm ply
veneered
with mahogany

Cork pin up
board

9 mm ply
shelves

Plastic
veneer

18 mm ply
plastic veneered

SECTION B-B

47   Counter with glass screen

76

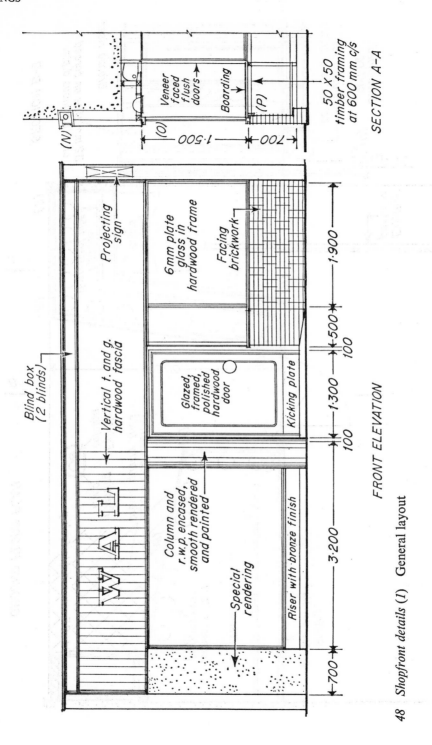

SECTION A-A

50 x 50 timber framing at 600 mm c/s

Veneer faced flush doors

Boarding

(N) (O) 1·500 (P) 700

FRONT ELEVATION

Blind box (2 blinds)

Projecting sign

6mm plate glass in hardwood frame

Facing brickwork

WALL

Vertical t. and g. hardwood fascia

Glazed, framed, polished hardwood door

Kicking plate

Column and r.w.p. encased, smooth rendered and painted

Special rendering

Riser with bronze finish

1·900 500 100 1·300 100 3·200 700

48 Shopfront details (1) General layout

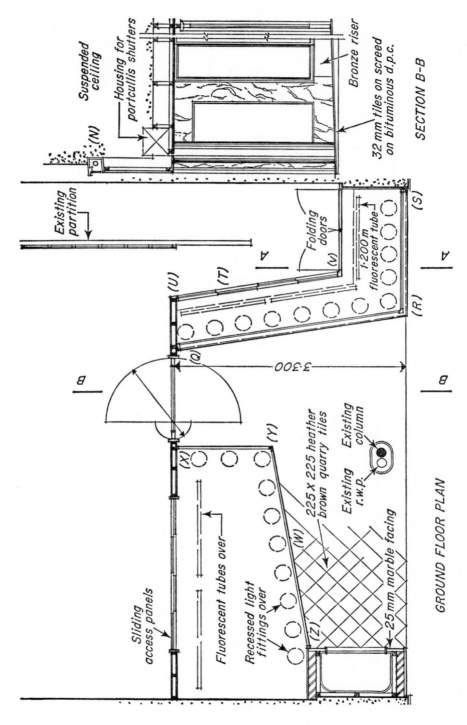

SECTION B-B

Suspended ceiling

Housing for portcullis shutters

(N)

Bronze riser

32 mm tiles on screed on bituminous d.p.c.

Existing partition

Folding doors

(S)

(v)

1·200 m fluorescent tube

A — A

(U)

(T)

(R)

B — B

(Q)

3·300

225 x 225 heather brown quarry tiles

Existing column

Existing r.w.p.

(Y)

(X)

25 mm marble facing

(W)

Sliding access panels

Fluorescent tubes over

Recessed light fittings over

(Z)

GROUND FLOOR PLAN

49 Shopfront details (2) General layout

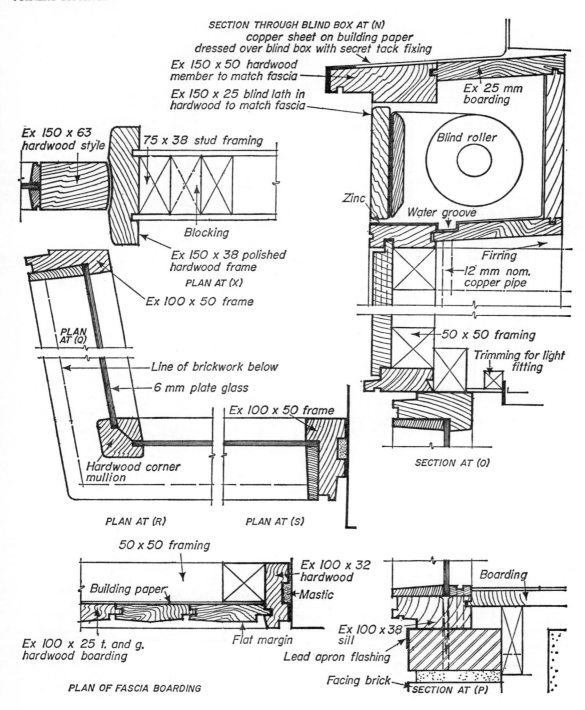

SECTION THROUGH BLIND BOX AT (N)
*copper sheet on building paper
dressed over blind box with secret tack fixing*

*Ex 150 x 50 hardwood
member to match fascia*

*Ex 150 x 25 blind lath in
hardwood to match fascia*

*Ex 25 mm
boarding*

Blind roller

*Ex 150 x 63
hardwood style*

75 x 38 stud framing

Zinc

Water groove

Blocking

*Ex 150 x 38 polished
hardwood frame*

Firring

*12 mm nom.
copper pipe*

PLAN AT (X)

Ex 100 x 50 frame

PLAN
AT (Q)

Line of brickwork below

6 mm plate glass

50 x 50 framing

*Trimming for light
fitting*

Ex 100 x 50 frame

*Hardwood corner
mullion*

SECTION AT (O)

PLAN AT (R)

PLAN AT (S)

50 x 50 framing

*Ex 100 x 32
hardwood*

Boarding

Building paper

Mastic

*Ex 100 x 25 t. and g.
hardwood boarding*

Flat margin

*Ex 100 x 38
sill*

Lead apron flashing

Facing brick

SECTION AT (P)

PLAN OF FASCIA BOARDING

50   Shopfront details (3)

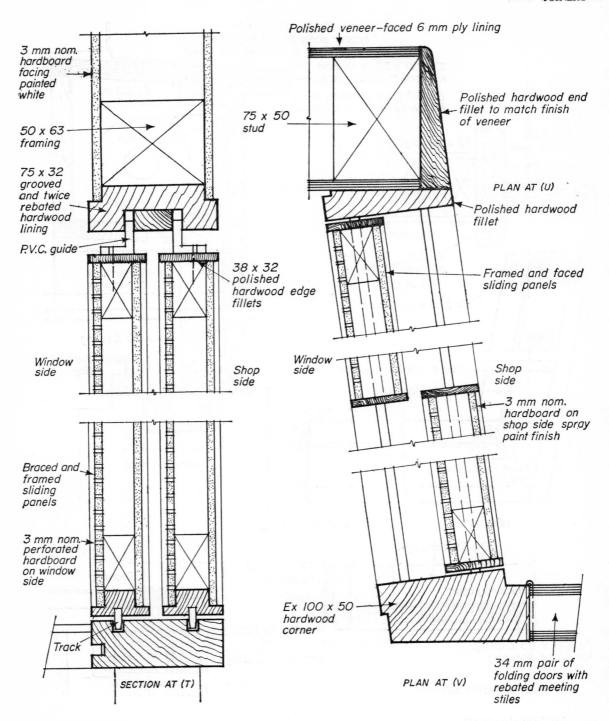

3 mm nom. hardboard facing painted white

50 x 63 framing

75 x 32 grooved and twice rebated hardwood lining

P.V.C. guide

38 x 32 polished hardwood edge fillets

Window side

Shop side

Braced and framed sliding panels

3 mm nom. perforated hardboard on window side

Track

SECTION AT (T)

Polished veneer–faced 6 mm ply lining

75 x 50 stud

Polished hardwood end fillet to match finish of veneer

PLAN AT (U)

Polished hardwood fillet

Framed and faced sliding panels

Window side

Shop side

3 mm nom. hardboard on shop side spray paint finish

Ex 100 x 50 hardwood corner

PLAN AT (V)

34 mm pair of folding doors with rebated meeting stiles

51 Shopfront details (4)

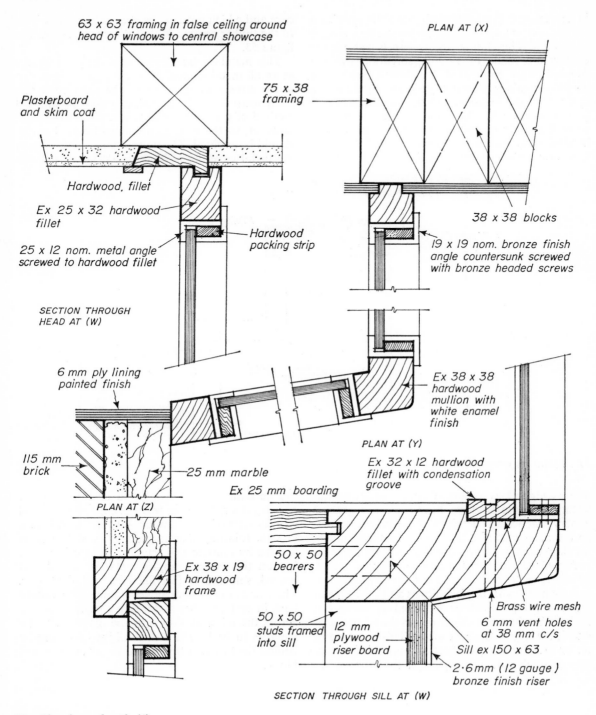

63 x 63 framing in false ceiling around head of windows to central showcase

Plasterboard and skim coat

75 x 38 framing

PLAN AT (X)

Hardwood, fillet

Ex 25 x 32 hardwood fillet

Hardwood packing strip

25 x I2 nom. metal angle screwed to hardwood fillet

38 x 38 blocks

19 x 19 nom. bronze finish angle countersunk screwed with bronze headed screws

SECTION THROUGH HEAD AT (W)

6 mm ply lining painted finish

Ex 38 x 38 hardwood mullion with white enamel finish

115 mm brick

25 mm marble

PLAN AT (Y)

Ex 25 mm boarding

Ex 32 x I2 hardwood fillet with condensation groove

PLAN AT (Z)

Ex 38 x I9 hardwood frame

50 x 50 bearers

Brass wire mesh

6 mm vent holes at 38 mm c/s

50 x 50 studs framed into sill

12 mm plywood riser board

Sill ex I50 x 63

2·6 mm (I2 gauge) bronze finish riser

SECTION THROUGH SILL AT (W)

52   Shopfront details (5)

in bronze and fixed reversed. Note the provision for the carrying away of condensation by a groove in the sill. The sliding access panels behind the display are made of 19 mm softwood framing covered with perforated hardboard, and with hardwood edging. Metal angle guides hold the top and a fibre guide secured to the panel slides in a groove in the sill. The blind box is the normal wood framed box zinc lined with a blind lath in hardwood to match the fascia. Shop fitting is a specialized trade embodying light metal work as

core and which moulds the sheet and presses it on to the timber centre. A typical section is shown in figure 53.

This metal-on-wood section is not as expensive as an all metal section. It is light, quite rigid, due to the strengthening effect of the solid core, and comparatively easily jointed. It is thus the simplest method of getting a metal finish. There are limits, however, to the profile and sharp internal angles should be avoided. The normal maximum girth of the metal covering is 30 mm, but larger sections

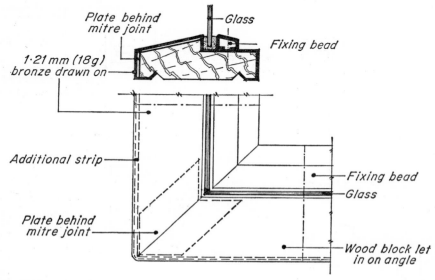

53   *Metal on wood sections*

well as high class joinery. Certain woodworking techniques used in shop fitting are not general joinery practice and details of these techniques can be found in specialist textbooks. Metal members for shop window frames and similar parts are often preferred to wood. Members entirely of metal, however, are expensive and not easily jointed except by metal working techniques and the range of sections being rolled or extruded is somewhat limited. Sections are therefore produced made of wood, covered with sheet metal. This sheet is put on by drawing the flat sheet and moulded timber core through a die slightly larger than the timber

can be built up by putting two or three smaller ones together. Note the way the edge of the metal strip is secured to the wood by turning it into a groove. Jointing of these metal-on-wood sections is done by mortice and tenon in the timber core, but on the external angles metal is mitred and brazed, soldered or just filled and polished over. The wood core at such angles is jointed by cutting back in each member and fitting a piece of timber across the mitre as shown in the diagram. If the metal is to be brazed a shielding strip should be behind the face and this would be set in the wood block.

3 Doors

A door is a moving part of a building and will be subjected to constant use and often abuse throughout its life. Therefore it must be carefully designed and detailed and well made from good materials. It must also be remembered that conditions of temperature and humidity will often be different in the rooms or spaces on each side of the door, which will produce a tendency for the door to warp or twist. The detailing must counteract this.

A door will either be of unframed, framed, or flush construction. The unframed door, consists of tongue and grooved boarding suitably jointed. Framed construction consists of an outer frame of timber, with infill either solid or glazed, to the various panels outlined by the framing. A flush door is formed by the application of sheet material such as hardboard or plywood on a suitable core.

PERFORMANCE SPECIFICATION

Function

A door is a moveable barrier to an opening in a building. Doors may be hung to swing, to slide, to fold or to revolve and the various arrangements as shown in plan form in figures 54 and 55.

Durability

Proper maintenance allied to the choice of good materials with good design and workmanship will ensure satisfactory durability throughout the life of the building, and these criteria also apply to all building components, including doors. Timber doors may need special consideration, in particular, external doors, and regular painting or clear treatment is necessary.

Weather protection

In the case of external doors, this is concerned with the exclusion of air and water. Penetration tests are often carried out by manufacturers and new British Standards are under consideration which will include this requirement. The top and bottom of the door is particularly vulnerable and special precautions in the form of throating and provision of weather bars should be taken. Figure 56 shows details of an external pre-hung door set suitable for an air and water penetration test.

Outward opening doors should, wherever possible, be set back into the opening and be provided with a projecting weather fillet to the head of the frame. Where possible the edges of the meeting styles of doors hung in pairs should be rebated. Doors should, as far as possible, be draught proof, and the use of some form of additional protection in the form of weatherstripping at the rebate is a wise precaution.

Sound and thermal insulation

With regard to thermal insulation the loss of heat through a closed door is minimal, and if the door is left open, the problem is one of human relations, and not building technology. For good sound insulation doors must be 'solid' with tight seals at all edges. Special doors are required if the criterion is high, and more important, the passage of sound between the door and frame must be restricted. Where the specification requirements are high for both sound and thermal insulation then two sets of doors with an intervening space, or vestibule, will be necessary.

Fire resistance

Precautions in respect of an outbreak of fire fall into three categories.

1 Structural fire precautions: being concerned with restricting the spread of the fire within the building. A door is regarded as a weak point in respect of fire resistance and for this reason the position and construction of doors is controlled by the Building Regulations in respect of

For side hung doors, determine the inside and outside faces, then, in relation to this, describe the direction of opening as clockwise or anti-clockwise.

For sliding doors, many variations are possible, the arrangement being determined by the choice of track as indicated.

Outside

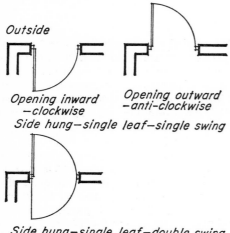

*Opening inward
—clockwise*   *Opening outward
—anti-clockwise*
Side hung—single leaf—single swing

Side hung—single leaf—double swing

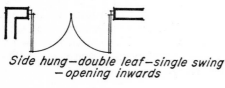

*Side hung—double leaf—single swing
—opening outwards*

*Side hung—double leaf—single swing
— opening inwards*

Outside

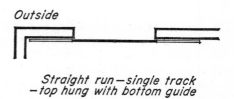

*Straight run—single track
—top hung with bottom guide*

*Straight run—single track
—sliding in cavity*

Straight run—double track—top hung

Straight run—triple track—top hung

Curved track—sliding on return wall

The sliding door can also be arranged to fold by pivoting the doors in pairs. A range of sliding, folding, internal doors is sometimes referred to as a folding partition.

Side hung—double leaf—double swing

54   Methods of hanging doors (1)

Outside

*Curved track sliding on return wall
—with pass door*

Three leaf—sliding folding door

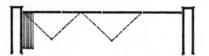

Four leaf—sliding folding door

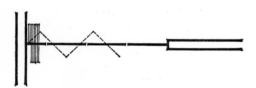

*Centre hung folding sliding door
with half leaf*

*Folded
position*

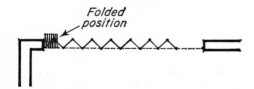

*Collapsible; on top track and bottom guide
as for a metal folding shutter gate*

*Flexible; on top track—used as an
internal partition or space divider*

REVOLVING DOORS

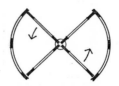

*1   Revolving position
—for draught exclusion*

*2   Leaves folded flat
to give clear passage*

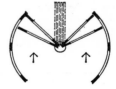

*3 Leaves collapsing against
pressure from crowd*

Revolving doors are used to form a draught-proof
lobby and are collapsible by hand to form a clear
opening. They can also be made automatically
collapsible by pressure from a crowd in case of
panic through fire or disturbance.

55   Methods of hanging doors (2)

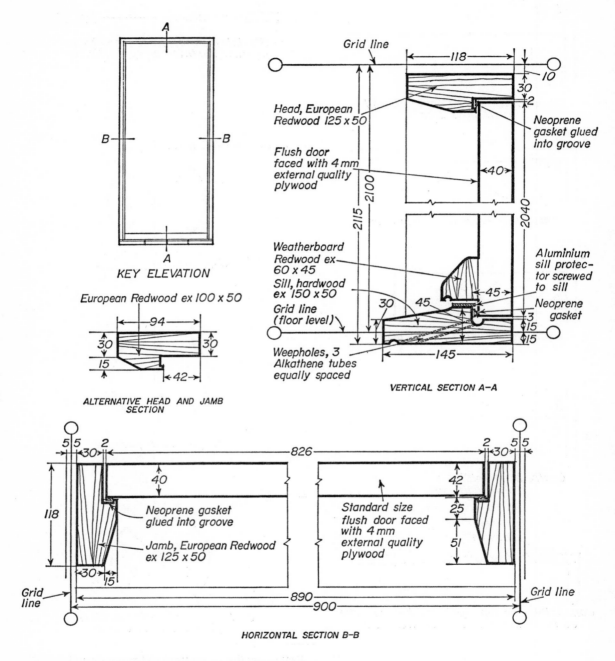

KEY ELEVATION

European Redwood ex 100 x 50

ALTERNATIVE HEAD AND JAMB
SECTION

Grid line

Head, European
Redwood 125 x 50

Flush door
faced with 4 mm
external quality
plywood

Neoprene
gasket glued
into groove

Weatherboard
Redwood ex
60 x 45

Sill, hardwood
ex 150 x 50

Grid line
(floor level)

Weepholes, 3
Alkathene tubes
equally spaced

Aluminium
sill protec-
tor screwed
to sill

Neoprene
gasket

VERTICAL SECTION A–A

Neoprene gasket
glued into groove

Jamb, European Redwood
ex 125 x 50

Standard size
flush door faced
with 4 mm
external quality
plywood

Grid
line

Grid line

HORIZONTAL SECTION B–B

56   *External prehung door set to satisfy air and water penetration test*

fire resistance. Specially constructed timber doors will resist the spread of fire for periods up to 1 hour. See figure 74, page 100.

2 Means of escape: to enable the occupants to leave the building in safety. Adequate width, correct direction of opening and method of hanging are all relevant factors in the consideration of a door as a means of escape. There are various legislative requirements appropriate to different types of buildings and the Local Fire Officer will always advise on any particular situation.

3 To restrict the movement of smoke throughout a public building during an outbreak of fire, it will be necessary to install *smoke-stop* doors (and screens) at strategic points, and in particular at the tops of stairways. These doors must be self-closing but need not necessarily be *fire resistant* doors; they must have a good fit in the rebates.

Strength and stability

A door is called upon to resist a number of stresses that will vary according to its use and position. Normal closing and opening, banging, slamming, bumping from articles being carried through and even kicking are to be expected.

In addition to these factors, the door must withstand stresses due to the variation in humidity that occur through changes in weather conditions and artificial conditions within the building.

The strength of the door is dependant on its method of construction and in respect of framed timber doors the strength is dependant on the joints used. Large sections of timber will give general solidity but the jambs will have to withstand greater internal stresses due to moisture movement. Flush doors on the other hand depend upon their total construction, since the facing is in the form of a *stressed skin*.

In addition to the air and water penetration tests already mentioned further research is being carried out with a view to devising tests for a future British Standard. The tests are concerned with resistance to torsion, heavy body impact, hard body impact, slamming and sound reduction.

UNFRAMED DOORS

These are doors made from a number of vertical tongued and grooved V jointed boards, known as *matchboarding*, which is held firm by means of horizontal members called ledges and strengthened by diagonal members known as braces. They are a traditional and much used method of construction for inexpensive exterior doors and for temporary doors. Framing, in the form of styles and a top rail, strengthens the construction and gives a door which, if properly made, has further proved itself by tradition and is much used for factory type buildings. BS 459 : Part 4 specifies the quality, construction and sizes of ledged and braced doors, and framed ledged and braced doors for general use, as follows:

Specification

The matchboard which must be tongued and grooved and jointed on both sides to be 16 mm thick and in the case of the ledged and braced doors there must be three horizontal ledges and two parallel (diagonal) braces nailed or stapled together. When nailing is used, two 50 mm nails, staggered at each ledge, and one at each brace driven below the surface and clinched tight, must be used. Alternatively the boards may be stapled to the ledges and braces with 1·63 mm (16 gauge) clinching staples 32 mm long driven below the surface by mechanically operated tools. The width of the matchboard (excluding the tongues) must be not less than 70 mm and not more than 114 mm.

Where the door is framed, the rails must be through tenoned into the styles, with haunched and wedged tenons to top and bottom rails, pinned by a hardwood dowel or non-ferrous metal star dowel. The joints must be additionally secured by adhesive or by bedding in red or white lead paint. Where weather resistant adhesive is used, the pin or dowel may be omitted. A manufacturing tolerance of 2 mm is allowable in the finished size of the door. Figures 57 and 58 show a ledged and braced door and a framed ledged and braced door to B.S.

Ledged (and battened) door

This is the simplest form of door, being in effect a number of tongued and grooved boards strengthened by a horizontal timber known as a ledge.

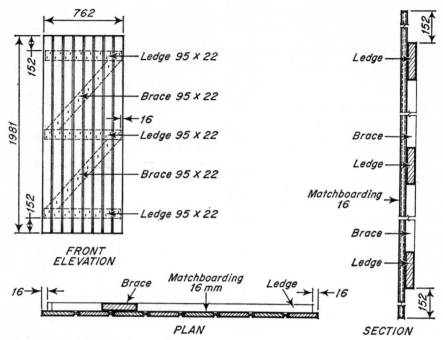

57 Details of ledged and braced door to BS 459   part 4

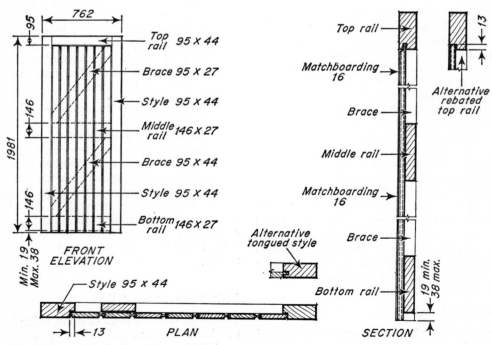

58 Details of framed, ledged and braced door to BS 459: Part 4

The ledged and battened door is mostly used for temporary work since after a time, if subjected to heavy use, it would tend to distort diagonally. This type of door is shown in figure 59 in heavier construction than the minimum laid down in the BS.

the brace must be upwards from the hanging style, so that the outer end of the brace supports the top free corner of the door. This is because the brace works in compression (not in tension) and if it is put on the other way round the joints between the battens would tend to open and the door would

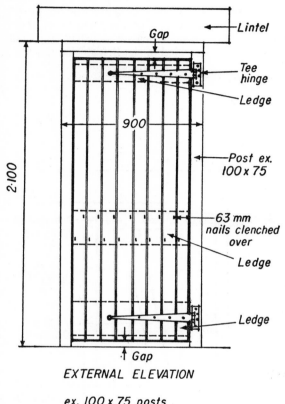

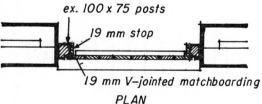

59 Ledged and battened door

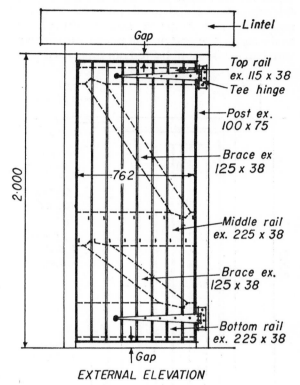

60 Ledged, braced and battened door

Ledged, braced (and battened) door

This is a more satisfactory form of construction since the diagonal braces prevent the distortion of the door. Figure 60 shows this type of door, which is often used for out-buildings. The direction of

drop on its hinges. Since there is not enough thickness of timber on the edge of the door to accommodate the screws for butt hinges, this type of door is hung on tee hinges over the face of the battens.

FRAMED, LEDGED, BRACED (AND BATTENED) DOOR

This is a refinement of the ledged and battened type and has the addition of styles, framed to top, bottom and middle rails. An example is shown in figure 61. The styles and top rail are the same thickness. Bottom and middle rails plus the thickness of the battens, are the same total thickness as the styles. The bottom and middle rails are cut with barefaced tenon, the top rail being fixed with a through, haunched tenon. The battens extend from the top rail to the ground over the middle and bottom rails in order to shed water from the face of the door. The door can be hung on strap or tee hinges, but since there is an outer frame the door can also be hung on butt hinges. Large garage or warehouse doors are made using the same principles of framing, battening and bracing shown for this type of door. The illustrations of these types of doors are of heavier construction than the minimum specified in the British Standard.

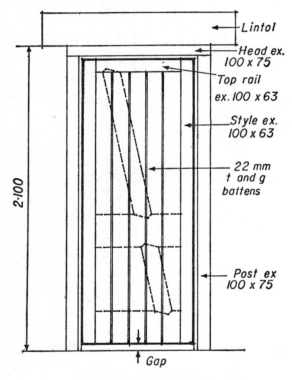

EXTERNAL ELEVATION

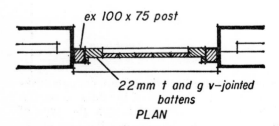

PLAN

61 Framed, ledged and braced door

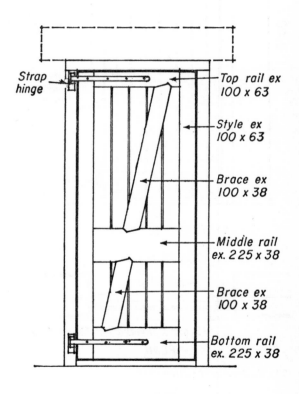

INTERNAL ELEVATION

The timber sizes shown are nominal

FRAMED DOORS

A framed or panelled door is a traditional form of construction. Its success depends on the correct proportions of the framing, the use of good quality well seasoned timber, and accurate framing up with properly made joints. The proportions of the panels must be carefully considered so that the door contributes to the architectural qualities of the building.

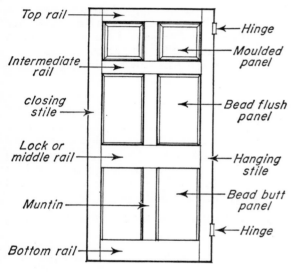

ELEVATION

62   Panelled door

The door illustrated in figure 62 has a *composite* elevation to illustrate the various forms of panel to be found in doors of this type. The horizontal rails are framed into the styles using various types of mortice and tenon joints fully illustrated in figure 29, page 54.

The vertical middle rail or *muntin* is stub-tenoned into the horizontal rails. To prevent any tendency for the rails to deform, the styles are grooved and the tenons haunched into them.

The styles (or stiles) should not be too narrow, or difficulty may be experienced in fitting suitable furniture without destroying the framing effect, and the bottom rail must be deep enough to allow proper jointing. Any excessive cutting away of the framing, particularly at the joints to fit bolts and

locks, will seriously weaken the construction and these points should be checked at the design stage, by the designer considering the application of the furniture, at the same time as the method of framing.

STANDARD PANELLED AND GLAZED WOOD DOORS

Minimum standards for framed, panelled and glazed factory made interior and exterior wood doors are set down in BS 459 : Part I : 1954 (amendments up to 1967). The specification provides for the patterns, dimensions and construction of the doors as follows:

Specification

Timber for framing and the plywood for panels to conform with BS 1186 : *Quality of Timber in Joinery. Exterior* quality plywood to be used for exterior doors.

Sizes

A guide to the types and sizes of the doors covered by the standard specification is given below:

Type	Height		Width	Finished thickness
Interior	1981 mm	×	610 mm ⎫ 686 mm ⎬ 762 mm ⎪ 838 mm ⎭	35 mm
Exterior	1981 mm	×	762 mm ⎫ 838 mm ⎬	44 mm
Glazed	1981 mm	×	762 mm ⎫ 838 mm ⎬ 914 mm ⎭	44 mm
Garage	1981 mm	×	2134 mm	44 mm

NB   In all references to BS 459, approximate metric equivalents correct to the nearest mm are given in the text. Until the appropriate British Standards are revised, however, the imperial units (given in the Standard) must be regarded as the correct dimension.

Framing

The option of dowelled or mortice and tenon joints is given for framing. The Standard specifies the finished sizes of the framing and the thickness of the plywood panels for all the types listed in the schedule. Where dowels are used they are to be of hardwood, minimum 16 mm diameter, equally spaced at not more than 57 mm centre to centre, with a minimum of three dowels in bottom and lock rail and a minimum of two for the top rail.

Where the framing is morticed and tenoned the doors must have through haunched and wedged tenons to top and bottom and one other (middle) rail. If there are more intermediate rails these are stub-tenoned (minimum 25 mm) into the styles.

For solid panels, the plywood is framed into grooves to fit tightly, the panels being cut to fit, 2 mm less in width than the grooved opening.

For glazed panels for exterior doors the opening is rebated out of the solid one side; with mitred glazing beads loosely pinned in position for delivery. All mouldings are scribed at the joints.

The adhesive used must comply with either BS 745: *Animal glue*; BS 1204: *Synthetic Resin Adhesive*; or BS 1444: *Cold Setting Casein Glue*. A manufacturing tolerance of 2 mm is allowed on the heights and widths of the finished sizes of component parts. The diagrammatic form of each of the joints mentioned is shown in 'Joints' starting on page 44.

Furniture

The doors can be supplied fitted with locks to the requirements of the purchaser, and the exterior doors prepared to receive a standard letter plate to BS 2911: *Letter Plates*.

The standard positions for butt hinges is specified.

Finish

The British Standard relates to joinery 'in the white', and if the doors are delivered unprimed they should be handled carefully and stored in dry conditions. Knotting and priming should be carried out as soon as possible and before fixing in position.

Figure 63 illustrates the BS designs for single

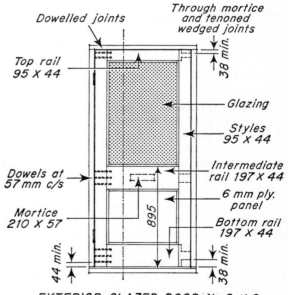

INTERIOR UNGLAZED DOOR No. 1

EXTERIOR GLAZED DOOR No. 2 X G

63 *Panelled and glazed wood doors: BS 459*

panel interior door and a standard glazed door. In addition to the two types illustrated the Standard includes three and four panelled doors and exterior doors with glazing bars. The standard garage doors have six panels.

It will be seen that the British Standard specifies minimum requirements and the panelled and framed doors described are used generally for low cost buildings.

FLUSH DOORS

BS 459 : Part 2 : 1962 (amendments to 1968) sets down the requirements for exterior and interior factory made flush doors in timber, in terms of standard dimensional design. There is no provision regarding strength or stability, since the Standard does not require any particular form of construction. Thus the reputation of, and method of construction used by the manufacturer is all important in respect of quality.

Specification

The quality (though not the type) of timber to be used is specified in detail with regard to the following matters: moisture content, amount of sapwood that may be accepted; freedom of the timber from decay and insect attack; the limitation of checks, splits and shakes; the plugging of knot holes and other defects, and the treatment of pitch pockets, ie a small cavity containing a resinous substance.

It is useful to note that pin-worm holes are permissible – under certain circumstances, providing that it can be established that the holes are made by the pinhole borer (ambrosia) beetle and no other insect. To make the diagnosis, reference should be made to the *Forest Products Research Leaflet No. 17.* The plywood facing must be in accordance with BS 1186 : *Quality of Timber*: with Moisture resistant exterior type for both sides of exterior doors. The direction of grain on the face veneer will normally be vertical. This is important where the door is to receive a clear finish.

Hardboard for facings must be to the requirements of BS 1142 : *Fibre Building Boards.*

The choice of adhesives to be used are BS 745 : *Animal Glue* or BS 1444 : *Cold Set-ting Casein Glue* or BS 1204 : *Synthetic Resin Adhesives.*

Where lippings are provided, they are to be solid, fixed to both vertical edges of the door, and measure at least 7 mm on face.

Sizes

The standard sizes are given below:

Type	Height	Width	Finished thickness
Interior	1981 mm	610 mm 686 mm 762 mm 838 mm	35 mm
Exterior	1981 mm	762 mm 838 mm	44 mm

Furniture

Provision for locks, letter plate and hinges are standardized.

Finish

The Standard specification relates to the doors, at the time of despatch from the factory, with an untreated surface. The doors should be protected from exposure to the weather to prevent deterioration during transport and storage, and after fixing. Where flush doors have to be stored on site, they must be kept protected and in dry condition – stacked horizontally on level bearers, not less than 3 cross bearers to each pile of doors. Doors should not be stacked leaning.

The use of flush doors is now almost universal in all types of buildings and there is a large range of types available reflecting considerable variation in price, quality and finish. Flush doors are a component which can be manufactured by methods using a high degree of mechanization with flow-line production techniques and automation.

Solid core

The laminated solid core door is the most expensive form of construction but gives a quality door of high sound insulation which will withstand heavy use over a long period of time. It is illustrated in figure 64. The core laminations are laid alternately to balance stresses, and thus reduce the risk of distortion. Western red cedar is a suitable timber for use in the core since it has a small moisture movement which is an important advantage where the door is subjected to changing temperature and humidity. Hardwood veneers for this class of door would be specially selected and matched for figure of grain.

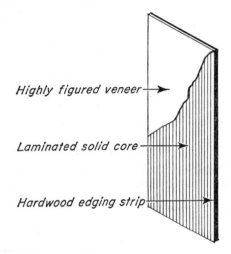

64 Solid core flush door

Semi-solid core

The semi-solid framed core medium cost door should contain 50 per cent timber, and is best constructed on the *stressed skin* principle, using the plywood to give a construction of great strength and rigidity. The edges of the door are normally lipped in hardwood to protect and cover the edges of the plywood. This type of door will also probably be veneered in hardwood, and a typical example is shown in figure 65.

Skeleton frame

The skeleton frame door shown in figure 66 is a less expensive method of framing which produces a door suitable for low cost contracts. This class of door would be faced with hardboard or plywood for painting.

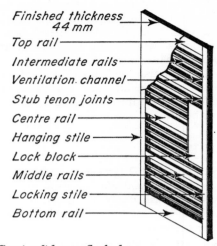

65 Semi-solid core flush door

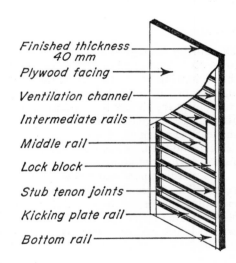

66 Skeleton framed flush door

Cellular core

There are various proprietary methods of producing a suitable cellular core such as a hardboard 'eggbox' or lattice construction. Both of these are illustrated in figures 67 and 68. Expanded cellular paper-board, extruded wood chipboard, flaxboard, and a method of utilizing timber 'shavings' in the form of precision cut spirals, are also commonly used for the core. Whichever form of construction is used it must avoid the defect of surface undulation where the 'ripple effect' reflecting the construction of the core is seen on the face of the door. The cost of these doors is related

is also used in the furniture industry. The method and type of lipping is also a guide to the cost of the door; the cheapest range will be unlipped, the medium range will be lipped on the vertical edges, either with parana pine or hardwood, and the most expensive range will have a matching hardwood lipping to all edges. It is in any case neces-

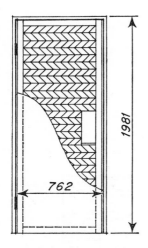

35 MM INTERIOR FLUSH DOOR
—expanded cellular board infill

*Dimensions correct
to nearest mm*

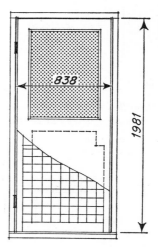

44 MM EXTERIOR FLUSH DOOR
— hardboard lattice core

67   *Cellular core*

68   *Lattice core*

to the type of facing that is used, and in ascending order of cost the range is as follows:

1 Painted hardboard.
2 Inexpensive plywood facing for painting.
3 A medium cost plywood facing finished at the factory with a clear finish. This type of clear finish has the double advantage of sealing the timber and enhancing the grain of the facing.
4 A sliced cut figured hardwood veneer plywood of timbers such as sapele, teak, oak, walnut and afrormosia, finished and protected at the factory by a clear lacquer.

The technique of utilizing a grain printing process to reproduce hardwood figure, either on hardboard or an inexpensive plywood is now also used in the manufacture of flush doors. This technique

sary to lip exterior doors on all edges for weather protection. It is important that a highly finished component such as a flush door, manufactured under strictly controlled conditions, should be carefully stored and handled on site. Manufacturers will not usually guarantee doors unless they are stored flat and dry, protected until ready for use, and not hung in a damp or freshly plastered building.

DOOR FRAMES AND LININGS

Doors are hung on either frames or linings within an opening, the difference being that a lining provides a covering to the reveals (sides) and soffit (upper surface) of an opening. A frame should always be strong enough to support the door without help from the main structure of the building;

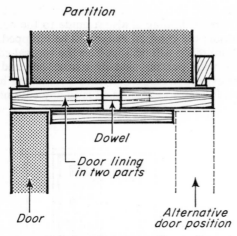

Partition

Dowel

Door lining
in two parts

Door

Alternative
door position

69   Dowelled door lining to allow adjustment
for various thicknesses of partition

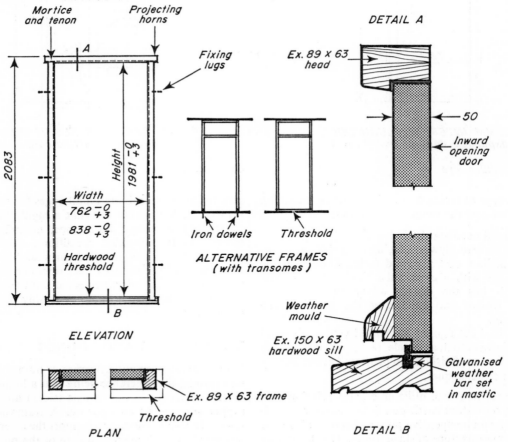

Mortice
and tenon

Projecting
horns

Fixing
lugs

2083

Height $\frac{-0}{+3}$
1981

Width
762 $\frac{-0}{+3}$

838 $\frac{-0}{+3}$

Hardwood
threshold

A

B

ELEVATION

Iron dawels

Threshold

ALTERNATIVE FRAMES
(with transomes)

Ex. 89 × 63 frame

Threshold

PLAN

DETAIL A

Ex. 89 × 63
head

50

Inward
opening
door

Weather
mould

Ex. 150 × 63
hardwood sill

Galvanised
weather
bar set
in mastic

DETAIL B

70   Timber door frames

a lining on the other hand is supported to a certain extent by the construction surrounding the opening. Neither frame nor lining must support any construction other than the door.

The size of the opening within the frame should allow between 2 mm and 3 mm clearance for hanging and adjusting the door. Rebates to receive the door should be minimum 12 mm deep, the rebate can either be recessed into a frame from the solid, or usually formed by a planted stop on the surface of a lining. A planted stop has the following advantages:

1 It makes a more economical use of timber.
2 Providing it is only temporarily pinned in position it can be adjusted on site to suit the door after it is hung.
3 Doors can be hung on either side of the stop, making the 'handing' of linings unnecessary.
4 Linings can be prefabricated in two separate halves, loosely dowelled together so that they can be adjusted on site to fit varying widths of partition. The planted stop fixed on site will then cover the gap between the two parts of the lining. An example of this construction is shown in figure 69.

Frames and linings appropriate to panelled and flush standard doors are described in BS 1567: 1953 and standard sections for an inward opening external door shown in figure 70.

The backs of frames should be protected against moisture penetration by priming paint before fixing.

Frames are now usually 'built in' as the work proceeds. Temporary strutting is necessary until the walling is built and metal cramps or lugs, as shown in figure 71, should be screwed to the back of the frame so as to coincide with the joints in the masonry, say three lugs to each side of the opening. Projecting 'horns' on the frame can also be built in to assist in restraining the frame. If a threshold is not fitted, metal dowels protruding from the foot of the post should be let into the step. The joint between door frame and the masonry opening should be raked out to a depth of say 12 mm and pointed with a suitable mastic. The mastic will probably be gun applied, and the width of mastic filling to the joint should be at least 6 mm or it will be ineffective. A detail is shown in figure 72.

Linings, on the other hand, must be fixed after the opening is formed. Timber pallet pieces (elm

is preferable) are built into the brickwork or blockwork joints and the lining screwed or nailed to these. In good class work the screws would be counter sunk and pelleted in timber matching the

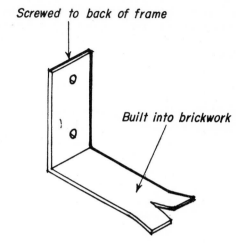

Screwed to back of frame

Built into brickwork

71   *Fixing cramp*

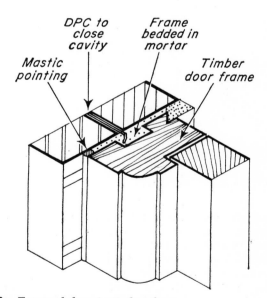

Mastic pointing

DPC to close cavity

Frame bedded in mortar

Timber door frame

72   *External door in timber frame*

frame to conceal the screw head. It may be necessary, particularly if the opening is wide, to fix the lining at the soffit also.

If the wall is plastered it is necessary to provide

7—C.F.

architraves (cover strips) to cover the joint between the lining and the plasterwork.

STANDARD TRIM

For low cost contracts *standard trim* sections as covered by BS 584 : 1967 : *Specification for wood trim*, would be of suitable section. The architrave sections are shown in figure 73.

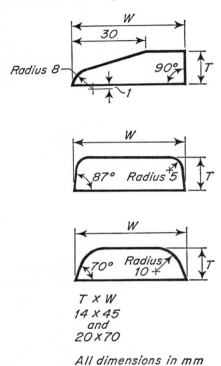

All dimensions in mm

73 Standard architraves: BS 584

Architrave details are shown in figures 84 and 85. Care should be taken to ensure that the thickness of the architrave is greater than the thickness of the skirting in order to avoid an awkward detail at the architrave-skirting junction. Traditionally a block of timber known as an architrave block was fixed at this point, against which both architrave and skirting butted.

The BS trim can be specified to be delivered at one of two alternative levels of moisture content, (a) 14 to 17 per cent where the conditions are such that the moisture content can be substantially maintained until completion of the building, or (b) not greater than 20 per cent.

The lower moisture content will be preferable since it will reduce the risk of movement and twisting of the trim after fixing.

FIRE RESISTANT DOORS

Buildings are divided into compartments separated by fire resisting barriers as defined in the Building Regulations and it is often necessary to provide for the passage of people through these barriers in which case fire resisting doors (which have *metal*, not plastic hinges) or shutters are necessary. Openings may also have to be made in floors in the form of trap doors and although this will not be a common procedure the rules apply.

Doors in walls separating flats or maisonettes from common access areas and doors between houses and small garages may be of one of two types – (a) single leaf opening one way, or (b) double leaf, each leaf opening in the opposite direction. Such doors must satisfy BS 476 : *Fire Tests on Building Materials and Structures*, in the following particulars:

1 Freedom from collapse – 30 minutes (half hour fire resistance)
2 Resistance to passage of flame – 20 minutes
3 Resistance to passage of heat – no requirement. The doors must also be self-closing by means of an automatic device, but in this case the use of rising butts is permitted as a method of automatic closing.

In other types of building, doors in 'protected shafts' where the doors open to a hall or corridor (providing that the surrounding walls are of the required period of fire resistance) may consist of one of the following types:

1 Single leaf, opening one way
2 Double leaf, each leaf opening in the opposite direction
3 Single leaf double swing
4 Double leaf double swing.

The double swing doors must have clearance between door and frame as small as is practicable. All fire resisting doors must be self-closing and doors may not be hung on hinges which are made of combustible material. Fusible links are permitted and these are usually fitted in connection with doors hung on a descending track. A fusible link 'fails' at high temperature, allowing automatic door mechanism to operate. The regulations require that if such doors are used in protected shafts then a normal door must be provided in the same opening. If there are two doors in an opening it is sufficient if the required fire resistance is achieved by both doors taken together.

FIRE-CHECK FLUSH DOORS

Fire check flush doors and wood and metal frames are specified in BS 459 : Part 3 : 1951 (amendments to 1968). The doors can be manufactured to give half hour fire resistance, or one hour fire resistance in accordance with the requirements of the Building Regulations relative to the use and position of the doors. Doors made and fixed in accordance with the Specification will provide an effective barrier against the passage of fire for the period stated. Doors of this type of construction are termed *fire-check* doors.

Specification

Timber and plywood in accordance with BS 1186 : *Quality of Timber in Joinery*; plasterboard to comply with BS 1230 : *Gypsum Plasterboard*; Asbestos wall board or asbestos insulation board is permitted in accordance with BS 3536. However, it must be noted that ordinary asbestos sheeting to BS 690 : *Asbestos Cement Sheet*; is not suitable.

Hardboard must be in accordance with BS 1142 : *Fibre Building Boards*; Adhesives to be BS 745 : *Animal Glues* or BS 1204 : *Synthetic Resin Adhesives* or BS 1444 : *Cold Setting Casein Glue*. For external doors, either gap-filling or close contact synthetic resin adhesives must be used.

Sizes and construction

838 mm or 914 mm are standard widths, with a standard height of 1981 mm.

Half hour type doors	One hour type doors
Minimum finished thickness 44 mm. Styles, top and bottom rails to be not less than 38 mm thick and 95 mm wide rebated both sides 25 mm to receive the protective plasterboard infill.	Minimum finished thickness 54 mm. Framing as for half hour type.
Middle rail 38 mm thick and 165 mm wide.	
Intermediate rails not less than 44 mm wide. Protective infil panels of 9 mm thick plasterboard fitted into the rebates and nailed to the framework.	Protective infill of plasterboard as for half hour type.
	Asbestos wall board or insulating board 5 mm thick glued over the whole area of the face of the door. The board to be applied in one piece and no metal fastenings to be used.
Plywood or hardboard facing 3 mm thick glued over the whole of the area of the face of the door – no metal fixings to be used.	Plywood or hardboard facing as for half hour type.
Doors may be used without lippings, but where these are required they must be no more than 9 mm on face and glued to the styles and rails. The lippings may be either tongued and grooved or straight profile on cross section – no metal fixings to be used. Lipping can be on one or both vertical edges, or all four edges.	Lippings as for half hour type, but must be tongued and glued, into grooves in the styles and rails.
External doors must be lipped on all four edges.	

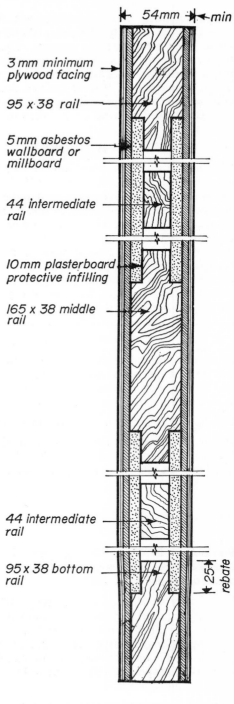

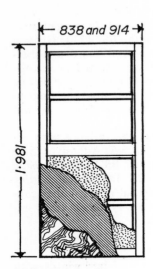

ELEVATION with facing
materials cut away

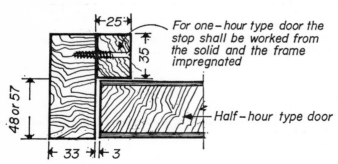

25

For one-hour type door the
stop shall be worked from
the solid and the frame
impregnated

35

48 or 57

Half-hour type door

33 — 3

TIMBER DOOR FRAME
minimum dimensions

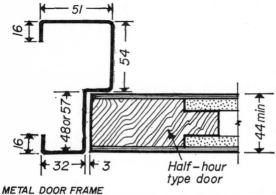

51

16

54

48 or 57

16

44 min

32 — 3

Half-hour
type door

METAL DOOR FRAME
minimum dimensions

74 *Fire check doors: BS 459: Part 3*

3 mm minimum
plywood facing

95 x 38 rail

5 mm asbestos
wallboard or
millboard

44 intermediate
rail

10 mm plasterboard
protective infilling

165 x 38 middle
rail

44 intermediate
rail

95 x 38 bottom
rail

54mm — min

25
rebate

SECTION one-hour type check
flush door

Doors are to be marked on the hanging style to BS 459 : Part 3 : *Half Hour* or *One Hour* as appropriate. Typical details of fire-check doors and frames to BS 459 is shown in figure 74. The dimensions are given to the nearest mm.

Frames in wood to have 25 mm rebate as shown in the diagram, and if this is formed by a stop, it

in mind, since locks with a small back set will be unsuitable. Since, to be effective, fire-check doors must be kept closed, self-closing springs, or falling butt hinges must be specified.

The British Standard specifies two types of timber fire-check doors which can be mass produced reasonably easily, but any door in its frame,

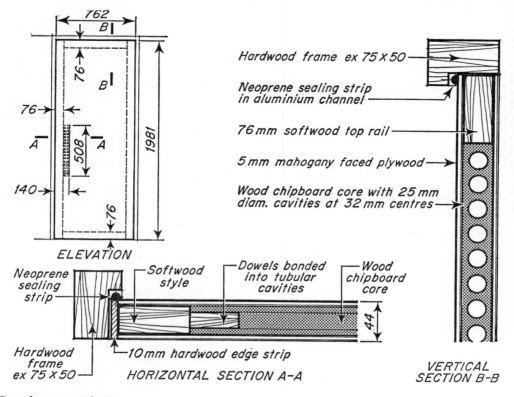

75   *Sound resistant door*

is to be fixed by 38 mm long No. 8 screws spaced 76 mm from each end and not more than 610 mm apart. The one hour type door must have the frames rebated out of the solid, and pressure impregnated with 15 to 18 per cent solution of mono-ammonium phosphate in water. Maximum clearance between door and frame when hung to be 3 mm. Metal frames to BS 1245 : *Metal Door Frames*, with one pair of hinges for half hour doors but 1½ pairs of hinges for 1 hour doors.

The type of fastening to be used will be determined by the use of the door. Where locks are required the large rebate of the frame must be borne

which has been shown by test in accordance with BS 476 : Part I : *Fire Tests on Building Materials* to give a similar performance to the doors described in the Standard, can be used as a fire-check door for the appropriate period.

SOUND RESISTANT DOORS

A type of flush door which would be expected to give a sound reduction of 37 decibels (dB) is shown in figure 75. To achieve this reduction in practical terms the door must be hung as shown in a hardwood frame, with sealing strips at the rebate, and

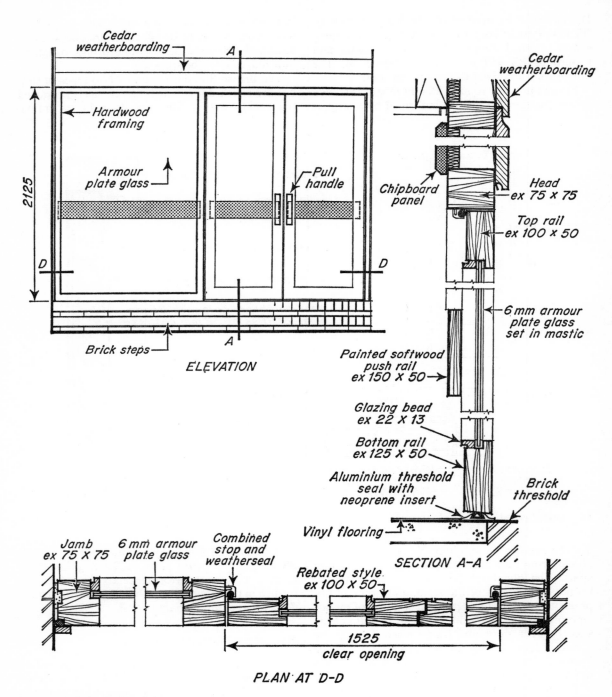

Hardwood
framing

Armour
plate glass

Pull
handle

2125

Brick steps

ELEVATION

Cedar
weatherboarding

Chipboard
panel

Head
ex 75 X 75

Top rail
ex 100 X 50

6 mm armour
plate glass
set in mastic

Painted softwood
push rail
ex 150 X 50

Glazing bead
ex 22 X 13

Bottom rail
ex 125 X 50

Aluminium threshold
seal with
neoprene insert

Vinyl flooring

Brick
threshold

SECTION A-A

Jamb
ex 75 X 75

6 mm armour
plate glass

Combined
stop and
weatherseal

Rebated style
ex 100 X 50

1525
clear opening

PLAN AT D-D

76   Hardwood glazed doors

102

the frame must be adequately secured to the walling, which should be at least 190 mm thick solid masonry to achieve the reduction indicated. The dB reduction required to eliminate a normal conversation from one side of a construction to another would be 28 dB. This is a normalized level difference represented by the door in its frame as shown, well fitted in the wall. The figure takes into account the combination of, and the different dB ratings for door and wall.

GLAZED DOORS

In addition to the standard panelled glazed door previously described, purpose made glazed doors are very much used so that persons passing through can see if anyone is coming from the opposite direction. Where these doors are used in entrances, as they often are, a very heavy use is made of them and sound construction is essential. Figure 76 shows an example of a pair of glazed doors in hardwood as part of a glazed entrance screen detail. Points to emphasize are the weather stripping by neoprene gaskets in extruded aluminium sections at the threshold, and the extruded aluminium weather stripped door stops. Further details of this type of weatherstripping are given on page 123.

Since this type of door will be in constant use it is sensible to use a floor spring as a means of controlling the movement. The floor spring can be fitted with a device which checks the doors open at 90°.

Another example of glazed door construction is shown in figure 77. This is a range of doors formed from extruded aluminium sections and is suitable for an hotel or department store entrance. The profiles are neat and points to note are the draught-proofing by woven pile strip and the different methods of securing the glazing in the door and fanlight.

GLASS DOORS

Figure 78 illustrates a toughened plate glass door and side screen of the type fitted at the entrance to shops and showrooms. The door is controlled by an adjustable top centre pivot hung on a double action floor spring. A special lock will be fitted in the top and bottom metal rails with the lock keepers set into the hardwood frame and concrete floor. The attractive feature of this type of door is its transparency, but it is sometimes difficult to know when the door is open, and for this reason some form of decoration may be fixed to the door to indicate its position.

LOUVRED DOORS

This is a form of door which is now much used both internally for decorative purposes and externally where permanent ventilation is required. In the example shown in figure 79 the louvres are housed into a vertical louvre style which is then shop glued within the panel formed by the main framing of the door. The edges of the louvres, because of their projection in front of the face of the door, are chamfered off at the corners. The louvre slats are set at 45° and fixed so that there is a minimum overlap of 3 mm. The door is shown closing against an extruded aluminium threshold.

FLEXIBLE DOORS

This type of door is used where it is not possible for the user to open the door in the normal way. The most usual applications are in industrial buildings, warehousing or hospitals where the user may be pushing or driving a trolley or carrying bulky packages. It is a comparatively inexpensive alternative to installing automatic opening and closing devices. The door is composed of a flexible membrane of either reinforced rubber or neoprene, or where complete vision is desired for safety in operation, and the use is not excessive, transparent or translucent plastic sheet. In any case, because of the risk of collision, this type of door would be fitted with a clear plastic vision panel.

The door is designed to open on impact, the flexibility of the sheeting taking the force out of the 'collision', and allowing the user to pass through. The doors then close automatically, being controlled by jamb spring hinges. The door illustrated in figure 80 is a lightweight door formed by a steel angle supporting frame at the head and hinged side, from which is hung a flexible sheet of 8 mm reinforced rubber clamped into the heel of the angle by means of a steel flat. The hinges are double action vertical spring type. For larger doors up to say 4·000 m high by 4·000 m wide the framing would be of steel tubing with the spring mechanism made as a separate detachable unit, and arranged to slide inside the vertical tube framing from the

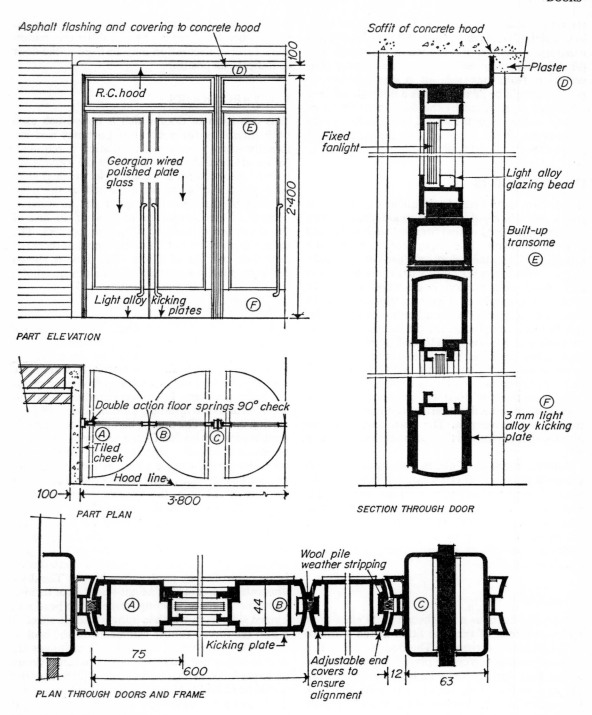

Asphalt flashing and covering to concrete hood

R.C. hood

(D)

(E)

Georgian wired polished plate glass

Light alloy kicking plates

(F)

100

2·400

PART ELEVATION

Double action floor springs 90° check

Tiled cheek

(A) (B) (C)

Hood line

100→ 3·800

PART PLAN

Soffit of concrete hood

Plaster (D)

Fixed fanlight

Light alloy glazing bead

Built-up transome (E)

(F)

3 mm light alloy kicking plate

SECTION THROUGH DOOR

Wool pile weather stripping

(A) 44 (B) (C)

Kicking plate

75

600

Adjustable end covers to ensure alignment

12

63

PLAN THROUGH DOORS AND FRAME

77 Glazed aluminium doors

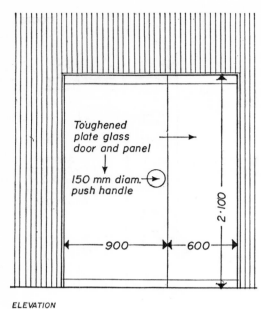

ELEVATION

- Toughened plate glass door and panel
- 150 mm diam. push handle

900   600

2·100

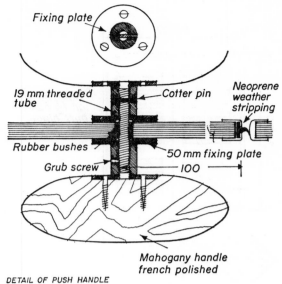

DETAIL OF PUSH HANDLE

- Fixing plate
- 19 mm threaded tube
- Cotter pin
- Neoprene weather stripping
- Rubber bushes
- 50 mm fixing plate
- Grub screw
- 100
- Mahogany handle french polished

25 mm nom. sapele boarding

75 x 38 nom. softwood frame

38 x 200 nom. sapele frame

Hardwood fixing block

Metal top rail finished in satin chrome

12 mm toughened plate glass

3 mm synthetic – resin floor

9 mm cork tiles cover plate

Double action floor spring

SECTION THROUGH FIXED PANEL

SECTION THROUGH DOOR

78   Glass door

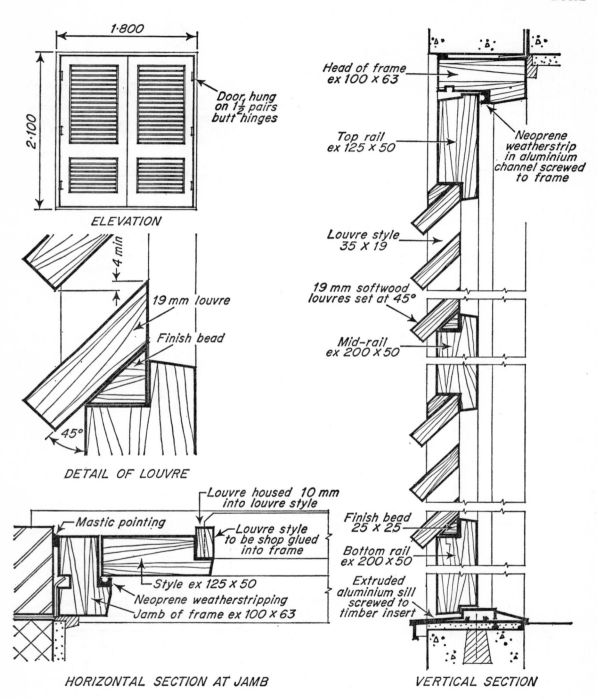

1·800

2·100

Door, hung
on 1½ pairs
butt hinges

ELEVATION

4 min

19 mm louvre

Finish bead

45°

DETAIL OF LOUVRE

Head of frame
ex 100 × 63

Top rail
ex 125 × 50

Louvre style
35 × 19

19 mm softwood
louvres set at 45°

Mid-rail
ex 200 × 50

Neoprene
weatherstrip
in aluminium
channel screwed
to frame

Louvre housed 10 mm
into louvre style

Mastic pointing

Louvre style
to be shop glued
into frame

Style ex 125 × 50
Neoprene weatherstripping
Jamb of frame ex 100 × 63

HORIZONTAL SECTION AT JAMB

Finish bead
25 × 25

Bottom rail
ex 200 × 50

Extruded
aluminium sill
screwed to
timber insert

VERTICAL SECTION

79   Timber louvre door

106

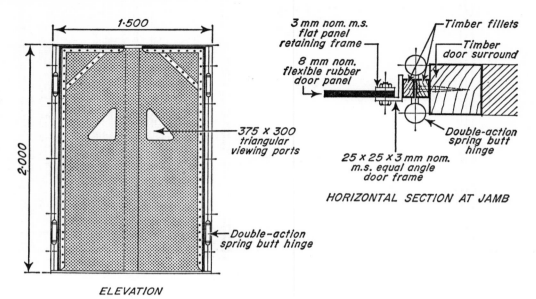

80   Lightweight flexible rubber doors

top. The heaviest doors are suitable for openings which are used by large vehicles and other heavy industrial transport.

BRONZE DOORS

In complete contrast a pair of purpose made, monumental cast bronze doors is shown in figures 81 and 82. The doors are set round a rolled steel channel framing which is *rawlbolted* into the main structure of the building. The doors swing on single action floor springs. The separate moulded sections forming the door frame are clipped back to the main steelwork by metal straps, and are also 'tucked in' to the stone surround to the opening. These doors are examples of fine craftsmanship in a traditional setting and would be a dominant element in any architectural composition.

VESTIBULE DOORS

Figures 83 and 84 show the application of a pair of purpose made hardwood doors to close off a vestibule for extra security when the building is shut up for the night. Teak would be a suitable timber to use in this instance. A pair of hardwood glazed doors form the main entrance doors to the building. A special feature of these doors is the *rounded corner* detail at the junction of the styles and rails. Toughened glass should, of course, be used in this situation. The *night doors* are a form of folding door. Each side of the opening having a pair of doors hung leaf on leaf. Note that the method of hanging is devised so that the edges of the doors do not show and the outer door forms a decorative hardwood lining to the sides of the vestibule during the day. The entrance doors are hung on double action floor springs to allow the doors to act as a means of escape in the case of fire during the time that the building is in use, and the fact that the line of swing impedes the outer doors does not matter since the two sets of doors will not be in use at the same time. Each of the night doors will be hung on 1½ pairs (3 to each door) of substantial brass hinges. The doors are an example of good class joinery work and will have to be carefully made and well hung to avoid trouble in use, since the stress on the hinges to the outer doors will be considerable.

SLIDING AND SLIDING-FOLDING DOORS

These types of doors are now much more used and providing that the problems of manipulation and

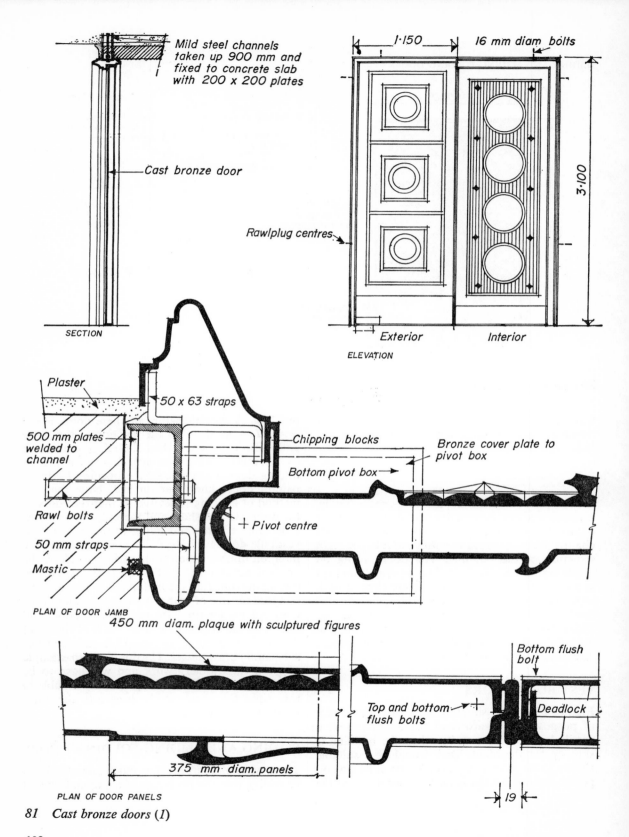

Mild steel channels
taken up 900 mm and
fixed to concrete slab
with 200 x 200 plates

Cast bronze door

SECTION

1·150   16 mm diam bolts

Rawlplug centres

3·100

Exterior   Interior

ELEVATION

Plaster

50 x 63 straps

500 mm plates
welded to
channel

Chipping blocks

Bronze cover plate to
pivot box

Bottom pivot box

Rawl bolts

Pivot centre

50 mm straps

Mastic

PLAN OF DOOR JAMB

450 mm diam. plaque with sculptured figures

Bottom flush
bolt

Top and bottom
flush bolts

Deadlock

375 mm diam. panels

PLAN OF DOOR PANELS

19

81   Cast bronze doors (1)

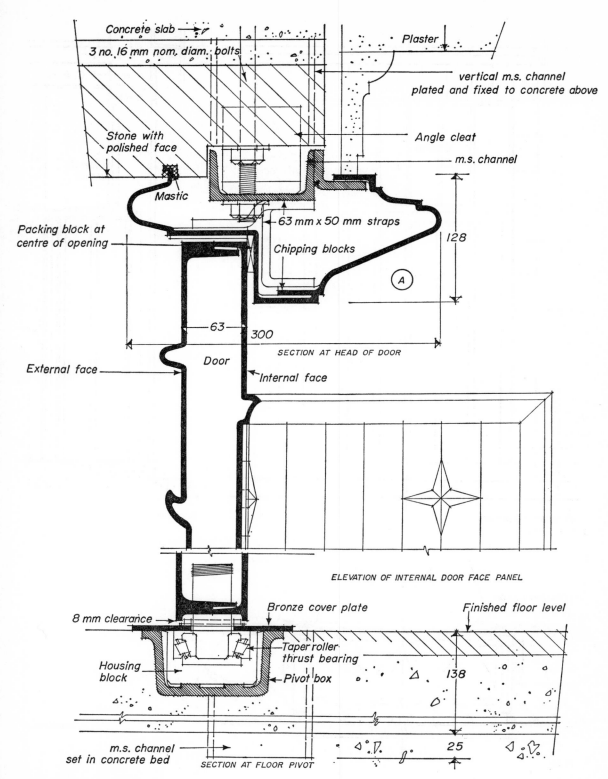

Concrete slab

3 no. 16 mm nom. diam. bolts

Plaster

vertical m.s. channel
plated and fixed to concrete above

Stone with
polished face

Angle cleat

m.s. channel

Mastic

63 mm x 50 mm straps

A

128

Packing block at
centre of opening

Chipping blocks

63   300

SECTION AT HEAD OF DOOR

External face

Door

Internal face

ELEVATION OF INTERNAL DOOR FACE PANEL

8 mm clearance

Bronze cover plate

Finished floor level

Housing
block

Taper roller
thrust bearing

Pivot box

138

m.s. channel
set in concrete bed

25

SECTION AT FLOOR PIVOT

82 *Cast bronze doors (2)*

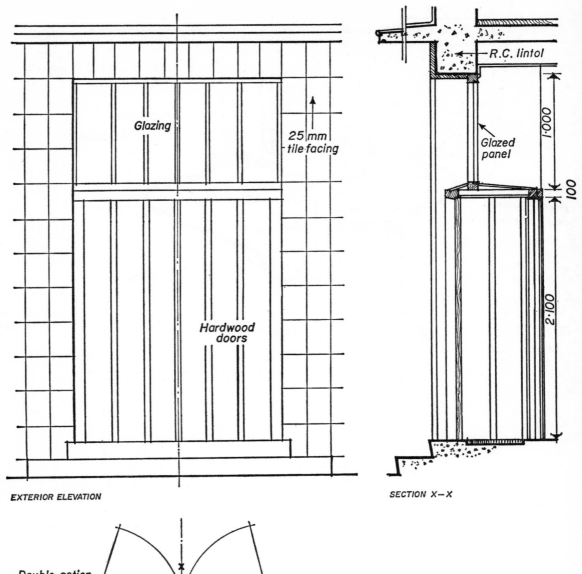

Glazing

25 mm
tile facing

Hardwood
doors

EXTERIOR ELEVATION

R.C. lintol

Glazed
panel

1·000

100

2·100

SECTION X—X

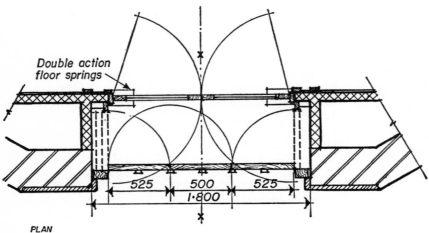

Double action
floor springs

525   500   525

1·800

PLAN

83   Vestibule doors (1)

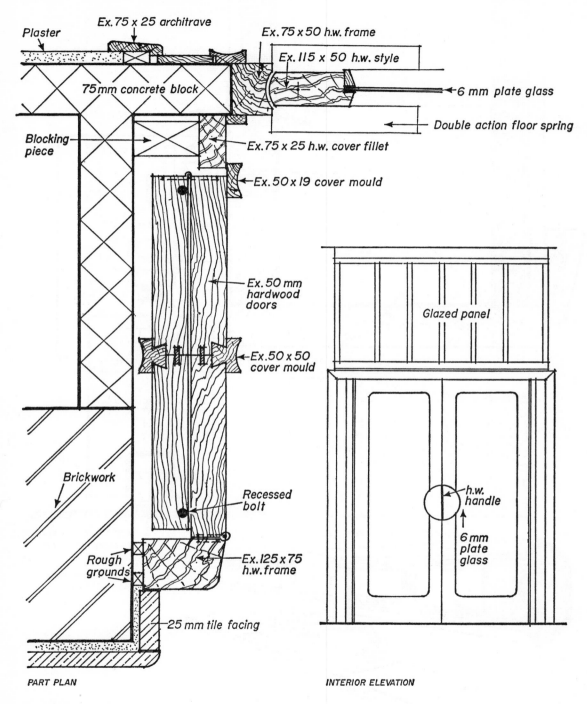

Plaster

Ex.75 x 25 architrave

Ex.75 x 50 h.w. frame

Ex.115 x 50 h.w. style

75mm concrete block

←6 mm plate glass

Blocking piece

←——— Double action floor spring

Ex.75 x 25 h.w. cover fillet

←Ex.50 x 19 cover mould

Ex.50 mm hardwood doors

Glazed panel

Ex.50 x 50 cover mould

Brickwork

Recessed bolt

h.w. handle

6 mm plate glass

Rough grounds

Ex.125 x 75 h.w. frame

25 mm tile facing

PART PLAN

INTERIOR ELEVATION

84   Vestibule doors (2)

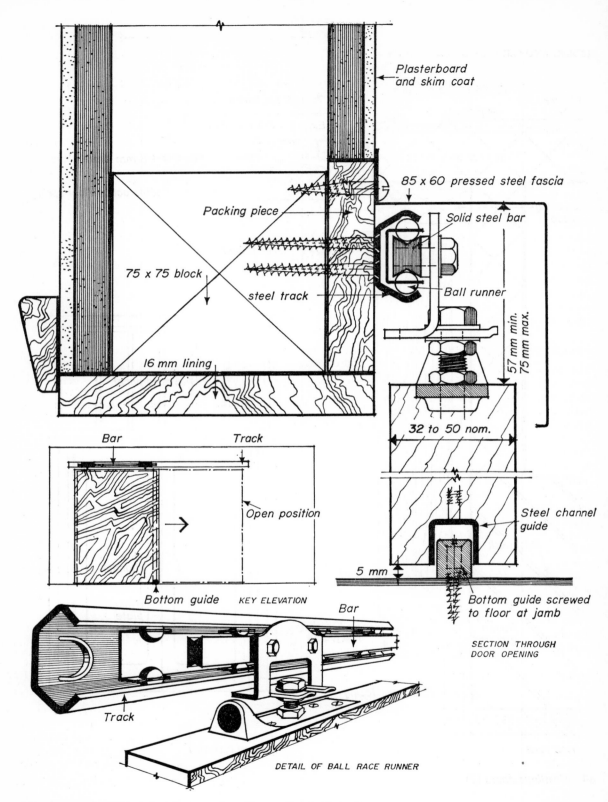

Plasterboard and skim coat

85 x 60 pressed steel fascia

Packing piece

Solid steel bar

75 x 75 block

steel track

Ball runner

57 mm min. 75 mm max.

16 mm lining

32 to 50 nom.

Bar

Track

Open position

Steel channel guide

5 mm

Bottom guide

KEY ELEVATION

Bottom guide screwed to floor at jamb

SECTION THROUGH DOOR OPENING

Bar

Track

DETAIL OF BALL RACE RUNNER

85 Sliding gear for internal door. Straight track, single leaf

maintenance are understood the doors will work satisfactorily throughout their life. It must be emphasized, however, that the working parts of the doors must be treated like machinery and must be regularly maintained. It should also be borne in mind that the more complex the mechanism the greater chance of failure. A straight sliding single leaf door is the simplest and cheapest but takes up most space when open. Increasing the number of leaves saves space but complicates the mechanism. Folding systems take up the least space of all but require the most complex hanging gear. The weight of the doors can be taken on wheels or rollers at the base or alternatively suspended from hangers on a track at the head of a door. A neater finish can usually be obtained by the bottom rollers but general opinion is that top track is the most efficient method of hanging.

Straight track sliding: single leaf

The track system chosen as an example of this type of action is suitable for interior doors not exceeding a width of 1200 mm and operating on a 'ball runner' principle. The details are shown in figure 85. The linear ball bearing motion is provided by a sliding inner bar grooved to receive chrome steel ball bearings and running between a vee section galvanized steel outer track. The ball bearings are located by a retainer cage. This type of gear, which will operate on doors weighing between 55 Kg and 90 Kg, is very reliable and prevents lifting or rocking of the doors when in use. The illustration shows an internal door in a house and this type of gear is often used where there is not sufficient space to allow a door to swing. The bottom of the door is controlled by a small nylon guide screwed to the floor at one side of the opening, so that a floor channel is not required and the fixing is suitable for carpeted interiors. It is also possible to fix this gear in the cavity of a double partition which makes a very neat detail.

Straight track sliding: double leaf

Figure 86 shows a simple two leaf arrangement for garage doors with double top track. Note that each leaf requires two hangers each having four wheels and running in a steel track of box like section. The track is supported on special brackets of malleable iron or forged steel The heavier the door the larger the track. The biggest being 150 mm by 125 mm, nominal, which would be capable of supporting doors weighing up to about 1500 Kg. There should be about 13 mm clearance between the doors and between the door and the wall. The bottom of the doors is held in place by malleable iron guides running in a steel channel let into the floor. The design of the track should prevent outward movement and so avoid any tendency for the doors to jam. The bottom rollers should also be so arranged that any dirt that gets into the channel will be ploughed out rather than pressed down. There are many alternative designs for track and channel guides. The leaves of the door are normally secured with bolts into the floor with an outside fastening on the end leaf by means of various kinds of locking bar or jamb bolt used with a padlock. Special cylinder locks are also available. In the example shown there is no frame or timber trim owing to the necessity for adequate clearance, but a wooden fastening post is screwed to the wall to close the gap between wall and inner door when in the closed position. The clearance required between the faces of the straight track doors can cause difficulties in respect of draught proofing and weathering.

Curved track

Here the doors are all in one plane and can fit close to each other and be rebated. One disadvantage, however, is that an area of the side walls of a width equal to the door opening has to be kept free to allow the doors to slide over the face. Hangers and guides as used with straight tracks are combined with back flap hinges to control the movement of the doors. The width of the doors should be restricted to a maximum of 900 mm. The minimum curve of track for light doors is in the region of 600 mm. The end leaf can be free swinging for use as a pass door and can be secured with an ordinary cylinder lock to a rebated door post. This makes a convenient arrangement where the suite of doors is used mainly for pedestrian traffic and only occasionally for vehicular access. Figure 87 illustrates a set of doors on a curved track suitable for a garage door opening. The top track is secured to a timber bearer plugged to the inside face of the lintel spanning the door opening. The hangers which are attached to the back flap hinges have nylon wheels and a ball bearing action. The curved section of the track must be supported across the

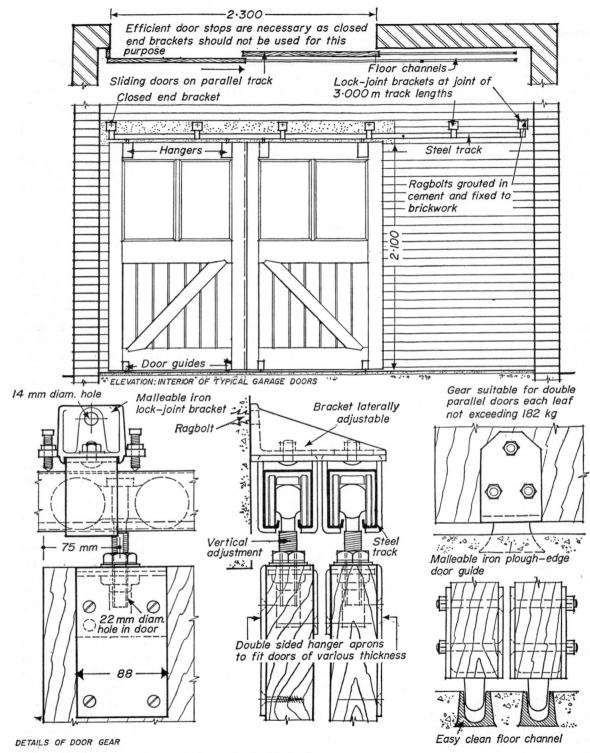

2·300

Efficient door stops are necessary as closed end brackets should not be used for this purpose

Sliding doors on parallel track

Floor channels

Closed end bracket

Lock-joint brackets at joint of 3·000 m track lengths

Hangers

Steel track

Ragbolts grouted in cement and fixed to brickwork

2·100

Door guides

ELEVATION: INTERIOR OF TYPICAL GARAGE DOORS

14 mm diam. hole

Malleable iron lock-joint bracket

Ragbolt

Bracket laterally adjustable

Gear suitable for double parallel doors each leaf not exceeding 182 kg

75 mm

Vertical adjustment

Steel track

22 mm diam. hole in door

Malleable iron plough-edge door guide

88

Double sided hanger aprons to fit doors of various thickness

Easy clean floor channel

DETAILS OF DOOR GEAR

86 Sliding garage doors. Straight track, double leaf

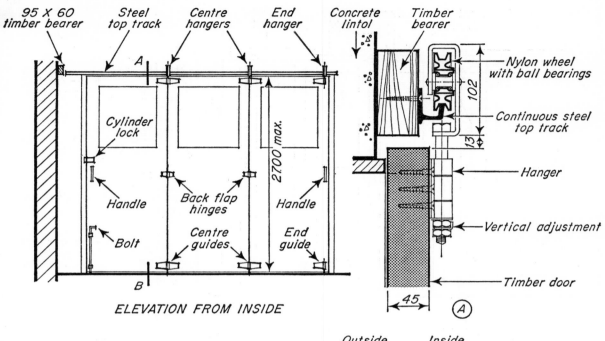

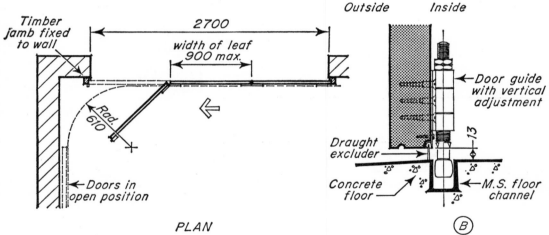

87   Top hung sliding doors

corner and this is usually done by packing out a short straight length of timber bearer at the correct angle. The radius of the curved track is governed by the distance between the return wall and the jamb of the opening and various radius curves can be fitted. A finished door thickness of 45 mm is the most suitable and the doors are located at floor level in the bottom channel by means of adjustable

nylon rollers. A swing or pass door is shown, and a roller bolt steers the swing door round the corner To fasten the doors, the swing door is secured by a cylinder lock.

Folding doors

The sliding, folding systems are the most sophisticated in terms of track and hanging. They take up

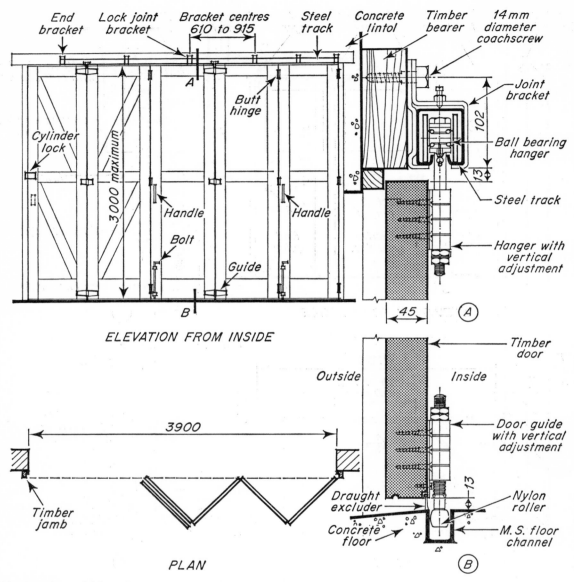

ELEVATION FROM INSIDE

PLAN

88 *Top hung folding doors*

less space and can be made to fit more closely at the head. The track, hangers and guides are all similar in principle to those used for the sliding curved type of door except that each pair of doors swings inwards from the hanger. Framed and filled in sliding doors should be of robust construction and should not be less than 45 mm finished thickness. The top rail should be at least 150 mm deep to

allow adequate fixing for the hangers. In the case of very large garage or warehouse doors and doors for industrial use, greater thickness and strength is often necessary. If the sliding folding range of doors is designed with an odd number of leaves, one leaf can swing and be used as a pass door. Figure 88 shows a set of top hung doors of framed, ledged and braced construction and suitable for

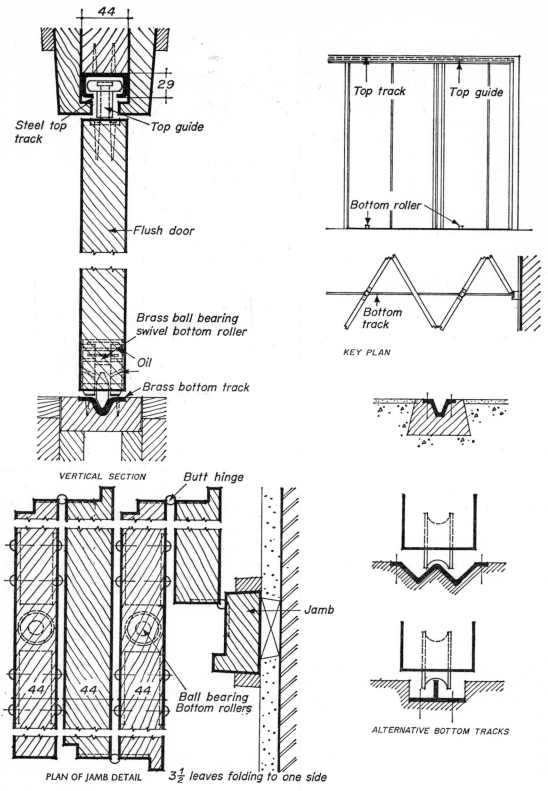

44

29

Steel top track

Top guide

Flush door

Brass ball bearing swivel bottom roller

Oil

Brass bottom track

VERTICAL SECTION

Butt hinge

Jamb

44   44   44

Ball bearing Bottom rollers

PLAN OF JAMB DETAIL

$3\frac{1}{2}$ leaves folding to one side

Top track   Top guide

Bottom roller

Bottom track

KEY PLAN

ALTERNATIVE BOTTOM TRACKS

89   *Folding partition*

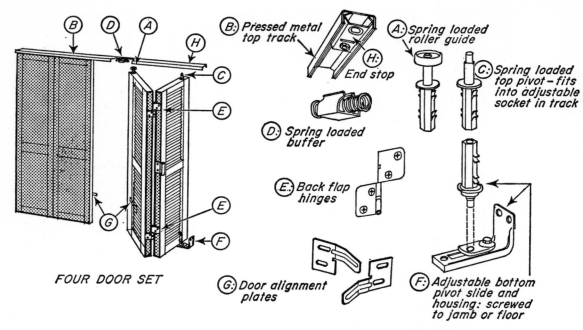

FOUR DOOR SET

B: Pressed metal top track.

H: End stop

A: Spring loaded roller guide

C: Spring loaded top pivot – fits into adjustable socket in track

D: Spring loaded buffer

E: Back flap hinges

F: Adjustable bottom pivot slide and housing: screwed to jamb or floor

G: Door alignment plates

DOOR FURNITURE

90   Louvred folding partition

industrial use in say a warehouse or factory. The top track is of U section galvanized steel and the runners or hangers have ball bearing action. The door is restrained at the floor level in the usual way by nylon rollers running in a shallow floor channel. Note also the draught stripping at the threshold. Back flap hinges are usual but will be seen at alternative joints on the outside elevation and if this is to be avoided then (100 mm) butt hinges can be used as shown.

FOLDING PARTITION

The sliding folding system of doors is often used in the construction of a room divider. Figure 89 shows a centre hung sliding folding partition used for this purpose. A half leaf is necessary against the frame on one side. The particular example illustrates the use of bottom track and rollers with a top guide. The requirements for bottom track are, however, contradictory since the track giving the least break in the floor surface is least likely to restrain the door properly.

LOUVRED FOLDING PARTITION

This type of partition shown in figure 90 has become popular for use as a room divider or decorative screen. Many firms make this type of door as standard at much less cost than doors of similar construction could be purpose made. Decorative timbers such as North American clear pine or Luan mahogany are used. The rails are dowelled and the louvre slats notched into the styles. This type of door is also suitable for built-in storage units and wardrobes, where maximum access is required.

The use of top and bottom pivots leaves the threshold completely clear, and a spring loaded roller guide is fixed to the top leading corner of each pair of doors to ensure smooth running in the track. Special back flap hinges are used and door alignment plates guide the doors together on the closing style of each pair of doors. If the four panels shown were hung to fold one way, then a different type of track would be required.

COLLAPSIBLE PARTITION

This type of collapsible sliding door or partition has almost become standard construction for use as a space divider in houses, and small community buildings. The partition illustrated in figure 91 is made up of an aluminium alloy collapsible frame over which is stretched leathercloth or similar material. These partitions are top hung and do not require a floor fixing or channel, and an important point to note is the minimum amount of space taken up when the doors are folded back.

FIXING JAMB DETAIL

CLOSING JAMB DETAIL

HEAD DETAIL

91 Collapsible doors

OVERHEAD DOORS

This type of door is known colloquially as an *up and over* door. It opens into a horizontal position overhead and is particularly useful for garages and wherever floor space is restricted. The type illustrated in figure 92 pivots on a balance spring, and is formed by cedar weatherboarding in an aluminium edge frame. The maximum size opening for a door of this type is in the region of 2·500 m wide and 2·100 m high. As the door moves from the vertical to the horizontal position, nylon wheels which are fitted to the top corners of the door run along the steel track at high level, the action of the door being balanced by special springs positioned as shown.

REVOLVING DOORS

Since this type of door requires special fittings and mechanism it is manufactured by specialist firms. The designer has freedom in the design of the leaves of the door and the curved casing. There are various patent methods of collapsing these doors so that a direct through access is possible when desired. The leaves should always be made to collapse in an outward direction in an emergency, and the door should be glazed, using safety glass. For a four compartment door an overall diameter of 1·800 m to 2·100 m is usual. Where luggage has to pass through the doors as in hotel entrances the larger diameter is essential. A four compartment door with associated joinery work is shown in figure 93. Where space is limited a three compartment revolving door can be used and in this case the diameter can be reduced to 1·500 m. It is good practice to place an auxilliary swing door in close proximity to the revolving door and where the revolving doors are used in association with steps at an entrance the first riser should be at least 1·000 m away from the sweep of the doors.

PATIO DOOR

An increasing use of the garden as additional living space has brought about the need for a well designed and draught proof sliding door for domestic use. Figure 94 gives an example of a reversible sliding door of aluminium construction produced to manufacturers' standard sizes for economy.

The illustration shows a combination of fixed light and sliding door in anodized extruded aluminium section. The doors are 'reversible' when fixing for either right or left hand opening, and are factory glazed with a sealed double glass unit

119

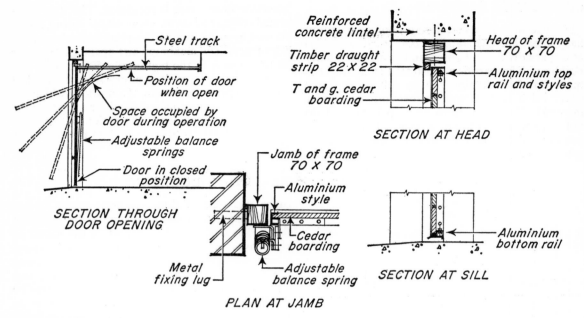

Labels in figure:
- Steel track
- Position of door when open
- Space occupied by door during operation
- Adjustable balance springs
- Door in closed position
- SECTION THROUGH DOOR OPENING
- Reinforced concrete lintel
- Timber draught strip 22·X·22
- T and g. cedar boarding
- Head of frame 70 X 70
- Aluminium top rail and styles
- SECTION AT HEAD
- Jamb of frame 70 X 70
- Aluminium style
- Cedar boarding
- Adjustable balance spring
- Metal fixing lug
- PLAN AT JAMB
- Aluminium bottom rail
- SECTION AT SILL

92 'Up and over' door

set in vinyl glazing channel. The sliding portion rolls on nylon ball bearing rollers and the door is weather stripped with silicone treated woven wool pile. The fixed panel is sealed with a vinyl membrane, and the aluminium frames are bedded and sealed into timber subframes by a suitable gun applied mastic.

Security is always an important consideration, in particular with a door which slides to open, and this particular example has an adjustable plate which prevents the door being lifted out, in addition to a cylinder lock and pull handle.

AUTOMATIC CONTROL OF DOORS

Doors can be controlled in terms of opening and closing by use of various types of automatic equipment. A fully automated system will incorporate a device which acts as the initial sensing control such as a push-button, a sensitized mat or a photo-electric beam. This initial sensor will be followed by a timing device connected to the motorization apparatus which causes the doors to move. Alternatively the motorization can be operated by remote control from a central point such as a security cabin. The timing apparatus can

vary from a simple cut-out to complex electronic control with programmed instructions to incorporate variable time delays for closing and opening doors in series as circumstances or security requires. It is essential that all automatic control devices allow the doors to be moved by hand in the event of a power failure. The motor gear usually takes its initial power from electricity which is then used to generate hydraulic or pneumatic pressure to cause the doors to move as signalled. The equipment should be capable of incorporating a checking action which slows the doors down towards closing in order to avoid clashing and rebound. A further refinement should be a repeat cycle of opening and closing should the door meet any obstruction.

Specialist advice should be sought on this type of gear since automation techniques are rapidly developing, and more sophisticated control is possible.

Automatic control may be required in hospitals, hotels, shops, offices or security buildings, and both swing doors and sliding doors can be controlled. Briefly, for the swing door the control will be as follows, a master control with time delay for setting the time that the door is held open, and a

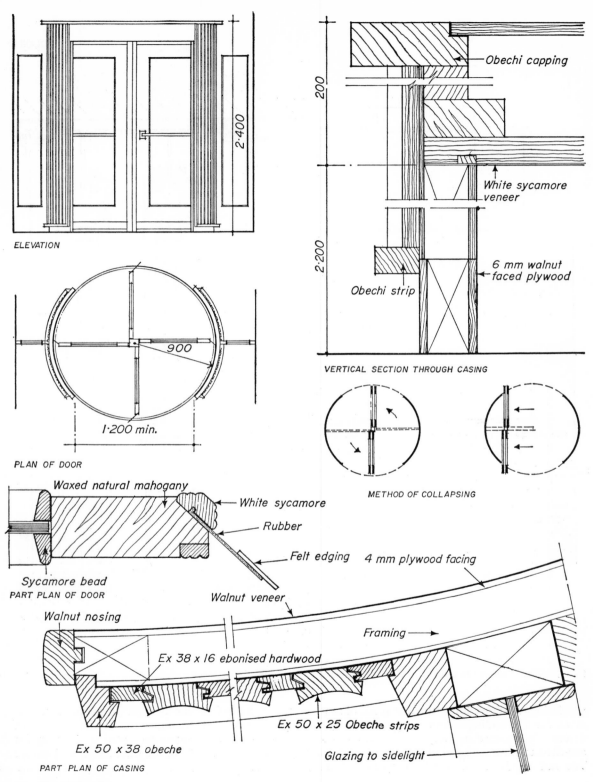

ELEVATION

PLAN OF DOOR

1·200 min.

900

2·400

VERTICAL SECTION THROUGH CASING

Obechi capping

White sycamore veneer

6 mm walnut faced plywood

Obechi strip

200

2·200

METHOD OF COLLAPSING

Waxed natural mahogany

White sycamore

Rubber

Felt edging

Sycamore bead

PART PLAN OF DOOR

Walnut veneer

4 mm plywood facing

Walnut nosing

Framing

Ex 38 x 16 ebonised hardwood

Ex 50 x 25 Obeche strips

Ex 50 x 38 obeche

Glazing to sidelight

PART PLAN OF CASING

93 *Revolving door*

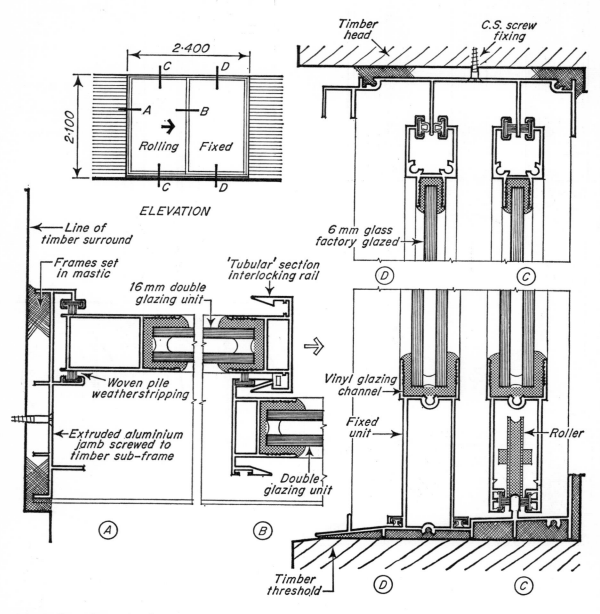

2·400

C   D

A   B

Rolling   Fixed

2·100

ELEVATION

Line of
timber surround

Frames set
in mastic

16 mm double
glazing unit

'Tubular' section
interlocking rail

Woven pile
weatherstripping

Extruded aluminium
jamb screwed to
timber sub-frame

Double
glazing unit

Timber
head

C.S. screw
fixing

6 mm glass
factory glazed

D   C

Vinyl glazing
channel

Fixed
unit

Roller

Timber
threshold

D   C

A   B

94 Rolling aluminium door

regulating resistance for setting the speed of movement for the sliding doors. The leaves may be
driven electro mechanically by a driving wheel
attached to a moving rail at the top of each leaf.
The rail regulates the width of opening, brakes

the door before the end of its movement, and
makes electrical disconnection at the end of the
movement. The maximum speed of opening for
a sliding door will be in the region of 1 m per
second.

WEATHER STRIPPING

Apart from the weather stripping details illustrated in the drawings, figures 95–99 show further applications of this technique which is a valuable method of reducing air filtration (draughts) at the threshold and closing style of a door. A point to bear in mind is that as buildings in general become better heated the occupants tend to feel draughts where previously there was no discomfort.

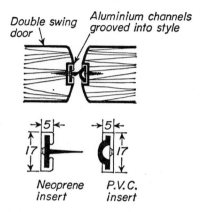

95 *Timber swinging doors*

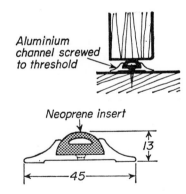

96 *Timber door with flush threshold*

95 shows a method of weather stripping the meeting styles of a pair of double swing timber doors. The neoprene insert is available with tongues

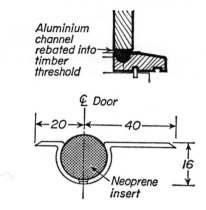

97 *Timber door with rebated threshold*

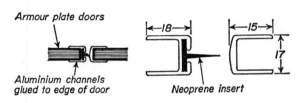

98 *Glass doors*

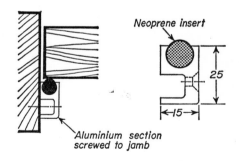

99 *Timber door stop*

The particular type of weather stripping shown consists of extruded aluminium sections secured to the door or threshold which grip a neoprene strip or pad which in turn is compressed into the gap between the frame or threshold and door.

A double swing external door is a particularly difficult situation since the weather stripping must not impede the smooth action of the door. Figure

suitable to seal gaps from 4 mm to 10 mm wide. The neoprene tongue closes and compresses against a strip of PVC in a similar extruded aluminium channel section, both extrusions being fitted into a groove in the face of the styles. Weather stripping of the top rail of the door can also be carried out by using this type of weather stripping. Figure 96 shows a method of weather stripping at the threshold. This will withstand very heavy foot traffic and is ideal provided the 13 mm upstand is not inconvenient. An alternative is shown in figure 97 where the upstand is reduced by cutting a rebate in the threshold. This detail gives a small underdoor gap and gives an unobstructed threshold. Toughened glass doors can be weather stripped by fixing an extruded channel with neoprene insert around the closing edges of the doors. The channel is secured by adhesive and is cut away to accommodate locks or a kicking plate to the base of the door. The neoprene tongue would seal against the glass, but the plain channel provides a symmetrical detail, as shown in figure 98.

A combined stop and compression seal is shown in detail in figure 99. This type of seal is used where an airtight or dust proof seal is required as in a computer room. The door must be sealed all round and top and bottom bolts should be fitted to hold the doors close against the seal.

4 Windows

DESIGN

A window is an opening designed primarily to let light or air into a building. It will also provide a view of what is inside, or outside if this is part of the design requirements. A window opening will normally be fitted with glass or similar transparent material—usually in a frame—to keep out the weather. The following list gives, in broad outline, the main points to be considered in connection with window design:

(a) Choosing the correct positions of the opening with due regard to both aesthetic and functional needs.

(b) Choosing the correct materials and proportions for the frame, so that it fulfils satisfactorily both technical and aesthetic requirements.

(c) Choosing correctly the weight and type of glass for the infil.

(d) Arranging the right part of the window to open, both in respect of proportion of opening and position and type of opening frame in order to admit the correct amount of fresh air for adequate ventilation.

(e) Determining whether or not the window opening when glazed will have any special requirements in respect of sound or heat insulation.

(f) Making sure that the method of manufacture and jointing will satisfactorily withstand the elements for an agreed period of time.

(g) Ensuring that the junction between the fixed and moving parts of the frame, and the junction between the outer frame and the window opening are satisfactory in practical terms, and will remain weathertight throughout their expected life (which should be defined).

(h) Ensuring that the completed product will fulfil all the current applicable statutory regulations and requirements.

(i) Doing all this within an agreed cost limit.

It will be seen that a large number of technical and aesthetic decisions must be correctly taken to produce a satisfactory component and that windows are a most important building element in respect of giving architectural character to a façade, and controlling the comfort conditions in the room which they light and ventilate. The more important design points are summarized in the following paragraphs.

PERFORMANCE STANDARDS

Lighting

The matter of lighting, both natural daylight and artificial lighting, is part of the fundamental design procedure for a building. Work should be carried out in greater detail at each stage of the design so that the lighting effect of each window has been fully considered before production drawings are made.

The window must light a room efficiently by providing the right amount of daylight in the right place with due regard to the use of the room. Where illumination of the room is a critical factor, the amount of light falling on the working surface at any given point should be calculated. Calculation of illumination levels in respect of daylight is a complex matter and students are referred to *MBC: E and S*, chapter 4, 'Daylighting'.

It is however, not only a matter of providing the right area of window, but the shape and position also affect the distribution of light in the room, together with the amount of obstruction caused by the mullions and transomes.

The contrast between the light area of the window and the dark area of the wall in shadow, in which the window is placed, is an important factor. Too sharp a contrast creates glare. A good illustration of these points, which may be helpful, is to consider the traditional Georgian arrangement of tall windows with wide-splayed internal reveals painted a light colour, which reflect the light well and lessen the contrast between the window and wall. The windows, if they go down to the floor, distribute light over a large area of floor, which

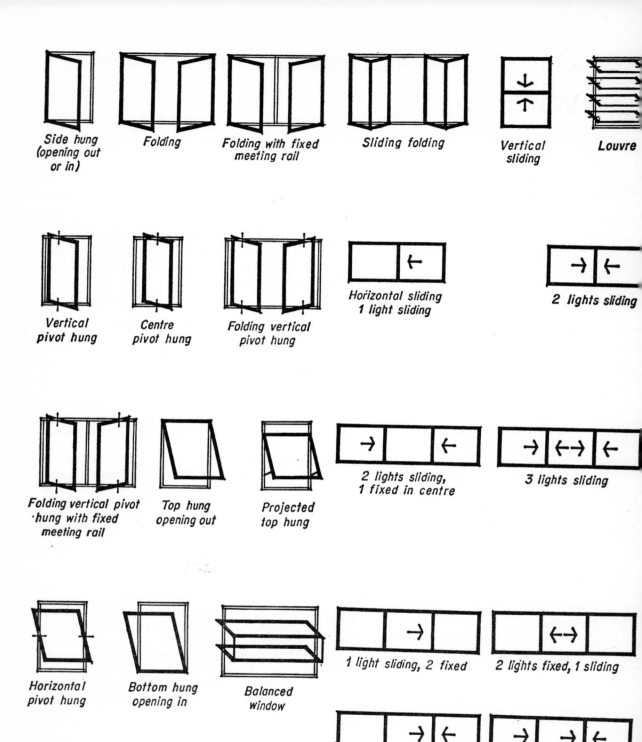

Side hung
(opening out
or in)

Folding

Folding with fixed
meeting rail

Sliding folding

Vertical
sliding

Louvre

Vertical
pivot hung

Centre
pivot hung

Folding vertical
pivot hung

Horizontal sliding
1 light sliding

2 lights sliding

Folding vertical pivot
·hung with fixed
meeting rail

Top hung
opening out

Projected
top hung

2 lights sliding,
1 fixed in centre

3 lights sliding

Horizontal
pivot hung

Bottom hung
opening in

Balanced
window

1 light sliding, 2 fixed

2 lights fixed, 1 sliding

2 lights sliding,
1 fixed at side

3 lights sliding

100   Types of window casements

again gives valuable reflection into the room. Similarly, when they are carried up to near the ceiling, the same effect is produced at high level. Rather than concentrating the window area into one wide opening, a number of openings are used, spaced out so as to avoid areas of deep shade in the corners of the room. Glazing bars of narrow section are also splayed, so that the inclined surfaces are lighted and only a thin edge is in complete shade and dark. The good illumination given by these windows, without an excessive window area, should be noted.

Ventilation

Window openings should be arranged to give an amount of ventilation most suited to the use of the room or space served by the window. This may require a large amount of opening, to give a very rapid change of air or alternatively a small opening which gives a regulated and controlled slow change of air. The question of air movement is considered in more detail in *MBC: E and S*, chapter 3. It may be desirable to provide one or more types of ventilation in the same window. Figure 100 shows the alternative ways of providing opening lights, or casements in a window.

In respect of the *handing* of a side hung casement window the following convention is followed: The opening casement is right or left hand according to the side on which the casement occurs looking from the *outside*. The casement is always hinged on the outside of the frame. Most working drawings show a view of the casement as seen from the outside as shown in figure 101. The metric is the reverse of the accepted convention for imperial windows. Note that the apex of the triangle showing the convention for opening always indicates the hinged side of the opening light.

In terms of ventilation the vertical sliding sash window is a good example of efficient design. The opening which is variable according to the position of the sash gives ventilation at high level by letting out the used air and is normally protected by the arch or lintel at this point. The sash can also be opened at the bottom for letting in fresh air, the variation in sash position being infinite to half the total area of the window opening. The opening is easy to operate provided that the window is well made and well balanced. Bottom hung, *opening in* and top hung, *opening out* windows are also an

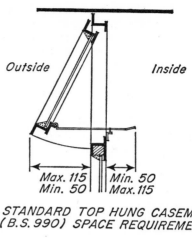

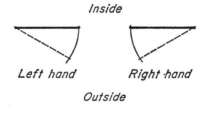

STANDARD TOP HUNG CASEMENT (B.S. 990) SPACE REQUIREMENTS

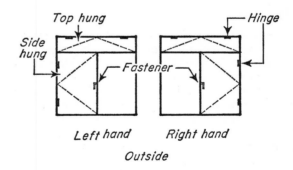

101 Handing of casements

efficient means of ventilation. The side hung opening casement does not provide draught proof ventilation since the vertical slit causes a concentrated air stream. In most windows a small top hung opening is usually provided for slow or night ventilation in addition to the side hung casements.

One particular aspect of natural ventilation – that of habitable rooms – is covered by the Building Regulations. The term *habitable room* in this context includes all living rooms, bedrooms, kitchens and sculleries. A habitable room is required to have a minimum of one or more ventilation openings whose total area is equal to not less than one twentieth of the floor area of the room and that some part of the area is not less than 1·750 m above the floor. The ventilation must be direct to the open air. The regulations make it clear however that windows are not the only acceptable means of natural ventilation. A door, for instance, if opening directly to the open air, and fulfilling certain other conditions (see Building Regulations K 4, paragraph 4) is considered to be a ventilation opening.

Mechanical ventilation is also permitted, apart from window openings. The Building Regulations also deal with the ventilation of larders in detail.

Apart from empirical data quoted in the Building Regulations, it is not easy to say in precise terms how much opening should be provided to give a certain ventilation rate because this is dependent on wind pressure and *stack effect*. Stack effect occurs mainly in winter, when warm air escapes from the upper part of the room and is replaced by cold, and therefore heavier air from outside.

Appearance

The pattern of windows on the façade is known as the *fenestration*, and this is a very important element in the design of a building being second only in architectural importance to the overall form or mass of the building. Important factors in the fenestration pattern are the subdivision of the window, the proportion of the panes and the recessing or the projection of the window opening. It is important to remember that the lines of sight from windows which afford a good prospect or view should be unobstructed. There should also be clear lines of sight from standing or sitting positions unobstructed by transomes or mullions.

Weather resistance

New British Standards are under consideration which will attempt to define and measure in quantitative terms the requirements of a closed window in respect of resistance to water and air penetration. Provision of water checks is important and grooves in the frame and sash are necessary to prevent

water being driven through the gap by difference of air pressures. A consideration of the sections recommended by the British Woodwork Manufacturers Association shows the careful thought that is required to produce a window section that will successfully resist water penetration. This type of *double rebated* timber section is shown in figure 107, page 131. The twin capillary groove between head and casement prevent water gaining access by capillary attraction and the groove and chamfer between the bottom rail of the casement and the sill is designed to prevent driving rain being blown into the room under the casement. The sill is throated to catch the water blown under the sill and to allow it to drip clear of the face of the building. The sill is also *weathered*, that is to say, the

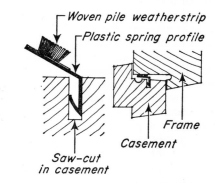

102 Details of woven pile weatherstrip to casements

sloping surface is angled away from the building to take away the water which runs down the face of the glass. The opening casement is also protected by means of a drip mould which projects over the opening. The casement must be fixed so as to give an efficient tight fit against the edge of the rebates on the frame to prevent draughts. Metal window sections can be provided with effective seals in the form of compressible strips of synthetic rubber, or neoprene. With timber, spring strips of metal alloy can be used, but these are probably most effective in curing draughty old windows rather than for use in new windows. A further application of weather stripping by the use of a patented flexible plastic strip section with a tufted polypropylene pile is shown in figure 102.

This type of draught proofing, or *weather stripping* as it is called, helps to provide an even temperature and increases comfort conditions by reducing unwanted air infiltration (draughts). With timber windows, in particular after much use, gaps up to 3 mm may appear between the casement and frame and use of some form of flexible seal at these points is most useful. In respect of metal windows, the opening light may not fit perfectly evenly within its frame. The method of operation of an opening light has a bearing in the importance of including weather stripping. For instance, a reversible (pivot) window is more difficult to make accurately than a side hung casement and thus the

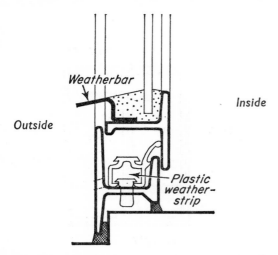

103   *Detail of inward opening casement at sill*

pivot window should always be weather stripped. The most difficult window to weatherseal is an inward opening casement, and an example of weather stripping technique using neoprene strip is shown used in conjunction with an inward opening metal casement in figure 103.

Maintenance and cleaning

Good watertight windows which are provided with ventilating openings are a complex piece of construction and need careful maintenance. It is important to consider this factor at the design stage and to bear in mind that a thoughtful building owner will usually be prepared to do more regular maintenance in return for increased comfort. Buildings which are likely to get rough usage and are impersonal in terms of maintenance should

rely on simple detailing without too many refinements.

Cleaning is also a very important consideration. In multi-storey buildings with large areas of glazing special cradles cantilevered from the face of the building may be necessary, but wherever possible, windows should be designed so that all parts can be cleaned from the inside. This will probably require special hinges or the choice of an inward opening type of window usually a pivot. In pivoted

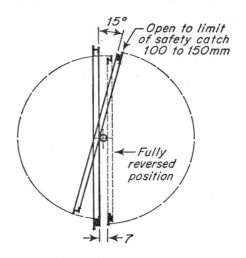

104   *Reversible window-space requirements*

windows the design of the pivot hinge should allow the window to turn through 180°. This is illustrated in figure 104, and adequate space must be allowed in the design of the building where this type of window is used. The effect of fitting an extending hinge or *easy-clean* hinge is shown in figure 105. The space requirements for a standard top hung casement is shown in figure 101.

TIMBER WINDOWS

Standard timber windows

Timber lends itself to the manufacture of inexpensive windows, but factors such as movement with variations in moisture content and the tendency for sapwood to rot, must be taken into consideration. See *MBC: Materials*, chapter 2.

Examples of typical standard timber windows are shown in figure 106 naming the various parts

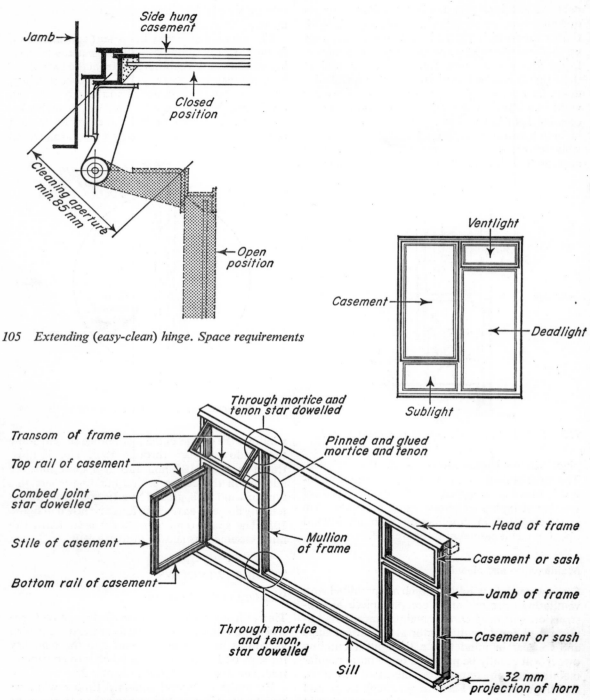

Jamb

Side hung casement

Closed position

Cleaning aperture min.85 mm

Open position

105 *Extending (easy-clean) hinge. Space requirements*

Ventlight

Casement

Deadlight

Sublight

Through mortice and tenon star dowelled

Transom of frame

Top rail of casement

Pinned and glued mortice and tenon

Combed joint star dowelled

Stile of casement

Mullion of frame

Head of frame

Casement or sash

Bottom rail of casement

Jamb of frame

Casement or sash

Through mortice and tenon, star dowelled

Sill

32 mm projection of horn

106 *Typical factory-assembled casement window. Single glazing*

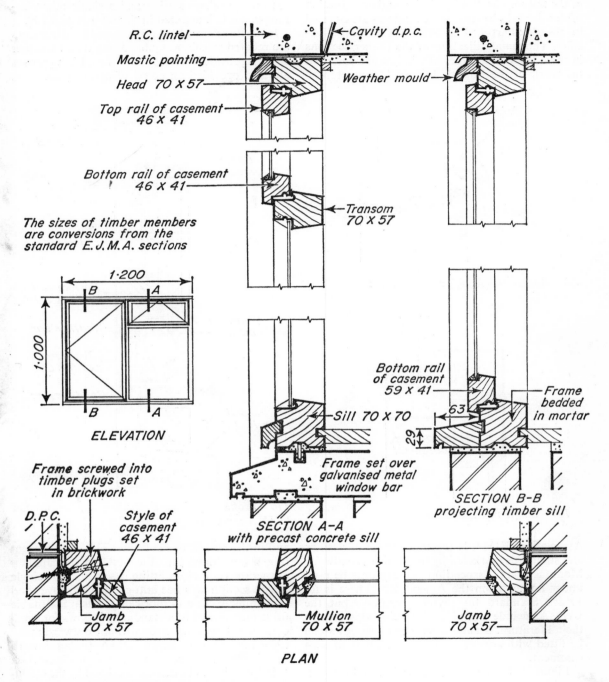

R.C. lintel

Cavity d.p.c.

Mastic pointing

Head 70 X 57

Weather mould

Top rail of casement
46 X 41

Bottom rail of casement
46 X 41

Transom
70 X 57

The sizes of timber members
are conversions from the
standard E.J.M.A. sections

1·200

B   A

1·000

B   A

ELEVATION

Bottom rail
of casement
59 X 41

Frame
bedded
in mortar

63

29

Sill 70 X 70

Frame screwed into
timber plugs set
in brickwork

D.P.C.

Style of
casement
46 X 41

Frame set over
galvanised metal
window bar

SECTION A-A
with precast concrete sill

SECTION B-B
projecting timber sill

Jamb
70 X 57

Mullion
70 X 57

Jamb
70 X 57

PLAN

107   Standard casement windows (EJMA section)

of the frame. The quality, design and construction of standard timber casement windows are covered in BS 644 : Part I : 1951 : *Wood Casement Windows*. The standardization of the timber sections in these traditional types of window are based on the work of the English Joinery Manufacturers'

the double rebate section and a single rebate arrangement is illustrated in figures 108 and 109.

In the BS section, both opening and fixed members are rebated so that a double draught and weather check is provided. Half round anti-capillary grooves are also provided on edges of opening members

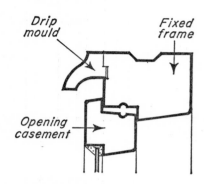

108   Double rebated (lipped) casement

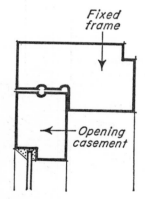

109   Single rebated casement

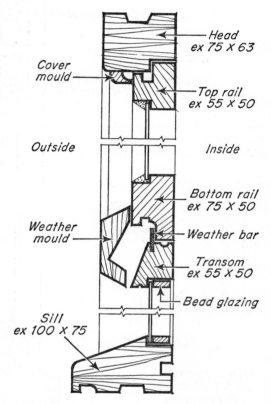

110   Profiles of inward opening timber window (*EJMA sections*)

Association. EJMA is the trade name of designs and standards marketed by the British Woodwork Manufacturers' Association and can only be used under licence from the Association. There is no British Standard for pivoted windows but the BWMA include a standard range of this type in their literature. Standard casement windows can be fitted with *easy-clean* hinges, one pair to each casement.

Figure 107 shows a typical window manufactured from BS sections. These sections are based on the *double rebated* principle. The difference between

and in the reveals of the frame. This is to prevent rain being drawn into the building by capillary attraction via a close fitting casement. The single rebate section also has anti-capillary grooves and is a simple section to fabricate. Thus it is suitable for production of non-standard windows for small contracts. For comparison with the outward opening casement a standard EJMA timber inward opening casement section is shown in figure 110. Windows should be delivered primed by the manufacturer. It is important to specify a high-quality primer, otherwise this coat becomes chalky before

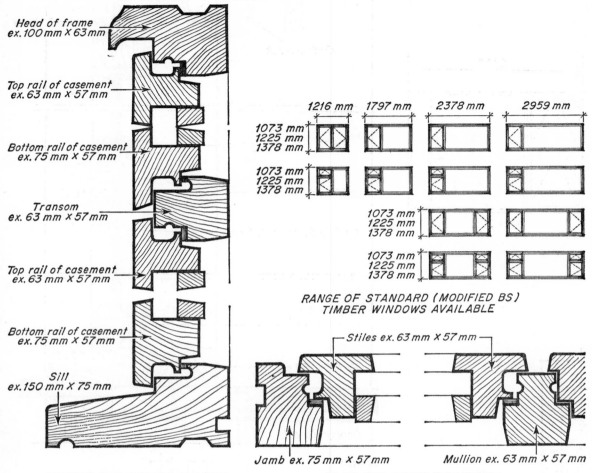

Head of frame
ex. 100 mm × 63 mm

Top rail of casement
ex. 63 mm × 57 mm

Bottom rail of casement
ex. 75 mm × 57 mm

Transom
ex. 63 mm × 57 mm

Top rail of casement
ex. 63 mm × 57 mm

Bottom rail of casement
ex. 75 mm × 57 mm

Sill
ex. 150 mm × 75 mm

SECTION FOR DOUBLE GLAZING

RANGE OF STANDARD (MODIFIED BS)
TIMBER WINDOWS AVAILABLE

Stiles ex. 63 mm × 57 mm

Jamb ex. 75 mm × 57 mm

Mullion ex. 63 mm × 57 mm

PLAN FOR DOUBLE GLAZING

111   Double glazing

the undercoat and other coats are applied, the vital point being that the life of a paint system depends upon the first coat, see chapter 17. The frames should be stored upright and under cover before fixing. It is not, in theory, a good thing to 'build in' window frames as the walling proceeds as it tends to distort or damage the frames unless extra care is taken. It is now, however, almost universal practice except on the highest class of work where the *second fixing* method is used. With this latter technique the opening is formed first and the window frames fitted afterwards. The British Standard windows shown, and windows made with sections, modified from the BS, are supplied from stock by approved manufacturers. These windows are highly competitive in price.

A selection from a range of modified BS windows prepared for double glazing is shown in figure 111.

In respect of the production of a modular co-ordinated range of timber windows, the BWMA await the revision of the relevant British Standards.

Double rebated casement

A non-standard window constructed on the double rebate, or lipped casement principle, is shown in figure 112. These sections must be carefully made

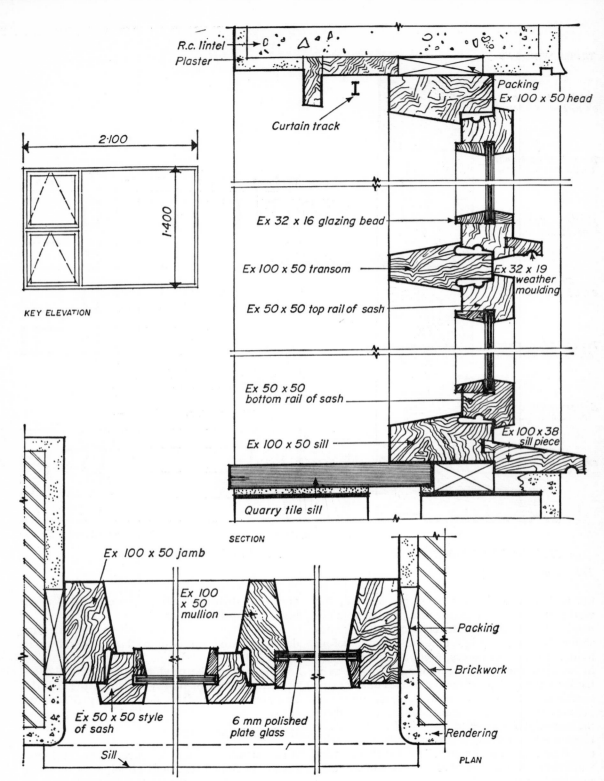

KEY ELEVATION

2·100

1·400

R.c. lintel

Plaster

Curtain track

Packing
Ex 100 x 50 head

Ex 32 x 16 glazing bead

Ex 100 x 50 transom

Ex 32 x 19 weather moulding

Ex 50 x 50 top rail of sash

Ex 50 x 50 bottom rail of sash

Ex 100 x 50 sill

Ex 100 x 38 sill piece

Quarry tile sill

SECTION

Ex 100 x 50 jamb

Ex 100 x 50 mullion

Packing

Brickwork

Ex 50 x 50 style of sash

6 mm polished plate glass

Rendering

Sill

PLAN

112   Double rebated casement

to be a good fit on the comparatively small areas of timber that are in contact when the casement is closed. Another point to note here, is that the two top hung opening lights are one above the other which means that the detail at the transom between the two openers must be very carefully considered. The additional weather moulding is very necessary at this point, otherwise the rain would run down the glass on the upper casement and be blown into the unprotected top rebate of the lower casement. Another point to notice is that the window is fixed (by screwing) to timber packing pieces plugged to the brickwork, which is a technique suitable where the window is part of the *second fixing* operations, being placed and secured in position after the opening is formed. The frame is set well forward in the opening and this leaves space for the formation of a *blind box* on the soffit, so that curtains may be hung within the window opening.

Inward opening casement

Figure 113 shows details of a lipped or double rebated casement window, inward opening and hung folding. This is to say, the two lock styles are rebated together and there is no centre mullion against which the casements would normally close. Inward opening is convenient for cleaning but inconvenient for conventional curtains. This type of window is much used on the continent and is meant to be either shut or fully open. The example is arranged on the inside of the wall thickness so that each casement can fold back, out of the way, against the wall. Note the zinc sheet covering dressed on a timber sill, also a continental detail which is quite satisfactory provided the ends are turned up against the brickwork and tucked in. The metal balustrade has a bottom rail so that the sill is not perforated by the fixing of the balusters. The sill details for an inward opening casement, always need special consideration because the rebate is reversed and rain will enter unless a water-bar or weather board is used. The channel water-bar shown gives double protection from driving rain and the outer flange is provided with draining holes at intervals.

Horizontal pivot window

There is no British Standard for this type of window, but most manufacturers approved under EJMA licence produce a 'standard' range for manufacture for delivery from stock. Other types of timber windows not covered by BS, eg inward opening casements, casements for double glazing and double casements, are also made to manufacturers' standard ranges.

Figure 114 shows a horizontal pivot hung timber window – the word *horizontal* refers to the placing of the hinges, which are opposed horizontally. The hinges of a vertical pivot hung window would be one above the other in a vertical line. The success of a pivot window depend upon the friction action of the hinge which should be strong enough to hold the window firmly in any open position. The pivot hung window is very much used because it gives a neat appearance to the façade of a building and provides good control of ventilation. There may be some difficulty in respect of hanging curtains or blinds on the inside of the window if the frame is set back into the window reveal. The example is shown fixed as far as possible towards the front of the brickwork opening and secured by rustproofed metal lugs. These lugs are screwed to the back of the frame and 'built in' as the brickwork is carried up when the opening is formed, as shown on the plan in figure 114. The opening casement is secured in this example by an espagnolette bolt which holds the casement to the frame at four points.

Double sash pivot window

The horizontally pivoted double sash has for a long time been developed by window specialists on the continent and is now produced by several manufacturers for use in this country. Details of such a window are shown in figure 115. The outer sash is secured to the inner sash and hinged so that the space between can be cleaned. The joint between the two sashes is not airtight, in fact the simple locking device is also a spacer to ensure that external air can circulate through the space. The air circulation should be enough to evaporate any condensation within the space but not sufficient to have any serious overall cooling effect. To separate the two sashes they have to be rotated through 180°. Accordian pleated, or venetian blinds can be fixed in the space and operated from the side with cords. These windows, being balanced, can be made to a large size, limiting factors being the distance the top swings into the room and the

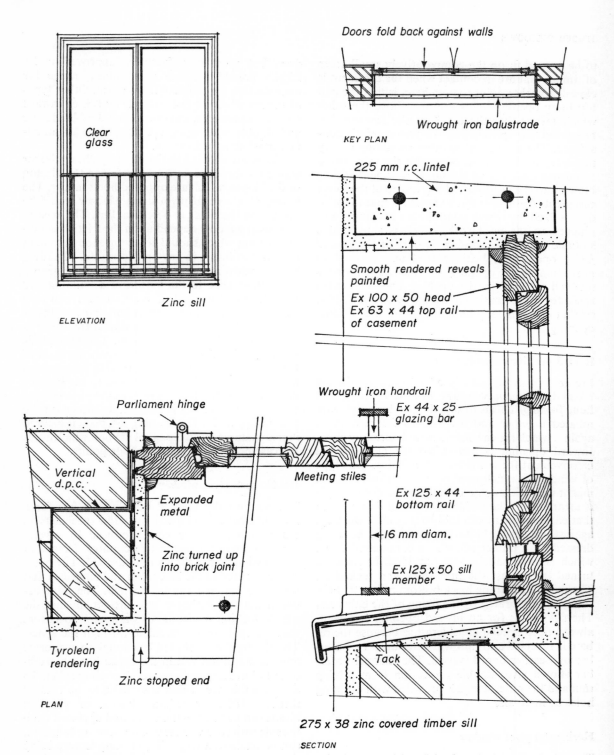

Clear
glass

Zinc sill

ELEVATION

Doors fold back against walls

Wrought iron balustrade

KEY PLAN

225 mm r.c. lintel

Smooth rendered reveals
painted

Ex 100 x 50 head

Ex 63 x 44 top rail
of casement

Wrought iron handrail

Ex 44 x 25
glazing bar

Meeting stiles

Ex 125 x 44
bottom rail

16 mm diam.

Ex 125 x 50 sill
member

Tack

275 x 38 zinc covered timber sill

SECTION

Parliament hinge

Vertical
d.p.c.

Expanded
metal

Zinc turned up
into brick joint

Tyrolean
rendering

Zinc stopped end

PLAN

113   Inward opening casement

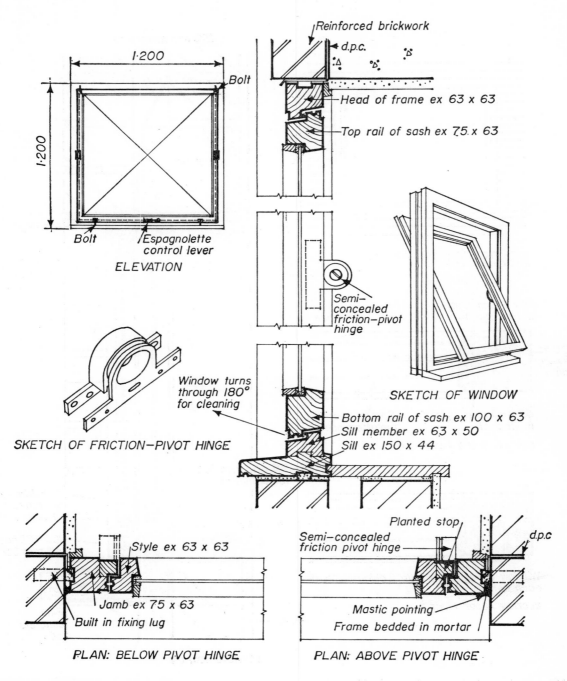

1·200

Bolt

1·200

Bolt

Espagnolette control lever

ELEVATION

Reinforced brickwork

d.p.c.

Head of frame ex 63 x 63

Top rail of sash ex 75 x 63

Semi-concealed friction–pivot hinge

SKETCH OF WINDOW

Window turns through 180° for cleaning

SKETCH OF FRICTION–PIVOT HINGE

Bottom rail of sash ex 100 x 63
Sill member ex 63 x 50
Sill ex 150 x 44

Style ex 63 x 63

Jamb ex 75 x 63

Built in fixing lug

PLAN: BELOW PIVOT HINGE

Planted stop

Semi–concealed friction pivot hinge

d.p.c

Mastic pointing

Frame bedded in mortar

PLAN: ABOVE PIVOT HINGE

114   *Horizontal pivot hung: timber window*

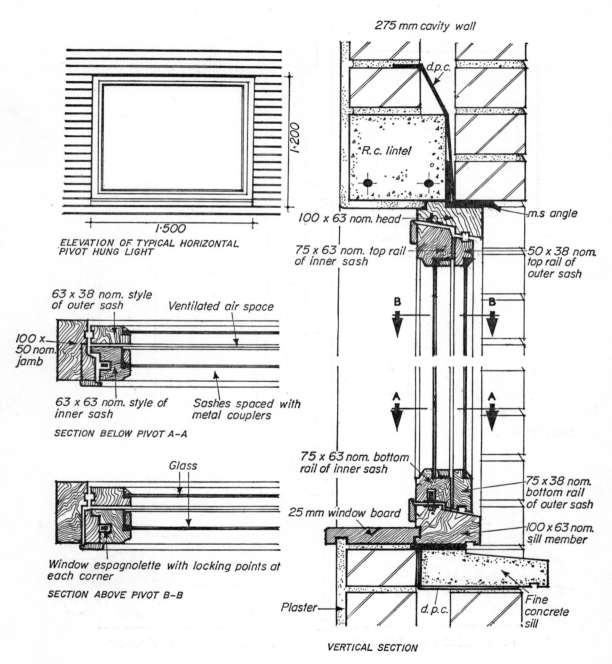

ELEVATION OF TYPICAL HORIZONTAL
PIVOT HUNG LIGHT

1·200

1·500

63 x 38 nom. style
of outer sash

Ventilated air space

100 x
50 nom.
jamb

63 x 63 nom. style of
inner sash

Sashes spaced with
metal couplers

SECTION BELOW PIVOT A–A

Glass

Window espagnolette with locking points at
each corner

SECTION ABOVE PIVOT B–B

275 mm cavity wall

d.p.c.

R.c. lintel

m.s angle

100 x 63 nom. head

75 x 63 nom. top rail
of inner sash

50 x 38 nom.
top rail of
outer sash

B   B

A   A

75 x 63 nom. bottom
rail of inner sash

75 x 38 nom.
bottom rail
of outer sash

25 mm window board

100 x 63 nom.
sill member

Plaster

d.p.c.

Fine
concrete
sill

VERTICAL SECTION

115   Horizontal pivot window – double sash

extra cost of plate glass. The window can be fastened with a mortice turn button into the sill, but larger windows need securing at all corners by an espagnolette bolt set in a groove on three sides and operated by one handle. The pivot mechanism holds the sash in any desired open position by friction. Note the traditional method of *weathering* the window opening, shown in figure 115, by means of a mild steel angle to support the outer leaf of brickwork and a sheet lead cavity *tray*. The lead must be carried over the metal angle to catch any water which may run down inside the cavity from a saturated outer leaf. This construction can now be effected using a specially fabricated all metal section which replaces the inner RC lintel, the cavity dpc and the mild steel angle.

Sliding and sliding-folding windows

In detailing sliding and sliding-folding windows bottom rollers are usually preferred to top track since the track is more difficult to conceal. Provision for draught exclusion is very important and this can be provided quite easily on the vertical edges. On the sill and head, however, there are many difficulties in particular with sliding windows. Where the window is sliding-folding however it is more easily draughtproofed as the final closing of the sash and shooting of the fixing bolts near the hinges can be ranged to clamp the sashes against the sill and at the head.

Horizontal sliding-folding window

Figure 116 shows details of a sliding-folding window. The sashes (nominal thickness 50 mm) are supported on bottom runners which incorporate the hinge and run on special hard brass or sherardized steel track screwed into the sill. There is ample provision for adjusting the rebate and sill and head as well as the jambs to ensure a close fit. Outward opening lights are most common as they do not interfere with curtaining and are easier to make weather-proof. The frame is shown nailed into fixing blocks built into the brickwork.

Horizontal sliding window

Straight sliding windows are more common and providing access to a terrace they should really be called sliding doors but the distinction is not important. Several alternative track arrangements are possible, the simplest is where single sliding windows are used, each sliding frame passes a fixed light of similar size. This reduces the amount of track and the joints between the opening sashes. A typical example is shown in figure 117. In this case the timber posts or *mullions* support the lintel above. One large fixed light is fixed direct to the mullions in a rebate and the sliding window passes behind the mullion and fixed light. This simplifies the joint at the jambs and enables the top track to be fixed on a packing at the side of the lintel. The door is carried on rollers running on a track let into the floor. The larger sashes are nominal 63 mm thick with 150 mm styles and bottom rail and with 100 mm top rail. Cavity sealed double glazing is used in the example. The weight of these sashes is considerable so 8 rollers are used. For single glazing and smaller sashes 2 rollers should be sufficient. The precautions to exclude draught include at one side a phosphor-bronze weather strip against which the sash closes. At the other side a felt strip fixed to the mullion is pressed by a hardwood stop which can be scribed to fit close. At the top is another weather strip fixed to the head and which rubs against the top rail as it closes. As an alternative to the phosphor-bronze weathering shown, the detail could be draught and weather-proofed by the use of wool-pile or neoprene weather stripping in extruded aluminium sections. A metal water bar is fixed to the floor runner and a cover strip which can be scribed and fixed with cups and screws overlaps this.

Vertical sliding sash

The quality, design and construction of standard *double hung* sash windows is covered by BS 644 : Part 2 : 1958 : *English Type* and Part 3 : 1951 : *Scottish Type*.

The frames are either (a) *cased*, by being formed into a box like construction to receive weights, which when guided by pulleys and with cords attached to the sashes, will counter balance the sashes holding them open at any given position; or (b) *solid* frames, where the outer frame or style serves as a guide to the sashes which are grooved to receive special spiral balance springs. For larger windows (other than domestic types) the groove to receive the balance spring would be made in the frame and not in the sash.

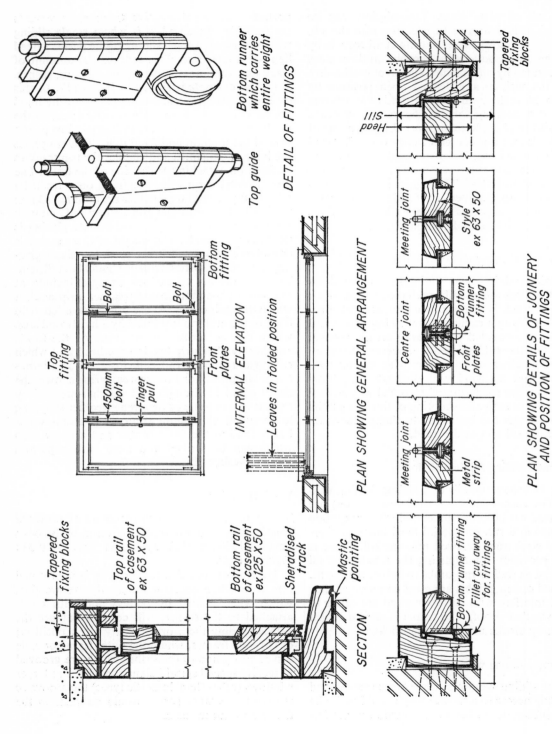

Bottom runner which carries entire weight

Top guide

DETAIL OF FITTINGS

Tapered fixing blocks

Head

Sill

Meeting joint

Style ex 63 x 50

Centre joint

Bottom runner fitting

Front plates

Meeting joint

Metal strip

PLAN SHOWING DETAILS OF JOINERY AND POSITION OF FITTINGS

Top fitting

Bolt

Bolt

450mm bolt

Finger pull

Bottom fitting

Front plates

INTERNAL ELEVATION

Leaves in folded position

PLAN SHOWING GENERAL ARRANGEMENT

Tapered fixing blocks

Top rail of casement ex 63 x 50

Bottom rail of casement ex 125 x 50

Sheradised track

Mastic pointing

SECTION

Bottom runner fitting

Fillet cut away for fittings

116   Sliding-folding wooden windows

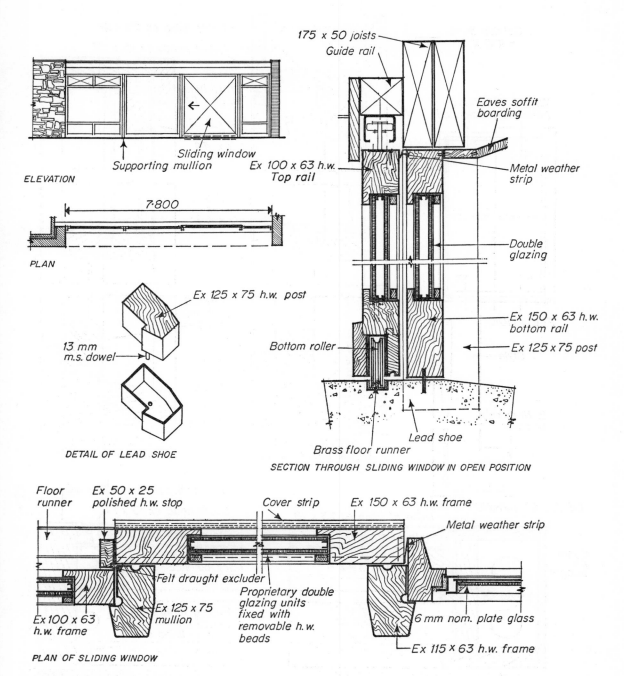

ELEVATION

Sliding window

Supporting mullion

Ex 100 x 63 h.w.
Top rail

7·800

PLAN

Ex 125 x 75 h.w. post

13 mm
m.s. dowel

DETAIL OF LEAD SHOE

175 x 50 joists

Guide rail

Eaves soffit
boarding

Metal weather
strip

Double
glazing

Ex 150 x 63 h.w.
bottom rail

Ex 125 x 75 post

Bottom roller

Lead shoe

Brass floor runner

SECTION THROUGH SLIDING WINDOW IN OPEN POSITION

Floor
runner

Ex 50 x 25
polished h.w. stop

Cover strip

Ex 150 x 63 h.w. frame

Metal weather strip

Felt draught excluder

Ex 125 x 75
mullion

Proprietary double
glazing units
fixed with
removable h.w.
beads

6 mm nom. plate glass

Ex 100 x 63
h.w. frame

Ex 115 x 63 h.w. frame

PLAN OF SLIDING WINDOW

117   Sliding window

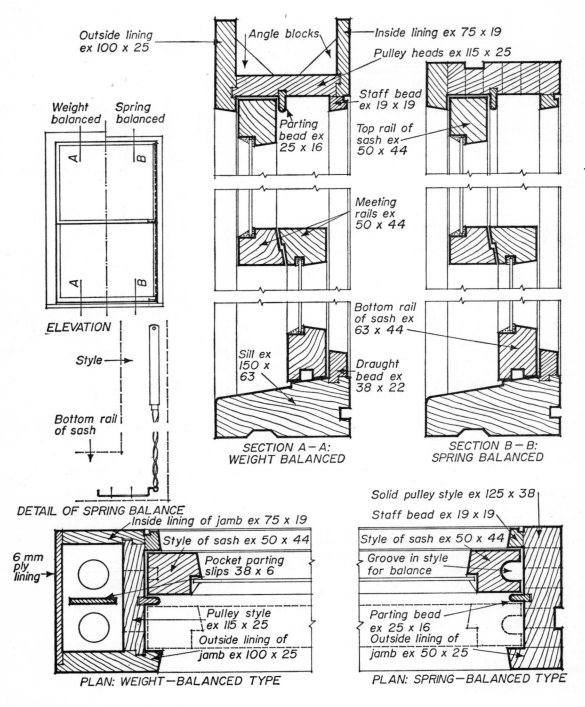

Weight balanced   Spring balanced

A   B

A   B

ELEVATION

Style →

Bottom rail of sash

DETAIL OF SPRING BALANCE

Outside lining ex 100 x 25

Angle blocks

Inside lining ex 75 x 19

Pulley heads ex 115 x 25

Staff bead ex 19 x 19

Top rail of sash ex 50 x 44

Parting bead ex 25 x 16

Meeting rails ex 50 x 44

Bottom rail of sash ex 63 x 44

Sill ex 150 x 63

Draught bead ex 38 x 22

SECTION A – A: WEIGHT BALANCED

SECTION B – B: SPRING BALANCED

6 mm ply lining →

Inside lining of jamb ex 75 x 19

Style of sash ex 50 x 44

Pocket parting slips 38 x 6

Pulley style ex 115 x 25

Outside lining of jamb ex 100 x 25

PLAN: WEIGHT—BALANCED TYPE

Solid pulley style ex 125 x 38

Staff bead ex 19 x 19

Style of sash ex 50 x 44

Groove in style for balance

Parting bead ex 25 x 16

Outside lining of jamb ex 50 x 25

PLAN: SPRING—BALANCED TYPE

118   Standard timber sash windows

Figure 118 shows a typical arrangement for a domestic type window showing both cased and solid frames. The weight-balanced types are now obsolete in new construction but were traditionally much used, and still require to be maintained.

Fixing timber windows

Figure 119a–e illustrates various methods of locating timber windows in openings in the following types of construction

1 traditional load bearing cavity walling
2 monolithic concrete construction
3 timber framed construction.

The window frames should not be called upon to take any load from the structure; the opening being 'self-supporting'. It is not altogether easy to ensure that the frame is relieved of load if the frame is built into the opening as the main work of construction proceeds. On the other hand, this method ensures a good fit for the window. Where the window is placed in position after the opening is formed there may be difficulties in ensuring correct tolerances, but there is likely to be less damage to the frame.

Wood windows should always be fixed to the dry leaf of cavity walling or otherwise be protected by a vertical damp proof course. There should always be a vertical dpc between the wet and the dry leaf in a cavity wall. The face of the gap between the woodwork and the brickwork should be sealed with a suitable strip of mastic. Rebates for glazing should be at least 9 mm deep. The glass is usually put in with putty formed to a triangular bead with a putty knife. For a higher class of work, weathered timber beads scribed or mitred at the corners can be pinned in with brass pins or screwed with brass screws. The glass in this case should have putty 'back and front' to allow for even support. For more detailed notes on glazing see chapter 5. The sill must be weathered at a sufficient slope to throw off the water and *throated* with a groove near the front on its underside so that the water will drip off and not run back to the bed of the sill. Sills are usually pointed in mastic and may have a water bar to act as an additional check against the penetration of moisture at this point, and to locate the sill horizontally.

The *throating* or *drip* must be able to shed water without obstruction on to a well-sloped tile, stone or metal sill beneath. Alternatively, it may shed the water clear of the wall where the frame is fixed close to the outer face of the wall.

Sills are very subject to defects caused by dampness. Either the weathering is not sufficiently steep to shed the water, or water can get back to the bed of the sill because the drip does not function, or because the slope of a concrete or stone sub-sill allows the water to run back instead of outwards. These are points to watch carefully. Paint cannot be relied upon to protect timber at this critical point, and it will be noted that BS 1186 does not permit sapwood in timber sills.

The head is not so troublesome usually, but the dpc in a cavity above must catch water running down the inside surface of the outside skin and conduct it properly to the outside of the head.

Window frames should be secured to walls by means of metal lugs or, alternatively, screwed in place into plastic or similar plugs cast or drilled into the surrounding masonry. The frames should be bedded in cement mortar with the external joint sealed by the application of the correct mastic.

Points to note about the various details shown are as follows:

(a) The head of the opening is supported by two reinforced concrete lintels, the inner one splayed to close the cavity over the frame.

The *cavity tray* or *cavity flashing* (shown dotted) will preferably be of lead, but is acceptable in good quality bituminous felt. This cavity dpc is carried under the soffit of the outer lintel and a drip is formed in the cement render finish.

The timber sill which should preferably be of hardwood is projected over the external rendering. This projection should be a minimum 35 mm and preferably 50 mm in order to shed water clear of the face of the building. If this simple fundamental principle is ignored – for whatever reason – and water allowed to permeate the wall below the opening due to there being no projecting sill, then at best, disfiguring staining will result and, at worst, severe deterioration of the fabric.

At the jamb the dpc is turned into the groove into the timber frame. The frame would be set in mortar by 'buttering' the opening as the brickwork is built. The frame is built in as the work proceeds.

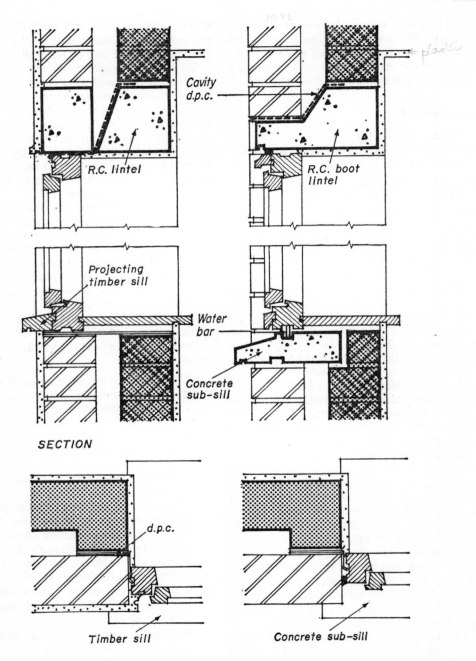

SECTION

PLAN

(a) *Load bearing brickwork*

(b) *Reinforced concrete 'boot' lintel with concrete sub-sill*

119 Timber windows

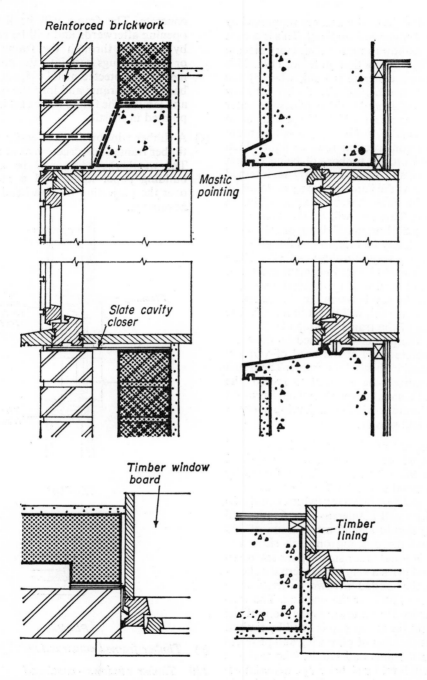

(c) *Reinforced brickwork projecting timber*   (d) *Monolithic concrete*

119 Timber windows – continued

(b) Both leaves of the cavity wall are supported by a reinforced concrete *boot* lintel. This is a neat detail which allows a more satisfactory placing of the cavity flashing than in figure 119a. This detail shows a concrete sub-sill, whereby the bottom sill member of the timber window frame has a drip mould which guides the water on to the concrete sill which protects the main structure. This is more expensive but more satisfactory construction than in figure 119a which relies on the timber sill being of first class quality and being regularly maintained by painting. At the jamb the cavity is closed by return of the inner leaf brickwork against a vertical dpc. This dpc will be the same material used as the horizontal damp proof course and will probably be bituminous felt asbestos based or with a very thin sheet metal core. The window frame will be set in cement mortar at the jamb and head whilst the metal water bar which seals the gap between the timber frame and the concrete sill, will be set in mastic. The outer edges of the frame will also be pointed in mastic. The plaster is returned on the soffit of the concrete lintel at the head of window and is 'tucked in' behind the frame. The frame may alternatively be grooved to receive the plaster and a small cover strip would prevent a view of the crack which will develop between the frame and plaster.

(c) Here the inner leaf of the walling is supported by a splayed or reinforced concrete lintel whilst the outer brickwork is reinforced by expanded metal strips for 3 or 4 courses over the opening. The reinforcing (which could also be done by small diameter – say 6 mm mild steel rods) should extend a minimum of 225 mm beyond the opening on each side. The technique is suitable for small spans say up to 3·000 m and gives a very neat external appearance since the bonded brickwork carries on in an unbroken line over the opening. The window frame here is set towards the front of the opening and the cavity gap is lined by timber. This saves the cost of plastering and provides fixings for curtains and blinds. The cavity is sealed at sill level by slate or dpc material because of the difficulty of setting a water bar in brickwork.

(d) The walling construction here is of reinforced concrete. The frame will be fitted into the opening afterwards and will be secured either by screwing through the frame into plastic or timber plugs cast into the concrete or by means of protected metal strips screwed to the back of the frame and into the concrete soffit and jambs. The frame will be set in mortar and pointed in mastic.

(e) A timber window is most easily screwed into timber framed construction as illustrated here. The weatherboarding will be backed by a building paper lining and a metal flashing over the projecting window head would be an advantage.

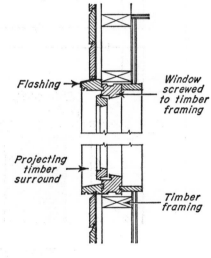

Flashing →

Window screwed to timber framing

Projecting timber surround →

Timber framing

SECTION

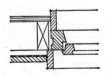

PLAN

(e) *Timber framed construction*

119 Timber windows – continued

In general, timber windows will be screwed or nailed to plugs or secured by means of metal fixing lugs, at the jambs only. Larger windows will also be secured at the head but the sill will almost always be used to locate but not to secure the window. The minimum number of fixing points will be 4 for a window say 600 mm square up to 8 for a window say 1800 mm square.

Figure 120a and b shows the location of timber windows with projecting surrounds set in a tile hung opening.

METAL WINDOWS

Steel and aluminium are the most common metals used in the manufacture of window sections. Where cost, in terms of permanency and freedom from maintenance, can be justified bronze is a material which can be used as an alternative. Stainless steel is a material which is eminently suitable for use for window frames and its rapid development as a building material for more general use may make it the window material of the future.

Steel windows

Galvanized hot rolled steel provides a material from which an economical range of windows with reasonable maintenance costs can be produced. White hot steel ingots are passed through rollers to form a billet of steel some 50 mm square 1200 mm long. The billet is then re-heated and 're-rolled' through a further series of rollers under very heavy pressure which produces the correct section profile from which the window frame is welded up. Sections are then normally galvanized by dipping in molten zinc. Regular painting is nevertheless essential.

Standard steel windows

The relevant main British Standards in respect of metal windows are as follows:

BS 990 : 1967 : *Steel Windows Generally for Domestic and Similar Buildings*
BS 1787 : 1957 : *Steel Windows for Industrial Buildings*
BS 2503 : 1954 : *Steel Windows for Agricultural Use*
BS 1285 : 1963 : *Wood Surrounds for Steel Windows and Doors.*

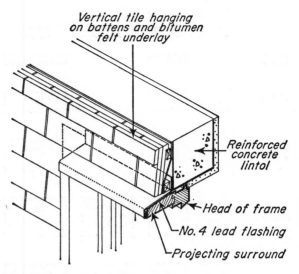

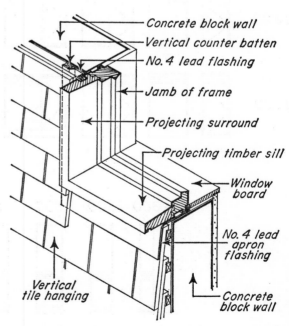

(a) *Detail at sill and jamb*

(b) *Detail at head*

120 *Projecting timber window surrounds*

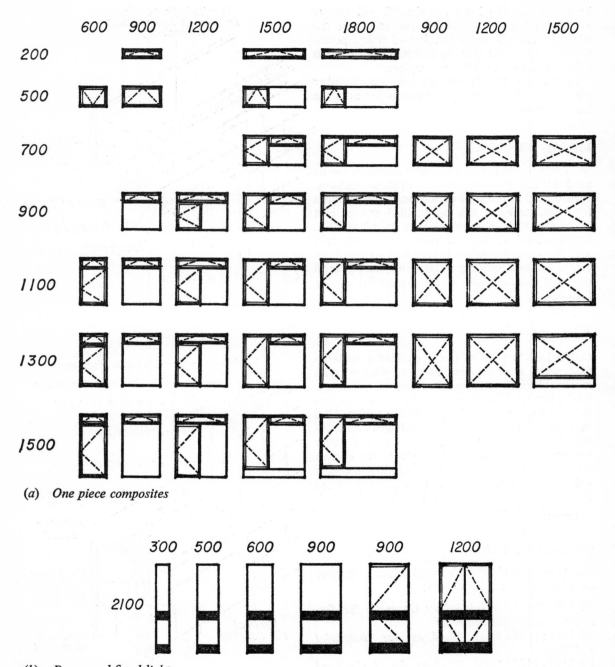

(a) *One piece composites*

(b) *Doors and fixed lights*

121   Selection from the range of module 100 steel windows

148

'Module 4' windows

Module 4 sizes based on BS 990 are not dimensionally co-ordinated. The window sizes are based on multiples of 102 mm, the vertical increments being basically 203 mm and the horizontal increments 305 mm. Top hung casements are normally 203 mm high.

'Module 100' standard windows

This is the dimensionally co-ordinated range of standard steel windows. A range of basic spaces for the window are shown in figure 7. Single or multi-pane window units will fit into these spaces.

sections and coupling arrangements used to form composite windows are shown in figure 124. The standard range includes fixed lights, side hung casements opening outwards, horizontally pivoted reversible casements and top hung casements opening outwards, with a selection of casement *doors* opening outwards. Windows and *doors* may be coupled together by the use of vertical coupling bars (*mullions*) and horizontal bars (*transoms*), and by the use of filler panels to form composite assemblies. There are limits to the sizes to which composites may be made, both in respect of the difficulties associated with the manufacturing tolerances and by reference to designated wind

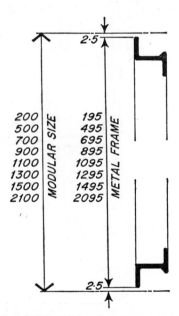

122 *Relationship of metal frames to modular size*

123 *Relationship of metal frames in timber surrounds to modular size*

A selection of windows from this range is shown in figure 121. Figures 122 and 123 show the relationship of the metal frames to the modular size, and also the relationship of the metal frames in timber surrounds to the modular size.

The *Module 100* metric range is the *standard* window and the *Module 4* is a *special* window available to order.

Typical details illustrating the standard steel

loadings. Advice should thus be obtained from the window manufacturers when these questions arise. The windows are manufactured from *test guaranteed* steel. The main frames of the windows are constructed from bars, cut to length and mitred, with all corners welded solid. Intermediate bars are tenoned and riveted to the outer frames, and to each other. The windows are hot-dip galvanized after manufacture. A tolerance of 2 mm

149

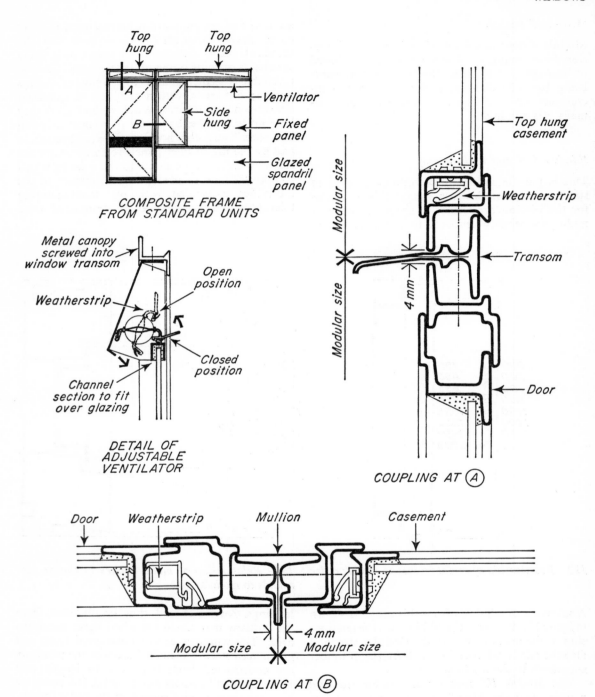

Top hung

Top hung

A

B

Side hung

Ventilator

Fixed panel

Glazed spandril panel

COMPOSITE FRAME
FROM STANDARD UNITS

Metal canopy
screwed into
window transom

Weatherstrip

Open
position

Channel
section to fit
over glazing

Closed
position

DETAIL OF
ADJUSTABLE
VENTILATOR

Top hung
casement

Weatherstrip

Modular size

Transom

Modular size

4 mm

Door

COUPLING AT Ⓐ

Door   Weatherstrip   Mullion   Casement

4 mm

Modular size   Modular size

COUPLING AT Ⓑ

124   *Coupling of standard steel sections*

above or below ($\pm$) the standard dimensions is allowable and a fitting allowance of 2·5 mm all round the window is allowed between the outside window size and the basic dimensions of the openings to receive the window units.

Side hung casements are hung on projecting friction hinges without a stay. They are made of steel and are welded or riveted to the frames. The hinge pins are either rust proofed steel or aluminium alloy. The friction hinge is adjusted by the manufacturer at his works to require a given pressure on the handle to move the casement, and the hinge can be adjusted in-situ. When the casement is open to 90° the projecting arm gives a clear distance between the frame and casement of not less than 85 mm as shown in figure 105, page 130. This will allow both sides of the glass to be cleaned from inside the window which is an important factor in reducing maintenance costs where the window is used in multi-storey buildings. If so ordered side hung casements can alternatively be supplied with non-friction hinges and peg stays. The side hung casement will also be provided with a lever handle providing limited or *crack* ventilation by means of a notch, engaging on a striking plate which is bevelled. Side hung (and top hung) casements are not weather stripped as standard, but if ordered specially the weather stripping is carried out in a suitable plastic, ie PVC.

The horizontally pivoted casements are fully reversible and are weather stripped by synthetic rubber. This type of window also permits cleaning of the outside face of the glass from the inside of the building and also the cleaning of all the adjoining glass areas within arms reach. Thus with careful design the whole of the glazing to a multi-storey building can be cleaned with safety from the inside, with considerable savings in maintenance costs. The glass in a reversible window can also be replaced from inside the building. The hinges for reversible casements are of the friction type, so adjusted as to hold the casement in any position. Automatic safety devices (releasable by hand) limit the initial opening of the casement to approximately 15°, which, depending on the height of the window, will mean that the window projects into the room from 100 mm to 150 mm. When the safety device is released, the window can be reversed, pivoted through 180°. There is then a further safety catch which can be operated to hold the window firmly in the reversed position whilst

maintenance or cleaning take place. This is shown in figure 104, page 129.

For the standard range of windows, handles are made in the following alternative finishes; hot pressed brass; nickel chromium plated on brass, or on zinc based alloy; and various aluminium alloys. Handles are detachable and can be replaced without disturbing the glass.

The whole range of windows to this BS is manufactured from only 12 basic steel sections, thus by standardization, and the application of industrial techniques of large scale manufacture, an acceptable and comparatively inexpensive range of windows giving a choice over a wide range of types and sizes can be produced.

Standard steel windows for agricultural buildings

In order to provide an inexpensive window, for an inexpensive building type, a limited standard range of windows is produced, covered by BS 2503. Three standard sizes are made with small panes of glass, each type incorporating an inward opening bottom hung hopper ventilator. The rolled steel sections used are similar to those specified in BS 990.

Standard steel windows for industrial buildings

BS 1787, which is due for revision, covers this type of window. A point to bear in mind is that there are other forms of sidewall glazing in metal frames which have an industrial application.

Purpose made steel window sections

A range of weather stripped *universal* steel sections is produced known as *W20* from which purpose made windows can be manufactured. The rolled section is heavier than that used for the BS 990 window and the maximum permissible sizes for the basic types of window made from these sections is given in table 2.

A detail of the section is shown in figure 125. Basic units of purpose made windows are coupled together by mullions and transomes, to form composite units in the same way as a standard window, but it is usual to employ a specialist sub-contractor to fix purpose made windows. Purpose made windows are usually fitted with good quality handles and other furniture, possibly of bronze.

Method of opening	Size of Section	Height plus width	Height	Width
Side hung	Normal	2600	1900	700
	Heavy	3300	2600	900
Folding	Normal	3200	1900	1300
	Heavy	3900	2400	1800
Vertically	Normal	2900	1900	1100
Pivoted	Heavy	3900	2600	1400
Folding vertically	Normal	3600	1800	1800
Pivoted	Heavy	4700	2400	2300
Top hung	Normal	2600	1500	1500
	Heavy	3200	1800	1800
Horizontally	Normal	2600	1500	1500
Centre hung	Heavy	3200	1800	1800
Bottom hung	Normal	2600	1500	1500
	Heavy	3200	1800	1800

Table 2   Extreme sizes of ventilators made of steel W20 Universal Section (dimensions in mm)

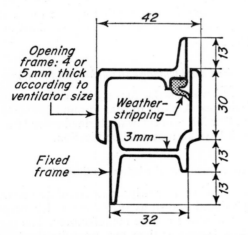

125   W20 steel section for purpose made windows

The basic spaces for purpose made steel windows are shown in figure 126 from which the preferred range of *W20* windows will be manufactured for use in dimensionally co-ordinated buildings.

Fixing steel windows

The windows are fixed by means of counter-sunk screws accommodated in pre-drilled holes in the web of the sections. The position of the fixings for standard windows are indicated in BS 990 and vary from 2 to 12 points of fixing per window depending on the size of the frame. The types of fixing are as follows:

1 Wood screws, not less than (3·25 mm) 10 gauge for fixing into proprietary plastic or fibre plugs in pre-drilled holes in precast concrete surround or in-situ concrete openings.
2 Short counter-sunk screw and nut for securing the frame – before building in – to steel lugs set in the joints of brick or masonry openings. The lug has elongated slots to allow adjustment to accommodate variation in joint positions.
3 Self tapping screw for fixing to pressed metal sub-frames.

Where fixed direct into the opening, the metal windows are set in a waterproof cement fillet, which is *buttered* to the jambs of the opening before the window is offered into position. The space between the frame and the opening is then pointed in a suitable mastic, and the inside reveal usually plastered.

Typical fixing details are shown in figure 127. Three examples of the arrangement of a metal frame within a surround are shown in figure 128.

(a) shows the use of a pressed steel combined lintel and cavity flashing at the head, and a pressed metal surround. This type of surround is described in BS 1422 : 1956 : *Steel Sub-frames, Sills and Window Boards for Metal Windows*.
(b) shows a purpose made slate surround into which is fixed small cross section hardwood fillets to receive the steel window. The surround serves as sill, head and window board.
(c) is an alternative to this where the slate is expressed only in the external face of the building.

Timber surrounds

Where a superior type of fixing is required the metal window can be set into a timber sub-frame, which is then fixed into the opening by means of built-in lugs or screwing into plugs. Standard sub-frames are detailed in BS 1285 : 1963 : *Wood Surrounds for Steel Windows and Doors.*

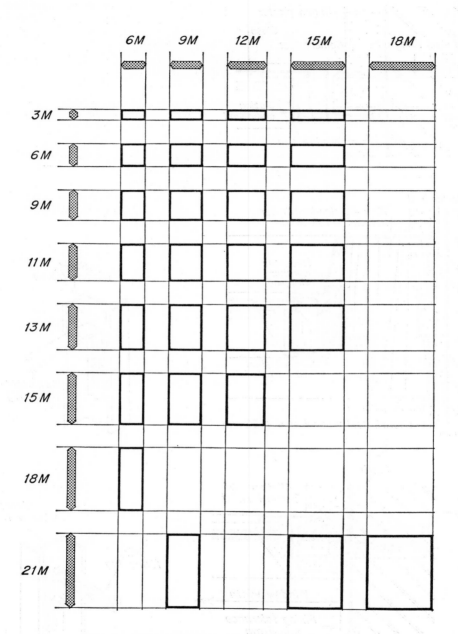

M = 1 module of 100 mm and refers to the size
of opening into which the window fits

126   Basic spaces for purpose-made steel windows

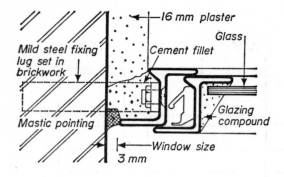

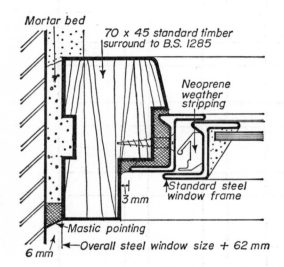

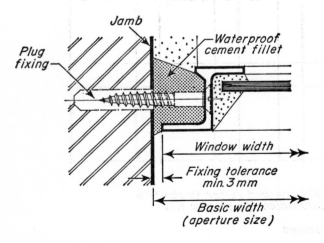

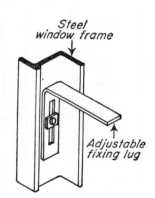

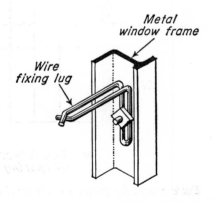

127 *Typical metal window fixing details*

Alternative types of adjustable fixing lug

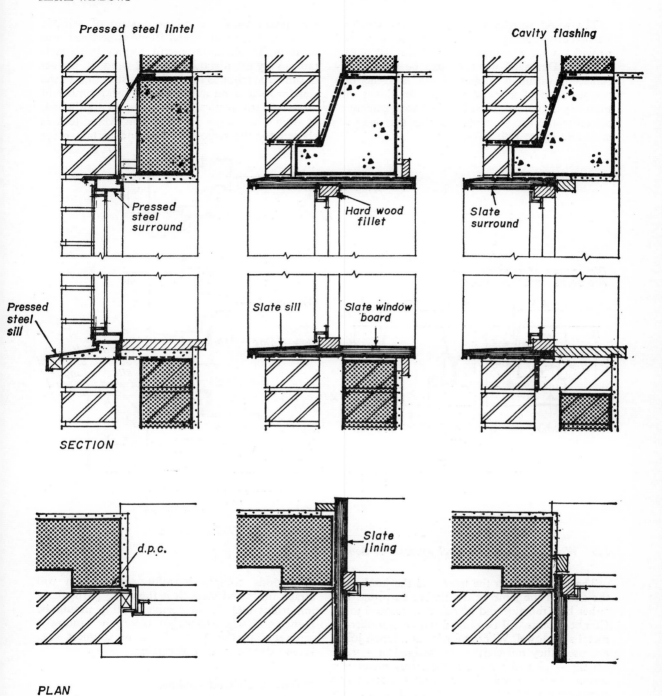

Pressed steel lintel

Cavity flashing

Pressed steel surround

Hard wood fillet

Slate surround

Pressed steel sill

SECTION

Slate sill

Slate window board

d.p.c.

Slate lining

PLAN

128   *Metal windows in brickwork openings*

The wood surround will protect the window, particularly during transport to the site, and provides a more satisfactory bed for the mastic sealants. Damaged windows can be more easily replaced, within a timber frame and the thin apppearance of a metal window set direct into masonry is avoided. Details of the arrangement of a steel window in a standard timber surround are shown in figure 129.

are spread with a continuous strip of suitable mastic and then the metal frame is screwed into position, 32 mm counter-sunk screws, being suitable. Very often standard metal windows are set in timber surrounds of similar construction to the standard surround described but using timber of non-standard section, very often in hardwood. It should be borne in mind that where teak is chosen for the surround, this, and certain other

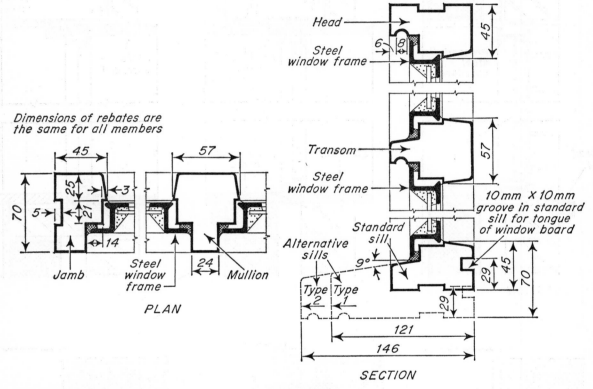

129   Wood surrounds for steel windows or doors: BS 1285

The joint between the head and the jamb, and the sill and the jamb in the timber surround will either be a mortice and tenon, or a combed joint. Combed joints will be pinned with a non-ferrous metal star dowel. Where mortice and tenon joints are used they must either be wedged or – more usually – pinned with a non-ferrous metal star dowel. Both combed joints and mortice and tenon joints are also glued. In order to produce a watertight joint between the timber surround and the metal frame, the rebates of the frame after priming

hardwoods contain harmful acids which will attack untreated steel. It is therefore particularly important that the protective coating should be made good, where damaged, before the window is screwed into the frame. Brass or stainless steel screws should be used for fixing.

Purpose made steel windows

Where floor to ceiling glazing is required and purpose-made metal windows are indicated the

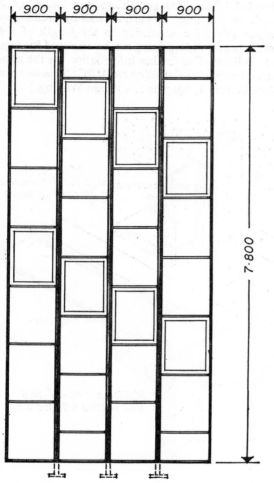

150 x 150 mm m.s. base plates welded on to mullions

KEY ELEVATION

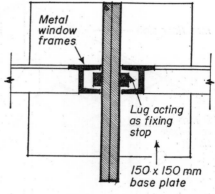

2 no. 175 x 10 m.s. flat section, drilled, tapp   and secured by countersunk screws

Metal window frames

Lug acting as fixing stop

150 x 150 mm base plate

DETAIL OF MULLION: CONCEALED FIXING STOPS

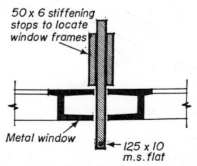

50 x 6 stiffening stops to locate window frames

Metal window

125 x 10 m.s. flat

PLAN OF BUILT—UP MULLION, EXPOSED FIXING STOPS

130   Large metal windows

mullions are usually the primary structural members. Figure 130 shows such a window detailed to have substantial mullions. Each mullion is 175 mm deep with a total height of 7·800 m. The problems of jointing mullions of this kind can be solved in several ways. In the example the stops are concealed so that the mullion is built up of two lines of 9 mm thick steel flats lapping each other and screwed together. This facilitates erection and reduces the parts to a convenient length for galvanizing. In the example shown the feet and tops of the mullions are cast into an in-situ concrete sill and head. This is a simple technique for the window fixer and for the contractor but it is not easy

157

to get a good finish on the in-situ concrete sill. Precast sills with joints on the mullion lines are an alternative technique but moisture penetration must be avoided at the joints where it will attack the foot of the mullion. It is, of course, possible to joint mullions at intermediate supports such as floor and landing levels as in curtain walling tech-

bedded joints. Box stanchions can be designed such as are used in curtain walling techniques which allow for expansion in the length of the window and sliding fixing can be arranged for tops of mullions. For further information on the construction of glazed walling see *MBC: Structure and Fabric*, Part 1, chapter 5, Curtain Walling.

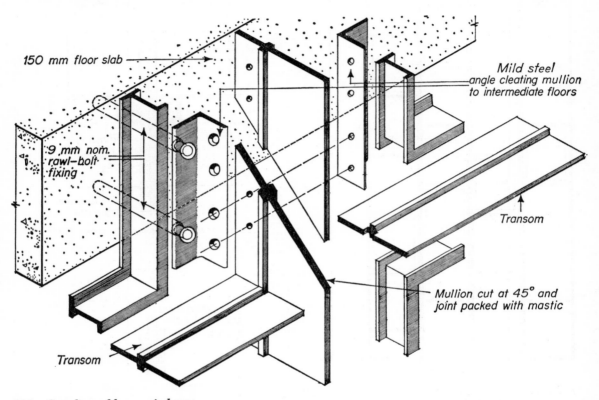

131   Coupling of large windows

niques. The fixing plate is shown on the detail in figure 131. The splayed cut gives a neat water tight joint which must be well sealed with mastic. In erecting large windows of this kind sashes may be coupled together with transoms if they are not structural, and built from the sill up, fixing to one side. The first mullion is placed and the next vertical range of sashes and so on across the total width. Expansion in large metal windows is a problem which must be overcome. The larger structural members are the chief cause of trouble as the expansion of the smaller member such as the sashes can be taken up in the many mastic

Pressed metal frames

Metal pressings first came into the building industry in the use of standard door frames, which proved strong, quick to erect, and clean in outline.

Skirtings, stair treads, risers, window frames and shelving have been made of pressed sheet metal for some time. Now doors, particularly lift doors, large window frames, and many other elements are produced.

Mild steel sheet is used mostly in a range of gauges, 26 gauge for angle bead, 20 gauge for door frames, 12, 14 and 16 gauge for window frames and sometimes 10 gauge, approximately 3 mm thick, where greater strength and rigidity is required. Sheets up to 3·000 m × 1·300 m are used, depending on the size of the press or folder the manufacturer has.

Typical profiles of pressed steel sections are shown in figure 132. Folds can be made through any angle up to 105°, that is forming an angle of not less than 75°, but a stiffened edge can be made by pressing a fold down flat. This is called a *bar fold*. Surfaces of the member must be flat planes: Sharp angles cannot be obtained, the minimum outside radius being usually 2 mm for 16 gauge and 5 mm for 10 gauge. Minimum width of any face is from 12 mm for 16 gauge sheet to 20 mm for 10 gauge. Sections are usually open for most of one side, this being necessary for connections, fixing stiffening cross-members, etc. If a member is to be formed with the fourth side mostly closed, it is necessary to form it with a false fold as shown.

Cutting is done by mechanical saws or by grinding wheels, or by burning. Sheet metal is also cut by knife in a guillotine. Burning is now precise enough to be used for cutting square mortices for a square member to pass through. Holes, including small mortices, are of course formed by drilling or punching. The latter may cause some deformation of the metal member which, if there are many holes, may accumulate to measurable increase in length and width. Running joints are made with sleeves, bedded in mastic and tapped and screwed with counter-sunk screws, as shown in the diagram. Junctions between members are formed by scribing the end of the stopping member to the profile of the continuing member, filling it with a shaped cleat and screwing it to the continuing member, with a good supply of mastic packed in the joint. It will be seen how the use of a simple rectangular profile simplifies the junction. Complicated profiles call for a complicated cleat and may present difficulties in screwing up. Similarly, the scribing can only be done against flat planes; but, most important of all, the stopping members should be smaller than the continuing member so that it is quite clear of the slightly rounded angles of the continuing member. This is shown in the same diagram. The joint of mullion to sill is made in the same way, the end of the mullion being filled with a cleat and being well filled with mastic before screwing up. It is essential that the cleat be solid behind the front edge of the mullion, so that the

mastic is squeezed between the two metal faces and there is no cavity to hold moisture. In some cases it may be more convenient to make a joint in the sill at each mullion; the latter will then continue down with the sill scribed to it. Figure 133 shows typical sill and mullion sections. If the front or back face of a frame of pressed-steel members is to be in one plane, it is necessary to form the angles by mitring and welding, and forming site joints with sleeves in the lengths of the members as shown in figure 133.

Large members can be built up out of several pressings. This is satisfactory if the joints can be masked by the sashes, or hidden on internal angles.

Where long members are used – tall mullion or a long sill – it is important to ensure that the arris is dead straight and the planes are true. What may look satisfactory in elevation may look very bad when seen from directly below or from one side, where it is easy to get 'an eye along the edge'. To get this trueness it is essential that the metal be thick enough to keep its folded shape and that it is carefully fixed. The architect can get the latter put right, but if the metal is too thin any remedy is rather expensive.

Aluminium windows

The use of aluminium windows has increased very much over the past few years. Aluminium alloy is an attractive and adaptable material, which produces windows to a very high degree of accuracy and with a high standard of finish. Because of its lightness it is particularly suitable for use in the manufacture of both horizontal and vertical sliding windows; frames which are to receive double glazing; and reversible pivot windows. Aluminium sections can be very easily weather stripped, and where this is carefully designed, a remarkable degree of sound insulation is obtained as a bonus to the draught and weatherproofing.

Aluminium window sections are extruded by forcing under extreme pressure, a heated billet of aluminium through a die of the desired profile. With this technique it is a simple matter to incorporate grooves in the section during extrusion to accommodate efficient weather stripping material. Aluminium windows are either supplied *mill*, that

159

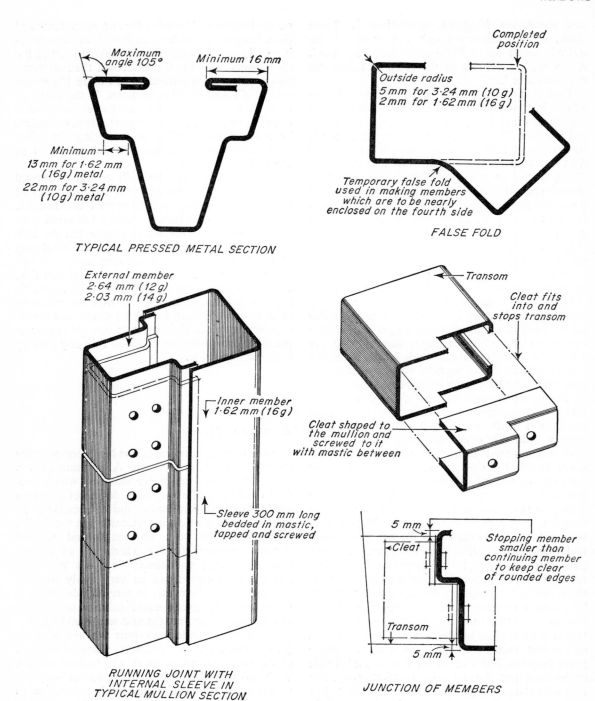

Maximum angle 105°

Minimum 16 mm

Minimum
13 mm for 1·62 mm
(16g) metal
22 mm for 3·24 mm
(10g) metal

TYPICAL PRESSED METAL SECTION

Completed position

Outside radius
5 mm for 3·24 mm (10 g)
2 mm for 1·62 mm (16 g)

Temporary false fold
used in making members
which are to be nearly
enclosed on the fourth side

FALSE FOLD

External member
2·64 mm (12g)
2·03 mm (14g)

Inner member
1·62 mm (16g)

Sleeve 300 mm long
bedded in mastic,
tapped and screwed

RUNNING JOINT WITH
INTERNAL SLEEVE IN
TYPICAL MULLION SECTION

Transom

Cleat fits
into and
stops transom

Cleat shaped to
the mullion and
screwed to it
with mastic between

5 mm

Cleat

Stopping member
smaller than
continuing member
to keep clear
of rounded edges

Transom

5 mm

JUNCTION OF MEMBERS

132   Pressed metal frames (1)

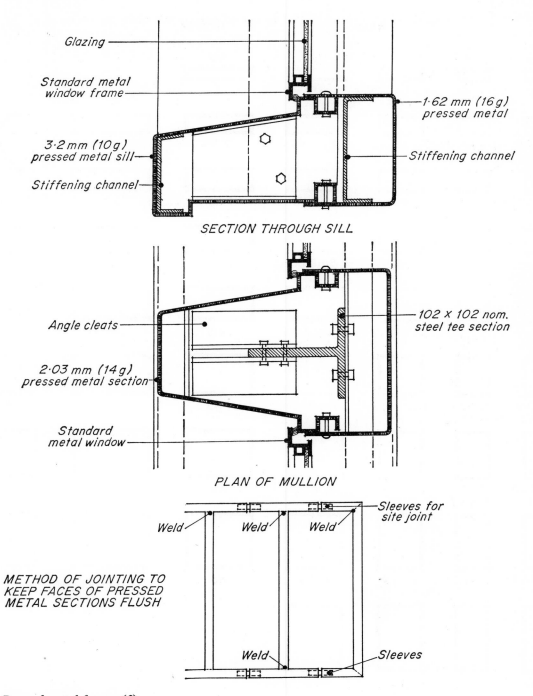

Glazing

Standard metal
window frame

1·62 mm (16 g)
pressed metal

3·2 mm (10 g)
pressed metal sill

Stiffening channel

Stiffening channel

SECTION THROUGH SILL

Angle cleats

102 x 102 nom.
steel tee section

2·03 mm (14 g)
pressed metal section

Standard
metal window

PLAN OF MULLION

Sleeves for
site joint

Weld

Weld

Weld

METHOD OF JOINTING TO
KEEP FACES OF PRESSED
METAL SECTIONS FLUSH

Weld

Sleeves

133   *Pressed metal frames (2)*

M = 1 module of 100 mm, and refers to size of opening into which the window fits

	6M	9M	12M	15M	18M	21M	24M
3M	T:B	T:B	T:B	T:B	T		
5M	T:B:HP	T:B:HP:HS	T:B:HP:HS	T:B:HP:HS	T:HS	HS	HS
6M	T:B:HP	T:B:HP:HS	T:B:HP:HS	T:B:HP:HS	T:HS	HS	HS
7M	T:B:HP	T:B:HP:HS	T:B:HP:HS	T:B:HP:HS	T:HS	HS	HS
9M	C:T:HP VS	C*:T:VP HP/R:VS:HS	T:HP/R:VS HS	T:HP/R:HS	T:HS	HS	HS
11M	C:T:VP HP:VS	C*:T:VP HP/R:VS:HS	T:VP:HP/R VS:HS	T:HP/R:HS	T:HS	HS	HS
13M	C:VP:HP VS	C*:VP HP/R:VS	VP:HP/R VS:HS	HP/R:VS HS	HS	HS	HS
15M	C:VP:VS	VP:VS	VP:VS	VS:HS	HS	HS	HS
18M	C:VS	VS	VS	VS			

134   *Basic spaces and ranges of aluminium windows*

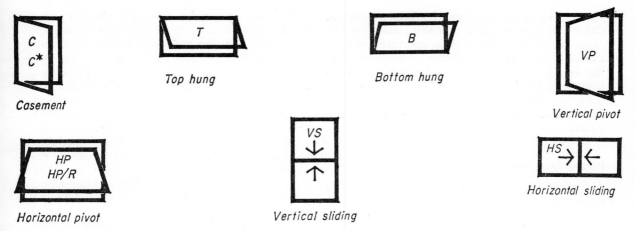

134 *Basic spaces and ranges of aluminium windows – continued*

is, natural finish, or anodized. The *mill* finish should be allowed to weather naturally and provided the atmosphere is not industrially corrosive then this will be satisfactory. Natural finish aluminium can of course be painted provided that a zinc chromate primer is used, though a painted finish on aluminium seems to be a contradiction in economic terms.

If it is desired to enhance the appearance of the window, then anodizing should be specified to be carried out in accordance with BS 3987:1967: *Anodizing for Exterior Architectural Work.*

Anodizing is comparatively expensive at the present time, but produces a beautiful finish on the metal, particularly if polished. Colour anodizing can be carried out, but particular care in respect of choice of colour should be observed since certain colours will not remain *light-fast*. In order to retain its attractiveness, anodized aluminium requires regular cleaning – with soap and water.

Mill finish windows will normally be despatched from the factory unprotected and must be cleaned down by the Contractor just before the scaffolding is dismantled. Where windows are anodized they should be coated by a film of wax and then protected by strong self-adhesive tape on all the visible and exposed surfaces. The Contractor can then easily remove the tape and polish the wax away to give a finished surface. This should not of course be done until there is no risk of damage by following trades.

The manufacture of the frames and opening sashes follows the methods generally used for steel windows, the corner jamb being electrically welded and using mechanical mortice and tenon joints for glazing bars and intermediate members and riveting or screwing for the fixing of the fittings. The maximum sizes for primary ventilators will depend upon the cross-sectional strength of the extruded sections.

Allowances for expansion of aluminium members are made roughly the same as for steel windows. One factor which should not be overlooked when aluminium windows are used is the necessity for great care in handling and treatment on site. Members are not so strong as steel and will not support scaffold poles or boards etc., and aluminium will show ill-effects at once. Preferably they should not be fixed until all the structural work and wet finishes are completed and should be protectively wrapped before dispatch and carefully stored on the site. They should be kept very clean during the progress of the work as cement or plaster will adhere to the surface and will leave a mark on bright aluminium.

Basic spaces

The Aluminium Window Association have produced a chart of the basic spaces and ranges in which it is intended that dimensionally co-ordinated aluminium windows will be made. The spaces – shown in figure 134, are in accordance with the information given in BS 4330 in respect of controlling dimensions in modular co-ordination. The spaces indicate aperture sizes, and when

163

work on joints, tolerances etc., has been completed, details showing sections and work sizes for the range of windows to fit these apertures, will be available from the manufacturers. (Note that at the time of printing the sizes have not been confirmed by BSI.) In addition to the sizes shown there is a range 21 M high suitable for vertical sliding sashes, single or double doors and sliding doors.

Bottom hung window

A domestic scale bottom hung opening inwards aluminium window is shown in figure 135. This type of window is useful where draught-free ventilation at low level is desirable. The sections are extruded from aluminium alloys HE 9P and HV 9P in accordance with BS 1476 : 1963 : *Wrought Aluminium and Aluminium Alloys*. Note the dovetailed grooves to receive the neoprene insert to act as weather stripping. The lengths of weather stripping *clip in* and can be removed for replacement if they become damaged or worn over the life of the window. The hinges have nylon bushed stainless steel pins and the opening casement is returned on hinged side arms which can be released to allow the window to fall back for cleaning and maintenance.

The figure shows examples of both single and double glazing. The glass which is put into the frame from the inside is bedded in suitable glazing compound and in the case of the single glazing the inner glazing bead which is extruded aluminium section, is clipped over, and retained by a nylon stud fixed to the frame. The alternative is an extruded aluminium section bead screwed to the frame. Note the mastic pointing at the head and the sill and the weather bar which protects the vulnerable joint at the base of the inward opening casement.

It is interesting to compare the profile of the extruded aluminium sections used in this window with the mild steel rolled sections used in the standard steel window illustrated in figure 124, page 150.

Vertical sliding sash

A fully framed purpose-made aluminium double hung sash window of sophisticated design is shown in figure 136, page 166.

The alloy used is the same as for the extrusions for the bottom hung sash illustrated previously. The corners for this window, however, are mechanically jointed by screw and spline, since the box section cannot be satisfactorily welded. The sashes are controlled by special spring balances and are held by continuous extruded plastic guides which are designed to prevent any uneven response during movement. Note the very effective polypropylene weather stripping which is clipped into the fixed frame in such a way that it can be replaced after damage or wear during use. The meeting rails have a positive interlocking action which ensures good security by preventing the release of the catch from the outside.

The form of the extruded sash section is such that it will accommodate proprietary double glazing units up to 14 mm overall thickness. The glazing is *internal*, that is to say the glass is fixed from inside the building which is an important factor in cost and ease of maintenance. The front edges of the glass are bedded in polysulphide glazing compound; each sheet being located by small spacing blocks within the frame, to give the correct balance all round. The glass is secured by an extruded aluminium *clip-on* bead with a *push in* vinyl glazing trim to complete the glazing procedure.

Two very neat design points incorporated in the extruded sections are the gap left to receive a window pole, and the continuous neat recess on the lower rail of the outer sash to act as a sash pull.

A window of this type could be made up to a maximum height of 2·440 m and a maximum width of 1·525 m with the limitation that the perimeter measurement must not exceed 7·625 m, which means that the maximum width and height cannot be used in the same window. The basic spaces relative to this type (VS) of window are shown in figure 134.

The following points should also be noted. The rain screen principle of design has been used to prevent water being blown under the bottom sash. The pressure created within the hollow inverted U section of the bottom rail in conditions of high wind and rain, has a screening effect which helps to prevent rain penetration – the higher the pressure, the more positive the screening effect. The sashes are factory glazed so that the helical spring balances can be adjusted to the correct tension by taking into account the variations in weight of

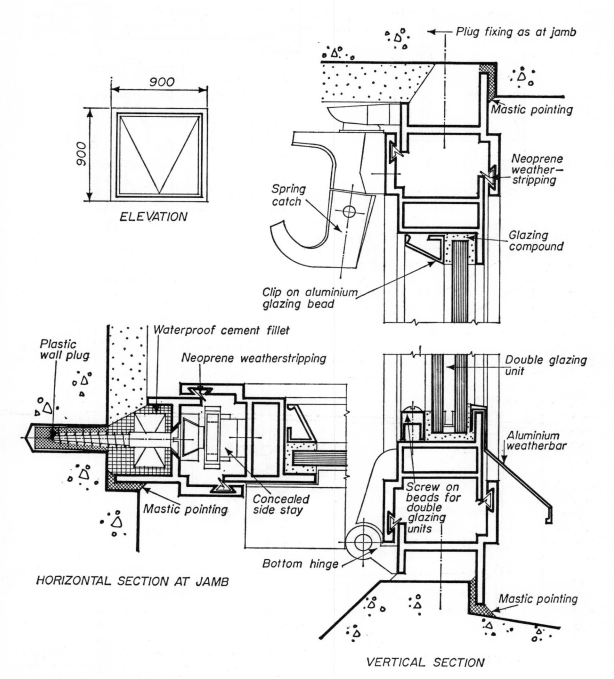

900

900

ELEVATION

Plug fixing as at jamb

Mastic pointing

Neoprene weather–stripping

Spring catch

Glazing compound

Clip on aluminium glazing bead

Plastic wall plug

Waterproof cement fillet

Neoprene weatherstripping

Double glazing unit

Aluminium weatherbar

Screw on beads for double glazing units

Mastic pointing

Concealed side stay

Bottom hinge

Mastic pointing

HORIZONTAL SECTION AT JAMB

VERTICAL SECTION

135   Aluminium window: bottom hung, opening inwards

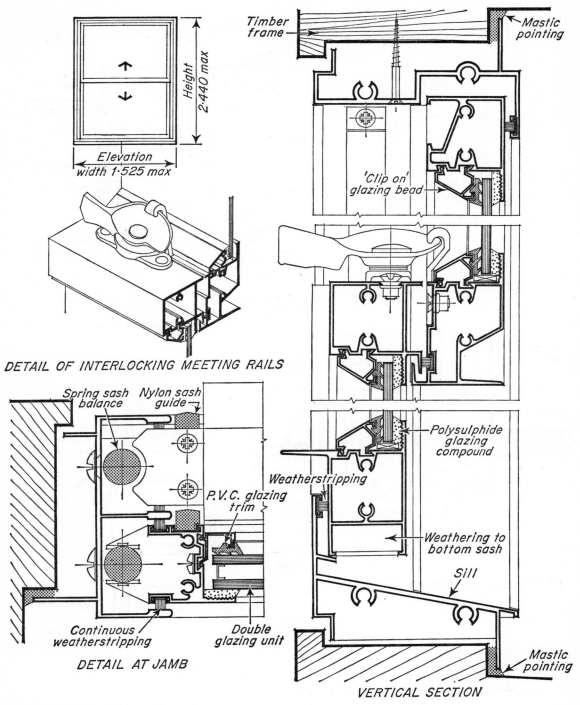

Height 2·440 max

Elevation width 1·525 max

Timber frame

Mastic pointing

'Clip on' glazing bead

DETAIL OF INTERLOCKING MEETING RAILS

Spring sash balance

Nylon sash guide

P.V.C. glazing trim

Polysulphide glazing compound

Weatherstripping

Weathering to bottom sash

Sill

Continuous weatherstripping

Double glazing unit

DETAIL AT JAMB

Mastic pointing

VERTICAL SECTION

136   *Aluminium sliding sash window*

glass. The nylon sash guides are to prevent crab-bing – or sideways motion of the sash during opening. This is a fault which occurs with loosely fitting sashes and causes the sash to become jammed. The U-shaped tube outline seen on the sections is part of the continuous extrusion and receives long self tapping screws which con-nect the horizontal and vertical members of the frame. The timber frame is built into the opening and the complete factory glazed window fixed later.

Horizontal sliding window

Figure 137 shows a purpose made horizontal sliding window in aluminium which is made in a range of sizes to comply with the basic space re-commendations for aluminium windows shown in figure 134. The horizontal sliding window is a type much used in commercial buildings, schools, and hospitals, being particularly suitable for high rise development. The window is detailed so that both sashes can be cleaned from the inside without re-moval, and a feature to note is the nylon skids upon which the sashes run. In large windows using say 6 mm glass, or heavier, or in double glazed windows nylon rollers would be used as an alter-native, as shown. The windows are fixed into the opening by the use of purpose made brackets which *twist lock* into position in the frame and are then screwed or shot fired into the concrete or brickwork. The tracks are fixed into the opening first and then the pre-assembled window at a later date. Alternatively the window can be set in a timber surround. A point to remember in respect of fixing aluminium is that ordinary steel or brass screws should not be used otherwise bi-metallic corrosion will be set up. This window has a security bolt which locks the window in the partially open posi-tion, and this is a point that must be watched with all horizontal sliding windows.

The window will be factory glazed, the glass being sealed into the frames by reusable neoprene gaskets.

The problem of weather resistance is difficult to overcome with a horizontal sliding type of opening light and much careful thought has been given to this problem in the example shown, which is de-signed to conform with the forthcoming British Standard on resistance to wind and water pene-tration. Woven pile double weather stripping is incorporated at the head, sill, and meeting style of the window panes and the PVC jamb sections en-sure a good weather seal. Note also the use of the PVC channels which isolate the weather stripping and nylon skids from the aluminium frame. This use of PVC reduces friction and resists the deterio-rating action due to accumulation of dust and grit.

Horizontal sliding window in timber surround

Figure 138 gives an example of a standard alu-minium horizontal sliding window in a timber surround which is competitive in price with a standard timber window. The timber surround provides the basic construction with the opening part of the window in aluminium. This window is made in the standard metric range of sizes to fit the openings shown in figure 134. The figure illus-trates a 1300 mm high window inserted over a deep middle rail to give a 2100 mm composite unit. Note that the actual frame size of the window will be 5 mm less than the aperture size subject to a manu-facturing tolerance of ± 3 mm. The metric sizes are in multiples of a basic module of 100 mm and are derived from the preferred dimensions in Ap-pendix A of BS 4330: *Recommendations for the Co-ordination of Controlling Dimensions in Build-ing*. The timber frames, which should be vacuum treated with preservative, and afterwards primed, will be built into the opening in the usual way. Then when all the wet trades are completed the head and sill of the aluminium component are set in mastic and screwed in position. The sashes are factory glazed with 3 mm or 4 mm glass according to overall size.

'Built up' aluminium window

The detail of a large window in aluminium is shown in figure 139. The dimensions here neces-sitate substantial structural members which in the form of transoms span the full width of the open-ing to avoid obstruction to the windows below. Steel sections are used for the main members and built up to give an arrangement which also sup-ports the pressed aluminium casings. The heavier lower transom also supports a heater. This is a good example of a large but relatively simple pro-file in pressed aluminium. The external exposed members are in hardwood.

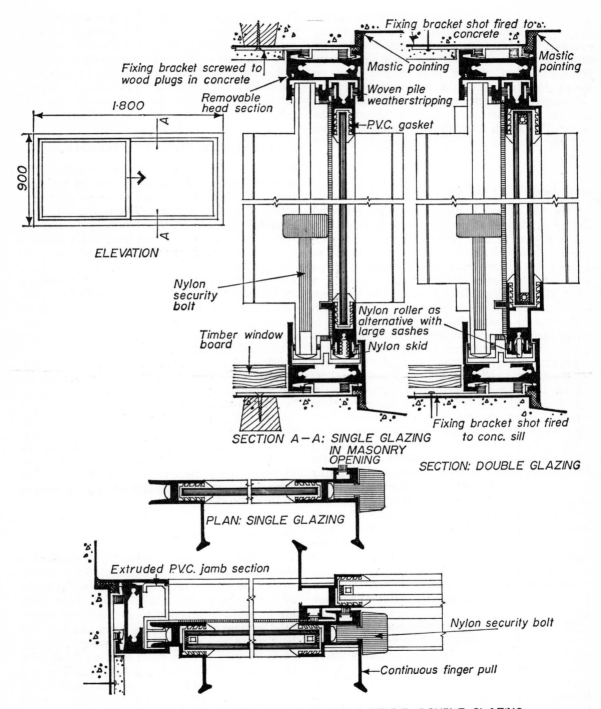

Fixing bracket shot fired to concrete

Fixing bracket screwed to wood plugs in concrete

Mastic pointing

Mastic pointing

Removable head section

Woven pile weatherstripping

P.V.C. gasket

1·800

900

ELEVATION

Nylon security bolt

Nylon roller as alternative with large sashes

Nylon skid

Timber window board

Fixing bracket shot fired to conc. sill

SECTION A—A: SINGLE GLAZING IN MASONRY OPENING

SECTION: DOUBLE GLAZING

PLAN: SINGLE GLAZING

Extruded P.V.C. jamb section

Nylon security bolt

Continuous finger pull

PLAN AT JAMB AND INTERLOCKING MEETING STYLE: DOUBLE GLAZING

137 Purpose-made aluminium horizontal sliding window

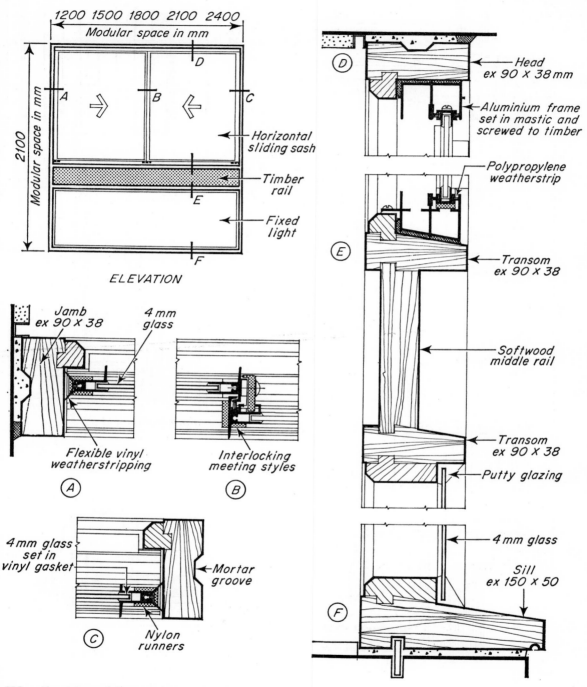

1200 1500 1800 2100 2400

Modular space in mm

2100

Modular space in mm

A → B ← C

D

Horizontal
sliding sash

Timber
rail

E

Fixed
light

F

ELEVATION

Jamb
ex 90 x 38

4 mm
glass

Flexible vinyl
weatherstripping

Ⓐ

Interlocking
meeting styles

Ⓑ

4 mm glass
set in
vinyl gasket

Mortar
groove

Ⓒ

Nylon
runners

Head
ex 90 x 38 mm

Aluminium frame
set in mastic and
screwed to timber

Ⓓ

Polypropylene
weatherstrip

Ⓔ

Transom
ex 90 x 38

Softwood
middle rail

Transom
ex 90 x 38

Putty glazing

4 mm glass

Sill
ex 150 x 50

Ⓕ

138   Aluminium sliding window in timber frame

169

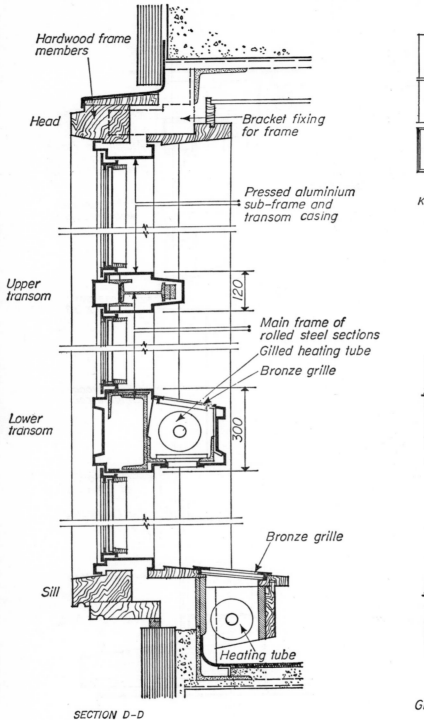

Hardwood frame members

Head

Bracket fixing for frame

Pressed aluminium sub-frame and transom casing

Upper transom

120

Main frame of rolled steel sections

Gilled heating tube

Bronze grille

Lower transom

300

Bronze grille

Sill

Heating tube

SECTION D-D

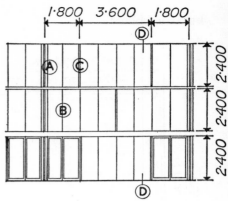

1·800 3·600 1·800

2·400 2·400

2·400

2·400

Ⓐ Ⓒ Ⓓ

Ⓑ

Ⓓ

KEY ELEVATION

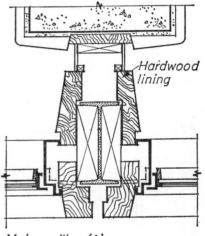

Hardwood lining

Main mullion (A)

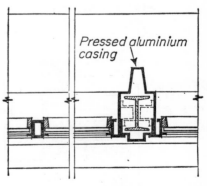

Pressed aluminium casing

Glazing Bar (B) Intermediate mullion (C)

139   Large metal window

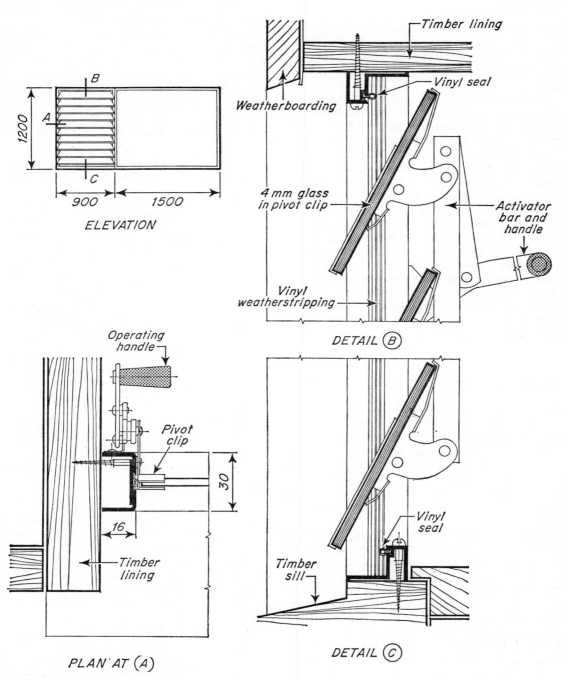

ELEVATION

B

A

C

1200

900   1500

Timber lining

Weatherboarding

Vinyl seal

4 mm glass
in pivot clip

Activator
bar and
handle

Vinyl
weatherstripping

DETAIL B

Operating
handle

Pivot
clip

30

16

Timber
lining

PLAN AT A

Vinyl
seal

Timber
sill

DETAIL C

140   Louvre window

Louvre window

This type of window (see figure 140), originated in the tropics, and has gained popularity elsewhere. Many industrialized Building Systems also include this method of ventilation in their standard range.

The louvre consists of a number of horizontal panes of glass gripped in a U-shaped aluminium or plastics extruded section at each end, and pivoted on an aluminium vertical channel which is secured within the window opening. The blades of glass are connected at the top and bottom to a lever bar for opening. Ventilation can be varied from 1 to 95 per cent of the net louvred area.

It is important to realize that the weathering of a louvre window depends on the overlap of the glass blades and the precise interlocking of the mechanism which holds the blades in position. In very exposed positions the blades may flex and cause concern regarding the possibility of the penetration of driving rain, clear widths should not exceed 1066 mm to minimize this. A louvre window is often used for cross ventilation between rooms such as over a door, or in a partitioning system.

MASTIC JOINTING

A mastic seal to a joint is used where some degree of movement is likely to occur, usually between dissimilar materials, such as between metal and timber, or brickwork and timber. The function of a mastic is to accommodate the movement and at the same time maintain a weatherproof seal. A mastic can also be used where it is required to provide a seal against draughts, dust or fumes.

It will be seen that a mastic will only fulfil these functions if it satisfies an exacting set of requirements. One material cannot of course satisfy all conditions so it is important to choose the right material for the job. The various types of mastic and their uses are discussed in *MBC: Materials*, chapter 15, and for the use of mastics in respect of curtain walling, etc, see *MBC: Structure and Fabric*, Part 1. Having made the correct choice of mastic it is essential that the joint is designed so that unreasonable demands are not made on the jointing material in its effort to accommodate the movement. The practical application of mastic

seals in connection with bedding and fixing window frames is shown in figure 141.

The method of applying the mastic is largely dependent upon the type of sub-frame or surround into which the frame is to be set. Where metal frames are to be set into wood surrounds a continuous ribbon of mastic applied in the external and internal rebate of the surround will ensure a perfect seal when the frame is placed in position. Any surplus mastic can be removed by a rag

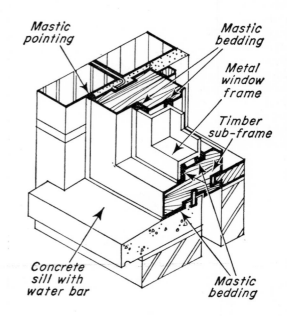

141   Standard metal window in timber sub-frame

soaked in mastic cleaner or smoothed with a moistened finger. The external vertical joint between the timber sub-frame or surround and the brick or masonry jambs of the window opening are particularly subject to differential rates of expansion and contraction. It is therefore, essential that these joints be pointed with a mastic which will accommodate this movement of the joint.

Water bars should be bedded in mastic and a ribbon of mastic applied to the rebate on the underside of the sill of the wood surround, before this is placed into position. Care should be taken that the two surfaces with which the mastic will be in contact are dry and free from dust. The vertical joints between sub-frame and window opening should be grouted in a weak cement mix, raked out to a depth of not less than 12 mm and, when dry, pointed with mastic. With old property where a mastic joint has not been used a deep, wide cavity may exist; in this case the joint should either be packed with hemp to within 12 mm of surface before pointing with mastic, or grouted with a weak cement, raked out and pointed.

Figure 142 shows the use of mastic for the joints between frames and loose mullions (or transom rails) in metal windows.

With composite windows a certain amount of movement is inevitable at the junction of the fixed frames and the mullions or transoms. It is therefore essential, and is indeed now common practice, to seal these joints with mastic. It is recommended that a ribbon of mastic for the internal and external joint be applied either to the fixed frame or to the mullion or transom as convenient during assembly.

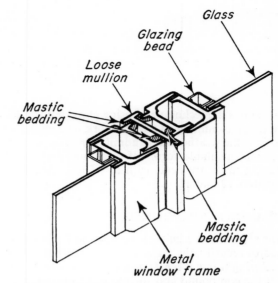

142   Metal window with loose mullion

5 Glazing

Glazing is the technique of using glass or a similar material as infilling to a framework or opening to exclude the weather but to admit light. The properties and available forms of glass and preformed glazing units are dealt with in *MBC: Materials*, chapters 12 and 16.

GLAZING COMPOUNDS

The selection of a suitable compound for bedding and/or securing the glass, depends on whether the enclosing frame is metal or timber and whether or not the compound and surround is to be painted.

Glazing materials are classified in CP 152 : 1966: *Glazing and Fixing of Glass for Buildings*, as follows:

Group 1
Glazing compounds which require protective treatment and regular maintenance, (a) linseed oil putty to BS 544, (b) metal casement putty and (c) flexible glazing compounds.

Group 2
Glazing compounds which do not require protective treatment or regular maintenance, (d) non-setting compounds for gun, knife or strip application (synthetic rubbers), (e) sealants for gun application (polysulphides), (f) strip sections of plastics or synthetic rubber designed for use between bead and glass in bead glazing and (g) gaskets of synthetic rubber – fabricated to a suitable profile to give a continuous weathertight seal between glass and surround.

Mastics are dealt with in *MBC: Materials*, chapter 16.

METHODS OF GLAZING

The following alternative methods are in general use:

1 Putty glazing without beads – by bedding the glass in glazing compound and securing with sprigs (in timber frames) or spring clips (in metal frames) and building up a front angle in glazing compound. Putty glazing is a suitable technique where comparatively small panes are to be fixed, but for large panes in exposed areas, the glass should be secured by beads. For very exposed positions the maximum length plus breadth of a pane of glass for glazing without beads should not exceed 1800 mm. This can be increased to a maximum of 2400 mm for more sheltered conditions.

2 With beads – the glass is set in glazing compound and the bead, which may be of timber or metal, is bedded on glazing compound and secured to the frame. For internal situations, the glass can be bedded in wash-leather or other suitable resilient material if special resistance to shock is required as in a glazed door.

3 With gaskets (gaskets rely on the pressure of the gasket against the glass to provide the weather seal) there is usually some form of removable strip to provide the final 'closure' of the seal, and special tools may be required to hold the gasket ready to receive the glass.

4 A combination of gasket and glazing compound in which the glass is set in spacing blocks, with glazing compound on the front edge of the glass against the rebate, then the glass is secured by means of a 'press in' PVC glazing strip internally. This method applies principally to factory glazing in say aluminium frames.

THERMAL EXPANSION

It is always necessary to allow clearance between the edge of the glass and the surrounding frame to allow for fitting, fixing and thermal movement. The terms used in connection with the measurement of the glass and opening are illustrated in figure 143.

Clearances for coloured glass and heat absorbing glass should be greater than those allowed for clear glass. Glass which is exposed to the full heat of the sun for long periods will show considerable movement. In all these cases it is important also that as little as possible of the edge of the glass is shielded since this area remains cold and the glass may crack because of an excessive temperature range across its surface.

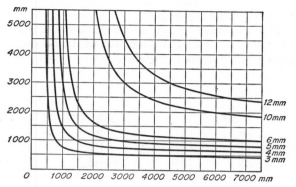

144   Float glass

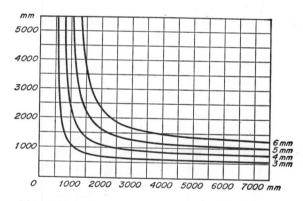

145   Sheet glass

various parts of the country can be obtained from the Meteorological Office. From this figure the maximum wind loading can be calculated. The glass factor is then obtained by using a formula

143   Terms used in the measurement of glass

SAFE GLAZING SIZES/ THICKNESS OF GLASS

Figures 144 and 145 show minimum thicknesses for float glass and sheet glass respectively for varying widths and lengths of panes in a typical exposure (1000 N/m²).

For unusual conditions, the glass size is determined by reference to the degree of exposure and the type of glass and method of fixing. This calculation should be carried out at the design stage. The calculation requires the speed of the wind in the area of the site to be determined. Figures for maximum wind speeds appropriate to

which takes into account the size of the pane and the relationship between the length to the breadth of the pane.

By reference to tables which relate the thickness of glass to the wind loading, by taking into account the glass factor, the safe glazing thickness can be obtained. CP 152 gives examples of calculations for various types of glass.

The risk of accidental (or wilful) damage and breakage is a criterion that, unfortunately, is of increasing importance and where there is risk of injury special care should be taken. This matter is more fully discussed in *MBC: Materials*, chapter 12.

SIZE OF REBATE AND GLASS CLEARANCE

In timber or metal frames the thickness of the back putty should not be less than 2 mm for linseed oil putty or metal casement putty, and 3 mm for non-setting compounds.

The minimum depth of rebate for external glazing often depends on the area of the pane of glass and the degree of exposure to which the glass say, up to 0·2 m² in area, the glass should always be set on small blocks of resilient material to locate the pane properly within the surround. The blocks used around the sides and top of the window are termed location blocks and those at the base are termed setting blocks. Setting blocks can be small pieces of lead, hardwood, nylon or unplasticized PVC. Each block should be wider than the glass or double glazing and generally from

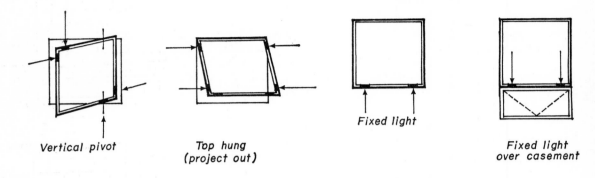

Vertical pivot

Top hung
(project out)

Fixed light

Fixed light
over casement

(min. 75 mm from corner of frame)

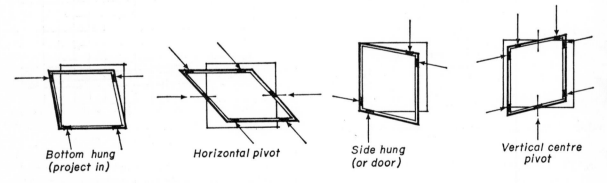

Bottom hung
(project in)

Horizontal pivot

Side hung
(or door)

Vertical centre
pivot

146   Positions of setting and location blocks

is subjected; as a guide the minimum depth is 5 mm, the maximum 10 mm and the optimum for normal conditions 8 mm. The maximum depth is usually used in connection with non-setting glazing compounds. The minimum clearance between glass and frame whether of metal or wood is 2 mm all round, but for special heat absorbing or dark coloured glass the clearance should be from 3 mm to 5 mm all round, depending on the size of the pane. In all cases except for small panes,

25 mm to 75 mm long. The exception is a vertical pivot window when the block should not be less than 150 mm long. Location blocks are usually about 25 mm long. The position of setting and location blocks is shown in figure 146.

Setting and location blocks support the sides and edges of the glass so that it can be set accurately within the rebates in respect of edge tolerances. In addition to these blocks, in the cases where non-setting glazing compound is used and where there is danger of the glazing being displaced by wind pressure, distance pieces should be placed between the back edge of the glass and the rebate as shown in figure 147.

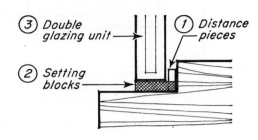

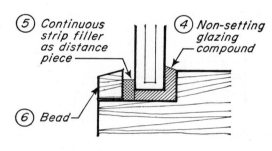

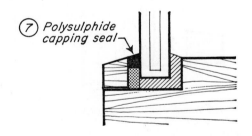

147   Glazing in a double glazed unit

The distance pieces, which should be of plasticized PVC, are usually 25 mm long and of a depth to give a cover of 3 mm of mastic. The distance pieces should be under slight compression when the beads are fixed. In no case should a distance piece be placed to coincide with a setting or location block. The figure also shows the application of the glazing and sealing compounds in connection with a double glazed unit.

GLAZING IN TIMBER FRAMES

The following techniques are considered: (1) glazing with putty in softwood frames, (2) glazing with beads in softwood and hardwood frames.

1 Glazing with putty in softwood frames

The most common glazing compound in use in this situation is linseed oil putty to BS 544. It sets, partly by absorption of the oil in the surround, and partly by oxidation. Thus, to prevent excessive and premature absorption of the oil into the frame, particularly with softwood, it is necessary to prime the rebates and beads. The primer should conform with BS 2521 : *Ready Mixed Oil-based Priming Paints*, or be aluminium based. Unprimed softwood will absorb too much oil and failure will result due to lack of adhesion of the putty. A frame which has been fully sealed will have the opposite effect, by retarding absorption of the oil, the setting of the putty will be delayed.

The putty must be protected with paint, which should be applied as soon as possible after the initial hardening of the surface of the putty. As an alternative to linseed oil putty, flexible glazing compounds in strip form can be used; this type needs protecting by paint after initial setting. The aim of painting over linseed oil putty is to maintain it in good condition, and to prevent long term shrinkage and cracking which allows water to penetrate into the timber section, which will cause paint failure and eventual decay. The rebate is first puttied. This is called the *bedding putty* and the glass is then pressed into position and secured with glazier's sprigs. These fixings should be spaced at about 450 mm apart around the perimeter of the frame. On pressing in the glass a certain amount of bedding putty is pressed out and the remaining putty is called the *back putty*, which should be about 2 mm thick between the glass and rebate. The glass is then 'front puttied' and the putty should be stopped about 2 mm from the sight line of the rebate so that when the paint is applied it is carried over the glass up to the sight line and so seals the edge of the putty to the glass. The front putty should be sloped at an angle to prevent the accumulation of water at this vulnerable point. The technique is indicated in figures 107, 110, 113 and 116.

The putty should be left about 14 days before painting to ensure that it has begun to harden. The putty used for glazing the wood frames is a linseed oil putty composed of whiting and boiled linseed oil, and since, as previously noted, the setting action of the putty is caused by the surrounding timbers soaking up the oil content, this explains why such putty is not suitable for glazing in metal frames.

2 Glazing with beads in softwood and hardwood frames

The beads should preferably be of hardwood and secured by panel pins, or preferably by brass counter sunk screws and cups. For double glazed units, panel pins are dangerous and cups and screws should always be used. Pins should be not more than say 75 mm from each corner, and at maximum, say, 225 mm centres. The mastic in which the bead is bedded must be of good quality, and applied generously, otherwise a failure in this respect will lead to water penetration. The beads should be primed on the back to prevent initial absorption of binder from the putty and subsequent absorption of rainwater, with consequent decay or early paint failure.

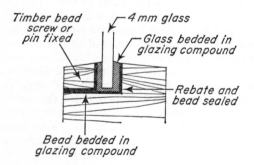

148   Single glazing with external bead

Figure 148 shows an example of single glazing with external bead. The rebate and beads are first sealed with a proprietary sealing compound applied by brush, the glass is then set into the opening using setting blocks at quarter points and distance pieces to restrain movement.

The glass is then bedded in glazing compound and the bead screwed or pinned in position on a fillet of sealant usually applied by gun. For internal bead glazing, the bedding for the bead

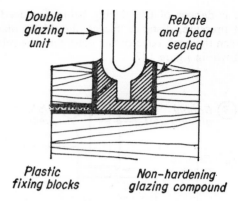

149   Internal bead glazing using double glazed units

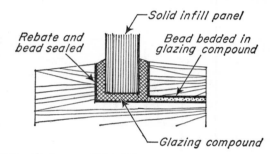

150   Fixing a solid infill panel

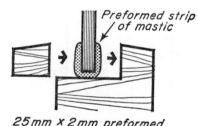

25 mm × 2 mm preformed strip of 'reinforced' mastic wrapped around edge of glass

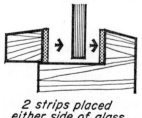

2 strips placed either side of glass and secured by bead

151   Glazing to internal doors or screens

can be omitted. An example using double glazed units is shown in figure 149. The fixing of a solid infill panel such as plywood is shown in figure 150. Figure 151 shows the method of bead glazing for a door. The beads may either be external or internal.

GLAZING IN METAL FRAMES

1 Glazing with putty

This method is again very similar to that described under the technique for wood frames but, as no absorption of the oil in the putty can

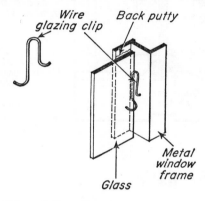

152   Wire glazing clip

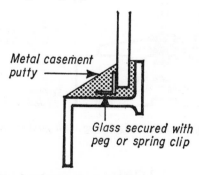

153   Single glazing in metal frames

take place, a special type of glazing compound is used containing a hardening agent. The glazing compound should be left for about 14 days in order to harden before painting commences. A wire clip of the type used to retain the glass before the front putty is applied is shown in figure 152. Single and double glazing in metal frames is shown in figures 153 and 154.

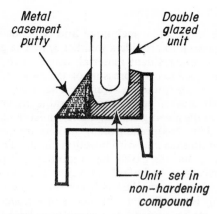

154   Double glazing in metal frames

2 Glazing with beads

A group 2 glazing compound is used in conjunction with bead glazing in metal frames. Metal beads are fixed either by means of screws into threaded holes or by clipping over protruding studs in the frame. These techniques are illustrated in figures 155 and 156.

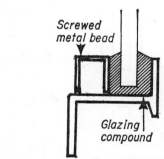

155   Metal beads fixed by screws

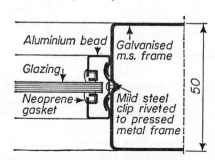

156   Metal beads fixed by clipping over protruding studs

179

GASKET GLAZING

This is a specialist technique and depends upon compression to provide a weather seal. The gasket is made in a resilient material, usually neoprene, and designed to exert pressure on the panes of glass and the surrounding frame. The seal, when properly made, permits considerable movement between the glazing and surround whilst remaining water tight. Neoprene glazing gaskets are made in one continuous unit with injection moulded corner pieces so that the gasket has a jointless periphery. It is necessary to be able to adjust the 'pressure' whilst the pane of glass is being set in the gasket and this is usually done by means of a *zipper* strip which applies positive and continuous pressure to the glass or panel when in position, but allows comparatively easy re-glazing when removed. The removal and fixing of the zipper strip is done by a special tool. With experienced workmen, gasket glazing, though more expensive than bead or putty glazing, is a quick and neat method, and is very suitable for factory assembly of units, in connection with Industrialized Building systems.

the seal. Figure 158 shows a different application of a gasket seal suitable for use in connection with both glazing and solid infill panelling to a timber frame.

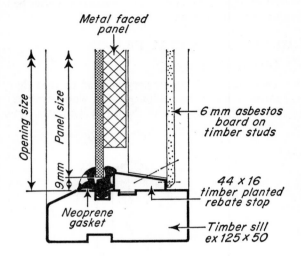

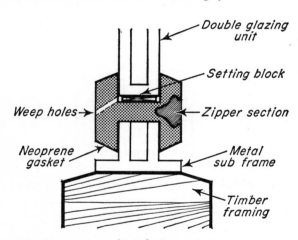

157 Neoprene gasket glazing system

Figure 157 shows a typical application of a neoprene gasket glazing system. The gasket is snapped over the metal subframe, which is first screwed to the timber lining or framing to the window opening. The glass is then placed in the bottom gasket channel and entered into the jambs with spatulas.

The locking strips are then inserted to complete

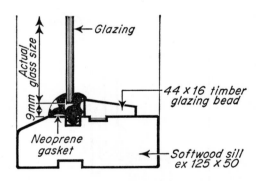

158 Infill panel and glazing with gasket seal

DOUBLE GLAZING

In practical terms double glazing in fixed lights does not present any difficulty provided that enough depth can be allowed for the glazing bead or putty plus the additional thickness of the unit. For heat insulation glazing with units of two panes of glass with an hermetically-sealed airspace between is the simplest and the least expensive method. Opening lights with double glazing should not be to extreme sizes owing to the considerable extra weight of glass. Double glazing is installed in order to cut down the heat loss through a glazed opening, and also under certain circumstances to improve sound insulation. It is obviously sensible building economics to give the same careful consideration to heat loss through windows as through walls since the window area in many types of building is equal to, and sometimes even greater than, the solid walling or infill panels. The reduction in the space between the sheets of glass will mean a decrease in the efficiency of the unit, with a consequent increase in the heat loss.

The following figures, with reference to factory-made hermetically-sealed double glazing units, will give a comparison of the effectiveness of the insulation compared with the width of air space.

Air space	Heat loss reduction compared with single glazing
12 mm	48 per cent
6 mm	42 per cent
5 mm	40 per cent

There are several methods of providing double glazing, of which the following are the most typical:

1 Double glazing units

These are factory-made hermetically-sealed units of two types;

(a) Two panes of clear sheet glass spaced at, say, 5 to 12 mm apart, with the internal air dried so that condensation will not occur in the cavity, and with the edges of the glass fixed together to seal the unit permanently into a continuous piece of glass. A unit should have an edge clearance of 3 mm all round in fixing to allow for manufacturing tolerance. This type of unit is made to a standard range of stock sizes, designed to fit standard window frames, or within the size range 250 mm × 400 mm to 1250 mm × 1750 mm. The types of glass used will determine the overall thickness of the unit, which will vary between 9 mm and 30 mm. This type of sealed unit is indicated in figures 149 and 154.

(b) A unit in which a dry cell of air is sealed between two panes of glass, which are separated by a metal spacer, protected by a metal edge

tape for protection as shown in figure 159. This type of unit is purpose made, and the following glass thickness and air space width are typical:

Glass	Air space
3 mm	5 mm
4 mm	6 and 12 mm
6 mm	6 and 12 mm
10 or 12 mm	12 mm

Maximum sizes vary, according to the type of glass and air space, from a maximum of, say, 3000 × 6000 mm using 9 mm glass and a 12 mm air space to, say, 750 × 750 mm with 3 mm sheet and a 3 mm air space.

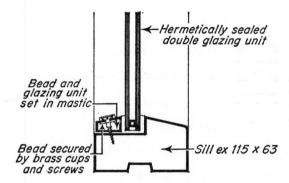

159   Double glazed sealed fixed unit

Two different types of glass can of course be used, one on each side of the same unit, to answer particular user requirements. To allow for manufacturing tolerances, the larger units should have an edge clearance for fixing in the rebate of 5 mm. The metal spacer can be in tube form, which contains a predetermined amount of selected desiccant which will absorb any moisture left between the panes.

Fixing double glazing units

For fixing the units in timber frames by bead glazing, figure 160 shows the terms used in connection with the tolerances and sizes of rebate applicable to the various thicknesses of units as detailed below.

Seal depth

The correct size of the edge seal varies with the

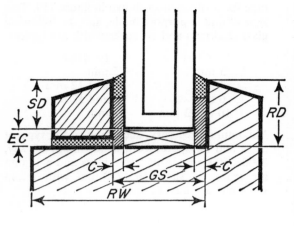

glazing compound

distance pieces

setting block

SD   seal depth

C   front and back clearances

GS   glazing space

RD   rebate depth

RW   rebate width

EC   edge clearance

160   Terms

width of the air space and the area of the unit, from 11 mm with a unit having a 5 mm air space to 29 mm for units having a 12 mm air space.

Clearances

The standard front and back face clearance is 3 mm and the edge clearance is 3 mm for units up to 4 m² and 6 mm for units up to 8·4 m², and for special heat absorbing glasses. For units over 8·4 m² or 25 mm thick, check the clearances required with the manufacturers at design stage.

Rebate depth

This is the minimum seal depth plus the edge

clearance and will vary from 16 mm to 32 mm according to the unit.

If front 'puttying' is used in timber frames, the unit must not exceed an area of 2·3 m² and a poly-sulphide sealant must be used – *not* linseed oil putty. For glazing the units in metal frames a non-hardening compound must always be used for bedding and edge filling. Front puttying (as an alternative to bead glazing) is permissible for units up to 11 mm thick – and not exceeding 2·3 m². Units larger than this require to be secured by beads. Whichever method of glazing is used, the technique must prevent the edges of the units being in continuous contact with trapped water, or there is a danger that the seal will be damaged. Thus the contractor must follow carefully the glazing procedures recommended.[1]

As site and exposure conditions vary widely it is important that the glazing compounds should be carefully chosen. Note that two or more bedding or weathering materials may have to be used in the fixing of a unit. More detailed information should be sought from the manufacturers, whose recommendations should always be followed, since the handling and fixing of a double glazing unit calls for considerable care and skill, and breakages are not only expensive but will probably cause frustrating delays. Methods other than those described are continually being developed for retaining glass – double glazed units included – in buildings. These developments are reported in the technical press as they become available.

2 Double windows

Two separate window frames, each single glazed, and fitted separately to the window openings as shown in figure 161. This type of construction is suitable where sound insulation is the main consideration. To achieve maximum sound insulation, the space between the glass should be as wide as possible, at least 100 mm and preferably 200 mm, and the frames should be separated. The sound insulation is further improved by lining the rebates with a sound absorbent sheet material and the use of as heavy a glass as possible. The windows should be hung to give access to the cavity for maintenance and cleaning.

[1] More information can be obtained from the Insulation Glazing Association, 6 Mount Row, London W.1.

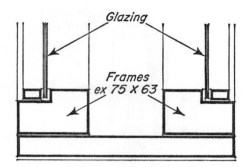

161   *Double window*

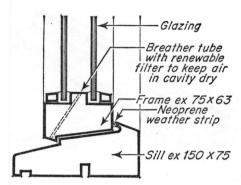

163   *Single frame double glazed*

3 Coupled windows (twin frames separately glazed)

This method is a variation of the double window. Two frames are used, each single glazed, and coupled together, The whole unit opens to provide ventilation, whilst the secondary frame is either hinged or completely removable for cleaning. This principle is illustrated in figure 162 and a pivot window of this type is illustrated in figure 115.

5 Converted single glazing

There are many well advertised proprietary systems on the market which will convert existing windows to 'double glazing'. Most systems attach the second pane of glass by means of aluminium or plastic channels, clipped or screwed to the original framing.

PATENT GLAZING

This is a form of dry glazing and is used both in vertical cladding, north light roof construction and continuous roof glazing in conjunction with roof sheeting. Patent glazing bars are manufactured in steel and aluminium. The steel must be fully protected either by covering with an extruded jointless lead or a PVC sheath. The aluminium bar may either have lead or aluminium *wings*. Bars are also made to accommodate double glazing units. The maximum size of the panes of glass in patent glazing is concerned primarily with problems of safety and handling rather than on maximum manufacturing sizes available. The width of the pane becomes the centre to centre measurement of the glazing bar (plus tolerances) and the length of the pane is dependent on the *span* of the glazing bar. Bars are made in different depths to accommodate the differing weights of glass at various spans. Bars at 600 mm centres can be regarded as convenient maxima. Figure 164a–d illustrates various types of bar.

The inverted T section supports the glass over the required span whilst the wings secure the glass in position. A gasket, shown in the form of an

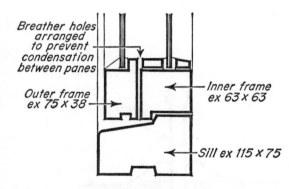

162   *Twin frames separately glazed*

4 Dual glazing (single frame, double glazed)

One timber frame carrying two sheets of glass, fixed separately. The air space between the frames should be allowed to 'breathe' to the outside to prevent condensation, since a complete seal is in any case a practical impossibility. In addition to this precaution, one sheet of glass should be removable for periodic cleaning. This type of double glazing is shown in figure 163.

183

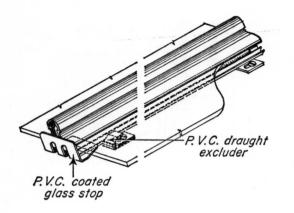

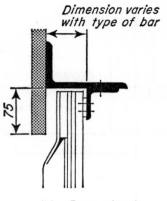

(b) *Fixing detail*

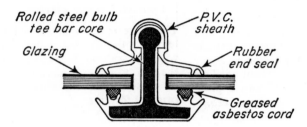

(a) *PVC covered glazing bar*

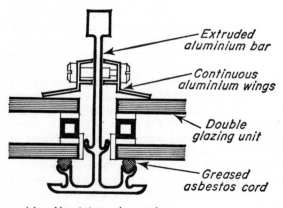

(c) *Aluminium glazing bar*

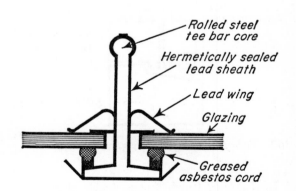

(d) *Lead covered glazing bar*

164 Patent glazing

asbestos cord, seals the joint. The profile of the bar has condensation grooves as an integral part of the extension. A special *shoe* or stop is required at the foot of each bar to prevent the glass sliding out. Patent glazing is an economic and flexible method of dry construction which requires very little maintenance.

Figure 165 shows the use of patent glazing in the

184

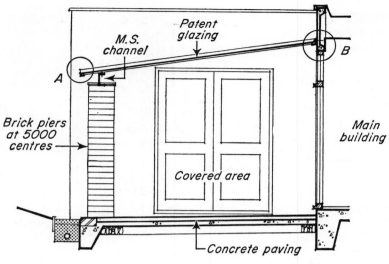

KEY SECTION

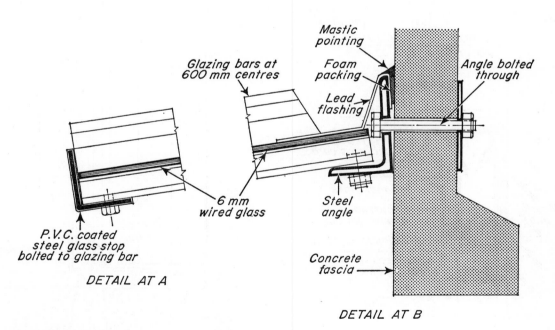

DETAIL AT A

DETAIL AT B

165   *Glazed covered area*

formation of a glazed covered way. This type of construction is currently used to give covered outside teaching spaces in many schools.

Patent glazing in the form of vertical cladding is shown in figure 166.

185

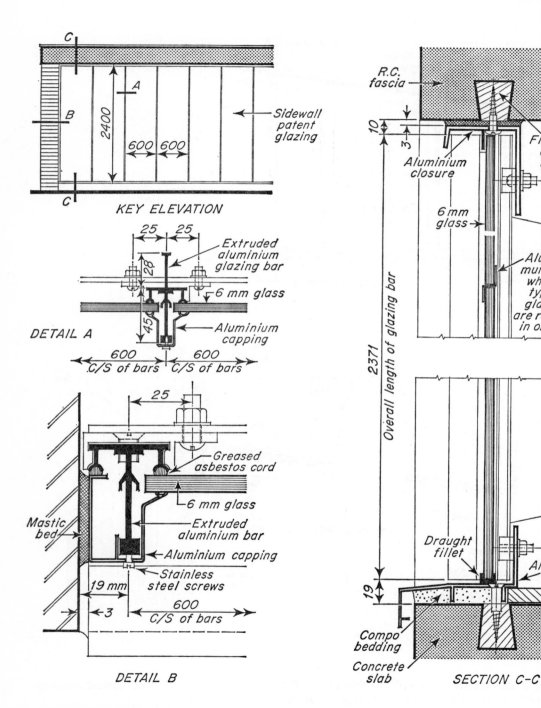

KEY ELEVATION

2400

600 600

Sidewall patent glazing

DETAIL A

25 25

28

45

Extruded aluminium glazing bar

6 mm glass

Aluminium capping

600
C/S of bars

600
C/S of bars

DETAIL B

25

Greased asbestos cord

6 mm glass

Extruded aluminium bar

Aluminium capping

Stainless steel screws

Mastic bed

19 mm

3

600
C/S of bars

SECTION C-C

R.C. fascia

10

3

Aluminium closure

6 mm glass

2371

Overall length of glazing bar

Fixing plugs at head and sill

Aluminium muntin used where two types of glass are required in one tier

2400

Draught fillet

19

Aluminium sill

Compo bedding

Concrete slab

166   *Vertical patent glazing*

6 Roof lights

The provision of natural lighting units for roofs, usually by dry glazing techniques in the form of dome lights, monitors, skylights and lantern lights, has become a specialist matter. Since the roof light is situated on the most vulnerable and exposed part of a building, formidable problems of weather resistance have to be overcome. A system of roof lights must, in addition to being completely weatherproof, be burglar proof and strong enough to withstand roof dead loads, provide for the escape of condensation and smoke in the event of fire, be easy to replace and inexpensive to maintain.

METAL FRAMED ROOF LIGHT

Figure 167 shows a form of roof light constructed from a rolled steel, hot-dip galvanized frame into which is set wired glass in non-hardening glazing compound using setting blocks to allow thermal movement. The roof light is either fixed or openable. The latter is illustrated, having a pressed steel hood to protect the opening. It is always difficult to guarantee that rain will not be blown into a building when an opening type roof light is used and for this reason the opening end of the light should always be placed with its back to the direction of the prevailing wind.

Many manufacturers have a detail which incorporates a louvre flap or 'hit and miss' ventilator in the upstand, which means that the top of the roof light can remain fixed, whilst ventilation can be obtained from the side. This is a slightly easier weathering problem. Some manufacturers also incorporate a temperature operated catch on the opening section which provides an automatic vent in case of fire.

DOME LIGHTS

These are made in glass or plastics. The glass domes are usually either circular or rectangular on plan and have wired glass in most cases secured by means of special clips. Upstand curbs are of concrete or wood, galvanized steel or aluminium.

Dome lights in various plastics are now popular. They are available in clear and opaque acrylic (PMMA) and glass fibre reinforced polyester resin (GRP). The glass fibre tested in accordance with BS 476: Part 3 must give an 'External FAA' designation. Solar energy transmittance and glare control can be achieved by the use of special bronze tinted acrylic. Figure 168 illustrates a selection from a range of dome lights made in a number of very pleasing forms, on a dimensionally co-ordinated 300 mm module.

In figure 169 the dome light is shown fixed to a pre-formed GRP base. The foam strip and clamp fixing detail provides a good weather seal and allows thermal movement to take place without damaging the dome light or surrounding structure. Condensation falls into the gutter formed by the upstand and the moisture then drains away through the plastic edge strip. Insulation can be improved by the placing of the roof lights one over the other to make a double skin construction.

Insurance companies are now demanding very high standards of security for construction and manufacturers are aware of this and provide security fixings for their products. Figure 169 gives an example of this. The L clamps shown are easily fixed but once in position they are permanently locked and should it be required to release the top component it will be necessary to saw through the clamps above the base.

Traditional timber skylight and lantern light

A traditional form of fixed skylight and a timber lantern light are shown. This form of construction has now largely been superseded by the forms of dome lights and lantern lights previously illustrated, but the traditional form will be found in large numbers on existing buildings and a knowledge of its construction will help in determining

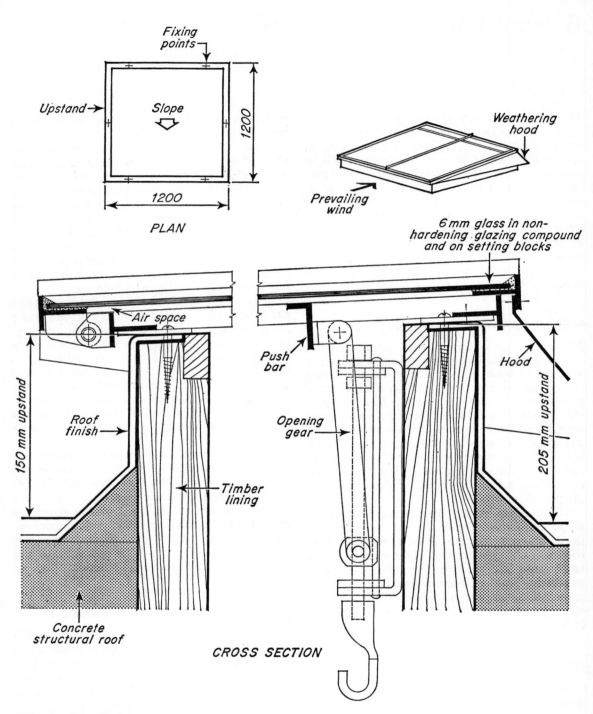

Fixing points

Upstand →

Slope

1200

1200

PLAN

Weathering hood

Prevailing wind

6 mm glass in non-hardening glazing compound and on setting blocks

Air space

Push bar

Hood

150 mm upstand

Roof finish →

205 mm upstand

Opening gear →

Timber lining

Concrete structural roof

CROSS SECTION

167   Steel roof light

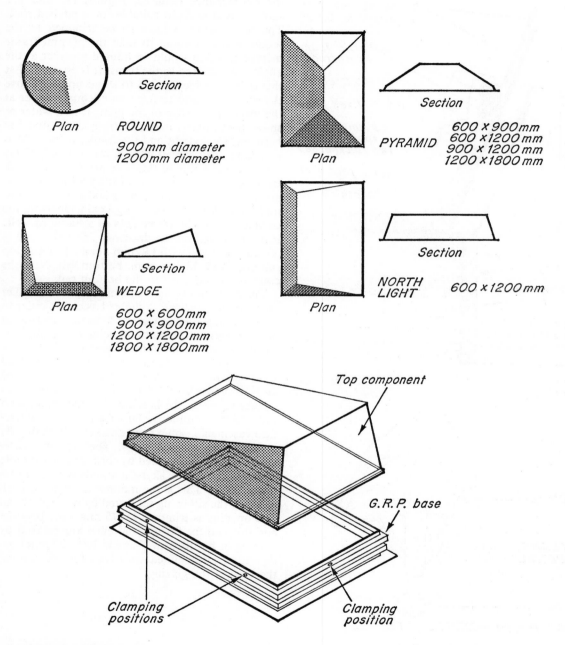

ROUND

900 mm diameter
1200 mm diameter

PYRAMID

600 × 900 mm
600 × 1200 mm
900 × 1200 mm
1200 × 1800 mm

WEDGE

600 × 600 mm
900 × 900 mm
1200 × 1200 mm
1800 × 1800 mm

NORTH LIGHT

600 × 1200 mm

Section

Plan

Top component

G.R.P. base

Clamping positions

Clamping position

168   *Plastic dome lights (1)*

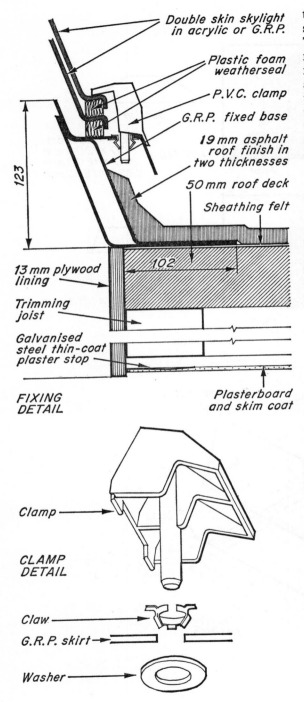

Double skin skylight in acrylic or G.R.P.

Plastic foam weatherseal

P.V.C. clamp

G.R.P. fixed base

19 mm asphalt roof finish in two thicknesses

50 mm roof deck

Sheathing felt

123

102

13 mm plywood lining

Trimming joist

Galvanised steel thin-coat plaster stop

Plasterboard and skim coat

FIXING DETAIL

Clamp

CLAMP DETAIL

Claw

G.R.P. skirt

Washer

the maintenance required. Figures 170 and 171 show a fixed skylight suitable for a pitched roof. The roof members have to be trimmed to the requisite size opening to take the 50 mm frame members, which would be housed together at the angles and secured to the trims. It is essential that this frame is wide enough to stand up well above the roof finish and to form an adequate gutter at the top or back edge of the light. If not, water or snow, particularly, may penetrate at the junction between the skylight and the frame. If the light is hinged to open, penetration of rain is highly likely and opening lights of this type are to be avoided. In the detail the thickness of the roof is not great and it has been possible, using 300×50 mm framing, to make the lower edge coincide with the ceiling so that the frame acts as a lining as well; it is so marked on the drawing. The light itself is 50 mm softwood with 150 mm nom. styles and top rail and 175×38 mm nom. bottom rail. Note the condensation groove to the bottom rail.

The roof lantern light shown in figure 172 takes the form of 4 inclined skylights basically similar to the skylight shown in figure 170 but is constructed out of styles and rails, these being cut angular or truncated on plan. These separate lights are tongued together and the joints protected by lead secured with a wood roll. They are supported on a framework of 100×100 mm timbers which themselves form the heads and corner posts with 100×75 mm mullions. This frames a set of vertical casements, some fixed and some horizontally pivoted with planted stops. The opening casements would be operated by cords or other remote control. The whole skylight stands on a 125 mm timber curb. This is the minimum height of curb to avoid the sill being saturated by rain splashing. The opening is trimmed by 75 mm wide trimmer and this and the firrings and curb are masked by a lining of hardboard. There is 100×20 mm condensation gutter lined with lead formed around the base of the glazing.

169   *Plastic dome lights (2)*

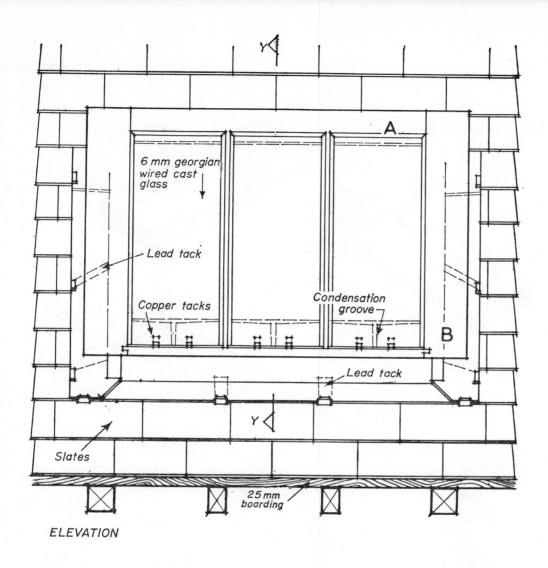

6 mm georgian
wired cast
glass

A

Lead tack

Copper tacks

Condensation
groove

B

Lead tack

Slates

Y

25 mm
boarding

ELEVATION

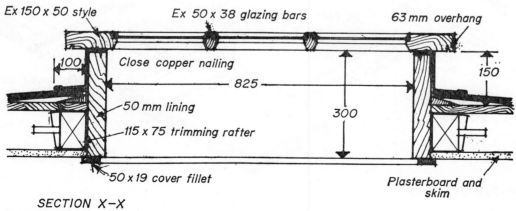

Ex 150 x 50 style

Ex 50 x 38 glazing bars

63 mm overhang

100

Close copper nailing

150

825

50 mm lining

300

115 x 75 trimming rafter

50 x 19 cover fillet

Plasterboard and
skim

SECTION X–X

170   Skylight (1)

191

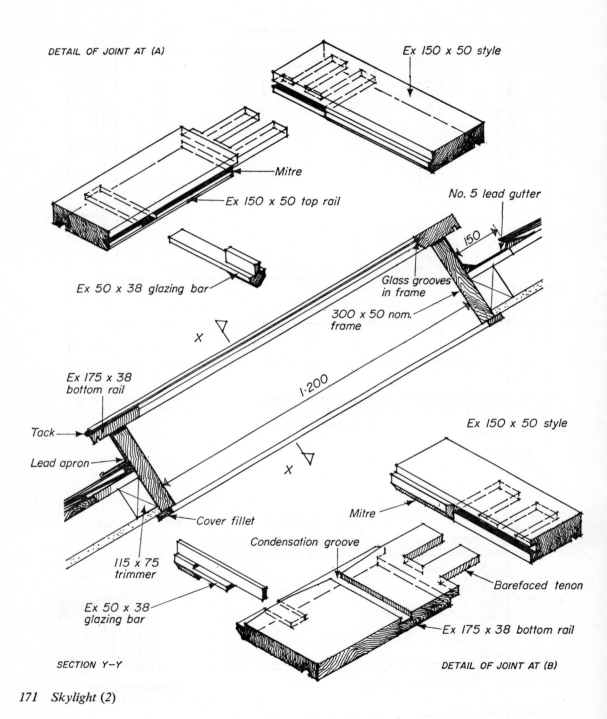

DETAIL OF JOINT AT (A)

Ex 150 x 50 style

Mitre

Ex 150 x 50 top rail

Ex 50 x 38 glazing bar

No. 5 lead gutter

150

Glass grooves
in frame

300 x 50 nom.
frame

1·200

Ex 175 x 38
bottom rail

Tack

Lead apron

X

X

Cover fillet

Ex 150 x 50 style

Mitre

Condensation groove

115 x 75
trimmer

Barefaced tenon

Ex 50 x 38
glazing bar

Ex 175 x 38 bottom rail

SECTION Y–Y

DETAIL OF JOINT AT (B)

171   Skylight (2)

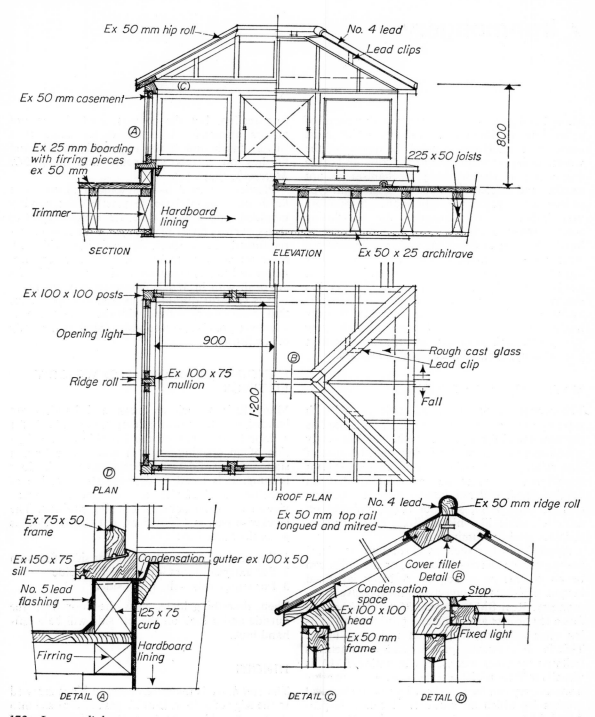

Ex 50 mm hip roll

No. 4 lead

Lead clips

Ex 50 mm casement

(C)

(A)

800

Ex 25 mm boarding
with firring pieces
ex 50 mm

225 x 50 joists

Trimmer

Hardboard
lining

SECTION

ELEVATION

Ex 50 x 25 architrave

Ex 100 x 100 posts

Opening light

900

(B)

Rough cast glass
Lead clip

Ridge roll

Ex 100 x 75
mullion

1·200

Fall

(D)

PLAN

ROOF PLAN

No. 4 lead

Ex 50 mm ridge roll

Ex 75 x 50
frame

Ex 50 mm top rail
tongued and mitred

Ex 150 x 75
sill

Condensation gutter ex 100 x 50

Cover fillet
Detail (B)

No. 5 lead
flashing

Condensation
space
Ex 100 x 100
head

Stop

125 x 75
curb

Fixed light

Firring

Hardboard
lining

Ex 50 mm
frame

DETAIL (A)

DETAIL (C)

DETAIL (D)

172 Lantern light

7 Ironmongery

Many building components are 'working parts' of a building, ie doors and windows, which must open and shut. However good the quality of the workmanship, it will fail in its function and cause annoyance if the working mechanism is not durable and efficient. The choice of the right type of ironmongery, and the right quality, is therefore very important. For instance, the self-closing mechanism of a door into a shop may operate hundreds of times every day and in a department store perhaps a million times a year. The door must be easy for a child to push open, but it must not be opened by the wind. Thus the specification which ironmongery is required to fulfil is a formidable one. Ironmongery can be divided broadly into two types of fittings: (1) fittings which allow movement, such as hinges, and (2) fittings which give security, such as locks, bolts and bars.

MATERIALS AND FINISHES

The strongest lock fittings are made of steel with wearing parts of special bronzes. Brass is used as the base metal for a plated finish. The less costly aluminium alloys are also widely used because of their relative freedom from corrosion and pleasant appearance. It must be remembered that an applied finish will not last so long as regularly cleaned *matt finish*, *satin* or *bright* polishes on durable metals like nickel-silver, brass, bronze, stainless steel or aluminium.

Applied finishes such as chromium or nickel plating can be electro-deposited, or the finish can be an enamel or a lacquer. A black japanned lacquer finish is common for inexpensive ironmongery. Real BMA (*Bronze Metal Antique*) is a finish for bronze and gunmetal produced by heating after polishing to give an iridescent finish. This is an expensive process and is sometimes imitated by other means, but imitation BMA is visually inferior to the real thing. Aluminium alloy ironmongery can be anodized. This is an electrical process by which an anti-corrosive film is produced. The metal can be stained with colour be-

fore sealing, but the colours available are not always attractive. Uncoloured anodizing is a 'silver' finish and looks very well. Metals and finishes on metals are dealt with in *MBC: Materials*, chapter 9.

Plastics are used in ironmongery mostly as a finish on a metal base, ie plastic door handles moulded onto a metal core. Items not subject to stress, such as finger plates, can be made from unreinforced plastic sheet. Some fittings which receive much wear, such as sliding stays for casements and some hinges, are made in nylon. Plastics are dealt with in *MBC: Materials*, chapter 13.

It is vital for durability, as well as appearance, that ironmongery is fixed with the correct screws, wherever possible, of the same metal as the body of the fitting.

HANGING OF DOORS AND WINDOW FITTINGS

Many fittings such as locks and handles are handed, which means that they are specifically for a door hung either on the left side or the right side of an opening, so it is essential to have a standard way of describing on which side the door is hung. It is usual to describe the direction of opening as clockwise or anti-clockwise when viewed from the outward opening position. The clockwise part is self-evident, but the 'outside' is generally agreed as:

1 For internal doors – the corridor side of a room
2 For external doors – the 'open air' side
3 For cupboards – the room side.

Then, describing locks, view the door from the outside and a lock on the left side will be a left-hand lock.

HINGES

The *butt hinge* is the most common hinge screwed to the edge of a door. Butt hinges are recessed into the frame and into the door. Normally one pair of

75 mm or 100 mm butts suits a standard internal door; external and other heavier doors might well have 1½ pairs, ie three 100 mm butts. Butt hinges are made in steel, brass with steel pins, brass with brass pins, or in nylon. Rising butts lift the door as it opens so as to clear the carpet, and this type of hinge is in some degree self-closing. Rising butts must be 'handed'. A falling butt hinge is also available which will keep a door in the open position.

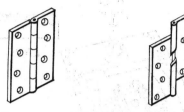

173   Butt hinge and rising butt

Tee hinges of cross-garnets are used for heavy doors of the ledged type.

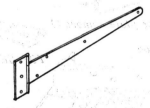

174   Tee hinge

With lift-off butts or pin hinges the door can be taken down without unscrewing the hinge and this type of hinge is therefore always used for doors that are pre-hung and assembled in the factory.

Back-flap hinges are for screwing on the face of the work where the timber is too thin to screw into the edge, or where appearance is not important. They make a strong job when used on internal joinery fittings.

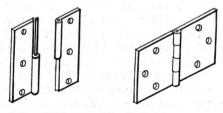

175   Lift-off hinge and back-flap hinge

The parliament hinge is used to enable a door to fold back. It projects from the face of the timber. The centre hinge is used where it can be fixed to the top or to the side of a fitting.

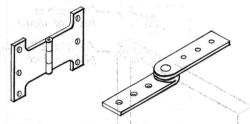

176   Parliament hinge and centre hinge

The cranked hinge is necessary for lipped or re-bated casements and is usually made with the two halves separate so that a pin fixing can be used in assembling the casements in factory production of windows.

The offset or *Easy-clean* hinge is used to allow the outside of windows to be cleaned when open at 90°.

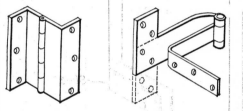

177   Cranked hinge and offset hinge (easy-clean)

The counter flap hinge is set in flush with the face of the work – its name being indicative of its use. The strap hinge is similarly used but has a projecting knuckle.

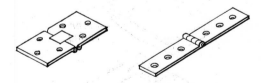

178   Counter flap and strap hinge

DOOR SPRINGS

For the control of swing doors, pivoted floor springs are the best, but they are expensive. The component consists of a strong spring contained in a metal box; a *shoe* which is attached to the base of the door; and a top pivot. The assembly is shown in figure 179. The box is fitted into the floor thickness so that the cover plate is flush with the finished floor level. For this reason the use of a floor spring is somewhat restricted, since many types of floor and threshold construction do not permit easy cutting away to receive the box. The adjustable pivot plate or top centre is fixed to the head of the frame and top of the door, and is adjusted up and down by a screw. The lower pivot is connected to the shoe, which is in turn firmly fixed

Pin plate in head of frame

Adjustable bearing plate in door

Shoe

Top plate

Spindle

Floor spring

Loose box

179   Typical installation of floor spring

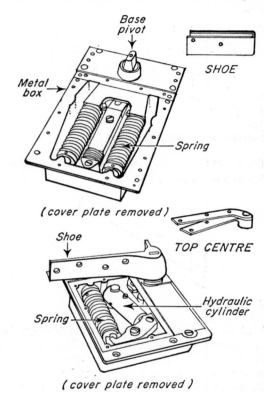

180   Double and single action floor springs

to the bottom of the door and to the side of the door at the base. The spring should have an hydraulic check which slows down the door at a point where it still has, say, 150 mm to travel before closing. This avoids banging or injury to a person following behind. Floor springs are illustrated in figure 180. The hydraulic check mechanism is seen in the figure as a cylinder attached by a lever arm to the strong metal springs. Double action (swinging both ways) and single action (swinging one way only) floor springs are shown.

The cover plates which are available in a variety of finishes to match the general ironmongery specification, have been omitted for clarity. To ensure the smooth working of a double swing door in conjunction with a floor spring, it is important that both the closing and fixed edges of the door are profiled to the correct radius. The recommended dimensions are given in figure 181.

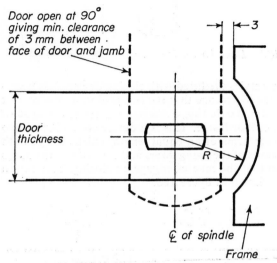

Door heels and their radii for standard applications

Door thickness	40	44	50	64
Heel radius R	32	35	38	48

181   Door heels and their radii

DOOR CLOSERS

There are several alternative methods for checking and controlling the opening and closing of doors. For swing doors there are various types of spring hinges. Figure 182 illustrates a patented type of hinge controlled by a small but powerful horizontal spring held in a metal cylinder at the back of the face plate. The cylinder or cylinders have to be housed into mortices cut into the frame and are covered by the face plate. The moving part of the hinge clips round both sides of the door in a shallow housing and is screwed firmly into position so that there are no projecting knuckles or plates. Both double and single action hinges are illus-

trated, the former controlled by two springs, the latter by one. This type of hinge is not made with a check action.

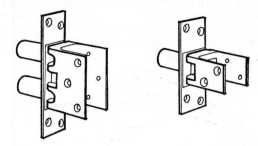

182   Single and double barrel, double action Hawgood spring hinges

Another type of spring hinge is illustrated in figure 183. This is similar in form to a butt hinge but has a large knuckle, the hinges are obtainable with double action or single action as shown. The spring, which is contained in the vertical metal cylinder, is adjustable by means of a *Tommy* bar in the hole at the top of the cylinder. This adjustment controls the momentum of the closing action. Spring hinges of this type can be obtained in matching pairs, the top hinge acting as the spring, the bottom hinge being made to provide a check action.

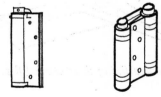

183   Single and double action spring hinges

The closing action of doors hung on ordinary butt hinges can be controlled by the fixing of check mechanisms on the top of the face of the door and the door frame head. There is a very wide range of this type of overhead door closer which provides a combined closing and check action control. This type of closer is adjustable to balance the weight of the door and is much less expensive than the pivot floor spring control. The overhead closer is available in double and single action patterns; handed and reversible. Three alternative

197

methods of fixing are shown. Figure 184 shows an example of a closer in a pleasantly designed case, for surface fixing to the opening face of the door. Figure 185 shows the same spring, but for fixing to the closing face of the door, and figure 186 shows a closer which fits into the thickness of the door at the top and is thus concealed with the exception of the projecting arm.

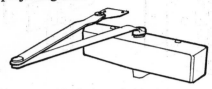

184   Hydraulic check, single action door check, surface fixing to opening face

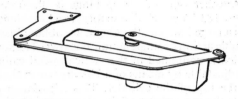

185   Hydraulic check, single action door check, surface fixing to closing face

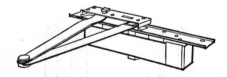

186   Concealed fixing door check (fits into thickness of door)

DOOR CHECKS

The door closer fittings so far described control the whole of the movement of the door, but perhaps a more universal requirement is to prevent the slamming of the door. Figure 187 shows such a device which by engaging a wheel attached to a cantilevered arm, causes the movement of the door to be checked. This type of check would be used in conjunction with a spring hinge which works in conjunction with the check to achieve final and positive closing.

Where pairs of doors which have rebated meet-

187   Door holder (to prevent door slamming)

ing styles are fitted with closing devices it is necessary to arrange that the leaves close in the correct order. To do this, a *selector* is fitted to the head of the door frame. This is a device consisting of two lever arms of an equal length which engage both leaves of the swing doors and can control the doors so that the rebates engage on closing. This action is shown in figure 188.

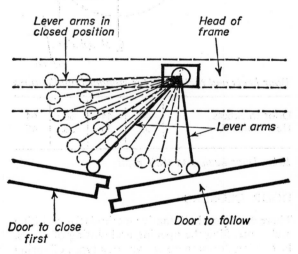

188   Door selector

LOCKS AND LATCHES

Locking gear contains complex mechanism and very great care must be exercised in the specification of the appropriate quality. The specifier must be quite clear as to the precise requirements since in general terms cost is proportionate to security. It is important to realize that, apart from the convenience of the user, the insurance company required to cover the contents of the building will be concerned with security whilst the local authority will be concerned with providing easy means of escape in case of fire. These two conditions are not always easy to reconcile.

There are four basic types of lock and latch. All others are variations of these.

1 *Dead lock* The dead lock illustrated in figure 189 has a single bolt which is pushed out and drawn back by operation of a key only; it is used for store rooms and other places where simple security is required. For additional security a dead lock is used with another type of fastening, such as a latch.

189 Mortice dead lock

2 *Latch* The latch illustrated in figure 190 has a bolt held in the extended position by a spring and which is drawn back to allow the door to open by the turning of a handle only. This keeps a door in the shut position without providing security.

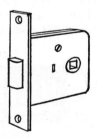

190 Upright mortice latch

3 *Two bolt lock set* The two bolt lock illustrated in figure 191 combines the previous two types of fastening in one lock case, and is probably the best lock for general use. The spring latch operated by a handle serves for all general purposes; the dead bolt operated by a key from either side permits the door to be locked when needed. A mortice lock of this type is preferred for security by insurance companies because of the separate dead bolt. It is such a common type of lock that it is not necessary in specifying to use the term *two bolt*. Reference to a lock set implies two bolts.

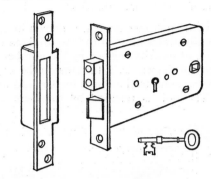

191 Horizontal mortice lock

4 *Night latch* A rim night latch, illustrated in figure 192, has a spring bolt operated by a handle on the inside and a key on the outside. When going out the door can be 'pulled to' behind the user, but a key is necessary for re-entering the premises. This gives a sense of security, but ordinary night latches do not provide a great deal of security, since by cutting a hole in the glass or wood panel of a door the

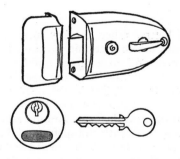

192 Cylinder rim latch

inside handle can be turned. This can be done in a few seconds by an expert. Also the spring bolt or latch in ordinary latches can be pushed back by a knife. On the other hand, cylinder latches are small and easily fitted and take a small key which adds to their convenience in use and many special kinds of cylinder latches have been developed to overcome the defects referred to. A knob or thumb slide, operated from the inside, will hold the bolt open or shut when needed and the key will then not operate. When fitted with these devices the cylinder lock is a most useful additional security.

A lock, with latch mechanism, is shown in figure 193. This illustrates most of the essential features. A measure of security is given by the number and complexity of the wards. If the cuts on the key bit do not correspond to the wards the key cannot be turned. The bolt is released by tumblers, or a

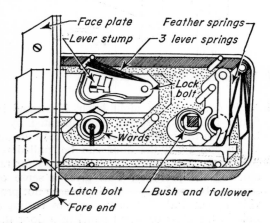

193   Horizontal mortice lock showing component parts

system of levers. When the key turns, the levers have to be lifted to a certain position before the bolt will pass and so a larger number of levers gives greater security. The tumbler mechanism (pin tumblers) is applied in the normal cylinder lock as shown in figure 194. The V-cuts on the key have to lift the pins the exact amount so that their tops become flush with the surface of the rotable plug to enable the latter to be turned and the latch to operate. There are many thousands of combinations of pin positions, which gives many thousands of 'differs' or locks requiring different keys. It is important when writing the specification for the locks to be clear as to what differs are needed. In a house there is usually no point in having different room locks; in fact it is convenient, in the event of a room key being lost, to be able to

use another from an adjoining room. However, on the other hand, in a building such as an hotel all room keys must differ. For this type of building locks which differ can be opened by a master key, or a number of locks, perhaps all on one floor, can be opened by a sub-master key. There is a large range of mastering 'possibles' to suit all requirements and the technique of arranging the mastering of the keys in the most convenient way is known as *suiteing*. Each group of keys being called a *suite*.

There are two methods of fixing for locks in general use. The four types of lock described are, in most cases, manufactured to be suitable for either method of fixing. The choice is whether to fix the lock on the face of the door or whether to set the lock into the thickness of the door. Where the lock is screwed to the inside face of the door it is referred to as a rim lock or rim latch. Where a lock is set into a mortice within the thickness of the door it is known as a mortice lock or mortice latch. Obviously the rim fixing is cheaper, but less secure and less neat. On the other hand, mortice fixing is not suitable for very thin doors. 13 mm thick locks will suit 35 mm finished thickness doors. 16 mm locks suit 40 mm doors, which is the recommended thickness. Many modifications of the four types of lock described can be studied in merchants' showrooms and in manufacturers' catalogues, so it is only necessary here to make special mention of one or two types which may need clarification. Dead bolts are sometimes designed to have *double throw*. This means that the bolt goes further into the staple when the key is turned a second time; this gives added security.

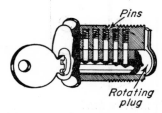

194   Cylinder lock showing pin tumbler mechanism

A dead bolt for a sliding door requires a claw or hook bolt as illustrated in figure 195.

Where pairs of doors with rebated meeting stiles are used, it is necessary to fit a rebated mortice lock as illustrated in figure 196. Here the fore-

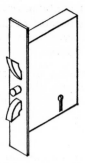

195   *Double hook bolt for sliding doors*

196   *Rebated mortice lock*

197   *Cupboard lock*

bined lock-latch set which needs only two holes to be drilled has been produced. This type of lock, which is now in common use, has the locking mechanism in the knob, and is usually referred to as a *knob set*. A typical example is shown in figure 198.

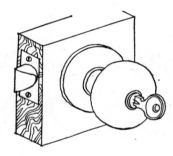

198   *Knob set*

end of the lock case is cranked to fit the rebate on the stiles.

The normal mortice lock is made 'horizontal', ie suitable for a deep mortice into the middle rail of the door, and this type of lock is illustrated in figure 193. Where a lock must fit into a narrow style it is made 'upright'. This type of lock, which is illustrated in figure 190, has a comparatively narrow case. In a lock (lock and latch) set, the keyhole and spindle mortice are in line vertically in a vertical mortice lock, and the keyhole and spindle mortice are in line horizontally in a horizontal mortice lock. The horizontal set is usually used in conjunction with knob furniture, and the vertical set with lever handle furniture. Drawer and cupboard locks are usually for a flush fixing. This means that they are let into the inside face of the work, so that the outside of the lock is flush with the inside face of the timber. The cover plate is usually extended round the side to give a neat finish. Figure 197 shows a typical cupboard lock. Simplication of the fixing is an attractive proposition as mortice cutting takes a long time. A com-

Ball catches and roller catches are used for cupboards and because they are inexpensive they have also been used for the doors to living rooms in place of a latch. They are, however, very noisy and tend to give trouble in adjustment unless the projection can be easily altered to suit any change in the gap between door and frame.

LEVER HANDLES AND KNOBS

Knobs should not be used where the backset of the lock is less than, say, 60 mm. The backset is the distance from the outer face of the fore-end of the lock to the centre of the key hole. The reason for this is if a knob-set is fixed too near the door frame the user will suffer damaged knuckles when operating the knob. The question of the fixing of the knob in relation to the spindle and rose requires some special consideration.

There are many methods of fixing knob furniture, several of which are patented. The two basic variants are

1 A spindle which is 'fixed' to the knob by a grub screw or patented fixing so that the pull of the knob is resisted directly by the spindle. This is a strong and most satisfactory method but requires exact and careful fitting.
2 'Floating' or free spindle which slides on to the knob and which relies for its fixing by screwing the rose to the face of the door. This type is easily fitted but a disadvantage is that when used

with mortice locks only short screws can be used to secure the rose because of the thickness of the lock case. These screws may work loose even in the best quality doors.

An 'exploded' drawing of a knob and spindle fixing is shown in figure 199.

Knob furniture provides a neat, unobtrusive and strong specification well suited to resist rough usage. Knob furniture is available in various alloys. Bronze is the most expensive but most hard wearing, but aluminium, because of its pleasant appearance and relatively low cost, is very popular.

Lever furniture must be well designed and

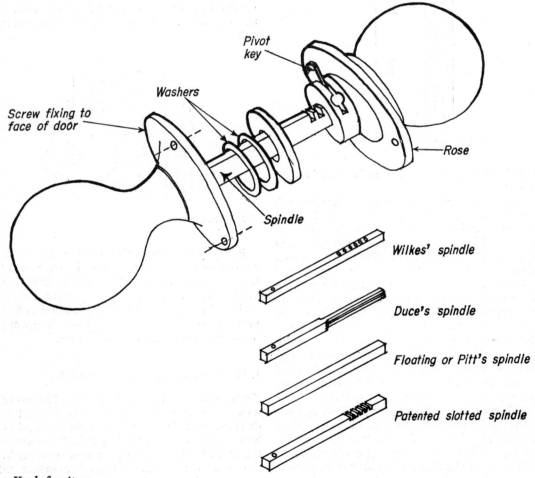

Pivot key

Washers

Screw fixing to face of door

Rose

Spindle

Wilkes' spindle

Duce's spindle

Floating or Pitt's spindle

Patented slotted spindle

199 *Knob furniture*

strongly constructed since the lever arm produces considerable strain on the lock or latch mechanism.

Where upright mortice locks are specified, lever furniture is essential because the distance of the spindle from the edge of the door is small. Most British lever furniture is of the floating spindle type in which the handles take the pull of the door through the handle plates or roses. Lever handles sometimes have, in place of a rose, a handle plate which allows the screws to be fixed beyond the mortice and so ensures that the fixing screws will not foul the lock case. This, of course, makes a stronger fixing. British lever handles often embody a spring to counterbalance the weight of the handle as British locks do not normally have strong springs on the latch. Continental locks have a strong latch spring and so their handles also operate on this. This point should be borne in mind when considering using continental lever handles on British locks. In a vertical mortice lock the spindle for the lever handle or knob is vertically above the key hole. This means that a specifier can choose between lever furniture which has a long handle plate incorporating a key hole and a lever handle with a small handle plate and a separate key escutcheon plate. The key escutcheon plate is used as a cover plate for the key hole. In order to hide the large number of screws which are necessary for fixing door furniture of this kind, several different types of cover plate have been produced. The cover plate will either clip over or be screwed over the fixing plates. The screw type are usually better but can only be used where circular roses are specified since the clip on types tend to give trouble in use unless very well

designed. A drawing of a lever handle showing the fixing is given in figure 200.

Lever furniture is available in a very wide range of materials. The choice of stainless steel, bronze, aluminium alloy, plastic covered metal, or nylon, will depend on considerations of first cost, appearance, type of use and subsequent maintenance costs.

DOOR SCHEDULE

A schedule of all the items of door furniture is usually prepared for each job. A typical schedule is illustrated in chapter 11, figure 243, page 252.

BURGLAR PROTECTION

BS 3621 : 1963 : *Specification for Thief Resistant Locks for Hinged Doors,* was prepared at the request of the police and the insurance companies to ensure a minimum degree of security against professional intrusion. However, it must be borne in mind that locks must be properly fitted for them to be acceptable and the Burglary Surveyors employed by the insurance companies may require a higher degree of security than offered by BS 3621. For situations of high security risk the specifier would be wise to contact the insurance company's surveyor for advice.

WINDOW FASTENINGS

Window fastenings, such as casement turns, sash fasteners and stays, are illustrated with the window details where appropriate in chapter 4. Typical examples of these are shown in figure 201 and need no further reference. The use of pegs and stays to regulate the opening of side hung casements is now being largely superseded by the use of friction hinges. The cam opener illustrated in figure 202 is now largely used on top hung steel window casements. Other forms of casement stay are shown in figure 203. Of particular note is the roller stay for use on bottom hung casements which open inwards; and on horizontal centre pivot hung windows to control the projection of the top part of the window into the room.

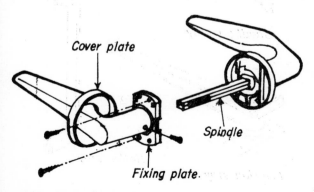

200   *Lever furniture*

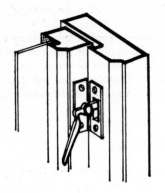

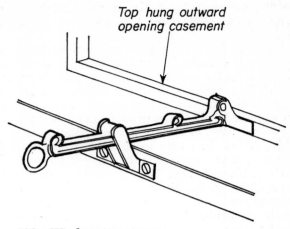

Top hung outward
opening casement

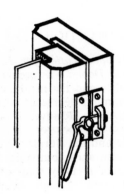

202   Window cam opener

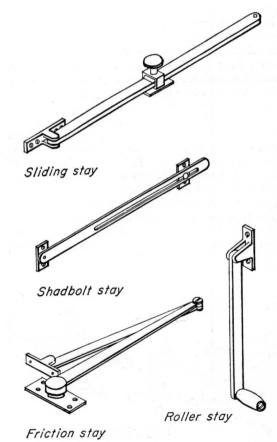

Sliding stay

Shadbolt stay

Friction stay

Roller stay

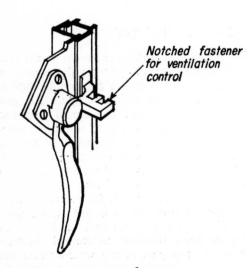

Notched fastener
for ventilation
control

201   Casement turns or fasteners

203   Casement stays

Bolts

Bolts are used as well as locks in additional security for doors and windows. They are usually fixed at the top and bottom of doors and should always have a socket to receive the shoot of the bolt. This is particularly important at the threshold. The diameter of the shoot, the type of metal used and the method of fixing of the bolt are an indication of its strength. The most common type of bolt is the barrel bolt, which has a round or *barrel*-like shoot on a back plate for surface fixing, as shown in figure 204. The shoot runs in a guide

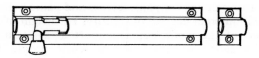

204   Barrel bolt

and is slid home into a metal keep. This type of bolt is inexpensive and easy to fix. For better class work a flush lever bolt is used, as shown in figure 205. This is more expensive and takes more time

205   Lever bolt

to fix. It is recessed into a shallow housing in the door until the face plate is flush with the surface of the timber. It is operated by a thumb slide or a lever action. A particular type of bolt which is used for minimizing the twisting of a door or window is the cremorne bolt, as shown in figure 206. This bolt extends the full height of the door or window so that when the handle is turned the top bolt slides upwards and the bottom bolt slides

downwards to give top and bottom fixing. A variation of a cremorne bolt is an espagnolette. This type of bolt provides centre fixing as well as

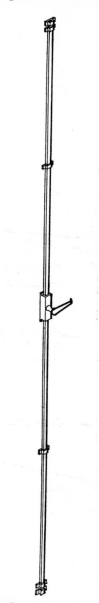

206   Cremorne bolt

fixing at the top and bottom. The centre fixing is commonly a lock. Espagnolettes may be surface or flush fitted as required. See figure 114, page 137.

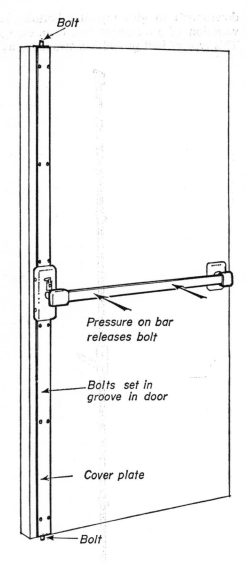

Bolt

Pressure on bar
releases bolt

Bolts set in
groove in door

Cover plate

Bolt

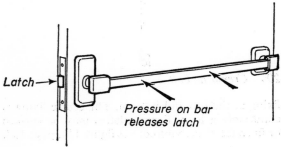

Latch

Pressure on bar
releases latch

Fire regulations for public buildings do not permit the use of ordinary locks on doors which are classified as means of escape in case of fire. To overcome this difficulty a panic latch or bolt is used. A panic latch is used on single doors and consists of a cross bar which is pushed against a latch to release it. A locking knob is often fixed to the outside of the door to enable two-way traffic to operate. A panic bolt will have a striking plate at the top and bottom of the door so that the door is held in three places, and thus gives a greater degree of security than a panic latch. A mortice panic bolt which is let into the face of the door for neatness is shown in figure 207. There are various designs of panic latches and panic bolts to suit different degrees of security. The height of the bar of the panic bolt is important since in an emergency it must operate when people fall against it. A generally acceptable height for the bar above the floor is 1050 mm.

CUPBOARD CATCHES

There are very many designs and types of cupboard catches as reference to the manufacturers' catalogues will indicate. The specifier must decide on the exact requirements before choosing the most suitable catch, depending for instance, on

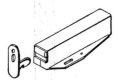

208   Cupboard catch

whether or not the catch is used in conjunction with some form of handle. Catches should be arranged, if possible, both at the top and bottom of a cupboard door since they will then act as a form of restraint to prevent the door warping. A cupboard interior catch which eliminates the need for door furniture is illustrated in figure 208. When the door is pressed it springs open and when the door is pushed closed it clicks shut.

207   Panic bolts

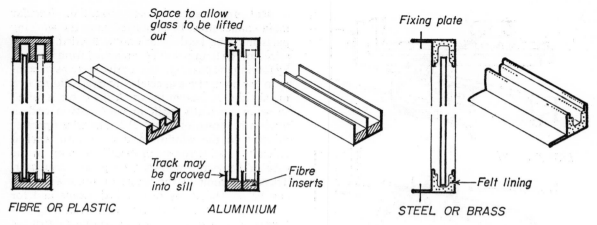

209 *Track for glass*

SLIDING GEAR

Sliding gear for doors and windows has been described separately with the fittings illustrated in the appropriate chapter. Sliding gear for cupboard doors is available in a very wide range. Small cupboard or bookcase fronts of plate glass with polished edges can be fitted directly into the channels of fibre, metal or plastic made in single, double or triple section. Thin plastic-faced sheet, or plywood, can also run in most of these tracks. Typical sections of this type of track are shown in figure 209. For larger plate glass doors a metal section track is provided in aluminium or brass which incorporates small wheels or ball bearings that run on a bottom track to take the extra weight of glass. For larger plywood or block-board, or framed cupboard doors, a fibre track with sliders is manufactured. The track is grooved into the sill, the sliders being morticed into the under edge of the door. This type of track is also made in nylon and an example is illustrated in figure 210. As an alternative to this there are a number of small ball-bearing roller fittings, for running on a bottom track, which are illustrated in figure 211. These run easily and so are used where the door is tall in proportion to its width and which might jam in a simple channel track.

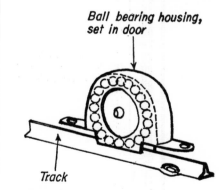

211 *Ballbearing roller*

WINDOW OPENING GEAR

The rod and worm gear type of control has been traditional for large and heavy windows – it is suitable where cost is the main consideration and

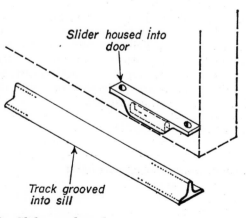

210 *Sliders and track*

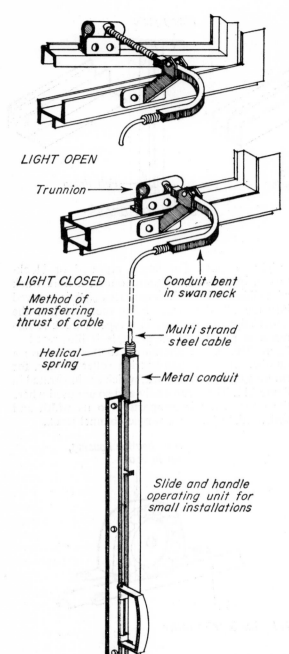

LIGHT OPEN

Trunnion

LIGHT CLOSED

Conduit bent in swan neck

Method of transferring thrust of cable

Multi strand steel cable

Helical spring

Metal conduit

Slide and handle operating unit for small installations

a neat appearance is not essential. Regular maintenance must be organized since the working parts must be kept clean and well oiled. If they seize up, the fixings will be wrenched from the wall by forcing the gearing. Alternative systems in common use comprise a special wire cable sliding in a metal tube. A system in which the cable is wired to serve efficiently both in compression and in tension is shown in figure 212. The wire operates directly on the window and is in turn worked either by a slide for small installations or, in the case of heavier windows, by a geared regulator. There is a limit to the range of windows which can be controlled by mechanical means and for very large installations travelling over long distances electrical or hydraulic systems must be used. This type of system is, however, uneconomical for small installations.

Electrical control

For this type of control a motor is installed at the receiving end which will drive a local installation of cable gear. The main push-button control can be situated in a convenient central position and is coupled to a forward and reverse contactor. The switching off of the current in both directions is by micro-switches at the receiving end.

Hydraulic control

This is effected by a small bore copper or nylon tubing filled with oil. A pump, either hand or electrically operated, delivers the requisite pressure to small hydraulic rams positioned in the actual opening gear. In this system a single operating position can be used to control a large number of opening lights remotely situated both from the operating position and from each other. Because of their neat appearance both electric and hydraulic systems are preferable provided that their initial cost can be justified.

212   *Remote control for opening lights*

8 Balustrades

FABRICATION OF BALUSTRADES

The making up of metal building components relies on the techniques of forming, fitting and jointing of metal parts and work on finishing to the surface of the metal when the component is complete.

Metals for building work are produced in forms suitable for casting, extruding or rolling. These techniques and various methods of forming and jointing metals are detailed in *MBC: Materials*, chapter 9.

The making of metal components involves one or more of the processes or operations referred to, and the design of the component should take account of these as well as of the physical properties of the metals involved. Bolting and riveting are traditional methods of metal jointing. Ordinary semi-circular headed rivets are used for industrial work, but for decorative work the head is usually cleaned off or a pin is used in place of a rivet. The top of the pin being concealed by the finishing process. Mortice and tenon joints are used in open work such as grilles or balustrading.

Drilling and tapping to receive screws is also used, not only for site jointing but in the metal workshop. Self-tapping screws are used for much commercial sheet metal work as they are quick, cheap, and look presentable from the face side.

Various metalwork details related to a composite metal balustrade are shown in figure 213.

For cladding steel with bronze strips special taper headed screws may be used as shown at 'A'. The screws will be in the same bronze as the strip and the heads left slightly proud to be cleaned off. The buffing up will drag the metal over the joint between the screw head and the strip so that no line is discernible. For specialist work special screws are made in the same metal as the cladding.

Details 'B' and 'D' show the make up of the balusters and rails forming the balustrade infill panel. The half lap joint in the rail is secured by countersunk screws and the baluster is screwed and *riveted* between the rails.

Detail 'C' shows the joint between two sections in a hollow bronze handrail. The rail is plugged by means of a solid steel core which is screwed up from below by say 9 mm countersunk screws.

Detail 'E' shows the junction of the square supporting standard and the lower rail. In effect the upright standard passes through the rail and is screwed in place – the heads of the screws being afterwards removed.

Detail 'F' shows an alternative infill between the standards by using 6 mm toughened glass. The glass is protected and secured at each corner by small steel clips which are screwed to the main uprights. The glass is shown bedded in washleather to accommodate movement. This is the traditional way though now glazing compound would probably be used.

BUILDING REGULATION REQUIREMENTS

The regulations cover stairway flights and landings at each floor level. With regard to the provision of handrails, it is always necessary to provide a hand rail on one side and for stairs more than 1070 mm wide a handrail must be provided at each side. Any balcony or other external area which is above ground floor level and is likely to be used for work other than maintenance must also have a guard rail. The height of handrails and balustrades are shown in figure 214. The metric dimensions given are those taken from the MOHLG Building Regulations 1965: *Metric Equivalents of Dimensions*: 1968, HMSO. The Building Regulations differentiate between *Private Stairways* and *Common Stairways*. A private stairway is a stairway in a single dwelling and a common stairway is a stairway in buildings designed for occupation as separate dwellings by more than one family. Thus the regulations refer only to stairways constructed in dwellings and not to stairways in public buildings. Schedule 5 of the Building Regulations, which covers rules for the calculation of loading, refers in rule 4 to the permissible imposed lateral loads

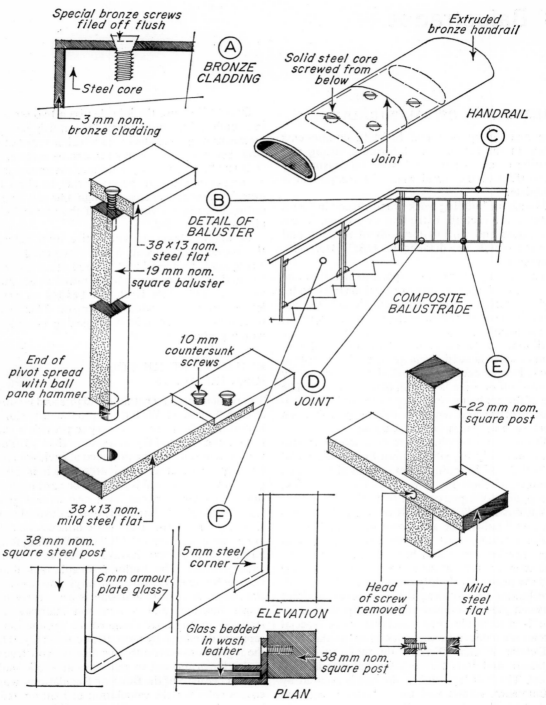

Special bronze screws filed off flush

(A) BRONZE CLADDING

Steel core

3 mm nom. bronze cladding

Extruded bronze handrail

Solid steel core screwed from below

Joint

HANDRAIL

(C)

(B) DETAIL OF BALUSTER

38 × 13 nom. steel flat

19 mm nom. square baluster

COMPOSITE BALUSTRADE

(E)

10 mm countersunk screws

(D) JOINT

End of pivot spread with ball pane hammer

38 × 13 nom. mild steel flat

(F)

22 mm nom. square post

38 mm nom. square steel post

5 mm steel corner

6 mm armour plate glass

ELEVATION

Head of screw removed

Mild steel flat

Glass bedded in wash leather

38 mm nom. square post

PLAN

213 Metalwork joints

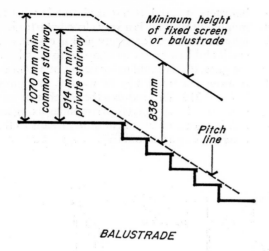

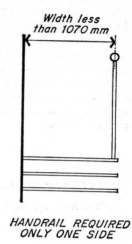

BALUSTRADE

HANDRAIL REQUIRED
ONLY ONE SIDE

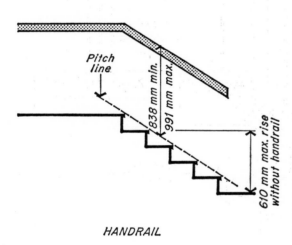

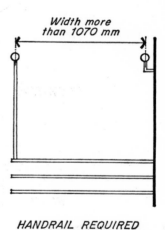

HANDRAIL

HANDRAIL REQUIRED
BOTH SIDES

Dimensions are to the nearest millimetre

214   Guarding of stairways

on parapets, balustrades and railings. The regulations require that balustrades to light access stairs used only for inspection or maintenance shall be designed to withstand a minimum lateral imposed load, ie horizontal thrust at handrail level of 218·9 N/m run.

Balustrades to stairs in connection with maisonettes, 'one family' houses and private balconies must be able to withstand a thrust of 364·8 N/m run. If the stairway is designed to form part of a building intended to be used as a stadium or a similar place where people will congregate in considerable numbers the balustrade must withstand a horizontal thrust of 2·92 kN/m run. This figure also applies, of course, to railings and safety barriers and in view of past experience of dangerous failure this is an important figure.

Stairways in connection with all other buildings

must be designed so that the balustrade will withstand a horizontal thrust of 729·7 N/m run. In the case of a private balcony used in connection with flats, maisonettes, dormitories, hospital wards or hotel sitting rooms and not exceeding 2·79 m² in area the balustrade must withstand a horizontal thrust of 364·8 N/m run. The reason for these regulations is that poorly designed and constructed stairways have been responsible for a large proportion of accidents.

balusters are used, two to each tread with a 50×19 mm handrail. This is a very close balustrade which may be required for safety and is essential where small children might be tempted to crawl through the gaps. If this could never occur, one 19 mm nom. baluster per tread may be used as in figures 216, 217 and 218. This reduces the number of mortices in the treads and therefore simplifies fixing and the making good of the finish of the treads to the balusters. Using a bottom rail to support intermediate

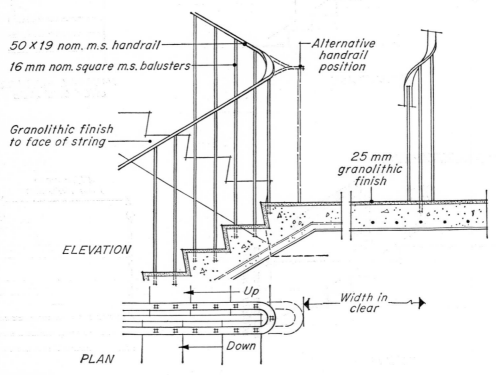

215 Metal balustrade (1)

METAL BALUSTRADES

Various forms of metal balustrading using vertical balusters are shown in figures 215 and 216.

The simplest form of balustrade consists of square or round balusters and a metal rail. This metal rail may be the handrail or the core rail for a wood or more elaborate metal handrail. The size of the members depends upon the number and the need for rigidity if stiffening is not provided by other means. In figure 215, 16 mm nom. square

balusters with a standard every third or fourth tread gives an easier fixing detail as shown in figure 216. Standards should be 25 mm nom. square and balusters would be in 13 mm nom. tube, or rod. The bottom and core rail would be 50×10 mm nom. mild steel flat section. Arrangement of the balusters and particularly the handrail will be affected by the planning of the staircase at the turn. There are several arrangements of turn shown in figures 215–18. The alternatives depend upon the size of the stair well and the arrangement of the

212

steps which are themselves governed by the space that can be allocated to the stair at the design stage. It is very important that ample space be allowed at this part of the staircase. A tight turn not only makes difficulties for the manufacturer of the balustrade and handrail but also makes the neat detailing of the steps difficult to achieve and results in an inconvenient arrangement for the users of the staircase. The most common arrangement for a turn is a half space landing as shown in figure

fire, the important dimension is the measurement 'in the clear' between the inside of the handrail and the wall or handrail on the other side. In figure 215 the intersections of the sloping soffit of the stairs are not in line with the junction of the landing. A better arrangement of this detail is shown in figures 216 and 217. Here the soffits coincide at a point which can conveniently be made the face of the edge of the landing. This simplifies the detailing of the staircase, particularly if expensive finishes like

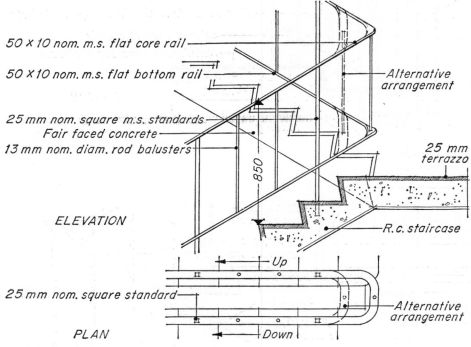

216   Metal balustrade (2)

215 where the faces of risers in both upper and lower flights are opposite or almost opposite each other on plan. The handrail has to drop the equivalent of two risers at the turn so unless the well is wide or the handrail can be extended on to the landing, as shown dotted, a very sharp ramp will be needed. There are two points to be borne in mind, a wide well loses space across the staircase but, on the other hand, extending the handrail on to the landing as shown loses space on the width of the landing. These considerations are important, since on staircases used for means of escape in case of

marble are used as facings both to the string of the staircase and the edge of the landing. The setting back of the top riser in the lower flight makes the staircase much more pleasant to use and it permits a pause in descending before embarking on the next flight. The handrails also intersect at a level to suit a proper height above the landing. The arrangement shown in figure 216 also permits an easy ramp at the turn and one well suited to forming in a metal section. If more space can be taken up on the landing, as shown in figure 217, it is possible to arrange the handrail without a wreath, so

213

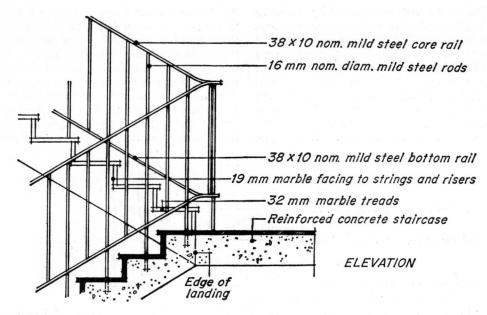

38 × 10 nom. mild steel core rail

16 mm nom. diam. mild steel rods

38 × 10 nom. mild steel bottom rail

19 mm marble facing to strings and risers

32 mm marble treads

Reinforced concrete staircase

ELEVATION

Edge of
landing

217   *Metal balustrade* (3)

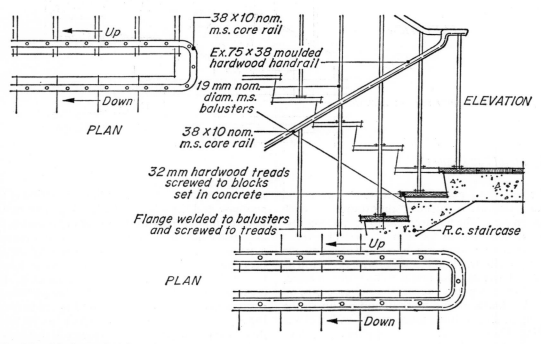

38 × 10 nom.
m.s. core rail

Ex. 75 × 38 moulded
hardwood handrail

19 mm nom.
diam. m.s.
balusters

38 × 10 nom.
m.s. core rail

32 mm hardwood treads
screwed to blocks
set in concrete

Flange welded to balusters
and screwed to treads

R.c. staircase

ELEVATION

← Up

← Down

PLAN

← Up

PLAN

← Down

218   *Metal balustrade* (4)

214

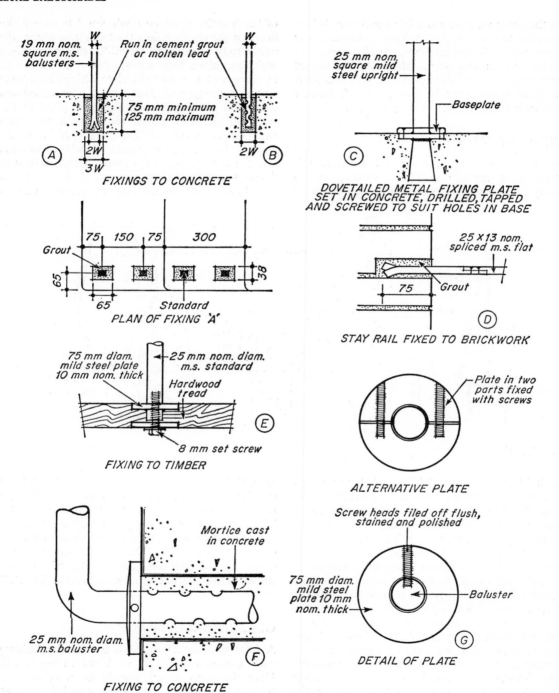

A

19 mm nom. square m.s. balusters

W

Run in cement grout or molten lead

75 mm minimum 125 mm maximum

2W
3W

W

B

2W

FIXINGS TO CONCRETE

Grout

75 | 150 | 75 | 300

65

65

Standard

38

PLAN OF FIXING 'A'

75 mm diam. mild steel plate 10 mm nom. thick

25 mm nom. diam. m.s. standard

Hardwood tread

E

8 mm set screw

FIXING TO TIMBER

Mortice cast in concrete

25 mm nom. diam. m.s. baluster

F

FIXING TO CONCRETE

25 mm nom. square mild steel upright

Baseplate

C

DOVETAILED METAL FIXING PLATE SET IN CONCRETE, DRILLED, TAPPED AND SCREWED TO SUIT HOLES IN BASE

25 x 13 nom. spliced m.s. flat

75

Grout

D

STAY RAIL FIXED TO BRICKWORK

Plate in two parts fixed with screws

ALTERNATIVE PLATE

Screw heads filed off flush, stained and polished

75 mm diam. mild steel plate 10 mm nom. thick

Baluster

G

DETAIL OF PLATE

219   *Metal balustrade fixing*

that the turns on plan are made separately before the bends to the two slopes. This arrangement is also shown by dotted line in figure 215. Space can also be saved in this way as shown by the dotted line in figure 216 but this involves a very considerable drop which may be dangerous. A further balustrade detail is shown in figure 218.

FIXING DETAILS

General fixing details for metal balustrading is shown in figures 219 and 220. Balustrades are usually fabricated in the workshop in lengths of

of the mortice must be made good to match the finish of the treads unless the technique allows the treads to be faced later. Detail 'C' shows a method which permits a little adjustment in all directions by the use of a cover base plate which also covers up any making good. This plate can be drilled and tapped in position to suit the base plate of the standard and with power tools this is comparatively easy. A method of fixing a stay rail to brickwork is shown. A short length of rail is grouted in and the flat section rail is then spliced on to it as detailed at 'D'. Fixing to wood is simpler but a large bearing area to resist lateral pressure is neces-

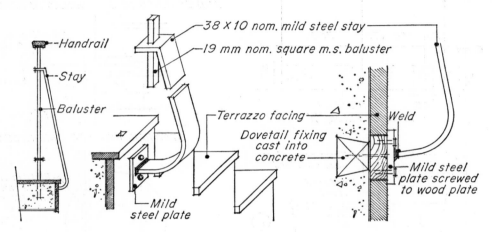

220   Metal balustrade fixing

one flight and one turn. The turn helps to stiffen the balustrade. Where there are no turns to give lateral bracing special stays may be needed as shown in figure 220. These special stays are fixed into the edge of the flight of stairs. The balustrades are usually fixed to the structure by setting the standards into a mortice or by screwing through a base plate set on the face of the structure. Where a standard is split or ragged a mortice should have the dimensions shown at 'A' (figure 219). It is, however, more common to cut indents in the standard as shown alternatively at 'B'. To allow for tolerance in fixing and for ease of fixing generally mortices are preferably wide in the direction of the flight. Mortices are usually run in with cement grout though fixers prefer molten lead as the joint is then rigid within a few minutes. The mouth

sary. Detail 'E' shows a base plate on the end of a standard let into a hardwood tread and the plate on the underside is held in place and makes the joint rigid, by a set screw, up into the end of the standard. A detail for securing a baluster into concrete is shown at 'F'. Collars or cover plates to cover up the making good of the mortice are shown in two alternative constructions in detail 'G'.

GLAZED BALUSTRADE

A detail of a metal balustrade to a landing balcony with a glass panel infill is shown in figure 221. Here the glass, which should be toughened, is framed in a small angle frame which is then attached to the uprights.

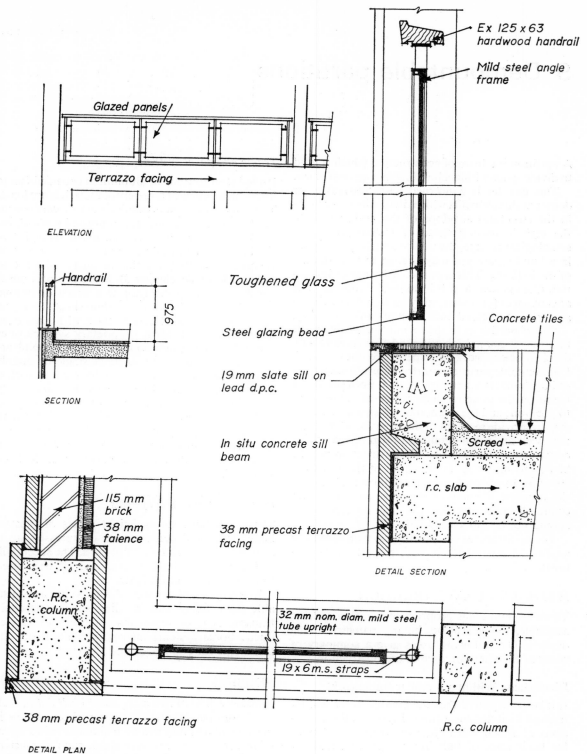

Glazed panels

Terrazzo facing →

ELEVATION

Handrail

975

SECTION

Ex 125 x 63 hardwood handrail

Mild steel angle frame

Toughened glass

Steel glazing bead

19 mm slate sill on lead d.p.c.

In situ concrete sill beam

38 mm precast terrazzo facing

Concrete tiles

Screed

r.c. slab

DETAIL SECTION

115 mm brick

38 mm faience

R.c. column

38 mm precast terrazzo facing

32 mm nom. diam. mild steel tube upright

19 x 6 m.s. straps

R.c. column

DETAIL PLAN

221 **Balustrade with glass panels**

9 Demountable partitions

A partition is a form of construction which is used to divide space within a building in a vertical plane.

This chapter is concerned with 'moveable' or demountable elements which divide the space within the structural envelope of the building. With the ever increasing speed of technological and sociological change, the uses to which spaces within a building are put may change during the life of the building. This is particularly true of Industrial, Commercial and Educational buildings. The advantage of future flexibility must, however, be set against the increased initial cost of demountability.

Dwarf partitions in the form of moveable walls up to say 2·000 m high and used as screens to subdivide office or workshop space, are not included. Demountable partition construction and suspended ceiling design is often inter-related. Both should be based on the same modular frame of reference as to position; and the method of construction necessary to provide restraint of the partition at the head may well affect the detail and form of the ceiling construction. Both forms of construction will be 'dry', relying on an interlocking of the parts for stability. In order to meet reasonable cost targets, the number of components must be kept to an economic minimum and the erection techniques should not be too specialized.

The performance of a partition system should be studied in general terms with respect to the following criteria.

METHODS OF CONSTRUCTION

There are numerous proprietary partition systems available, many systems having patented fixing devices. The following notes give a summary of some of the alternative types of construction.

Dimensions: Within a modular framework

It is to be expected that the manufacturer will introduce modular co-ordinated systems, the dimensions of which will follow the recommendations for basic sizes of building components and assemblies set out in BS 4011.

Frame and panel systems

Rolled steel sections or aluminium extruded frame into which panels of a variety of materials are fixed. The panels may be a cellular core of cardboard, or solid core of flaxboard, compressed straw slabs, chipboard, plywood, asbestos wood or foamed plastics and may be faced with hardboard; hardwood veneer; laminated plastic, or metal sheet (see *MBC: Materials*, chapter 3). More complex panel construction may incorporate a single or double skin of pressed steel or aluminium sheet. This type of double skin panel may be filled with glass fibre or mineral wool. Most proprietary systems offer a number of permutations of glazed to solid arrangements and are available as single or double glazed units. The glass is usually secured with a gasket type of fixing. The finishes also vary widely according to considerations of first cost, and maintenance costs. The choice of finish is from an inexpensive material to receive paint, such as hardboard, to self finished decorative laminated plastics or metals which may be stove enamelled or anodized.

Post and panel (Unit) systems

These will have storey height sheets of plasterboard 'egg box' construction, compressed straw slab, wood-wool slab or chipboard. The sheets will be faced with a suitable veneer, and will be secured to timber or metal uprights.

Many systems have special details such as adjustable floor fixing and levelling shoes, telescopic transom rails or removable pilasters to service ducts. Some systems incorporate 'hook on' attachments for cupboards and shelving.

FINISHES

Finishes will be of two categories: 1 *self finish*, such as decorative laminated plastic sheet, which is permanent and requires no maintenance in respect of re-decoration or 2 *base finish*, such as plasterboard, which will be ready to receive a painted finish and will thus require normal maintenance. In choosing the appropriate finish, consideration must be given to initial cost, cost in use, and consistency of surface treatment throughout the building.

PROVISION FOR SERVICES

Provision of space for the normal electric wiring and telephone cables, within a partition is not difficult, but large service ducts for heating and other mains services are not compatible with partition design, and of course, pipework within the partition will seriously inhibit demountability. Wherever possible, the structural envelope should be designed to accommodate major service runs with numerous connection points into the partition (or ceiling) system.

FIRE RESISTANCE

The fire resistance qualities of a partition construction are of primary importance. In particular, since partitions are normally associated with building types having a high occupancy. When a fire occurs, the danger arises both from within the building and in the risk of the spread of fire from one building to the other. The various fire regulations are concerned to limit this spread, the risk of which is related to (a) the use of the building, (b) the resistance of the constructional elements, (c) the resistance of the surface finishes to the spread of flame, (d) the size of the building, and (e) the degree of isolation between the various parts of the building.

The requirements of the Building Regulations (covering England and Wales) are summarized below in respect of the types of partition under consideration.

Notional period of fire resistance

Most systems will give a notional period of fire resistance of $\frac{1}{2}$ to 1 hour, which will be adequate for most situations. The fire rating and considerations of means of escape from the building will, however, be fundamental to the choice of system and the Building Regulations and other Statutes relevant to particular building types should be studied carefully to determine their particular requirements.

Surface spread of flame

Section E14: Building Regulations

Pur-pose group	Building type	Classification		
		Small rooms	Other rooms	Circu-lation spaces
I	Small residential	3	1	1
II	Institutional	1	0	0
III	Other residential	3	1	0
IV to VIII	All other building types	3	1	0

Table 3 Minimum rating for surface spread of flame on wall surfaces

The Building Regulations make no particular reference to demountable partitions, the applicable figures given above being prescribed for structure and permanent finish.

Group I is the normal two storey house (with or without a basement).
Group II – Institutional – is a home which provides sleeping accommodation for small children or people suffering from certain disabilities.
Groups IV to VIII include offices, shops, factories and similar buildings.

A description of the classifications of rate of spread of flame is also applicable to ceilings and is given on page 228. A 'small room' for purpose groups I to III is defined as a room with a floor area not exceeding 3·720 m² and for the other purpose groups a 'small room' is a room with a floor area not exceeding 27·870 m². Since the size of a building is a very important factor the Building Regulations put forward the idea of a large building being split up into self-contained units, or compartments where walls and floors will contain the fire without endangering the remainder of the building. Partition systems will normally be used within the structural envelope of the building and so the stringent structural fire precautions contained in the Building Regulations in respect of compartment walls (walls which divide a building up into fire-resistant units) will not apply. Note that the Building Regulations do not apply in

Scotland and in the Inner London area. The regulations in the London area are, however, in essence similar to Section E14 of the Building Regulations, their general objective being to reduce the amount of exposed combustible material in a building. The requirements of the Building Standards (Scotland) Regulations 1963 are summarized below.

No specific mention is made of demountable partitions although regulation 25, which refers to 'separating wall', could be applied. However, the general interpretation by the majority of Scottish authorities is that demountable partitioning is not an element of structure and therefore need only comply with the surface spread of flame standards which are set out in Section 57 of the Regulations. Four grades are specified in the Regulations as follows: Grade A which is equivalent to Class 0, Grade B which is the same as Class 1, and Grade C which is equivalent to Classes 2 or 3. Grade D covers all other classes. Corridor partitions are required to comply with Grade A (Class 0) whilst the internal faces of office walls fall within the requirements of Grade C (Class 2 or 3).

Unlike the Building Regulations for England and Wales, the Scottish standards include a section on *means of escape* and part 5, sections 42 to 46, clearly defines the requirements but once again no mention is made of demountable partition in relation to the division of office areas.

Fire Authorities

In addition to the controls so far mentioned, the Fire Authorities have to be satisfied on the means of escape in case of fire under certain statutes according to the type of building, eg Offices, Shops and Railway Premises Act 1963 which is universally applicable. Section 28 deals with *means of escape* and reads as follows: 'All premises to which this Act applies shall be provided with such means of escape in case of fire for the persons employed to work therein as may reasonably be required in the circumstances of the case.' This phrasing needs some interpretation but, providing that the necessary *compartment* walls and floors comply with the relevant section of the Building Regulations, most Authorities rule that a demountable partition is a temporary fitting not required to protect escape routes. Nevertheless, some stipulate that certain corridor partitions must have a *half hour* standard

of *fire resistance* while others only require this standard if the length of a corridor is more than 18 m from a fire exit or if the partitions are used in a single staircase building. In these instances additional fire doors will often be necessary.

SOUND INSULATION

A demountable partition is an element of construction which by its nature is vulnerable to the passage of sound, and to expect a lightweight site-assembled structure to provide a very high standard of sound insulation is to some extent contradictory as explained below.

The matter of sound control should be considered at the design stage so that 'noise producing' rooms and rooms requiring quiet can be, as far as possible, remote from each other. In order to solve the problem of insulating the occupants of a room against unwanted noise, air and structure borne sound and external noise from whatever source must be considered. Airborne sound is created by fluctuations in air pressure which are perceived by the ear as sound. These sound waves strike the surface of a partition and cause it to vibrate – in turn vibrating the air in the opposite side. The sound insulation afforded is the degree to which the intensity of the noise is reduced in the process. The heavier and denser a partition, the more difficult it is to vibrate but it is equally important for the materials to have a degree of elasticity – to 'give' with the sound like a loosened drum skin. For example, two 13 mm panels set each side of a 50 mm deep framework will produce a higher standard of insulation than a single panel of equal weight. The sound insulation value is assessed by comparative measurements of sound pressure on opposite sides of a barrier and these noise levels are normally measured on a decibel (dB) scale. This scale is not a measure of sound intensity but is a way of expressing the difference of intensity between one sound and another. The decibel is expressed in terms of familiar sounds in the list below to give a general guide to the relevant levels of sound in respect of partition design.

Quiet conversation	30 dB
Conference room	50 dB
Normal conversation	60 dB
Office machine room	80 dB
(Heavy lorry at 6·000 m)	100 dB
(Sound becomes painful)	140 dB

All sounds differ in pitch and intensity and BS 2750 : 1956 has been established for comparative acoustic testing – this test provides the arithmetical average decibel reduction over the range of 100 to 3150 Hz (cycles per second) and all partition systems should be tested to this standard. It is possible to flatter performance figures by testing over a more limited frequency range or by testing single panels in isolation rather than a panel and its framing components, and an apparent gain of 4 to 5 decibels can be incorrectly claimed. Site conditions are very much more difficult than the controlled conditions of the laboratory and, although measured figures are useful for comparison, a poorer acoustic performance on site is almost inevitable. Doors, sliding hatches, ventilators, and every junction with the structure are all potentially points of serious sound leaks. It is also important that ceiling voids, continuous lighting troughs and heating ducts are adequately baffled.

In some systems, sophisticated constructions, such as resilient air seals at abutments to walls and ceilings, are incorporated to assist in sound reduction and to take up possible dimensional inaccuracies in the enveloping structure and, in general terms, acoustics are improved with refined detailing.

The standard of insulation against external noise is governed by the size and position of the windows. With single glazed windows of 'average' size, the net reduction of noise would be say 10 dB, and with sealed double windows – designed for acoustic and not thermal insulation – the reduction could be as high as 45 dB, so that it is between these two ranges that sound reduction would be required, in the partition system. Since the awareness of noise is to some extent a subjective matter the question of acceptable background noise is important. An intruding noise will not be a nuisance unless it approaches the general loudness of the background.

One irritating source of noise, that of door slamming can easily be prevented by the fitting of automatic door closers, and rubber seals.

Rooms which require good sound insulation such as directors' offices, interview rooms, libraries, sick rooms and rest rooms will require partitions which give a sound reduction of 45 dB between them and other rooms. On the other hand, rooms in which background noise is acceptable such as general offices will be satisfactory if a 30 dB re-duction factor is obtained through the partitions. In general terms, provided that the cost of more sophisticated detailing is acceptable, partitions giving a 45 dB insulation level can be obtained. The 'average' solid, full height partition will give 30 dB whilst a half glazed partition with single glazing will not give more than a 25 dB reduction.

DEMOUNTABILITY

Changing demands over the life span of a building may require the reorganization of the internal space and so far as this factor is applicable, it is advantageous to be able to take down (demount) and re-erect a partition system. In these circumstances the enveloping structure of external wall, structural floor and ceiling are considered to be permanent and fixed construction, with the elements which divide the space within the building being capable of re-arrangement to provide variable layout.

The option of demountability is a most significant factor in respect of initial cost and the effect it will have on the fulfilment of the other requirements of the performance specification. Taking down a partition and re-erecting in a new position may involve adaptation to the lighting and heating systems, and will almost certainly necessitate redecoration and possible repairs to flooring and wall surfaces.

The greater the degree of demountability required the more difficult it is to provide adequate sound insulation and satisfactory provision for services within the partition. A demountable partition system which provides a high degree of sound insulation will be expensive, both in first cost, and cost of re-assembly, since the jointing technique will be complex. A system which gives demountability only at junction points such as doors, abutments and intersections will, however, be less expensive than a partition which by reason of more sophisticated jointing techniques can be demounted at each panel on the planning module.

Figure 222 shows examples of two alternative methods of obtaining flexibility.

(a) by the use of an H section vertical member into which the partition panel fits. The sequence of erection with this type of partition is to fix the wall channel at the abutment and then continue – panel – post – panel, the panels being fitted from the side. The demountability is therefore at junction points only.

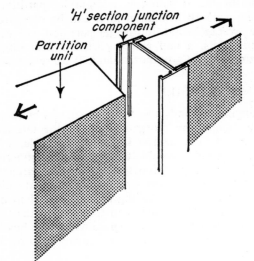

PARTITION DEMOUNTABLE AT DOORS, ABUTMENTS AND INTERSECTIONS ONLY

(a)   The use of an 'H' section

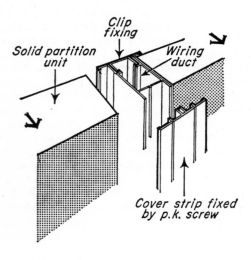

PARTITION DEMOUNTABLE AT EACH MODULE

(b)   The use of a 'breakdown' post

222   Two methods of obtaining flexibility

222

(b) by the use of a 'breakdown' post. The post is in 3 sections so that the panels can be fitted from the front or rear and that demountability is at each module. Note also the opportunity to use the column as a vertical duct for wiring.

CONSTRUCTION

Frame and panel systems

Figure 223 shows an example of a simple concealed fixing frame and panel system.

The frame is of anodized aluminium alloy to BS 1615, the panels can be designed to fit any module using standard sheets. The infill panels are sandwich construction with a core of polystyrene, or flax board or similar material according to the required performance specification faced with hardboard and finished with decorative PVC sheet, decorative laminated plastic or hardwood veneers. The total thickness of the panel is nom. 50 mm. As with most partition systems the doors are pre-hung, in this case on nylon washered, aluminium built hinges and have a rubber strip air seal around the perimeter of the frame. Note the use of PVC glazing beads which fit neatly into the I section frame and the 'clip on' cornice and skirting trim.

The junction at floor and ceiling is most important, particularly in respect of partitions which must have a high sound reduction factor. Here a foam rubber sealing strip is used.

A more sophisticated system is shown in figure 224. This is a modular ceiling and partitioning system with integrated storage and accessories. The ceiling grid has a dimensional relationship with the partitioning providing complete flexibility within the discipline of a modular layout. The framework to the ceiling is of extruded aluminium alloy channels suspended from the structure by rod or strap hangers attached to the main span members of the ceiling.

Notched and turned aluminium connecting members are fixed to the spine framework at module points. The junction of the spine and intermediate members is concealed by a plastic boss. The grid is designed to receive any proprietary acoustic boards or tile ceiling. Ceiling and partition modules are standard 1·220 m. The partition system has a maximum height of 3·050 m with a 51 mm overall thickness. Panel cores are flax,

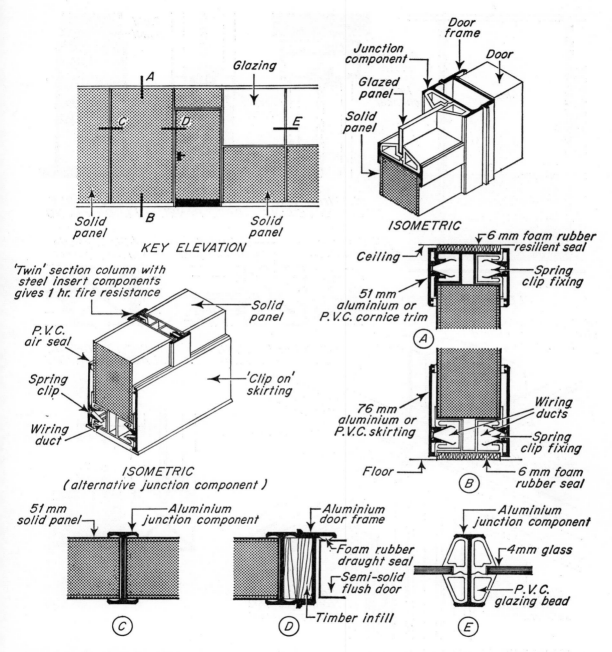

Glazing

A

C **D** **E**

B

Solid panel

Solid panel

KEY ELEVATION

Door frame

Junction component

Door

Glazed panel

Solid panel

ISOMETRIC

'Twin' section column with steel insert components gives 1 hr. fire resistance

Solid panel

P.V.C. air seal

Spring clip

'Clip on' skirting

Wiring duct

ISOMETRIC (alternative junction component)

6 mm foam rubber resilient seal

Ceiling

Spring clip fixing

51 mm aluminium or P.V.C. cornice trim

Ⓐ

Wiring ducts

76 mm aluminium or P.V.C. skirting

Spring clip fixing

Floor

Ⓑ

6 mm foam rubber seal

51 mm solid panel

Aluminium junction component

Ⓒ

Aluminium door frame

Foam rubber draught seal

Semi-solid flush door

Timber infill

Ⓓ

Aluminium junction component

4mm glass

P.V.C. glazing bead

Ⓔ

223 *A simple concealed fixing frame and panel system*

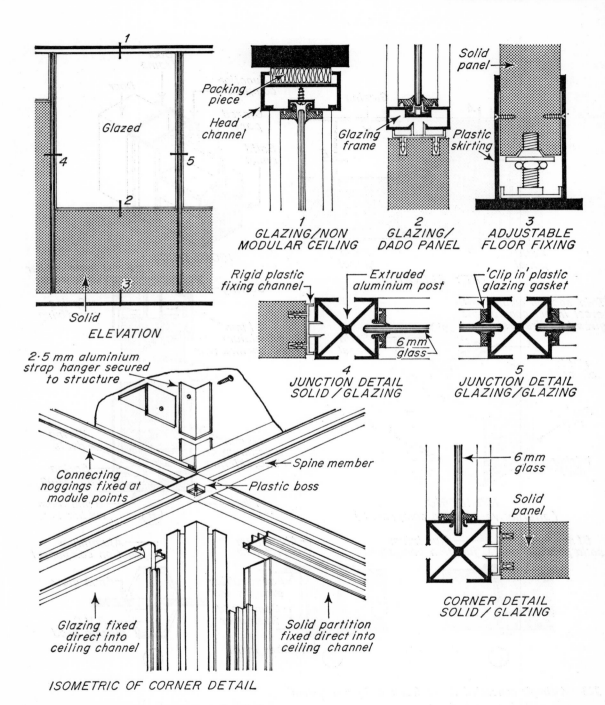

ELEVATION

Glazed

Solid

4   5

2

1

3

Packing piece

Head channel

Glazing frame

Plastic skirting

Solid panel

1
GLAZING/NON
MODULAR CEILING

2
GLAZING/
DADO PANEL

3
ADJUSTABLE
FLOOR FIXING

Rigid plastic
fixing channel

Extruded
aluminium post

'Clip in' plastic
glazing gasket

6 mm
glass

4
JUNCTION DETAIL
SOLID / GLAZING

5
JUNCTION DETAIL
GLAZING/GLAZING

2·5 mm aluminium
strap hanger secured
to structure

Connecting
noggings fixed at
module points

Spine member

Plastic boss

Glazing fixed
direct into
ceiling channel

Solid partition
fixed direct into
ceiling channel

ISOMETRIC OF CORNER DETAIL

6 mm
glass

Solid
panel

CORNER DETAIL
SOLID / GLAZING

224   A more sophisticated system than 223

chipboard or expanded polystyrene faced with 3 mm hardboard or asbestos board and finished in PVC, laminate or hardwood veneer. The glazing is into extruded plastic beads with glass up to 6 mm thick. One feature of this system is the design of various special brackets which screw clip into the cruciform framing to provide anchorage

Post and panel system

An example of this form of construction is shown in figure 225. This partition uses a hardboard or asbestos faced timber lipped compressed straw slab panel of total thickness 58 mm nom. There is a dry tongued joint between the edges of the panels and posts and the units are housed at floor and

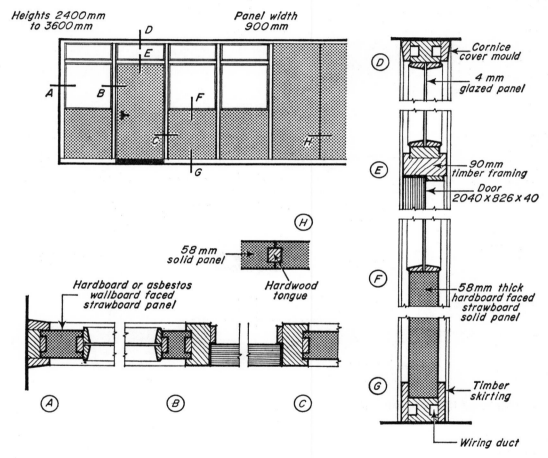

Heights 2400mm to 3600mm

Panel width 900mm

D

E

A

B

F

C

G

H

58 mm solid panel

Hardwood tongue

Hardboard or asbestos wallboard faced strawboard panel

A   B   C

D — Cornice cover mould

— 4 mm glazed panel

E — 90mm timber framing

— Door 2040 x 826 x 40

F — 58mm thick hardboard faced strawboard solid panel

G — Timber skirting

— Wiring duct

225   Post and panel system

for such items as shelves, coathooks, pinboards, and chalkboard. Storage cabinets can also be clipped and hung from the framing, provided that the rigidity of the supports to the ceiling is checked.

Storey height (or normal height) doors are supplied prehung and complete with furniture.

ceiling positions by means of timber plates. The partition uses a standard 900 mm wide panel and a 100 mm post, and can be built to a height of 2400 mm and 3600 mm. The asbestos faced panel gives a Class I spread of flame rating, the hardboard faced a Class III with half hour fire resistance.

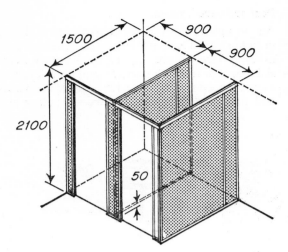

WC partitions

This used to be a much neglected field of design, but there are now many proprietary systems on the market providing not only standard WC cubicles but also prefabricated compartments, showers, clothes lockers, and changing cubicles. Figure 226 shows an example of a surfaced paper laminate covered plywood cubicle.

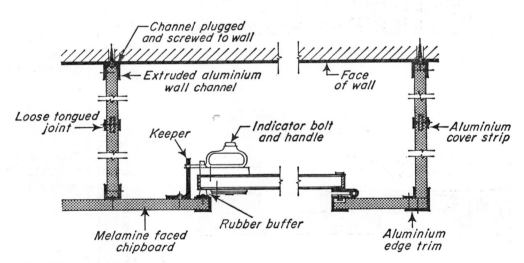

226   Prefabricated WC compartment

10 Suspended ceilings

A suspended ceiling is defined in BS 3589 : 1963 : *Glossary of General Building Terms* as 'a ceiling hung at a distance from the floor or roof above and not bearing on the walls'.

The method of construction may vary widely, from a jointless ceiling constructed on a foundation of expanded metal, or a PVC sheet stretched between bearers, to a ceiling of small infill panels of suitable building board supported on a lightweight metal frame. The ceiling may incorporate lighting, heating or ventilation services as part of the construction.

The functional requirements of suspended ceiling construction are considered under the following headings: access; weight; acoustic properties; fire properties; and cost.

ACCESS

The space between the suspended ceiling and roof or floor over is used as a horizontal service duct where heating pipes, water and waste pipes and all types of wiring and cable work can be easily and freely run. Thus the question of easy access to the duct for maintenance purposes, is of primary importance. A modular panel, which can be removed over the whole area of the ceiling, thus becomes the easiest and the most complete means of access. The consideration of the direction of the services and the amount of access required will help to determine the type of suspended ceiling most suitable. Narrow strips which can be removed over certain areas will give access to parallel service runs, whilst jointless ceilings will be satisfactory where one or two pre-determined access points are acceptable.

A ceiling system which gives full access may lead to an uneconomic design of the service runs. There is also the risk that the ceiling may be damaged if too many panels are removed.

WEIGHT

Because, by definition, the ceiling is suspended from the main structure, it is important to keep the weight of the construction to a minimum. The jointless ceilings using traditional techniques and finished by a skim coat of plaster is the heaviest form of suspended ceiling, weighing between 20 and 50 kg/m². The 'panel and frame' construction will be much lighter, most proprietary systems weighing between 5 and 15 kg/m². The construction must, however, always be designed to be strong enough to support the weight of lighting fittings, and this loading should always be calculated for each individual scheme. A strip ceiling is also a very light form of construction, weighing between 3 and 5 kg/m².

ACOUSTIC PROPERTIES

These are concerned with both sound absorption and sound insulation. Suspended ceilings will act as a sound absorbent surface provided that absorbent or perforated panels are used. The sound insulating properties of a suspended ceiling system are not usually very high and unless partitions are carried up to the structural floor above, sound will pass over the partitions from room to room. The structural floor is the main sound barrier in this context, although the space between the ceiling and structure contributes in some measure to the sound insulation of the whole construction.

There is a wide range of sheet material available which are suitable for use as infill to the frame as panel ceilings. Usually the sheets are textured, perforated or embossed to increase sound absorbency, but re-decoration by painting will reduce the acoustic properties of such a material over a period of time (see *MBC: Materials*, chapter 1 and chapter 17 in this volume).

FIRE PROPERTIES

The surface of the ceiling can constitute a considerable fire hazard in respect of the spread of flame. The Building Regulation (E14) controls the surface of a ceiling according to its location (and the particular purpose group of the building) in respect of the ease with which the surface may allow flame to spread over its surface.

The classifications in respect of rate of 'spread of flame' are as follows:

Class 1 a surface of very low flame spread.
Class 2 a surface of low flame spread.
Class 3 a surface of medium flame spread.
Class 4 a surface of rapid flame spread.

These four classifications are those given in BS 476. The British Standard classification was, however, not considered adequate in all cases and the Building Regulations introduce a further class designated '0' which is defined as follows:

(a) non-combustible throughout.
(b) Comprise a base or background which is non-combustible with the addition of a surface (a layer of combustible material) not exceeding 0·8 mm thick, so that the spread of flame rating of the combined product is not lower than *Class 1*.
(c) Comprise a base or background which is combustible but with any exposed face finished with a layer of not less than 3·2 mm thick of non-combustible material, so that the spread of flame rating of the combined product is not lower than *Class 1*.

For the purposes of fire risk, the Building Regulations divide the space inside a building into three categories, namely: small rooms; other rooms; and circulation spaces. Table 4 is a summary of the regulations in respect of spread of flame

Pur-pose groups		Small rooms	Other rooms	Circu-lation spaces
I	Small residential	3	3	3
II	Institutional	1	1	0
III	Other residential	3	1	0
IV to VIII	Office, shop, factory, place of assembly, place for storage of goods and all other buildings	3	1	0

Table 4   Minimum class of surface spread of flame designation for ceilings

The terms used in the above table are defined on p. 219.

to ceilings in the purpose groups of buildings indicated.

If it is intended that a suspended ceiling shall contribute to the overall fire resistance of the floor construction of which it may be said to form a part, the suspended ceiling construction must fulfil the criteria set down in Table B to Regulation E5. These include the height of the building, and whether or not the floor is a compartment floor and the total period of fire resistance required. Table 5 gives details of the contribution to fire resistance of various suspended ceilings.

The inference from the table is that the type of suspended ceiling relying on separate tiles within

Height of building	Type of floor	Fire resistance of floor	Description of suspended ceilings and class of surface spread of flame
Less than 15·240 m	Non-compartment	1 hour or less	Surface of ceiling exposed *within* the cavity not lower than *Class 1*
	Compartment	Less than 1 hour	
	Compartment	1 hour	As above but *Class 0*, and with supports and fixings not combustible
15·240 m or more	Any	1 hour or less	Surface of ceiling exposed *within* the cavity, not lower than *Class 0* and *jointless*. Supports and fixings not combustible
Any	Any	More than 1 hour	Ceiling of non-combustible construction and *jointless*; supports and fixings not combustible

Table 5   Suspended ceilings

a framework of metal angles or Ts is not allowed as a factor contributing to the fire resistance of the total floor construction in buildings more than 15·24 m high where the period required is 1 hour, or in buildings of any type where the period required is more than 1 hour. In the latter circumstances the ceiling construction must be jointless. However, it must be borne in mind that the Regulation is concerned only with the contribution made by suspended ceilings to the fire resistance of the total floor construction. The question of the protection afforded by suspended ceilings to structural steelwork is a separate consideration.

COST

The comparative installation costs, costs in use and subsequent maintenance costs for the systems under examination must be considered at the design stage of a project.

METHODS OF CONSTRUCTION

1 Jointless

(a) Lath and plaster supported and suspended on metal framework and hangers.
(b) PVC membrane stretched over a frame.
(c) Plasterboard and skim, or suitable building board with cover strips supported on timber framework and suspended from the floor above, by timber (or more usually) by metal or wire hangers. See chapter 13.

Jointless ceilings, with the exception of the PVC membrane type, are usually non-proprietary and rely on traditional materials and methods. They are relatively low cost and give a good fire resistance. The slowness of the wet construction where plastering is used is, however, a disadvantage.

2 Frame and panel

Infill panels of fibreboard tiles; asbestos tiles; mineral wool tiles; metal trays or plastic tiles dropped to a suspended framework of metal angles and tees. There are various methods of securing the panels and framing.

The erection of a frame and panel ceiling is speedy and clean, and this type of ceiling is usually easily demountable.

3 Strip ceiling

(a) Profiled aluminium strips.
(b) PVC strips on metal cores.

4 Service ceiling

Suspended ceilings in which the services form an integral part of the construction fall into the following categories:

(a) Fully illuminated ceilings, having infill panels of translucent plastic which form the diffusers for the light fittings suspended above them. The diffusers may be plain face, three dimensional, corrugated, embossed or 'egg box' construction.
  This type of ceiling should not be confused with the use of modular light fittings, which fit into the grid spacing of the panel, and frame type of ceiling discussed previously.
(b) Ceiling panels which incorporate low temperature heating elements, or small bore hot water circuits, usually in conjunction with sound absorbing panels.
(c) Ceilings in which the whole of the space above is used as a plenum chamber for the circulation and direction of hot or cold air.
(d) A fully 'service' integrated ceiling which gives an element of construction providing heat, light and sound absorption. This arrangement, though expensive, permits the ultimate in flexibility of use of the space below.

The detailed consideration of the technical aspects of the 'service' ceilings is a specialist matter outside the scope of this volume.

CONSTRUCTIONAL DETAILS

There are many proprietary suspended ceiling systems available and some typical details are shown as follows:

Jointless plaster

The ceiling shown in figure 227 is a suspended plaster ceiling on metal lathing.

Two methods of securing the hangers to support the lath are shown.

It is possible to construct neat access panels by using purpose made trap doors as shown in figure 228.

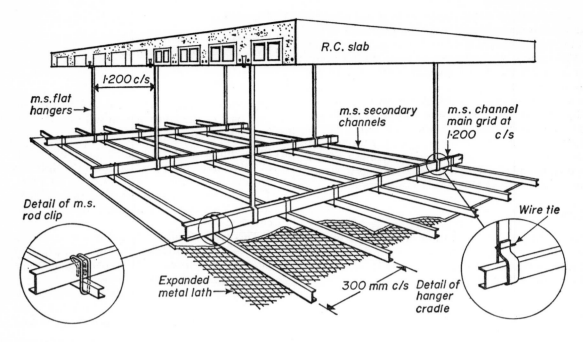

R.C. slab

1·200 c/s

m.s. flat
hangers

m.s. secondary
channels

m.s. channel
main grid at
1·200 c/s

Detail of m.s.
rod clip

Wire tie

Expanded
metal lath

300 mm c/s

Detail of
hanger
cradle

227   *Suspended plaster ceiling*

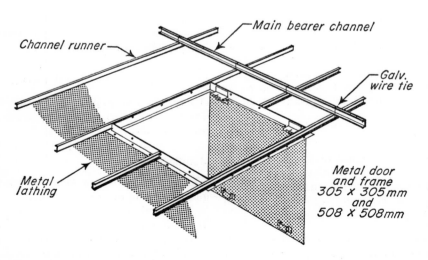

Channel runner

Main bearer channel

Galv.
wire tie

Metal
lathing

Metal door
and frame
305 x 305 mm
and
508 x 508 mm

228   *Prefabricated access door to suspended ceiling*

A suspended plaster ceiling of the type shown using vermiculite plaster 15 mm thick will weigh 20 kg/m², including the suspension, with a fire rating of 2 to 4 hours, depending on the thickness of plaster.

Jointless PVC

An example of the application of the use of a PVC foil membrane, stretched to form a suspended ceiling is shown in figure 229. This type of ceiling can be installed in one sheet 0·2 mm thick, forming a panel up to 7·500 m × 6·000 m nom. The

occupancies except on circulation routes and for parts of buildings housing the sick or aged.

Frame and panel ceilings

The method of suspending the ceiling membrane is similar with each type of panel and consists of:

1 *Hangers*

Metal straps, rods or angles which hang vertically from the main floor or roof construction to support and 'level up' the suspension system.

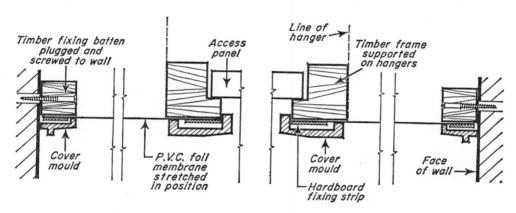

MEMBRANE CEILING

229   Jointless PVC

method is adaptable to any shape of room and will accommodate any size of access panel or light fitting.

The finish of the PVC foil is semi-matt, and does not require decoration. Where a higher degree of sound absorption is required, a special perforated foil with a loose backing of absorbent quilt is used.

The Agrément Certificate report on the construction states that since the ceilings melt at too low a temperature to be classified by reference to BS 476 : Part I, it cannot comply with the restriction on the spread of flame requirements. In the opinion of the Agrément Board, provided the structure above the ceiling conforms in respect of spread of flame, it would be reasonable to seek a relaxation from the requirements of the Building Regulations to permit the use of the ceiling on most

Various methods of securing the hangers to the main floor construction are shown in figure 230.

2 *Bearers*

These are the main supporting sections connected to the hangers and to which the subsidiary horizontal runner supports are fixed. The use of bearers enables the hangers to be at wider centres than the basic ceiling module. There are many ingenious proprietary methods of attaching the runners and hangers.

3 *Runners*

These are the supporting members which are in contact with the ceiling panels. They are usually of aluminium T or Z section. The runners span in the opposite direction to the bearers.

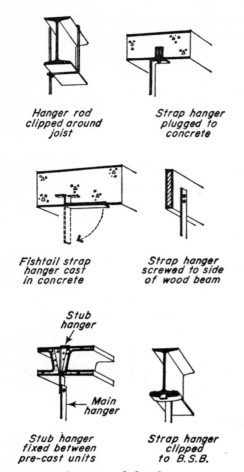

Hanger rod
clipped around
joist

Strap hanger
plugged to
concrete

Fishtail strap
hanger cast
in concrete

Strap hanger
screwed to side
of wood beam

Stub
hanger

Main
hanger

Stub hanger
fixed between
pre-cast units

Strap hanger
clipped
to B.S.B.

230   Hangers for suspended ceilings

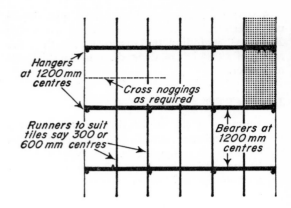

231   Plan layout of suspended ceiling

panels being lifted by wind pressure (say in an entrance hall) they can be left loose and are thus very easy to remove where the void above is used as a duct. Where they require to be held down, a wire or spring metal clip is slotted into the web of the T to hold the panel down from above.

4 Noggings

These are subsidiary cross members which span in the same direction as the bearers but in the same plane as the runners in order to complete the framework. Runners and noggings can either be concealed or exposed.

A typical layout is shown in figure 231.

Typical methods of securing the ceiling panel into the suspension system are illustrated as follows:

(a) Exposed fixing

Here the ceiling panel or tile drops into the suspended framework formed by the extruded aluminium T section. Unless there is a risk of the

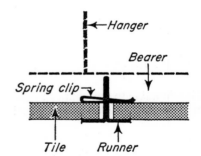

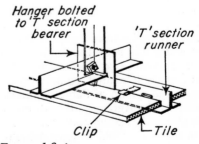

(a)   Exposed fixing

232   Typical methods of securing the ceiling panel

(b) *Concealed fixing*

This is a concealed type fixing since the method of support is not visible from below. The diagram shows the grooved tiles slotted into the Z section runner. An alternative form of concealed fixing using a tongued and grooved tile is shown in figure 233

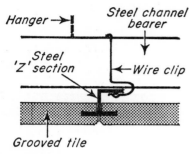

(b) *Concealed fixing*

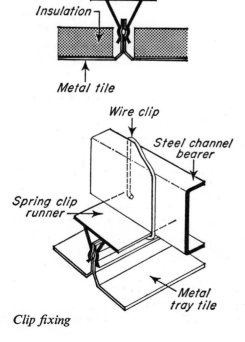

(c) *Clip fixing*

(c) *Clip fixing*

In this detail a special runner is used which holds the metal tray in position. The tray will be perforated and will probably have an infill of mineral wool or similar inert, sound absorbent material.

(d) *Screw fixing*

This detail shows two alternative forms of securing the ceiling panels by direct screw fixing.

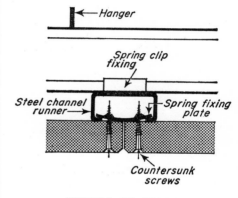

METHOD OF FIXING

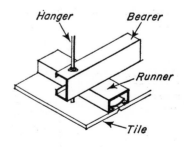

(d) *Screw fixing*

A large range of building boards are suitable for infill panels as follows:

Aluminium sheet and tiles
Asbestos cement flat sheets

Asbestos insulation board
Corkboard
Expanded plastics
Fibrous plaster tiles
Hardboard
Metal sheet and tiles
Mineral fibre boards
Plasterboard, cut sheets or tiles
Plasterboard faced with PVC sheet
(See chapter 13)

Plywood
Resin bonded glass fibre
Vermiculite slabs
Wood fibre boards

For details of the sizes and physical properties of these materials see *MBC: Materials*. Details of a concealed suspension system with fibre board tiles are shown in figure 233.

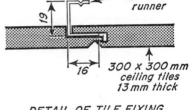

DETAIL OF TILE FIXING

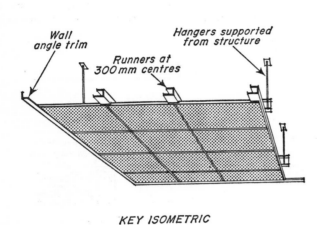

KEY ISOMETRIC

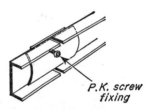

DETAIL OF SPLICED JOINT IN BEARER

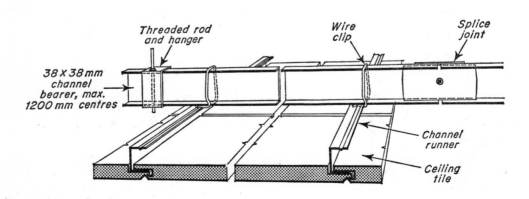

DETAIL OF SUSPENSION SYSTEM

233 *Concealed fixing of suspended ceiling tiles*

11 Industrialized system building

The industrialization of the building process is the increasing utilization of factory techniques of production in relation to the total process of building. The number of skilled and semi-skilled workers available to the building industry, even in times of economic stability, is inadequate to meet the total volume of new building required. It is necessary for industrial techniques of design and construction to be applied, particularly in respect of those building types which have come to be recognized as a social necessity such as housing, hospitals, and school buildings. The methods and materials used in industrialized systems of building are a development of rationalized traditional good practice to the point where prefabricated factory made components are a dominant feature. Because of adverse weather, building site conditions are generally poor so that the transference of operations from the site to the factory has obvious advantages. Where a building process is industrialized, a greater proportion of the work is carried out in the controlled environment of the factory. Industrial building techniques are able to make more efficient use of manpower with increased productivity under the better working conditions in the factory, and controlled production of components will produce a high standard of finish since the procedures are linked to factory rather than to site inspection.

In order to be commercially successful, a building system must have an assured long term market with continuity of demand backed by sufficient capital for development. It must also have a long term development programme and be based on sensible cost limits. Pre-ordering and the bulk purchase of materials is an integral part of industrialized building and an important characteristic of the manufacturing process is an increase in economy in direct proportion to the length of the production run. Efficient industrialization is achieved by the co-ordinated development of design procedures, production processes and erection techniques. Examples of the early industrialization of building were the introduction of standard parts for fixing, such as the nail and the screw, and then the development of standard parts for cladding, such as the standard window and door. With advanced technology, production processes, and handling equipment larger units can now be made and components previously considered separately can now be grouped together. For example, a door with door frame and door furniture delivered to the site pre-hung and pre-finished; factory glazed windows; complete wall panels either in timber or concrete; roof trusses which fold up for transporting to the site; hot and cold water systems and associated pipework to form complete plumbing units for use as service cores. Industrialization is not exclusively concerned with changes of method on site or in the factory but it involves a new attitude to design and construction which concerns client, architect, administrator, manufacturer and contractor. Traditionally, it is generally true, perhaps surprisingly, that the construction industry is the only major industry where design and construction are carried out under different management control. Industrialization breaks down these traditional divisions of responsibility in the building process and this tends to favour the mutually exclusive organization.

Because of the reliance on pre-planning it is necessary that instructions should be given on as long a term as possible. Project approval should be received at least two years in advance of the starting date and in the public sector an advance programme should indicate the likely level of approval for periods of five years. Uncertainties and delays are very serious in the case of industrialized building since the system is less flexible than traditional methods. The Agrément method of approval of new components has much to commend it, in that objective information is provided at an early stage to enable architects and contractors to consider new products. In this respect also, the uniformity of requirement represented by the Building Regulations favours the more widespread use of industrialized techniques. It is interesting to note that, in this respect, Part F (Thermal) and Part E (Fire Regulations) are in the form of a performance specification giving more freedom of choice to the designer providing the conditions are met.

Industrialized systems require large investment in building research with specialist knowledge of the techniques of factory production, site organization and mechanization. Research into the optimum economic levels for the production of building components is required to give a sound basis on which to plan the proper scale for building programmes. New ways of assessing user requirements and the development of drawings, specifications and contractual procedures, particularly applicable to industrialized building are also necessary.

A common factor running through the design process is the size or dimension of the component. Following from this the key to industrialization in building is a rational approach to the co-ordination of dimensions. There is now a new opportunity for progress on an international scale with the introduction of metrication. Handling equipment for components assumes special importance, particularly in respect of heavy units both within the factory, factory to site and on the site. The limits of road and rail transport assume growing importance as the use of factory made components increases and the problems of off-site assembly and packaging are of paramount importance.

'OPEN' AND 'CLOSED' SYSTEMS

In connection with industrialized building the terms *open system* and *closed system* are used. Sometimes the term *method building* is used and this is a technique in which inter-related factory produced components are used in a manner which combines freedom of design for each individual building, with the maximum use of standard components. In a *closed* system of building the components are not inter-changeable with any other system or method and thus the building is formed from components specifically designed for and applicable to the particular building type in question, for example schools or housing.

The designer's choice is governed by the variations allowed within the system but the system is developed to meet precisely the requirements of its users. The idea of client participation at the design stage and close co-operation with the component manufacturers should produce a *closed* system

building which fulfils its function within exacting economic limits. An *open* system of building is where components are inter-changeable with other systems, and the aim of an open system of building is to produce a complete range of standard components which are inter-changeable over a wide range of building types. This inter-change-ability could well be the result of the acceptance of dimensional co-ordination (see chapter 1). The *open* system being one for which components are chosen within the agreed range of dimensions from components available on the open market. Thus the designer's choice is wide and limited only by his experience and knowledge of the market. Both *open* and *closed* systems can incorporate traditional forms of construction such as brick-work but this tends to detract from the efficiency of the system as such. Since site works take up a large proportion of construction time and effort, these operations should be rationalized as far as possible. Many systems of building which started as *closed* systems are likely to become *open* systems mainly through the application of dimensional co-ordination, where it is obviously an advantage to be able to combine various systems in respect of the supply of components and fittings.

CLIENT SPONSORED AND CONTRACTOR SPONSORED SYSTEMS

Systems of building have been developed and sponsored by both client organizations and contractors' organizations. In the case of client sponsored systems, because of the necessity for a large and continuing building programme, and in order to make a particular system viable, various local authorities (which may include new towns and government departments) have created between themselves associations for the development of a particular system of building. An association of this kind is called a consortium and its members are able to exchange information on building problems, engage in bulk purchase of materials and support the joint use of a particular building technique. Examples of client sponsored systems are those of the various consortia of local authorities for schools and similar buildings such as CLASP, SEAC and SCOLA. In the case of the contractor sponsored or proprietary system the contractor will provide a specialist erection service. In the case of a client sponsored system the contract is put out to competitive tender in accordance with normal procedure. Systems are sub-divided into light systems using steel and timber or heavy systems using storey height concrete panels and classified *high* or *low* according to the number of storeys that can be constructed.

Many proprietary low rise (1 to 3 storeys) housing systems are currently in use. Because of the importance of providing sufficient good housing the National Building Agency has been formed. This is an independent advisory body whose main function is to promote the use of improved techniques of design, management and site operation in both public and private house building. The Agency is managed by a board of directors appointed by the Government and represents a wide range of professional, industrial and administrative experience. The National Building Agency provides an advisory service to local authorities, contractors or architects on such subjects as work-study, project planning, plant utilization, production control and management accounting. The Agency also investigates system building for housing and issues an appraisal certificate to the selected systems. The National Building Agency's appraisal certificates are subject to review periodically and systems are added and occasionally withdrawn. Low rise housing systems generally, are based on a basic construction of either precast or in-situ concrete, steel framing, or timber framing or a combination of these materials. In each case the system attempts to make the maximum use of dry construction, sometimes in conjunction with traditional materials such as in-situ concrete or brickwork, but in rationalization of traditional building methods aims at reducing site labour and at the same time increasing the speed of erection. It is claimed for one system that 6 men can erect a house completely in fourteen days. The systems use as much off-site fabrication of components as possible but in different ways depending on the particular skills or facilities of the manufacturers. Some examples of the pre-fabrication of various component parts from a selection of the systems is given below:

1 Pre-cast, pre-finished, storey height concrete external wall units.
2 Long-span, pre-stressed concrete floor unit panels.

3 Pre-cast storey height flank and cross wall panels.
4 Pre-cast concrete internal partition wall panels ready to receive decoration.
5 Non-loadbearing in-fill panels of timber framing complete with pre-hung and glazed windows, pre-hung doors and with flashings in place.
6 Pre-formed plumbing units for warm air heating and hot water supply.
7 Pre-formed first floor sections with timber joists and chipboard finish.
8 Double storey height timber framing with plywood sheathing, with a selection of external cladding materials such as tile hanging, metal panels, weather boarding or glass fibre panels.
9 Pre-formed service units incorporating hot and cold water storage, electric service duct, soil and waste stack and the heating unit.
10 Prefabricated internal timber framed partitions with engineering and plumbing service ducts and pre-hung doors and frames.

Most of the systems incorporate in-situ solid concrete ground floor slabs, sometimes in modified raft form with edge beams. Framed construction has the usual concrete pad foundations. Most roof forms are still traditional pitch with some form of tiling and prefabricated timber trusses. Some of the more flexible systems, although designed principally for housing have been used for other building types.

Many proprietary systems have also been developed for medium rise (3 to 5 storeys) and high rise housing. High rise systems can of course be conveniently adapted to low rise dwellings particularly in mixed development. Most systems are based on pre-cast concrete units and use storey height wall panels, floor panels, and even room sized elements, which require specialist plant and equipment. Some of these types of heavy prefabrication were originally used and developed on the continent in France and in Denmark and Sweden. The construction of high rise buildings is a complex technical problem and where large units are used the question of site jointing is of paramount importance.

In addition to building systems for housing there are a wide range of proprietary contractor sponsored systems which have been developed for schools, commercial buildings and industrial buildings. Some form of concrete, steel or timber frame or frame and panel construction is used. The systems are based on a structural grid and the recommendations of BS 4330 for the co-ordination of controlling dimensions in building are now relevant to these systems.

CONSORTIA SYSTEMS

There are several client sponsored local authority consortium systems currently in use at this time. Most of the systems were developed from the need to build schools quickly and of course they can be, and are, modified for other types of local authority building such as training centres, old peoples homes, libraries, fire and police stations and office building. The main consortia are briefly described below:

Consortium of Local Authorities Special Programme (CLASP)

This system was originally established in 1956 to develop and control a prefabricated system of building aimed at reducing the amount of labour used on site. The use of prefabricated techniques in particular for school buildings was pioneered immediately after the end of the war in 1945. In particular, the CLASP system was required to solve a specific problem, namely the design of school buildings for sites which were liable to mining subsidence. It should be noted that CLASP like the other Consortia has no formal legal organization, and it does not therefore enter into contracts. Individual members or sponsoring authorities negotiate tenders for components on behalf of the Consortia from contractors and suppliers. The various components are then included in the Bill of Quantities as prime cost (PC) items. The actual orders for the components are placed through the general contractor for each separate contract. CLASP utilizes a light steel frame with steel lattice floor and roof beams. The roof deck is of prefabricated timber, and the floors are also of timber construction either prefabricated or in-situ. The cladding materials are chosen from pre-cast concrete slabs with exposed aggregate facing or tile hanging, protected metal sheeting or timber boarding on timber cladding frames. The window frames are factory glazed with gasket glazing. Opening lights are in metal frames. The CLASP construction described can be

used up to 4 storeys in height. The system has a development group and a contracts group for component supply contracts and programming. The system is extremely well documented, being illustrated in a series of excellent handbooks. A *Planning Handbook* illustrates the design disciplines, and a *Technical Handbook* gives detailed information for working drawings. An *Administration Handbook* is provided for use of architects and consultants in pre-contract procedure and an *Assembly Handbook* is used as a guide to the erection process and on site. CLASP has been used on the continent and in South Africa.

Second Consortium of Local Authorities (SCOLA)

This Consortium was established in 1961. SCOLA Mark II has a pin jointed light steel frame with square section steel columns supported on a modified form of raft foundation for single storey buildings or reinforced concrete strip foundations for multi-storey buildings. The system is designed to be built up to 4 storeys. The roof construction is steel channel edge reinforced woodwool slab with a felt or asphalt finish. Suspended floors are pre-cast concrete panels on steel lattice beams. Various lightweight dry cladding can be used such as tile hanging, protected metal sheeting or timber boarding. Brickwork can be used as an alternative cladding. The window walling is of metal frame with various types of opening light incorporated. The internal partitioning is of dry plasterboard units and ceilings are of asbestos or mineral board slabs. The Consortium obtains quotations for the supply, and fix and supply only items which are then included in the Bills of Quantities as PC items. The Consortium has developed the use of computers and automatic data processing in the preparation of Bills of Quantities and a computer is also used in the design and manufacturing documentation of the steel window walling, see page 243.

Consortium for Method Building

This Consortium is concerned with a whole range of local authority building types. The headquarters are in Somerset.

The Organization of North West Authorities for Rationalized Design (ONWARD)

This is a recent formation concerned with a wide range of building types but excluding housing.

South Eastern Architects Collaboration (SEAC)

This Consortium is based in Hertfordshire and is concerned with a wide range of buildings to the cost levels dictated by local authority programmes. It was established in 1963 and is based on the use of modular principles to incorporate proprietary commercial components. The Consortium has developed the use of computers and automatic data processing for Bills of Quantities.

INNOVATIONS

The above list is not exhaustive, and in addition to the main consortia there are also consortia concerned with bulk purchasing, in particular of kitchen equipment and science equipment and furniture for schools. The type of consortia mentioned have been instrumental in bringing about many innovations in system building which are now accepted as commonplace. For example, the use of dry construction wherever possible above foundations; the use of suspended ceiling acting as a fire barrier and the use of the space above for services; storey height window wall assembly and an agreement on dimensional co-ordination within the system. This pre-dates by several years the current dimensional co-ordination in respect of the change to metric.

The following points are given for general consideration in respect of industrialized system building:

1 The user has a finished product carefully developed as a result of widely based studies and proto-type testing.
2 Production drawings are simplified. The content of the drawing becoming more diagrammatic and less pictorial.
3 The known production run will permit early cost planning and encourage experiment with contractual methods to reduce costs.
4 Orders for components can be placed well in advance so that effective control of production and delivery can be maintained.
5 Assembly on site can be rationalized so that more economic use is made of mechanical plant and manpower.
6 Use of components encourages performance testing so that modifications can be fed back to designers and manufacturers.

The aim of standardization is not to produce standard buildings in the architectural sense but to create a standardized system of construction made from interchangeable parts of good design and high quality which can be used to fabricate a great variety of building.

A point to note is that following the change to metric all building which is Government controlled through the various consortia will have the same metric dimensional basis. This will follow the recommendations in respect of dimensional co-ordination discussed in chapter 1.

DOCUMENTATION

The consortia systems are very well documented providing a comprehensive manual of data sheets in various forms. To illustrate the method of working of a consortia system in respect of job drawing procedure the following information is based on the SCOLA system of building. The documentation is divided into five main sections which can be grouped or bound separately. If required the sheets can be intermixed, eg component drawings and specifications.

The sections of the manual are:

Design data

A series of information sheets to illustrate the principles, limitations and range of the system. These do not include detail component assembly information but do include composite axonometrics and isometrics. The design data sheets give information under the following headings:

Job drawing production
Site investigation and foundations
Steel frame
External walls
Partitions
Suspended floors
Stairs
Ceilings and blindboxes
Flat roof
Deck, finish, rooflights, tank rooms, fans, flues
Ironmongery
Doors, internal

Floor finishes
Services: Heating
Services: Electrical
Fixtures and equipment
Sanitary equipment

Assembly details

Standard drawings of combinations of components or units, fully annotated and coded. These cross reference to the design data sheet ranges and component sheets.

Component drawings

A series of information sheets to illustrate consortium components, used for tendering or prepared from specialist shop drawings, or components provided by the general contractor.

Specification sheets

Component specifications state the standards which have to be met set out in regularized format so that individual items can be pinpointed, eg material, quality, dimensions, tolerances, finish. General specification items are also included in this section.

Schedule of rates

Unit prices for all consortium components set out in standard format.

Procedure sheets

A series of information sheets to illustrate SCOLA job drawing procedure and job procedure from brief to completion, advance schedule procedure and coding procedure.

Job drawings

In addition to the relevant standard drawings and details appropriate to all projects the following drawings are required, particular to each contract:

Design drawings

These are prepared in order to obtain committee, planning, ministry, regulation and other statutory approvals.
To obtain approval to steel layout by specialist manufacturer and to establish the cost plan.

Basic layout drawings

Ground floor layout plan
Upper floor layout plan(s)
Elevations

Site layout drawings

Block plan
Site layout plan
Site works + drainage adjacent to building
Site landscaping layout

Subsidiary layout drawings

Foundation plan
Ground floor slab plan
Roof steel layout
Upper floor steel layout(s)
Upper floor slab plan(s)
Partition plan(s)
Ceiling plan(s)
Heating + Mechanical ventilation plan(s)
Gas + cold water services
Electrical layout

Schedules

Elevations
Internal door schedule
External door schedule
Ironmongery schedule – internal doors
Ironmongery schedule – external doors
Sanitary fittings schedule
Room fittings : furniture schedule
Finishes schedule
Internal decoration schedule
External decoration schedule

Examples of a selection from the above list of drawings is shown in figures 234 to 244 prepared for a particular schools project in Shropshire.
It should be noted that the drawings take the form

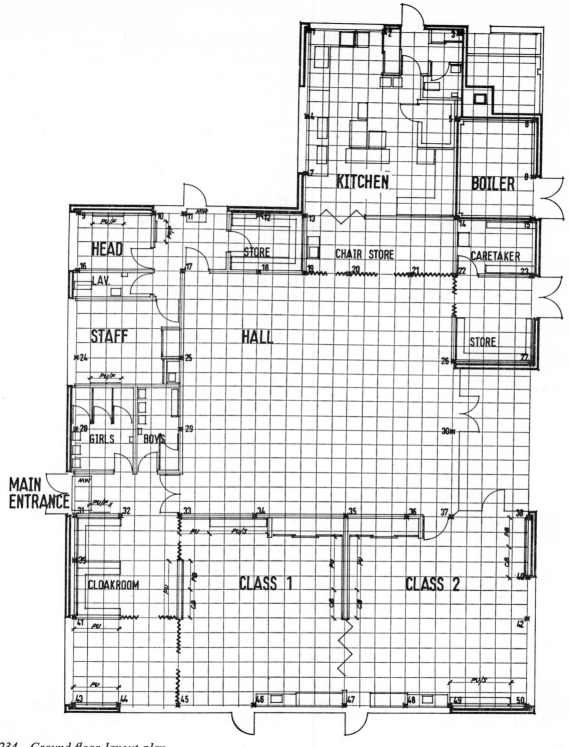

234 Ground floor layout plan

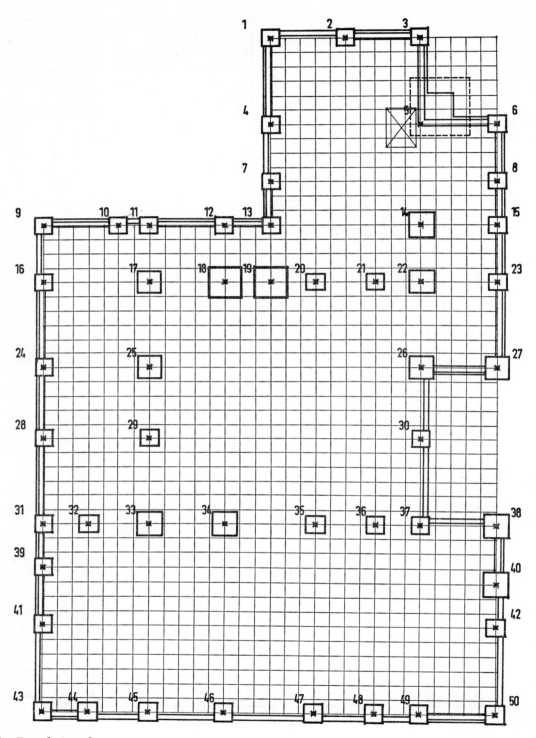

235   *Foundation plan*

of coded charts which relate to standard detail sheets and assemblies upon which the contractor develops his erection procedure. By using a system of *copy negatives* upon which subsequent information can be superimposed the basic negatives are re-used throughout the drawing procedure so that the completed layout plan is produced in stages. This saves a considerable amount of drawing office time. The following information is contained on the drawings:

Ground floor layout plan – figure 234 shows the plans of the building with reference to the modular grid, and the disposition of the fittings and fixtures within the building.

Foundation plan – figure 235 shows the pad foundations for the stanchions and the ground beam or strip foundations for the infill panels. The stanchions are numbered and the drawing is read in conjunction with a schedule which gives the plan dimensions and depths of each foundation pad, as shown in figure 236.

Roof steel layout – figures 237 and 238. These drawings show the coded roof steelwork at two levels. The position of the roof lights is also shown and the roof bracing is indicated.

Ceiling plan – figure 239 shows the grid of the suspended ceiling. The coding indicates the type of construction required for the recess in the ceiling to receive the window blind.

The roof plan is shown in figure 240, indicating the rainwater outlet positions and roof falls, together with the trimming required for the roof lights.

The coded elevations are shown on figure 241 and 242. The types of opening are coded and the dimensions are indicated by stating the number of modules.

A typical door and frame schedule is given in figure 243, and an *ironmongery schedule* is shown in figure 244.

For each project, the contractor is supplied with the standard detail sheets and assembly details, standard documentation and drawings and schedules particular to the contract.

Coding

Various systems of coding are used to relate the components required to the manufacturing processes. In respect of the coding for the elevational glazed cladding, the following procedure based on computer techniques is adopted:

The manufacturers receive the coded elevations from the architect and quantity surveyor. The code is an alpha numeric code which is designed to give sufficient manufacturing details to allow the manufacturer to produce an accurate quotation.

Input data sheet for computer

The architect indicates on the elevational drawing the bay number, the modular size of each part of the window walling, and specifies by initial or a number the types of glass or infill and the method of opening of the windows. This is shown in figure 245 for a typical bay. The detail of the construction is shown in figure 246 to explain the system, but of course this drawing would not be produced in practice.

The quantity surveyor translates this information on to a computer input data sheet using a code devised by the manufacturer. A specimen input data sheet using the SCOLA system of coding is given in figure 247.

The construction is 'separated' into three parts for purpose of coding, so that the coding is carried out in three sections as follows: 1 unit; 2 horizontal members and 3 vertical members.

1 Unit section, which includes the top hung window unit, the projecting top hung window unit and the dado infill panel. The bay number location reference (4) is given and the column headed 1 is used to indicate the type of opening light; top hung (T) in this case. The (T) also indicates the type of opening control unless a standard alternative is coded later. Columns 2 and 3 give the modular length of the opening light (12 modules), and columns 4 and 5 give the modular height of the opening light (04 modules). Columns 6, 7, 8 and 9 are to indicate optional variations of construction which may be associated with the top hung ventilator such as type of bead for glazing; weather stripping, fly screens, or a variation on the standard cam opener. In the example the top hung light is required to be weather stripped (W). Column 10 codes the thickness of glass (or infill panel), 3 mm coded (1) in this example. Column codes

STANCHION NO.	PLAN DIMENSION 'A'	DEPTH DIMENSION 'B'	STANCHION NO.	PLAN DIMENSION 'A'	DEPTH DIMENSION 'B'
1	750	225	26	975	675
2	750	225	27	975	675
3	750	225	28	750	225
4	750	225	29	750	225
5	SPECIAL	SPECIAL	30	750	225
6	750	525	31	750	225
7	750	225	32	750	225
8	750	525	33	1125	675
9	750	525	34	1125	675
10	750	525	35	750	225
11	750	225	36	750	225
12	750	225	37	750	225
13	750	525	38	1125	675
14	1050	675	39	750	525
15	750	225	40	1125	675
16	750	225	41	750	525
17	975	675	42	750	225
18	1275	675	43	750	525
19	1275	675	44	750	525
20	750	225	45	750	225
21	750	225	46	750	225
22	1050	675	47	750	225
23	750	225	48	750	225
24	750	225	49	750	525
25	975	675	50	750	525

236   *Schedule*

244

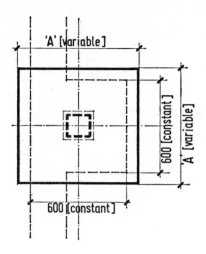

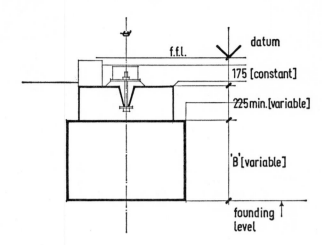

PLAN   SECTION

236 – continued

the type of glass, clear sheet (0) in this case. The procedure is repeated for each of the other 'units' in the bay: (F) for the fixed light, (P) for the projecting top hung window and (F) for the 'fixed light' with infill forming the dado construction.

2 Horizontal members. This coding indicates the horizontal components associated with the bay in addition to the units already coded, such as flashings, transom and sill. The bay which forms part of the full elevation is located by code (0108) and the columns headed 1 and 2 are used to code the component, in this case a particular type of flashing (AF). Columns 3, 4 and 5 are used to give the modular length of the component part. The remaining component parts indicated on the example are head member (HCH), the transom above the projecting top hung window (TR) and the sill member (GC).

3 Vertical members. This coding shows the vertical component types required, in this case a mullion. The bay is first located (4) and the columns headed 1 and 2 are used to indicate the mullion and its width (M3), the columns headed 3, 4 and 5 give the modular height of the mullion (024).

There are very many more alternative components available, each with a separate code or

initial and it will be seen from the example that it is possible, by a simple coding, to translate a drawing to provide numerical rather than dimensional information, so that the information can be processed by *mechanical* means – in this case, a computer. The coding having been set down on the input data sheet, the computer programme is punched on tape from this after certain other coded information has been included by the manufacturer. The manufacturer in this instance checks the architect's drawings against the data sheets since errors in coding can be costly to put right.

The computer produces a priced print-out giving the following information:

1 For each unit section (ie fixed or opening light) the computer prints out a repeat of the data sheet with the addition of a particular coding relevant to the manufacturer's processing.
2 The computer checks the total area in modules against the sum of the units in modules and accepts the data if the end figure is zero.
3 The computer also costs the infill materials which may be glazed or sheet material and prints in words the specification for the infill.
4 The computer gives the cost of each item as *supply only* or *supply and fix* as required.

245

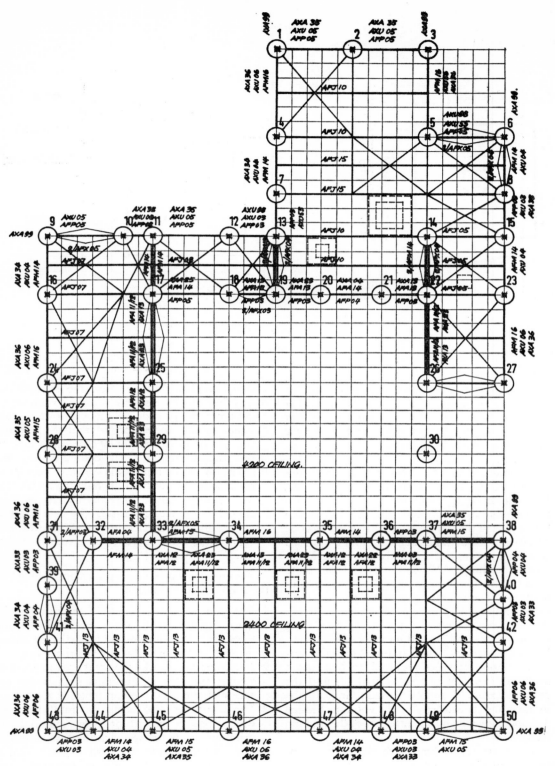

237 Roof steel layout

246

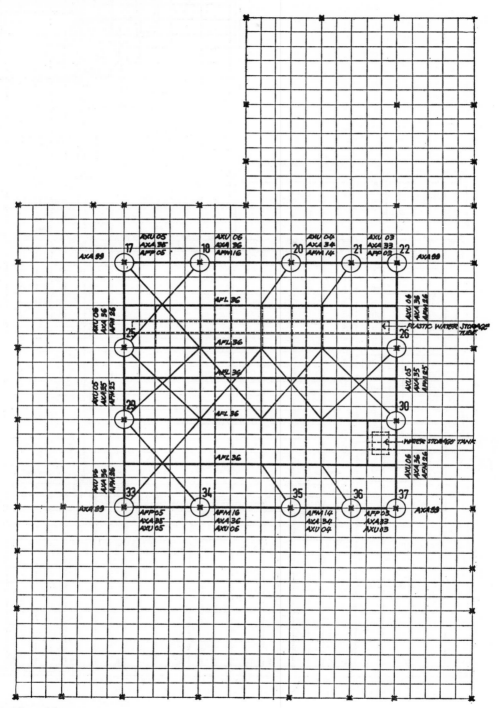

238   Roof steel layout

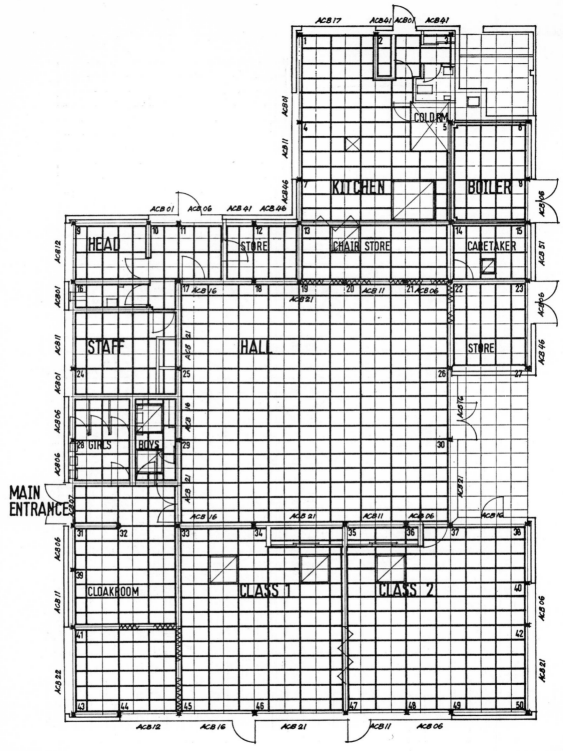

239 *Ceiling plan*

248

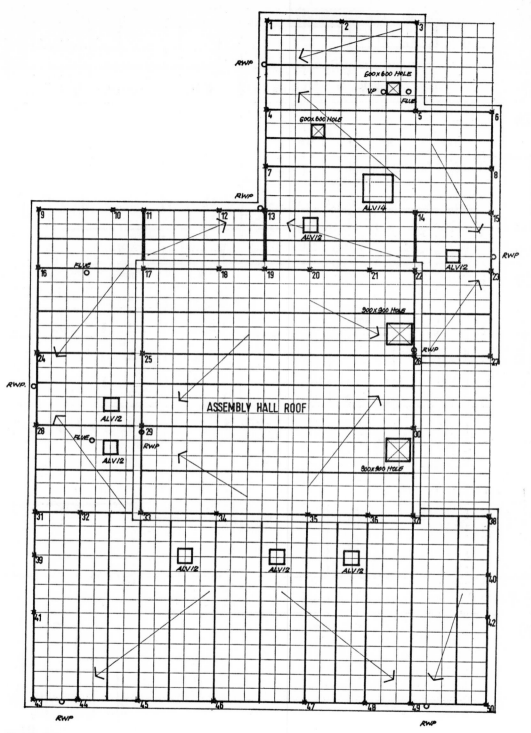

240   Roof plan

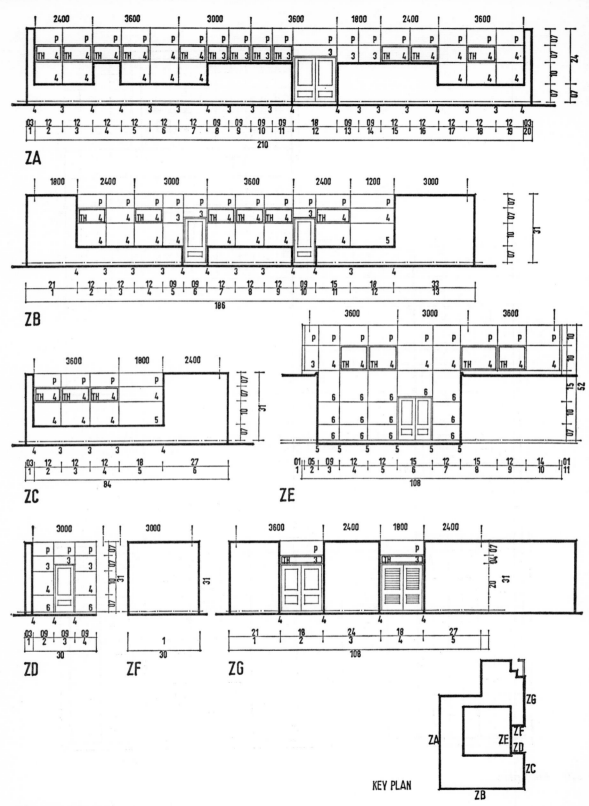

ZA

ZB

ZC

ZE

ZD

ZF

ZG

KEY PLAN

241 Coded elevations

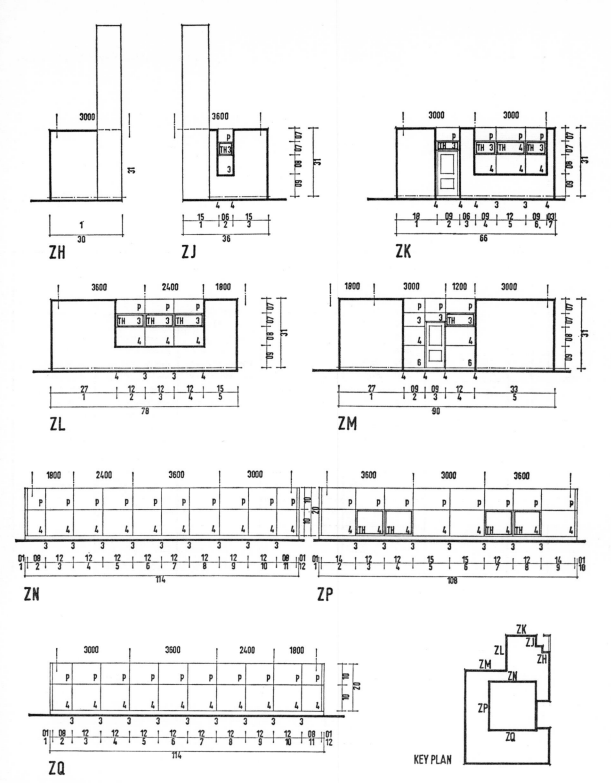

242 *Coded elevations*

DOOR GROUP	DOOR NO.	JOB SPECIAL	DOOR-FRAME SET	DOOR PANEL	FRAME PANEL	DOOR FINISH	FRAME FINISH
	1		ADC 274		LOUVRES TO DETAIL DRG. E·935	POLYURETHENE	WHITE GLOSS
	2		ADC 278		4mm CLEAR GLASS	POLYURETHENE	WHITE GLOSS
	3		ADC 262	6mm 'ARMOURPLATE'	6mm 'ARMOURPLATE'	WHITE GLOSS	WHITE GLOSS
	4		ADC 244		4mm CLEAR GLASS	POLYURETHENE	WHITE GLOSS
	5		ADC 264		4mm CLEAR GLASS	POLYURETHENE	WHITE GLOSS
	6		ADC 244		4mm CLEAR GLASS	POLYURETHENE	WHITE GLOSS
	7		ADC 254		4mm CLEAR GLASS	POLYURETHENE	WHITE GLOSS
DOUBLE	8		ADR 242	6mm 'ARMOURPLATE'	6mm 'ARMOURPLATE'	WHITE GLOSS	WHITE GLOSS
	9			6mm 'ARMOURPLATE'		WHITE GLOSS	WHITE GLOSS
	10		ADC 272	6mm 'ARMOURPLATE'	6mm 'ARMOURPLATE'	WHITE GLOSS	WHITE GLOSS
	11		ADC 244		4mm CLEAR GLASS	POLYURETHENE	WHITE GLOSS
	12		ADC 260	6mm 'ARMOURPLATE'	4mm CLEAR GLASS	WHITE GLOSS	WHITE GLOSS
	13		ADC 234		VENEERED PLY. PANEL	POLYURETHENE	WHITE GLOSS

243   *Typical door and frame schedule (part)*

Ironmongery schedule (part)

DOOR GROUP PREFIX LETTERS			INTERNAL DOORS													EXTERNAL DOORS coded XD												
DOOR NUMBERS			1	2	3	4	5	6	7	8	9	10	11	12	13	1	2	3	4	5	6	7	8	9	10	11	12	13
Common suiting Master keying	REFERENCE NUMBERS	AZA								DOUBLE						DOUBLE			DOUBLE		DOUBLE		DOUBLE					
UPRIGHT LOCKS	WITH ONE KEY	100																										
	LOCKS TO PASS	101	1	1	1		1					1	1	1														
	WITH TWO KEYS	102																										
	REBATED COMPONENTS	103																										
	ROLLER BOLT, ONE KEY	104																										
	ROLLER BOLT, LOCKS TO PASS	105																										
	ROLLER BOLT, TWO KEYS	106																										
	ROLLER BOLT REBATED COMP'S	107																										
UPRIGHT DEADLOCK	WITH ONE KEY	112																										
	LOCKS TO PASS	113								1						1		1	1	1		1		1			1	1	1
	WITH TWO KEYS	114																										
	REBATED COMPONENTS	115														1		1	1	1		1		1			1	1	1
LEVER HANDLES	PAIR ON ROSE	130																										
	PAIR ON BACKPLATE, KEYHOLE	131	1	1	1		1					1	1	1														
	PAIR ON BACKPLATE, NO KEYHOLE	132																										
	ESCUTCHEONS	133								2						2		2	2	2		2		2			2	2	2
PULL HANDLES	150 mm CENTRES FIXING	134																										
	225 mm CENTRES	135					1	1	1	1					1	1	1	1	1	1	1	1	1	1	1	1	1	1
	300 mm CENTRES	136																										
FINGER PLATES	300 x 75	140				1		1	1	1	1				1	1	1	1	1	1	1	1	1	1	1	1	1	1
KICKING PLATES	625 mm WIDE	141												1														
	725 mm	142				1	1	1	1	2	2		1															
	775 mm	143	1	1	2						2		2								1	1					1	1
	825 mm	144													1	1	1	1		1	1	1	1				1
	875 mm	145																										
FLUSH AND BARREL BOLTS	PAIR FLUSH BOLTS	150								1						1			1		1		1					
	SOCKET FOR WOOD	151																										
	SOCKET FOR CONCRETE	152																										
	PAIR BARREL BOLTS	153																										
OVERHEAD CLOSERS	FOR EXTERNAL DOORS OPEN OUT	160																										
	FOR INTERNAL DOORS	161				1		1	1				1	1														
	DOOR SELECTOR	162																										
	OVERHEAD LIMITING STAY	163														1	1	1	1	1	1	1	1	1	1	1	1	1
DOOR STOPS	FOR TIMBER	170																										
	FOR CONCRETE	171			1						1	1	1	1														
	POST MOUNTED DOOR HOLDER	172																										
	CABIN HOOK	173																										
LETTER BOX	LETTER BOX	174																									1		
HAT AND COAT HOOKS	ALUMINIUM	180																										
	NYLON COATED SECRET FIX	181																										
	PAIR NYLON COATED SECRET FIX	182																										
	NYLON COATED SCREW FIX	183																										

244   Ironmongery schedule (part)

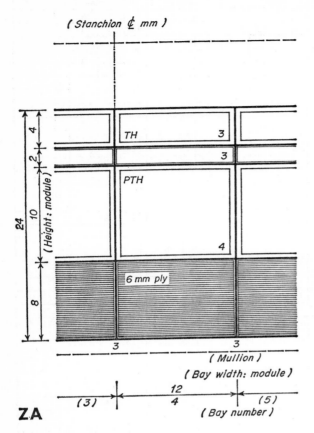

ZA

245 SCOLA window unit

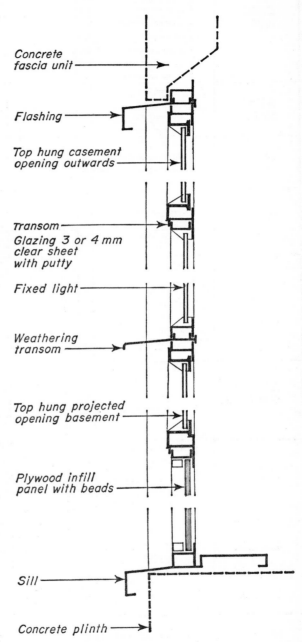

246 Detail of the construction

5 The computer gives details of glazed and infill material in the form of a summary in accordance with the Standard Method of Measurement for the use of the quantity surveyor.

6 Information is also given on painting quantities.

7 A printed summary sheet of costs is produced. This is done by means of reference to a basic unit cost 'with additions' so that variations in price can be dealt with without alteration to the punched tape.

8 The cost per square metre of the elevation is given which allows comparisons of cost relevant to the type of construction.

Minor alterations to design, such as the reduction of the number of window opening lights can be accommodated after the computer *print out* has been done, but this is documented by means of

EXAMPLE OF CODING   Job No.

Contract Ref.   ELEVATION **ZA**   AREA *1096*

Location Ref.	Spec ial	1	2	3	4	5	6	7	8	9	10	11		Archts Ref.	REMARKS
							U SECTION								
4	T	1	2	0	4		W				1	0			
	F	1	2	0	2						1	0			
	P	1	2	1	0		W				2	0			
	F	1	2	0	8		B				4	7			7 = plywood infill
	?														
							H SECTION								
0108	A	F	2	1	2										
0108	H	C	H	2	1	0									
4	T	R	0	1	2										
0108	G	C	2	1	0										
							V SECTION								
4	M	3	0	2	4										
5	M	3	0	2	4										

247   *Specimen input data sheet*

handwritten variation sheets. Major variations necessitate reprogramming and since this is expensive, it is an *on cost* charge to the client. Thus, the principle of preplanning in this context makes obvious economic good sense. After the computer print out, no further work is done by the manufacturers until a letter of intention to proceed (from the client) or a contractor's order is received. The computer is then required to translate the print out into manufacturing documents. These manufacturing documents are in the form of coded sheets and are used in the works for manufacture.

In respect of manufacturing procedure all frames for the window units are *bars* in the form of rolled steel sections until they reach the end of the main processing. They are then ready to be welded together to form the various completed frame units.

The documents produced by the computer for manufacturing are as follows:

1 Coding of the machining document: this gives detailed information with regard to the drilling required on each length of bar.
2 Welding document: this gives details of quantities and references to the elevational coding.
3 *After galvanizing* and despatch document: this gives instructions in respect of assembling the various components for each job.

The above manufacturing documents are in respect of fixed lights and similar documentation is produced for opening lights, plus additional information on hinges and fixings. There is also a *parts list* for each job based on numbers of units per elevation, which is used for despatch purposes, and, in addition, a bay location document for the site fixers, which gives all the details of the openings required to complete each elevation. There are no *working drawings* in the traditional sense, either for manufacturing details or for fixing on site.

FINISHES

12 Floorings

BS 3589 : 1963 *Glossary of general building terms* defines flooring as 'the upper layer providing a finished surface to a floor, which latter provides a lower load-bearing surface'. References include:

Floor finishes for houses and other non-industrial buildings, National Building Studies Bulletin 11, HMSO
Floor finishes, Architects' Journal Information Library
Floor finishes, *Specification*, The Architectural Press Ltd
Flooring, D. Phillips, A Design Centre Publication Macdonald and Co (Publishers) Ltd
Floors, Factory Building Study 3, HMSO
Flooring for industrial buildings, The Engineering Equipment Users' Association, Constable and Co Ltd

Other references, including British Standards and Codes of Practice, are given under the respective headings.

PERFORMANCE CRITERIA

Selection of floorings is facilitated by the *UPEC system* adopted by the Agrément Board which grades *premises*, and gives details of tests for grading the *performance* of various types of floorings under four headings. See table 4. A flooring is considered suitable if its grading under each performance heading is not numerically lower than that of the premises in which it is intended to be used.

Other factors which must be taken into account in selecting floorings include: appearance, comfort criteria, and cost.

We now consider in turn: Wear; Cleaning and surface protection; 'Comfort' criteria; Special requirements; Costs.

Wear

Good resistance to wear caused by pedestrians and vehicles is almost always a primary requirement –

Deteriorating Agent	Classification	Gradings of 'Premises' and 'Performance of Floorings'
Walking	U (*usure*)	1 – 5
Indentation and impact wear	P (*poinçonnement*)	1 – 3
Water	E (*eau*)	0 – 3
Chemicals	C (*chemiques*)	0 – 3

Table 4   UPEC classifications

surfaces are often deemed to be worn out when quite superficial deterioration mars their appearance.

Wear is greatest where traffic is concentrated, where it starts, stops, and in particular where it turns, and it is an advantage if floorings can be renewed locally in such areas. It is often economical to eliminate causes of serious deterioration such as badly designed legs to furniture and steel tyred trucks. Gravel and other gritty paving should be separated from entrances to buildings by hard paving. Immediately inside buildings grit and moisture, which are particularly damaging to materials such as magnesium oxychloride, should be removed from footwear by door mats wide enough to ensure that both feet make contact with them.

The effective lives of most floorings depend very much on how well they are looked after and in selecting materials it is most important to know how much effort and care will be expended in cleaning and maintenance when the building is in use.

Cleaning and surface protection

Floor Maintenance: Materials, their cost and usage, J. K. P. Edwards, Butterworths is a good reference. The tables of flooring materials on pages 272–309 recommend treatments for each material. It is important that the correct treatments are applied. For example, polishes and seals which contain solvents damage rubber and mastic asphalt and unsuitable detergents can cause considerable harm to some floorings. Manufacturers' instructions should be carefully followed and tried out on small areas. Instructions should be displayed for the maintenance staff to read.

In deciding upon floorings it should be borne in mind that if too many different treatments are required in one building wrong treatments are more likely to be given to some surfaces.

In design of buildings it is important to realize that it is often difficult to clean and treat floors without scraping and dirtying the lower parts of walls and fixed furniture. These parts should therefore be hard and easily cleaned.

Smoothness, which makes floorings easier to keep clean, is obtained by fine abrasion; pores can then be filled and the final polish given by a polish or seal.

Polishes

Wax polish protects surfaces from abrasion partly by absorbing grit but is too soft for heavy traffic. The finish looks well after buffing. Too many layers of polish darken surfaces and become slippery and require periodic removal and renewal. Solvent wax polishes are not suitable on rubber, mastic asphalt, thermoplastic tiles and similar materials and they may attack the adhesives used for fixing tiles which are themselves resistant to solvents.

Water-wax and/or synthetic resin emulsions can be used on all floorings although water-sensitive materials should be sealed first. They are easy to apply, eg with a mop, and may provide gloss without buffing. Gloss can also be obtained without slipperiness.

Seals

The original seal used on wood flooring was *button polish* (*shellac*) which is fairly easily scratched and stained. Modern seals give good protection for long periods before requiring renewal but they do not penetrate surfaces and are too rigid for application on flexible floorings.

Surfaces to be sealed must be dirt, dust and wax-free. Slow curing, up to forty-eight hours, is a disadvantage in buildings such as hospitals. Regular cleaning with soap or detergent and water is usually sufficient to maintain seals in good condition for long periods. Floor seals include:

Oleo-resinous These one-can products, made from a drying oil such as tung oil and a phenolic or other resin, are easily applied, but drying by atmospheric oxidation is rather slow. They are usually yellowish in colour. Being soft they show wear more readily than other seals, but worn patches are easily made good.

Epoxy ester Similar to oleo-resinous seals but they are more glossy and harder wearing.

Resin solutions These consist of resins in volatile solvents. They are quick drying but less hard than other seals.

One-can urea formaldehyde – self cure These seals are more transparent and wear better than the foregoing. However, like those mentioned below, they tend to stick wood blocks and strips together and cause cumulative movement. One way of stopping this is by waxing floors before they are sanded.

Two-can modified urea formaldehyde – organic solvent An acid hardener is mixed in immediately before use of two-can seals. This finish is of excellent appearance and hard wearing, although difficult to repair if allowed to wear through. Penetration is insufficient on terrazzo, quarries and clay tiles.

One-can polyurethane – moisture curing Humid conditions are necessary to form a hard yet flexible coating which is suitable for timber, cork and magnesium oxychloride. It is too difficult to remove from linoleum and penetration is insufficient on terrazzo, quarries and clay tiles.

Two-can polyurethane (also available pigmented) has excellent resistance to wear and staining but is slow hardening. It is unsuitable on terrazzo, quarries and clay tiles.

Two-can epoxy resin This type is rather slow in hardening and is usually yellowish, but has excellent resistance to wear and staining.

Synthetic rubber seals These are suitable for the same uses but are generally cheaper than two-can polyurethanes and give good all round performance.

Water based seals usually consist of acrylic polymer resins. They are recommended for use on thermoplastic and vinyl-asbestos tiles, flexible PVC, rubber, porous linoleum, terrazzo, marble and asphalt.

Sodium silicate and silicofluoride dressings are suitable only on concrete floorings. See page 276.

'Comfort' criteria

Although to some extent subjective, comfort assessments are influenced by the temperature, resilience, colour, pattern and texture of the floor, by the temperature and humidity of the atmosphere and by the footwear and activities of the users.

The properties which affect the 'comfort' of floors are:
1 sound control
2 resilience
3 freedom from slipperiness
4 warmth
5 appearance.

Softness, quietness, resilience and warmth tend to go together, for example in cork. At the other extreme, hardness, noisiness and coldness are associated for example in concrete and clay tiles.

1 Sound control

Soft floorings which are not masked by furniture can contribute to the absorption of air-borne sound in a room. Thus at the middle frequency of 500 Hz coefficients for carpets on felt vary from 0·25 to 0·50 according to thickness. (For comparison the absorption of *acoustic* ceiling tiles is 0·70 to 0·90 according to type.)

Soft floorings also absorb impact sound and reduce its transmission through floors. *Floating floors* comprising panels of tongued and grooved strip or boards, or heavy screeds on resilient underlays, reduce the transmission of impact sound if they are isolated at their edges from surrounding walls and columns. See *MBC: E and S*, chapter 6.

Floor finishes are generally of little value in reducing the transmission of air-borne sound through floors – the extent to which this occurs depending mainly upon the mass of the floor as a whole and that of the surrounding walls.

2 Resilience

'Dead' floors are tiring to walk on and resilience is particularly necessary for dancing, gymnastic and similar activities. Thus, wood is more resilient than concrete and wood strips laid on joists or battens are more comfortable than wood blocks laid on concrete. On the other hand, very deep pile carpet is tiring to the feet.

3 Freedom from slipperiness

Slipping on floors is a major cause of injuries in buildings, in particular to children, physically handicapped and elderly persons. Accidents are more likely to occur in badly lit conditions, at sharp corners, thresholds and on stairs and ramps, on surfaces made uneven or polished by wear or where the degree of slipperiness suddenly changes. Unexpected conditions are dangerous, eg where polish is transferred on footwear from a polished surface on to materials such as terrazzo and where a floor which is dull in appearance is slippery. Gloss and slipperiness are not related. Moisture, dirt and grease reduce friction and are particularly hazardous on rubber, PVC and some clay tiles.

Stair treads of hard stones, terrazzo and timber require non-slip nosings or insets. Resistance to slip is increased by frequent joints, as in mosaic, by embossed surfaces and by the temporary depression of soft materials such as cork. It is important that inherent non-slip properties should not be lost by too liberal application of wax polish, especially on timber and linoleum. Non-slip floor seals are often preferable.

4 Warmth

Effective 'warmth' depends upon the temperature of a surface, its thermal conductivity, thermal capacity, the temperature of the air near the surface and on whether shoes are worn. Dampness reduces the thermal insulation of porous floorings and increases the transfer of heat from shoe to floor. Parts of the body not in contact with floors are cooled by radiation to cold surfaces. Contrariwise hot floors can be uncomfortable and floor warming should not raise the surface temperature above 25°C.

5 Appearance

Floor coverings are an important factor in determining the 'scale' of a room and whether it is gay or formal, warm or cold and so on.

Floor finishes are often condemned because they have lost a surface pattern, faded or worn unevenly. Monochromes, especially black and white and glossy surfaces show the slightest mark whereas marbled, jaspé and similar patterns help to camouflage even marks made by black rubber soles.

Patterns and colours should be chosen from large samples. To ensure matching throughout a contract the material should be obtained in one batch and a proportion of additional material should be ordered for future repairs.

Special requirements

Industrial floors

Typical requirements are high resistance to impact, trucking, thermal shock and constant wet conditions.

Underfloor warming

Generally underfloor warming which does not cause discomfort to occupants does not present insuperable problems. Stones, ceramics and concrete which have high thermal capacity are ideal but manufacturers of other floor finishes and of adhesives should be consulted. Some organic materials soften, embrittle or shrink, especially if they are overlaid with carpets or similar insulation.

Resistance to water

Where floor surfaces are likely to be constantly wet the choice of floorings excludes magnesite, linoleum, cork-carpet, wood products, most composition blocks, and all adhesives.

Floors in shower baths and other wet floors require tanking, usually with mastic asphalt.

Resistance to freezing

External paving must be frostproof, eg mastic asphalt, tarmacadam, fully vitrified ceramics and good quality stones and concrete.

Freedom from dusting

Dust arising from abrasion must be avoided particularly where precision work is performed. Concrete floorings tend to produce dust. Ceramic tiles do not, but care must be taken in selecting the jointing material.

Resistance to chemicals

No flooring or jointing material can resist all possible combinations of chemical attack, and in buildings such as food processing factories and laboratories spillage should either be avoided or arrangements made for its prompt removal. In such situations paviors and vitrified ceramic tiles with chemical resistant bedding mortars and jointing materials combine high resistance to chemicals with resistance to trucking and thermal shock. Floors should be laid to a fall of 1 in 60, or up to 1 in 40 where dangers of slipping or of trucks rolling, do not arise. A chemical resistant membrane, eg of acid resistant mastic asphalt or polythene sheet may be required below the flooring as a second line of defence.

Valuable references are BRS Digest 120 *Corrosion-resistant floors in industrial buildings* and CP 202: 1971 *Tile flooring and slab flooring.*

Fire properties

Floors do not generally present a serious fire hazard, but non-combustible floorings may be required in escape routes.

Resistance to sparking

Sparks can arise from impact by metals on hard surfaces or from friction on electrically non-conductive materials such as PVC and rubber. Where gases with a low flash point occur, as in operating theatres, electrically conductive materials must be used. Expert advice should be sought for specific cases. *Anti-static precautions: flooring in anaesthetising areas* MOH Hospital Technical Memorandum no. 2, 1965 deals with the subject.

Ordinary grades of ceramic tiles, PVC, rubber, cork and asphalt and some sealing treatments are poor conductors of electricity but conductive grades are available. Terrazzo is often used as an electrically conductive floor. Electrical bonding by copper strips or by a special adhesive or coating on the underside of floorings is required to give uniform conductivity throughout a floor. Floor polishes or seals must not be allowed to reduce anti-static properties.

X-ray resistance

Ordinary floorings do not resist X-rays and a lead or other resistant barrier may be needed.

Costs of floorings

Initial costs of floorings vary as much as 50 to 1 but differences in serviceable lives can be of the same order. Low initial cost is often associated with rapid deterioration, high maintenance costs and high *cost-in-use*. The fact that timber, composition blocks, terrazzo, cork and natural stones being homogeneous throughout their thickness can be resurfaced, substantially reduces their cost-in-use.

THE BASE

Generally, bases must be rigid and stable: few, if any, finishes can withstand constant movement. They must be level (see page 267), and for thin floor coverings which mirror the slightest irregularities they must be smooth.

Bases for floorings which will transmit or be damaged by moisture must be sufficiently dry. BRS Digest 18 describes a simple apparatus comprising a hygrometer which measures the relative humidity of a small volume of air enclosed so it is in equilibrium with the surface. If the reading taken after at least four hours (preferably 12 hours) is in the range 75 to 80 per cent it is safe to lay all floorings. This section deals with damp-proofing requirements in 'solid' concrete floors and 'suspended' timber floors at ground level where no water pressure exists.

Solid floors at ground level

References are:
CP 102 : 1963   *Protection of buildings against water from the ground*
CP 204 : 1965   *In-situ floor finishes*
BRS Digest 54   *Damp proofing solid floors.*

Dampness may lead to uncomfortably humid atmospheric conditions, a 'cold floor', surface discolouration, and decay of organic materials in underlays, adhesives and floorings. Rising damp, either as liquid or vapour which penetrates through flooring units or through the joints between them is often only remarked upon when condensation appears on the underside of an impervious mat, or where water which evaporates leaves salts on a surface. Incidentally, perishable materials may remain sound where they are able to 'breathe' but decay rapidly if moisture is trapped by superimposed impervious materials.

Concrete and cement/sand screeds are not vapour-proof even if a waterproofing admixture is included in their composition. Only mastic asphalt and pitch mastic are completely vapour-proof. Table 5 gives damp-proofing requirements for floorings on solid floors. According to their position damp-proof membranes are called:
(i)   sub-base membranes
(ii)   sandwich membranes   or
(iii)   surface membranes.

(i)   *Sub-base membranes*

Damp-proof films with lapped joints can be laid on a sub-grade blinded with fine material before the base concrete is laid. CP 102 states that poly-isobutylene film can provide a vapour seal and polythene film at least 0·13 mm thick with lapped joints is of value under thermoplastic and vinyl-asbestos tiles, although it does not always afford sufficient protection to water-sensitive materials such as magnesium oxychloride, PVA emulsion-cement, flexible PVC, cork and timber.

The membrane must be below base concrete which includes heating elements but in other cases because it takes about four weeks for every 25 mm thickness of concrete to dry out, it is usually best to place the membrane above the base concrete.

(ii)   *Sandwich membranes*

These are laid between a concrete base and a screed. Four examples are:
(a)   *Hot bitumen or coal-tar pitch* at least 3 mm thick and soft enough to avoid brittleness in cold weather, without being tacky in hot weather. (Softening points should be 50–55°C and 35–45°C respectively.) If the concrete is too damp or dusty pinholes may develop in the membrane. It should be primed with bitumen solution or emulsion for a hot bitumen membrane, or with a solution of coal-tar pitch for a hot pitch membrane.

263

Floor finishes	Resistance of finish to damp	Minimum damp-resisting requirements[1]
16 mm mastic asphalt 16 mm pitch mastic	No material, dimensional or adhesion failure	No additional protection normally required[2]
Concrete including terrazzo Clay tiles	No material, dimensional or adhesion failure if sulphates are not present	A sandwich membrane is recommended on wet sites[2]
Cement/rubber latex Cement/bitumen Composition blocks laid in cement mortar	No material or dimensional failure Generally no adhesion failure	
Wood blocks dipped and laid in hot soft bitumen or coal-tar pitch covering whole area	Material, dimensional and adhesion failure may occur in wet conditions	
Thermoplastic tiles PVC, vinyl-asbestos tiles	In wet conditions dimensional and adhesion failure may occur. Thermoplastic tiles may be attacked by dissolved salts	
Magnesium oxychloride	Softens and disintegrates in wet conditions	A sandwich membrane is essential
PVA emulsion/cement	Expands when damp	
Rubber and flexible PVC Linoleum and cork carpet Cork tiles	Loses adhesion and expands when damp	
Wood blocks laid in cold adhesive Wood strip and boards Chipboard	Expands and may rot	

[1] Damp-proof membranes must be continuous with damp-proof courses in walls
[2] A damp-proof membrane is always required below floor warming

Table 5   Damp-proofing requirements for floorings on solid floors
(Includes information from BRS Digest 54)

(b)   Three coats of *bitumen solution, bitumen-rubber emulsion* or *tar-rubber emulsion* at least 0·5 mm thick.

(c)   *Bitumen sheet* damp-proof course to BS 743 with sealed joints.

(d)   *Plastic films* as for sub-base membranes.

(iii)   *Surface membranes*

Damp-proof underlays or floor finishes of 16 mm mastic asphalt and pitch mastic are water and vapour-proof and eliminate the need to wait for base concrete and screeds to dry. Pitch-epoxy resin coatings are slightly permeable to water vapour and are not able to 'bridge' cracks which may form in the surface to which they are applied.

Suspended timber floors at ground floor level

A properly constructed floor comprising tongued and grooved timber boards on joists, supported on sleeper walls or piers with damp-proof courses, built off a concrete slab laid on hardcore can provide a dry floor if there is adequate sub-floor ventilation to remove water vapour which rises through the site concrete (see *MBC: S and F* part 1). However, the thermal insulation provided by the boards must be supplemented by insulating boards or quilt or by reflective foil.

Floor screeds

References are:

BRS Digest 104, *Floor screeds*, HMSO

MPBW Advisory Leaflet 5, *Laying floor screeds*, HMSO.

Screeds to receive floorings are laid, usually on a concrete base, for one or more of the following purposes:

1 To provide a degree of level and smoothness to suit a particular flooring, where this is not provided by the structural base with or without a *levelling compound* applied to it.
2 To raise levels.
3 To provide falls. To maintain a minimum stipulated thickness most parts of the screeded area will be wastefully thick and where possible it is better to form falls in the structural base.
4 To accommodate services. Ideally services should be readily accessible and cracking is likely to occur where screeds are reduced in thickness above embedded pipes.
5 To accommodate floor warming installations.
6 To provide thermal insulation.
7 To provide insulation against transmission of impact sound, in the form of *floating screeds*.
8 To provide a nailable base for certain floorings.
9 To form part of the structure of certain precast concrete floor systems.

Generally, if floor finishes are liable to be damaged by damp, a damp-proof membrane is necessary, see page 263.

Screeds on timber bases

Screeds would not normally be laid on timber bases but if they are the timber must be rigid, dry and adequately ventilated below. The upper surface of timber must be protected by bitumen felt or building paper and wire netting or light expanded metal should be fixed at about 200 mm centres and so that no part of the mesh rises more than 6 mm above the surface of the timber.

Screeds are considered in the following order:
Concrete screeds:
cement: dense aggregate
modified cement and sand screeds
lightweight concrete screeds
Synthetic anhydrite screeds.

Cement: dense aggregate screeds

The thickness of cement: dense aggregate screeds must relate to their strength, the degree of bond with the base and where applicable the strength of the base. Screeds which are *monolithic* with sound bases can be very thin. Those which are laid separately must be thicker and *unbonded* screeds, in particular *floating* screeds on compressible layers, must be sufficiently thick to be strong in their own right. They are also more liable to crack and curl upwards at the edges of slabs. Screeds are described under these headings:

1 *Monolithic screeds* (on green concrete)
2 *Bonded screeds* (on hardened concrete)
3 *Unbonded screeds*

1 *Monolithic screeds* By laying screeds on green concrete within three hours of placing, differential shrinkage between the screed and base is minimized and success is guaranteed. However, an early decision to lay monolithically must be made and the screed must be protected during subsequent building operations.

2 *Bonded screeds on hardened concrete* The fact that cement aggregate screeds often fail to bond fully to hardened concrete bases may be acceptable for light duty floors, very thick screeds and where the floor finish is of rigid units such as quarries and in such cases the concrete base need only be brushed with a stiff broom just before it hardens. To obtain maximum bond the aggregate in the base concrete must be exposed without loosening the large particles. This can be done by water spray and brushing the unhardened concrete, but after the normal delay before laying the screed the dirty surface is usually very difficult to clean and mechanical hacking[1] just before laying the screed is preferable.

[1] It is not practicable to hack precast concrete units and screeds should be considered to be 'partially bonded'.

Whether the surface is prepared to give partial or maximum bond it should be thoroughly cleaned and wetted (preferably overnight), any surplus water removed, and not more than twenty minutes before laying the screed a thin coat of cement grout should be well brushed into the damp surface of the base. Alternatively, a proprietary *bonding agent* can be used, but it remains necessary to remove surface laitance and to wet concrete before it is applied. Agents based on polyvinyl acetate, however, are not suitable in persistently damp conditions.

3 *Unbonded screeds* These screeds must be at least 50 mm thick as shown in table 6. Greater thicknesses are necessary for heated screeds and for those laid on resilient layers. Great care should be taken in the design and laying of screeds which incorporate floor warming installations. For those including electrical cables *The Electric Floor Warming Design Manual*, obtainable from the Electricity Council, 30 Millbank, London, SW 1, should be consulted.

Type	Base	Thickness mm	Bay size*
Monolithic	Concrete less than 3 hours old†	12 – 25	—
Bonded	Sound, clean concrete more than 3 hours old but not including water repellent admixture	40* min	15 m² max and length not exceeding 1½ × width for screeds to receive thick finishes and heated screeds only – see page 267
Unbonded	Damp-proof membrane or concrete which is weak, contaminated or includes water repellent admixture	50 min *unheated* 65 min *heated*	
	Resilient quilt for *floating floor*	65 min *unheated* 75 min *heated*	

* Joints must also be provided in monolithic and bonded screeds over movement joints in the structure.
† Where bays are very small, eg for terrazzo, minimum thickness can be 25 mm.

Table 6 Thicknesses and bay sizes for dense concrete screeds

'*Floating screeds*' for sound insulation must be at least 65 mm thick and 75 mm thick if they are heated. Wire mesh will not prevent curling but it may restrain drying shrinkage. Resilient layers with a nominal thickness of 25 mm should not be reduced to less than 10 mm under the dead load of the floor and they must be turned upwards at their edges so the screed is isolated from walls and columns. Adjacent edges of quilts should be closely butted and great care must be taken to prevent mortar from seeping into or bridging the insulation at any point.

Materials for cement:dense aggregate screeds Portland cement to BS 12 *Portland cement (ordinary and rapid hardening)* is usually satisfactory. Aggregate should comply with BS 882, 1201 *Aggregates from natural sources for concrete (including granolithic)* and BS 1199 *Building sands from natural sources*, zones 1, 2 or 3.

To minimize drying shrinkage, the most common cause of failure, the cement:aggregate ratio should not exceed 1:3 and the driest mix which can be thoroughly compacted with the means available should be used. A sample squeezed in the hand should ball together without water being forced out. Low water:cement ratios become practicable by the use of workability aids and mechanical compaction.

Mixes Suitable mix proportions by weight are:

Thickness of screed mm	Cement	Fine Aggregate (dry sand or crushed stone graded 5 mm down)	Coarse aggregate (graded 10 down)
up to 40	1	3* – 4½	–
40 to 75	1	1½	3
over 75			

* The richer 1 : 3 mix is preferred for screeds for thin floorings such as PVC (vinyl)-asbestos and flexible vinyl tiles

Where weight batching is not practicable, cement should be batched by whole bags, accurate gauge boxes should be used for measuring the aggregate and proportions should be adjusted to compensate for *bulking* (see *MCB: Materials*, page 158).

Mixing Thorough mixing is most important to obtain optimum strength, and a mechanical mixer is advisable.

Laying It used to be thought preferable to lay all screeds in bays to control shrinkage cracking but drying from the upper surface of screeds often caused bays to curl upwards at their edges and it was necessary either to relay or to grind down the raised parts in order to prevent them showing through thin floorings such as vinyl sheet and tiles. It is now realized that if *bonded* screeds for thin floorings (other than heated screeds), are laid in strips about 3 m wide (2 m wide for lightweight concrete screeds) random cracks can be easily repaired. However, *bonded* and *unbonded* screeds to receive thick floorings, and those including heating, should be laid alternately in bays 'chess board fashion' with close butt vertical joints. Adjacent bays should be laid at intervals of at least twenty-four hours, the edges of the first laid bays being wetted and brushed with cement grout. Shrinkage will accommodate local thermal expansion and expansion joints need only be provided to coincide with those which occur in the structure.

Screeds must be thoroughly compacted preferably with a beam vibrator, particular attention being paid to edges of bays and especially to the corners. Where trowelling is required to give a true surface it should be delayed for some hours when it will be accompanied by a ringing sound. Premature or excessive trowelling brings laitance to the surface which will craze and dust. For some finishes a screedboarded or a wood floated surface suffices, but a very smooth trowelled surface is necessary for thin floorings such as linoleum and vinyl sheet.

The tolerances for level given for floor finishes in CP 204 would apply to screeds for thin finishes. Acceptable deviations from datum could be ± 15 mm over large open areas and local variations in level ± 3 mm in any 3 m. Differences of level between adjacent bays should not exceed ± 1 mm, and less where thin flexible floor coverings will be laid.

Curing The screed must be kept well above freezing point until it is hard and kept damp for at least seven days until it is strong enough to withstand the stresses arising from drying shrinkage.

Drying The slower the rate of drying the lower is the risk of cracking and curling, and the temptation to accelerate drying must be resisted for at least the first four weeks. Water sensitive finishes should not be laid until screeds are sufficiently dry. A rough rule is to allow four weeks for every 25 mm of screed (or concrete) above the damp-proof membrane in normal weather but the test described in BRS Digest 18 and CP 203 should be used (see page 263). Drying by underfloor warming should not commence for at least four weeks and then only at a reduced temperature. It is important to note that drying will not occur below the elements while the heating is in operation.

Modified cement and sand screeds

Proprietary screeds which include metallic soaps or other water repellents dry slowly but those which contain emulsions of bitumen, polyvinyl acetate, acrylic resins and/or synthetic rubbers are usually thinner than cement/sand screeds and dry more quickly. Screeds of this type may set quickly, adhere well and be laid to a feather edge, resist cracking and some are *self smoothing*.

Lightweight concrete screeds

Screeds of aerated, lightweight aggregate or no-fines concretes[1] are particularly useful in saving weight where thick screeds are required to provide falls or to accommodate services. Broadly, thermal insulation improves, strength reduces and shrinkage increases with increasing density. No-fines concrete, however, has low shrinkage. Table 7 gives recommended thicknesses and other information.

Synthetic anhydrite screeds

Screeds of 1 synthetic anhydrite (anhydrous calcium sulphate : 2½ specially graded aggregate (by volume) can be laid to minimum thicknesses of 25 mm for normal use, 30 mm for electric floor warming and 40 mm on compressible layers. Although more costly for equal thicknesses than cement/sand screeds:

(a) the base need not be prepared to provide bond
(b) almost all the water used combines as water of crystallization and moisture-sensitive floorings can sometimes be laid as soon as ten days after the screed is laid.

[1] Lightweight concretes are discussed in *MBC: Materials*, chapter 8.

Type	Usual minimum thickness mm	Remarks
Aerated	40 plus 15–20 *monolithic* dense topping on screeds less than 1280 kg/m³ and if heavy wear is likely before floor finish is laid	Mixing and laying should be done by specialist firms
Lightweight aggregate 'weak' eg exfoliated vermiculite, perlite	50 plus 15–20 *monolithic* dense topping*	Mixing and laying should be done in strict accordance with the aggregate manufacturers' instructions eg: *Bonded* screeds are laid on fresh neat cement grout 'Weak' mixes should not be tamped or vibrated
'strong' eg expanded clay, shale or slate, foamed slag, sintered pulverized fuel ash (pfa)	40 including 10 *monolithic* dense topping* if floor finish cannot distribute point loads sufficiently	*Note* Absorbent aggregates are slow in drying but pfa *no-fines* mixes dry more quickly than dense mixes
No-fines eg 1 Portland cement : 10 sintered pfa (*Lytag*) 6 mm single size (by volume)	25 *bonded* or 51 (including reinforcement) *unbonded* plus 10 dense topping* in each case	

* Not richer than 1 cement : 4 sand to minimize risk of shrinkage cracking

Table 7   Lightweight concrete screeds

(c) very low drying shrinkage means that screeds can be laid in large areas without cracking or curling

On the other hand, synthetic anhydrite loses strength in damp conditions and bases must be dry before screeds are laid. If the calcium sulphate dries out before it is thoroughly hydrated dustiness and low strength may result.

Dry underlay systems on concrete bases

A proprietary dry floating floor to receive non-rigid light duty floorings consists of 6 or 8 mm sheets of hardboard with rebated edges which are bonded with PVA adhesive when they are laid mesh side up on 13, 16 or 19 mm heat tempered bitumen insulating fibre building board which is laid loose on the subfloor. 2 mm gaps should be left between adjoining insulating boards, 10 mm gaps around rooms and 3 mm gaps between rooms and every 10 m in corridors. Joints between hardboards and

insulating boards should not coincide. Subfloors should be dry and reasonably smooth, although the insulating board accepts a degree of unevenness. The boards should be stored flat on the site for a few days to allow them to adjust to the ambient humidity.

Alternatively, chipboards with t and g joints to all edges are laid on foamed polystyrene boards, at least 12 mm thick, separated from the base by polythene foil. Chipboards should be not more than 610 mm wide with end joints staggered. If 12 mm gaps are left adjacent to all walls, columns etc. the system has some value in reducing the transmission of impact sound.

TYPES OF FLOORINGS

The range of floorings includes materials as diverse as wool, cork, plastics, timber, granite and steel with widely differing appearance, performance and initial and maintenance costs. Common types of materials are either: **A** *Laid while 'plastic'* or **B** *'Preformed'*.

A Floorings laid while 'plastic' See page 270

A I *Without joints*

1 Mastic asphalt
2 Pitch mastic
3 Cement rubber-latex
4 Cement-bitumen emulsion
5 Cement-resin
6 Polyurethane resin
7 Epoxide resin
8 Polyester resin

See text page 270 and table 9 pages 272–5

A II *With joints*

1 Concrete floorings
  (i) Plain
  (ii) Granolithic
  (iii) Terrazzo
2 Magnesium oxychloride (magnesite)

See text page 270 and table 11 pages 278–9

B Preformed floorings See page 280

B I *Sheet supplied rolled*

  Adhesives
1 Linoleum
2 Cork carpet
3 Printed linoleum
4 Flexible vinyl
5 Rubber

See text page 280 and table 13 pages 286–9

B II *Boards* (other than timber)

1 Plywood
2 Chipboard
3 Hardboard

See text page 280 and table 14 pages 290–1

B III *Timber floorings*

1 Blocks
2 Blocks, end grain
3 Boards
4 Strip
5 Overlay strip
6 Parquet
7 Parquet panels
8 Mosaic

(Plywood – see B II *Boards*)

See text page 280 and table 15 pages 292–5

B IV *Clay and precast concrete floorings*

1 Bricks
2 Paviors
3 Quarries
4 Vitrified ceramic floor tiles
5 Fully vitrified ceramic floor tiles
6 Mosaic
7 Concrete, precast
8 Terrazzo, precast

See text page 282 and table 16 pages 296–299

B V *Composition blocks*
See table 17 pages 300–1

B VI *Stones*

1 Granites
2 Sandstones
3 Limestones
4 Marbles
  (mosaic see B IV *Clay and precast concrete floorings* table 16)
5 Slates
6 Quartzite

See text page 284 and table 18 pages 302–3

B VII *Other tile and slab floorings*

1 Linoleum
2 Cork
3 Rubber
4 Thermoplastic ('asphalt') tiles
5 Thermoplastic vinylized tiles
6 Vinyl-asbestos
7 Flexible vinyls
8 Asbestos-cement
9 Mastic asphalt
10 Cast iron
11 Steel

See table 19 pages 304–9

B VIII *Glass mosaic* See table 16, page 298

B IX *Carpets and felts* See text page 284

A Floorings laid while 'plastic'

A I *Without joints* see table 9

These floorings are able to move sufficiently at ordinary temperatures to accommodate slight structural movements without cracking. The following notes supplement the information given in table 9.

1 *Mastic asphalt* Grades are:

I *'Special hard'* – for ambient temperatures 25 to 35°C, schools, showrooms, etc.

II *'Light duty'* – more liable to indentation.

III *'Medium industrial'* – not resistant to heavy trucking.

IV *'Industrial-factory'* – resistant to heavy trucking and thermal shock. Special grades are: coloured, for use at low and high temperatures eg over floor warming installations, for chemical and mineral oil resistance, non-slip, anti-static and spark-free grades.

An isolating membrane laid loose with lapped joints is essential for mastic asphalt up to 20 mm thick on bases of: timber; concrete or screeds of porous or open texture or containing fine cracks or which have received a surface treatment, eg sodium silicate

A membrane is also required for any thickness of mastic asphalt on timber, roofs and on bases which would cause 'blowing' or which would cause the mastic to cool too rapidly during laying and where a polished surface is required. Membranes can be black sheathing felt complying with BS 747 *Roofing felts* (*bitumen and fluxed pitch*), Type 4A (i) or *glass fibre sheathing* where the base concrete is in direct contact with the ground.

Mastic asphalt should be heated to a temperature between 200 and 220°C preferably in a mechanically agitated mixer, as near the point of laying as possible to minimize cooling before it is laid.

Slight shrinkage occurs during cooling and thermal shock causes cracking, particularly of Grade I material. During laying and for 3 or 4 days the ambient temperature should be 5 to 10°C.

2 *Pitch mastic* Generally properties and laying are similar to those for mastic asphalt.

3 *Cement rubber-latex.*

4 *Cement-bitumen emulsion.*

5 *Cement-resin.*

6–8 *Resin-based in-situ floorings* These recently much developed materials, are characterized by toughness, resistance to abrasion and most chemicals, and give dustless and easily cleaned surfaces. Some products are self-levelling to a degree although their high cost precludes their use in sufficient thickness to make levelling screeds unnecessary. Bright colours and coloured flakes suspended in a clear matrix are available.

A II *Floorings laid while plastic, with joints*

Floorings which shrink or are inflexible and which should be laid with joints to accommodate movement include concrete and magnesium oxychloride.

1 *Concrete floorings* Concrete finishes must be of high quality concrete, the principles for obtaining which are stated in *MBC Materials*, chapter 8. Good appearance, resistance to abrasion and avoidance of cracking, dusting, loss of bond with the base and other defects demand careful specification and supervision and skilled workmanship by specialist layers. In particular, aggregate should be clean and well graded, water : cement ratio should be low, mixing, compaction and curing should be thorough. Resistance to wear depends to a large extent on the skill displayed in trowelling. Over-trowelling brings laitance to the surface leading to *dusting*. Adequate temperature, while maintaining the requisite water content, must be maintained for at least seven days' curing and the flooring must not be brought into use until it is sufficiently strong.

Concrete finishes can be classed as either *integral finishes* on concrete slabs or *applied toppings* laid *monolithically* with, *bonded* to, or *unbonded* to the base. Structural slabs, such as domestic garage floors, at least 100 mm thick, can be finished by a tamping beam, float, trowel or by mechanical surfacers, as soon as the concrete has been thoroughly compacted and is sufficiently stiff to avoid an excess of laitance being brought to the surface.

Toppings may be of *plain*, *granolithic* or *terrazzo* concrete and will normally be laid on concrete bases. Falls should be formed in the base concrete so the thickness of the finish is uniform. Thicknesses above 40 mm should be laid in two courses, both at least 20 mm thick, the upper course immediately following the first course.

Services should be laid in the base concrete or in ducts, rather than in the concrete topping.

(i) *Plain* concrete toppings with ordinary aggregates provide utilitarian finishes for light and medium duty. They should be laid as recommended for granolithic finishes.

Information concerning granolithic and terrazzo finishes is summarized in table 11, page 278.

(ii) *Granolithic* Useful references are *A specification for granolithic floor toppings laid on in-situ concrete* (Cement and Concrete Association) and BRS Digest 47.

Granolithic is a utilitarian finish in which superior resistance to abrasion is a primary requirement and aggregate must be hard and tough. Coarse aggregate should comply with BS 1201 : 1965 *Aggregates for granolithic concrete floor finishes* and the fine aggregate should comply with BS 1198–1200 : 1955 *Building sands from natural sources.* (Crushed material may contain dust and it requires more mixing water to give a workable mix.) Proportions of topping granolithic should be 1 : 1 : 2 (by weight) subject to small adjustments to compensate for *bulking* of sand and to obtain a satisfactory overall grading from 10 mm down. Mixing should be done by machine.

The methods for laying are similar to those for screeds and thicknesses depend upon similar considerations, although here functional requirements are often considerably more exacting.

Monolithic finish As with screeds the best adhesion to the base is obtained by laying granolithic within three hours of the base having been placed or sooner in hot weather. It must be emphasized that the description 'monolithic' cannot apply to finishes laid at a later stage. Although an early decision to adopt the method, and protection during subsequent building operations are essential CP 204 advises that 'the method should be adopted whenever possible'.

For floors in contact with the ground a monolithic finish becomes possible if the damp-proof membrane is laid on blinding below the base concrete. For suspended in-situ floors the finish can be taken to contribute to the structural thickness. Monolithic finishes need be only 10–25 mm thick.

Bonded finish ('separate construction') The rules for obtaining the maximum bond between screeds and concrete bases more than three hours old apply to granolithic finishes and they should be strictly observed. See page 265.

Unbonded finish Where finishes are laid on concrete bases which are contaminated with oil, or containing a water repellent, or where they are laid on separating membranes a thickness up to 75 mm is needed, but even with prolonged damp curing the possibility of slabs curling upwards at their edges must be accepted.

Joints Granolithic should be laid in bays of the sizes given in table 8, the lengths of which should not exceed $1\frac{1}{2} \times$ widths. Vertical butt joints should occur over construction joints in the base and movement joints must be provided to correspond with any in the base.

Construction	Thickness mm	Maximum bay size m²
Monolithic	10 – 25 max	30 on concrete base 150 mm thick 15 on concrete base 100 mm thick
Bonded *floors* *stairs* treads and risers where forms are used risers where forms are not used	40 min 20 min 15 min	15 and length not exceeding $1\frac{1}{2} \times$ width
Unbonded	up to 75	2

Table 8 Thicknesses and bay sizes for granolithic floorings

Finishing surfaces After the topping has been levelled and fully compacted, and is set, it must be trowelled at least three times during the next 6 to 10 hours to produce a hard and dense surface free from laitance, and with as much coarse aggregate just below the surface as possible. Usually about two hours after the first trowelling the surface should be retrowelled to close any pores, laitance which arises being removed and not trowelled back into the surface. The final trowelling, usually being the third and sometimes the fourth, is delayed until considerable pressure is needed to make an impression on the surface.

Material, form and references	Base	Properties	Appearance
1 Mastic asphalt Binder – natural and/or derivative bitumen Aggregate – 'natural rock' or crushed limestone, or coarse siliceous grit for acid-resisting grade Mineral fillers and grit Pigments – optional BS 1076 : 1956 Table 2 *Limestone aggregate* BS 1410 : 1959 *Natural rock asphalt aggregate* BS 1451 : 1956 *Coloured limestone aggregate* CP 204 : 1970[1] : Section 4	1 Floated and slightly coarsened concrete 2 Wood boards No damp-proof membrane required in an unheated floor	Wear varies with aggregate – good to excellent. Non-dusting Hardness – indented by point loads – special grade required in hot positions, eg over underfloor heating Resilience – low but tolerates slight movement if laid on sheathing felt Slippery – if wet or polished Warmth – moderate Quiet – moderate Water and vapour proof Chemical resistance – damaged by oils, greases, acids, sugar solutions – but special grades available. High resistance to alkalis at normal temperatures	Colours – natural black, dark red and brown. Green is costly Textures – matt, polished (Heavily gritted material is less easily polished)
2 Pitch mastic Binder – coal tar-pitch Aggregate – limestone or siliceous grit Chalk – up to 15 per cent Pigments – optional BS 1450 : 1963 *Black pitch mastic flooring* BS 3672 : 1963 *Coloured pitch mastic flooring* CP 204 : 1965[1] : Section 5	Floated and slightly coarsened concrete (not timber) No dpm required	Similar to mastic asphalt but superior resistance to mineral oils and inferior resistance to alkalis More brittle at low temperatures and softer at high temperatures – not suitable over floor warming	As mastic asphalt
3 Cement rubber-latex Binder – rubber latex – natural or synthetic and Portland or high alumina cement Pigments Aggregate – cork, rubber, wood and/or stone Mineral fillers CP 204 : 1970[1] : Section 6	1 Floated concrete 2 Timber, if strong, rigid and thoroughly seasoned 3 Other firm strong bases A dpm is required	Wear – good resistance Resilience – more comfortable than concrete Non-slip, moderately warm and quiet Water resistance – low to medium Good resistance to burns Resistant to dilute alkalis Resistance to oils and greases: natural rubber – low synthetic rubber – good Suitable over floor warming Good adhesion to base	Colours – wide range Texture – smooth Pattern – with marble aggregate resembles terrazzo if buffed
4 Cement-bitumen emulsion		Wear – good resistance, non-dusting	Colours – black and dark colours

Table 9   A I Flooring laid while 'plastic' – without joints (continued overleaf)

TABLE 9

Thickness mm	Laying	Surface treatment		Average Cost factor[2]
		Initial	Maintenance	
15 min – underlays 15 – 20 – Grades I and II 20 – 30 – Grade III 35 – 50 – Grade IV	Materials must not be over-heated Float in one coat for ordinary thicknesses Metal armouring may be incorporated in mastic asphalt Thicknesses up to 19 mm are laid on black sheathing felt or glass fibre sheeting where the base is in direct contact with the ground	Matt finish – trowel with fine sand or stone dust Polished finish – apply special water-wax emul-sion (not polishes which contain solvents)	Sweep – avoid oiled sweeping compounds Wash – warm water and neu-tral detergent, or small quan-tity of washing soda for very dirty floors. Rinse Non-solvent polish can be applied Strip occasionally	18
May require to be thicker than mastic asphalt for equivalent uses	An isolating membrane is essential on a timber base and on concrete which con-tains fine cracks, is porous or of open texture Adequate ventilation is neces-sary to remove toxic fumes from pitch mastic	As mastic asphalt May be buffed to expose aggregate		18
6 – 13 Can be laid to 'feather edge'	Dampen absorptive concrete Prime with latex and cement for heavy-duty, fix galva-nized wire netting on timber bases Apply finish by trowel as soon as priming coat has set	May be buffed (in two stages) to remove laitance and expose the aggregate Non-oil emulsion polish only	Sweep frequently, avoid oiled sweeping com-pounds Wash – warm water and mild soap. Do not over-scrub Non-solvent polish on natural rubber type flooring	25
13	Prime screed Apply finish by trowel	——	Sweep Wash	14

Material, form and references	Base	Properties	Appearance

Aggregate – sand and crushed granite	See previous page	Resilience – more comfortable than concrete
		High resistance to burns
		Resistance to:
		    solvents – very low
		    acids and oils – low
		    alkalis – high
		Suitable over floor heating	

5 Cement – resin Binder – cement and polyester resin Aggregate – sand, crushed stone etc		Wear – good resistance Resilience – very low Fairly good resistance to acids, alkalis and oils Non-slip Suitable over floor heating	Texture – slight
6 Polyurethane resin Binder – polyurethane resin Vinyl chips or other fillers One and two-part types	Screed Rigid plywood A dpm is required	Wear – good resistance Non-slip Resilience – good Good resistance to water and oils Moderate resistance to acids and alkalis Low resistance to burns Normally suitable over floor heating	Colours – wide range Texture – 'orange peel' with chips Pattern – plain or chips in transparent binder
7 Epoxide resin Binder – epoxide resin Hardener Aggregate Mineral fillers	Screed – must be level (particularly for self-levelling grades), clean and free from laitance Rigid plywood A dpm is required	Wear – high resistance particularly for trowelled type 'Trucking grades' available Non-dusting Adhesion to base – excellent – good for repairs to existing floors Has chemical set and hardens within 48 hours Excellent resistance to water, acids, alkalis, oils and some solvents Can be resilient and non-slip High resistance to burns Can be suitable over floor heating Some anti-static grades available	Depends upon pigments and aggregates used Self-levelling grades tend to be glossy
8 Polyester resin Binder – polyester resin Catalyst Aggregates, fillers, glass fibres Pigments	Screed – must be level Rigid plywood A dpm is required	Wear – good resistance Resilience – very low Good resistance to water, acids, oils Moderate resistance to alkalis High resistance to burns Not suitable over floor heating Resin may shrink and hair-crack in curing	Colours – wide range

General considerations in selecting, laying and maintenance are discussed on page 270.

Table 9 A I Flooring laid while 'plastic' – without joints

TABLE 9

Thickness mm	Laying	Surface Treatment		Average cost factor[2]
		Initial	Maintenance	
Can be laid to 'feather edge'			Do not use strong detergents for about six months	
3 – 10	Apply by trowel	—	Sweep Wash	18
2 – 3	Various specialized methods	—	Sweep Wash Wax polish is un-necessary and makes it diffi-cult to 'reglaze' worn parts	35–40
2 self-levelling grades 2 sprayed grades 3 – 6 trowelled grades	Prime surface Fill hollows with epoxy resin – sand Spread or trowel Some grades can be sprayed using specialized equipment	Two coats of wax or silicone polish should be applied on self-levelling grades Surfaces of some grades can be ground to re-semble terrazzo	Sweep Wash with soap or detergent Polish to main-tain good ap-pearance of self-levelling grades	50–70
2 – 6	Trowel	Surface can be ground to re-semble terrazzo	Sweep Wash – warm water and soap or detergent Polish – poly-acrylate non-slip emulsion	36–46

[1] General reference: CP 204 : 1970 In situ flooring
[2] Approximate cost relationships for typical floorings 'as laid', based on granolithic = 10

Granolithic must be protected against drying winds and strong sunlight and as soon as it is sufficiently hard it should be protected continuously for seven days, or longer in cold weather, with:

1 canvas, straw mats or 50 mm of sand kept damp,
2 impervious sheets securely held in position, lapped 75 mm and overlapping the edges of slabs. This method is necessary for coloured concrete.
3 a proprietary curing medium.

Drying should be delayed as long as possible to reduce the likelihood of shrinkage cracking. Artificial heating should not be used for at least six weeks and then temperature should be increased slowly. Steel wheeled trollies should not use floors for at least 28 days.

Non-slip properties can be obtained by trowelling in non-slip granules, or later, surfaces can be mechanically or chemically roughened.

Hard materials such as ferrous aggregate, and surface applications of solutions of sodium silicate, magnesium or zinc silico-fluoride improve resistance to abrasion but oleoresinous seals are more effective. Surface treatments applied in accordance with CP 204 and the manufacturers' instructions can be effective on newly hardened concrete, or on old floors if they are clean and dry.

(iii)   *Terrazzo* (Properties and requirements are summarized in table 11). – In-situ terrazzo floor toppings are described in CP 204 : 1965 *In-situ finishes*. Information on the subject can be obtained from The National Federation of Terrazzo-mosaic Specialists, 111 Wardour Street, London, WC 1.

This 'quality' floor (and wall) finish although initially costly provides a hard wearing washable surface in a very wide range of colour combinations. It consists of white or coloured cement with crushed marble aggregate, laid usually on a screed on a concrete base and later ground and polished. It can be slippery when wet or where floor polish is transferred to it from adjacent floorings. For safety the finish should not be smoother than 'fine grit'. Carborundum or bauxite grit can be incorporated in, or trowelled into, mixes. Non-slip inlays are often included in the front edges of stair treads. If polish is ever used, it should be wax-free.

Terrazzo is often used in entrance halls to public buildings, food shops, lavatories and in hospitals. It is especially suitable for anti-static floors, see page 262.

The principles for obtaining sound granolithic finishes apply generally to terrazzo. It can be laid in three ways, ie *monolithically* on a green concrete base or on a screed which may be either *bonded* or *unbonded* to a concrete base, The thickness of screeds must be greater and panel sizes smaller as bond with the base reduces, see table 10.

Construction	Thickness[1] minimum mm	Panel size[2] maximum m^2
Monolithic	15	dividing strips over all construction joints
Bonded *floors*	15 on 25 mm screed	1
stairs treads risers strings	15 10 6	
walls and skirtings	6 on 12 mm render	
Unbonded	15 on 50 mm screed	

[1] thickness should be greater if maximum aggregate size exceeds 10 mm
[2] length of panel should not exceed twice the width. Re-entrant angles must be avoided.

Table 10   Thicknesses and panel sizes for terrazzo finishes

Monolithic construction – To ensure complete adhesion and to minimize the likelihood of shrinkage cracking, where possible terrazzo should be laid directly on structural concrete bases within three hours of their having been placed, and after they have been brushed with a stiff broom to remove water and laitance. Panels of monolithically laid terrazzo can be larger than with other methods of laying but difficulties may arise in protecting the finish from following trades and the method is not widely used.

Bonded construction Where terrazzo is not laid directly on green concrete it must be laid on a screed preferably within three hours of its having been laid. If the screed is older (it should not be older than 48 hours), a neat cement slurry should be brushed into the surface immediately before laying the terrazzo.

Unbonded construction Where the base is hard, or bond is prevented by contamination or water repellents, the terrazzo topping must be laid as described for bonded construction but on a screed at least 50 mm thick, reinforced with light mesh reinforcement and laid on a bitumen felt. Building paper or polythene separating layer lapped 50 mm at the joints.

Toppings The marble aggregate should be clean, angular – not elongated or flaky, and free from dust. Nominal sizes are:

Italian code	Nominal sizes
	mm
$\frac{1}{5}$	2 – 5
$\frac{1}{6}$	4 – 6
2	5 – 9
3	9 – 19
4	12 – 20
5	22 – 25

These sizes can be used individually or in combinations, eg for a fine mix 1 part 3–5 mm : 1 to $1\frac{1}{2}$ parts 5–6 mm. The larger the size of aggregate the less risk of cracking and particles less than 3 mm should not be used. The cement : aggregate ratio varies with the grading and maximum size of the aggregate, but should not exceed 1 : 2 by volume.

Toppings may either be laid as mixes which include all the aggregate or by the *seminar method* as mixes containing only fine aggregate into the upper surfaces of which the larger particles are beaten and rolled in. Metal, ebonite or plastics strips should be securely anchored in the screed to divide toppings into panels, see table 10, and wherever cracks are likely to form due to structural movements. Expansion and contraction joints in the main structure must, of course, be carried through the flooring and be suitably finished on the surface. After tamping, compaction with a heavy roller, trowelling, and removal of laitance to achieve a dense surface with a regular distribution of aggregate and a minimum of cement matrix visible, the flooring must be damp cured. (See *Granolithic flooring*.) Canvas, hessian and sawdust curing media are very liable to stain terrazzo and where white or coloured cement is used plastics sheets are essential.

Finishing surfaces Terrazzo is sometimes sufficiently hard for grinding and polishing within four days of laying. It is best done by machine except for small areas, and in the following sequence: Grind with coarse abrasive stone with water; wash the floor; clean out voids and fill them with neat cement paste. Damp cure and keep the floor free from excessive temperature changes for at least three days before polishing with a fine abrasive stone with water.

Where possible artificial heat should not be turned on in the building for 6 to 8 weeks and the temperature should then be increased slowly.

Heavy traffic should not be allowed on the floor for at least two days.

Maintenance and cleaning Before opening to traffic, terrazzo should be scrubbed with an acid and alkali-free soap and allowed to stand overnight. The following day the surface should be scrubbed vigorously with hot water and rinsed. Subsequently surfaces should be kept clean with soft soap. Strong detergents should not be used and some disinfectants contain phenols and cresols which stain terrazzo.

A II 2 *Magnesium oxychloride* (magnesite) Properties and requirements are summarized in table 11. This comparatively low-cost finish consisting of calcined magnesite, wood or mineral fillers, pigments and sometimes silica, talc or powdered asbestos, gauged with a solution of magnesium chloride, can be laid in plain colours and in mottled and terrazzo effects. However, colours are dull and the material has been largely supplanted by preformed floorings. If the surface is protected by oil or wax, resistance to wear is

Material, form and references	Base	Properties	Appearance
1 Concrete finishes (i) *Plain* (ii) *Granolithic* *Cement*: usually Portland cement BS 12: 1958 *Aggregate*: BS 1201 : 1965 *Aggregates for granolithic concrete floor finishes*; BS 1198–1200 : 1955 *Building sands from natural sources* CP 204 : 1970 : Section 2 *In-situ floor finishes*	Concrete (Not timber)	Cold, hard, noisy Subject to 'dusting' Resistant to alkalis, mineral oils and many salts Slippery when wet if abrasive is not incorporated in surface. Rounded aggregate is more slippery than angular aggregate	Grey, utilitarian
(iii) *Terrazzo* *Cement*: usually white or coloured Portland cement *Aggregate*: marble or spar CP 204 : 1970 : Section 3 *In-situ floor finishes*		Cold, hard, noisy Slippery when wet, if machine polished, washed with soap, or if polish is applied Does not 'dust'	Resembles a mosaic of polished marble chippings divided into panels by strips
2 Magnesium oxychloride (Magnesite) Calcined magnesite and magnesium chloride with wood or mineral and asbestos fillers and pigments to comply with: BS 776 : 1963 *Materials for magnesium oxychloride (magnesite) flooring* and BS 1014 : 1961 *Pigments or cement magnesium oxychloride and concrete* CP 204 : 1970 : Section 7 *In-situ floor finishes*	1 Dry and non-porous concrete, tiles, etc 2 Timber flooring with galvanized wire netting fixed to it	Moderately hard, warm and quiet 'Dusts' if not protected Slippery if highly polished but abrasive can be incorporated Deteriorates in damp conditions Tends to 'sweat' Not recommended with underfloor warming	White and plain colours, mottled and terrazzo effects

General considerations in selecting and laying these floorings are discussed on page 270.

Table 11 A II Floorings laid while 'plastic' – with joints

moderate to high and the flooring is free from dusting. It is slippery if highly polished but abrasive grit can be incorporated in the finish to give a non-slip surface. Wood-fillers make the flooring moderately warm and resilient. Magnesium oxychloride is not seriously affected by alkalis, non-drying oils, fats, greases and organic solvents, but it gradually disintegrates if it is continuously exposed to water or to acids and salts.

Magnesium chloride absorbs moisture from the air and 'sweating' may occur in humid atmospheres. It corrodes metals and stains plaster and

TABLE 11

Thickness mm	Laying	Surface treatment		Approximate cost factors[1]
		Initial	*Maintenance*	
10 – 25 *monolithic* 40 *bonded* 75 *unbonded*	Trowelled when set and well compacted in bays defined by dividing strips Damp cured	When flooring is dry a pigmented oleoresinous seal can be applied	Sweep and wash	5 (19 mm cement: sand) 10 (19 mm garnolithic)
12 min terrazzo* laid *monolithically* on structural concrete base 15 min terrazzo* topping laid *monolithically* on 25 mm screed bonded to base or on lightly reinforced 50 mm screed on isolating membrane * Greater thicknesses needed if aggregate is larger than 10 mm	Trowelled and well compacted in bays defined by dividing strips Damp cured Surface ground, filled, cured and reground	See *Terrazzo Tiles* page 300		54 – 60
10 – 65 on concrete 15 – 45 on timber	Isolate from plaster and metals (punch home nails in boards, and fill) Trowelled in one or two coats preferably in bays defined by dividing strips Damp cured	Proprietary dressing	Sweep Damp mop mild alkaline soap may be used occasionally Do not use household cleaning powders or sweeping powders Wax polish	15 – 25

[1] Approximate cost relationships for typical floorings 'as laid', based on granolithic = 10

should be separated from them by at least 25 mm of uncracked, dense concrete or by a bituminous coating. It is difficult to ensure that floor warming systems remain fully coated and CP 204: 1970 *In-situ floor finishes* does not recommend their inclusion in magnesite.

Magnesium oxychloride can also be used as an underlay for thin sheet and tile floorings.

Concrete bases should be finished reasonably free from ridges and hollows but be slightly roughened with a stiff broom. They should be thoroughly dry when the finish is laid. Galvanized wire netting should be laid on timber bases and fixed at about 200 mm centres with galvanized clout nails. Other nails should be left proud of the base at the same centres.

One coat work is generally 10 to 25 mm thick, and thicknesses greater than 40 mm are laid in two coats, each being not more than 20 mm thick. CP 204 recommends that 6 mm plastics or hardwood dividing strips should be incorporated at not more than 7600 mm centres.

Drying must be delayed for at least 24 hours and light traffic should not be permitted for three days, or longer in cold weather. Heavy traffic should not be permitted for some weeks. Maintenance involves sweeping, damp mopping and treatment with a polish or seal.

B Preformed floorings

B I *Sheet supplied rolled* (See table 13, page 286.) These preformed materials can be laid rapidly with few joints (and these can be welded in (vinyl) PVC sheets). Being thin, a level and very smooth base is needed, although smoothness is less important with materials which have resilient backings. The wear performance of thin materials depends upon the flatness of the base, their thickness, the type and intensity of traffic and on maintenance. Edges of sheets must be protected.

All resilient materials are more flexible and easier to handle and bond to the base when they are warm. The base must be clean, dust-free and dry. Sheet floorings require damp-proof membranes in solid ground floors. Some of them will rot in damp conditions and adhesives will fail. Adhesives prevent sheets curling up at the edges, discourage creep and generally improve performance and appearance of thin floorings.

Adhesives must hold various different materials in place while resisting the stresses imposed by traffic and by movements of the flooring and base. It is important to know that no adhesive can act as a damp-proof membrane.

Water-based adhesives, eg starch, casein and lignin are lowest in cost but their brittleness limits their use to porous materials such as linoleum, cork and fabric-backed PVC in dry conditions. The gum-spirit adhesives are also fairly low in cost and suitable for porous surfaces but although insoluble in water some products are attacked in damp conditions.

Bitumen emulsions and solvent solutions are suitable for thermoplastic and vinyl-asbestos tiles but not for all types of flexible PVC floorings. Synthetic latex adhesives can withstand normal damp and alkaline conditions. Natural and synthetic rubber-resin solutions used for laying rubber floorings must be applied to both the base and flooring and allowed an exact drying time before the surfaces are brought together. Although more costly than the aqueous products they have very high immediate and final bond strengths.

Floorings should not be washed until adhesive is thoroughly hard.

B II *Boards* (See table 14, page 290.)

Suitable boards of appropriate thickness can perform the dual function of supporting traffic and other loads between joist or batten or over other supports and providing a wearing surface of good appearance with few joints.

B III *Timber floorings* (See table 15, page 292.)

General references are:
CP 201 : Part 1 : 1967 *Wood flooring* (*Board, strip, block and mosaic.*)
Timbers for flooring, FPR Bulletin 40, HMSO
Timber floorings, The Timber Research and Development Association (TRADA)
BRS Digest 18, *Design of timber floors to prevent dry rot*, HMSO
MBC : *Materials*, chapter 2, *Timber*.

Timbers of widely differing properties, appearance and costs can be used in various ways in buildings of almost all types, whether they be residential, educational, industrial or public. Timber is hard wearing (resistance in any one species increases with density), and resilient, more so where fixed on joists or battens rather than a solid base. Resistance to acids and alkalis varies from moderate to high, but polishes and in particular seals, provide protection from them, and also from staining, dirt and water. Timber flooring must be correctly seasoned and also designed to accommodate the moisture movement which is inevitable in service. To prevent fungal attack, timber which is not exclusively heartwood of an inherently durable species must be kept with a sufficiently low moisture content, or be treated with a preservative.

Some timbers which are suitable over floor warming are listed in table 12, but they are not recommended where carpets with insulating underfelts are to be used.

Quarter sawn timber has less movement in its

width, gives better wear and may have more attractive appearance than plain-sawn timber. However, its high cost is unlikely to be justified except in cases such as softwood gymnasium floors, where freedom from splintering is essential. End grain timber is even more resistant to wear than quarter sawn timber.

A notable advantage of timber flooring is that it can be repeatedly resurfaced, provided any tongues or dowels are well below the surface.

Moisture content of timber BS 1297 : 1970 *Grading and sizing of softwood flooring* specifies a maximum moisture content of 22 per cent for air-dried timber and 15 per cent for kiln-dried timber. CP 201 gives 18 per cent. If considerable shrinkage is to be avoided where flooring is installed in modern buildings lower moisture contents requiring kiln seasoning are necessary. Moisture contents likely to occur in service are:

No heating	14 – 18%
Intermittent heating	12 – 15%
Continuous heating	11 – 12%
High degree of central heating	10%
Over underfloor heating	7 – 9%

Selection of timber Table 12 based on FPRL Bulletin no. 40 classifies some timbers for uses as strip, boards or blocks (but not end grain blocks) in respect of wear and other properties.

Specialist subcontractors should be consulted, as both availability and cost vary considerably.

Timber	Industrial	Pedestrian	RS	G	CA	FH	B	D	SM
African mahogany		LP				FH			
African walnut								D	
Afrormosia		NP			CA	FH			
Afzelia		NP			CA	FH			
Agba		LP				FH			
Brush, box	HI		RS		CA				
Burma teak		NP				FH			
Douglas fir		LP		G					
East African olive								D	
European beech	LI	HP		G					
European birch		LP							
European oak		HP			CA		B	D	
Greenheart	HI								
Guarea		NP		G		FH	B		
Gurjun		NP		G	CA				
Idigbo		LP							
Iroko		NP			CA	FH			
Japanese maple	HI		RS	G			B		
Keruing		NP		G	CA				
Loliondo	LI	HP		G		FH	B		SM
Missanda	LI	HP				FH			SM
Muhuhu	HI	HP				FH		D	SM
Muninga		NP		G		FH			
Niangon		LP							
Opepe		NP			CA	FH			
Panga panga		HP				FH		D	SM
Parana pine		LP							
Purpleheart		HP						D	
Redwood		LP							
Rhodesian teak	HI	HP			CA	FH	B	D	SM
Rock maple	HI	HP	RS	G			B		
Sapele		NP		G			B	D	
Scots pine		LP							
Utile		NP							
Wallaba	HI								
Western hemlock		LP		G					
Yew								D	

HI	*Heavy duty industrial* including trucking and other impact loads as in factories, mills, workshops and warehouses.
LI	*Light duty industrial* including trucking of a light nature, eg clothing and food processing establishments.
HP	*Heavy pedestrian* Intensities of more than 2000 persons per day, usually concentrated in traffic lanes, eg in public institutions, barracks and corridors in large schools and colleges.
NP	*Normal pedestrian* Intensities of less than 2000 person per day, eg in assembly halls, school and college classrooms, hospitals, shops and offices
LP	*Light pedestrian* Residential and domestic buildings, small classrooms and offices
RS	*Roller skating rinks*
G	*Gymnasia* (softwoods rift sawn only)
CA	*High impermeability to chemicals and acids*
FH	*Suitable over floor heating*
B	*Ballrooms*
D	*Decorative*
SM	*Small movement*

Table 12 Timbers for flooring

The base Timber must be protected from moisture by damp-proof membranes in solid ground floors, and by damp-proof courses and ventilation below suspended floors (see *MBC: Structure and fabric, part 1*). Timber fillets embedded in concrete are required to be either treated in accordance with BS 3452 : 1962 *Copper-chrome water-borne wood preservatives and their application*, or pressure impregnated with copper-chrome-arsenate. Any surfaces which are exposed by cutting must be thoroughly treated with a 10 per cent aqueous solution of the preservative.

The relative humidity of air trapped on the surface of concrete infill between fillets should not exceed 75 – 80 per cent when wood flooring is laid.

Laying Good quality flooring should not be delivered to a site, or fixed before windows are completely glazed, the heating installation has been tested and the building has been maintained at its normal temperature with correct ventilation for at least a week.

A gap must be left for expansion between timber flooring and walls and columns. This can be concealed by a skirting which should not be fixed to the flooring. Where underfloor heating is installed the flooring should be laid in contact with the concrete filling between fillets to obtain maximum thermal transmittance.

Surface treatment See CP 209 : 1963 *Care and maintenance of floor surfaces Part 1 – Wooden flooring.*

Good appearance and cleanliness of floors is obtained by fine sanding and filling the pores of the wood to reduce absorption. *Wax polish* gives good appearance but is soft and requires frequent renewal. *Button polish* (*shellac*) provides a filler coat before wax polishing but is too easily scratched and stained to serve as a durable finish.

Seals – see page 260 – are preferable for heavy duty, or where liquids are likely to be splashed. They are very tough and normally only require to be kept clean during a long life which can be prolonged by applications of resin-emulsion polish. Ordinary paste wax polish on sealed floors makes them dangerously slippery.

Penetrating or *dust-allaying* oils hold dirt and are only suitable for heavy duty and where appearance is unimportant.

B IV *Clay and precast concrete floorings*

Information concerning these floorings is summarized in table 16, page 296. Both clay and concrete products are hard, noisy and 'cold', have high thermal conductivity and capacity and are suitable over under-floor warming installations. Concrete products are lower in cost but the better clay products have the following advantages:

(i) very high resistance to chemicals, except hydrofluoric acid and strong hot caustic alkaline solutions

(ii) they are harder and more resistant to abrasion than concrete products and are 'non-dusting'

(iii) colours are permanent and can be very intense, and tiles can be glazed.

(iv) there is a much wider range of sizes, shapes, textures and colours.

Thermal movement of clay products is about half, and the modulus of elasticity about 1·5 to 3 times that of concrete products.

Bedding systems CP 202: 1971 *Tile flooring and slab flooring* describes methods for laying various units on different bases and for stated conditions of use.

(i) *Bedding in cement : sand mortar bonded to the base* This traditional method is for heavy traffic. Concrete bases should be at least four weeks' old and screeds at least two weeks' old. They should not contain water repellent admixtures. After dipping the more absorptive units in clean water, but not soaking them, they are drained and then bedded on 1 cement:3 to 4 clean sand which should be at least 15 mm thick for tiles of 10 mm or less and up to 20 mm thick for thicker units. To improve adhesion a light dusting of dry cement can be trowelled into the upper surface of the bedding or either a slurry of neat cement or a cement-based adhesive can be applied to the backs of the tiles before they are laid. The backs of concrete tiles are usually painted with neat cement slurry.

Unfortunately, where units are bonded rigidly to bases, loss of bond with 'arching' or 'ridging', particularly of the thinner units, sometimes occurs, for one or more of the following reasons:

1 Shrinkage of the concrete base in drying. (Defects are likely to show in the first twelve months.)

2 Shrinkage of the concrete base in cold weather. (Thermal movement of concrete is two to three times that of fired clay.)

3 Rapid local thermal expansion of tiles caused by steam or hot water hosing.

4 Creep deflection of concrete structural floors.

The expansion of ceramics, particularly the less dense materials, with absorption of moisture which occurs most rapidly in the first weeks after they leave the kiln (see *MBC: Materials*, chapter 6) may contribute to compressive stresses in tiling.

The risk of 'arching' and 'ridging' of tiles which are bonded to subfloors can be reduced by providing *movement joints* as described below, and by the following methods of laying, which permit some relative movement between tiles and subfloor.

(ii) *Separating layer method* This method is

suitable internally on true and smooth concrete bases. Units can be laid as above but on a bedding mix 15 mm thick and at least as thick as units up to 25 mm thick, separated from the base by poly-thene foil,[1] bitumen felt[2] or building paper[3] with 100 mm lapped joints or by damp-proof mem-branes.

(iii) *'Thick-bed', semi-dry method* To prevent bond with reasonably level concrete bases damped if necessary to reduce suction, a lean mix, 1 cement : 4 sand containing only sufficient water so it retains its shape when squeezed in the hand, is tamped down at least 25 mm thick. For a bed-ding thicker than 40 mm a 1 cement : 1½ dry, 10 mm 'down' coarse aggregate : 3 dry sand mix (by weight) should be used. (If proportions are batched by volume bulking of sand should be allowed for.) A slurry of 1 cement : 1 fine sand of creamy consistency is applied about 3 mm thick immediately before the units are well beaten down. The backs of concrete tiles are painted with a 1 : 1 slurry. Joints should be grouted within four hours of laying.

(iv) *'Thin-bed', cement based adhesive method* On a sufficiently level, and dry base, dry tiles are well tamped on an adhesive which should comply

[1] 500 grade for most conditions
[2] BS 747
[3] BS 1521

with Appendix B of CP 212, Part 1 and be not more than 5 mm thick. The method is not recom-mended on screeds over underfloor heating. This, and the following proprietary products, should be used in strict accordance with the manufacturer's instructions.

(v) *Bedding in rubber-latex cement mortar* This method is practicable on any base, including metal decking. The mortar, which resembles rubber-latex cement flooring, accepts some movement and is resistant to mildly corrosive conditions.

(vi) *Bedding in bitumen emulsion : sand* The base is primed with the compound (BS 3940 *Adhesives based on bitumen or coal tar*) which is spread to a minimum thickness of about 10 mm.

Joints Joints must be sufficiently wide to accom-modate some movement and variations in size of units, ie at least 3 mm wide for ordinary units up to about 152 mm square and up to about 15 mm for larger and less accurate units. It is important that joints are completely filled in order to prevent penetration of liquids, to support their top edges and evenly distribute stresses between units. When the bedding has set ordinary joints are grouted with 1 cement : 1 fine dry sand, by volume, and those in mosaic with neat cement.

Movement joints should be taken through the tiles and bedding as indicated in figure 248. They are topped with an elastic but suitably hard sealant

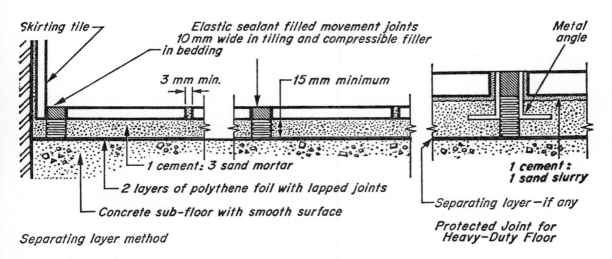

248   *Laying of clay and precast concrete flooring*

(see CP 202 and *MBC: Materials*, chapter 16). Compressible back-up materials are used to control the depth of sealant and the way it deforms, and fillers are used to fill the remaining joint. Sometimes one material fulfils both functions. They must be compatible with the sealant. A barrier such as polyethylene film may be needed to prevent elastic sealants sticking to the back-up or filler material.

Clay units CP 202 recommends that where units are bedded 'solid', movement joints should be provided to perimeters,[1] over supporting beams and walls, and at 4·5 m centres. However, units bedded on a semi-dry mix, at ground level and which will not be subjected to large and rapid changes in temperature or humidity, usually do not require perimeter joints in floors which do not exceed 6 m in any direction. In such floors any intermediate joints can be at 9 m centres.

Concrete units – laid by any method – require perimeter joints[1] where floors exceed 15 m in any direction and intermediate joints at 15 m centres.

B V *Composition blocks* (See table 17, page 300)

B VI *Stones* (See table 18, page 300)

Stones are hard, 'cold' and noisy but very suitable for underfloor warming. They have good resistance to oils but may be stained if they are not sealed.

B VII *Other tiles and slabs* (See table 19, page 304)
These units include heavy-duty cast iron slabs, semi-rigid materials such as compressed cork and thermoplastic tiles and tiles cut from sheet materials which are also provided in rolls.

B VIII *Glass mosaic* (See table 16, page 298)

B IX *Carpets and felts*
References include:

Product selection for architects: Carpets, RIBA Journal, January 1970
BS 3655 : 1963 *Code for informative labelling of carpets, carpeting and rugs* deals with size, construction, fibre content and cleansing.

---

[1] Where movement joints are required to perimeters they should also be provided around columns, machine bases, etc.

284

BS 4223 : 1967 specifies *A method for the determination of constructional details of carpets with a yarn pile*
BS 4334 : 1968 *Selected tests for carpets*
also: BSs 4051, 4052 and 4098.

Carpets vary widely in quality, which is generally related to initial cost. Low initial cost is often associated with high *cost-in-use*. It should be noted that durability and deterioration in appearance are not directly related. The materials used for pile, backing and underlay all influence performance. A high pile is not always an advantage in wear but the weight of pile, including that woven into the backing, and the number of tufts per 100 mm² are guides to durability.

With correct and regular maintenance the better quality carpets are extremely durable, but all carpets are damaged by grit, by rubber soles and pointed heels to shoes, and by pointed legs to furniture.

Use-category gradings adopted by *The British Carpet Centre* and *The Consumer Council* are valuable aids in the selection of carpets.

The BCC system grades Axminster and Wilton woven carpets produced in this country and non-woven carpets manufactured by members of *The Federation of British Carpet Manufacturers* as suitable for:
1 Light domestic, eg bedrooms,
2 Light to medium domestic,
3 General domestic and/or light 'contract' use,
4 Heavy domestic and/or medium 'contract' use,
5 Luxury domestic and/or heavy 'contract' use. (Carpets in this category usually have only one stated use.)
The *'Teltag' system* of *The Consumer Council*, which employs BS tests, and quality control in manufacture, grades carpets from all sources as suitable for:
1 Light use, eg bedrooms,
2 Anywhere in the home, except hall and stairs,
3 Anywhere in the home,
4 Anywhere in the home – extra quality,
5 Special uses.
In addition 'merit points' are awarded for fastness to light and to shampooing and for resistance to crushing.

Types of carpets Machine made carpets (hand made carpets are not considered here) are either *woven* or *tufted*:

Woven carpets In Axminster-type carpets the pile is woven with the backing and is always cut, the method permitting a large number of colours to be used. In Wiltons the pile is woven into the backing; the number of colours is restricted. Plain coloured woven carpets are usually Wiltons and their pile is usually denser than Axminsters.

Woven carpets are made in *body widths* of 457 mm to about 1 m and *broadloom widths* up to 4·572 m in thicknesses of 6 to 19 mm.

Tufted carpets Here the looped or cut pile is stitched into a jute backing and secured with latex. Patch repairs are more easily made than with woven carpets. A good quality carpet may have a PVC primary backing and an expanded PVC secondary backing, both of which include glass fibre reinforcement.

Types of pile *Cut pile* has a matt appearance, but tends to *shade* and *track*. *Cording* or *loop pile* does not shade and the irregular appearance of *cut loop* minimizes tread marks and shading.

Types of fibres Fibres which are used alone or in various combinations include:

Wool fibres are resilient and warm and do not soil easily. They do not ignite easily and are self-extinguishing, but wool is costly and is attacked by moths if it is not specially protected. A '*Woolmark*' is awarded to pure wool carpets of specified quality.

Nylon is strong, tough and very hard wearing, but is less soft and resilient than wool. It soils but is easily cleaned, and it melts at high temperatures.

Polypropylene, although cheap, has comparable durability to nylon and cleans well. It is difficult to dye and tends to flatten quickly.

Acrylic is not as soft as wool but is resilient, wears well and is easily cleaned.

Rayon has low strength and resilience but is cheap and provides bulk in carpets.

Organic fibres can be treated to render them anti-static but:

Stainless steel fibres are included in some carpets to eliminate static electricity which can arise when all animal or synthetic fibres are walked on.

Felts These consist of fibres needled into a jute hessian backing.

Fixing

The base should be smooth, level and without gaps. Good quality resilient underlays, either separate or integral, add considerably to the lives of carpets and reduce the downward transmission of impact noise.

After being well stretched, carpets should be fixed at their edges by tacks or by angled pins on *gripper strips*. Carpet to carpet joins can be made by sewing, or by adhesive strips.

Some felts are stuck to subfloors, but animal hair carpet tiles bind together at their contacting edges and do not require to be stuck down.

Aluminium or brass extrusions are used to protect the edges of carpets at junctions with other floorings.

Maintenance

Stains should be removed immediately. Vacuum cleaning is necessary at intervals varying widely with use, and less frequently, dry cleaning or shampooing, which are best done *in-situ*, are required.

Material, form and references[1]	Base	Properties	Appearances

1 Linoleum
Powdered cork, fillers, pigments, oxidized linseed oil and resins pressed on jute canvas or cork
Also on bitumen felt in 2·5 and 3·2 mm thicknesses only
Available sealed with polyurethane and butadiene copolymers
 	
BS 810 : 1966 *Sheet linoleum (calendered type) and cork carpet*
BS 1863 : 1952 *Felt backed linoleum*
	1 *Concrete screed* – with steel trowelled finish and levelling compound if required
	
	hardboard (with rebated edges on polythene film, on sand) A dpm is essential in solid ground floors
	
	2 *Wood boards* (at ground level protected by dpcs and ventilated below)
	existing boards – if sanded and filled lay flooring on paper felt, or preferably treat as:
	new boards – should be t and g preferably strip width. Cover with 4·8 mm standard hardboard or 4 mm resin-bonded plywood in sheets not larger than 1 m² laid breaking joint and fixed with ring nails or self-clinching staples at 150 mm centres over the whole area.
	Paper felt may prevent nails or staples 'grinning' through flooring
		Wear – low to high resistance, increases with thickness. *Hardened grades* have good resistance to sharp point loads and to burns
		Resilience: high for thicker grades
		Cannot be bent to small radii
		Quiet and warm
		Slippery if highly polished
		Resists oils and weak acids but deteriorates in damp conditions
		Attacked by alkalis
			Colours –
			  large range
			Patterns –
			  plain, jaspé, moiré, granite, marble, geometrical
			
			Textures – semi-matt

2 Cork carpet Granulated cork, pigments, oxidized linseed oil and resins pressed on jute canvas BS 810 : 1966 *Sheet linoleum (calendered type) and cork carpet*		Wear – moderate if well maintained in light domestic use Not suitable where excessive soiling is likely Softer, more resilient, quieter and warmer than linoleum Non-slip even when wet or polished Resists occasional water and weak acids Low resistance to alkalis and burns	Colours – medium to dark cork colour and shades of green, red and brown Texture – open
3 Felt base or **printed 'linoleum'** Paint finish or thin vinyl film on bituminous felt	3 *Chipboards* – as floor finish See table 14 4 *Mastic asphalt* – as floor finish See table 9 5 *Clay and concrete tiles, stone slabs etc* – If in contact with the ground and there is no dpm, surface with 13 mm mastic asphalt.	Wear – low resistance but sufficient for very light duty or temporary work Cracks at low temperatures Not suitable over underfloor warming	Colours – various Patterns – various Texture – glossy
4 Flexible vinyl – homogeneous Mainly PVC binder with varying contents of fillers, plasticizers and pigments	If dry but irregular, apply levelling compound	Wear – moderate to high. Resistance varies with vinyl content and thickness Resilience – varies similarly	Colours – very wide range Patterns – very wide range including vinyl chips in clear vinyl

Table 13   B I Sheet supplied rolled (continued overleaf)

TABLE 13

Typical sizes			Laying	Surface treatment		Average cost factors[2]
Thickness mm	Width mm	Length m		Initial	Maintenance	
2·0 2·5 3·2 4·5 6·0 6·7	1830 2000	9 27	Keep at room temperature for at least 48 hours before fixing Lay on adhesive For cheap work on boards, lay loose with edges lapped. Trim edges and tack down after sheet has expanded	If not factory-finished with a hard seal, clean with mild soap or detergent (not with abrasives or strongly alkaline soap or detergent). Rinse and dry Apply suitable seal (later removing any factory dressing) Apply water-wax or spirit-wax polish	Sweep Damp mop with mild soap or neutral detergent Burnish polish and only occasionally renew sparingly, or maintain seal	21 28 (4·5 mm)
3·2 4·5 6·0	1830	15	Keep rolled at room temperature for at least 48 hours Must be bonded to base	Wash, rinse and dry as linoleum Suitable seals reduce dirt being ingrained	Generally as for linoleum but removal of grit is very important and polish 'build-up' is difficult to remove	23 (4·5 mm)
1·0			Normally laid loose	None required	Damp mop	2
			Must be bonded to base	Water-wax emulsion polish (non-solvent type)	Damp mop Burnish polish and renew sparingly, only occasionally	24 – 33 (2 mm)

Material, form and references[1]	Base	Properties	Appearances
Non-slip grade contains aluminium oxide grains BS 3261 : 1960 *Flexible PVC flooring*	6 *Metal decking*	Moderately warm and quiet High resistance to surface water Tends to shrink More resistant to chemicals, oils, alcohols etc and less easily stained than linoleum and vinyl-asbestos tiles Cigarettes may char	Texture – matt to glossy and embossed simulations of travertine marble, mosaic, timber, etc
Flexible vinyl – backed Cork, foamed plastics, needled felt or inorganic backings '*Cushion vinyl*' has a thin foam interlayer '*Foam-backed vinyl*' has a thick foam backing		Very quiet with resilient backings but surface may be punctured and backings may lose resilience with age Inorganic fibre felt improves dimensional stability	
5 **Rubber** Natural or synthetic rubber vulcanized, with fillers and pigments, in some cases on fabric backing Available with foamed-rubber base BS 1711 : 1951 *Solid rubber flooring* BS 3187 : 1959 *Electrically conducting rubber flooring* BS 3398 : 1961 *Anti-static rubber flooring*		Wear – good resistance increases with thickness. Heavy duty quality (black) Very resilient and quiet especially with foamed-rubber base Smooth types slippery when wet Warm Good resistance to water, weak acids but natural rubber is damaged by oils, fats and solvents Damaged by ultra-violet radiation Emits rubber odour, particularly over underfloor heating Special grade required over underfloor heating	Colours – very wide range and black and white Patterns – plain, marbled, mottled etc Textures – matt to glossy, studded, grooved, rough texture

General considerations in selecting, laying and maintaining sheet floorings are discussed on page 280

Table 13   B I Sheet supplied rolled

TABLE 13

Typical sizes			Laying	Surface treatment		Average cost factors[2]
Thickness mm	Width mm	Length m		Initial	Maintenance	
1·1	910	11	Joints can be welded in-situ	Do not seal		44 (foam backed)
1·6	1220	27				
2·0	1370					
2·5	1830					
3·2						
┌ 3·0						
*⟨ 3·9						
└ 4·5						
* with resilient backings						
3·8 light domestic floors 4·8 6·4	910 1370 1830	15 — 30	Must be bonded to minimize creep caused by wheeled traffic	Water-wax emulsion polish applied sparingly (non-solvent type only)	Damp (not wet) mop with mild soap (Not with alkaline or abrasive soap, detergents not having a soap base or 'cleaning agents') Burnish polish and renew sparingly occasionally only Strip polish when 'build-up' becomes excessive	45 (4·8 mm) 56 (6 mm wide-ribbed surface)
12·7 to order						
4·5 with foamed backing						

[1] General reference: CP 203 : 1969 Sheet and tile flooring
[2] Approximate cost relationship for typical floorings 'as laid', based on granolithic = 10

Material, form and references[1]	Base	Properties	Appearance
1 Plywood Resin bonded plies Face-ply at least 3 mm thick T and g boards available BS 1455 : 1963 *Plywood manufactured from tropical hardwoods* CP 201 : 1951 *Timber flooring*	*Full support* Boarded floor Sand bed Expanded plastics boards *Partial support* thicker boards only on:	Wear – moderate, resistance varies with timber and life is determined by thickness of the top ply Moderately warm and quiet – but thin boards 'drum' if not fixed overall to base	Pattern – Normally rotary cut timber
2 Chipboard Wood chips bonded with synthetic resin and compressed Density not less than 640 kg/m² Sanded or sealed finish Available with edges t and g or grooved for loose tongues BS 2604 : 1963 *Resin-bonded wood chipboard*	Joists or battens with noggings to support ends of boards without tongues Compressible quilt t and g boards (only) laid loose as floating floor	Wear – Moderate to good resistance Low resistance to water	Colour – warm yellow Pattern – as wood chips
3 Hardboard Wood fibres compressed Preferably *tempered hardboard* BS 1142 : 1961 *Fibre building boards*	Sub-floors must be dry	Wear – moderate resistance Properties of tempered hardboard similar to plywood	Colours – natural browns and integrally coloured yellow, green or red

Table 14   B II Boards (Timber boards see table 15)

TABLE 14

Typical sizes[2]			Laying[3]	Surface treatment		Average cost factors[4]
Thickness mm	Width mm	Length mm		Initial	Maintenance	
4 fully supported	1220	2440	Panel pins where appropriate	As wood blocks		19 (6 mm)
13 supported at 460 mm centres	1220	2440	Face grain must be at right angles to main supporting members			
16 supported at 610 mm centres	1220	2440	50 mm nails should be inserted at 150 mm centres	See page 292		28 (13 mm)
12 fully supported	1220	2440	*On sanded boards* Lost head nails at 400 mm centres punched home and holes filled	Fill open texture of untreated boards and apply plastics seal	Damp mop Renew seal when necessary	21 (12 mm)
18 supported at 400 mm centres	1220	2440	*On joists or battens* Lost head nails at 400 mm centres punched home or can be glued			
22 supported at 600 mm centres	1220	2440	Fill holes Leave expansion gap below skirtings			23 (18 mm)
4·8 fully supported	1220	1220	Wet backs of boards and store flat for 48 h (72 h for tempered hardboard) *On sanded boards*: nail with 25 mm lost head panel pins at 150 mm centres at edges and at 200 mm centres on lines 400 mm apart *On smooth concrete*: bond with adhesive	Can be sealed	Damp mop Polish regularly (must be non-slip type) Renew seal when necessary	14

[1] General reference: *MBC Materials*, chapter 3
[2] Thicknesses and spans between supports relate to domestic loadings
[3] Edges of boards must be protected. Boards can, in suitable qualities, be used as bases for thin floor finishes, but they are considered here as floorings in their own right
[4] Approximate cost relationships for typical floorings 'as laid', based on granolithic = 10

Form of unit and references[1]	Base	Properties	Appearance
1 Blocks Hardwood and softwood units tongued and grooved or dowelled BS 1187 : 1959 *Wood blocks* *(interlocking)*	Floated screed on dry concrete slab	Moderately resilient, warm and quiet Not suitable in damp conditions or where wide variations in atmospheric humidity occur The greater moisture movement of timber across the grain than that along the grain is balanced by alternating lengths and widths of blocks thereby avoiding accumulated movement across a floor	Colours – as timbers; some timbers darken and others fade with age Joint patterns *basket* – square and open *herringbone* – square, single and double *brick bonds*
2 Blocks – end grain Usually softwood impregnated with preservative for wet conditions of use	Level concrete	Exceptional resistance to wear and impact Brittle objects if dropped are less likely to break than on other industrial floorings	Utilitarian
3 Boards Usually softwood Nominal widths more than 102 mm Should be tongued and grooved to increase strength and fire-resistance and for draught proofing	Joists or battens Maximum spans for softwood boards or strip for domestic loadings:	More resilient than blocks If timber is not correctly seasoned cupping of plain sawn boards more than 165 mm wide and shrinkage gaps between boards are likely to be pronounced	Good appearance requires first-class material, laying techniques and maintenance

Finished thickness of board or strip	T and g Min. face width (net) 89 mm	Plain edged Min. face width 146 mm
14·29	457	356
16·67	533	406
19·84	610	457
26·99	762	533
33·34	914	610

BS 1297 : 1970 *Grading and sizing of softwood flooring*

(Building Regulations 1965)

Form of unit and references	Base	Properties	Appearance
4 Strip Hardwoods and softwoods. Up to 102 mm wide with tongued and grooved edges and ends – long lengths		As t and g boards	Joint pattern – Narrow widths (sometimes random) and long random lengths

Table 15 B III Timber floorings (continued overleaf)

TABLE 15

Typical sizes			Laying	Surface treatment[2]		Average cost factors[3]
Thickness mm	Width mm	Length mm		Initial	Maintenance	
21	75	229 305	(1) Screed primed and blocks laid in hot bitumen, or (2) blocks laid in cold adhesive 13 mm gaps or cork strips under skirtings 13 mm cork strips sometimes recommended to divide floor into bays	Stop if required, sand, stain or dye if required and seal with oleoresinous solvent-based seal (eg polyurethane) or apply wax polish Floor seal or plastics polish is necessary to protect softwoods Non-slip gymnasium oil for gymnasia (only)	Wipe seal with damp (not wet) cloth or apply wax polish Renew seal (surface must be wax-free). Polyurethane seals can be patch repaired Renew wax polish When badly worn resurface by sanding (Effective wearing surface is determined by depth of tongues or dowels below the surface	40 (softwood) 43 – 79 (hardwood)
63 — 114	76	102 127 229	Blocks dipped in hot soft pitch and laid with close joints or laid dry and grouted	Usually none but hard grit can be rolled into bituminous dressing	Sweep	33 (63 mm)
21 28 BS 1297 t and g flooring	13 137	Random 1800 min 3000 min average in any one delivery	Boards cramped Header joints to bear on joists or battens and be staggered at least two boards' width in both directions *Softwood boards* Fix with brads, punch in and stop two brads per bearer for boards up to 178mm wide, three brads for wider boards *Hardwood boards* Secret nail through tongue and nail or screw through face and stop or pellet	As I Blocks	As I Blocks	22 (25 mm ordinary softwood t and g)
19 25	51 63 76 89 102 less 13 mm as laid	Random	Strips cramped Secret nail at 50° just above tongues to all bearers T and g header joints need be supported by noggings only for heavy duty floor			50 – 80 (25 mm hardwood t and g)

Form of unit and reference[1]	Base	Properties	Appearance
– short lengths – (reduce price slightly) BS 1297 : 1970 *Grading and sizing of softwood flooring*	Floated concrete	Resilience etc as for blocks	Narrow widths and short random lengths
5 Overlay strip Hardwood Tongued and grooved edges, ends may be tongued and grooved	Sound, sanded, softwood flooring or softwood flooring with underlay	Suitable for light duty	Joint pattern – as end-matched hardwood strip
6 Parquet Selected hardwoods square or t and g edges Units for laying may comprise components glued together at their edges	Thoroughly seasoned and level boards – preferably overlaid with 4 mm resin-bonded plywood or 4·8 mm hardboard	Suitable for light domestic duty only	Exotic and costly woods can be used in parquet thickness Patterns, including elaborate marquetry, are independent of base
7 Parquet panels 6 mm hardwood parquet mounted on laminated softwood Tongued and grooved on all edges	1 Joists or battens 2 Screed	Composite construction gives wear properties equivalent to strip	As end-matched hardwood strip
8 Mosaic Hardwood butt-edged 'fingers' bonded to a base of scrim, felt or perforated aluminium foil or overlaid with membrane which is stripped off after laying BS 4050 : 1966 *Wood mosaic flooring*	Floated screed, 4 mm resin-bonded plywood or 4·8 mm hardboard	Similar to blocks Smaller units and basket pattern localize moisture movement	Generally supplied in less exotic hardwoods than parquet Joint pattern – Usually basket weave in 114 or 150 mm square units each comprising five or six 'fingers' respectively

Plywood, chipboard and **hardboard** see page 290

General considerations in selecting, laying and maintaining timber floorings are discussed on page 280.

Table 15   B III Timber floorings

TABLE 15

| Typical sizes | | | Laying | Surface treatment[2] | | Average cost factor[3] |
Thickness mm	Width mm	Length mm		Initial	Maintenance	
25	76 less 13 mm as laid	Random 230 — 610	As I Blocks	As I Blocks	As I Blocks	
9 — 16	up to 76	Random	Glued and secret pinned along tongued edges Laid at an angle with boards if no underlay is used			46 – 55
5 — 10	51 76 89	Various	Glued and pinned Pins punched home and holes filled	As I Blocks or can be french polished for light duty	As I Blocks or revise french polish	90 (6 mm)
25 — 32	305 and 610 squares for laying		1 Glue tongues and nail through tongues if necessary 2 Bedded in hot bitumen 3 Some interlocking products can be laid loose, eg as removable dance floor on carpet	Products without-shop finishes treated as *blocks*		
10 — 16	305 and 457 squares for laying		Bonded with cold adhesive and rolled Any surface overlay removed Gaps below skirtings and cork expansion strips as for wood blocks			34 – 60 (10 mm)

[1] General reference: CP 201: Part I: 1967 *Flooring of wood and wood products*
[2] See CP 209: 1963 *Care and maintenance of floor surfaces* Part I: Wooden flooring
[3] Approximate cost relationships for typical floorings 'as laid', based on granolithic = 10

Material, form and references[1]	Base	Properties	Appearance
1 Bricks Manufactured from un-refined clays, pressed and burnt Intended primarily for walling BS 3921 : 1965 *Bricks and blocks of fired brickearth, clay or shale* BS 3679 : 1963 *Acid resisting bricks and tiles*	*Internally* – concrete *Externally* – (i) for vehicular traffic – concrete (ii) for pedestrian traffic – rammed earth or hard-core	Best products (eg *Engineering bricks Classes A and B* (BS 3921) have excellent resistance to wear, impact, chemicals and frost) For external use '*Special quality*' (BS 3921) bricks must be specified	Colours – wide range Joint patterns – brick bonds and unbonded, with wide joints Texture – usually plain
2 Paviors (i) Manufactured as for *Engineering bricks*	Concrete or screed finished to suit method of laying	As *Engineering bricks* but without frogs	
(ii) Manufactured from refined clay and fired at very high temperature		Most paviors have resistance to chemicals and wear superior to that of quarries	Colours – red, buff, cream, brown Texture – plain, ribbed, chequered and roughened
3 Quarries Manufactured from un-refined clays, pressed and burnt BS 1286 : 1945 (amended 1967) *Clay tiles for flooring – Type A*	A damp-proof membrane may be needed to prevent water vapour passing through joints and through porous units and to prevent water evaporating from the surface leaving salt deposits	Similar to equivalent bricks. Some have harder surfaces than the interiors Wear resistance good to excellent, especially for red and blue quarries *Slipperiness*: moderate to good *Maximum water absorption* (BS 1286): Class 1 6 per cent Class 2 10 per cent *Size tolerance* (BS 1286): ±4·5 mm – units 229 × 229 mm ±3·2 mm – smaller units	Colours – natural clay colours, ie red and in certain sizes, brown, blue and buff. Slight variations are characteristic Texture – slightly irregular Joint patterns – usually square bond. Wide joints are necessary for less accurate quarries
4 Vitrified ceramic floor tiles[2] Manufactured from refined clays, of more uniform composition than used for quarries and which include fluxes to increase vitrification Non-slip tiles contain silicon carbide The clay is ground, pressed and fired at high temperatures		More accurate size and shape and more uniform colours than above units Smooth surface Greater resistance to wear, oils, fats and chemicals including alkalis and to frost than quarries Electrically conductive grades are available *Slipperiness*: moderate when dry and oil, grease and wax free	Colours – black, white and wide range of monochromes and mingled colours Textures – *Matt* develops sheen with wear. Available with non-slip silicon carbide surface and a glazed tile is textured with sand

Table 16   B IV Clay and precast concrete floorings – (continued overleaf)

TABLE 16

| Sizes[4] | | | Laying | Surface treatment | | Average cost factor[5] |
Thickness mm	Width mm	Length mm		Initial	Maintenance	

65
 	
or can be laid *brick-on edge* or *brick-on-end*
	102·5	215	*Externally*:
			  pedestrian traffic –
			    units may be bedded
			    in sand or weak
			    mortar
			  heavy traffic – units
			    bedded on 16–19 mm
			    cement : sand mor-
			    tar on concrete base
				Clean off and pro-
				  tect as for quarries
					Sweep	30 – 60

19
—
51
	95
	108
	114
	124
		190
		216
		241
		251
			Internally:
			  See page 282
			  Remove cement stains
			    with proprietary fluid
				As *Bricks*
				
				Externally as *Bricks*
				Internally as *Vitrified tiles*
						60
						
						70

19
16 or
22
29
32
38 or
51
 	
also diagonal halves, sills, stairtreads, etc
	102
	76 or
	152
	203
	229
	}
	305
		102
		}
		152
		203
		229
		305
			Methods of laying
			See page 282
			
			    Thickness
			    of bedding
			    mm
			Mortar on
			 – concrete 15–20
			 – separating
			 layer 15–25
			
			Semi-dry mix 25 min
				Clean immediately
				  with sand or saw-
				  dust
				Wash repeatedly with
				  water until any
				  efflorescence ceases
				Protect with white-
				  wood sawdust
				  during works
					Wash with warm
					  water and neutral
					  sulphate-free de-
					  tergent
					(Soap residues
					  cause slipperiness
					  and hold dirt)
					Rinse thoroughly
					  with clean water
					
					(Do not use oiled
					  sweeping com-
					  pounds)
						30 – 50

8·5 {
 	
10
11
13
18–24 }
 	
12·7 {
 	
13
	76
	102
	152
	100
	100
	150
	25
	51
	76
	152
	60
		76
		102
		152
		100*
		200*
		150*
		
		152
		
		250*
			*Cement-based
			adhesive* 5 max
				Polishes, linseed oils and other seals are not
				absorbed. They tend to make surfaces
				slippery and more difficult to clean
						60

Material, form and references[1]	Base	Properties	Appearance
BS 1286 *Type B – Class 2*: 1945	As previous page	*Water absorption:* (BS 1286) 5 per cent max (Typical products 1–2 per cent) *Size tolerance* (BS 1286): ± 2·4 mm	*Ribbed, studded, panelled and granulated* *Glazed* – not suitable for heavy duty Joint patterns – geometrical. Accurate size and shape of tiles permits narrower joints than quarries
5 **Fully vitrified ceramic tiles**[2] Manufactured to give a higher degree of vitrification than *vitrified ceramic floor tiles Class 2* BS 1286: *Type B Class 1*: 1945		Similar to vitrified ceramic tiles but are virtually impervious and have excellent resistance to chemicals and staining *Water absorption:* (BS 1286) 0·3 per cent max (Typical products absorb appreciably less)	Colours – wider range than for vitrified ceramic tiles Textures and joint patterns – as for vitrified ceramic tiles
6 **Mosaic** Tesserae, usually of vitrified or fully vitrified ceramic are supplied bonded to paper in sheets up to 800 mm square. (Also available in glass and marble)		Similar to equivalent tiles of equal thickness *Slipperiness:* Rice grain clay tesserae and recessed joints reduce slipperiness for bare feet. Flush joints can be dusted with silicon carbide abrasive Glass suitable only for light pedestrian traffic	Colours – as tiles Texture of tesserae – Glazed, matt rice grain and incorporating abrasive. (The latter can be used as non-slip insets in terrazzo or marble stair treads Joint patterns – Normally regular but special patterns can be ordered
7 **Concrete – precast** Ordinary or coloured cement and aggregate hydraulically pressed Heavy duty tiles have hard stone or metal aggregate and/or abrasive included in surface BS 368: 1956 *Precast concrete flags* BS 1197: 1955 *Concrete flooring tiles and fittings*	Flags for pedestrian traffic may be laid on rammed earth or hardcore	Properties vary widely Better products benefit by quality control, hydraulic pressing etc, are 'pre-shrunk' and have high resistance to wear, but inferior products may craze and 'dust' Resistance to chemicals varies with density Not suitable for chemical-resisting floors Accurate size (tolerance ± 0·8 mm on length and breadth)	Colours – given by natural grey, white and pigmented cements and by aggregates when exposed in manufacture, by wear or by weathering Textures – plain, ribbed and containing abrasives

Table 16   B IV Clay and precast concrete floorings (continued overleaf)

TABLE 16

Sizes[4]			Laying	Surface treatment		Average cost factors[5]
Thickness mm	Width mm	Length mm		Initial	Maintenance	
15 { 19 22·2 } 32 } 17·5 18	52 115 152 254 250	240 152 254 250*	After bedding mortar has set, completely fill joints with 1 cement:1 fine sand grout[3] and point joints wider than 6 mm with 1 cement:3 fine sand[3]. Remove surplus with dry cement. (not sawdust)	As previous page	As previous page	
* imported tiles also diagonal halves, hexagonal and other shapes, sills, stairtread tiles etc			Damp cure for at least 3 days Movement joints See page 283 Light foot traffic should not be allowed for three or four days			80
4 — 10	13 – 5 sided squares, hexagons etc		Bed on 9 mm of 1 cement : 2 sand[3]. When the bedding is hard, the paper is stripped and joints are grouted as with neat cement Movement joints See page 283			100
16 19 25	151 227 303	151 227 303	As for similar clay products see above and page 282 but the backs of concrete tiles or slabs are brushed with neat cement slurry immediately before they are laid	May be sealed to prevent oil stains	Scrub with detergent in hot water and with mild scouring powder if dirt is engrained	30 – 50
also hexagons and other shaped *tiles*						60 (industrial)

51 {
—
63 {
	457	610
		762
		915
			Mortar for slabs 1 : 4 to 6, semi-dry mix or 1 cement : 1 lime : 5 to 6 sand
			Movement joints
			See page 283
						17 (flags)

flags						

Material, form and references[1]	Base	Properties	Appearance
8 **Terrazzo – precast tiles** Hydraulically pressed concrete tiles, faced with marble aggregate in white or coloured cement matrix about 10 mm thick (abrasive may be incorporated) Surface ground BS 4131 : 1967 *Terrazzo tiles* BS 4337 : 1968 *Precast terrazzo units* (*other than tiles*) eg stair treads and risers	Concrete	Properties generally as for high quality precast concrete units Similar to in-situ terrazzo, but tiles benefit from factory production as above	Colours – wide range Joint pattern – can be inconspicuous or colours of tiles can be alternated Appearance similar to in-situ terrazzo but very large aggregate is sometimes used in a matrix of smaller particles and cement Liable to staining by some timbers, rope and straw

General considerations in selecting, laying and maintenance are discussed on page 282.

[1] *General references*: CP 202 : 1971 *Tile flooring and slab flooring*; BRS Digest 79 *Clay tile flooring, MBC Materials, Ceramics* chapter 5, *Bricks* chapter 6, *Concrete* chapter 8

Table 16   B IV Clay and precast concrete floorings

Composition blocks	Concrete or screed	Properties	Appearance
Composition blocks Various combinations of cement and drying oil or PVC binder, chalk, sawdust, wood flour, inert aggregate, and pigments pressed into blocks and cured Blocks have dovetailed keys on underside CP 202 : 1959 *Tile flooring and slab flooring*	Concrete or screed A dpm is recommended on wet sites and is essential below floor warming	Good resistance to wear Heavy duty blocks incorporate white spar chippings Resilience low. Very good resistance to indentation Moderately warm Slippery only if highly polished Very good resistance to vegetable oils Good resistance to water, alkalis, acids, animal and mineral oils	Colours – rather dark Black and four colours on grey cement base Seven colours on white cement base Patterns – basket, herringbone and brick bond

Table 17   B V Composition blocks

1 Granites	1 Internally	Properties	Appearance
1 **Granites** eg Cornish BS 435 : 1931 *Granite and whinstone kerbs, channels, quadrants and setts*	1 *Internally* and for heavy-duty externally – concrete	Excellent resistance to wear, impact, frost and chemicals Slippery when polished, eg by wear Impervious to water and water vapour Resistant to staining	Colours – grey, red, pink, blue, black Pattern – mosaic of crystals Texture – from rockface to glossy

Table 18   B VI Stones (continued overleaf)

Typical sizes[4]			Laying	Surface treatment		Average cost factors[5]
Thickness mm	Width mm	Length mm		Initial	Maintenance	
19 22 25·5 32 38 300 and 500 max width hexagons	200 225 300 400 500	200 225 300 400 500	As above but with dividing strips (see in-situ terrazzo) between groups of tiles	Usually ground after laying to remove any lipping edges Protect with non-staining sawdust Scrub with non-alkaline non-acid soap and allow to stand overnight Rinse with hot water Can be protected against staining with suitable seal	Wash with warm water and occasionally fine abrasive powder. Use soap only if it is thoroughly rinsed off Do not apply polish or allow to become contaminated with soap or wax Do not use oiled sweeping compounds or disinfectants containing phenols and cresols	70

[2] Geometrical shapes sometimes called tessellated tiles
[3] Mixes by volume
[4] Subject to specified tolerances
[5] Approximate cost relationships for typical floorings 'as laid', based on granolithic = 10

10 and 16 Also accessories	52 63	157 190	Bed on 13 mm 1 cement : 3 sand Joints grouted with proprietary mortar Cure with wet sawdust	Sand Seal	Sweep with damp sawdust Wash with soap and water Rinse Apply proprietary polish Can be resurfaced by sanding	36 (10 mm) 43 (16 mm)

40 and setts	up to about 1830 × 910		*Internally* and for heavy-duty externally	Clean	Scrub with water and neutral sulphate-free detergent Rinse Surface may need to be roughened after many years	(310–560

Material, form and references	Base	Properties	Appearance
2 Sandstones eg 'York stone' type (usually riven) Darley Dale Forest of Dean BS 706 : 1936 *Sandstone kerbs, channels, quadrants and setts*	2 *Externally* for pedestrian traffic only: Sound hard-core or compacted soil	Wide range of density and hardness Some varieties eg 'York stones' have very high resistance to wear and frost and are 'non-slip' More absorbent stones readily stained Sandstones are attacked by sulphates washed from limestones in towns	Colours – grey, buff, brown, pink, red Texture – from rough-sawn to smooth. Riven surfaces may have mica particles
3 Limestones eg Portland Hopton Wood Kotah		Some varieties have high resistance to wear and frost Resistant to alkalis but not acids More absorbent varieties readily stained Hard varieties slippery when worn	Colours – grey, buff, white Texture – from sawn to high (integral) polish
4 Marbles and hard limestones commonly called *marbles* eg Swedish green Dove Sicilian Travertine	Granite, slate and quartzite are impervious but a dpm in bases at ground level may be needed to prevent salt deposits on joints	Many varieties are very hard but superficial scratching by footwear tends to obscure bright colours and markings	Colours and Markings – very wide range Texture – from sanded to very high (integral) polish Pattern – slabs or mosaic
5 Slates usually riven and edges sawn eg North Wales Westmorland Lancashire BS 680: 1944 *Roofing slates*		Very good resistance to abrasion Riven surfaces of coarser slates are non-slip but polished smooth surfaces are slippery when wet Impervious to water and water vapour Stained by oils and greases if not sealed	Colours – green, blue, purple, black, greys (seals intensify colour) Texture – riven, sawn, sanded, rubbed or finely polished
6 Quartzite eg Norwegian		Excellent resistance to abrasion and chemicals Riven surfaces are non-slip wet or dry Resistant to staining Dirt is not absorbed but riven surface holds dirt	Colours – grey, green, buff, yellow Texture – riven

General considerations in selecting, laying and maintenance are discussed on page 284

Table 18   B VI Stones

TABLE 18

Typical sizes		Laying	Surface treatment		Average cost factors[1]
Thickness mm	Length and width mm		Initial	Maintenance	
40–75 and setts	up to about 3050 × 1220	Bed on 13–76 mm 1 cement : 3 sand on concrete base	Clean Seals prevent staining but are not recommended by CP 202 Polish can make smooth surfaces dangerously slippery	Scrub with water and where necessary, a suitable neutral, sulphate-free pumice powder or detergent	110
15–40 50	300–600 squares up to about 1500 × 600	Externally: for light pedestrian traffic only: bed on weak cement or sand on compacted subsoil or hardcore If base is impervious, bed should be drained to prevent frost-heave			110
15–30 and mosaic – see table 15	up to about 1500 × 900			Scrub with warm water and sulphate-free non-caustic detergent Rinse Do not use soap (causes slipperiness), or oiled sweeping compounds	270 – 370 (19 mm)
6–13 19–25 32–40	457 × 229 381 × 381 1500 × 900	Movement joints as concrete units page 283			250 – 270 (19 mm)
Due to natural camber, riven slates require to be thicker than sawn slates, and may not be suitable in large sizes					
10–20	152–229-mm sided squares and oblongs Random sizes up to 900 mm long				135 (19 mm)

General references: CP 202 : 1971 Tile flooring and slab flooring, MBC Materials, chapter 4
[1] Approximate cost relationships for typical floorings 'as laid', based on granolithic = 10

Material, form and references	Base	Properties	Appearance
1 **Linoleum**	As sheet linoleum page 286		Pattern can be provided by varying sizes and direction of tiles
2 **Cork** granulated cork (no fillers) bonded by natural or artificial resins under heat and pressure Square, or tongued and grooved edges for tiles 8 mm thick and upwards Available with thin vinyl film surface Common densities: 480 and 560 kg/m^3 CP 203 : 1969 *Sheet and tile flooring*	Trowelled screed Paper felt underlay on boarding A dpm is essential in solid ground floors	Wear – good resistance especially high density grade tiles, but damaged by stiletto heels or badly designed furniture. Dirt becomes ingrained and cork is readily stained if not protected Resilient Very quiet and warm Non-slip – even when wet or polished Moderate resistance to acids Low resistance to alkalis Not suitable in damp conditions	Colour – honey to dark brown and dyed colours Pattern – cork granules Appearance deteriorates if maintenance is neglected
3 **Rubber** (i) Cut from sheet Some tiles contain fibre reinforcement	As sheet rubber page 288		Colours – as sheet but heavy duty tiles usually black Pattern – can be provided by varying direction and sizes of tiles
(ii) Moulded with dovetailed grooves on underside and bold grooves or ribs on upper surface Interlocking or plain edges BS 1711 : 1951 *Solid rubber flooring* CP 203 : 1969 *Sheet and tile flooring*	Tiles laid into screed or mastic asphalt on concrete – a dpm is not required	As sheet but non-slip Suitable for heavy duty public circulation areas Grease resistant grade available	Texture – smooth, studded bold ribbed, and other anti-slip grooved textures

Table 19 B VII Other tile and slab floorings (continued overleaf)

TABLE 19

Typical sizes[1]		Laying[2]	Surface treatment		Average cost factors[3]
Thickness mm	Width and length mm		Initial	Maintenance	
As sheet	229 305 up to 914	As sheet linoleum but must be bonded to base	As sheet linoleum page 287		21 (3·2 mm)
3 5 8 25 stair treads	229 305 —	Keep tiles at room temperature for at least 48 hours Fix with adhesive and headless steel pins If pinning is not practicable 'load' tiles until adhesive has set	After fine sanding ordinary tiles, apply flexible seal or heavy grade solvent wax polish If great care has been taken in laying, sanding of prefinished tiles may not be necessary Water emulsion polish can be applied on sealed tiles	Sweep frequently Damp (not wet) mop with detergent or mild (non-alkaline) soap Revive polish or seal periodically Smooth surface and colour can be restored by sanding	32 (6 mm)
As page 289 6 13 ribbed	229 – 914 914 × 1829	As sheet rubber page 289			44 (5 mm)
10 20	457 914	On fresh screed: Sand/cement applied to backs On old screed or mastic asphalt: tiles bedded in latex/ cement	—	Sweep and vacuum Wash occasionally Can be polished (non-solvent type)	50

Material, form and references	Base	Properties	Appearance
4 Thermoplastic ('asphalt tiles' – standard) (not to be confused with 'vinyl' tiles which are also thermoplastic, or with mastic asphalt tiles) Bitumen or non-vinyl resin binder, mineral fillers, asbestos fibres and pigments BS 2592 : 1955 *Thermoplastic flooring tiles, sometimes known as asphalt tiles* CP 203 : 1969 *Sheet and tile flooring*	As for 'Sheets supplied in rolls' – but not wood boards	Wear – moderate resistance Rather noisy Hard at lower temperatures and crack if not uniformly bedded Surface temperature with floor warming must not exceed 27°C (they soften at higher temperatures) Resistant to alcohol and water Moderate resistance to alkalis May be attacked by dissolved salts Poor resistance to solvents, acids, oils and greases Slippery if highly polished	Colours – limited range of dark colours (darker colours are cheapest) Patterns – plain or marbled
5 Thermoplastic – 'Vinylized' thermoplastic tiles with vinyl content BS 2592 : 1955 CP 203 : 1969 *Sheet and tile flooring*	A dpm is essential where rising moisture is severe	Slightly flexible and more resistant to wear, oils and greases than ordinary thermoplastic tiles	Colours – wider range than ordinary thermoplastic tiles
6 Vinyl asbestos vinyl (usually PVC) binder, asbestos fibres, fillers and pigments BS 3260 : 1960 *PVC (vinyl) asbestos floor tiles* CP 203 : 1969 *Sheet and tile flooring*		Properties intermediate between thermoplastic tiles and flexible vinyl tiles	Colours – brighter than thermoplastic tiles Textures – include 'travertine'
7 Flexible vinyl material as flexible vinyl sheet Tiles are not suitable where welded joints are required BS 3261 : 1960 *Flexible PVC flooring* CP 203 : 1969 *Sheet and tile flooring*	As for flexible vinyl sheet page 286		Colours – as sheet material Pattern – can be provided by varying direction and size of tiles

Table 19   B VII Other tile and slab floorings (continued overleaf)

TABLE 19

Typical sizes[1]		Laying[2]	Surface treatment		Average cost factors[3]
Thickness mm	Width and length mm		Initial	Maintenance	
2·5 3·2 4·8	229	Usually warmed to make them more flexible before laying on a suitable adhesive Thermoplastic tiles may crack at low temperatures if not uniformly bedded	Water-wax emulsion polish only (not polish containing solvents) Seals should not be used	After at least two weeks wash with mild soap or neutral detergent (*not* alkaline cleaners) Remove stains with fine steel wool and cleaning powder Burnish and apply polish sparingly	9 – 14 (3·2 mm)
2·5 3·0	229				21 (3·0 mm)
1·6 2·0 2·5 3·2	229 305				24 (3·2 mm)
1·1 1·5 2·0 2·5 3·0 3·2	229 300 305 457 914				24 – 33 (2 mm)

Material, form and references	Base	ʁperties	Appearance
8 Asbestos-cement Portland cement and asbestos fibres *Semi-compressed tiles* (BS 690 : 1963) – suitable for roof terraces *Fully-compressed tiles* (BS 4036 : 1966) – suitable for roller skating rinks etc	Floated concrete or screed on concrete	resistance moderate good ʒh resistance to water and alkalis ᴍoderate resistance to acids Low resistance to animal and vegetable oils	Light grey – standard
9 Mastic-asphalt – preformed as in-situ material but tiles are pressed BS 1324 : 1962 *Asphalt tiles for paving and flooring (natural rock asphalt)*		Generally as for in-situ flooring but preformed tiles are denser Acid resisting grade available	Colours – black, brown, dark red Texture – plain or chequered
10 Cast iron plates and grids	ꞓrete	Hard, cold and noisy Extremely resistant to metal tyred trucks, impact and molten metal spillage High resistance to acids and alkalis Suitable for heavy duty industrial floors	*Plates* – plain, studded, ribbed *Grids* – with hexagonal holes
11 Steel 'Anch lates' – trays pr d from 10 swg (ᴍm) sheet. ꞇgues turned down om slots in face ꞷrm 'anchors'. Available unfilled or filled with concrete	Concrete	As cast iron	Steel plates with bedding mortar exposed in slots

T le 19   B VII Other tile and slab floorings

TABLE 19

Typical sizes[1]		Laying[2]	Surface treatment		Average cost factors[3]
Thickness mm	Width and length mm		Initial	Maintenance	
8 25	305	Flexible bedding compound	—	Wash and sweep	15
16 – 51 {	114 × 229 203 254	Bedded in mortar or bitumen Often laid with tight joints	As in-situ mastic asphalt page 273		21
6·3 25·4 over flange *Squares* 22·2–25·4 *Triangles*	229 × 229 305 × 152 and 305 mm 305 mm sides	Bedded in 19–76 mm 1 cement : 1½ sand : 3 gravel, 6·3–3·2 mm Damp cure for at least 3 days and delay use for 5 days	—	Sweep and scrub	50
12·7	305 × 152 and 305 mm	Holes filled with 1 cement : 1 granite, 3·2 mm Cure as above			
22–50	305 × 152, 305 and 457 mm	Plates 'buttered' on underside and laid, with anchors downwards in 38 mm bed of stiff 1 cement : 2 sand : 1½ gravel Cure as above	—	Sweep and scrub	74

[1] Preformed skirtings and other fittings are available in some materials
[2] Adhesives should be those recommended by the manufacturer of the flooring and should be used as they advise. (No adhesive is effective as a damp-proof membrane)
[3] Approximate cost relationships for typical floorings 'as laid', based on granolithic = 10

13 Plastering

The term *plastering* is usually applied to internal wall and ceiling finishes which give jointless, hygienic, easily decorated, and usually smooth surfaces, often on uneven backgrounds (external plastering is usually called *external rendering* – see chapter 14). Plasterwork may also be required to provide thermal insulation, fire resistance, and to contribute to sound insulation by sealing porous materials such as no-fines concrete. Special plasters are used to absorb sound within rooms and others to insulate against the passage of X-rays. (*Asbestos spray*, which provides thermal insulation, fire protection and sound absorption, is described in *MBC Materials*, chapter 10.)

This chapter deals with *In-situ plasterwork* and with *Precast plasterwork* including *fibrous plaster* and *glass-fibre reinforced plaster*. See page 327.

In-situ plasterwork

References include: BS 4049 : 1966 *Glossary of terms applicable to internal plastering, external rendering and floor screeding*.
CP 211 : 1966 *Internal plastering*.

In-situ plastering is a wet and messy process and today, brickwork, blockwork and concrete are often left unplastered, or lined with preformed boards which, however, present problems in concealing joints, or in making them aesthetically and hygienically acceptable.

In-situ plasterwork is considered under the following headings:

1 Properties of plaster finishes
2 Materials for plastering
3 Backgrounds
4 Mixes and application of plasters

1 PROPERTIES OF PLASTER FINISHES

Thermal insulation

Plaster finishes are relatively thin and make a correspondingly small contribution to the thermal insulation of ordinary buildings.

Condensation

Gypsum lightweight plasters, lime plasters and to a lesser extent sanded gypsum plasters with permeable decorative treatments absorb temporary condensation but in conditions which give rise to permanent condensation all plasters may become saturated and lose their thermal insulation value. Gypsum lightweight plaster having a low thermal capacity, warms up quickly and having superior thermal resistance tends to keep the surface temperature above the dew point of the air so that condensation does not occur.

Sound absorption

This is a property of a surface which affects the volume and character of sound in a room. See *MBC: Environment and Services* and *Materials* volumes. It is most important to understand that although sound absorbent finishes reduce the level of sound in transmitting rooms their effect on sound insulation between rooms is negligible. Ordinary plasters have low values for sound absorption – from 1 to 3 per cent, but special *acoustic plasters* have values up to 25 per cent (see page 316).

Sound insulation

The effectiveness of a solid and airtight sound barrier increases with its mass but, being thin, plaster finishes contribute significant mass only to lightweight elements. Plaster can also improve sound insulation by sealing the surfaces of porous barriers, in particular no-fines concrete, the result usually being most favourable when plaster is applied directly rather than being separated from the surface by battens.

Fire protection

Normal plasters are *non-combustible*[1], have no *spread of flame*[1], do not evolve smoke, and where adhesion to surfaces is good they contribute to the fire resistance of elements. Gypsum plaster is particularly effective and lightweight aggregates provide better fire resistance than sand. See page 315.

Corrosion of metals

Lime and Portland cement mixes which contain uncarbonated lime, or gypsum plaster mixes to which substantial proportions of lime have been added afford protection to ferrous metals, but when they are persistently damp they corrode lead and aluminium. Some *anhydrous Class C* and *Keene's Class D*[2] gypsum plasters containing a salt accelerator have an acid reaction and when they are damp tend to corrode metals. Salts resulting from the use of sea sand or from frost-proofing admixtures such as calcium chloride mixed with Portland cement, also tend to increase the corrosion of metals.

Hardness

In housing a fairly soft finish may be preferred, but in public buildings, and more so in factories, plaster finishes on walls and in particular dados and arrises must often be very hard. Arrises were formerly often plastered for about 76 mm on each return in *Keene's plaster*[2] where the main surfaces were in soft lime plaster. Today, the metal angle beads often used to protect vunerable corners also provide a line for the plasterer to work to. Finishing coats are given on page 325 in ascending order of hardness.

Texture

Smooth trowelled surfaces comprising either neat gypsum or gypsum including a fine grade of exfoliated vermiculite are the most common, but texture can be provided by manipulation of a trowel or other tools or by including sand in the finish.

Suitability for decoration

Mixes containing lime or cement are alkaline and

[1] BS 476 see *MBC: Materials*, chapter 1.
[2] BS 1191 : 1967 *Gypsum building plasters*, see page 313.

unless they are dry and likely to remain so, an alkali resisting sealer or primer is necessary, see page 17. Gypsum plasters are not chemically aggressive to decorative or protective treatments, and in particular *Classes C* and *D* can give smooth finishes suitable for high gloss paint.

Gloss, semi-impervious finishes and wallpapers should not be applied on surfaces which are not dry (see page 356) but although newly applied *Class B* plaster can be safely dried by moderate artificial heat if there is through-ventilation, or by the use of a dehumidifier, *Classes C and D* must not dry quickly.

2 MATERIALS FOR PLASTERING

These comprise binding materials, workability agents, page 313; aggregates, page 314; water, page 314; ancillary materials and premixed plasters, page 315.

Binding materials

The main materials and their more common uses are:

1 *Gypsum plasters* (calcium sulphate) for undercoats and finishing coats
2 *Portland cement*[3] – for undercoats and very hard and water resistant finishing coats
3 *Organic binders* – for single coats on true backgrounds
4 *Limes*[3] – for undercoats and finishing coats but rarely used as binders today.

1 Gypsum plasters

Gypsum (calcium sulphate), plasters which have been in general use in this country during this century are made by pulverizing and driving off more or less of the chemically combined water from natural gypsum rock which is essentially $CaSO_4$. $2H_2O$. The resulting powder is white, or coloured pink or grey by impurities which do not affect the properties of the product. BS 1191 : 1967 – Part 1 *Gypsum Building Plasters* describes four classes.

When water is added to gypsum plaster it sets and hardens into a crystalline solid, heat being evolved as it recombines with water and reverts to the dihydrate form of calcium sulphate. The reaction is *hydraulic*, ie it does not require air.

[3] see *MBC: Materials*, chapter 7.

Gypsum plasters expand slightly in setting, and while this is beneficial in forming castings from moulds and in filling cracks, the movement can cause failure in adhesion on non-rigid backgrounds such as plasterboards and smooth backgrounds such as concrete on which it is important to use *Class B* (BS 1191) *Board plaster* which has *low setting expansion*. Premature drying out of *Class C – Anhydrous plaster* and *Class D – Keene's plaster* sometimes lead to *delayed expansion* with consequent disruption of plaster. Unlike Portland cement and limes, gypsum plasters undergo negligible drying shrinkage. It is not necessary to wait for one coat to dry and crack before applying the following coat and surfaces can be trowelled to a very smooth finish without crazing. Gypsum plasters are not strongly alkaline and 'the provisions of BS 1191 virtually exclude from most types of calcium sulphate plaster those salts which are likely to lead to appreciable efflorescence' (National Building Study 2 *Painting new plaster and cement* HMSO). The rate of early strength development is superior to that of Portland cement and the final strength of a 1 plaster:1 sand mix is about the same as a 1 Portland cement:3 sand mix. Gypsum is slightly soluble in water and breaks down in persistently damp conditions so that it is not suitable for use externally.

Lime, particularly site-slaked, non-hydraulic, high calcium (fat) lime, improves the workability of gypsum plasters and may be added to all *Class A, B* and some *Class C* plasters. The factory-made *dry hydrate* which is usually employed should be *soaked overnight*, ie steeped in water for at least 24 hours to improve its *fatness* before use. Lime also counteracts any acidity and tendency to corrode metals by soluble salt or acid accelerators in *Class C* plasters.

Gypsum plaster which has already set seriously accelerates the setting of fresh gypsum plasters, and plasterer's tools and equipment should be kept free of set material. Setting is also accelerated by organic matter, and sand should comply with BS 1198 to ensure cleanliness. *Class B* plasters are accelerated by lime.

Gypsum plaster can be safely applied to dry backgrounds containing Portland cement but the two materials must never be mixed as the formation of sulpho-aluminates disrupts the plaster.

In fires gypsum plaster containing only inorganic material is *non-combustible* and does not evolve smoke or spread flame. The outer surface dehydrates first but provides an insulating layer until all the water of crystallization (about 21 per cent) is expelled. Disintegration occurs at a temperature above 110°C. Adhesion is good and various combinations of gypsum products protect steel members for $\frac{1}{2}$ to 4 hours (see page 320).

The choice of a suitable type of gypsum plaster from BS 1191 : 1967 *Gypsum building plasters* is determined by the nature of the background and by the smoothness and hardness required of the finish. (Hardness increases from *Class A* to *Class D*.)

Class A Hemi-hydrate calcium sulphate plaster (commonly called *Plaster of Paris*) results when three-quarters of the water of crystallization contained in the mineral gypsum is driven off in manufacture. Because *Class A* sets quickly its uses are limited to small areas of stopping and filling and to casting in moulds, eg as *fibrous plaster* (see page 327). Formerly non-hydraulic lime plaster was gauged with Plaster of Paris to give it early strength and hardness.

Trade names include:
  CB Stucco pink or grey
  SNB and CBD casting plasters
  Fine and superfine casting plasters

Class B Retarded Hemi-hydrate plaster in which retarders have been added to Plaster of Paris to delay the set is the most generally useful gypsum plaster. Setting times are adjusted in manufacture to give relatively slow setting for undercoats and a more rapid set for finishing coats. Non-hydraulic (*fat*) limes added to *Class B* finish coats accelerate setting but improve working qualities and reduce the hardness of the surface. Mixes should never be retempered after the initial stiffening has taken place.

BS 1191 : Part 1 specifies:

Type a *Browning* and *Metal lathing* grades including haired plasters suitable for sanded undercoats

Type b *Wall finish* or *Finish* plaster for final coats to be used neat or gauged with up to 25 per cent lime by volume

Board finish plaster which is intended for use neat as a one coat finish on boards

Trade names of *Class B* plasters include: *Thistle*

312

Class C   Anhydrous gypsum plaster

In this case gypsum is calcined at a higher temperature so that all the water of crystallization is driven off leaving *Anhydrous calcium sulphate* ($CaSO_4$). Due to the presence of a small proportion of calcium sulphate hemihydrate, setting is in two stages. The initial set is rapid and it may not be possible to apply fresh plaster before it has taken place. However, within one hour of mixing the plaster it can be *retempered* (*knocked back*), and the relatively slow final set of *Class C* plasters gives the plasterer adequate time to obtain a good flat finish, or if required, textural effects by the manipulation of special floats, sponges, brushes and other tools. On the other hand, slow setting means that care must be taken to avoid drying out before hydration of the plaster is complete, with the danger of *delayed expansion* later.

Class C plasters are not suitable on plasterboards or other boards but are used as a final coat on most gypsum or Portland cement sanded undercoats. They are applied neat, or with the addition of up to 25 per cent thoroughly slaked lime putty (by volume), or of sand if a rough texture is required.

Trade names include:
Sirapite

Class D   Keene's plaster (or 'cement')

As with *Class C* all the water of crystallization is driven off in manufacture so that the product is anhydrous. The slow continuous set and working properties allow it to be scoured with a cross-grained float and brought to a surface smooth enough for a high quality gloss paint finish. Even greater hardness makes Keene's plaster suitable for dados and it was used for exposed arrises where the general surfaces were plastered with a softer plaster. Today metal trim (see page 315) is commonly used to strengthen arrises. Important uses of Keene's plaster are for squash rackets courts and refrigerated stores.

The plaster is sold only as a finishing coat type for use neat, preferably on strong cement/sand undercoats and never on backgrounds such as plasterboards or insulating fibreboards. It should not be mixed with lime, or normally be retempered after one hour from the time of adding water to the plaster.

Trade names include:
Fine Keene's cement
White Keene's cement
Standard and fine Polar white gypsum cements

2   Portland cement

Portland cement is sometimes used as a binder in undercoats and in finishing coats where an exceptionally hard surface is required. Too rapid drying increases the likelihood of cracking and of efflorescent salts penetrating, but shrinkage must be substantially complete before a further coat is applied. See *MBC: Materials*, page 139.

3   Organic binders

These are used in *Scandinavian thin-wall or veneer type* single coat plasters, see page 324.

4   Limes

Plasters in which limes are the only binders are rarely used today. Fat lime (BS 890 : 1966) is non-hydraulic and hardens very slowly in moist conditions. Any surfaces in contact with air harden first and retard the hardening of the interior. Final strength is very low. Sand reduces the tendency for shrinkage cracks to appear on surfaces, but fat lime plaster must be applied in several coats each being allowed to dry slowly so that shrinkage movement is divided into stages. Hydraulic lime/sand mixes are similar to Portland cement/lime/sand mixes, but weaker. See *MBC: Materials*, page 137.

Workability agents

Workability agents comprise non-hydraulic lime and plasticizers based on organic materials.

Non-hydraulic (fat) lime is most plastic in the form of well matured site-slaked lime, but factory produced *dry hydrate* which is usually employed is improved by *soaking overnight*. Fat lime also reduces the strength of Portland cement and gypsum mixes. In the former it distributes shrinkage stresses by *creep*, reducing the tendency for visible cracks to form, and it retains the water which is essential for thorough hydration.

Organic based plasticizers, available in liquid and powder forms, entrain air which improves the workability of mixes.

313

Aggregates

The usual aggregates for plastering are *sand*, or lightweight *expanded perlite* and/or *exfoliated vermiculite* (see premixed plasters, opposite page).

Sand

BSs 1198 and 1199 : 1955 describe *Building sands from natural sources*. Sand obtained from a river or sandpit or by crushing sand, gravel or other stones is used in plaster undercoats, and sometimes in finishing coats for textural effect. It reduces the shrinkage of plasters containing Portland cement and lime.

Impurities – may adversely affect the rates of setting and hardening, reduce strength and cause *cracking*, *flaking*, *blowing*, *popping* and *pitting* of plaster. *Iron* which is present in most sands, in some forms affects the set of gypsum plasters. If sand is dark or reddish a trial mix should be made up. *Iron pyrites* expands in taking up oxygen and may cause stains. *Coal dust* may cause popping, pitting or blowing and excessive proportions of *flaky material* reduce strength. *Calcium carbonate* may retard the set of *Class C* and *D* gypsum plasters which contain accelerators. *Salts*, in particular *sea salt*, may affect the setting of Portland cement and gypsum plasters, lead to dampness and corrosion of metals and to efflorescence in the completed work. *Animal and vegetable matter* may retard or even prevent setting especially of Portland cement. If the colour of liquid tested as laid down in BS 812 clause 22 is darker than the standard colour 'the purchaser should request satisfactory evidence of the general performance of the material'. *Clay* (as distinct from *silt* which is very finely divided sand), increases drying shrinkage, reduces adhesion and final strength. It may accelerate the setting of *Class B* gypsum plaster but retards the setting of Portland cement and counteracts the action of accelerators used in the manufacture of *Class C* and *D* gypsum plasters. BS 1198 limits the content by weight of clay, fine silt and fine dust to 5 per cent for natural sand or crushed gravel sand and 10 per cent for crushed stone sand.

  With experience, a fair idea of the quality of a sand can be obtained by simple site tests. For example, when rubbed between the fingers sand should not ball too readily or leave stains to show impurities under a magnifying glass. A layer of silt will form after about 15 minutes on top of sand shaken with water in a glass bottle; clay takes much longer to settle. Too much iron oxide is indicated by persistent red cloudiness.

Grading A well graded sand in which the voids between the larger particles are filled by smaller particles makes for easy working and reduces the shrinkage of Portland cement and lime mixes. BS 1198 gives percentages by weight passing BS sieves for two types of sand suitable for gypsum undercoats, and a third grade for internal finishing coats of gypsum as follows:

BS Sieve	Gypsum undercoats		Gypsum fiinishing coats
	Type 1	Type 2	Type 3
5 mm	100	100	100
no. 7	90 – 100	90 – 100	100
no. 14	70 – 100	70 – 100	90 – 100
no. 25	40 – 80	40 – 100	55 – 100
no. 52	5 – 40	5 – 50	5 – 50
no. 100	0 – 10[1]	0 – 10[1]	0 – 10[1]

[1] Higher proportions of certain crushed stone material may be satisfactory.

A 5 per cent total tolerance, which can be split up between the sieves, is allowed for each type. Samples of about 0·5 kg must be carefully taken from the bulk and dried before sieving. The undercoat mixes given in table 21, page 326 are for BS 1198 *Type 1 sands*. *Type 2 sands* being finer, require more water to obtain a workable mix and as this reduces the strength of plaster, one third less sand should be used. For *Portland cement based plasters* BS 1199 gives a grading for cement/lime external renderings, internal cement plastering and lime plaster undercoats, see page 332. It shows the BS 1198 grading, *Type 3*, as being suitable for lime finishing coats.

Water

Water must be free from excessive proportions of salts and other impurities and if not suitable for drinking its suitability for plastering should be checked by analysis.

Ancillary materials

Fibres CP 211 states that goat hair is the most suitable animal hair for reinforcing plaster undercoats at the rate of 5 kg/m³, but 'at works' clean vegetable or synthetic fibres are usually incorporated in so-called *'haired' plasters*.

Bonding agents – applied to 'difficult' backgrounds give improved adhesion for plaster.

Scrim – with a mesh just large enough for plaster to pass through is an open weave fabric of hessian, cotton or corrosion-resistant metal which is used to reinforce plaster at joints between boards and slabs and in other positions where local stresses occur.

Metal beads Metal angle and casing beads are described in BS 1246 : 1959, *Metal skirtings, picture rails and beads.*

Galvanized wire netting – for use in plaster which is described by BS 1485:1948 should be 22 swg (0·71 mm) with a mesh not exceeding 51 mm.

Plasterboards see page 318.

Metal lathing see page 323.

Premixed plasters

We consider under this heading:
1 Premixed gypsum/lightweight aggregate plasters
2 Thin-wall (thin-coat) plasters
3 Acoustic plasters
4 X-ray resistant plasters

1 *Premixed gypsum/lightweight aggregate plasters*
These plasters described by BS 1191 : Part 2 : 1967 *Premixed lightweight plasters* contain *exfoliated vermiculite* produced by heating a form of mica, and/or *expanded perlite* which is produced by heating a siliceous volcanic glass.

Compared with sanded plaster mixes, premixed lightweight plasters have the advantages of being clean and accurately proportioned. The wet mix is only about half the weight of sanded plaster and the dry weight about one third. Also the thermal insulation provided by premixed plasters is better than that of sanded mixes. Thus:

Plaster	Density kg/m³	Thermal conductivity (k) W/m deg C
Gypsum/perlite *browning grade*	572	0·162
Gypsum/perlite/vermiculite *metal lathing grade*	675	0·188
Gypsum/vermiculite *bonding grade*	658	0·218
Gypsum/sand	1826	0·577

It follows that pattern staining and condensation are less likely to occur, and lightweight plasters being more absorptive than sanded plasters, condensation is less likely to show on surfaces in conditions of temporary condensation. Gypsum/vermiculite plasters adhere particularly well even to difficult backgrounds such as smooth concrete. Lightweight plaster is softer than sanded plaster but being more resilient it can accept light blows without damage and absorb movements of the background where sanded mixes would crack or lose adhesion to the background.

Lightweight aggregates also improve the *fire resistance* of gypsum plaster. For example, 2 hours fire resistance is provided to a steel column by steel lathing with 38 mm thick sanded plaster or 19 mm thick lightweight plaster.

2 *Thin-wall (thin-coat) plasters*
See *single coat finishes*, page 324.

3 *X-ray resistant plasters*
These pre-mixed gypsum plasters supplied *rough* or *haired* for undercoats and as a finish, contain a barytes aggregate. Backgrounds must be prepared, and the plaster mixed and applied in very strict accordance with the manufacturers' recommendations to ensure the calculated minimum thickness and freedom from cracking.

A trade name is *Barytite X-ray plaster.*

4 *'Acoustic' plaster*

These proprietary plasters comprising *Class B* retarded hemi-hydrate plaster ready-mixed with a porous aggregate, should be applied in two coats

315

each 6 mm thick, and for maximum sound absorption be finished with a cork or carpet surfaced float to give a rough open texture. Poor suction of backgrounds, too much water in a mix, over trowelling and thick paint coatings all reduce surface porosity and the resulting sound absorption. Decoration should consist of two thin sprayed coats of diluted emulsion paint or water-bound distemper.

Average coefficients of sound absorption for ordinary and *acoustic* plasters are:

	Frequency, cycles per second (Hz)		
	125	500	2000
Gypsum, cement or lime plasters on a solid background	0·02	0·02	0·04
12·7 mm thick acoustic plaster on haired retarded hemi-hydrate plaster	0·10	0·20	0·30

Unlike most other sound absorbent finishes *acoustic plaster* is jointless, non-combustible and can be applied to irregularly shaped surfaces. It is not suitable where knocks and abrasions are likely to occur, eg low soffits and on walls up to a height of about 2 m. A trade name is *Deekoosto*.

3 BACKGROUNDS

Properties

Backgrounds are considered under the following headings: movements, key, strength, suction, efflorescence and accuracy.

Movements

Differences in the movement of plaster and background arising from structural settlements or from changes in temperature[1] or moisture content[1] of backgrounds particularly at junctions between dissimilar backgrounds can be considerable and often cause cracking and loss of adhesion of plaster. The unrestrained thermal movement of gypsum plaster is greater than that of most backgrounds, and about twice that of brickwork and concrete.

[1] See *MBC: Materials,* chapter 1.

A straight cut through plaster is the simplest way to avoid irregular and disfiguring cracks due to differences in movement at changes in background or plane, eg at junctions between blockwork and concrete and between walls and ceilings. Alternatively metal *plaster stop beads* provide an efficient and inconspicuous controlled joint. Where the expected movement is very small the plaster undercoat can be reinforced with 90 mm wide jute scrim or with a 76 mm wide strip of expanded metal. Narrow widths of different backgrounds can be bridged by expanded metal, fixed for example to blockwork on each side of a concrete column. Spacers should be used to ensure a good key for the plaster, and building paper should be interposed to prevent the plaster bonding to the background being bridged.

Key

Voids in surfaces into which plaster can penetrate and interlock provide the most effective means of supporting the weight of plaster and resisting the effects of thermal and drying movements,[1] and for strong undercoats an effective mechanical key is essential. Wood-wool slabs, porous bricks, no-fines concrete and metal lathing provide good mechanical keys. *Bonding agents* consisting of emulsions of polyvinyl acetate (PVA) and other polymers provide good adhesion for plaster on dense and smooth concrete, glazed bricks and tiles and firm and clean painted surfaces if applied strictly in accordance with the manufacturers' instructions.

Bituminous bonding agents resist damp penetration, but they are not recommended to be used on soffits.

Strength

A background should be at least as strong and not less rigid than the plaster which is to be applied to it. It must be strong enough to restrain the drying shrinkage of Portland cement[2] and any setting expansion of gypsum plasters.

Suction

Absorptive backgrounds reduce the water : plaster ratio, which, as in the case of Portland cement mixes, increases the density and therefore the

[2] See *MBC: Materials,* chapters 1 and 2.

strength of the product. Thus, a 1 gypsum plaster : 3 sand mix on a high suction background has about the same strength as a $1:1\frac{1}{2}$ mix on a low suction background. However, an excessively absorptive background such as aerated concrete may remove water from plaster so rapidly that there is insufficient time to compact and level a surface so the adhesion is permanently weakened. Prevention of loss of water by excessive wetting of backgrounds such as aerated concrete may lead to drying-shrinkage of the concrete with consequent cracking, or to efflorescence. To reduce suction while avoiding these defects, a polyvinyl acetate emulsion bonding agent may be applied to the surfaces, or a water-retaining ingredient added to the plaster, ie either fat lime putty (BS 890) on the site, or cellulostic material as included in some proprietary plasters.

Efflorescence

Clay bricks and blocks contain efflorescent salts (see MBC: Materials, chapters 1 and 6), which may be brought forward to the surface of the wall when any water contained in them dries out. If the background is dry before plastering, and any efflorescence on plaster surfaces is brushed off before decorations are applied, there is little likelihood of trouble, but if clay brickwork or blockwork is not dry it is advisable to use an undercoat which will provide a barrier to salts. Cement based undercoats, in particular aerated cement/sand mixes, are more effective barriers than undercoats based on gypsum plaster.

Accuracy of backgrounds

On dimensionally true backgrounds one coat is usually sufficient but to obtain a true surface on an irregular background a greater thickness and hence number of coats of plaster are applied. Thus on well fixed plasterboards one set coat, and on ordinary brickwork and blockwork two coats (render and set coats) are normally required. On backgrounds which are irregular and out of plumb and line, dubbing out of depressions and three coats (ie: render, float and set coats) are necessary.

Types of backgrounds

The more common backgrounds and their preparation for plastering are discussed here:

1 Clay brickwork and blockwork
2 Concretes
3 Boards
4 Wood-wool slabs
5 Compressed straw building slabs
6 Cork slabs
7 Metal lathing
8 Dovetailed bitumen-impregnated fibre sheets
9 Wood laths

1 Clay brickwork and blockwork

The more porous clay bricks and blocks usually give a good 'natural' key, and raking out mortar joints gives a valuable key. Some bricks and blocks are manufactured with a mechanical key but dense bricks such as clay engineering bricks (BS 3921 : 1965) are usually smooth and should be treated generally as dense concrete. (Bricks and blocks are described in MBC: Materials, chapter 6 and Mortars in chapter 15.)

Before plastering, local projections should be trimmed off, dust and loose particles removed and deep impressions dubbed out. Bricks and blocks and any Portland cement/lime dubbing out should be allowed to dry and shrink and salts should be brushed off without the use of water, which would bring further salts forward when it dried out.

2 Concretes

The properties of concrete backgrounds vary widely. (Concretes are described in MBC: Materials, chapter 8.) Problems in plastering are concerned with drying shrinkage, lack of key or suction and differences between thermal movements of concrete and plaster. We now consider (i) dense, (ii) lightweight and (iii) no-fines concrete backgrounds.

(i) Dense concretes

The drying shrinkage of dense concretes varies from low to high according to quality. Any traces of mould oil reduce suction and should be removed with a suitable detergent and washed off with clean water. Where the suction of concrete surfaces is pronounced a clean water brush should be applied before plastering commences. A mechanical key can be obtained by the use of surface retarders on the formwork or by special linings

317

which provide dovetailed grooves and this is essential for undercoats with high drying shrinkage. Hacking, even if done thoroughly over the whole surface and from two directions, is of doubtful value. Other pretreatments which are sometimes recommended are *bonding agents* and *spatterdash coats* (thrown on) of 1 Portland cement: 2–3 coarse sand or proprietary mixtures which should be allowed to harden before plastering.

In most cases, an undercoat of premixed *lightweight bonding plaster* followed by a coat of premixed *lightweight finish plaster* adheres well. If the accuracy of a surface permits, one coat of neat *Class B Board finish plaster* can be applied, even on smooth concrete, while *thin-wall plasters* can be used on very accurate surfaces. In damp situations, or where plaster will be subject to rough use Portland cement undercoats should be applied on an additional bonding coat usually based on PVA or other polymers, having the manufacturers' assurance as to suitability.

(ii) *Lightweight concretes*

Aerated (cellular) concretes and those containing lightweight aggregates have high drying shrinkage and should be allowed to shrink before being plastered. Suction of products varies widely and specifications should always be obtained from the manufacturers of blocks, or for in-situ concrete from the manufacturers of the aggregate.

(iii) *No-fines concrete*

No-fines concrete provides a good mechanical key but has low to moderate drying shrinkage and suction according to the aggregate employed. Where lightweight aggregates are used, specifications for plastering should be obtained from the manufacturers of the aggregate.

3 *Boards*

Boards suitable for plastering are: (a) *plasterboards*, (b) *asbestos boards*, (c) *plastics boards* and (d) *insulating fibre building boards*.

Boards must be evenly supported and stored flat in dry conditions. Fixing methods, including details such as the widths of gaps between boards, should accord with the manufacturers' recommendations. Boards must be fixed at all edges and intermediately, to give a firm and level surface, particularly where single coat plastering is intended.

Boards should be staggered to break the joints, and to avoid unsightly cracks the latter should be reinforced, except joints between *gypsum laths* which are fixed in one plane (or alternatively a straight cut can be made in the plaster). Joint reinforcement should preferably be jute scrim, not less than 90 mm wide. If galvanized wire scrim is used cut ends should be painted. Joints are covered with the same plaster which will be used directly on the boards, the reinforcement is pressed into it, avoiding overlapping, and the plaster trowelled as flat as possible. Plastering should follow when the joints have set, but before they have dried out, and before boards become dirty or damaged. Boards having excessive suction should be sealed with one or two coats of suitable PVA emulsion. Mixes containing lime are unsuitable for direct application on boards and mixes containing Portland cement must never be used. See table 21.

3a *Plasterboards*

These boards, described in BS 1230 : 1955 *Gypsum plasterboard* (amended October 1968) comprise a solid or cellular gypsum plaster core which sometimes contains a small proportion of fibres, surfaced with heavy paper. Plasterboards are a low cost and very common form of internal wall and ceiling lining which can either be plastered or decorated direct. A proprietary partition unit comprises two plasterboards separated by an 'egg crate' cellular core and another product consists of two thick plaster boards (*gypsum planks*) stuck back to back.

The long edges of boards are bound, and shaped as shown in figure 249, but ends of boards are cut exposing the plaster core.

Properties Plasterboard is a *stressed skin* construction. As the *strength* lies mainly in the paper liners and as the strength of the paper in the machine direction is about twice that across it, it is important that plasterboard should be fixed with the bound edges running across joists or other supports. Boards have a *density* of about 849 kg/m³. *Moisture movement* is low.

Although the paper liners are *combustible* plasterboards satisfy the requirements of the *Building Regulations* 1965 for *Class 0 surfaces* because the paper surface does not exceed 0·8 mm thick and is on a *non-combustible* base, while the *spread of flame* rating of the combined product is

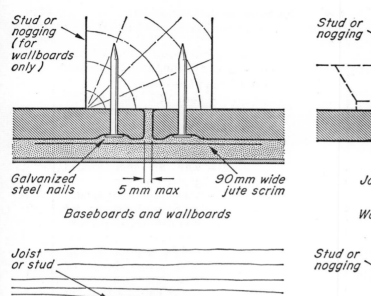

Stud or nogging (for wallboards only)

Galvanized steel nails

5 mm max

90 mm wide jute scrim

Baseboards and wallboards

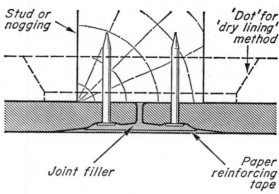

Stud or nogging

'Dot' for 'dry lining' method

Joint filler

Paper reinforcing tape

Wallboards with tapered edges

Joist or stud

3 mm max

Gypsum laths

BOARDS FOR PLASTERING
–on grey paper surfaces

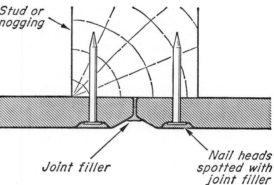

Stud or nogging

Joint filler

Nail heads spotted with joint filler

Wallboards with bevelled edges

BOARDS FOR DECORATION DIRECT
–on ivory paper surfaces

The plasterboards are shown 12·7 mm thick which is suitable for support by joists, studs or dots and dabs at 610 mm maximum centres. Supports should be at least 50 mm wide.

Boards for plastering Two-coat plaster is shown. (If one coat only is used it should be at least 5 mm thick.) Joints in gypsum laths require scrim at all wall/wall and wall/ceiling junctions.

Boards for decoration direct The tapered edges (exaggerated for clarity) are finished with *paper joint tape* firmly embedded in *joint finish* (not shown), followed by a wider band each having the edges feathered out. A thin slurry of *finisher* is then applied over the whole surface to equalize suction between the joints and boards. For ceilings a very common and simple method is to butt square edge boards closely together and smooth joints with a filler. A proprietary, flexible, textured paint is then applied over the whole surface (not shown).

249 *Plasterboard edge joints*

not inferior to *Class 1* (BS 476 : 1953). If suitably fixed, plasterboards can contribute usefully to the *fire resistance* of separating and structural elements. For example:

319

Non-loadbearing partitions

Fire resistance hours

1 *Steel or timber frames faced each side with*:

(a) 12·7 mm *gypsum wallboard*
    – unplastered

(b) 9·5 mm *gypsum lath*
    – with 4·7 mm neat gypsum plaster $\frac{1}{2}$

(a) Two layers of 9·5 mm *gypsum plasterboard* fixed to break joint or 19 mm *gypsum plank*
    – unplastered   1

(b) 9·5 mm *gypsum lath*:
    – with 12·7 mm sanded gypsum plaster
    – with 9·5 mm lightweight gypsum plaster   1

    – with 15·9 mm lightweight gypsum plaster

(c) 19·0 mm *gypsum plank*:
    – with 9·7 mm lightweight gypsum plaster $1\frac{1}{2}$

    – with 15·9 mm lightweight gypsum plaster

(d) 9·5 mm *gypsum lath*:
    – with 25·4 mm lightweight gypsum plaster   2

2 *Cellular core plasterboard partitions*

(a) 57·0 mm thick comprising two 9·5 mm *gypsum plasterboards*
    – unplastered $\frac{1}{2}$

(b) 63 mm thick comprising two 12·7 mm *gypsum plasterboards*:
    – with 12·7 mm sanded gypsum plaster each side   1

    – with 15·9 mm lightweight plaster each side   2

3 *Solid plasterboard partitions*

(a) 19·0 mm *gypsum plank*
    – with 22·2 mm lightweight plaster each side

(b) Three layers of 19 mm *gypsum plank* bonded with neat gypsum plaster   2
    – unplastered

Encasures to steel stanchions
(weight not less than 44·8 kg/m)

Fire resistance hours

Gypsum plasterboard with 1·6 mm (16 swg) wire binding at 102 mm pitch:

(a) 9·5 mm *plasterboard*
    – with 2·7 mm sanded gypsum plaster

(b) 19 mm *gypsum plank*
    – with 6·35 mm gypsum plaster   1

    – with 9·5 mm sanded gypsum plaster $1\frac{1}{2}$

    – with 12·7 mm sanded gypsum plaster or 9·5 mm lightweight plaster   2

    – with 31·75 mm lightweight gypsum plaster with corner beads or with light mesh reinforcement 12·7–19·0 mm below the surface   4

Types of plasterboards The types of plasterboards contained in BS 1230 are described here with the sizes which were available from 1 April 1970 (figures in bold type are dimensionally co-ordinated basic sizes. The other lengths will be progressively withdrawn.)

Gypsum wallboard This has one side with a cream or ivory finish ready for decoration direct with paint. The back, recognized by the double thickness of paper along the longitudinal edges, has a grey liner paper suitable to receive an appropriate gypsum plaster. The edges are square, rounded, tapered or bevelled. The shallow depressions formed by adjacent tapered edges are intended to be filled with plaster reinforced with *wallboard joint tape* and brought to a flush finish. See figure 249.

Dimensions
Thicknesses: 9·5 (except bevelled) 12·7 mm
Widths: **600**   **900** **1200** mm
Lengths: **1800** 2350 **2400** 2700 **3000** mm

Gypsum lath is a narrow plasterboard with rounded edges which is designed to receive gypsum plaster on one side only. The small size makes for easy handling and when correctly fixed movement is distributed over a larger number of longitudinal joints. Also the extra thickness of plaster at joints makes cracking less likely so they require to be reinforced with scrim only at internal and external angles.

Dimensions
Thicknesses: 9·5 mm   12·7 mm
Widths: 406 mm
Lengths: **1200** 1219 1372 mm

Gypsum baseboard is designed to receive gypsum plaster on either side. The edges are usually square but rounded edges are available.

Dimensions
Thickness: 9·5 mm
Width: 914 mm
Lengths: 800 **1200** 1219 1372 mm

Gypsum plank is a narrow board with surfaces suitable for plaster or decoration direct. Its greater thickness is useful where additional strength, sound insulation or fire protection is required.

Dimensions
Thickness: 19 mm
Width: **600** mm
Lengths: 2350 **2400 2700 3000** mm

Insulating gypsum plasterboards All types of plasterboard are available with a sheet of bright aluminium foil on one side. If the foil is fixed facing an enclosed cavity it provides thermal insulation by reflection so that the thermal conductance of the board with an adjacent cavity is 12·3 W/m² deg C for 9·5 mm boards and 13·9 W/m² deg C for 12·7 mm boards.

PVC faced plasterboards Plasterboards (not described in BS 1230) are available with both heavy and light gauge PVC veneers in plain colours and printed designs with smooth or textured surfaces. They have a *Class 1 surface spread of flame* (BS 476 : Part 1 : 1953[1]) and can be washed with a solution of mild detergent or with soapy water.

Perforated and slotted plasterboards These boards are usually fixed with a glass-fibre or mineral wool backing to increase sound absorption.

Fixing plasterboards The thickness of boards must relate to the span between fixings, thus:

Plasterboards should be fixed with their longitudinal edges at right angles to joists or other supports. All four edges of wallboards and baseboards should have a minimum bearing of 25 mm,

[1] To be reissued as Part 7.

51 mm wide noggings for edge support being inserted between the main framing where required. Plaster laths should be fixed with longitudinal edges at right angles to the main supports, 'breaking joint' on each course and with 3 mm gaps between their edges.

Thickness of board mm	Maximum centres of joists, studs and battens (spans for plaster 'ribbons' for dry linings are given in **bold** type	
	Walls mm	Ceilings mm
9·5	381 **457**	457
12·7	457 **610**	610

Fixing by nails Nails should be 14 swg (2 mm) galvanized, and with small flat heads and smooth shanks, 32 mm long for 9·5 mm thick boards and 38 mm long for 12·7 mm thick boards. Nails should be driven slightly below the surface without breaking the paper, starting from the centre of the boards, at 152 mm centres for ceilings, 203 mm centres for walls and partitions, and at 102 mm centres 13 mm from all edges.

Fixing as 'dry linings' The expression *dry lining* is applied to the fixing of *gypsum tapered edge wallboards* to walls by plaster dabs or on battens so that a true and jointless surface is obtained as described in *BRS Digest 9* and *MPBW Advisory Leaflet 64*. On walls which are reasonably true in line an allowance of 19 mm should suffice for the thickness of the finish. The method has the advantages of being 'dry' and rapid, particularly if cutting of boards is minimized. Efflorescence problems are eliminated and the cavity improves thermal insulation particularly where foil-backed boards are used. (On the other hand, on walls of bricks or blocks, sound insulation is lower than that provided by wet applied plaster.) Heavy objects can be fixed by drilling a hole in the plasterboard and injecting plaster to form a solid mass in the cavity behind, into which, when the plaster has hardened, a hole can be drilled for a plug and screw.

In the method of fixing advocated by British Gypsum Ltd, 76 × 51 mm *dots* of thin bitumen-impregnated fibreboard are bedded in *Board finish*

plaster at 457 mm centres horizontally (to suit 914 mm wide boards) and about 1067 mm centres vertically – their purpose being to *straighten* the wall and to provide a temporary means of fixing the boards. When the dots are firm, neat *Board Finish plaster* dabs, slightly thicker than the dots, of trowel length and 51–76 mm wide are applied with gaps of 51–76 mm between them. One vertical line of dabs is required at the centre of each 914 mm wide board with others set in about 25 mm from each vertical edge. Dabs are also applied horizontally between the top and bottom dots. Each wallboard which should be at least 26 mm shorter than the floor–ceiling height is pressed back against the dots and lifted gently with a foot-operated wedge until it is tight to the ceiling. The board is then secured to the outer dots by double-headed galvanized nails which can be removed and re-used when the plaster dabs have set.

The depressions formed by the tapered edges of adjacent boards are filled with proprietary *joint filler* and a special 44 mm wide *paper tape* is pressed into it. A further application of filler is used to bring the surface flush with the face of the boards and when this is hard a *joint finish* is laid in two applications in a band 203 to 254 mm wide and the edges are feathered out with a sponge. Finally, a very thin slurry of joint finish is spread over the entire board surface to remove differences in texture between the jointed areas and the plasterboards. Cut edges are less easily concealed and should be chamfered with a *Surform* type tool and be placed at internal angles. Metal reinforced tape is available for external angles which require special protection.

Preparation for plaster All joints of square-edged plasterboards, and wall to ceiling and wall to wall junctions (including external angles) between *gypsum laths*, are reinforced with 90 mm jute scrim bedded in neat *board plaster*. Boards should not be wetted before they are plastered.

3b Asbestos boards
(See *MBC*: *Materials*, chapter 3.)

Asbestos *insulating boards* and *wallboards* (BS 3536 : 1962), unlike *semi-* and *fully-compressed asbestos cement boards* are suitable for plastering if porosity is reduced with suitable primers.

3c Expanded plastics boards
(See *MBC*: *Materials*, chapter 3.)

Boards such as expanded polystyrene and foamed polyurethane, have low suction and provide adequate key for appropriate types of plaster. They have low resistance to impact and should be fully bonded to a firm background.

3d Insulating fibre building boards
(See *MBC*: *Materials*, chapter 3.)

These boards, described in BS 1142 : 1961 provide better thermal insulation than plasterboards but are combustible, have high moisture movement and are liable to fungal attack in damp conditions. They can be nailed to joists, battens or studs as follows:

Thickness of board, mm	Maximum centres of supports, mm
12·7 (1220 mm wide)	405
12·7 (915 mm wide)	455
19·0 and thicker	610

Alternatively, boards can be used as permanent formwork to concrete structures.

Insulating fibre building boards should be wetted before fixing to give a 'shrink fit' but they must dry before plastering or the bond between plaster and board may fail. The 'rough' side provides the better key for suitable gypsum plasters.

All joints must be scrimmed. (FIDOR recommend wire mesh.)

4 Wood-wool slabs
(See *MBC*: *Materials*, chapter 3.)

As described in BS 1105 : 1963 have low suction and provide a good key. Although they have high moisture movement, if they are dry when they are fixed the likelihood of shrinkage damaging the plaster is small. They may be fixed as *permanent formwork* for concrete, or nailed with sufficiently long nails. Joints between slabs should be reinforced in accordance with the manufacturers' instructions.

5 Compressed straw building slabs (Stramit) BS 4045 : 1966. (See *MBC*: *Materials*, chapter 3.)

Slabs must be kept dry. *Plaslin* slabs have plaster liners on both sides and plain paper liners treated with a PVA bonding agent provide a good mechanical key. Joints between slabs should be scrimmed.

6 Cork slabs

Cork has low suction and a variable key but pre-mixed gypsum lightweight bonding coats adhere well. With certain methods of fixing slabs, joints may require to be reinforced.

7 Metal lathing

Provides a mechanical key for general surfaces or locally where changes in background materials occur. Metal lathing being a good conductor of heat, ordinary plaster is liable to show *pattern staining*[1] but plaster on metal lathing can provide a good standard of *fire resistance* (see *MBC: S and F Part 2*). The lathing should be protected from corrosion by galvanizing[2] or by bituminous paint (see chapter 17, page 352). BS 1369:1947 *Metal lathing (steel) for plastering* describes the following types:

Plain expanded metal
Expanded metal with integral ribs
Expanded metal with attached ribs
Perforated expanded metal
Dovetailed expanded metal

Plain expanded metal with diamond shaped mesh having at least two strands per 29 mm and an aperture not less than 5 mm wide is the commonest type. It should weigh not less than 1·62 kg/m² for sanded plasters and 1·22 kg/m² for premixed lightweight gypsum plasters and be fixed to supports at 356 mm centres with the long way of the mesh across the supports. The strands of the mesh should slope inwards and downwards from the face on vertical surfaces, and on soffits the strands in adjacent sheets should all face in one direction.

It should be tensioned as tightly as possible and fixed with galvanized nails at 102 mm centres driven at an angle across the grain of timber, or with wire or suitable clips to steelwork. Edges of adjacent sheets should be lapped 26 mm over supports and wired together at 102 mm centres with 18 swg (1·2 mm) galvanized wire. To avoid rust stains appearing through the plaster, the ends of sheets and wire should be bent back from the face of the work. To ensure continuity of the key for plaster over wide supports rods or strips should be fixed between the supports and the lathing. A spiral of 3·2 mm wire at 305 mm pitch is commonly used as a spacer around steelwork and to increase the rigidity of the lathing. A lighter gauge is suitable where the lathing is fixed at frequent centres and is required only to give a key.

Plastering on expanded metal As normally fixed, metal lathing lacks rigidity and is less able than 'solid' backgrounds to restrain the drying shrinkage of cement undercoats which tend to crack and expose the lathing to corrosion. Cement undercoats are necessary in damp conditions or where cement or *Keene's Class D* (BS 1191) finishes are to be applied, but for other gypsum finishes a *Class B metal lathing grade*[3] undercoat and float coat is to be preferred and for *lightweight gypsum finishes* a *gypsum lightweight metal lathing* undercoat and float coat is usually required. Three coats are essential to obtain a smooth and true finish.

8 Dovetailed bitumen-impregnated fibre sheet (*Newtonite lathing*)

This is particularly suitable for fixing to existing walls where a barrier to damp is required. The manufacturers' advice should be obtained as to its suitability and methods of use.

9 Wood laths

These are unlikely to be used today except possibly for repairing old plasterwork. They should comply with BS 1317:1946 *Wood laths for plastering*.

4 MIXES AND APPLICATION OF PLASTERS

Adhesion requires intimate contact between surfaces, air must be expelled by force during or after applications, and for finishes subject to high drying shrinkage or to constant temperature changes a mechanical key is essential. *Bonding agents* (see pages 315–17) are useful in less exacting stress conditions. Generally no coat should be stronger than the background or the undercoat on which it is applied. Table on page 325 gives approximate thicknesses of plaster coats on common backgrounds. Table on page 326 gives typical plastering systems for premixed-lightweight and site mixed *Class B*, BS 1191 gypsum based plasters, and table on page 327 gives systems for use with Portland cement based undercoats.

[1] See *MBC: Materials*, chapter 1.
[2] See *MBC: Materials*, chapter 9.

[3] The *metal lathing grade* contains a rust inhibitor which dispenses with the need to add lime for this purpose.

The number of coats required depends upon the rigidity of a background, the 'truth' of the background and that required of the finish, and to some extent upon the type of plaster which is used. In the past, on most backgrounds after *dubbing out* any depressions, three coats of plaster were required. Today backgrounds tend to be more accurate, and while three coats are still needed to obtain a level surface on metal lathing, two coats not less than 13 mm thick can give a surface with not more than about 3 mm deviation in a length of 1830 mm (about 1 in 600) on backgrounds which reach a good standard in line and plumb. Thinner plaster is bound to closely follow the contours of backgrounds, but on very accurate backgrounds a single coat is often considered to be sufficient.

We now consider single coat and multi-coat finishes:

Single coat finishes

Single coats are bound to follow the contours of backgrounds and only well fixed plasterboards, compressed straw slabs, some cellular plastics boards, good quality concrete slabs and in-situ concrete are sufficiently true.

Single coat finishes comprise:

(a)   *Class B Retarded hemi-hydrate low setting-expansion board plasters* (see page 312).

Skim coats in these plasters should be at least 5 mm thick.

(b)   *'Thin-wall' plasters*

These have gypsum and/or organic binders. Less labour is involved in handling and application, it is possible to spray a surface and level it later and there is less water to dry out, although to secure these advantages backgrounds must be very true.

(i)   *Gypsum based thin-wall plasters*   These can be applied in an economical thickness of 2 to 3 mm.

(ii)   *'Scandinavian', 'Swedish sand putty'* or *'veneer type' thin-wall plasters*. On exceptionally accurate backgrounds a thickness of 1 to 2 mm is sufficient. Bond is good. The semi-liquid is normally sprayed on (although small areas can be applied by hand), and levelled with a broad spatula which can have a long handle to obviate the need for scaffolding.

A trade name is *Breplasta*.

Multi-coat finishes

We now consider:
1   the first undercoat
2   the second undercoat (where applicable)
3   the final coat

1   *The first undercoat*

Before applying the first undercoat it is necessary to *dub out* any depressions. Cement and gypsum plaster undercoats must be pressed well into the background which should provide a good key. Lime reduces adhesion and should never be added to first coats on plasterboards or other boards.

Undercoats must be scratched with a crossed undercut key for a cement of gypsum second undercoat and scratched for a final coat of those plasters.

Undercoats are of the following types:

Cement based undercoats – (see table 22), are necessary in damp conditions and to hold back water and less effectively, water vapour. Water repellent admixtures can help. 1 Portland cement : 3 sand (by volume) is usual on rigid and well keyed backgrounds for cement, *Keene's* and *Class C* gypsum plasters which require a strong undercoat. Cement based undercoats are suitable for *Class B* gypsum and for Scandinavian thin-wall plasters.

Gypsum based undercoats – (see table 21) adhere better than Portland cement mixes, particularly *Premixed bonding grade lightweight gypsum plaster*; also they do not shrink in drying.

Organic based undercoats   On accurate backgrounds a *backing grade* plaster may be necessary to 'true up' surfaces and normally two coats of *finish grade* are applied with an interval of twenty-four hours. A *rendering grade* is available for use on less accurate backgrounds with the advantage of greater speed over cement and gypsum based first coats.

2   *The second undercoat*

Before this coat is applied Portland cement based first coats should be allowed to develop sufficient strength before being allowed to dry and shrink. Gypsum based first coats should have set but not dried out when the second undercoat is applied.

The second undercoat must be ruled to a plane surface, if necessary consolidated with a wood float, and keyed to receive the final coat.

3 The final coat

Finishing coats must set at a rate which enables the plaster to be applied and finished level and smooth as a base for decoration. It must then provide the required degree of hardness. Finishes must be not stronger than undercoats and otherwise be compatible with them – see tables 21 and 22.

Types of finishes are now described in order of increasing hardness from (a) – (g):

(a) *Lime putty* which is a paste of water and hydrated lime could be applied on any normal undercoat but strength develops extremely slowly and is insufficient for modern buildings. The addition of sand decreases shrinkage. If lime is slaked from quicklime the process must be thorough to avoid *popping* and *pitting* of reactive particles. *Soaking overnight* improves workability.

(b) *1 lime putty* : $\frac{1}{4}$*–1 Class B plaster (BS 1191)* : *0–1 sand (by volume)*. With the higher gypsum plaster content mixes are moderately strong and provided the surface is not over-trowelled the gypsum restrains the shrinkage of the lime. The mix could be applied on most normal undercoats but not on Portland cement : fat lime : sand mixes.

(c) *Premixed gypsum lightweight plasters*. These finishes (see page 315) are intended for use on gypsum lightweight plaster undercoats.

(d) *Class B (BS 1191) gypsum plaster*. The addition of up to 25 per cent lime putty (by volume) slightly reduces hardness and improves workability but accelerates setting.

Backgrounds	First undercoat mm	Second undercoat mm	Final coat mm	Total mm
Plasterboards and insulating fibre building boards	—	—	5	5 minimum
	8	—	2	10 minimum
Concrete	—	—	2–3	2–3[1] – Class B Board finish[2] or 'Thin-wall' plaster on very true close texture surfaces only
	8	—	2	10 maximum*
Most brickwork and block-work	11	—	2	13 maximum*
No-fines concrete	11	6	2	19 maximum*
Metal lathing	4	4	2	10[3] approx. – Lightweight gypsum plasters
	8[3]	3	2	13[3] approx. – Other plasters
Wood-wool slabs	11	—	2	13
Expanded polystyrene	8	—	2	10 approx. – on ceilings
	11	—	2	13 minimum – on walls
Backgrounds treated with bonding agents	—	—	2–3	2–3⎫ Class B Board finish plaster
	8	—	2	10⎭

[1] Thickness should be obtained from the manufacturer
[2] A bonding treatment may be needed on some concretes
[3] Thickness measured from face of lathing
* The greater the thickness the smaller the strain to cause failure

Table 20 *Approximate thicknesses of gypsum based plaster coats on common backgrounds*
Greater thicknesses may be necessary on inaccurate backgrounds, or for increased sound insulation or fire resistance.

Premixed lightweight aggregate plaster (BS 1191 Part 2)		Background[1]	Site-mixed plasters		Finish coat
Finish coat	Undercoat(s)		Undercoats(s)		Class B (BS 1191 Part 1) plaster
			Class B (BS 1191 Part 1) plaster	Type 1[2] (BS 1191) sand	
—	—	Boards True concrete surfaces Expanded plastics boards	—		Board finish plaster – neat (or 'Thin-wall' plaster)
—	—	Aerated concrete slabs and block-work	not recommended		—
Finish grade (b1)	Bonding grade (a3)	Compressed straw slabs[3] Glazed surfaces treated with bonding agent Close texture lightweight aggregate concrete[3,7] Dense concrete[3] Clay engineering brickwork[3]	1 Browning grade (a1)	1½ (1)	Finish grade – neat or with up to 25 per cent lime putty
	Metal lathing grade (a2)	Plasterboards (grey side) Insulating fibre building boards	1 Haired browning grade (a1)	1½ (1)	
		Expanded plastics boards		1½[4] (2–3)[4]	
		Metal lathing[5]	1 Metal lathing grade (a2)	1½ (1) render	
				2 (1½) float	
	Browning grade (a1)	Wood wool slabs[6]			
		Dense clay brickwork with joints raked[3] – other than engineering brickwork Dense clay blockwork Calcium silicate and concrete brickwork No-fines concrete[7] Open-textured lightweight aggregate concrete[7]	1 Browning grade (a1)	2 (1½)	
		Normal clay brickwork and block-work		2–3[4] (1½–2)[4]	

[1] For description and preparation of backgrounds, see page 316
[2] If BS 1198 type 2 sand is used the proportions of sand should be reduced as indicated in parentheses
[3] May require bonding agent
[4] According to plaster manufacturers' instructions
[5] Two undercoats are required
[6] Two undercoats may be necessary
[7] Manufacturers of lightweight aggregates should be consulted

Table 21   Premixed plasters and site-mixed plasters based on Class B (BS 1191) gypsum plasters (mixes by volume)

The mixes shown are intended as a guide only and should be confirmed with the plaster manufacturer in each case.

Background	Undercoat[1]	Finish coat	
		Portland cement based	Gypsum based (BS 1191)
Strong brickwork with raked joints Strong no-fines concrete	1 PC : 3 S	Any Portland cement based finish not stronger than the undercoat	Keene's – Class D – neat
Clay, calcium silicate and concrete brickwork Clay and concrete blockwork Strong no-fines concrete	1 PC : ¼ L : 3 S		Classes B or C – neat or with up to 25 per cent lime
Backgrounds as above No-fines concrete – moderate strength Aerated concrete	1 PC : 1 L : 5–6 S 1 PC : 5–6 S with plasticizer 1 Masonry cement : 4½ S		
Backgrounds as above Metal lathing	1 PC : 2 L : 8–9 S 1 PC : 7–8 S with plasticizer 1 Masonry cement : 6 S		

[1] Undercoats containing cement or lime are not normally suitable on engineering brickwork, dense concrete, close textured lightweight aggregate concrete, and they are not suitable on boards
PC – Portland cement   L – Non-hydraulic lime putty   S – Sand – BS 1199

Table 22   Plaster mixes with Portland cement based undercoats (by volume)

(e) *Class C – Anhydrous (BS 1191) gypsum plaster* is very slightly harder than *Class B* plasters. They set slowly and can be retempered allowing ample time for finishing. The addition of up to 25 per cent lime makes for easy application.

(f) *Class D – Keene's (BS 1191) gypsum plaster* has a more gradual set and can be brought to an even smoother finish than *Class C*.

(g) *Cement : lime : sand mixes.* These finishes would normally be used internally only for extremely heavy duty, where dampness cannot be avoided and where a non-alkaline and craze-free surface is not essential. A rich mix such as 1 Portland cement : 0–¼ lime putty : 3 sand (by volume) gives maximum hardness on an undercoat of the same mix and strength. Increases in the lime : sand ratio reduce hardness and the associated tendency to crack and craze.

Precast plasterwork

On the continent, partition blocks made from gypsum plaster and straw are common. In Australia sisal fibre reinforced slabs 11 mm thick of storey height and 12 m long are used extensively as an inner leaf in framed construction requiring support only at 450–600 mm centres. In this country precast plaster takes the form of: *Bellrock* partition units which have outer surfaces of plaster with a honeycomb core, *fibrous plaster* and *glass fibre-reinforced plaster*.

FIBROUS PLASTER

Fibrous plaster (or '*stick and rag work*') (not to be confused with plaster which contains fibres), is precast *Plaster of Paris* reinforced with jute scrim, wood laths and occasionally with wire netting. Plane surfaces are superior to those which can normally be obtained in trowelled work although distortion can present some difficulty in accurate matching of adjoining units. Flexible moulds enable intricate detail to be cast, and at low cost for quantity production. For internal use standard louvres for air bricks and encasures for columns and beams are made in fibrous plaster.

327

Units of fibrous plaster can be made in any size which is convenient for conveyance to the site and for fixing. Fixing is rapid and simple, usually by nails to timber grounds, or by galvanized wire fixed to metal grids. Wads of scrim soaked in plaster are used to reinforce fixings where additional strength is required. Only nail holes and joints require to be made good with plaster, so that the process on the site is almost completely dry.

GLASS-FIBRE REINFORCED GYPSUM

The BRS has developed spraying and pressing techniques for the manufacture of *glass-fibre re-* *inforced gypsum (grg)* products such as partition units, slabs for use instead of floor boards, and diamond shaped pyramidal panels which can be bolted together to form a dome. Although unsuitable in damp conditions, glass-fibre reinforced gypsum products have good strength properties, fracture is quasi-plastic rather than brittle and there is no loss of strength after 6 months at 40 per cent RH and 18°C. Fire resistance is excellent and moisture expansion is low. Table 23 compares the properties of an asbestos cement sheet with those of a glass-fibre reinforced gypsum plaster board.

	Flexural strength N/mm^2	Tensile strength N/mm^2	Impact strength N/mm^2	Moisture expansion per cent	Fire resistance
Asbestos cement[1] sheet	28	14	1·75–2·50	0·2	Poor
Glass fibre[2]-reinforced gypsum plaster board	24–35	12–18	44–53	0·02	Excellent

[1] 10–15% asbestos: ordinary Portland cement by weight. See *MBC: Materials,* chapter 10.
[2] 6–10% glass fibre: gypsum plaster by weight

Table 23   Comparison of the properties of an asbestos cement sheet and a glass-fibre reinforced gypsum plasterboard

14 Renderings

Renderings[1] modify the weather resistance, colour and texture of external wall surfaces. The recommendations in CP 221 : 1960 *External rendered finishes* should be followed.

We consider, in turn: 1 Durability and weather resistance; 2 Backgrounds; 3 Mixes; 4 The coats; 5 Application; 6 Detailing.

1 DURABILITY AND WEATHER-RESISTANCE

Differential drying and moisture movements, and thermal movements greater than occur internally, give rise to shear and/or tensile stresses between the background and rendering, or between coats. Ice reduces adhesion to backgrounds, and in persistently wet conditions sulphates derived from clay bricks or other sources attack Portland cement in mortar joints and in the rendering. Expansion of jointing material cracks renderings, further water enters and the deterioration becomes progressive.

In ordinary exposures moderately strong and dense cement: lime : sand rendering mixes provide satisfactory weather resistance. They absorb some rain, but when it stops it can evaporate freely if the outer surface is left unpainted. Incidentally, mixes containing lime are better able to retain water, which makes for thorough hydration of cement on absorptive backgrounds. However, dense renderings are necessary in severe exposures although they are particularly prone to *crazing*[2] and because they are strong their shrinkage is less easily restrained by the background and cracks result. Water which flows down the non-absorptive surface enters the cracks and is unable to

evaporate outwards so that a dense rendering can, in fact, reduce the weather resistance of a wall. In practice in severe exposures it often becomes necessary to fill cracks as they occur and to paint renderings.

2 BACKGROUNDS

Table 24 summarizes the main properties of common backgrounds. For good adhesion they must be rigid, free from dust, dirt, oil, grease, paint and efflorescence. Some suction is necessary to prevent the material sagging or sliding after application, and a spatterdash treatment is recommended where suction is high or irregular.

Physical adhesion is insufficient and an effective mechanical key must be provided. Mortar joints in brickwork and blockwork should be raked out to a depth of at least 13 mm and brushed clean. Smooth concrete should provide a dovetailed key from rubber formwork liners or by the use of surface retarders (see chapter 16, page 343). Hacking hardened concrete is a costly alternative while superficial treatments such as light *sparrow picking* are of little value.

No-fines concrete provides a good mechanical key and so do wood-wool slabs although here little restraint is afforded to thermal and moisture movements, and bitumen coated metal lathing should be fixed over them.

Renderings cannot 'bridge' structural movement joints and at junctions between dissimilar backgrounds, eg reinforced concrete columns and adjacent lightweight concrete infill panels, joints should be provided. Alternatively expanded metal can be used to prevent concentration of movement as described for plastering in chapter 13.

Renderings must not be stronger than the background, so that it may be necessary to apply strong renderings on expanded metal lathing fixed to battens which have been impregnated with preservative.

---

1 The term *rendering* is confusingly also applied to first coats on brickwork, blockwork and masonry internally.
2 *Crazing* is a surface network of fine cracks produced by the carbonation of cement laitance caused by overworking a surface or by evaporation of excess water. Disfigurement is less with mixes of lower cement content and with textured and scraped finishes.

Type	Properties			Remarks
	Suction	*Key or bond*	*Movement*	
Dense, strong and smooth, eg — high density bricksand blocks — dense concrete	Low to moderate	Poor. Mechanical key needed. Hacking may be needed even if brick joints are raked	Low to high. Clay materials may expand Concrete materials may shrink	The risk of efflorescence is lower than with more porous backgrounds
Moderately strong and porous, eg — most bricks and blocks	Moderate to high	Good if joints well raked out, keyed bricks are used, or if spatterdash or other bonding treatment is applied	Shrinkage moderate to high for materials other than clay brickwork or blockwork which may expand	If suction is high or irregular, a spatterdash treatment is recommended Risk of efflorescence with some products
Moderately weak and porous, eg — lightweight aggregate and aerated concretes — low strength bricks	Moderate to very high	Moderate to good	Shrinkage, low to high	Background should be dry, (and therefore 'preshrunk') Risk of efflorescence with some products Strong renderings may shear the background surface
No-fines concrete	Low to moderate according to aggregate type	Good mechanical key	Low to moderate	Sufficient strength to resist shrinkage stresses
Metal lathing (BS 1369)	—	Good	None if lathing is tightly stretched	Use a dense and relatively impervious mix for the first undercoat, and 'back plaster', if possible, to prevent rain penetration and to protect the lathing

Table 24 Backgrounds for renderings (Based on CP 221 : 1960)

3 MIXES

Table 25 recommends mutually compatible undercoat and final coat mixes for various backgrounds and exposures, and for four types of finish. It will be seen that 1 Portland cement : 1 lime : 5–6 sand is suitable for most purposes and is preferred for many purposes, the stronger mixes being recommended only for strong backgrounds or where they are needed to resist knocks and abrasion or to retain dry-dash.

330

Background (see table 24)	Type of finish	Type of mix* for given exposure conditions†			
		'Severe'		'Moderate' or 'Sheltered'	
		Undercoat(s)	Final coat	Undercoat(s)	Final coat
Dense, strong and smooth Moderately strong and porous	Wood float	1, 2 or 3	1 or 3	1, 3 or 4	1, 3 or 4
	TEXTURED (Including SCRAPED)	3	3	3 or 4	3 or 4
	ROUGHCAST	1, 2 or 3	as undercoats	1, 2 or 3	as undercoats
	DRY-DASH	1 or 2	2	1 or 2	2
Moderately weak and porous	Wood float				
	TEXTURED (Including SCRAPED)	3		3 or 4	
			as undercoats		as undercoats
	ROUGHCAST	3		3	
	DRY-DASH	2 or 3		2 or 3	
No-fines concrete	Wood float	1, 2 or 3	1, 2 or 3	1, 2, 3 or 4	1, 3 or 4
	TEXTURED (Including SCRAPED)	1, 2 or 3	3	2, 3 or 4	3 or 4
	ROUGHCAST	1, 2 or 3	1, 2 or 3	1, 2 or 3	1, 2 or 3
	DRY-DASH	1 or 2	2	1 or 2	2
Metal lathing	Wood float	1, 2 or 3	1 or 3	1, 2 or 3	1 or 3
	TEXTURED (Including SCRAPED) ROUGHCAST	1, 2 or 3	3	1, 2 or 3	3
	DRY-DASH	1 or 2	2	1 or 2	2

* MIXES:

Type 1 1 Portland cement : 0–¼ fat lime : 3 sand (by volume)

Type 2 1 Portland cement : ½ fat lime : 4–4½ sand (by volume)

Type 3 1 Portland cement : 1 fat lime : 5–6 sand (by volume)

Type 4 1 Portland cement : 2 fat lime : 8–9 sand (by volume)

Spatterdash – to provide a key – 1 Portland cement : 1½–2 sand (by volume); to overcome irregular suction on porous backgrounds – 1 Portland cement : 2–3 sand (by volume)

† *Exposure Gradings*

Severe Exposure to the full force of wind and rain, as with buildings on hills or near the coast, and tall buildings in towns.

Moderate Walls protected by eaves or other projections, and by neighbouring buildings, such as buildings in towns and suburbs.

Sheltered Walls in districts of low rainfall, and those in close proximity to other buildings, such as ground and first floor walling in towns.

Proprietary *masonry cement* : sand mixes may be used as alternatives to Types 3 and 4 but mix proportions should be in accordance with manufacturers' instructions.

Where renderings are required to resist moderate sulphate action, *sulphate-resisting Portland cement* may be used instead of the Portland cement given in the mixes above.

Sand to BS 1199 : 1955 – preferably Table 1 of the BS.

Where alternative sand contents are shown, (eg 4–4½, 5–6, and 8–9) the higher proportion should be used if the sand is well graded, and the lower content if the sand is coarse or uniformly fine.

Table 25 Recommended mixes for external renderings (Based on CP 221 : 1960)

The types of finish shown in capitals and the mixes shown in bold type in the table are those to be preferred in most circumstances.

Materials used in renderings include:

*Ordinary and rapid hardening Portland
    cements* BS 12
Sulphate-resisting Portland cement[1] BS 4027
Masonry cement
High alumina cement[2] BS 915
Limes BS 890

Plasticizers BRS tests have indicated that cement/sand mixes plasticized by air-entraining agents or mortar plasticizers sometimes have less satisfactory resistance to rain penetration than cement/lime/sand mixes of similar strength. Proprietary mixes based on masonry cement which contain a fine mineral filler in addition to an air-entraining agent were nearly as effective as cement/lime/sand mixes.

For the above materials see *MBC: Materials* chapter 7.

Sand should be clean, sharp and preferably comply with table 1 of BS 1199 : 1955 *Building sands from natural sources, Sands for external renderings, internal plastering with lime and Portland cement and floor screeds* which is quoted below:

BS sieve	Percentage by weight passing BS sieves
5 mm	100
no. 7	90 – 100
14	70 – 100
25	40 – 80
52	5 – 40
100	0 – 10[3]

Impurities – see Sand for plaster, page 314.

Natural aggregates other than sand BS 882 : 1965.

Pigments White or coloured Portland cements can be used in the finish coat or pigments can be added to ordinary Portland cement on the site.

[1] Sulphate-resisting cement is advisable for renderings, and mortars in chimneys, parapets and free-standing walls which are constructed with clay bricks of *ordinary quality* (BS 3921 : 1965)
[2] High alumina cement is used only where special conditions justify its high cost.
[3] In the case of certain crushed stones, higher proportions may be satisfactory.

Unfortunately the white film of calcium carbonate (*lime bloom*) which forms on drying, tends to give coloured renderings a faded look, more so on the darker colours.

Water should be free from salts and other deleterious substances.

Metal lathing (steel) for plastering BS 1369 : 1947.

4 THE COATS

One coat is rarely able to accommodate the irregularities of suction which occurs between small units or to prevent mortar joints 'grinning through'. One undercoat and a final coat are usually sufficient in moderate exposures but in severe exposures three coats are recommended A *spatterdash* (thrown-on) coat bonds well and evens out the suction on backgrounds, and applied as a continuous covering on relatively even surfaces it may be considered as being the first coat in a three-coat (but not in a two-coat) system.

Undercoats should be 10 to 16 mm thick. Final coats are normally 6 to 10 mm thick, but where they are machine applied, as little as 3 mm.

Undercoats

Undercoats can prevent rain penetrating, align or straighten uneven surfaces and prevent backgrounds 'grinning through', and they must provide uniformly moderate suction and good adhesion for the finishing coat. Mixes must be sufficiently strong to obtain a good key but if they are stronger than the background or a previously applied undercoat, cracking and loss of adhesion often occur.

Undercoats, if not left rough, should be scratched to provide a key. Each coat should be left to dry and shrink for at least two days in summer and a week in cold or wet weather, before the next coat is applied.

Undercoats (and spatterdash coats) which will be subject to moderate or severe exposures may benefit by the inclusion of water-repellent cement or a water-proofing admixture.

Finishing coats

Finishes, especially those rich in cement, containing fine sands or finished with a steel trowel are liable to surface crazing and unavoidable variations in surface texture give a patchy appearance.

Rain streaks are more obvious on smooth than on textured surfaces. Finishes considered in order of increasing durability, resistance to rain penetration and to irregular discolouration are:

Wood floated finishes

Renderings lightly patted with a wood or felt-faced float provide a uniform, flat surface free of scouring marks. Crazing, cracking and uneven weathering may result if too much cement and/or fine sand are used or if surfaces are overworked.

Scraped surfaces

A truly aligned, recently set finish is usually scraped with a steel straight-edge or old saw blade thereby removing 2 to 3 mm from the surface which includes the laitance which would tend to crack or craze. Scoring marks result where granular material is dragged across surfaces and coarse particles produce a 'travertine' effect.

Ornamental textures

During application and while a surface remains plastic (suction of undercoats must be low), combed, ribbed, stippled and the bold *English cottage texture* effects can be obtained.

Thrown finishes

These comprise *wet dash* and *dry dash*. A typical hand-thrown wet dash (or *roughcast*) is 6 to 13 mm cement coated aggregate thrown on a suitably matured undercoat. Dry proprietary compositions, obtainable in a wide variety of colours, give a range of textures (including *Tyrolean*), when they are machine applied. Some manufacturers provide premixed undercoats.

Dry-dash finishes result where 'dry' 6 to 13 mm pebbles (hence *pebbledash*), shingle or spar, are thrown on and lightly pressed into a freshly applied final coat of mortar so the aggregate is left substantially exposed. The final coat must be strong enough to hold the aggregate, ie not weaker than 1 cement : 1 lime : 6 sand.

5 APPLICATION

After 'slaking the thirst' of absorptive backgrounds but without saturating them, a high standard of workmanship is needed to produce functionally and visually satisfactory renderings. Force is necessary to expel air and bring the rendering into intimate contact with the background. Throwing on, manually or by machine, gives better adhesion than 'laying-on' with a trowel and is particularly advisable for first coats on smooth backgrounds.

Apart from *English cottage textures*, renderings should be applied from the top downwards. If work cannot be completed in one operation, straight *day joints* should be located at window heads, sills or other architectural features.

Work should not continue at freezing temperatures or when night frosts are likely. On the other hand, work should be done out of bright sunlight or drying winds, and in hot weather damp curing is recommended.

6 DETAILING

The following principles should be observed in detailing renderings:

1 Large areas should be avoided by providing movement joints where necessary.
2 Horizontal surfaces must be protected by flashings, copings and sills, with drips to throw water well clear of walls. Damp-proof courses should be provided below mortar jointed copings and sills. See figures 113, 119 and 250.

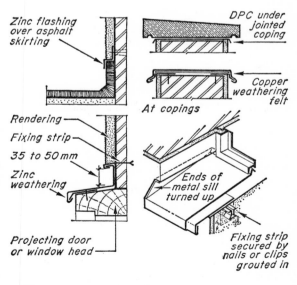

250 Protection of renderings

3 Where there is any possibility of water penetrating behind renderings, flashings and weep holes must be provided to conduct it outwards.

4 Parapets and free-standing walls should not be rendered on both sides and it is better not to render chimney stacks.

5 Renderings carried across damp-proof courses are a common cause of dampness in the lower parts of walls. Renderings on walls below dpcs are pushed off by salts from soils and water rises by capillary movement between the rendering and wall and by-passes the dpc.

15 Wall tiling and mosaics

Wall tiling and mosaic wall coverings consist of relatively thin and small units which are usually fixed by adhesion. They may be required to improve appearance or to improve resistance to abrasion or staining. Glazed tiles are particularly easy to clean and special epoxy based jointing grouts can be used where sterile conditions are essential. Materials include ceramics, concrete – including terrazzo, glass, stainless steel and plastics. In addition, quarries and tiles such as linoleum, cork and rubber which are intended primarily for flooring are often used for walls, particularly at dado level. Tiles which absorb sound include perforated and slotted insulating fibre building boards. The choice of materials which are durable externally is limited to high grade ceramics, concrete, glass and stainless steel.

Ceramic wall tiling

Ceramic, ie clay, wall tiles are resistant to staining and attack by chemicals and if properly fixed good clay tiles retain their natural colour and gloss indefinitely. They are hard and robust but should not be used, particularly on arrises, where collisions are likely to occur. Externally a frost resistant product is essential and where severe chemical attack may occur clay tiles should comply with BS 3679 : 1963 *Acid-resisting bricks and tiles* and the jointing material and possibly the bedding must be chemically resistant. See BRS Digest 120.

CERAMIC TILES FOR INTERIOR USE

Most ceramic tiles for interior use have an earthenware body made from a mixture of ball-clay, china clay, calcined flint and cobalt oxide which help to produce whiteness, and limestone to limit shrinkage in firing. Each ingredient is ground and mixed with water, the separate slurries being mixed together to form a *slip*. Water is extracted and the clay is pressed into packs which are dried and crushed. The resulting dust is moistened slightly and tiles formed by die-pressing have finer surfaces than can be obtained by other means. Firing in kilns at about 1100°C takes up to ten days.

A glaze ground to a fine powder and suspended in water is put on the *biscuit* which is fired again in a tunnel kiln. The tiles are then separated into *Specially selected tiles* which are free from all blemishes, and into *Standard quality tiles* which are adequate for many purposes.

Surfaces are: *high glaze* (glossy), *eggshell*, *satin* and *matt*.

Tiles are made in white and a very wide range of colours (*enamel glazes*). One manufacturer produces two hundred colours, thirty-five of which are available from stock. Mottled effects and patterns are also available.

It may not be easy to match old colours, even if the manufacturer's colour number or description is known but modern colour ranges are very consistent and a reasonable match should be obtainable. In the past, colour designs other than mottled effects had to be done by hand and their high cost, particularly where many colours are used, may still be justified for important work. Today, however, patterns are silk-screen or transfer printed, and some ripple-textured tiles are available at the same price as plain tiles. Some patterned tiles can be arranged in various ways and combinations to form larger patterns.

Tiles with a moulded face, termed *profiled* or

sculptured tiles, are available in a range of standard designs.

Sizes

BS 1281 : 1966 *Glazed ceramic tiles and tile fittings for internal walls* specifies properties and gives details of tests for warpage and curvature, water absorption and resistance to chemicals, impact and crazing. It gives the following *preferred nominal sizes*:

$152 \times 152 \times 5$ and 6 mm } tiles with cushion
$108 \times 108 \times 4$ and 6 mm } edges and spacer lugs
$152 \times 152 \times 10$ mm { tiles without cushion edges and spacer lugs

Great advances have been made in the control of sizes and the above lengths and widths are subject to tolerances of $+0.6$ per cent and -0.3 per cent with a maximum of ± 0.4 mm in any one order based on average dimensions of a batch of at least thirty-five tiles sampled as laid down in the British Standard.

In addition, BS 1281 recommends *basic sizes* (which include the tile and its share of the joint) for dimensionally coordinated tiles of:

$$100 \times 100 \text{ mm and } 200 \times 100 \text{ mm.}$$

Actual sizes which take into account manufacturing tolerances and an absolute minimum width of joint of 1.6 mm are 98×98 and 197.5×98 mm ± 0.5 mm on the lesser dimension and ± 1 mm on the greater dimension. Internal tiles are at present made in the following sizes:

Square tiles

$25.4 \times$ 9.5 mm
$50.8 \times 6.35, 9.5$ mm
$76.2 \times 6.35, 9.5$ mm
101.6×6.35 mm
$101.6 \times$ 9.5 mm (12.7 mm *three dimensional tiles*)
$107.95 \times 3.97, 6.35$ mm
$152.4 \times 4.76, 6.35, 9.5$ mm (15.9 mm *three dimensional tiles*)

Rectangles

$101.6 \times 12.7, 25.4, 50.8,$ $\times 6.35, 9.5$ mm
107.95×6.35 $\times 6.35$ mm
$152.4 \times 6.35, 12.7, 25.4, 50.8, 76.2 \times 6.35, 9.5$ mm

$152.4 \times 101.6 \times 9.5$ mm
$203.2 \times 101.6 \times 6.35, 9.5$ mm
$215.9 \times 107.95 \times 6.35$ mm
$217.5 \times 107.95 \times 6.35, 9.5$ mm

Hexagons

50.8, 57.15, 76.2, 101.6 measured from side to side $\times 9.5$ thick.

Fittings

Fittings are tiles which provide curved junctions at internal and external right angles and a finish to exposed edges of tiled areas. They include *round edge, cushion edge* and *attached angle* tiles, *beads* and *cappings*.

Round edge tiles are flat tiles with one edge, or two opposite or adjacent edges rounded, the latter being termed an *external angle tile*.

Cushion edge tiles have a very slight radius at the glazed edges, and must not be confused with round edge tiles.

Attached angle (or *combination*) *tiles* are flat tiles with a short return on one or two edges. They are glazed outside for external angles and inside for coves.

External angle (or *quadrant*) *beads* and *internal angle* (or *cove*) *beads* are made with maximum overall widths of 31.75 and 50.8 mm.

Cappings are 50.8 and 76.2 mm wide with one or two attached external angles to the long edges.

Angle beads, attached angles and cappings are made with external radii of 22 and 35 mm. Coves and attached angles are made with internal radii of 12.7 and 25.4 mm.

Accessories

Soap dishes, tumbler and tooth brush holders, coat hooks, toilet paper holders and other accessories are made to suit standard tile sizes.

EXTERNAL AND HEAVY-DUTY CERAMIC TILES

Externally in this country frost resistant tiles are essential. These may be internal tiles the surfaces of which have been treated with a water repellent or the pores of which are filled with wax. Alternatively, highly vitrified tiles (fired at about 1250°C), usually extruded and necessarily thicker than internal tiles, can be used. Some of the latter type are unglazed.

Heavy-duty tiles (not all of which are frost resistant), are often used internally for their decorative appearance and/or for hard wear. Applications include floorings, swimming pools and industrial uses such as vessel linings, eg stock chests in paper mills.

Available sizes include most of those given for internal wall tiles and in addition:

73×73
98×98
149×73
152×152
$\left.\right\} \times 10$ mm

102×102
152×51 and 76
241×114
250×60
$\left.\right\} \times 13$ mm

152×152
196×96
200×48
$203 \times 102*$
242×51 and 114
250×51
254×63 and 127
$\left.\right\} \times 16$ mm

220×40
228×73, 79, and 152
242×57
$\left.\right\} \times 20$ mm

203×203
228×228
305×203 and 228
$\left.\right\} \times 25$ mm

* This modular size includes one joint. Some tiles of this size are extruded in pairs back to back and must be separated before use.

Larger sizes up to $610 \times 304 \times 32$ mm are usually called *Ceramic wall facing tiles*.

Blocks can be purpose-made in glazed faience or unglazed terra-cotta – see *MBC: Materials*, chapter 5.

Fittings such as angle returns are made to suit some external tiles.

FIXING TILES

The relevant Codes of Practice are: CP 212 : Part 1 : 1963 *Internal ceramic wall tiling in normal conditions* and CP 212 : Part 2 : 1966 *External ceramic wall tiling and mosaics*.

Expert advice is available from the *British Ceramic Tile Council*, Federation House, Stoke-on-Trent, Staffordshire.

Almost all surfaces can be satisfactorily tiled but the method of fixing must be appropriate to the properties of the tiles and background, and to the climatic exposure and other service conditions. Bedding materials and joints have a very important bearing on success. Each of these factors is considered in turn:

Properties of tiles

Ceramic tiles are rigid and thermal movement can normally be ignored. New tiles, however, like bricks (see *MBC: Materials*, chapter 6), absorb moisture and expand when they are removed from the kiln, although this movement is likely to be partially complete when tiles are fixed. Reversible moisture movement is negligible.

Properties of backgrounds

Some backgrounds are too weak, in themselves or in their adhesion to a wall, to support tiling. Tiles, as distinct from slabs, are fixed by adhesion and movement of backgrounds is the most common cause of loss of bond and cracking of tiles. Such movements arise from structural deformations, including creep, and from changes in temperature and moisture content. Fixing should not be undertaken on certain calcium-silicate bricks, on dense concrete and in particular on lightweight aggregate and aerated concretes, until they have thoroughly dried and shrunk. Serious reversible movements may occur in fibreboards, chipboards and plywood. To avoid tiles being cracked by disparate movements of adjacent backgrounds, metal lathing or wire netting is sometimes fixed across the junction, but a movement joint in the tiling is recommended. Other properties of backgrounds which affect adhesion are mechanical key, porosity, suction and chemical characteristics. Soluble salts may be harmful, particularly sulphates if the background is constantly wet.

On some true backgrounds tiles can be fixed directly with a thin-bed adhesive. On backgrounds which are not plumb and level, however, and on expanded metal a *floated* or *rendering coat* of cement and sand (rather than plaster) should be provided.

Floated coat

Backgrounds must provide an effective key. Smooth surfaces must either be hacked to a depth of 3 mm over at least half the area, or a *bonding agent* may be used as advised by the manufacturers. Surfaces must be wetted to adjust suction before applying the floated coat.

The floated coats must be firmly applied but not overworked. They must be sufficiently strong, but not stronger than the background or the undercoat on which they are applied. The high drying shrinkage of unduly rich cement mixes may cause failure. Where appropriate, sulphate resisting Portland cement should be used and where severe sulphate concentration is likely to occur high alumina cement should be used.

If a greater thickness than 13 mm is needed to provide a level surface it should be built up in coats each not more than 10 mm thick, the undercoat being allowed to dry out and shrink before the following coat, which should not be stronger than the undercoat, is applied. Additions such as lime, and air entraining agents should only be used under strict control.

CP 212 Part 1 : 1963 and Part 2 : 1966 recommend mixes for floated coats on various backgrounds as shown in table 26.

Background		Floated coat§ **
Glazed bricks and tiles Sheets, boards and compressed straw slabs‡ Plasterwork (dry, strong and adherent)‡		None
Dense, strong and smooth	High density clay brickwork and blocks*† Dense concrete (pre-cast or in-situ)* Natural stone*†	1 Portland cement : 3 sand[1] to
Moderately strong and porous	Clay and concrete bricks – raked joints Hard sand lime bricks – raked joints† Medium density concrete – hacked	1 Portland cement : 4 sand[2]
Metal lathing No-fines concrete – dense or lightweight aggregate		
Moderately weak and porous	Lightweight aggregate concrete Aerated concrete Soft sandlime bricks – raked joints	1 Portland cement : 4 sand[1] to
Metal lathing on wood wool‡ or compressed straw slabs‡		1 Portland cement : 5 sand[2]

* May require hacking
† May require metal lathing or wire netting
‡ Not recommended externally
§ Alternatively, masonry cement and sand or air-entrained cement and sand mixes of equivalent strengths, can be used as recommended by manufacturers.
** Floated coat mixes must also suit the method of fixing to be adopted.

[1] and [2] To improve workability fat lime is sometimes added to cement : sand mixes as follows:
  [1] up to ¼ part; [2] up to ½ part. Thorough mixing is, however, essential.

Table 26 Floated coats for tiling on various backgrounds – mixes by volume

Methods of fixing

Tiles can be fixed in four ways depending upon the flatness and other characteristics of backgrounds. The advice of manufacturers of proprietary products should always be followed, particularly as to the time which should elapse between applying a float coat and fixing tiles. After fixing, external tiling should be protected from frost and rain.

1 The sand–cement (traditional) method

1 Portland cement : 3 to 4 sand (by volume) is usually suitable on Portland cement-based floated coats which have been scratched to provide a key (see table 26). Mixes stronger than 1 : 3 should not be used and although plasticizers, waterproofers, fungicides and other admixtures are sometimes useful it is most important to ascertain that they will not adversely affect adhesion. Tiles should preferably not be fixed until the floated coat is at least two weeks old and thoroughly dry. Immediately before tiling it must be wetted sufficiently to prevent loss of water from the bedding material. The more porous tiles should be soaked in clean water for at least half an hour, drained and stacked before use in the manner described in CP 212. Each tile should be 'buttered' with mortar over the whole of the back. Solid bedding is particularly important where mechanical damage is likely or where entrapped water might freeze. After tapping tiles firmly into position the bed thickness should not be less than 6·5 mm for tiles up to 152×152 mm and up to 9·5 mm for larger tiles. The surface should be cleaned off after 1 to 2 hours.

2 The cement-based mortar (thin-bed) method

CP 212 : 1963 : Appendix B gives performance standards for these adhesives. They are satisfactory for fixing tiles which are not deeply keyed on many backgrounds which are true and plumb to within $\pm 1·6$ mm in any distance of 3 m. Cement-based thin-bed adhesives are suitable both internally and externally, but not on wood-wool slabs, plasterwork, compressed straw slabs, plasterboards, glazed bricks or tiles.

Cement-based mortar can either be applied to walls with a notched trowel as a thin screed, or be 'buttered' over the backs of tiles so its thickness does not exceed 3 mm. Tiles must be dry when they are fixed.

3 The mastic adhesive (thin-bed) method

These proprietary mastics permit a joint thickness of about 2 mm. Some are flexible, and bond dry tiles even to surfaces such as chipboards, plaster work and glazed tiles. Some are suitable for service in hot or damp conditions. In all cases they should comply with CP 212:1963:Appendix A *Performance requirements for mastic adhesives (organic)* and be used in strict accordance with the manufacturers' instructions. Grouting or pointing should not be done for twenty-four hours after fixing, and preferably longer where tiles are fixed on low porosity backgrounds.

4 The thick-bed adhesive method

Adhesives are available which can accommodate irregularities up to about 13 mm in the length of a wall.

Joints

Joints must allow a degree of micro-movement. The jointing material must, therefore, not be too strong and the joint must not be too narrow. The spacer lugs on some tiles provide a sufficient and uniform width.

For small tiles on a stable background a minimum joint of 2 mm is recommended but wider joints are necessary for larger tiles and less stable backgrounds, eg 10 mm is recommended for some external tiles. Additionally, movement joints at least 6 mm wide should be provided in the bedding and tiling. Inside buildings they should occur at internal angles and at distances not exceeding 4·5 m vertically and horizontally. Externally, they should occur at storey heights, preferably where changes in structural materials take place, and vertically at about 3 m intervals. Movement joints in the structure must of course be carried through the floated coat, bedding and tiling.

Joints must be grouted or pointed, preferably with proprietary products, to prevent ingress of dirt, moisture and corrosive substances. The mix should be crushable; neat cement should never be used. For joints up to 5 mm wide the mix is brushed on as a grout, worked into the joints with a squeegee and 'pencilled in'. Wider joints are filled with a pointing tool. In both cases surplus material is removed as the work proceeds and when the mix is hard the tiling should be polished with a dry cloth. Movement joints should be filled with a suitable elastomeric mastic, see *MBC: Materials*, chapter 16.

Mosaics

Mosaic tesserae, typically $19 \times 19 \times 5$ mm, of glazed or unglazed ceramics, glass and marble are usually supplied glued face down on paper which is later removed, or with nylon strips, nylon net or similar material glued to their backs which will be embedded in the bedding mortar.

Floated coats should be provided as for tiles, to which a bedding mortar of 1 Portland cement : 3 to 4 clean sharp sand (by volume) is applied not more than 10 mm thick. Up to $\frac{1}{2}$ volume of hydrated lime can be added to the richer cement mix

provided it is thoroughly mixed in. The backs of paper faced mosaic should be pre-grouted to fill the joints between the tesserae, and differences in level of the backs of marble mosaic should be made out with 1 cement : 2 fine silver sand. The mosaic is then beaten into the bedding without delay. Nylon-backed and similar mosaics are grouted after fixing is completed.

Alternatively, mosaics can be fixed to floated backgrounds with cement-based *thin-bed* mortar not more than 3 mm thick or to backgrounds such as plaster with a mastic adhesive. *Thick-bed* adhesives are sometimes used.

After removing any paper facing and glue, and rubbing a grout over the mosaic it should be cleaned down.

Movement joints should be provided as for tiling.

16 Integral finishes on concrete

Structurally sound concrete[1] is essential, but many other criteria must be satisfied in order to achieve concrete surfaces which are aesthetically satisfactory. References include: *Recommendations for the production of high quality concrete surfaces*, Cement and Concrete Association Limited and *Guide to Exposed Concrete Finishes*, M. Gage, The Architectural Press Limited.

Colour can be provided by cements and aggregates, and some of the latter sparkle. Formwork imparts shapes and textures which can be modified mechanically and to a small degree chemically. Nevertheless, unless special precautions are taken, concrete may be patchy in colour and texture and defects such as the following may occur:

Efflorescence (or *lime bloom*) – is a persistent chalk film which may form rapidly on surfaces where lime liberated by cement and carried through concrete as it dries is carbonated by carbon dioxide from the air.

Crazing – is a pattern of fine, shallow cracks which often divide very smooth surfaces into areas about 5 to 25 mm across. It is associated with carbonation of 'wet' mixes which have not been adequately cured.

Honeycombing results from undersanded mixes, segregation if concrete is allowed to flow in the formwork, inadequate compaction or leakage of mortar from formwork.

Blow holes Small blow holes in surfaces are almost unavoidable but their number and size can be reduced by the use of absorptive linings (the use of vacuum forms prevents them).

Surfaces of uniform colour and texture are the most difficult to obtain, crazing and other defects are more apparent and runnels of water show as dirt stains in polluted atmospheres and of algae in clean air.

In so far as visual requirements affect the type of cement, type, size and grading of aggregate and the depth of cover required on reinforcement, the

[1] See *MBC: Materials*, chapter 8.

structural engineer must be consulted at an early stage, and special care must be taken to ensure:

(i) *Uniformity of batching and mixing* The colours of cements and aggregates vary and they should be obtained in large batches from the same sources. Variations in grading of aggregate, and water migration between parts having different mix proportions cause variations in colour. Because cement and sand adhere to the mixer drum and blades, the first batch of concrete should not be used for work which is to be exposed to view.

(ii) *Low water/cement ratio*—crazing is more likely to show where a high water/cement ratio both facilitates the migration of lime and reduces the density and strength of concrete. Absorbent formwork is not recommended as a means of reducing the water/cement ratio of surfaces – see (vii).

(iii) *Avoidance of segregation during handling, placing and compaction.* Placing should be in shallow layers, commence as soon as possible and proceed continuously until in-situ concrete has been placed between construction joints or moulds for precast work have been filled.

(iv) *Complete compaction* especially at vertical surfaces, where a slicing tool may be usefully employed to avoid honeycombing.

(v) *Correct positioning and design of construction joints in in-situ work* because they are always apparent, even after a surface has been bush hammered.

(vi) *Freedom from rust stains* Ends of binding wires should be turned inwards, and wire, nails and other ferrous debris must be removed from the formwork before concrete is placed.

(vii) *Limited and uniform suction of formwork surfaces* Absorbent formwork is generally more likely to cause variations in the colour of finished concrete surfaces than non-absorbent formwork (although it is less likely to cause *blow-holes*). Uniform suction can be obtained by applying a thin but complete coat of a *parting agent* to formwork, which can be done more evenly by spraying rather than by brushing. Straight oil often gives good results, particularly on impermeable formwork, but water in oil (not oil in water), or chemical release agents have the advantage of remaining effective for a number of uses. Good results have also been obtained by soaking formwork before concrete is placed in it and keeping it wet until the concrete has hardened.

(viii) *Leak-proof joints to formwork* Migration of water and entry of air through joints causes variations in colour and honeycombing. Butt joints, and even tongued and grooved joints, in timber should be sealed with foamed plastics strips. Joints in formwork constructed of materials which have less movement, such as plywood, plastics and steel, should be sealed with masking tape.

(ix) *Rigid formwork* Lack of rigidity causes distortion, and air which enters open joints discolours concrete.

We now consider integral surface finishes, first on in-situ concrete and then on precast concrete.

INTEGRAL FINISHES ON IN-SITU CONCRETE

1 Effects obtained from formwork or liners

Shapes, including complex shapes in high relief, can be formed by timber, steel or glass-fibre reinforced plastics (GRP). Almost any texture can be obtained, either from the formwork itself or from liners such as: hardboard, plywood, vacuum-formed plastics sheets, moulded rubber sheets, rigid cellular plastics or foamed polystyrene which is easily worked and removed when it has served its purpose; it can be used once only. Surface retarders can be applied to formwork to delay the setting of cement – see 3 (v). The tendency of glass-like surfaces to craze can be reduced by adding a water repellent to concrete mixes. Where a smooth finish is required formwork should be struck as soon as possible so that minor projections can be removed by rubbing down the whole surface with a planed end-grain wood block, or a rubber-faced float lubricated with water. Surface voids can then be stopped with fine mortar.

Board-marked surfaces In recent years sawn timber boards – sometimes sand-blasted to emphasize the grain – have been used as formwork. For a satisfactory impression on the concrete, absorbency should be reasonably uniform and edges and ends should be jointed with tongues. By chamfering the edges of the boards projecting fins can be formed on the concrete.

The aggregate transfer method conceals any variations there may be in the colour of the structural concrete. Selected aggregate is stuck to the rough side of peg-board type hardboard formwork liners which have been coated with water soluble cellulose-bound mortar. After the concrete has been placed and hardened, the peg-board is stripped, leaving the aggregate adhering to the concrete. The surface is then scrubbed to remove adhesive and sand.

2 Effects obtained in placing concrete

(i) *Hand-placed aggregate* Aggregate can be positioned by hand, or distributed over and then pressed into, horizontal slabs of 'green' concrete.

(ii) *'Sand-bed' method* On the site, this method is suitable only for soffits. Larger aggregate is embedded by hand in a layer of dry sand which has been spread evenly on the formwork. The backs of the stones are covered with 1 cement : 3 sand (parts by volume), followed by ordinary concrete. When the formwork is removed the sand falls away leaving the aggregate exposed in one plane on the surface. Vibration would displace stones and cause mortar to run through to the face.

(iii) *'Naturbetong'* This system, developed in Norway, exposes coarse aggregate so that it lies in one plane. Either dry coarse aggregate, which excludes materials smaller than 15 mm, is placed in the formwork and mortar is injected into it, or alternatively the aggregate is vibrated into mortar which has been placed in the formwork. The first method is generally more suitable for slender vertical elements and the second method for horizontal elements. After 12 to 20 hours the cement and fine aggregate is removed from the face by sand blasting.

3 Effects obtained after placing but before concrete has hardened

(i) *Floated and trowelled surfaces* The hand

operations for finishing horizontal surfaces are dealt with under *Floorings*, chapter 12.

(ii) *Rotary surfacers* can be used to give a smooth and reasonably level finish to flooring and other large horizontal surfaces.

(iii) *Screedboard tamped and rolled surfaces* Upper surfaces of slabs can be patterned in relief by dropping a screed board, or for a bolder texture a scaffold pole, on them at regular spacings. Notched screed boards can be drawn over a surface, or rollers or tampers with patterned surfaces can be used.

(iv) *Spraying* Where new concrete surfaces are not enclosed by formwork, cement and fine material can be removed with a water spray.

(v) *Brushing* 16 to 18 hours after casting ordinary Portland cement concrete and curing it at an air temperature of about 15°C, aggregate can be exposed by brushing vigorously while hosing with clean water. The damp surface is then brushed with a 10 per cent solution of hydrochloric acid and finally hosed with water. Where it will not be possible to obtain access to surfaces at such an early stage the setting of cement near surfaces can be safely delayed by spreading a *retarder* uniformly on the contact surfaces of formwork at the rate of coverage recommended by the manufacturer. If this is done, immediately after carefully removing the formwork, the aggregate can be exposed by brushing, followed by hosing down, and light brushing to remove remaining loose material.

(vi) *Scraping* Surfaces which are accessible soon after casting can be scraped, eg with an old saw blade.

4 Effects obtained on hardened concrete

(i) *Tooling* Hardened concrete surfaces can be worked with a point or other mason's tool. After at least three weeks the larger aggregate can be exposed by *bush hammering* which should be done uniformly and without chipping the aggregate. Tooled surfaces usually look best when they are either contained within smooth faced margins or carried round chamfered corners.

(ii) *Abrasive blasting* Interesting textures and modelling can be obtained by this method although like other mechanical treatments it emphasizes rather than conceals imperfections in concrete surfaces. It can be carried out at any time but more rapidly on green concrete. Precautions must, of course, be taken to avoid inhaling dust. Varying degrees of texture are given by sand, grit and shot. *Blast carving* of cellular concrete has been skilfully exploited by William Mitchell. Coarse aggregate which is harder than the matrix can be exposed to up to one-third of its mean size. It is worth noting that shot which lodges in cavities can cause stains.

(iii) *Grinding and polishing* Grinding is usually done 'wet' with a carborundum wheel, often to remove unintended projections, preferably 24 to 36 hours after striking formwork. Surface voids are stopped with fine mortar. Grinding and polishing after a further seven days or so, are costly and are usually confined to small areas. Terrazzo is always ground. See chapter 12.

INTEGRAL FINISHES ON PRE-CAST CONCRETE

The control which can be exercised over materials and processes, and the availability of techniques such as hydraulic pressing make for the production of superior products in the factory which can, and should, be thoroughly matured and thereby 'preshrunk' before use.

Most of the processes which have been described for finishes on in-situ concrete are applicable also to pre-cast concrete but techniques which are not practicable on the building site include the use of:

(i) *Special moulds*, eg stainless steel, vacuum-formed thermoplastics, plastics-glass-fibre, and for 'pre-cast' stone, rubber bearing the imprint of natural stones.

(ii) *Special mixes* (a) *non-homogeneous* By casting special mixes as a facing on ordinary concrete, the use of relatively costly aggregates and cements may become economic.
(b) *homogeneous* 'Faircrete' (John Laing Concrete Ltd) is a patented air-entrained concrete incorporating fibres with either dense or lightweight aggregate. It is extremely workable so that it gives a very faithful impression from formwork

and can readily be formed while it remains plastic, into complex and deeply profiled shapes. However, slump is negligible and such shapes are accurately retained.

(iii)   *Casting, either face up or face down – as convenient.*

(iv)   *Acid etching*   The surface should be wetted thoroughly before applying dilute hydrochloric acid which after five minutes should be well hosed off to prevent yellow stains.

(v)   *Splitting*   Exposes irregular surfaces which are free from efflorescence, the cause of pronounced crazing. In a process developed at the BRS, tubes which are incorporated in concrete slabs are inflated while the mix is still green to split them into two units with a contrast between the appearance of smooth grooves and irregular projecting ridges.

(vi)   *Mosaic*   Used as permanent shuttering, the tesserae are placed individually or mounted on paper in the base of the mould, the joints are grouted with 1 white or coloured cement : 5 sand (parts by volume) and the normal backing concrete is placed.

17 Thin surface-finishes

Finishes may be required to protect surfaces from rain, sunlight, abrasion, chemical liquids and fumes, micro-organisms, fungi, insects and fire. They may be required for hygiene, to reflect or diffuse light, to provide colour and/or pattern, to define areas visually or to absorb sound.

This chapter deals with thin surface-finishes under the following headings:

Painting

Painting is the application to surfaces of pigmented liquids or semi-liquids, which subsequently harden. We are concerned here mainly with site-applied finishes.

Useful references are:

BRS Digest 21 *New types of paints*, HMSO
BS 2015 : 1965 *A glossary of paint terms*, BSI
CP 231 : 1966 *Painting of buildings*, BSI
Introduction to paint technology, The Oil and Colour Chemists' Association.
Painting from A to Z, J. Lawrence, The Sutherland Publishing Co. Ltd.

COSTS OF PAINTING

Surface finishes represent up to five per cent of the initial cost of a typical building, but the recurring costs of materials, plant, labour and inconvenience occasioned by their maintenance may represent as much as twenty-five per cent of the cost of a building during its life. It follows that more costly but more durable finishes, in particular many factory-applied finishes, are often cheaper in the long run.

Because the cost of labour, plant, etc, greatly exceeds the cost of paint, using cheap and inferior paint or skimping the preparation of surfaces is false economy, and generally for external work an extra coat is a good investment. It is also sound economy to reinstate the surface of a paint film before it has deteriorated to the extent that it becomes necessary to remove the whole film, to repair any rotted timber and corroded metal, and to prepare, prime and paint the background.

LIVES OF PAINT SYSTEMS

Inside buildings the life of a paint film is usually thought to have ended when it is faded, dirty, chipped or scratched. Externally, protection is usually the main need. Table 27 gives life expectations for various protective systems applied to vertical surfaces, but lives may be much shorter:

on horizontal and inclined surfaces,
in abnormally corrosive atmospheres,
where the wrong system is adopted,
where preparation is inadequate,
where application techniques, or conditions during application were poor.

NUMBER OF COATS

The minimum number of coats for ordinary work are given below. The durability of an external paint film is usually directly related to its thickness.

Surface	Externally	Internally
New	4*	3*
Old paint in good condition	2	1

* Including primer.

Externally this should be at least 0·125 mm. A normal coat of paint rarely exceeds 0·05 mm thick,[1] and at least four coats are usually required.

[1] There is a temptation to apply paint in thick coats but they are more liable to form wrinkles. Also, in evaporating, solvents in paints tend to form pin-holes or to soften the outer layer. Paints which combine with oxygen from the atmosphere are therefore generally mechanically sounder where they are applied in thin coats.

A greater number of coats is justified on surfaces which are difficult to reach, which are not vertical, or face south.

Internally, a greater number of coats may be needed to provide acceptable opacity and a superior finish.

THE PAINT SYSTEM

Ordinary paint systems comprise: a primer, undercoat(s) and finishing coat(s), each of which performs a specific function, although in finishes such as emulsion paint two or more functions are performed by one material.

Primer

The primer must adhere to surfaces, including those which are shiny, chemically aggressive and those which move or are very hot. Suitable primers are used to seal porous surfaces which would cause loss of gloss in the finish, and to equalize suction on surfaces such as old plaster which has been repaired and would lead to a very uneven sheen or gloss. Various primers minimize *bleeding*, eg of bitumen, staining by resin or sapstained timber and attack by alkalis in the background.

On metals, etching and corrosion-inhibiting primers are important.

Undercoats

The first undercoat should follow as soon as the primer is hard.

Undercoats must provide obliteration, and adhere well to the primer and to each other. They should fill minute surface depressions and provide a good base so that the finishing coat will not 'sink' and lose its gloss. With paints containing synthetic ingredients it is no longer necessary to rub down

Type of coating (normal number of coats)	Background	Average life – years
Long-oil alkyd-based paint finishing systems with suitable primers and undercoats	timber	3 – 5
	ferrous metals	3 – 7
	aluminium concrete masonry renderings	3 – 8
Cement paint	brickwork, concrete, renderings	5
Special protective paints, eg micaceous, iron oxide, aluminium, coal-tar epoxy	steel – with thorough surface preparation	5 – 10
Thick PVC coatings Thin PVF films	galvanized sheet wood, asbestos cement, metals etc.	10 – 20
Thick coatings containing mineral aggregate	concrete renderings masonry	
Vitreous enamel	steel, cast iron, aluminium	at least 20

Table 27   Lives of protective systems on vertical surfaces
The shorter lives in the ranges given can be expected facing south and in severely polluted or marine atmospheres. Lives are even shorter on sloping surfaces and where materials and workmanship are poor.

newly applied coats to obtain a key, but 'flatting' of undercoats – preferably 'wet' – is necessary to obtain a first-class finish.

In applying coloured paint each succeeding coat should be readily distinguished, although the colour of the last undercoat should be near to, but lighter than the finishing coat, the latter often being less opaque than the undercoats.

Finishing coat

The finishing coat forms the final protection against the weather, chemical and mechanical damage, and finally determines texture and colour.

In diminishing order of smoothness surfaces can be described as: *full gloss*; *semi-gloss*; *eggshell* (*lustre, satin, velvet* or *suede*) – these have 'sheen'; *flat* or *matt*.

Gloss reflects light directly, so that its effect on surfaces illuminated with a point source of light is to accentuate the slightest irregularities.

Gloss and eggshell paints do not collect grime as readily as matt and textured paints, and give good protection. Resistance to moisture is good and some of them are suitable externally. Flat paints are usually permeable and partly 'hide' condensation.

Colour

British Standard Specifications for paints used in building employ the terminology of the *Munsell system*, ie *hue, value* and *chroma* (*HV/C*) defined in BS 1611 : 1953 *Glossary of colour terms used in science and industry*, as follows:

Hue – commonly referred to as 'colour', eg red, yellow, blue, green, etc.

Value (*reflectance value* or *lightness*) is a measure of the light reflected, irrespective of hue and chroma.

Chroma (*saturation* or *intensity*) is the intensity of a particular hue compared with a neutral grey of similar lightness.

A very wide range of paints of varying hues, values and chroma, including the 101 colours, black and white of BS 2660 : 1955 (amended 1966) *Colours for building and decorative paints*, is held in stock by paint manufacturers, and special paints can be made to order.

It is important to note that all colours 'fade' when exposed to short wave radiation and that many paints which are suitable for use inside buildings would not achieve a satisfactory *Paint Research Station 'colour permanency rating'* if they were used externally.

Because the finishing type of many modern paints, such as modified alkyds, is more durable than the undercoat type, externally two finish coats are sometimes applied *gloss on gloss*, one of them taking the place of the last (or only) undercoat. Internally, however, since the finish type paint tends to flow away from high spots the undercoat is required to give obliteration on rough surfaces.

COMPOSITION OF PAINTS

All paints contain a *binder* (or *medium*) which hardens. Other ingredients found in various paints include:

> *pigments, stainers, extenders, driers, catalysts* (or *hardeners*), *thinners* or *solvents* and *gelling agents*. Some water-thinned paints (see page 352) include *emulsifiers*.

The preparation, proportioning and mixing of paint ingredients was formerly done by the craftsman, but today most paint is provided ready for a stated use. Paints of the same brand and type can be intermixed to vary their colour and a suitable thinner may be added if it is required but otherwise no addition should be made to the factory product, and different brands should not be intermixed.

Binders (*media* or *vehicles*)

The binder must bind the other ingredients together, adhere to and sometimes penetrate or seal the surface. When the paint has been applied, the medium must harden at a rate suited to the method of application, whether by brush, roller, spray or by dipping.

Various hardening mechanisms of paints are set out in table 28. Common binders are glue, casein, natural drying-oils – now usually *modified*, natural or synthetic thermoplastic and thermosetting resins, bitumen and cement. The distinction between paints and plastics coatings is not clearly defined; most paints are now based on synthetic polymers, but some 'plastics coatings' are deposited from solution in the same way as cellulose paints.

Binder	Durability	Cost	Hardening mechanism
Cements	High	Low	Chemical moisture re-action
Glue and casein-bound non-washable distemper	Low	Low	Evaporation of water and gelling
Polymer emulsions	Medium/high	Medium	Evaporation of water and coalescence
Drying oils eg linseed, tung and soya – in washable distempers	Low	Low/medium	Evaporation of water and some oxidation
– in paints – straight oil and oleo-resinous	Low/medium	Low/medium	Evaporation of thinner, absorption of oxygen from air and polymerization
– oil modified resins, eg air-drying alkyds	Medium/high	Medium/high	
Natural resins uncombined with oils, ie shellac	Low	Medium	Evaporation of thinner and deposition of resin
Thermoplastics in solution, eg celluloses, vinyls, acrylics	Medium/high	Medium	Evaporation of solvents
Bitumen	Medium/high	Low/medium	
Chlorinated rubber	Medium/high	Medium	
Two-pack epoxides and polyurethanes Coal-tar epoxides	Medium/high	High	Evaporation of solvents and complex chemical change
Thermosetting polymers – some urea and melamine formaldehydes	Medium/high	Medium	Evaporation of any solvent present, crosslinking and oxidization
– alkyds	Medium	Medium	
– polyesters	High	High	Polymerization by catalyst
Plastisols[1]	High	High	Coalescence on heating
Organosols[1]	High	Medium	

[1] see plastics coatings , page 369.

Table 28   Types of binders and their hardening mechanisms

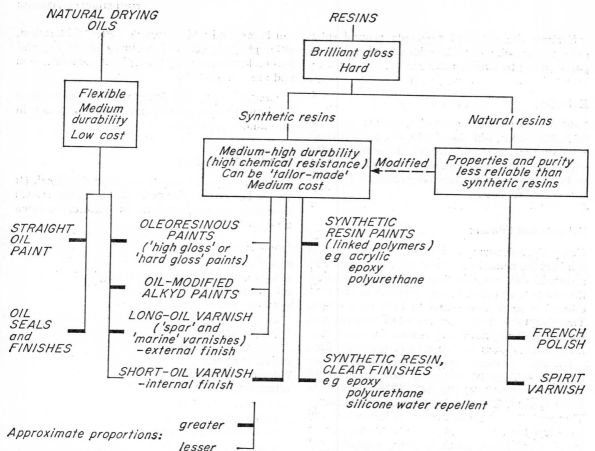

NATURAL DRYING OILS

Flexible
Medium durability
Low cost

STRAIGHT OIL PAINT

OIL SEALS and FINISHES

OLEORESINOUS PAINTS ('high gloss' or 'hard gloss' paints)

OIL-MODIFIED ALKYD PAINTS

LONG-OIL VARNISH ('spar' and 'marine' varnishes) – external finish

SHORT-OIL VARNISH – internal finish

RESINS

Brilliant gloss Hard

Synthetic resins

Medium-high durability (high chemical resistance) Can be 'tailor-made' Medium cost

Natural resins

Modified

Properties and purity less reliable than synthetic resins

SYNTHETIC RESIN PAINTS (linked polymers) e g acrylic epoxy polyurethane

SYNTHETIC RESIN, CLEAR FINISHES e g epoxy polyurethane silicone water repellent

FRENCH POLISH

SPIRIT VARNISH

Approximate proportions: greater / lesser

251 Oil and resin binders (or media)

Driers and catalysts

Paints which contain drying oils dry in two stages, first by evaporation of thinners and solvents, then by oxidization and polymerization of the oil. Driers catalyse and speed up the process of early drying.

Catalysts – or *hardeners* – either as a separate component, or incorporated in *single part* (or *single pack*) paints, induce an irreversible chemical change leading to hardening of non-oxidizing systems.

Pigments

Pigments are fine powders or flakes derived from organic and inorganic sources which impart colour to paints, together with opacity, 'body' and sometimes chemical resistance, rust inhibition and increased durability.

White pigments – Titanium dioxide the most common white pigment has excellent opacity and is available in *chalking* and *non-chalking* forms.

White lead (basic lead carbonate) combines well with oil and is easy to apply. The film is very elastic and highly resistant to penetration of moisture and weathers by *chalking*, providing a good surface for redecoration. However, sulphur gases in urban atmospheres turn white lead to black sulphide. Also lead compounds are poisonous and paint containing soluble lead must not be sprayed, or rubbed down 'dry'. It should not be used indoors – particularly in kitchens and nurseries – and never on toys!

Other white pigments include: *zinc sulphide* (lithopone), *antimony oxide* and *zinc oxide*.

Coloured pigments   All colours are available, although they are not all equally light-fast. For example iron oxides provide reds and browns and zinc and lead chromates give the brighter yellows.

349

Stainers are coloured pigments ground in a paint vehicle which can be added to already prepared paints to modify their colour.

Extenders

Extenders are finely ground minerals such as china clay, mica, whiting (chalk), silica and barium sulphate (barytes). They have little or no opacity when they are mixed with oil but give body, help to keep pigments in suspension, harden the film and reduce its cost.

Solvents and thinners

Generally, solvents are added in manufacture and thinners are sometimes added later to render oils, resin and wax miscible with each other, to adjust the viscosity of paint, to suit the method and conditions of application, and to help penetration. They evaporate during the drying of the paint and should leave no deleterious residue. Excessive thinning reduces gloss and density of the paint film.

Oil and oleo-resinous paints were traditionally thinned with turpentine, but now *white spirit (turpentine substitute)* (BS 245 : 1956 amended to 1963) is used. Bitumen is thinned with naphtha. Thinners such as those used in cellulose lacquers have low flash points and require special care in use. Cement paint, emulsion paint, washable and non-washable distempers are thinned with water and this non-combustible and cheap thinner is being used increasingly for factory-applied primers.

Other constituents

Flatting agents are sometimes added to reduce the gloss of the dried film.

Gelling agents   Gelled or thixotropic paints include ingredients which give 'false body' to gloss, semi-gloss and emulsion paints. They do not settle in the can and do not require stirring before use. More paint can be carried by the roller or brush and larger brushes can be used because they drip less than 'liquid' paints.

The movement of a roller or of the bristles of a brush breaks down the gel and the paint flows freely, although in so doing it tends to follow surface irregularities. The paint resumes its gelled condition after application so that heavier coats

can be applied which provide better obliteration, although thick coats of ordinary paints dry and harden less thoroughly throughout their thickness and are less durable.

Emulsifiers are included in washable distempers (oil-bound water paints), emulsion paints and in bituminous emulsions.

TYPES OF PAINTS

The main types of paints are now described. (It should be noted at this point that some terms such as *enamel, lacquer, synthetic* and *plastics* are often used loosely.)

Paints for general uses:

straight oil
oleo-resinous (*high-gloss* or *hard-gloss*)
oil-modified alkyd
synthetic resin
  acrylic resin
  polyurethane
  epoxy (epoxide) resin
cellulose nitrate
chlorinated rubber
bituminous
water-thinned paints
  limewash
  non-washable distemper
  washable distemper
  emulsion paints
  cement paints
  synthetic resin/aggregate finishes

Paints with special properties: page 353
  special properties in application
  special properties in service

Paints for general uses

Straight oil paints

These paints are uncommon today except as primers. BSs 2525–2532 : 1954 describe *Ready-mixed oil-based undercoating and finishing paints (exterior quality)*. Based on natural drying oils, usually thinned with white spirit, straight oil paints have relatively low flow properties, and gloss. The oil, which dries by the absorption of oxygen causing polymerization, is liable to *saponification* by alkalis of which Portland cement is a common source in building.

Drying oils include the following:

Linseed oil occurs in various forms:

Raw linseed oil (BS 243 : 1936 amended to 1952), produced by crushing flax seed pods, is yellow in colour. It is available as:

Boiled linseed oil (BS 259 : 1936), produced by heating raw oil in air for several days and adding driers, is much darker in colour, quicker drying and gives a film which is more resistant to moisture, harder and glossier than that provided by raw oil.

Pale boiled oil (BS 242 : 1936) bleached with Fuller's earth is suitable for delicate tints.

Stand oil produced by prolonged heating of a refined oil to a high viscosity is pale and flows well, giving a full gloss.

Blown oil is produced by blowing air through a heated oil so that it thickens, becomes much darker and dries faster.

Other natural drying oils – For light tints linseed oil has been largely superseded by tobacco oil, soya bean oil, dehydrated castor oil and others, which all show less yellowing on ageing.

Oleo-resinous paints (*high-gloss* or *hard-gloss* paints)

Oleo-resinous paints (sometimes misleadingly referred to as 'synthetic paints'), comprising drying oils reinforced with natural or synthetic resins, show a marked improvement in gloss, durability and other properties over straight oil paints, but like them oleo-resinous paints have been largely supplanted by oil-modified alkyd paints.

Oil-modified alkyd paints

These paints which are flexible and very durable are the most common type of high gloss paints. The resin never exists as a separate entity, but is 'built-in' by reacting a complex acid with a complex alcohol in the presence of a drying oil.

Synthetic resin paints

This description can be applied to paints which contain substantial proportions of synthetic resins, such as acrylics, polyurethane and epoxides.

Acrylic resin paints Polymethyl methacrylate which is water-white and holds colour well is the basis of some rapid drying and extremely durable factory finishes and emulsion paints.

Polyurethane paints Air-drying, single-part paints are used like alkyd gloss paints but have better resistance to water, alkalis and wear. Chemically-curing two-part polyurethane paints are hard, tough, have good resistance to chemicals, and may have better resistance to weather than epoxy paints. However, they do not adhere well to all surfaces and intercoat adhesion may be poor.

Epoxy (epoxide) resin paints

Single-pack epoxy ester paints are tougher and have better resistance to water, alkalis and possibly to abrasion than oil-modified alkyds. In this respect they are similar to the one-pack polyurethane paints.

Two-pack epoxy paints have excellent resistance to abrasion, severe alkaline attack, oils, fatty acids and solvents. Resistance to immersion in water and to continuous condensation is intrinsically poor although it can be improved by heat curing. Two-pack epoxides have great cohesive strength and for that reason must not be applied on plaster. Adhesion to concrete is excellent but steel must be grit blasted and an etching primer may be essential on other metals. They 'chalk' fairly rapidly externally, but further breakdown is slow.

After the catalyst is mixed into the paint the *pot life* is 24 hours or less. At 18°C the paint should be hard in six hours and have full chemical resistance in seven days but below 10°C the rate of cure is very slow or may cease completely.

Suitable uses include: floors, laboratory furniture and machinery.

Synthetic resin/aggregate finishes. See 6, page 353.

Cellulose nitrate paints (or 'lacquers')

These paints, based on cellulose nitrate compounds, contain suitable solvents, alkyd resins as plasticizers for flexibility and toughness, and resins for hardness and body. They dry by evaporation of the solvent without any chemical change.

Previously applied cellulose nitrate (and also oil-based) paints, would be lifted by brush-applied cellulose nitrate, and for this reason and because it dries very quickly, it is best applied by spraying.

Nitro-cellulose finishes contain less solids than oil or ole-oresinous paints so that more coats are required, but by applying a number of translucent coats graduated colour effects can be obtained.

The paint presents a serious fire risk in storage and during application and the hardened surface has *rapid spread of flame*. It is used for some factory finished components but on the building site its use is mainly confined to 'metallic finishes' on metal balustrades and shop front sections.

Chlorinated rubber paints

These finishes dry by solvent evaporation requiring specially formulated primers and undercoats to resist softening by the solvents in the following coat. The paints offer considerable resistance to a wide range of acids and alkalis, and to sulphur dioxide, white spirit and sea water, and are used in chemical factories, laboratories, gas works, dairies, swimming pools and in marine conditions. They resist mould growth, and resistance to moisture penetration is high, but they are not flexible and resistance to heat is poor. The range of colours is restricted by the requirement for the maximum chemical resistance. Chlorinated rubber paints can be applied by brush, roller or spray.

Bituminous paints

As the term is ordinarily understood, these paints are made from bitumen, asphaltum, pitch or resin, sometimes with heat-treated oil, and solvents. Bituminous paints are described by BS 3416 : 1961 – amended 1963, *Black bitumen coating solutions for cold application*, and BS 1070 : 1956 *Black paint (tar base)*. Bituminous products are black, or if pigmented, dark in colour, apart from those which include aluminium to reflect heat and reduce degradation by light. They are largely used for protecting steelwork from corrosion. Suitably formulated as thixotropic or heavy-duty paints, thicknesses up to 0·125 mm can be applied in one coat. They adhere well, are flexible and resist moisture and chemicals, but tend to disintegrate or crack in hot sunlight.

Bituminous paints contain strong solvents and should not, therefore, be applied over paints which contain oil other than red lead primers which are thoroughly hard. Conversely, oil paint is best not applied on bituminous paint – even if a sealer is used to stop the latter bleeding through, movement of bituminous paint is likely to lead to crazing. Special bituminous paints include BS 3416 : 1961 Type II, which must be free from toxic ingredients, for treating drinking water tanks.

Black Japan, made from a superior grade of bitumen cooked with oil and blended with copal varnish, provides a hard but elastic film which does not bleed, and is heat resisting.

Black varnish consisting of tar thinned with a solvent, often used for dipping rain water goods at works, is very cheap but difficult to overpaint satisfactorily.

Water-thinned paints

Water-thinned paints are generally less durable than other paints but easier to apply; a 178 mm brush, a roller or spray can be used. In warm weather they may dry very quickly but in cold and damp weather they may remain wet for many days. They are generally permeable to moisture and can be applied to surfaces which are not perfectly dry allowing them to dry out through the paint. The same formulation usually serves as primer, undercoat and finishing coat.

Paints which are thinned with water are:

1 *Limewash* The cheapest finish is slaked lime which has very little binding power and can often be brushed off with the hand. Traditionally, tallow added during slaking gave limewash a degree of durability for external use, although it 'chalked' rapidly with weathering.

2 *Non-washable distemper* (*ceiling* or *soft distemper*) which is whiting (chalk powder) mixed with *size* (dilute animal glue – BS 3357 : 1961) in hot water is described in BS 1053 : 1966 *Waterpaint and distemper for interior use*. It is the cheapest 'domestic' finish but when dry is easily rubbed off and is suitable only on ceilings. However, it gives a flatter matt surface than can be obtained in any other way and size being soluble, the finish can be easily washed off.

A solution of size with a little whiting (*clear-*

cole), is applied to surfaces to reduce and equalize their suction before non-washable distemper is applied. (It should never be used below washable distemper or emulsion paints.)

3   *Washable distemper* – also known as *oil-bound water paint*, or just *water paint* – is covered by BS 1053 : 1966 *Type A*. Consisting of an emulsified drying oil, glue or casein, with pigments and extenders, it is provided ready-for-use, or as a paste to be mixed with water or with *petrifying liquid* (a diluted form of medium). The latter helps to seal porous surfaces and to increase the durability of external finishes.

Washable distemper has a matt finish. It is cheaper than most emulsion paints. Hardening takes place slowly as the oil oxidizes and polymerizes and surfaces should not be washed for at least a month, but the best modern products then withstand moderate scrubbing and weather fairly well outdoors.

4   *Emulsion paints*   The description *emulsion paint* is applied in particular to paints which are bound with emulsions of vinyl, acrylic and polyurethane polymers. They harden quickly and provide *matt*, *sheen* or *lustre* surfaces. A few pigments are not light-fast externally but emulsion paints are tougher, more elastic, and although permeable they are more resistant to wear and weather than washable distemper, while being cheaper both to buy and apply than oil-based paints. Those incorporating vinyl caprone or vinyl versatate and those based wholly on acrylic polymers have the best resistance to alkalis.

Generally, emulsion paints can serve as primer (many adhere even to glossy backgrounds), undercoat(s) and finish coat. They are sometimes used as a primer and undercoats under oil-based paints, but it must be remembered that they are porous and an alkali-resistant primer/sealer may be required. Special primers may be needed on absorptive or powdery surfaces; in particular, on external masonry an oil-based sealer is essential.

5   *Cement paints* – consist of white Portland cement with or without pigments, water repellents, plasticizers and fillers. The need for alkali resistant pigments limits the colour range. A coarse texture and lack of 'flow' makes it difficult to avoid brush marks so that cement paint is not generally acceptable internally.

If it is used soon after water has been added (paint which has thickened must not be thinned), it adheres well to reasonably porous brickwork, concrete and renderings even if they are damp, but not to timber, metals or gypsum plaster or other types of paint. Absorptive surfaces should be dampened and old surfaces should be treated with a fungicidal wash if required.

Work must not proceed in wet or frosty weather, in a drying wind or direct sunlight. In hot weather each coat should be damped with a fine spray 6 to 12 hours after it has been applied.

6   *Synthetic resin/aggregate finishes*   Finishes of this type, although more costly than cement-based paints, are available in bright and light-fast colours, no water need be added, they are easy to apply and are more durable. Lives well in excess of ten years can be expected. Ingredients include water-emulsified synthetic resin binders and aggregates such as a hard granite derivative and mica which contribute to durability. One product is reinforced with nylon fibres.

Suitable backgrounds are clean, firm and dry brickwork, renderings, concrete and asbestos cement, in all cases constructed to prevent the ingress of water behind the finish. The paint manufacturer's advice should be followed at all stages, including the removal and inhibiting of mould and algae growths, and in sealing chalky or friable backgrounds with a *stabilizing solution*. White or light coloured paints of this type may be applied to mastic asphalt or bituminous felt roofings to reflect solar heat.

The paints are normally water repellent, but not water or vapour proof, allowing a wall to 'breathe'. Where a rain-proof finish is required, as on steelwork or porous 'solid' walls, a bituminous basecoat is needed.

Application should not proceed in wet or frosty weather. Surface finishes range from matt applied by brush, spray or roller, to textured and stippled.

Paints with special properties

Manufacturers should be consulted in selecting paints for special purposes.

Paints with special properties in application

Low-odour paints   It is rarely possible to do

more than minimize the odour of fresh paint. Masking odours can be a source of contamination.

Quick-drying paints   Some paints based on modified alkyd media, epoxy and polyurethane resins dry in 1 to 2 hours and those which dry by solvent evaporation such as chlorinated rubber and cellulose dry faster than oxidizing paints.

Paints for stoving   These are usually alkyd/ amino or epoxy based, intended for spray application and hardening at temperatures above 66°C in an oven or by infra-red radiation and are considerably harder than air-dried finishes. Urea and melamine formaldehyde resins blended with alkyd resin produce a colourless stoving enamel which is extremely hard and resistant to alkalis and solvents and is often used on refrigerators.

Paints with special properties in service

Water and chemical resistant paints   Paints which have superior resistance to chemical fumes and liquids include chlorinated rubber, bituminous, epoxy and polyurethane which have already been referred to. The two-part synthetic resin paints have greater resistance to chemicals than the one-part paints. Other chemical resistant paints include, *Neoprene* and *Hypalon*. Coal-tar-epoxy and polyurethane-pitch paints combine the good water, heat and chemical resistance of their constituents. Vinyl paints with special primers to secure adhesion give thin films, but in a sufficient number of coats they are chemically resistant while being flexible and tough.

Fire-retardant paints are available as oil-bound and water-borne finishes. They retard ignition, and particularly, spread of flame over surfaces. Some are *intumescent* and swell when heated forming an insulating porous coating.

Advice as to the efficacy of individual products in a given situation should be obtained from the Fire Research Station, Boreham Wood, Hertfordshire, which issues certificates of classification according to BS 476 – Part 1 : 1953.

Heat resistant paints   Typical high grade modern paints can be safely applied to surfaces such as hot water radiators, but manufacturers should be consulted as to the suitability of white and pale coloured paints. White silicone paints are very resistant to yellowing at high temperatures

and some formulations which combine silicone with phenolic, alkyd and epoxy resins, have excellent resistance to high temperatures. One type, pigmented with aluminium powder, withstands temperatures of 535°C in dry conditions and up to 400°C externally. The stoving necessary to polymerize the paint may conveniently be done when objects such as boilers and chimneys are in service.

Fungus-resisting paints   Wherever possible the damp conditions which give rise to the growth of moulds should be avoided, but paints which contain fungicides may be required in bakeries, breweries and textile mills. Fungicides which are toxic to humans must not be used where contamination of food or licking by children and animals might occur. Incidentally the life of a fungicide may be shorter than that of the paint in which it is incorporated.

Before painting on infected areas, they must be thoroughly dried and then treated with a fungicidal solution. Some of these cause discoloration and externally it is safer to use solutions of household bleach or industrial sodium hypochlorite.

Insecticidal paints   Paints can be formulated to kill insects on contact in specific environments but they should not be regarded as a primary means of dealing with this problem.

Permeable paints   Water thinned paints can be applied on damp plaster moisture from which they can dry out through the paint film, but claims that specially formulated synthetic resin finishes, including gloss finishes, are permeable to water vapour should be confirmed by practical tests.

Floor paints   One- and two-pack epoxy and polyurethane paints can improve the appearance of concrete and tiled floors and they are extremely tough and resistant to abrasion. Life, however, is determined by their limited thickness and factors such as bond with the base.

Multi-colour paints contain globules of colour which differ from the main paint and remain separate and float on the surface. When dry, the appearance is of flecks of colour on a background of another colour and there is a very slight texture which disguises minor surface irregularities. Multi-colour paints are suitable for spraying only.

Texture paints – sometimes called 'plastic'

paints, but not to be confused with plastics – are very heavily bodied paints with a consistency rather like plaster. The paint can be applied thickly to conceal irregularities in existing surfaces; soon after application it can be worked to form textures and relief patterns and when hard it can be carved.

Imitation stone paint has a fine crushed stone body which gives it an appearance resembling stone and added durability.

Anti-condensation paints have fillers such as cork, which provide some thermal insulation and absorption. If condensation is not too severe it may be prevented or at least rendered inconspicuous.

'Metallic' paints   These include minute flakes of metals usually in varnish or cellulose media – eg zinc in rust inhibiting paints; aluminium in wood primers and in protective and light reflecting top coats; copper in decorative paints.

Luminous paints   These specialized paints present problems in application which make them unsuitable for site use. There are three types:

Fluorescent paints absorb ultra-violet radiation and re-emit visible light.

Phosphorescent paints absorb energy and emit it as visible light which continues to glow after the source of stimulation has been removed.

Radio-active paints are self-luminous, normally phosphorescent paints in which radio-active compounds activate phosphor.

APPLICATION OF PAINT

Generally, painting should not proceed in wet, damp, or foggy weather, on surfaces below about 4°C, in direct sunlight or in dusty conditions. Each coat should be thoroughly dry before the next coat is applied. Good ventilation is required to dry paint and sometimes to remove noxious fumes. Humid conditions delay drying of ordinary paints and entrapped moisture reduces the adhesion, durability and gloss of finishes, and corrodes ferrous metals. On the other hand, moisture-curing polyurethane and cement paints – although they should not be applied in rain – are best cured in damp conditions.

On the building site, application may be by *brush*, *hand roller* or *spray*. In the factory, *dipping*, *flow coating*, *roller coating* and other time and labour saving techniques are possible.

Brush

Provided brushes are vigorously manipulated, they displace air and traces of dust and moisture from the surface, and give the best adhesion – which is particularly desirable in priming coats. However, skill is necessary to avoid brush marks and to maintain wet edges when applying paint on large areas.

Rollers

Rollers, which are wider than brushes, hold more paint, require less frequent recharging and save time on large plane surfaces, although a brush is still needed to finish to a line and to paint into internal angles.

Lambswool, mohair and nylon pile and synthetic sponge coverings all slightly stipple surfaces – even of gloss paint.

Spray

Good spraying equipment is costly – particularly the two-pack gun required for paints which harden by catalytic action – and areas which are not to be sprayed must be masked.

The electrostatic method directs and confines spray to the surface being painted, including otherwise inaccessible parts, but it is not easily adapted to site painting.

Lead paint is a health hazard and must not be sprayed, but generally spraying is economical on large areas and on details in relief. It is the only method for applying quick-drying paints such as cellulose, and it lends itself to the production of certain metallic and graded effects. The hot spray process reduces the viscosity of paints without adding solvent. Airless spray restricts overspray and increases productivity but often sufficient continuous work cannot be provided in buildings.

Dipping

Dipping is a rapid and economical method of

355

painting those components which allow for adequate drainage, but the requisite close control of the paint and process is not possible on the building site. Other factory processes, which enable excess paint to be recovered, include:

Flow coating in which paint is hosed onto the article and

Roller coating by machine of one or both sides of boards and often continuous lengths of metal sheet.

BACKGROUNDS

Backgrounds must be sound, generally dry, and be properly prepared.

Moisture content

Moisture in backgrounds, or trapped between surfaces and primers or between successive coats of paint, causes loss of adhesion and sometimes leads

to blisters in the paint film. Impervious finishes should not, therefore, be applied on damp surfaces unless there is an alternative route for moisture to escape freely. As a rough rule even in good conditions it takes about one week for every 5 mm thickness of wet construction to dry out completely.

The superficial appearance of a surface is not a reliable guide to the moisture content of a construction 'in depth'. Knowledge of the weather conditions during and after construction helps, but it is much better to measure the moisture content directly. Methods include: 1 *Electrical moisture meter.* 2 *Coloured indicator papers*, the significance of colour changes being assessed by reference to a standard colour sheet. Readings should be taken in the centre of a surface at least 300 mm square which has been covered overnight with a glass, metal or polythene sheet. 3 *Hygrometer.* BRS Digest 55 gives recommendations for decoration related to overnight readings of the relative humidity of air inequilibrium with a surface, which are summarized as follows:

Relative humidity per cent	Wall condition	Recommendation
100	Moisture on surface	If decoration *must* proceed wipe surface dry and use a specially formulated, porous, highly pigmented emulsion paint.
	No moisture on surface	If decoration *must* proceed use specially formulated emulsion paint as above, or white cement paint (but not on gypsum plaster).
90 – 75	Drying	As above, and as the surface becomes drier reasonable chance of success extends progressively to: 1 most emulsion paints 2 oil-bound and size-bound distempers 3 wallpaper 4 special types of permeable flat oil paints
Less than 75	Dry	Any treatment

Preparation

Inadequate preparation of backgrounds is a common cause of defective paintwork. Some surfaces require only to be brushed down but others need washing and scraping to remove dirt, dust, loose deposits or defective paint. Oils and stains must be removed by suitable solvents.

Surfaces must have sufficient 'key' for the type

of paint which is to be applied. Some proprietary washing solutions slightly etch surfaces while additional key can be provided by a chemical etching solution or by rubbing down with an abrasive. Copper, lead and existing paint containing lead must not be rubbed down dry and it is convenient to combine rubbing down with the washing operation. After rubbing down, etching and washing it is important to remove all residues with clean water. Surfaces must then be dry before ordinary paints are applied.

Previously painted surfaces

For good class work all surface-fixed ironmongery, fittings etc. should be removed before painting. Water soluble paints such as non-washable distemper must always be removed. If other paints have only slightly 'chalked' they provide a good base and key, and one or two coats of new paint usually restore their original condition.

Where a perfect appearance is required, small defects can be 'brought forward' by priming, filling and rubbing down so that the surface is brought into one plane. This, however, is laborious and for large areas where a perfect appearance is desired it is economical to remove all the old paint and treat the surface as being new.

Paint can be removed by:

Burning off – ie softening paint with a blowlamp and scraping.

Solvent and chemical removers An oil binder is most easily softened, water-thinned paints with a low oil content less readily, and chemically cured resins are very difficult to remove. It is clearly most important to remove all residues before repainting. Water rinseable and solvent rinseable paint removers are described in BS 3761:1964.

Solvent and chemical removers are not effective on structural steel due to its surface texture and the presence of rivets and bolts, and they are not suitable on gypsum plaster.

Steam stripping Softening with steam, followed by scraping, is the only economical way to remove some paint systems and varnishes but the equipment is bulky, the method is suitable only for flat surfaces and it may damage delicate backgrounds.

PAINTING ON VARIOUS BACKGROUNDS

The problems which are peculiar to various backgrounds are dealt with in CP 231 : 1966 *The painting of buildings*, and some of the more important points are considered here:

Woodwork

Wood changes size with variations in its moisture content; it is liable to attack by fungus, insects and fire. See *MBC*: *Materials*, chapter 2. Oils and resins contained in certain timbers, and differences between the densities of earlywood and latewood present other problems which are referred to later.

With the high proportion of sapwood (all of which is *non-durable* or worse) contained in much softwood now being imported, it is strongly recommended that softwood for external joinery should be treated with a paintable preservative. Self-draining details and a well maintained impervious paint system will minimize the movement of timber which cracks paint particularly at joints and allows water to enter.

Because moisture may cause loss of adhesion by paint, and because moisture vaporizing below paint forms blisters, at the time of painting the moisture content of timber should never exceed 18 per cent. To minimize moisture movement, however, its moisture content may require to be as little as 10 per cent for internal joinery. On the other hand it must be remembered that timber can be too dry for its situation.

To obtain a first-class paint finish, the finish on joinery itself must be of very good quality and the thirteen operations described below, which take at least five days to perform, may be needed. The 'minimum' treatment on ordinary softwoods – letters *A–E* – takes four days.

1 *Repair* Large, loose or resinous knots and other gross defects should be cut out and holes plugged with sound wood. Nails should be punched well below surfaces, especially externally.

2 *Rub down* To receive first class painted finishes even the best planed work must be rubbed down with a fine glass paper in the direction of the grain.

3 *Dust off*

4 *Wash with solvent* Oily woods such as teak, afrormosia, gurjun and makoré should be washed with a solvent such as white spirit.

5 *A* *Knot* Resin which is not sealed always tends to discolour paint even on old wood. If an aluminium primer/sealer is not used two thin coats of *knotting* (shellac in methylated spirit to BS 1336 : 1946) must be applied to knots and any other resinous parts of softwoods in an effort to prevent resin staining.

6 *Seal* Wood which has been exposed to the weather becomes absorbent and may require: two priming coats, the first well-thinned; the application of a thin coat of a long-oil oleo-resinous varnish; or treatment with boiled oil.

7 *B Prime* The traditional lead-based primer, usually pink in colour due to the inclusion of red lead, possesses the flexibility needed on wood backgrounds. BS 2521 and 2523 are relevant but some manufacturers recommend products with a slightly lower lead content. Emulsion primers, usually based on acrylic polymers, have the advantages of quick drying, freedom from toxic pigments and durability which is said to be equal to that of white lead.

Aluminium primers have an alkyd or oleo-resinous medium which adheres well, even on dense and non-absorbent latewood. They seal against 'bleeding' of resins in softwoods, dispensing with the need for shellac knotting. They are specially recommended on Douglas fir.

A full coat of primer should be vigorously brushed in, particular care being taken to fill end grain. Backs of members which will be in contact with external walls should receive at least two coats, preferably of *aluminium wood primer*.

A sound primer applied 'at works' protects joinery from moisture during transport and in storage on the site, but in fact works primers are often inferior and too thin to exclude rain. They should be carefully specified, and on the site damage should be touched up and an extra coat given if the works primer looks thin.

It is important to apply the primer at this stage to prevent loss of oil from stopping (8) and filling (9).

8 *C Stop* All cracks, nail holes and the like should be stopped, preferably with a proprietary *hard stopping*, or with *putty* (BS 544 : 1934) applied and finished with a knife. Water soluble stopping should not be used outdoors.

9 *Fill* To obtain a first-class smooth surface free even from minor irregularities, a filler is applied with a broad knife. Gypsum plaster or water soluble cellulose-based fillers are satisfactory internally but outdoors a waterproof proprietary paste filler must be used.

10 *Flat down* 'Flatting' with a suitable abrasive is necessary at this stage where a first class finish is required. For ordinary work only hard stopping needs to be rubbed down (this must be done 'wet' if stopping contains lead).

11 *D Apply undercoat(s)* At least two undercoats are needed for good quality work externally, and for first class work internally. Any stopping or filling should be hard.

Background	Exposure	Primer
Non-resinous woods	Externally and internal parts of window frames and sashes, reveals etc.	White lead in linseed oil with not more than 10 per cent red lead, aluminium wood primer or acrylic emulsion primer
	Internally	Leadless primers, eg acrylic emulsions
Resinous woods		Aluminium wood primer
Flat sawn timbers with wide variation between earlywood and latewood eg Douglas Fir	Internally and externally	Aluminium wood primer with leafing aluminium powder and a synthetic varnish medium is 'probably best'
Oily hardwoods washed with solvent eg Teak		Aluminium wood primer or special tenacious 'teak sealer'
Old and thin creosote		Aluminium sealer (two coats)
Thick creosote or bitumen	Externally	Re-apply existing finish

Table 29   Primers on wood

12 *Flat down undercoats* if a very high gloss finish is required.

13 *E Apply finishing coat(s)* Externally, and for superior quality internal finishes, greater durability is obtained by applying two coats of finishing type paint – one of which may be in substitution for an ordinary undercoat.

Metals

Metals often require to be protected from corrosion – see *MBC: Materials*, chapter 9. Paint can protect from rain and damp, separate dissimilar metals, and protect from contact with, or washings from, woods such as oak, teak and chestnut which contain acids, and form acid vapours.

Metals offer no suction for paint, and grease and fluxes which are often present should be removed with trichloroethylene.

Metalwork which is to be exposed to the weather must be carefully designed. It must be fully accessible for painting and welds should be ground smooth. Pockets and crevices which might retain water must be avoided especially in industrial and marine atmospheres, and where necessary holes should be provided to drain water away.

Ferrous metals

References include:
  BRS Digest 70 *Painting metals in buildings – 1 Iron and steel*
  CP 2008 : 1953 *Protection of iron and steel structures from corrosion*
  Protective painting of structural steel, F. Fancutt, FRIC, AMI and J. C. Hudson, DSc, DIC, ARCS, FIM., Chapman and Hall Ltd.

Ordinary ferrous metals are particularly difficult to protect from corrosion. Essentials are: very thorough preparation of surfaces, a specially formulated paint system including a rust-inhibiting primer, thick and impervious top coats and application by a skilled operative in dry conditions.

Ideal conditions are rarely achieved on the building site and unfortunately, although they are possible in the factory, in fact the ordinary factory primer is often applied over dirt and rust and is of poor quality.

In ordinary, *mild, inland exposures* two priming coats and at least two further coats of air-drying paint with a minimum thickness of 0·125 mm are necessary. (An equal thickness may be obtained with fewer coats of thixotropic or chemically-cured paints.)

In *severe exposures* where heavy industrial pollution occurs, or within two miles of a coast, no paint system is effective unless applied in the factory on galvanized or zinc sprayed metal. Alternatively, vitreous enamelled or plastics coated metal may be used.

Preparation Fancutt and Hudson have shown that thorough surface preparation increases the life of a paint film four to five times. At present the BRS is not able to recommend primers which are claimed to penetrate or react with rust and advise that the primer should be applied on bright metal. Mill scale and tightly adhering rust on pitted surfaces can only be completely removed by grit or shot blasting[1] or in a factory by acid pickling. Less serious rust, mill scale and old paint can be removed by hand or power tools, or by flame cleaning with oxyacetylene or butane gas (a blow lamp is not effective) followed by brushing. Pickling is effective in the factory, but the use of pickling jellies or pastes is not recommended on the site, where phosphoric acid washes are suitable although less effective than in the factory. (Treating metal with linseed oil while it is still hot after rolling, and weathering to remove rust and scale are no longer recommended.) Degreasing is also best done in the factory. On site, swabs soaked in white spirit should be used and changed frequently to avoid merely spreading grease over surfaces.

Priming Primers, or the first coats of systems such as zinc-rich and coal-tar epoxy paints which do not require separate primers, should be applied immediately the background has been prepared. Generally the temperature of the air should be above 5°C and its relative humidity not greater than 80 per cent. The temperature of the metal should always be above the dew point of the air. Condensation, including moisture from handling which may not be visible, will lead to corrosion later if it is trapped in the paint film. Flame cleaning has the advantage that it dries surfaces and suitably formulated primers should be applied while the metal is still warm (but not hot).

Brushing is recommended, but roller or spray

1 BS 4232 : 1967 *Surface finish of blast-cleaned steel for painting* describes three degrees of finish.

application of primers may be satisfactory on smooth surfaces, provided any tendency to rush the work is resisted. Paint runs away from arrises and a second primer coat is recommended on them. Also, because a second primer coat is of more value than an undercoat, it should be applied where there are specially corrosive conditions. and externally, except in inland areas having low rainfall.

For normal paint systems rust-inhibiting primers such as those listed below, are essential.

Red lead in oil, eg BS 2523 : 1966 – *Type B* and branded products also containing red iron oxide or graphite.

Metallic lead   Like red lead, metallic lead is a 'tolerant primer' ie it is excellent where preparation is not of a high standard and where the primer will not be immediately overpainted.

Calcium plumbate BS 3698 : 1964 specifies *Type A* – 48 per cent and *Type B* – 33 per cent calcium plumbate oil-based primers. Not all undercoats adhere well to these primers.

Non-toxic primers are now often required and these include:

Zinc chromate   Zinc chromate-in-oil primers are particularly useful for priming non-ferrous metals. Suitable formulations give good results on structural steel although generally red lead-in-oil primers are more effective.

Zinc dust   Two-pack zinc-rich epoxy resin-based paints are suitable for use on blast-cleaned metal.

Wash or etch primers   These are based on PV butyral resins and phosphoric acid with or without zinc chromate. Available in one- and two-pack forms they can be used as primers on steel which has been acid-pickled or blasted. 'Wash' means that these primers are very thin, and they provide protection for a short time only. Strictly they do not etch although they provide excellent adhesion.

Most other primers, including red (iron) oxide and aluminium, do not possess special rust-inhibiting properties.

Undercoats and finishes   Undercoat and finish type paints must be suited to the primer coat as well as to the conditions of exposure.

Paint systems suitable for various conditions of exposure can be taken from table 1 in BRS Digest 70. Examples which provide a high degree of protection include suitably formulated paints of the following types:

Oil modified alkyd
Exterior aluminium pigmented
Micaceous iron oxide
Bituminous and coal-tar with bituminous-aluminium finish
Coal-tar epoxy
Graphite and silica-graphite (for limited applications)

Chlorinated rubber, vinyl, two-pack epoxy and two-pack polyurethane coatings are resistant to severe chemical attack.

Non-ferrous metals

BRS Digest 71 *Painting metals in buildings 2 – Non-ferrous metals and coatings* is a reference.

Generally, non-ferrous metals do not require protection, but externally, zinc coatings on ferrous metals should be painted and aluminium alloys may require to be painted in certain industrial atmospheres, or near the sea.

Table 30 describes preparation and primers for site application. Ordinary undercoats and finishes are usually satisfactory.

The best quality finishes, for example most stoved paints and vinyl, acrylic and vitreous enamel coatings, must be applied 'at works'.

Bituminous surfaces

Bituminous surfaces are best painted with bituminous paint. Other types of paint can be applied if a specially formulated sealer is used, but only if the bituminous coating is hard and thin.

Insulating fibre building boards

Factory primed and ivory surfaced boards need no further priming. Ordinary boards can be primed with an oil-based primer to counteract suction and to prevent subsequent water paint raising the surface fibres.

Bitumen impregnated boards should be sealed with preferably two coats of aluminium sealer. Boards impregnated with fire retardant salts and asbestos-faced boards are usually best treated with an alkali-resistant primer.

New metal surface	Site preparation	Suitable primers
Aluminium and Aluminium Alloys[1] – smooth eg sheet, extrusions, alumin-ized steel	Phosphoric acid washes or Emery (*NOT* wire wool) with white spirit as lubricant or Solvent degreasing with white spirit or white spirit with equal parts of solvent naphtha	Etch-primer[2] plus zinc chromate (*NOT* lead-based primer)
– rough eg castings, aluminium spray	Smooth off nibs with emery paper Clean off dust and dirt	Zinc chromate
		One-pack etch-primer plus zinc chromate
Zinc – sheet, hot-dipped or electro galvanized[3]	Degrease with white spirit	Calcium plumbate direct, or etch-primer plus zinc chromate
	Weather for several months and wash	Zinc chromate or calcium plumbate
	Phosphoric acid washes and rinse thoroughly	Calcium plumbate
– sprayed or sherardized coatings	Smooth off nibs with emery paper Clean off dust and dirt	One-pack etch-primer preferably plus zinc chromate
Copper and Copper Alloys eg brasses and bronzes	Emery with white spirit (*DO NOT* weather or abrade dry[4]) Phosphoric acid treatments	If painting is essential: *In exposed conditions:* Etch-primer or aluminium pigmented primer *Internally:* Alkyd gloss paint may be applied direct
Lead[5]	Abrade wet (*NOT* dry)[6]	Alkyd gloss direct for small areas – otherwise do not paint
Cadmium coatings	Phosphate treatments (*DO NOT* weather)	Two-pack etch-primer
Chromium and nickel plating	Emery with white spirit	

Table 30   Site preparation and primers for new non-ferrous metals
(Information from BRS Digest 71 *Painting metals in buildings 2 – Non-ferrous metals and coatings,* and other sources)

[1] Aluminium should be protected from alkaline materials such as concrete by an alkali-resistant system (eg chlorinated rubber) or a bitumen-based paint.
[2] A special etch-primer with improved water resistance should be used if exposure to rain or dew is likely before later coats are applied.
[3] The insides of galvanized steel cisterns can be protected against corrosion with a non-toxic bituminous paint to BS 3416, Type II.
[4] Copper dust settling on surfaces can cause stains when they are subsequently painted.
[5] Graphite-based paints should not be applied directly on metals, particularly on lead.
[6] Lead dust is a health hazard.

Sound absorbent tiles and boards

To minimize loss of sound absorption properties paint should be as thin as possible and spray application which avoids paint build-up at the edges of channels or perforations, is preferable.

Hardboards

As with insulating fibreboards, some hardboards are primed or sealed at the factory but a primer-sealer should be used on untreated boards especially under water paints. Externally an aluminium flake primer is suitable. Wood primers are not suitable. Backs and edges should be painted.

Plastics

A tenacious primer is desirable and it may be necessary to rub down shiny surfaces. Paint manufacturers should be consulted in each case.

Paper

Lining paper, wall paper and paper faced boards usually provide uniform suction and if the paper is firmly adherent will accept water-borne paint or an oil-bound primer sealer. Patterned wallpapers should be tested to see if the pattern 'grins through'; if it does it is likely to be more economical to strip the paper and to hang lining paper if this is required.

Fabrics

Hessian, jute and other fabrics can be painted direct with emulsion paints. If the joints spring the problem should be referred to the paint manufacturer.

Plasterwork

Reference should be made to BRS Digests 55, 56 and 57 *Painting walls* 1, 2 and 3.

Trouble is likely to follow if an impervious paint is applied before drying of plaster and the structure are complete – a process which normally takes months, especially if the other side cannot dry freely. Distemper and emulsion paint, however, can be applied once the plaster is surface-dry, and an emulsion paint provides a base for a suitable impervious finish when drying is complete.

Dry gypsum plasters are chemically compatible with all except Portland cement paints. Two-pack epoxy paints should be used only after reference to the manufacturer.

If plasters or backgrounds may contain lime or Portland cement it is wise to check for alkalinity with moistened litmus paper and if they prove to be alkaline two coats of alkali-resistant primer should be applied before following with any paint which contains oil.

Sanded, retarded, hemi-hydrate plasters give a good key for paint but absorption is sometimes patchy and in continuously damp conditions they 'sweat out' causing paints to fail. In the light-weight form, they tend to be very smooth and in exceptional cases a special primer-sealer may be needed.

Anhydrous plasters and Keene's cement are harder and less porous than retarded hemi-hydrate plasters and are often finished to almost glass-like smoothness. If they dry too quickly the partially hydrated surface becomes powdery affording a poor key for paint and if 'delayed expansion' of the plaster occurs, breakdown can be complete.

Procedure on new plaster

The processes are:

1 Scrape, 2 Rub down, 3 Dust down, 4 Make good, 5 Prime and 6 Paint. Thus:

1 *Scrape* Plaster and mortar splashes should be carefully scraped off.

2 *Rub down* If it is necessary to rub down to remove irregularities care should be taken to avoid causing variations in the porosity of the surface leading to variations in the sheen of the paint.

3 *Dust down* to remove dust and any efflorescence. The latter must *not* be washed off.

4 *Make good and stop* with plaster of the same type as that used for the surface as a whole.

5 *Prime* Apply a coat of alkali-resistant primer on alkaline surfaces and a well thinned alkali-resisting or *plaster primer* on Keene's plaster. Formerly a *sharp primer following the trowel* (ie a primer with a very small oil content, applied within three hours of plastering being completed) was recommended on Keene's plaster. It was argued that the fresh plaster induced some suction and that this, together with the disturbance caused by the brush, gave good adhesion. In addition, the

sharp primer delayed the rate of drying of the plaster, thereby reducing the risk of a '*dry out*' followed by '*delayed expansion*' (see page 312). However, it must never be applied to alkaline surfaces and most proprietary primers are not suitable for 'following the trowel'.

Procedure on old plaster

If surfaces are damp the cause should be removed. Decorations affected by moulds or mildew should be stripped and a mould inhibitor, eg *ICI Mould Inhibitor* or *Santobrite*, should be applied. Unsound plaster should be removed and made good, and cracks and holes should be filled with new plaster of the same type and having the same finish as the old plaster.

Failures often arise because the adhesion of old paint is insufficient to hold fresh paint. Water-soluble paint must always be washed off and the surface allowed to dry. Other old paint which is in poor condition should be removed, or if this is not practicable it may be rubbed and scraped 'dry' and treated with a special penetrating and binding primer.

'*Binding down*', *penetrating* and alkali-resisting primers equalize suction and reduce patchiness in the finish, but on repaired surfaces lining paper (see page 369) may be needed to provide a uniform texture, particularly for gloss paint.

Backgrounds containing Portland cement

Alkalis in lime or Portland cement contained in a structure, rendering, mortar or plaster when carried in solution, cause chemical breakdown of paints containing oil, producing sticky or oily matter (*saponification*), and lime which diffuses from the substrate sometimes becomes 'fixed' in paint producing apparent bleaching. Efflorescent salts may penetrate permeable paints or 'push off' impervious paints during the drying out of concrete and brickwork.

Because new surfaces containing Portland cement are rarely completely dry and may accidentally become wet later, a non-saponifiable alkali-resistant primer is desirable under paints containing oil. Alkaline finishes such as cement and silicate paints are, of course, immune from saponification (but they may present difficulties if it is ever desired to over-paint them with paints containing oil). Ready-mixed synthetic resin/aggregate finishes are suitable and emulsion paints can usually be safely applied on these backgrounds – the first coat being well thinned.

Traces of mould oil must be scrubbed off concrete surfaces using detergent or a solvent which, in turn, must be rinsed away.

Asbestos-cement products which have not been steam cured are highly alkaline when they are new and their porosity is variable. If an impervious finish is applied on one side only, condensation may cause loss of adhesion while carbonation of the untreated reverse side often causes warping and cracking. Before being painted both sides of sheets should be exposed to air for at least ten days to reduce their moisture content and to allow carbonation to take place. Back painting is desirable if the sheet is not fully carbonated and if the finish is impervious. BRS Digest 38 (First series) and MPB and W Advisory leaflet 28 *Painting asbestos cement*, are useful references.

Brickwork and stonework

Clay bricks contain soluble salts and the mortar is usually alkaline so that generally these surfaces should be treated as for backgrounds containing Portland cement.

On dense and glazed bricks, strongly adhesive primers having penetrating binders are preferable, followed by any paint which is suited to the conditions of exposure. Alternatively, oil-modified alkyd gloss paints may be applied direct after repairing pointing and allowing it to dry out.

Clear finishes

Clear finishes, with or without added colour, enhance the natural appearance of wood and other surfaces, and protect them from knocks and the weather. This protection, however, is inferior to that afforded by opaque finishes.

Materials must be formulated to suit the conditions of use and the substrate. Internally, the main requirements are usually rapid drying, good appearance and resistance to staining and scratching, and a high gloss may be desired. Externally the need for protection limits the choice of materials.

The main clear finishes suitable for common backgrounds are:

Internal surfaces

Wood
   oil seals
   wax polish
   French polish
   short-oil varnishes
   spirit varnishes
   synthetic resin finishes
   cellulose lacquers

Paper
   water varnishes

Metals
   cellulose lacquers

External surfaces

Wood
   preservatives
   oil finishes
   fortified linseed oil
   long-oil varnishes
Brickwork, Stonework, Concrete
   water repellents

   synthetic resin
   finishes

Internal clear finishes on wood and metal are considered first.

Internal surfaces

Internal clear finishes on wood

In general, surfaces must be firm, clean and dry and first-class finishes can only be obtained on smooth surfaces where preparation is thorough. Operations in preparing wood surfaces include:

Bleaching

Lime treatment to give a grey effect and *fuming* to either lighten or darken.

Scraping along the grain.

Sand with garnet paper.

Stop holes and cracks, with hot beeswax, resin and orange lac, plaster of Paris or with whiting and a drying oil – both the latter being coloured to match the wood.

Fill pores (for a first class finish) – usually with a tinted oil-based filler.

Stain – to modify colour – with oil, varnish, wax, or with chemical water stains (which tend to raise the grain). Alternatively, stain may be included in the finish.

Clear finishes suitable for application on internal woodwork are:

1   *Oil seals*
These seals, a form of varnish, often based on tung oil, are used mainly for water and grease resistant, non-slip finishes on wood floors.

2   *Wax polishes*
Wax polish – a paste, liquid or emulsion based on beeswax or other waxes with turpentine or spirits – is fairly easily applied to new wood either directly or – to save time – after 'bodying in' with french polish. (It is also used to maintain all the other clear finishes.) Wax polish is relatively soft and more inclined to collect dirt than other finishes, it is 'whitened' by water and spirits and stained by ink and heat. However, it is not so prone to blooming, crazing or 'orange peeling' and is less likely to show scratches than other finishes. Further, repairs are relatively easy to carry out.

3   *Polymer-based emulsions*
Emulsion polishes based on PVA, acrylic resin and polyethylene are easy to apply and maintain.

4   *French polish*
French polish is costly to apply and is marked by heat, water and spirits. However, it is generally agreed to be the finest internal finish on wood, and it is fairly easy for a skilled polisher to match colours and to repair defects.

After any necessary preparation, the processes are:

Body in   – with lac (a resinous excretion of certain insects) and gums held in a rubber

Body up   – by thin applications of lac held in a rubber using linseed oil as a surface lubricant

Spirit off – polish with a pad of cotton wool soaked in methylated spirit and covered with chamois leather which slightly softens and levels the surface

5   *Cellulose lacquers*
Cellulose lacquers consist of nitro-cellulose with a plasticizer to counteract brittleness and with natural or synthetic resins where gloss is required. The appearance of a cellulose lacquer finish is similar to french polish, although being easier to apply, it is cheaper. Initially, cellulose is more resistant to water, but it is also attacked by spirits. Cellulose deteriorates by cracking so that it must be completely removed before it is renewed. For a

first class finish the preparation should be similar to that for french polish but here application must be by spraying in suitable conditions of temperature and humidity. The surface can be *pulled over* rather like the *spiriting off* of french polish, to give a final gloss. Nitro-cellulose is a serious fire risk and the Petroleum Regulations must be observed in storage and use.

6 Short-oil varnishes

These finishes have a low oil and a high resin content making for high gloss but reducing flexibility, so they tend to fail by cracking and are not suitable externally. Figure 251, page 349 shows the occurrence of oil and resin in various products. Oil varnishes are usually applied with a brush – a simpler proceeding than for french polish or cellulose, but they dry relatively slowly and tend to collect dust. Undercoats are sometimes rubbed down to obtain a first class finish.

Semi-gloss and matt varnishes containing wax *flatting agents* are used as finishes only.

7 Spirit varnishes

Spirit varnishes are made with resins such as shellac and dry quickly by the evaporation of solvents such as alcohol. They remain soluble in the solvent (hence *picture varnish* can be conveniently removed) and as with cellulose brush application of following coats is difficult. Spirit varnishes are cheap but having a high shellac content they are brittle and inclined to crack. ('Knotting' (see page 357) and french polish are forms of spirit varnishes with lower shellac contents.)

8 Water varnishes

The medium of emulsion paint is a form of water varnish which can be used to glaze emulsion paint or wallpapers.

9 Synthetic resin finishes

One- and two-pack finishes are made from phenol, formaldehyde resins, urea and melamine formaldehydes, polyurethane, polyester, coumarone, indene and epoxy resins together with thinners and catalysts (hardeners).

Although relatively costly, suitable synthetic resin finishes can satisfy one or more exacting requirements such as: extreme hardness; flexibility; resistance to high temperatures – including burning cigarettes; and resistance to water, grease, spirits, acids and alkalis. Synthetic resin finishes are particularly suitable for bar and shop counter

tops, laboratory benches and fume cupboards, but not generally for external use.

Surfaces must be free from wax polish and their preparation is similar to that for french polish and cellulose. Synthetic resins dry rapidly, so application must in most cases be by spray – special equipment being required for two-pack finishes.

Patch repairs are very difficult because synthetic resins cannot be removed by normal solvents.

Internal clear finishes on metals

Aluminium alloys, particularly those which are anodized, retain a bright and uniform appearance if they are kept clean, Regular wax polishing is required on copper based metals. Alternatively, cellulose finishes or two coats of *Incralac* or *BNF/CB lacquer* (see page 366) can be applied.

External surfaces

These are mainly applied to wood and sometimes to brickwork, stonework and concrete. Clear finishes lack pigments to filter the damaging ultraviolet radiation and are much less durable than paints.

External clear finishes on wood

Wood which is exposed to the weather often splits and develops a woolly or spongy surface which collects dirt and encourages mould growth; colours are washed out, and bleached by light and eventually all species of timber become grey. In addition, in wet conditions the less durable timbers are attacked by fungus. These effects are minimized by avoiding horizontal surfaces and cavities which could retain water. Table 31 is a useful summary.

Generally, a rather lower standard of surface preparation is acceptable for external than for internal finishes, but any stopping, or filling must be water resistant. Hammering of galvanized nails damages the zinc coating and they should be driven well below the surface to avoid rust stains.

Clear treatments which will help to preserve the natural appearance of timber are:

1 *Preservatives* The sapwood of all timbers and the heartwood of many timbers is readily attacked

365

by fungi and should be preserved if only in order to prevent discoloration by moulds.

2 *Water repellents* applied by brush, especially to end grain, or by dipping in a solution for at least ten seconds can prolong the 'new' appearance of timber for a few years by reducing the surface cracking which results from repeated wetting and drying. Linseed oil alone, is not recommended; it tends to remain sticky and to hold dirt and its effective life is only about six months. BRS Digest 21 states 'on timber cladding where a high gloss is not required, the appearance can be preserved and the cost of treatment and maintenance reduced by applying, instead of varnish, a single coat of linseed oil fortified with paraffin wax and a fungicide'.

3 *Stains* change the colour of wood and can revive the colour of bleached wood, and water resistant stains are valuable ultra-violet light filters. Some proprietary finishes which include all the above ingredients have preserved the natural colour of Western red cedar for four or more years.

4 *Varnishes*   Unlike the above finishes, varnishes attempt to seal timber against the entry of water, but it remains desirable to preserve the less durable wood (as recommended where timber is to be painted, see page 357). Short-oil varnishes, french polish and finishes based on urea formaldehyde, epoxide, vinyl and acrylic resins which contain little, or no oil are generally poor performers externally. Long-oil varnishes including *spar*, *marine* and *exterior varnishes* are the most durable clear and glossy finishes, but in spite of their superiority, even on plane and vertical surfaces four coats are unlikely to last more than three years, and fewer coats may deteriorate in a year or so.

Before timber is delivered to the site at least two coats should be applied on all surfaces – especially end grains and backs and at least two further coats should be applied on the site. Extra coats should be given to surfaces which face South, or which are not vertical.

Because unhardened varnishes are extremely sensitive to moisture they should not be applied in damp weather or where condensation might form on the film before it dries.

The appearance of white patches and slight flaking at edges is a signal to recoat surfaces before it becomes necessary to remove all the remaining varnish by the use of a solvent and scraper. Slight discoloration of timber may be removed with glass paper, oxalic acid or white spirit or it may be possible to conceal it by a water stain.

External clear finishes on brickwork, stonework and concrete

BRS Digest 90 (First series) and BRS Digest 56 discuss colourless waterproofing treatments for damp walls, some of which remain effective for up to ten years.

Impervious clear finishes are sometimes applied as a protection from soiling and to intensify the colour of marble or concrete, but no attempt should be made to waterproof pervious walling materials where there is no effective damp-proof course.

Water repellents line surface pores without filling them and encourage droplets to form, rather than a continuous film of water. An initial 'duck's back' effect is soon lost, but water repellency of *Silicone-based water repellents for masonry* (BS 3826 : 1967) – lasts for ten years or more. The latter materials are colourless, although a fugitive dye is sometimes added to assist in obtaining complete coverage in application. Water repellent fluids based on waxes, oils, fats or metallic soaps may retain dirt and cause a slight change in the tone and texture of some surfaces.

Surfaces should be free from cracks, reasonably dry, and free from efflorescence; salts deposited below the film may lead to spalling.

External clear finishes on metals

The only clear finish recommended by the British Non-ferrous Metals Research Association for site application on copper-based metals is *Incralac* which is based on an acrylic resin with a solvent, a corrosion inhibitor, ultra-violet light absorbers and a levelling agent. Metal must be thoroughly cleaned as recommended by the manufacturers of the lacquer. Application must be by spray, and in fine weather. Provided the finish is washed occasionally and not subject to excessive wear, three coats at least 0·025 mm thick have preserved the natural appearance of copper-based metals for five years in London.

BNF/CB lacquer, a two-pack polyurethane based finish is harder than *Incralac* but slow drying limits its use to the factory. Two coats give the

Finish	Initial treatment	Appearance of wood	Maintenance procedure	Maintenance period of surface finish	Cost of initial treatment	Maintenance cost
Coal tar oils	Vacuum/ pressure, hot and cold tank, steeping	Grain visible. Brown to black in colour, fading slightly with age	Brush down to remove surface dirt and brush apply	5–10 years only if original colour is required, otherwise no maintenance	Medium	Nil to low
	Brushing	Grain visible, light to dark brown	Brush down to remove surface dirt	3–5 years or according to colour	Low	Low
Waterborne preservatives	Vacuum/ pressure	Grain visible Greenish colour fading with age	Brush down to remove surface dirt	None, unless stained, painted or varnished	Medium	Nil
Organic solvent preservatives	Steeping, dipping, brushing	Grain visible, colour as desired	Brush down and re-apply	3 years or according to colour	Medium to high	Medium
Water repellents	One or two coats, but preferably dip applied	Grain and natural colour visible, becoming darker and rougher textured	Brush down and apply fresh material liberally	4 years or according to colour	Medium to high	Medium
Linseed oil with white spirit	Fibre saturation	Grain and colour unchanged	Brush down, sandpaper and re-apply	6 months	Low	High
Good quality exterior varnish	Four coats minimum	Grain and colour unchanged	Clean and stain bleached areas and apply two more coats	3 years or when a breakdown is imminent	Medium	Medium to high
Polyurethane* (2 pack)	Four coats minimum	Grain and colour unchanged	Completely remove gloss and re-apply	3 years or when a breakdown is imminent	High	High

* These finishes require controlled conditions during application and drying which are not readily obtained on building sites.

Table 31 External clear finishes on woodwork

Based on *Maintaining Exposed Woodwork*, Advisory Leaflet 62, Ministry of Public Building and Works – HMSO

367

requisite 0·025 mm thickness and full hardness can be obtained by stoving.

Vitreous enamel

Vitreous enamel (called *porcelain enamel* in USA) which is glass fused on steel, cast iron, aluminium or copper, is harder than cast-iron and extremely durable. It is attacked by strong alkalis but many enamelled steel advertisements are in good condition after 50 years' exposure externally in industrial climates. Where the finish coats of coloured enamel have been damaged the dark coloured ground coat usually remains intact but where it has also been damaged rust does not creep below it. Exterior finishes should comply with BS 1344 : 1947 : Part 1 (citric acid test) in respect of acid resistance. Designs, which can be in almost any colours, do not fade, stain or discolour.

Finishes can be *gloss, semi-gloss, textured* or *full-matt*. The latter two surfaces collect grime and should not be used externally.

Before enamelling, all fabrication should be completed. The object to be coated is thoroughly cleaned and raised to red heat. A finely pulverized *slip* made from a special form of glass, colour oxides and other ingredients is then sprayed on and flows and bonds with the metal. One-coat finishes are possible on aluminium. On steel at least two coats are required. The ground coat should cover the whole unit – including the back and edges – and for exterior work at least one further coat should do so.

Products should comply with the standards recommended by the Vitreous Enamel Development Council. For example, blemishes should not be visible when a unit is viewed at eye level from a distance of 1524 mm.

Applications

Wall infill panels – usually metal trays filled with an insulating material and with backs sealed with a vapour barrier;
Signs and advertisements;
Mullions, panels for lifts, escalators etc;
Kitchen furniture;
Chalkboards;
Steel rainwater goods;
Pressed steel and cast iron baths.

Plastics coatings

Plastics coatings on wood, metal and other substrates are warm and smooth to handle, easily cleaned and provide electrical insulation. Generally, they are thicker, tougher and more durable than ordinary paint coatings.

In particular, nylon and PVF coatings are extremely durable but not all plastics coatings are recommended outdoors – polythene, for example, loses its flexibility, and fades in time.

Plastics coatings are applied in the following ways:

1 Melt (or sinter) coatings

Metal articles are coated with powdered or molten plastics which are either self-curing or cured (sintered) by heat. Melt coatings are applied in several ways to give a homogeneous, smooth surfaced coating 0·26 to 1·0 mm thick.

Dipping Preheated objects are dipped into powder resins such as polythene, flexible PVC, nylon, CAB and epoxides. In a method used mainly for temporary protection of machine parts, cold objects are dipped into molten plastics such as ethyl cellulose. In the *fluidized-bed method*, air is blown through the powder to hold it in suspension.

Flock spraying Cold powder is sprayed onto preheated objects – where the powder is not self-curing the whole object is sintered after coating.

Electrostatic spraying Powder sprayed onto cold objects adheres by electrostatic charge and is then sintered.

Flame spraying A powdered resin such as nylon is melted in a flame gun and projected onto the object – a method liable to degrade the polymer.

Dusting After dipping in solvents and plasticizer, wood and metal objects are dusted with cellulose acetate powder – giving a hard, high gloss finish.

2 Paste coatings

Heated objects, including complex shapes such as wire mesh, are coated by dipping them in finely divided dispersions of resin in the form of either *organosols* or *plastisols* – which are then coalesced.

Organosols The resin particles are in a wholly or partly volatile organic liquid. These coatings are thinner and cheaper than:

Plastisols When heated, a plasticizer softens the resin – often PVC or a copolymer – which fuses to a continuous film with little loss of volatile matter. Pastes are spread on fabric, paper and other sheet backings, thickness being controlled by a 'knife'.

3 Solution coatings

Thin coatings – usually of PVC copolymers – can be sprayed on brickwork, concrete and open textured backgrounds such as wood-wool slabs to provide washable dust and vapour-proof barriers. Sprayed skins of this type span small cracks and are sufficiently flexible to accommodate structural movements. One formulation has been certified as having *Class 1 Spread of Flame* (BS 476 test).

Thin plastics coatings applied on aluminium sheet in the factory are more accurately described as a paint deposited from solution, rather than as a plastics coating.

4 Cast resin coatings

Cold, usually liquid, epoxides can be cast round articles which are stoved – usually in a factory. As no solvent is used hardening is rapid and thick coatings are possible.

5 Film and sheet coatings

PVC, ABS, polyurethane and PVF films and sheets can be bonded to asbestos cement, metals and other substrates. Extensive use is made of PVC coated steel for furniture, demountable partitions and external cladding.

Thick PVC films on galvanized steel may be expected to last externally for twenty years although with some colour change. PVF film, although costly, is extremely durable externally. 'Tubes' of cellulose acetate, cellulose nitrate or PVC softened by solvents before being placed over components of uniform section such as handrails, acquire a 'shrink fit' when the solvent evaporates.

Preformed coverings

Preformed coverings such as lining papers, wall papers, Lincrusta-Walton, fabrics and metal foils are considered here. They may save labour and time on the site and often provide the only economical way of obtaining complex patterns in colours on large areas. Light fastness varies considerably and few of these materials resist strong sunlight. Colours and patterns should be selected from large samples and in the lighting conditions in which they will be used. With the exception of suitable metal foils and special adhesives, these coverings are suitable only in dry conditions.

It is wise to follow the manufacturers' recommendations for hanging various coverings. Methods vary – thus for some materials, the adhesive is best applied to the wall rather than to the back of the hanging and some materials are best jointed by overlapping adjoining sheets, cutting through both thicknesses and then removing the surplus material.

The following types of thin preformed coverings are described:

Metal foils	Wood veneers
Lining papers	Cork
Expanded polystyrene (lining)	Leather
Wallpapers	Expanded polystyrene
Plastics-faced cloths	Textiles
Rollywood	Grasscloth etc.
Pinotex	Lincrusta-Walton
	Gilding

Metal foils are used for decorative and functional reasons. Underlinings of lead or aluminium foil (or of pitch coated paper) may be required to protect water-sensitive wall coverings while structures dry out from the reverse side. In other cases, metal foil on the inner surfaces of walls and ceilings can serve as a vapour barrier to prevent moisture from the building condensing within the structure.

A two-can epoxy varnish which sets independently of the air and in moist conditions is an effective adhesive for metal foils.

Lining papers are used as coverings on imperfect plaster and similar surfaces, to bridge hair-cracks and give even suction and texture for wall-papers and other thin coverings, and for paint. *Cross lining* is hung horizontally under wall paper to avoid coincidence of joints in the lining paper and wallpaper.

Colours vary from good white to dark brown.

Qualities are *common pulp* in weights from 165 to 365 kg per ream; *strong brown* – for badly cracked surfaces; *pitch coated* for damp walls, and *cotton backed* for surfaces which are liable to move – eg existing t and g boarding.

Lining papers are 559 and 762 mm × 11 m. There is no selvedge.

Expanded polystyrene is available in widths of 610 mm and thicknesses of 2 mm and 5 mm. In addition to having the merits of paper lining it provides some thermal insulation – often sufficient to prevent surface condensation. Here, suitable solvent-free adhesive is applied to the wall or ceiling.

Wallpapers

Wallpapers vary considerably in character and cost. Patterns have 'repeats' (the distance between identical motifs in any one vertical line) up to 2 m and the size of repeats must be taken into account in estimating quantities. A pattern where motifs are at the same level at the two edges of a paper is called a 'set pattern' and where this does not occur it is called a 'drop' pattern.

Machine-made wallpaper is described by BS 1248 : 1954 amended 1963. It covers 533 mm width as hung. Rolls are 10·5 m. ± 1½% long.

Examples include: *pulps*, having a pattern printed directly on paper; *embossed*; *duplex papers* which are two-ply papers; *ingrain* having fibres incorporated in the surface; *varnished* and *plastic emulsion coated* 'washable' papers and *mica surfaced papers* having sheen.

Finishes include *moirés*, a watered silk effect, and *metallic finishes*. Vinyl faced papers including those with gloss and metallic finishes are washable and most domestic stains can be removed. Papers faced with a thin film of PVC are costly, but provide maximum dirt resistance.

Flock papers have patterns in raised pile – produced by blowing wool or rayon fibres onto patterns printed in adhesive.

Anaglypta, wet-moulded in high relief from high quality cotton pulp, is provided in natural form or in one colour. It is very tough and the emboss gives the material a high degree of resilience so that it can be used on hair-cracked surfaces which move slightly. High relief patterns and wood textures are provided as panels up to 978 mm square.

Hand-printed paper

This is more costly and the patterns more 'exclusive' than machine printed paper. Colours tend to be denser and do not run downwards – a characteristic of rotary printing by machine. However, patterns are not always so accurate – presenting difficulty in hanging – and some colours are soluble in water.

English hand-printed paper is approximately 533 mm by 11 m long.

Hanging wallpapers

A crack-free, smooth and level background is important. Defective plaster should be 'made good' with plaster of the same type, lightly glass-papered and dusted. It should be dry, chemically neutral and have slight suction. Any efflorescent salts should be brushed off 'dry' and a liberal coat of well thinned alkali-resisting primer applied to the surface.

Old wallpaper should preferably be wetted and removed by a stripper. If it shows signs of mould growth, stripping is essential and the surface should be sterilized with a fungicidal wash.

Normally a coat of size is required to equalize and reduce the suction of plaster, but not foamed polystyrene.

Ordinary papers are pasted on the back with flour, starch or cellulose pastes, which provide good 'slip' properties during hanging. Heavy papers are best fixed either with flour or starch pastes with some *Dextrine* (a maize-based paste) added, or with a specially prepared *tub* paste. The addition of about 57 g of washing soda per bucket of paste neutralizes any acid which would darken metallic pigments on papers.

Depressions in the back of anaglypta may be filled with plaster, sawdust and glue size, before fixing, to increase the area for adhesion and the resistance to mechanical damage.

For the best results – especially with heavily grounded papers – edges should be trimmed with a straight edge and knife. In certain cases the edges should be slightly undercut. Before hanging, rolls must be carefully matched for colour.

In hanging, patterns should be matched at eye level to minimize the effects of inaccuracies in printing and of stretch in the paper. Allowing neither too long nor too short a time for the paste to wet the paper, and to reach a stage conducive to good adhesion, is a most important factor in paperhanging and good pattern matching depends very much on this.

Great care must be taken to avoid paste staining the face of the paper, especially flock papers and those with soluble pigments.

If drying is too rapid, the paper fibres are over-stretched and in drying do not shrink back to their original size, leaving the paper loose and blistered.

Plastics-faced cloths

Strong cotton cloths impregnated with PVC resist normal scratches and scuffing and 'domestic' chemicals and can be cleaned with warm water and mild soap.

They are produced in monochromes and in a large range of patterns, and with plain and textured surfaces, in various widths from 673 mm to 1321 mm.

Surfaces to receive cloths should be prepared as for wallpapers. The adhesive recommended by the manufacturer – which must be mould-inhibiting – may be applied either to the wall or to the back of the cloth.

Allowance of up to 26 mm/m in the length of some cloths must be made for shrinkage which may occur after hanging.

Other preformed coverings

Rollywood consisting of thin wood slats woven together with thread is applied to a liberally pasted wall which has been previously lined.

Pinotex is similar to *Rollywood* but has thin cylindrical slats.

Wood veneers often exotically figured, in varying widths and in lengths up to about 2 m are stocked in the order in which they were sliced from the log so that patterns can be made by matching adjacent veneers. Products mounted on paper, cloth and metal foil backings are easier to bend with than across the grain. An aluminium foil-backed wood veneer has a transparent vinyl coated face.

Textiles The very wide range of materials includes cottons, linen, jute, silk and synthetic fibres. Natural coloured and dyed hessians are available in close, medium and open weaves – either backed or with a paper, foamed plastic or PVA backing. Suitable unbacked materials can be fixed in folds or stretched taut on light frames or horizontal rails. Inexpensive textiles are fixed on surfaces lined with paper tinted to suit the colour of the fabric, paste being applied to the lining paper. Paste is applied to the back of backed materials. Good products can be cleaned with an upholstery fabric cleaner, a vacuum cleaner or by brushing lightly.

Cork is provided on a coloured paper backing 760 mm wide, the colour of which shows through the cork which is extremely thin. It should be hung on a lining paper like wallpaper.

Leather An economical size for cutting cowhide is about 915 mm by 760 mm. It is usually backed with padding such as polyether foam and mounted on blockboard or 6 mm hardboard 'invisibly' fixed to walls.

Expanded polystyrene This hanging, already described as a lining material, must be fixed with a PVA adhesive and painted with emulsion paint. Other adhesives and paints destroy it.

Grasscloth etc Grasses, honeysuckle and bamboos are held together with thread and mounted on backings. After careful trimming, the *cloths* are pasted on the back and applied to previously lined surfaces.

Lincrusta-Walton *Lincrusta* as it is normally called, is a composition of whiting, wood flour, lithopone, wax and resin with linseed oil as binder, pressed at high temperature on a kraft backing paper giving a more faithful reproduction from the mould than anaglypta. Units of Lincrusta are provided in natural putty colour for painting, and also in colours. Surfaces should be lined before Lincrusta is fixed with a heavy duty adhesive.

Gilding is the application of extremely thin *leaves* of silver, platinum, copper, aluminium, or in particular gold, to surfaces.

Gold leaf is provided in various shades and thicknesses. 23–25 carat English gold of 'double thickness' is used for the best work. Imitation gold tarnishes rapidly if it is not lacquered. A coat of weak parchment size enriches the colour of gold and from time to time the size can be removed together with the dirt adhering to it.

On surfaces other than glass, metal leaves either mounted on paper as a *transfer*, or loose, are applied on *gold size*, the tackiness of which, when the leaf is applied, determines the final lustre of the gilded surface.

Gilding with loose leaf is a very skilled process which requires still air conditions. The leaf is picked up and brought into contact with a gelatine size with a special brush (a *tip*) – which has been touched on the hair of the operator. On moulded surfaces the leaf is then dabbed and polished with a camel hair *dabber*.

Water gilding – leaf is floated on water on backgrounds of composition, the glue in which provides adhesion. The method, which gives a brilliant, join-free gold surface is rarely used today except for high class and intricate work such as making picture frames.

18 Roofings

CONSTRUCTION: THEORY

A roof is a major element of construction and the satisfactory solution of the aesthetic and technical problems associated with roofing is fundamental to the satisfactory performance of the building as a whole. Structural behaviour and roof structure are considered in *MBC: S and F* parts 1 and 2. Some of the more common terms used in connection with roofing are illustrated in figure 252.

it is important to note that a roof is defined as *flat* up to a pitch of 10 degrees to the horizontal (see BS 3589 : 1963 *Glossary of general building terms*). Where a flat roof is chosen, the appearance of the roof's surface is generally not so important, except that flat roofs can always be overlooked from higher levels and may be used for terraces and even vehicular traffic. Where a

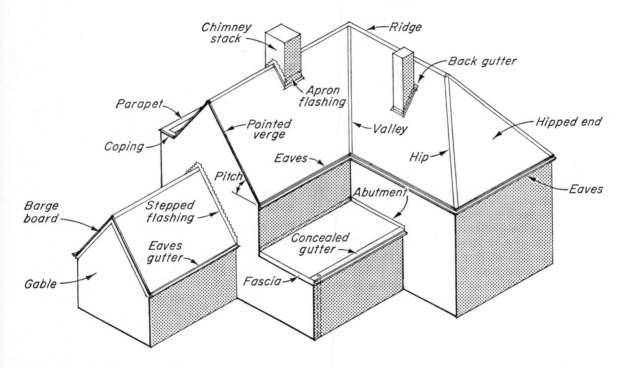

252 Terms used in connection with roofing

With regard to roof finishes the following list gives the more important factors which must be considered in order to decide on a suitable method of construction.

1 **Appearance** The degree of pitch of the roof surface is a primary design decision. A roof is generally described as either *flat* or *pitched* and

roof is pitched, the colour and texture of the materials used is a very important factor.

2 **Durability** In general terms a roof is more vulnerable to the effects of rain, snow, solar radiation and atmospheric pollution, than any other part of a building. Traditional pitched roof coverings such as tiles, slates, lead sheet

and thatch remain serviceable for many years but the more modern flat roof covering presents a difficult problem. The question of the rate at which water will 'run off' a roof is of fundamental importance. Pitched roofing has a high rate of 'run off' and, providing that the detailing in respect of overlap or jointing is satisfactory, the materials used to cover pitched roofs will be expected to have a long life. The 'run off' from a truly flat roof is very slow indeed and in practice most materials used for flat roof covering do not remain perfectly level and true after laying. As a result, water is very often retained in shallow pools on the finished roof surface. This is known as *ponding*. It is a prime cause of deterioration because local variations in temperature between the wet and dry areas of the roof cause differential thermal movement, which together with accumulations of acid left by evaporating rain cause a break-down in the roof surface. It is of course possible to design roofs to retain a considerable depth of water to protect and insulate the roof surface so that the roof benefits from freedom from diurnal temperature. The depth of water must however be sufficient to withstand evaporation and it must not be allowed to stagnate. Because this is difficult in practice, the most satisfactory method is to construct the roof deck so that it slopes or falls towards the roof outlet to a sufficient degree to shed the surface water whilst the outline of the roof still retains its flat appearance by the use of a horizontal fascia. A fall of 1 in 80, say is 12 mm in 1000 mm, is required for sheet metal covering and a similar fall is also the minimum for asphalt although a greater fall is desirable wherever possible.

3 **Weather exclusion** Roof coverings are required to prevent the entry of rain, snow and dust and to resist the effects of wind—both wind pressure and the effects of suction.

Rainfall Maps showing an index of driving rain are included in BRS Digest 23. It has been shown that rain penetration depends both on rain amount and wind speed and is governed more by maximum rain intensity rather than total duration or total quantity. This is of particular importance where the roof covering is in the form of separate heavy units made butt jointed as in tiles and slates. This type of cover-

ing depends upon the adequacy of the overlap of the units and the pitch of the roof to shed the water.

Wind pressure The effect of wind pressure upon a roof depends upon the angle of pitch and the degree of exposure of the roof slope. For a ridge type roof of between 20 degrees and 30 degrees pitch the suction will more or less be equally balanced on both roof slopes. On steeper pitches the negative pressure (the suction) is higher on the leeward side. For shallow pitched roofs up to 20 degrees a suction occurs on the windward side. Modern pitched roofs usually fall into this category and it is in this type of roof that suction may present a serious problem, and in particular where lightweight sheet coverings are used, on a lightweight timber decking. With this construction the roof deck should be securely anchored down and this can be done by making sure that sheeting is firmly fixed to the roof framing and then securing a wallplate by means of galvanized steel straps built in the brickwork. Severe air pressure tends to occur at eaves on a roof particularly in the case of projecting eaves used in conjunction with a low pitch. It is especially important to seal the edges of flat roof coverings to prevent wind entering below. BRS Digest 99, 101 and 105 are concerned with wind loading on buildings and BSCP 3 Chapter V part 2, should be studied.

4 **Fire resistance** For England and Wales (excluding the old LCC area) the Building Regulations 1965 include structural fire precautions for roofs in Part E. For Scotland the Building Standards (Scotland) Regulations 1963 include structural fire precautions for roofs. The London County Council Constructional Byelaws 1965, prevail in the area of the Greater London Council. BS 476 Part III : 1958 *External fire exposure roof tests* is used as the basis for the fire resistance requirements. The BS sets down tests for the measurement of resistance of external fire penetration and spread of flame for roofs. A tested specification receives a designation consisting of two letters, eg AA, AC, BB. The first letter relates to the resistance to external fire penetration and the second letter refers to the degree of spread of flame on the external surface Categories A to D are listed in each case. A building must be positioned at a particular

specified distance from the site boundary depending upon the fire specification of the roof and having regard to the use of the building. There are no limitations on roofs with a specification of Class AA, AB, AC.

5 **Thermal insulation** The Building Regulations specify that a thermal transmittance through a roof construction shall not be more than $1·42$ W/m² deg C for the roofs of dwellings. The Thermal Insulation (Industrial Buildings) Act 1957 require that the roof of an Industrial Building shall have a U value not greater than $1·71$ W/m² deg C at an internal temperature of $21·1°C$ but provision is made to allow the U value to increase as the temperature reduces, as shown below (interpolated values).

Internal temperature °C	U value of roof W/m² deg C
20	1·7
17·5	1·9
15·0	2·4
12·5	2·8
10·0	3·4
7·5	4·4
5·0	6·2

Thermal insulation may be provided in the roof in one of three ways as follows
(a) A layer of insulating material, external to the roof structure and placed immediately below the roof covering. In the case of slates or tiles this could be an insulating quilt laid over the rafters. In the case of a built-up felt roofing the insulation could be an insulating board placed immediately beneath the waterproof covering.
(b) Insulation may be obtained by means of the resistivity of the construction of the roof sub-structure. In respect of a flat roof, this would be in the form of a self-insulated roof deck and is an economic form of construction because one material performs both the function of insulation and support to the roof surface.
(c) An insulating lining beneath the structure. This type of construction may sometimes be advantageous when rapid changes of interior temperature are expected.

The most economic method of construction is where the insulation is external to the roof structure but immediately beneath the roof covering as described in (a) for the following reasons

(i) It insulates the structure and thus reduces stress due to temperature change.
(ii) It can be fully continuous and will thus eliminate cold spots in the construction.
(iii) It can control condensation by keeping all the construction including its internal surface warm and above the dew point. The matter of condensation and the necessity for vapour barriers under certain circumstances is discussed more fully later.
(iv) The insulation is simpler and conveniently supported by the structure itself without additional suspension. Where insulating linings are fixed beneath the sub-structure as in (c) there may be a liability to the risk of condensation within the roof.

6 **Condensation** The atmosphere contains water in the form of water vapour but the amount varies according to the temperature and the humidity. The temperature at which air is saturated is called *dew point* and warm air is able to contain more water vapour than cold air before it becomes saturated. Thus if air containing a given amount of water vapour is cooled there will be a temperature at which condensation of the water vapour into water droplets will occur. Surface condensation occurs when moisture laden air comes into contact with a surface which is at a temperature below the *dew point* of the air. In respect of roof construction surface condensation can be avoided by keeping the internal surface at a temperature above the *dew point* of the internal air. This is done by insulation. Surface condensation can also be avoided by reducing the moisture content of the air within the building or within the roof space and thus lowering its *dew point*. This is done by ventilation, thus the combination of ventilation and insulation is the best way of preventing surface condensation. Where the internal conditions are warm and humid the difference in the vapour pressure of the internal atmosphere and the cold external atmosphere may be such that the warm water vapour will move into and through the roof structure to the

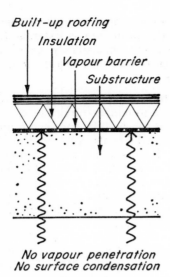

Built-up roofing

Insulation

Vapour barrier

Substructure

No vapour penetration
No surface condensation

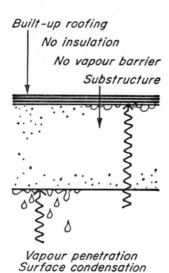

Built-up roofing

No insulation

No vapour barrier

Substructure

Vapour penetration
Surface condensation

253   Vapour barrier

coldest side and condense within the roof thickness. This form of condensation is known as *Interstitial condensation*. Where this type of condensation occurs the water will most likely cause the structure to deteriorate, and in very bad situations part of the moisture may drip back into the building. In such cases a vapour barrier is necessary to prevent this vapour

movement and the barrier should be positioned at a point where it remains at a temperature above the *dew point* of the vapour. The most suitable practical position is to place the vapour barrier on the warmest side of the insulation, since at this point it will prevent moisture vapour getting to a point within the construction where the temperature drop would cause the vapour to form condensation. This is illustrated in figure 253. In general terms it is advisable that where moisture sensitive materials are used for roof decking they should be sealed on all surfaces if they are to maintain stability in cases where condensation is likely.

7 **Cost** In calculating the cost in use of roof covering the cost of maintenance and periodical renewal must be taken into account. Although roof coverings can be replaced and repaired with less disturbance than most other parts of the structure failure will usually involve costly damage to the fabric and its contents. From a study cost analysis on various projects the water proofing element of a flat roofed building represents on an average 1·5% of the total cost per unit floor area. This figure applies to waterproofing in respect of built-up felt roofings and similar materials.

SYSTEMS OF CONSTRUCTION

Roof pitch

The roof shape will determine the range of materials from which the choice can be made for the roof finish. The basic form of the roof will either be flat or pitched or curved. Roofs having a fall of less than 10 degrees are technically termed flat roofs, and suitable materials for finishes are felt, asphalt and sheet metals such as copper or zinc. These materials will also be suitable for curved roof shapes. For pitched roofs materials which overlap each other such as slates and tiles or corrugated metal or asbestos are suitable. A material which will be satisfactory on a shallow pitch (or flat) roof will also be adequate on a steeper pitch. Modification of flat and sloping roof covering techniques can also be used as cladding for vertical surfaces, ie tiling, slating, and metal sheeting. BS 2717:1956 *Glossary of terms applicable to roof coverings* is a useful reference. Slates or tiles used on pitched roofs need only be supported at intervals by means of battens. Materials such as built-up felt and copper, or jointless materials such as asphalt normally used on flat roofs require continuous overall support in the form of a roof deck. Table 32 gives the more commonly used coverings related to the recommended roof pitch at which they are used.

Roof pitch is the angle of slope to the horizontal and can be shown as rise/span. This is expressed as a fraction for pitched roofs, because the relationship of rise to span is more easily used information for setting out on site. Note however that most trade literature in respect of pitched roofing materials indicates roof pitch as the angle of slope.

The minimum pitch at which a material can be used depends on many factors such as exposure to wind and weather, workmanship, design and type of joints in the roofing, porosity of the roof covering material and its tendency to laminate in frost, and the size of the unit.

For flat roofs the pitch is usually indicated by the 'fall' to which the material must be laid to shed water. The 'fall' is expressed as a relationship between the rise and given run of roof of say 1000 mm or 3000 mm.

As an example for pitched roofing, slates laid to an angle of $33\frac{1}{3}°$ would have a pitch of rise/span $= \frac{1}{3}$.

For flat roofs, asphalt laid to a deck at an angle of $\frac{3}{4}°$ would have a 'fall' expressed as 12 : 1000 which means that for every 1000 mm of roof deck the rise is 12 mm. Figure 254 illustrates the terms used.

Roof decking

There are two basic forms which the sub-structure or deck can take as follows

(i) *In situ monolithic* such as reinforced concrete slab or
(ii) *prefabricated decking and panel units* ranging from thin pre-cast concrete slabs, metal and asbestos cement decking units, to timber and man-made boards such as compressed straw and wood wool.

An in situ monolithic deck should be designed and constructed so that it does not break-up or crack in a manner which will affect the roof covering.

Roof covering	Angle	Pitch	Rise in 1000 mm run
Asphalt: lead and copper (with drips)	$\frac{3}{4}°$	1/160	12 mm
Built up bitumen felt: zinc (with drips)	1°	1/120	17 mm
Corrugated asbestos cement sheeting with sealed end laps	10°	1/11	180 mm
Copper and zinc (with welted end seams)	$13\frac{3}{4}°$	$\frac{1}{8}$	250 mm
Interlocking concrete tiles	$17\frac{1}{2}°$	1/6	333 mm
Corrugated asbestos cement sheeting with 150 mm end laps	$22\frac{1}{2}°$	1/5	400 mm
Slates: min. 300 mm wide	$26\frac{1}{2}°$	$\frac{1}{4}$	500 mm
Slates: min. 225 mm wide Single lap tiles	$33\frac{3}{3}° \atop 35°$ }	$\frac{1}{3}$	660 mm
Plain tiles: (BS CP 142 allows 35° for concrete)	40°	5/12	830 mm

Table 32

This may be achieved by providing suitable joints. Precise specification and careful site supervision is essential. Screeds which are used to provide

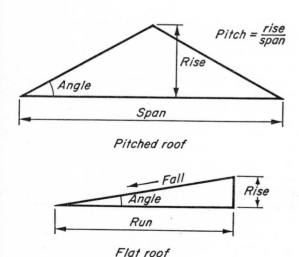

$$Pitch = \frac{rise}{span}$$

Pitched roof

Flat roof

254 'Pitch' and 'fall'

falls or insulation or to level an uneven surface should have adequate strength and adhesion to the material supporting them so that they function integrally and do not separate or give stresses which will affect the roof covering. In situ or reinforced concrete must be well cured and free from excess moisture or frost. The surface should be hard and smooth and clean without irregularities and preferably wood floated. Where it would otherwise be of open texture, it must be floated or screeded. Adequate crack control methods including movement joints must be provided in the sub-structure. Lightweight aggregates may be used in in situ concrete. The types generally in use are either prepared from manufactured materials such as foamed slag, expanded vermiculite, expanded clay, etc, or by using foaming or air entraining agents. Lightweight concrete should comply with requirements for ordinary concrete in respect of condition of surface. The water content should be kept to a minimum and sufficient time must be allowed for the water or foaming agent to dry out or disperse. The porous nature and high residual water content of lightweight concrete make it essential to take special precautions to disperse this trapped water so that it does not disrupt the roof finish. The more commonly used prefabricated decking and panel units are listed below

Pre-cast or pre-stressed concrete beams or slabs

Where this type of structural unit is used for a flat roof deck a 1 : 4 sand and cement screed of at least 25 mm thick is required. Drainage holes should be provided to prevent water being trapped in the construction after laying.

Lightweight concrete slabs

Where this type of slab is laid carefully a sand cement screed may not be required. A bitumen emulsion primer should however be applied to the top surface of the slabs as soon as possible after erection to prevent absorption of rainwater.

Asbestos cement decking

This is another useful material for flat roof decks, but is subject to movement due to change of temperature and moisture content. Great care should be taken in fixing to minimize these effects and the units should be inter-connected to prevent differential deflection. The hollow decking units are designed to accommodate supplementary insulation, say in the form of a glass fibre quilt or alternatively the asbestos decking can be covered with 12 mm wood fibre insulating boards in panels 1200 mm by 600 mm laid with staggered joints and bonded to the asbestos cement decking with hot bitumen compound.

Metal decking

This form of construction is suitable for both flat and pitched roofs and is usually laid complete with insulation and built up felt waterproofing as a composite roof construction by specialist sub-contractors. The decking may be of galvanized steel or aluminium formed by a continuous rolled process in a variety of profiles and gauges to suit most span and load requirements. Fibre insulation board, polystyrene, cork or other materials is used in sheet form to give any required insulation value. This insulation is protected by a bituminous felt vapour barrier where necessary. The decking units are fixed by hook bolts or shot firing to the steel supporting structure; the vapour barrier is bonded to the top surface of the metal decking followed by the insulating boards.

Timber boarding

The whole of the timber sub-structure should be constructed in accordance with BSCP 112 *Constructional use of timber in buildings*. The construction should minimize the effects of shrinkage, warping and displacement or relative movement of the timber and care should be taken to guard against all conditions which might allow decay through moisture already present in unseasoned timber or resulting from the ingress of water from other parts of the structure or from condensation. To avoid dry rot, ventilation should be provided between roof boarding and the ceiling. BSCP 144 Part I:1968 *Roof coverings* stresses the importance of ventilation in roof spaces to avoid fungal growth. Roof boarding should be well seasoned to avoid the tendency to shrink and cup. It should not be less than 25 mm thick and 100 mm wide and should be tongued and grooved. Arrises should be rounded, upstanding edges planed down and nail heads well sunk. The supporting roof construction should be rigid with joists at maximum 450 mm centres and the board fixed by nails at each edge to minimize the risk of curling. Boarding should be laid either in the direction of the fall of the roof or diagonally and the roof surface should be protected as far as possible from rain during the course of construction.

Plywood

It is essential to supply sufficient support to the plywood and there should be noggin pieces between the joists. Nailing should be at 150 mm centres and at all edges and at intermediate supports. Rafter centres and nail length, according to plywood thickness, are set out below:

Plywood thickness	Rafter centres	Nail length
8 mm	400 mm	38 mm
19 mm	600 mm	38 mm
12 mm	800 mm	50 mm
16 mm	1200 mm	50 mm

Wood-wool slabs

These should be the heavy duty type of slab fixed according to the manufacturers' instructions by clips or screwing to timber joists or steel purlins. The joints between the slabs should be filled with sand and cement and the slab should be topped with a 1 : 4 sand and cement screed 12 mm thick in bays not exceeding 9 m². On roof slopes of more than 20 degrees the screed may be omitted and a sand and cement slurry used instead. Where wood wool units are fixed direct to roof support the span should not exceed 600 mm and the bearing surface at the edge of each unit should not be less than 50 mm and fixed securely at every bearing point. Channel reinforced wood wool is often used to increase strength and span. The usual thickness is 50 mm. Note should be taken of the risk of condensation due to the direct conductivity of the steel reinforcing channels, and in order to counteract this, thicker slabs are available rebated at the joints to receive cork inserts to achieve continuity of insulation at each joint. Pre-screeded and pre-felted wood wool slabs are also available. The felt is a protective layer only and does not form part of a built-up felt system. The joints of this type of wood wool slab should be taped immediately the slabs are laid to prevent moisture

infiltration. The channel reinforced wood-wool slabs will span up to 4500 mm and so can be used as self-supporting decking.

Compressed straw slabs

These must be of roofing quality which means that they are covered on the external face with an impregnated liner making the unit shower proof for short periods. Each edge of all the units must be fully supported and fixed in accordance with the manufacturer's instructions. Straw board slabs should not be laid unless they can be covered (with built-up felt roofing) the same day. A sand and cement screed is not required but instead the joints are taped with strips of roofing felt bonded with hot bitumen compound before the first layer of felt is applied. Thus close co-ordination is essential during the fixing of the deck units and the application of the weather proofing and for this reason it is good practice to allow the deck and built-up roofing to be supplied and fixed by the specialist roofing sub-contractor.

Chipboard

This should be nailed to the joists and to noggins to support all edges. It is recommended that joints be taped with strips of roofing felt bonded with hot bitumen before the first layer of felt is applied. Chipboard does not in itself provide sufficient insulation and should be used in conjunction with an insulating quilt placed over the joists.

Non-structural insulation boards

Where the decking unit does not give sufficient thermal insulation (in particular in the case of the metal decking) a non-structural insulation board is used between the decking and the water-proofing. Vegetable fibre boards which include those made from wood or cane fibres or natural or regranulated cork, are suitable provided that they are adequately supported. As in the case of timber, care should be taken to guard against decay, particularly through moisture. Where this type of board is laid on concrete or similar materials and where there will be moisture vapour diffusion from within the building a vapour barrier is essential. Mineral fibre and granular boards include those made from glass or mineral fibres, mica or similar granules compressed and bonded with bitumen, synthetic resin or other material. When used with metal decking joints in the board must not be made over the trough of the deck or the board will collapse under normal maintenance traffic. Extruded polystyrene sheet is now a commonly used non-structural board and for all practical purposes is vapour proof. That is to say a vapour barrier can be omitted except in conditions of a very high humidity, ie as found in a laundry.

Wood boards, particle boards, wood-wool slabs and compressed straw slabs, fibre building boards, foamed plastic board are described in *MBC: Materials*. Lightweight concrete for screeds is also described in the *Materials* volume.

Screeds

Mention has been made of the necessity to screed certain decks to provide a smooth surface upon which to lay the roof waterproofing. The selection of a suitable mix and thickness of screed is very important and whilst the mix must be related to that of the sub-structure concrete, sand cement screed should not be normally richer than 1 part cement to 4 parts sand by volume. They should be of low workability and laid in areas not exceeding 9 m² even if they are reinforced. The minimum thickness should be 25 mm except where they are laid as topping on wood-wool slabs when the minimum thickness can be reduced to 13 mm. Additional insulation can be provided by using a lightweight concrete screed but in such cases entrapped water is always a problem and if allowed to remain may seriously reduce the thermal insulation value of the screed and may cause blistering of the roof finish where built-up felt, asphalt or single layer roofing is used. It is customary to provide a topping of 12 mm of sand cement immediately after lightweight concrete has been laid—this provides a surface which will shed water to pre-arranged temporary drainage holes in the roof structure. These drainage holes should pass through the screed and the roof deck at the lowest part of the roof and be positioned in any depression where water collects. The problems that may arise where water is trapped in a screed are more fully discussed on page 387.

MATERIALS FOR ROOF COVERING

Mastic asphalt

Mastic asphalt is a mixture of several materials and is prescribed for various purposes such as roofing, flooring and tanking by a series of British Standard Specifications. The specifications relevant to asphalt for roofing are as follows. BS 1162 *Mastic asphalt for roofing (natural rock asphalt aggregate)*; BS 988 *Mastic asphalt for roofing (limestone aggregate)*. Where the roof is liable to be used by vehicular traffic say for car parking, the British Standards are BS 1446 *Mastic asphalt (natural rock aggregate) for roads and footways* and BS 1447 *Mastic asphalt (limestone aggregate) for roads and footways*. As will be seen from the British Standards, asphalt consists of an asphaltic cement and an aggregate. The asphaltic cement will consist of bitumen from petroleum distillation or a blend of this bitumen with Trinidad Lake Asphalt. The choice is then between rock asphalt from Switzerland, France or Sicily which is a limestone naturally impregnated with about 6% bitumen or a natural ordinary crushed limestone. Mastic asphalt produced from the natural rock asphalt is lighter in colour but is about one-third more expensive than the crushed limestone material. The British Standards permit alternative percentages of Trinidad Lake asphalt which may be incorporated in the asphaltic cement. These are specified in BS 988 as Table III, columns 1, 2 and 3 and in BS 1162 as Table II, columns 1 and 2. The specifier should thus indicate which composition of asphaltic cement is required in accordance with the British Standards. The Code of Practice CP 144: *Roof coverings* Part 2 *Mastic asphalt* requires the use of black sheathing felt to BS 747 type 4A (i) as an isolating membrane under the asphalt. Black sheathing felt is available with either a bitumen or a pitch saturant. On wet construction decks the bitumen impregnated type must be employed whilst on decks of dry construction either the bitumen or the pitch impregnated type may be used.

Roofing asphalt can be used either to form a continuous waterproof covering over either, flat, pitched or curved surfaces and can be easily worked round pipes, roof lights and other roof projections. It can be laid on most types of rigid sub-structure such as concrete either precast or in situ, timber boarding or a variety of proprietary structural deck units.

Durability

Mastic asphalt when laid by a good specialist roofing sub-contractor on a sound base will not require major repairs for at least 60 years. When repairs are required they should always be carried out by a specialist. Eventually, exposed mastic asphalt is broken down by acids in the atmosphere and by ultra-violet radiation. So a special surfacing such as stone chippings, greatly increase the durability of the covering. Special surfacing is also necessary where there will be pedestrian or vehicular traffic.

Mastic asphalt is a dense material and being a very dark colour the uncovered material absorbs the heat very readily and especially where extra insulation is laid below the asphalt. To counteract this, a wide range of chippings is available for applying to the surface of asphalt roofing to give a high degree of self-reflectivity. Various coloured granites, white limestone, calcined flint and white spar usually in sizes up to 13 mm are the most widely used. Reflective chippings are suitable for use on roofs up to 10 degree pitch. They are embedded in a layer of bitumen dressing compound to form a textured surface.

Thermal insulation

This may be necessary to provide the insulation levels required in the Building Regulations in the case of housing and the Thermal Insulation (Industrial Buildings) Act 1957 in the case of factories. The U value obtained for constructions using 20 mm asphalt and top dressed with 10 mm mineral chippings with various forms of insulation are shown in table 33.

It should be remembered that insulation within the roof construction leads to a reduction in temperature variations in the roof structure, thereby minimizing thermal movement.

Vapour barrier

It is necessary to provide a vapour barrier on the warmest side of the insulation. The vapour barrier may consist of a layer of roofing felt with sealed laps but the best type incorporates an impermeable

Sub-structure	Insulation	U value (W/m² deg C)
150 mm solid concrete	25 mm cork slab	1·08
	20 mm fibre insulation board	1·53
	50 mm cellular concrete screed	1·25
125 mm hollow concrete beams with 25 mm sand and cement screed	13 mm fibre insulation board	1·53
	20 mm fibre insulation board	1·30
50 mm wood-wool slabs with 13 mm sand cement screed	Sub-structure acts as insulation	1·42
50 mm compressed straw slabs	Sub-structure acts as insulation	1·25
25 mm thick flax board	Sub-structure acts as insulation	1·70
25 mm deal boards	20 mm fibre insulation board	1·30
Metal decking	20 mm fibre insulation board	1·65

Table 33

metal foil. A good example of a proprietary vapour barrier supplied by specialist asphalt contractors consists of a sheet of aluminium foil protected by a coating of bitumen on both sides and reinforced with a sheet of glass fibre tissue. The vapour barrier should be folded back at least 225 mm over the outer edges of the insulating layer and the asphalt roofing bonded to the overlap as shown in figure 255.

Fire resistance

Asphalt for roofing achieves the designation AA under the test requirements of BS 746 Part 3 *External fire exposure roof tests*.

Application of asphalt

In-situ concrete, precast concrete beams and slabs, wood-wool slabs, timber construction, asbestos

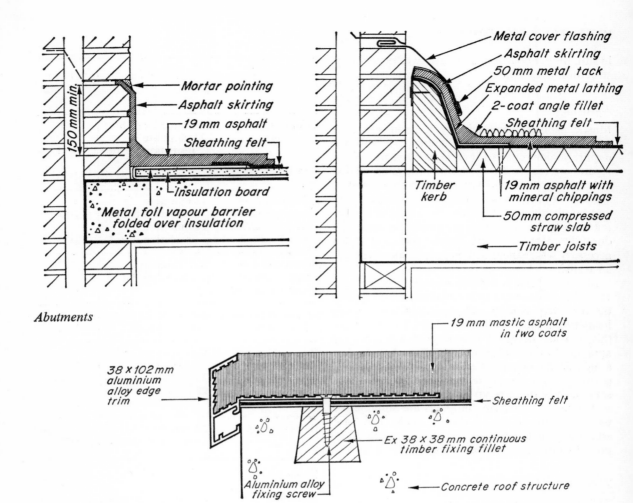

Mortar pointing

Asphalt skirting

150 mm min.

19 mm asphalt

Sheathing felt

Insulation board

Metal foil vapour barrier folded over insulation

Metal cover flashing

Asphalt skirting

50 mm metal tack

Expanded metal lathing

2-coat angle fillet

Sheathing felt

Timber kerb

19 mm asphalt with mineral chippings

50 mm compressed straw slab

Timber joists

Abutments

19 mm mastic asphalt in two coats

38 × 102 mm aluminium alloy edge trim

Sheathing felt

Ex 38 × 38 mm continuous timber fixing fillet

Aluminium alloy fixing screw

Concrete roof structure

Verge

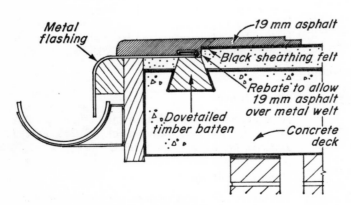

Metal flashing

19 mm asphalt

Black sheathing felt

Dovetailed timber batten

Rebate to allow 19 mm asphalt over metal welt

Concrete deck

Aluminium eaves trim to asphalt roofing

255   *Asphalt details: abutments, eaves and ver*

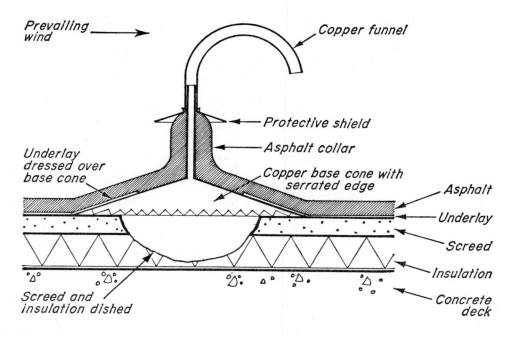

256 'Parovent' copper ventilator

cavity decking, compressed strawboard and metal decking are all suitable methods of construction for the sub-structure upon which asphalt may be laid. In all cases the sub-structure must be strong enough to prevent excessive deflection. And in particular where metal decking is used the deflection limit must be reduced 1/325 of the span instead of the more normal 1/240. For timber flax board, plywood, strawboard or metal decking a timber kerb is required to walls and timber surround to eaves and verges for the application of the asphalt finish. At walls and upstands timber kerbs should be fixed so as to leave an air space between the wall and the sub-structure as shown in figure 255. With a sub-structure formed of wood wool, strawboard, timber or plywood, provision must be made for ventilation between the roof deck and the ceiling. The sub-structure on which the asphalt is to be laid should be designed to ensure the rapid dispersal of rainwater and so falls not less than 1 in 80 should be provided. Any change in the direction of the roof surface in buildings shaped as letter T or L indicates the need for movement joints. Movement joints should be continuous through the entire structure, including

roof, walls and upstands, as shown in figure 260, which is similar in detail to those elaborated for built-up felt roofing in figure 272.

To assist in drying out screeds used in connection with concrete decks and to release trapped moisture, it is good practice to instal drying vents. A proprietary example is shown in figure 256.

On flat roofs up to 10 degrees pitch the roofing asphalt is laid with a wooden float in two coats breaking joint to a minimum thickness of 19 mm on an underlay of black sheathing felt laid loose with 50 mm lapped joints. Where there is thermal insulation material under the asphalt it is recommended that the surface be dressed with reflective mineral chippings to reduce the temperature induced in the asphalt by solar heat. For concrete or screeded sub-structure of 10 to 30 degrees pitch the asphalt is applied in two coats as before. On slopes of over 30 degrees the asphalt is applied without sheathing felt in three coats, the first coat being applied very thinly with a steel trowel. The second and third coats are then applied breaking joint to give a total thickness of not less than 22 mm. Where the asphalt is laid on vertical or sloping surfaces of more than 30 degrees a positive

383

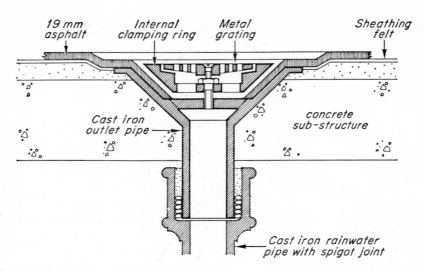

257   Asphalt details: cast iron rainwater outlet

key is required. In the case of sloping surfaces over 10 degrees formed in timber boarding a layer of black sheathing felt is nailed to the timber boards and bitumen clad expanded metal lathing

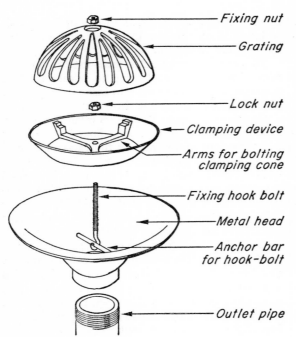

258   Asphalt details: spun steel rainwater outlet

is then fixed at 150 mm centres with galvanized clout nails or staples to form the key for the asphalt which is then applied in three coats. In all cases where the asphalt is laid on flat or slightly sloping roofs clean sharp sand is rubbed evenly over the surface of the asphalt whilst it is still hot. This breaks up the skin of the bitumen brought to the surface by the wooden float at the time of application. The object of this is to minimize the gradual crazing of the surface due to the action of the sun.

Details at abutments and edges are shown in the drawings as follows: figure 255 Abutments, eaves and verge; figure 257 Cast iron outlet with grille; figure 258 an alternative type of outlet made from gun metal or spun steel which has a domed grating and a clamping device which allows the grating to be tightened against the waterproofing; figure 259 Projections through roof; figure 260 Movement joint. Where there is continuous foot traffic, mastic asphalt can be protected with tiles or an in-situ screed as follows:

(a) *Concrete or asbestos cement tiles* Concrete tiles are approximately 300 mm × 300 mm × 25 mm thick, asbestos tiles are also 300 mm × 300 mm but usually available in two thicknesses 25 mm and 8 mm. They are lighter than the concrete tiles and thus can be used where weight is an important consideration. The tiles are laid in bays of maximum 9 m² with 25 mm joints

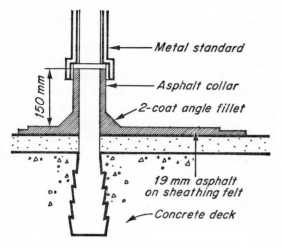

Metal standard

Asphalt collar

2-coat angle fillet

150 mm

19 mm asphalt
on sheathing felt

Concrete deck

Asphalt finish to metal standard

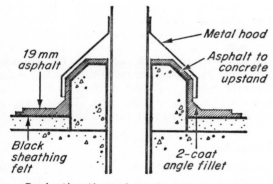

19 mm
asphalt

Metal hood

Asphalt to
concrete
upstand

Black
sheathing
felt

2-coat
angle fillet

Projection through roof with upstand

259   *Asphalt details: projections through roof*

laid in bays of not more than 9 m² with a 25 mm joint between the bays. The grooves and joints can be filled with hot bitumen compound on completion.

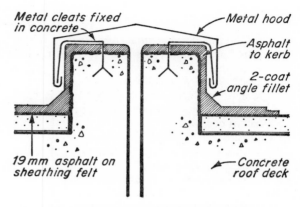

Metal cleats fixed
in concrete

Metal hood

Asphalt
to kerb

2-coat
angle fillet

19 mm asphalt on
sheathing felt

Concrete
roof deck

Twin kerb expansion joint

260   *Asphalt details: movement joint*

Bitumen felt roofing
('Built-up' roofing)

Terms

The following terms are commonly used in connection with multi-layer sheet roofing.

(i) *Built-up roofing*   two or more layers of bitumen roofing fused together on site with bitumen compound. For flat roofs, three layer specifications are recommended, and for pitched roofs, two layers are usual.

(ii) *Roof sub-structure*   the elements of the building on which the built-up roofing is directly laid.

(iii) *Vapour barrier*   a special material interposed between roof surface and the insulation to prevent transmission of moisture or moisture vapour into the insulation.

(iv) *Layer*   a single thickness of bitumen roofing. The word *ply* is not synonymous with layer but is a term sometimes used to denote the thickness of the bitumen sheet.

(v) *Under-layer*   an unexposed layer in a built-up roofing specification.

(vi) *Cap-sheet*   the exposed or final layer in a built-up roofing specification.

between the bays which are filled with bitumen compound. The tiles are set 25 mm back from the base of angle fillets and the margin is completed with bitumen compound. A bitumen primer is applied to the surface of the mastic asphalt roof covering and to the backs of the tiles and allowed to dry. The tiles are then bedded in hot bitumen bonding compound, taking care not to squeeze the compound upwards between the individual tiles.

(b) *Jointed screed.*   A cement and sand screed 25 mm thick is laid on a separating membrane of building paper and grooved into a 600 mm square tiled pattern. The screed should be

(vii) *Movement joint* break or joint in the roof sub-structure where relative movement of the elements of the structure would otherwise affect the roof covering. The movement may be of any origin, eg thermal, loading, wind loading, settlement, vibration, shrinkage or subsidence.

Materials

BS 747 is the *Specification for Roofing Felts.* There are three main types used in built-up felt roofing as detailed below.

BS Class 1 *Bitumen felt (fibre base)*

This material has great flexibility and is used extensively in specifications which are generally lowest in cost.

BS Class 2 *Bitumen felt (asbestos base)*

The asbestos base is relatively inert and provides improved fire resistance.

BS Class 3 *Bitumen felt (glass fibre base)*

This type of felt has high dimensional stability, is proof against decay and is used where the Specification calls for the highest quality.

The BS subdivides the classes according to the finish of the felt, eg

A	saturated	E mineral surfaced
B	fine sand surfaced	F reinforced
C	self finish	G venting base
D	coarse sand surfaced	layer

The use of the saturated felts are not recommended for the lower layers of the roof, and the reinforced felt listed is used as the underlayer beneath slates or tiles, over spars.

Each type of felt is further subdivided according to its weight per 11 m × 0·9 m roll. The heavier felts are normally used as a top layer and thus taking into account the different types, finishes and weights available, the Specifier has a wide choice of alternatives. The Felt Roofing Contractors Advisory Board, list 18 sample Specifications for typical conditions in their Booklet *Built-up Roofing* which is a very good reference.

It is usual to use a protective finish on the top layer of built-up felt roofing to give a reflective finish and protect the bitumen from sunlight or to provide a wearing surface. Stone chippings 10 mm to 13 mm size are often used bedded in bitumen and there is a wide range of types, Derbyshire, White Spar and Leicester Red granite being examples. If the roof is to withstand foot traffic the spar finish will not be suitable because of the danger of the sharp granules cutting the felt. Thus for promenade roofs special concrete or asbestos tiles should be used.

In general for roofs not taking foot traffic (except for maintenance) the main area will be stone chippings; edges and upstands will be in mineral surfaced felt and gutters in self finished felt.

Durability

Successful built-up felt roofing is dependent on the correct specification for each situation. Good materials, careful detailing and correct application are all necessary and so since supervision is difficult the contract should be carried out by a specialist contractor experienced in this type of work.

Thermal insulation

The requirements of the Building Regulations and The Thermal Insulation (Industrial Buildings) Act 1957 will apply (see page 375). An insulating material is often laid directly under the felt and this work should be part of the Felt Roofing Contract. Table 34 gives the U value in W/m^2 deg C for three-layer built-up felt roofing with various alternative forms of insulation. The roofing is top dressed with 10 mm mineral chippings.

Vapour barrier

Condensation is liable to occur on the internal surfaces of a roof construction within a building if the temperature and humidity of the air inside is appreciably higher than the outside temperature and humidity. Thus a vapour barrier will be required on the underside of the insulating layer below the built-up roofing. The barrier should incorporate an impermeable metal foil, and the type and application detailed in the notes on asphalt, page 381, is suitable for use with built-up felt roofing.

Fire resistance

External fire designations for various weatherproofing specifications are set out in the 'deemed to satisfy' section of The Building Standards (Scotland) Regulations 1963, and The Building Regulations 1965 for England and Wales.

Sub-structure	Insulation	U value (W/m² deg C)
150 mm solid concrete	20 mm fibre insulation board	1·48
	20 mm expanded polystyrene (extruded)	1·13
	50 mm cellular concrete screed	1·25
125 mm hollow concrete beams with 25 mm sand cement screed	13 mm fibre insulation board	1·53
	20 mm expanded polystyrene (extruded)	1·02
50 mm wood-wool slabs with 13 mm sand and cement screed	Sub-structure acts as insulation	1·42
50 mm compressed straw slabs	Sub-structure acts as insulation	1·25
25 mm flax board	Sub-structure acts as insulation	1·70
25 mm deal boards	20 mm fibre insulating board	1·30
Metal decking	20 mm fibre insulating boards	1·65
	20 mm expanded polystyrene (extruded)	1·19

Table 34

Where stone chippings are used as topping all felt roofs have the highest AA fire rating in respect of BS 476 Part 3. On pitched roofs the rating varies according to the type of felt in each layer and the combustibility of the roof deck. Asbestos felt has the best fire resistance and most Local Authorities require its use.

Application of built-up roofing

Hollow precast concrete beams or slabs, in-situ concrete, aerated concrete, wood wool slabs, compressed strawboard, timber construction or asbestos or metal decking are all suitable for the roof decking intended for built-up roofing. The use of these materials is more fully discussed on page 377. All built-up felt roofing should be carried out in accordance with the requirements of CP 144 Part I 1968 *Built-up bitumen felt*. It is necessary to provide falls to clear the water from a flat roof and a minimum of 17 mm in 1000 mm is recommended (1 degree slope). The first layer of roofing felt is fixed by nailing, or by full bonding or by partial bonding according to the nature of the sub-structure. Partial bonding to the deck prevents the formation of blisters between deck and the waterproofing due to vapour pressure, and gives a measure of freedom of movement in the roof deck.

BRS Digest 51 *Developments in roofing* discusses at length the problem of water vapour in the roof deck particularly in connection with lightweight screeds. The sources of screed moisture are as follows

(i)   mixing water
(ii) rain water during the drying out period and
(iii) condensation formed within the building.

The effect of a saturated screed is as follows
(i)   diminished thermal insulation
(ii) blistering and damage to water-proofing by vapour pressure
(iii) staining of internal decoration.

Experiments at the Building Research Station with an exposed aerated screed found that after four wet days and with subsequent shielding from further rain complete drying out needed 36 good summer days or 180 winter days. Research and long observation has revealed that nearly all roof blisters are caused by the entrapping of constructional moisture in the roof deck. Solar heat vapourizes this moisture and causes considerable pressure which weakens the bond between the roofing layers and the roof sub-structure. Ventilation of the roof deck can be obtained in several ways in connection with built-up felt roofing by: (i) deliberately isolating the first layer of felt by means of precisely graded granules on the underside. This first layer is of perforated glass fibre felt laid dry on the sub-structure and the

387

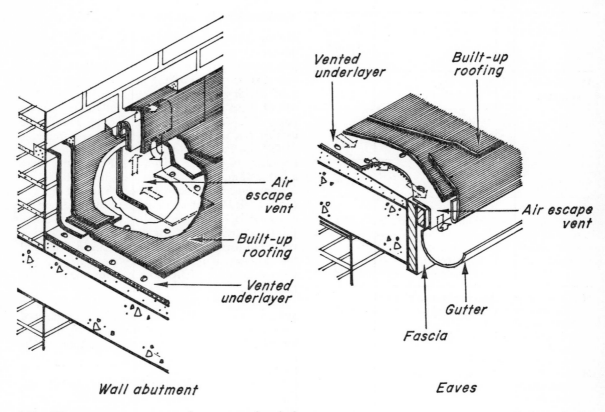

261   Water vapour pressure release: vented underlay

bonding bitumen of the upper layer penetrates the perforations automatically to give 10% bonding. Precautions must be taken to release pressure through special details at eaves and abutments as shown in figure 261. The specially prepared base sheet is known as a *vented underlayer* or *venting base layer*.

(ii) *partial bonding* or *frame bonding* where provision must be made for the release of pressure by the installation of special perimeter details. Figure 262 shows a typical pattern of partial bonding. Partial bonding, or vented underlay must always be used on a screeded finish; a vented underlay is in fact recommended for most roof decks (except timber boarding) due to the possibility of moisture being trapped during the course of construction.

(iii) installing proprietary plastic or metal breather vents spaced in accordance with the manufacturers' instructions with various types specially designed

to dry out wet screeds and/or to act as pressure release vents. Note that this type of ventilation is also suitable for asphalt roofing. In addition to the drying out of the screed, and the release of vapour pressure it is also necessary to ventilate the roof space where timber is used in the substructure.

BSCP 144 Part I:1968 *Built-up bitumen felt* states that where roofs of timber joists with timber boards, compressed straw slabs, flax board, particle board or plywood decks are constructed so that there is a space between ceiling and deck, this space must be ventilated to the open air to avoid fungal growth. Minimum ventilation is given by 300 mm² opening per 305 mm run on two opposite sides of the building. Provision must be made for a free air path from one side to the other. Where the width of the roof between openings is greater than 12 m the size of the openings should be doubled.

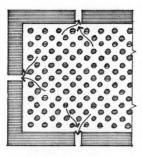

Spot sticking

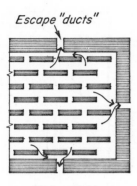

Escape "ducts"

Strip sticking

262   *Frame bonding*

Vents should be preferably located in the walls rather than roof. The ceiling below a ventilated roof space should be free from gaps and holes and have no vapour permeability.

The following are three typical examples of built-up felt roofing specifications.

1   *Timber deck*   built-up roofing with chipping finish. The first layer is laid, starting at and parallel to the lower edge or eaves, at right angles to the direction of fall, and secured by large headed galvanized clout nails spaced at 50 mm centres along the laps and stagger nailing at 150 mm centres over the sheet. First layer to be self finished asbestos base felt weighing not less than 13·6 kg per 10 m² roll. Second and third layers to be self finished fibre base felt weighing not less than 13·6 kg per 10 m² roll continuously bonded to the first layer and to each other with bitumen compound applied hot. All layers fixed breaking

joint 50 mm side laps, 75 mm end laps. Top surfaced with 10 mm diameter stone chippings, embedded in bitumen dressing compound and laid shoulder to shoulder.

2   *Fully bonded specification*   built-up roofing with mineral surface finish. Two layers asbestos based self finish felt weighing 27·2 kg per 20 m² and one layer asbestos based mineral surfaced felt weighing 36·2 kg per 10 m². The first layer fully bonded to the deck and subsequent layers continuously bonded with hot bitumen compound. The three layers laid breaking joint. 50 mm side laps, 75 mm end laps.

3   *Vented underlay specification*   built-up roofing with mineral surface finish. First layer glass fibre based mineral surfaced vented underlay weighing 31·8 kg per 10 m² (proprietary material) fixed to the roof deck simultaneously with the second layer and to the third layer with hot bitumen compound. The two top layers to be glass fibre based felt weighing 18·1 kg per 10 m². Surfaces to be covered with approved mineral chippings. All laps 50 mm, and to run with the slope of the roof.

In view of the very many alternative specifications possible in built-up felt roofing and the various weights and types of felt available, it is advisable to take advice from the specialist contractor regarding the intended specification with regard to suitability and cost. Typical details of three-layer built-up felt roofing are shown in the following figures. Figure 263 flashing to brick parapet; figure 264 detail at abutment; figure 265 detail showing a balustrade fixing; figure 266 welted apron to eaves; figure 267 welted apron to verge.

As an alternative to the welted drip shown at the verge, aluminium trim is available in various depths and profiles to receive the built-up felt and asphalt. A typical profile is shown in figure 268. The welted drip (figure 267) is formed by nailing the felt to a timber strip and returning the felt over the roof surface lapping with the roof covering according to the direction of the fall. The depth of the apron can be varied but will not be satisfactory if it is less than 50 mm. The aluminium trim is 'built-in' to the three-layer felt system as shown, and because of the possibility of electrolytic action between steel and aluminium, it is fixed with stainless steel or aluminium alloy screws at

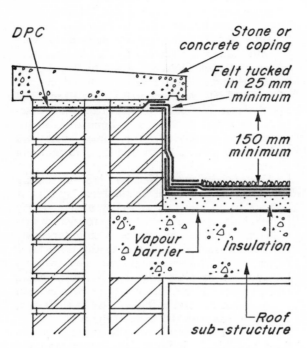

DPC

Stone or
concrete coping

Felt tucked
in 25 mm
minimum

150 mm
minimum

Vapour
barrier

Insulation

Roof
sub-structure

263   Built-up felt roofing: flashing to brick parapet

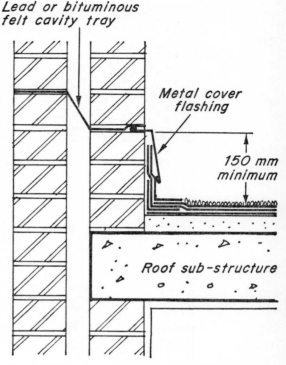

Lead or bituminous
felt cavity tray

Metal cover
flashing

150 mm
minimum

Roof sub-structure

264   Built-up felt roofing: detail of abutment

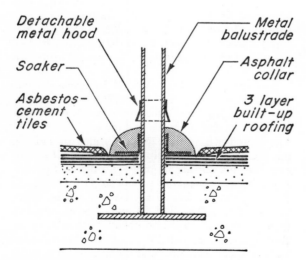

Detachable
metal hood

Soaker

Asbestos-
cement
tiles

Metal
balustrade

Asphalt
collar

3 layer
built-up
roofing

265   Built-up felt roofing: balustrade fixing

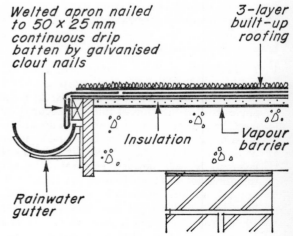

Welted apron nailed
to 50 x 25 mm
continuous drip
batten by galvanised
clout nails

3-layer
built-up
roofing

Insulation

Vapour
barrier

Rainwater
gutter

266   Built-up felt roofing: welted apron to eaves

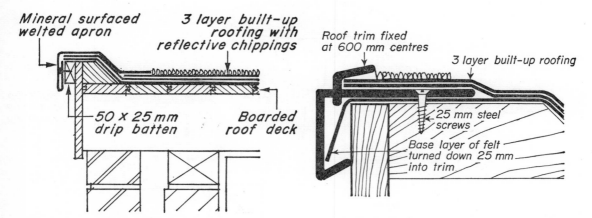

267 Built-up felt roofing: welted apron to verge

269 Built-up felt roofing: plastics eaves trim

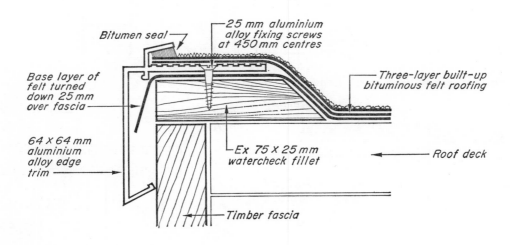

268 Built-up felt roofing: aluminium eaves trim

450 mm centres. The trim is produced in standard lengths of 3·050 m, the longer pieces are jointed by a spigot and a 3 mm gap should be left between each length to allow for expansion. A glass fibre reinforced polyester resin eaves trim is shown as an alternative detail figure 269. Since there is no possibility of electrolytic action galvanized steel screws can be used for fixing. Because of the low thermal expansion of this material, it is not necessary to leave a gap between the lengths of trim.

Built-up felt roofing will often be detailed to incorporate an internal or 'secret' gutter. A typical detail incorporating a plastic outlet component is shown in figure 270.

In order to prevent the failure of the roofing due to movement in the structure it is necessary to incorporate joints in the roof finish which will accommodate relative movement, figures 271, 272 and 273 illustrate suitable joints for minor, moderate and major movement respectively.

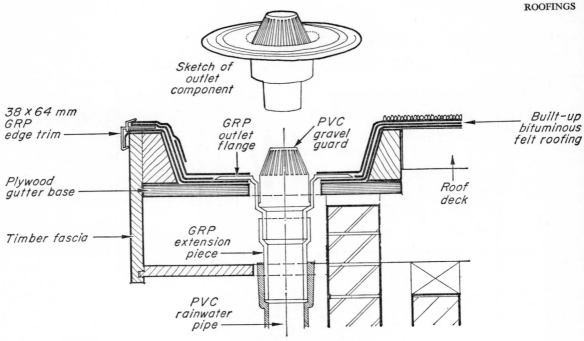

Sketch of outlet component

38 x 64 mm GRP edge trim

GRP outlet flange

PVC gravel guard

Built-up bituminous felt roofing

Plywood gutter base

Roof deck

Timber fascia

GRP extension piece

GRP outlet flange

PVC rainwater pipe

270   *Built-up felt roofing: plastic rainwater outlet to flat roof*

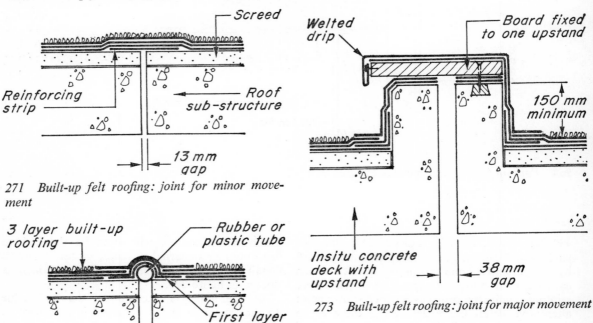

Screed

Welted drip

Board fixed to one upstand

Reinforcing strip

Roof sub-structure

150 mm minimum

13 mm gap

271   *Built-up felt roofing: joint for minor movement*

3 layer built-up roofing

Rubber or plastic tube

First layer reinforcing strip of felt

Insitu concrete deck with upstand

38 mm gap

273   *Built-up felt roofing: joint for major movement*

25 mm gap

272   *Built-up felt roofing: joint for moderate movement*

Single layer sheeting

Bitumen/asbestos

A proprietary sheet roofing composed of asbestos and bitumen is available, manufactured by the Nuralite Co Ltd. The material is applied in a one-layer technique and is laid either as roll-cap roofing, a 'twin-rib' system, or factory bonded to flaxboard, wood chipboard or plywood decking.

The roll-cap technique is a method of laying standard 2438 mm × 914 mm sheets to near flat or pitched roofs having a minimum fall of 17 mm per 1 m. The technique can be used on steeper pitches up to vertical. The finished appearance resembles the roll-cap technique as used for zinc, copper, lead or aluminium. The laying is carried out in accordance with CP 143 Part 8 1969. The roof has drips at 2300 mm across the slope and 32 mm × 44 mm wood rolls at 840 mm apart down the slope.

The 'twinrib' system is an application of the standard sheets to near flat or pitched roofs having a minimum fall of 12 mm in 1 m, up to vertical. The edges of the sheets are jointed impermeably by heat and pressure, using prefabricated cover strips. The sheets are secured to the decking by nailing or screwing at the top and through the base ribs and the centres of sheets secured by adhesive.

Prefabricated cover flashings and other roofing components are manufactured for use in conjunction with the sheets. These components are also available for use with corrugated roofing sheets, and patent glazing. The joints in the pre-fabricated decking systems are made by heat welding of a jointing strip. Manufacture and site installation of the flax board deck system is covered by Agrément Certificate No 69/29. Traditional *Nuralite* systems are normally fixed by the Contracting and Plumbing trades. The cost of the material compares favourably with that of other roofings of similar durability. Its appearance is initially black slowly weathering to mottled grey, and it has a thermal expansion slightly greater than copper but less than zinc or lead. The same manufacturers market the *Nuraphalte* system using 1219 mm square sheets. The sheets are 'joggled' on two adjacent sides in order to form overlap joints. The sheets are laid starting at the lowest point of the roof and arranged so that the joints are diagonal. *Nuralite* and *Nuraphalte* are guaranteed by the manufacturers for 25 years providing the materials are laid in accordance with their recommendations. CP 143 Part 8 1970 covers the recommendations for laying fully supported semi-rigid asbestos bitumen sheet roofs using the roll cap and rib systems.

Vinyl/Asbestos

This new material in use for roofing has been introduced by The Marley Company and is suitable for low pitched roofing (minimum fall 12 mm in 1 m). The sheeting is laid in one layer and the joints are solvent welded. It is necessary to vent roof decks where lightweight screeds are used to prevent the moisture and rain absorbed during the curing period causing the sheets to blister (as with built-up felt). Where insulation is provided immediately below the waterproof sheeting, the insulation accelerates the heat build-up from sunshine on top of the roof and so increases the vapour pressure and the need to ventilate.

The roof sheeting is cold bonded to the roof and breather vents and ducts are located at 6 m centres. The technique is illustrated in figure 274.

The breather vent, abutment duct detail and verge duct detail are illustrated in figures 275, 276 and 277 respectively. *Marleydek* is covered by Agrément Certificate No. 16.

Synthetic rubber/asbestos

This is a single layer system based on Du-Pont *Hypalon* synthetic rubber, laminated with asbestos. It is marketed under the trade name *Uniroof* and is covered by Agrément Certificate No 68/19. There are several other proprietary plastic membrane sheets available and manufacturers' advice should be sought regarding performance. In general the cost of a plastic or elastomer sheet roof is higher than for typical built-up bitumen felt systems.

Brushed or sprayed finishes

Elastomeric materials such as neoprene for brushing or spray application are known to be extremely durable but there is limited experience of their use as in situ roof coverings in this country. Advice should be obtained from the manufacturers and the materials should be laid by contractors appointed by them.

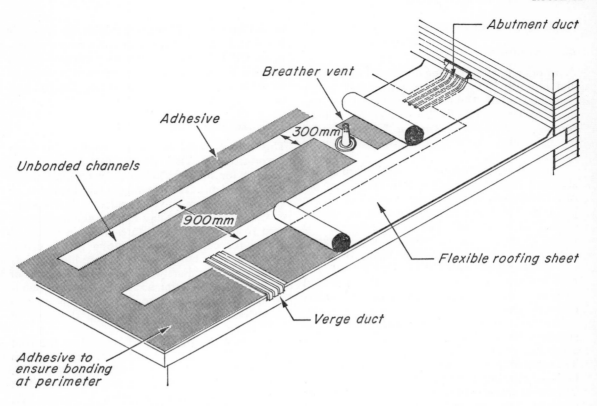

274 *Vinyl asbestos: roofing sheet details*

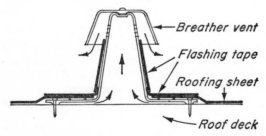

275 *Vinyl asbestos: detail of vent*

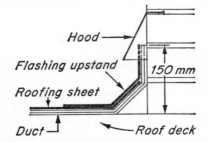

276 *Vinyl asbestos: abutment duct detail*

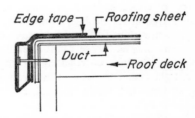

277 *Vinyl asbestos: verge duct detail*

Sheet metal roof covering

Durability

Fully supported sheet metal roofing has standing seams, rolls, drips and welted joints to connect the sheets. These roof coverings are durable provided access is restricted to maintenance personnel. For purposes such as escape in case of fire and for maintenance inspections duck boards should be provided to distribute weight evenly without restricting the flow of rainwater.

With the exception of lead, sheet metal roof coverings are much lighter than tiles and slates and differences in weight between copper, zinc and aluminium are not significant. Correctly laid lead and copper roof covering have given trouble-free protection for buildings for centuries but premature decay can result from bimetallic electrolytic action or in the presence of corrosive agents. For instance, timber such as Western Red Cedar and those treated with corrosive preservatives should not be used for the duck boards. Lead can be perforated by constant concentrated dripping of water from roofs upon which algae are growing. See *Corrosion of Metals: MBC: Materials*, chapter 9. Durability increases with the pitch of roofs and all the metal sheets can be fixed at any pitch or in the vertical plane.

Methods of fixing

The principles of fixing are the same for all sheet metals. Stresses which could arise from constant thermal movements will cause fatigue and should be minimized by reducing friction between the metal and the decking by providing joints at suitable centres designed to absorb movement. Sheet metals are laid in bays with their lengths in alignment with the fall of the roof. The sheets are turned up to form upstands against abutments and these are protected by cover flashings being taken into a raked joint in the case of brickwork or a raglet groove in the case of masonry or concrete. The cover flashing is retained by wedges and afterwards pointed. Joints in the direction of the fall are formed into rolls. Rolls with solid cores are preferable where there may be foot traffic and also on flat roofs since their greater height is an advantage. An alternative to the roll is a standing seam. Differences between the properties of the metal determine the techniques for laying, thus lead is malleable but roofing grades of copper and aluminium are less so and zinc is relatively stiff. In consequence lead can be formed into complex shapes by bossing, copper and aluminium can be formed into standing seams and welts while details in zinc roof covering are generally restricted to simple folds, the sheets being preformed before being placed in position. Joints across the fall are formed as follows

(a) in pitches up to 5 degrees as steps called *drips* – these are at least 50 mm high.

(b) pitches over 5 degrees as welts.

(c) for very steep pitches laps are satisfactory. Where the longitudinal joints are standing seams welts across the fall must be staggered to avoid the problem which arises if the corners of four sheets coincide.

Underlays

Underlays are required

(a) to allow free movement of the metal

(b) to prevent corrosion by screeds or timbers

(c) for sound deadening. Rain and hail can be very noisy on copper, aluminium and zinc sheets.

Lead, copper and zinc sheets should be laid on an inodorous felt (BS 747 Type 4A (ii) Brown no. 1 inodorous felt) butt jointed and fixed with clout nails. The same felt is suitable for aluminium which is laid over timber boarding but on other bases BS 747 Type 1C self-finished bituminous felt 13·6 kg per roll, should be used below aluminium. The underlay in this case should be laid with 75 mm laps sealed with cold bonding mastic and covered overall with waterproof building paper (BS 1521) to prevent possible adhesion between the metal and the underlay. Underlays should be dry when the roof coverings are laid, and this is particularly important in the case of inodorous felt.

Lead

This is described in CP 143 Part 11 : 1970 *Sheet roof and wall coverings – lead*. The metal is discussed in *MBC: Materials*, chapter 9. The use of this extremely durable roof covering is limited by its weight and high initial cost. It is however still widely valued for its malleability and consequent suitability for items such as flashings which require to be bossed into complex shapes. The use of lead for vertical cladding has been revived recently and the use of thin gauge metal premounted on panels is likely to increase. Fully supported lead sheet for roofing has an AA fire rating in respect of BS 476 Part 3 except where laid on plain edge boards when the rating is reduced to BA. The following table is a guide to the thicknesses of lead sheet suitable for various uses, and the appropriate code number.

Code No	Thickness in mm	Use
5	2·24	Roofing and gutter lining
6	2·50	
7	3·15	
4	1·80	Flashings and lead 'slates'
5	2·24	
3	1·25	Soakers
4	1·80	

A typical small lead flat roof is shown at 'C' in figure 278. The upstand flashing at each abutment is protected by a cover flashing secured by means of lead tacks and wedges, illustrated at A and B. The cover flashing is tucked at least 25 mm into the brickwork joint. The object of the cover flashing is to seal the joint between upstand and wall and at the same time, allow the covered sheet freedom to contract or expand.

The cost of lead has discouraged its use on new buildings but there are inumerable examples of traditional lead work in roofing which now may require maintenance. For this reason the various joints used in lead roofing are detailed in figure 279 so that the methods of construction may be understood.

A This is an enlargement of the construction of the drip shown in figure 278. The flat roof consists of plane surfaces slightly inclined and separated by low steps or *drips* to facilitate the run off at the joints where the ends of the lead sheets overlap.

B This is a development of the drip construction by the formation of a groove to resist capillary attraction.

C This is a welted seam for a joint running with the fall on steeply pitched surfaces or on vertical surfaces. The seam is made by fixing copper clips or tacks at about 600 mm centres at the junction of the sheets. The clips should be 'dead soft' temper and cut from 24 swg (0·559 mm sheet). The edges of the sheets are then turned up and dressed flat as shown.

D This is an alternative to the welted seam and is

in the form of a hollow roll of lead. This is a traditional detail extensively used on steep pitches in old buildings. It was common practice in the Middle Ages.

E, F and G These show a solid roll, made over a wood former. This joint is used on flat roofs, as shown in figure 278 or as a ridge joint. Wooden rolls of 38 mm to 50 mm diameter are fixed at the joint either by screwing through the roll or by using a double headed nail. The lead is then dressed as shown in G being formed well into the angles to obtain a firm joint.

Copper

CP 143 Part 12 1970 (metric units) describes *Sheet roof and wall coverings – copper:* and the relevant BS is 1569:1965 *Copper sheet and strip for building purposes.* Copper is strong in tension, tough, ductile and in suitable tempers it is malleable, but has negligible creep. See *MBC: Materials,* chapter 9. Roof sheets and flashings should be in dead soft temper. Welts and folds should be made with a minimum number of sharp blows rather than the succession of taps with which the plumber works with lead sheet. Half-hard temper metal is sometimes required for weatherings to window frames and copings. Like lead, copper is extremely durable. When exposed to most atmospheres a thin coating of basic sulphate of copper forms which in a number of years becomes green. This coating protects the underlying metal from continuing corrosion—even in industrial areas. Copper is not attacked by other metals. Fixings should be copper. The coefficient of linear expansion of copper is less than for lead, aluminium and zinc.

Fully supported copper sheet for roofing has a fire rating of AA in respect of BS 476. Sheets are usually supplied in 1·22 × 0·61 m, 1·83 × 0·91 m or 2·44 × 1·22 m sizes. Strip is supplied in coils. The usual gauge is 0·559 mm (24 swg) although a very satisfactory pre-formed roofing unit, with copper sheet, factory bonded to 50 mm compressed strawboard or 25 mm chipboard uses embossed copper sheet of 0·315 mm (30 swg).

Timber decking upon which copper roofing is to be laid should be free from 'spring' and preferably t and g of 25 mm nominal thickness. Heads of nails should be punched in, and the boarding

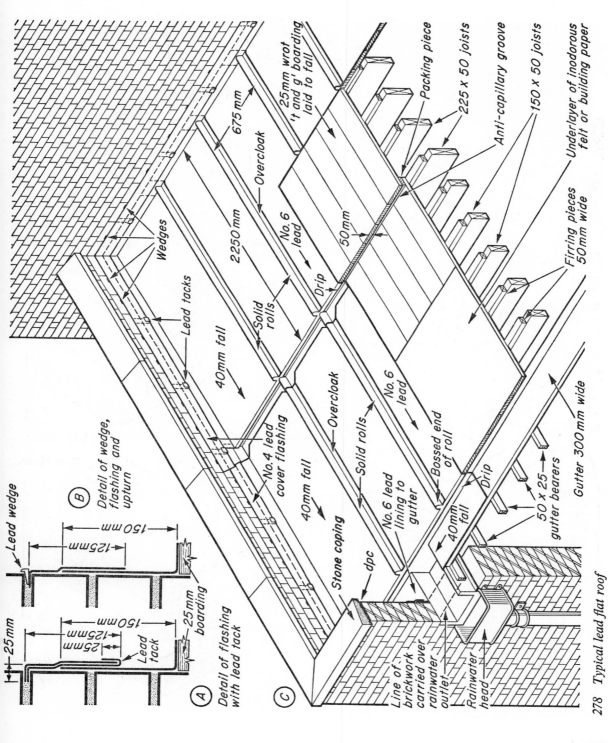

Lead wedge

(B) Detail of wedge, flashing and upturn

150 mm
125 mm
25 mm boarding

25 mm
150 mm
125 mm
25 mm
Lead tack

(A) Detail of flashing with lead tack

(C)

Wedges

Lead tacks

675 mm

Overcloak

2250 mm

No. 6 lead

40 mm fall

Solid rolls

Drip

25 mm wrot 't and g' boarding laid to fall

Packing piece

225 x 50 joists

Anti-capillary groove

150 x 50 joists

Underlayer of inodorous felt or building paper

50 mm

Firring pieces 50 mm wide

No. 4 lead cover flashing

40 mm fall

Stone coping

Overcloak

Solid rolls

No. 6 lead

dpc

No. 6 lead lining to gutter

Bossed end of roll

40 mm fall

Drip

Gutter 300 mm wide

50 x 25 gutter bearers

Line of brickwork carried over rainwater outlet

Rainwater head

278 Typical lead flat roof

397

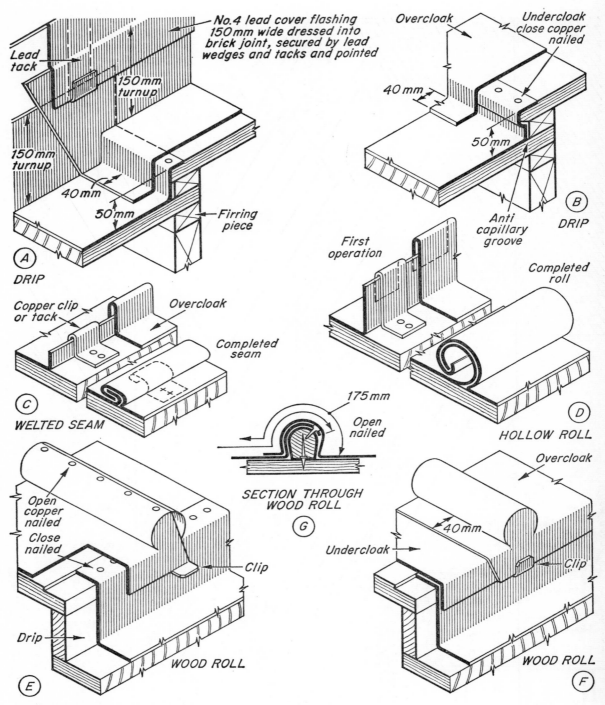

Lead tack

No.4 lead cover flashing 150 mm wide dressed into brick joint, secured by lead wedges and tacks and pointed

150 mm turnup

150 mm turnup

40 mm

50 mm

Firring piece

A DRIP

Overcloak

Undercloak close copper nailed

40 mm

50 mm

Anti capillary groove

B DRIP

Copper clip or tack

Overcloak

Completed seam

C WELTED SEAM

First operation

Completed roll

D HOLLOW ROLL

175 mm

Open nailed

SECTION THROUGH WOOD ROLL

G

Open copper nailed

Close nailed

Clip

Drip

WOOD ROLL

E

Overcloak

40 mm

Undercloak

Clip

WOOD ROLL

F

279   Joints used in lead roofing

laid either diagonally or in the direction of fall. Other dry decking materials are suitable providing that they are dimensionally stable. Concrete decks should be screeded, and preferably sealed with a coat of bitumen.

It is necessary to use an underlay of impregnated flax (inodorous) felt whatever the decking material. The underlay is secured to the deck by copper nails and laid butt jointed. The underlay lessens the possibility of 'wearing' the copper as it expands and contracts and deadens the drumming sound of rain. The minimum fall for copper roofing is 17 mm in 1 m and drips 63 mm deep, spaced not more than 3 m apart should be used in roofs of 5 degree pitch or lower.

There are two traditional methods of forming the longitudinal joints in copper roofing: 1 the standing seam, and 2 the batten or wood roll.

1 *Standing seam* The three processes in the formation of a standing seam in copper are shown in figure 280.
2 *Wood roll* This method used timber battens to form a shaped wooden core against which the edges of the sheet are turned up. A prepared capping strip is then welted to the flanges. The timber battens are screwed to the decking and the roof sheeting is secured to the battens by means of 50 mm wide copper strips. The four stages in the formation of a batten roll are shown in figure 281.

Transverse joints in each case are formed by double lock cross welts (or for very flat roofs— drips). The formation of a double lock cross welt is shown in figure 282 and the application of the standing seam method is shown in figure 283. Long strip 'economy' roofing can be used where the total distance between eaves and ridge does not exceed 8·500 m. Expansion cleats in the standing seam joint allow movement over this length.

A proprietary roofing material which utilizes an indented copper sheet (42 gauge) backed with bitumen and laid as a top layer of built-up felt roofing specification on an underlayer of asbestos or glass fibre based bitumen felt. This copper/bitumen roofing gives the appearance of traditional copper at less cost.

Zinc

CP 143: Part 5 describes *Zinc sheet Roof and Wall Coverings*. The metal is considered in

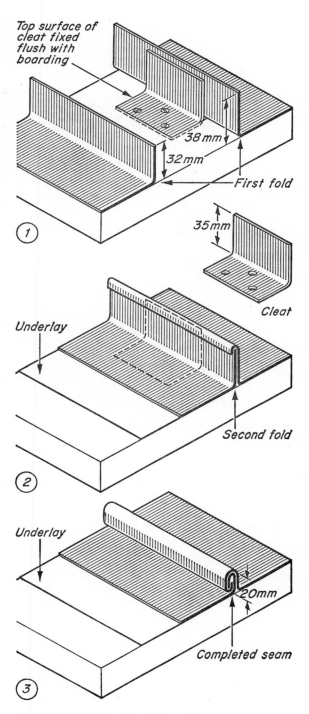

280 *Copper roofing: standing seam*

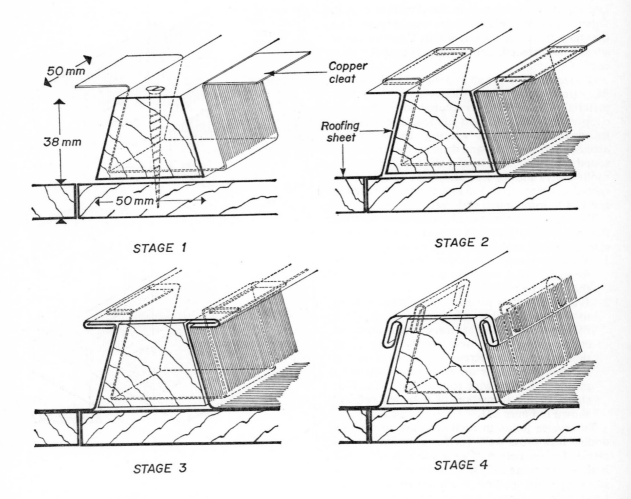

STAGE 1

STAGE 2

STAGE 3

STAGE 4

281   Copper roofing: batten roll

MBC: Materials, chapter 9. The minimum thickness of zinc sheet for roofing should not be less than 0·78 mm. In average urban conditions the maintenance free life of zinc roofing conforming to the CP should not be less than 40 years for a roof laid to the minimum fall of 1 in 80 (approx. 1°). In rural areas or by the sea, and with steeper pitches, the life will be longer. Zinc is attacked by acids and water must not be allowed to drain from Western Red Cedar shingles on to a zinc roof, nor should drainage from copper pipes discharge on to zinc. The coefficient of thermal expansion of zinc is greater than that of copper, but slightly less

than lead. Standard sizes of zinc sheet are 2400 mm × 920 mm and 2100 mm × 920 mm and as continuous strip in widths of up to 1 m. Zinc provides one of the lightest roof coverings which although less durable than lead or copper has the lowest first cost. Zinc sheet for roofing has a fire rating AA in respect of BS 476. Typical details to a flat roof covered in zinc sheet are shown in figure 284. The formation of the batten roll is shown at A and the treatment of the sheeting at the junction of a drip and roll is shown at B. Detail C shows the formation of a 'dog ear' at an internal corner and a detail of a holding down clip is shown at

D. Saddle pieces are formed on the ends of cappings at walls and drips as shown at E and where a roof abuts the wall at a drip, a corner piece is welted to the upper sheet as shown at F.

Aluminium

Since aluminium forms a protective oxide when exposed to the atmosphere the alloy used for roofing is normally extremely durable even in industrial and marine atmospheres. Precautions must however be taken to avoid a galvanic attack with other materials and aluminium should be protected from wet concrete and mortar. Timbers containing acid and preservatives are also dangerous to the sheeting. Fully supported aluminium sheet for roofing has a fire rating AA in respect of BS 476. The techniques of laying aluminium fully supported roof coverings are similar to those of copper, see CP 143 Part 7: 1965 *Sheet roof and wall coverings: aluminium,* which should be consulted for detailed information. Aluminium sheet for roofing should comply with BS 1470:1966 *Wrought aluminium and aluminium alloys for general engineering purposes – sheet and strip.* Aluminium is the lightest of roofing metals – it has ample strength and ductivity and creep is not significant. Hand forming is easiest in soft temper and high purity metal. It has a high reflectivity to solar heat. The durability of high purity aluminium is good in normal atmospheres provided it is washed by rain. However, it must not be used in contact with copper or copper alloys.

Fixings should be preferably of aluminium but where steel is used it should be galvanized. Water must not be allowed to drain on to aluminium from copper roofing and particularly not from copper expansion pipes.

Corrugated sheet roofing

Asbestos cement sheet

Asbestos cement is described in *MBC: Materials,* chapter 10. A comprehensive range of asbestos cement components in the form of corrugated sheets and accessories are available for use in the covering of pitched roofs. Although complex roof shapes can be covered by asbestos cement sheets, maximum economy is achieved where the

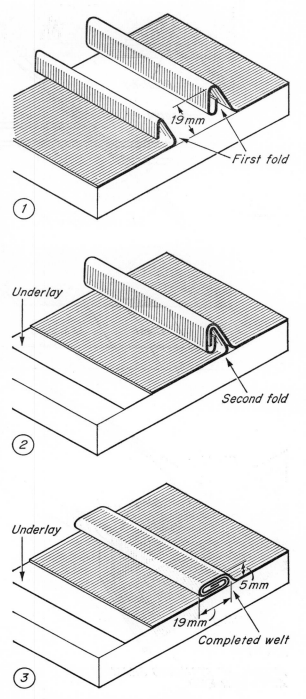

282 *Copper roofing: welted joint*

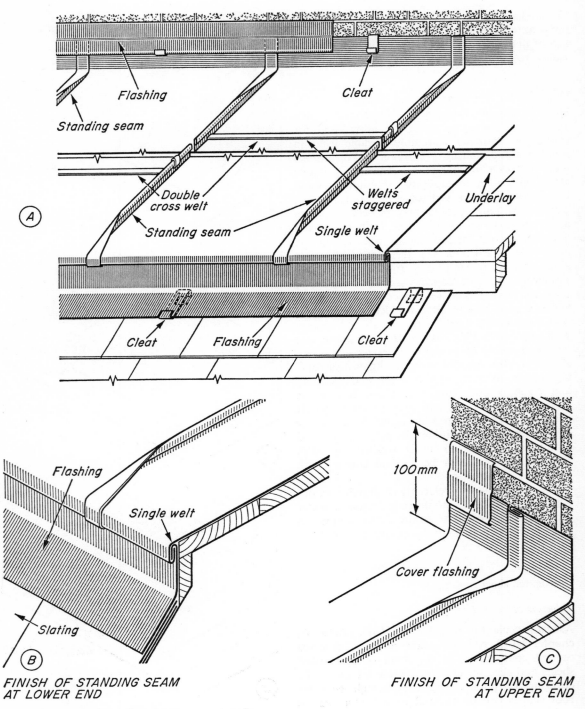

Flashing

Cleat

Standing seam

(A)

Double cross welt

Welts staggered

Underlay

Standing seam

Single welt

Cleat

Flashing

Cleat

Flashing

Single welt

Slating

(B)

FINISH OF STANDING SEAM
AT LOWER END

100 mm

Cover flashing

(C)

FINISH OF STANDING SEAM
AT UPPER END

283   Application of standing seam copper roofing

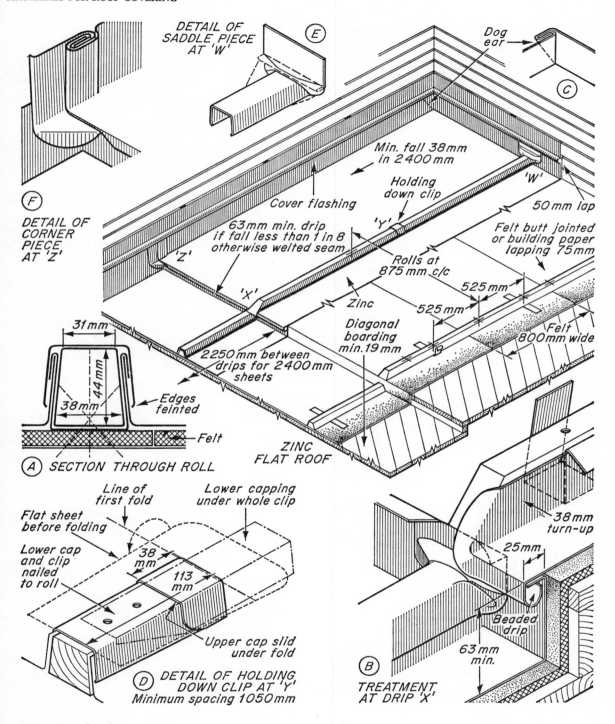

DETAIL OF
SADDLE PIECE
AT 'W'

E

Dog
ear

C

F

DETAIL OF
CORNER
PIECE
AT 'Z'

Min. fall 38mm
in 2400mm

Cover flashing

Holding
down clip

'W'

50 mm lap

63mm min. drip
if fall less than 1 in 8
otherwise welted seam

'Z'

'Y'

Felt butt jointed
or building paper
lapping 75mm

'X'

Rolls at
875 mm c/c

525 mm

Zinc

525 mm

Felt
800mm wide

2250 mm between
drips for 2400mm
sheets

Diagonal
boarding
min.19 mm

31 mm

44 mm

38 mm

Edges
feinted

Felt

A SECTION THROUGH ROLL

ZINC
FLAT ROOF

Line of
first fold

Lower capping
under whole clip

Flat sheet
before folding

Lower cap
and clip
nailed
to roll

38
mm

113
mm

38mm
turn-up

25mm

Upper cap slid
under fold

Beaded
drip

D DETAIL OF HOLDING
DOWN CLIP AT 'Y'
Minimum spacing 1050mm

63 mm
min.

B
TREATMENT
AT DRIP 'X'

284   Zinc details

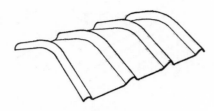

Cranked crown sheet

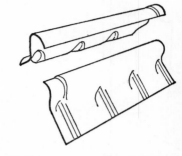

Adjustable close-fitting ridge

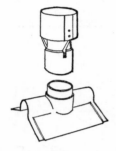

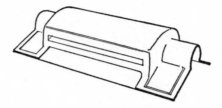

Ridge ventilator

Ridge soaker with
extractor ventilator

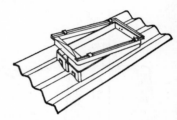

Roof light – opening type

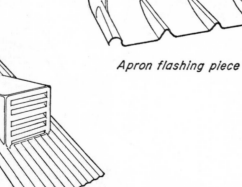

Apron flashing piece

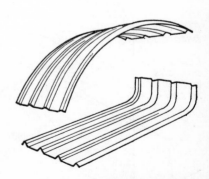

Dormer ventilator

Curved and curved-end tiles

285　Corrugated asbestos cement sheet roofing: accessories

BS type	Profile	Length in 152 mm increments	Roof pitch	Maximum purlin centres:mm
A	5·6 mm, 25 mm; 38 mm lap; 648 mm net cover; 762 mm nominal width	914 to 3048	10° min	914
B	6·3 mm, 54 mm; 70 mm lap 146 mm nominal; 1016 mm net cover; 1086 mm nominal width	914 to 3048	10° min	1372
C	6·3 mm, 51 mm; lap 339 mm 339 mm; 1016 mm net cover; 1092 mm nominal width	914 to 3048	10° min	1372
D	6·3 mm, 82 mm; lap 339 mm 339 mm; 1016 mm net cover; 1092 mm nominal width	914 to 3048	4° min	1676
E	9·5 mm, 89 mm; lap 381 mm 381 mm 12 mm; 1143 mm net cover; 1219 mm nominal width	1219 to 3048	4° min	1981

286   *Corrugated asbestos sheet roofing: profiles*

roof is simple in plan shape. The roof should also be planned so that the purlin spacing allows the use of standard sheets without cutting to waste. Figure 285 gives an idea of the range of accessories available for use with standard profile sheets. Note that certain of the roof ventilators can be used with soaker flanges and so dispense with the need of separate flashings. BS 690: 1963 *Asbestos cement slates, corrugated sheets and semi-compressed flat sheets* is the relevant British Standard and illustrates 14 profiles for use as roofing or vertical cladding sheets. Figure 286 gives a selective range of the more commonly used profiles for roof sheeting. Metal fixing accessories are covered by BS 1494:1964 Part I *Fixing for sheet roof and wall coverings*. Figure 287 illustrates a recently introduced profile giving a net cover of 1000 mm. Asbestos cement sheets may be coloured by factory applied processing in a range of subdued colours giving a high resistance to fading. Profiled translucent sheeting made from glass fibre reinforced polyester-resin and transparent sheets

from rigid pvc are manufactured for use with the various asbestos cement sheet sections to give a natural diffused daylighting, and are available clear, or in a range of colours. The thermal transmittance (U) through a single layer of unlined asbestos roof sheeting is approximately

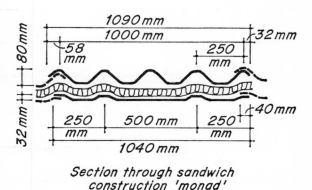

Section through sandwich construction 'monad'

287   *'Monad' asbestos cement sheet*

7·95 W/m² deg C. In order to fulfil the requirements of the Thermal Insulation (Industrial Buildings) Act 1957 the heat loss through the roof (excluding roof lights and openings) must not exceed the U values shown on page 375. The U values are in each case related to the given range of internal design temperatures shown. Thus it will be seen that an unlined asbestos roof will not be acceptable under this Act. The method of insulating asbestos cement roofs which meets the requirement of the Act and which does not require the use of additional supporting members is to incorporate a top corrugated sheet with an associated lining panel of asbestos cement. The cavity between the two layers of asbestos cement accommodates an additional insulant in the form of a glass fibre or mineral wool mat 25 mm thick which improves the insulation value of the structure and at the same time restricts the flow of free air circulating within the cavity. This system of construction thus improves insulation and helps to provide a reasonably dust tight covering. Insulated double cladding or sandwich construction as it is called can also be arranged with timber or asbestos cement spacer strips fixed above the purlin lines between the lining panels and the corrugated sheets. This method avoids any consolidation of the glass fibre infil by the superimposed weight of the top sheeting and so provides a further improved U value. Several types of sandwich construction are available and two typical profiles are illustrated in figure 288. By the use of timber spacer bands the U value can be improved from 1·08 W/m² deg C to 0·91 W/m² deg C. Roof lights are excluded from the requirements of Thermal Insulation (Industrial Buildings) Act but where it is considered necessary to provide insulated natural lighting panels in conjunction with the insulated roofing, hermetically sealed insulated rooflights or translucent lining panels are available. As an alternative to sandwich construction satisfactory thermal insulation can be obtained by 'under drawing' or lining the roof above or below the purlin by suitable rigid sheet of insulation material such as fibre building board.

Fixing for asbestos sheeting in general should not be too rigid since allowance must be made for slight movement. Usual fixings are various types of hook bolts which pass through the asbestos sheet and clip round steel or concrete purlins or drive screws into timber purlins or timber plugs in concrete purlins as shown in figure 289. In order to accommodate movement and render the detail weathertight a plastic washer with a separate dome shaped cap-seal is used, as shown in figure 290. Alternatively galvanized steel or bitumen washers are available. The minimum pitch of the roof will vary according to the profile of the sheet and the degree of exposure of the site. Sheets are designed to provide resistance to the penetration of rain at end and side laps without seals provided that the roof pitch is adequate and the site is not severely exposed. Where such conditions are fulfilled the base of the corrugations act as gutters and the rainwater will usually run down the roof slope without the risk of penetration into the interior. A shallow pitch or wind blowing at the slope of the roof may reduce the velocity of flow sufficient to cause a build-up of water which may

BS type		Thermal insulation 'U' approx.	
		Sandwich (25 mm glass fibre insulant)	Single skin
B		1·08 W/m²deg C	7·95 W/m²deg C
C		1·19 W/m²deg C	7·95 W/m²deg C

288   *Corrugated asbestos cement sheet roofing: insulated double cladding profiles*

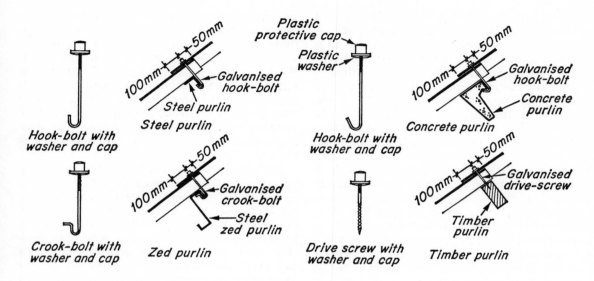

Hook-bolt with washer and cap

Steel purlin

50mm

100mm

Galvanised hook-bolt

Steel purlin

Plastic protective cap

Plastic washer

Hook-bolt with washer and cap

50mm

100mm

Galvanised hook-bolt

Concrete purlin

Concrete purlin

Crook-bolt with washer and cap

Zed purlin

50mm

100mm

Galvanised crook-bolt

Steel zed purlin

Drive screw with washer and cap

50mm

100mm

Galvanised drive-screw

Timber purlin

Timber purlin

289   Corrugated asbestos cement sheet roofing: purlin fixings

then be forced under the joints in the sheets. In such conditions or to prevent dust penetration it is necessary to seal the laps. The following roof pitches may be used as a guide.

Roof pitch Sheltered and normal sites	Lap treatment
over 22½°	150 mm unsealed end laps
15° to 22½°	150 mm sealed end laps (or 305 mm unsealed)
10° to 15°	150 mm sealed end laps and sealed side laps
4°	Sealed end and side laps to manufacturers' requirements

Exposed sites	
over 25°	150 mm unsealed end laps
17½° to 25°	150 mm sealed end laps
15° to 17½°	150 mm sealed end laps and sealed side laps
10° to 15°	350 mm sealed end laps and sealed side laps (extra fixings at end laps)

Plastic protective cap

Fixing nut

Plastic washer— shaped or flat

8 mm galvanised hook bolt

Hooked for steel angle

290   Detail of hook bolt

407

The 4° pitch is recommended only for a limited number of profiles and the manufacturers should be consulted to check suitability. Where it is necessary to use a mastic seal 8 mm extruded mastic strip should be used. The type and method of laying should be as directed by the manufacturers. It should be borne in mind however that the efficiency of the seal can be affected by the temperature in which it is laid and it is recommended that a routine check be made on the compression of mastic laid during winter months.

Laying procedure Sheets should be fixed in accordance with the recommendations made in CP 143 Part 6:1962 *Sheet roof or wall coverings.* Fixing holes should never be punched, they should always be drilled through the crown of the corrugations. Always use roof ladders to avoid damaging the roof sheets when fixing and provide properly constructed walkways or roof boards where it is necessary to give regular access to rooflights or other places likely to need periodical attention, and maintenance. See Safety Health and Welfare Regulations 1948.

All fixing accessories should be in accordance with BS 1494:196 *Specification of fixing accessories for building purposes* Part I.

Sheets are designed to be laid smooth side to the weather with a side lap of one corrugation.

The sheets are fastened on each side of the lap except at each intermediate purlin where one fixing only on the overlapping side is adequate. The laying procedure is shown in figure 291. Working upwards from the eaves sheets may be laid either from left to right or right to left. It is advisable to commence sheeting at the end away from the prevailing wind. The starter sheet and the last sheet to be fixed are laid unmitred; all other sheets require mitring where the overlap occurs as shown.

With insulated double cladding the fixing procedure is similar. The lining panels are first laid mitred as for the roofing sheets except that they are laid smooth side to the underside. The sheets are secured with a short bolt through the intermediate corrugation. Lining panels are then overlaid with a glass fibre or mineral wool insulating mat which should have a minimum 100 mm lap to all joints. The laying of the final covering sheet then proceeds as before. A typical double cladding unit is shown in figure 292. Figure 293 shows a typical roof sheeting arrangement using single skin construction suitable for a storage building. Detail A shows the finish at the eaves. The sheets should not have an unsupported overhang of more than 300 mm beyond the eaves purlin and the detail is completed by an eaves filler compo-

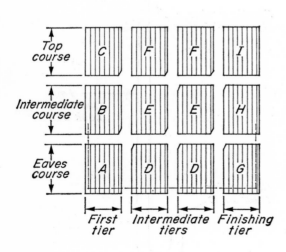

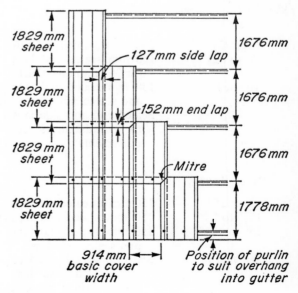

291   Corrugated asbestos cement sheet roofing: laying procedure

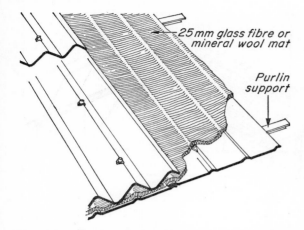

292 *Corrugated asbestos cement sheet roofing: laying procedure*

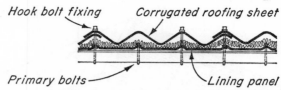

nent. (See also figure 294.) Details B and C show the method of construction where a translucent rooflight is used. The translucent sheet is un-mitred, and 13 mm diameter sealing strips are used at the end laps. Detail D shows a close fitting ridge. Because the ridge is in two parts, it is adjustable to suit various degrees of slope. An alternative apex detail is shown using a cranked crown sheet. The correct positioning of the top purlin is important and should be arranged so that the hook bolt fixing is not less than 100 mm from the end of the crown sheet.

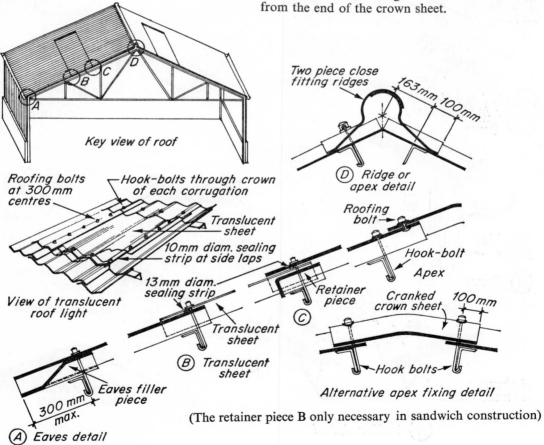

293 *Corrugated asbestos cement sheet roofing: single skin construction*

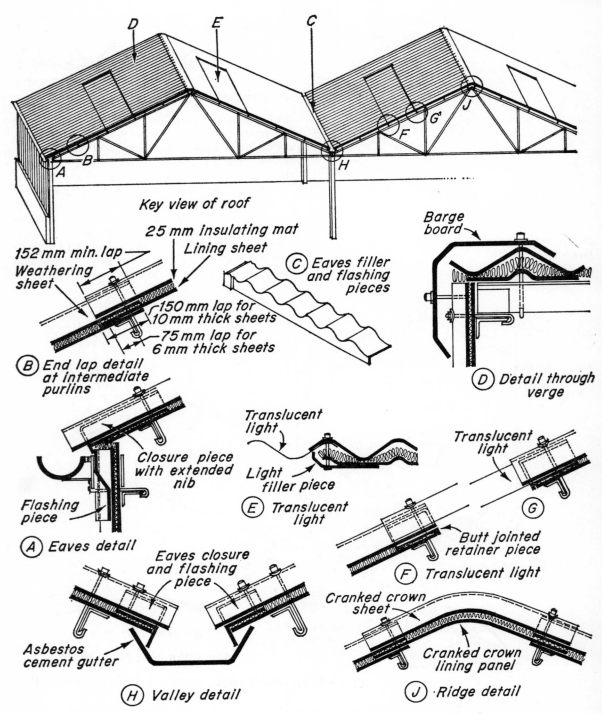

Key view of roof

152 mm min. lap

Weathering sheet

25 mm insulating mat

Lining sheet

150 mm lap for 10 mm thick sheets

75 mm lap for 6 mm thick sheets

Ⓑ **End lap detail at intermediate purlins**

Ⓒ **Eaves filler and flashing pieces**

Barge board

Ⓓ **Detail through verge**

Closure piece with extended nib

Flashing piece

Ⓐ **Eaves detail**

Translucent light

Light filler piece

Ⓔ **Translucent light**

Translucent light

Ⓖ

Butt jointed retainer piece

Ⓕ **Translucent light**

Eaves closure and flashing piece

Asbestos cement gutter

Ⓗ **Valley detail**

Cranked crown sheet

Cranked crown lining panel

Ⓙ **Ridge detail**

294 Corrugated asbestos cement sheet roofing: insulated double cladding fixing details

Figure 294 illustrates the use of insulated double cladding. The eaves detail at A indicates the use of eaves filler pieces and a method of fixing an asbestos gutter by means of front and back plates. B shows a typical end lap detail at an intermediate purlin. Detail D is a section through the roof verge and illustrates the barge board component which provides a neat finish between the vertical cladding and roof sheeting. Details E, F and G show the method of detailing the translucent roof sheeting. Note the use of the closure piece on the underside of the roof. H shows the use of a valley gutter and the method of flashing the sheets into the gutter. J gives the fixing of the cranked crown sheet and lining panel at the apex of the roof.

Aluminium

Corrugated and troughed aluminium sheets are dealt with in CP 143 Part I. BS 2855:1962. The alloy used for this type of roof covering is NS 3 H to BS 1470, and the sheets should comply with BS 2855 or BS 3428. The behaviour of aluminium when exposed to the atmosphere is discussed on page 401. Corrugated sheets are available with a plain finish or with a baked enamel finish. A small selection of the BS profiles available are illustrated in figure 295. Translucent plastic sheets of matching profiles are available. The minimum recommended gauges for durability related to the use of the aluminium sheeting is as follows:

Use	Swg
Heavy and marine industrial	18
Industrial	20
Light industrial	22
Agricultural	24

Fixing techniques are similar to those used for corrugated asbestos sheeting, in that hook bolts are used to secure the sheets to purlins but in addition, the side laps should be secured by bolts or rivets passing through the crown of the profile.

A comprehensive range of accessories is available in 20 and 22 swg, and aluminium alloy fixings are preferable although galvanized fittings may be acceptable in a non-polluted atmosphere. Flashings for aluminium roofing are preferably preformed and of $\frac{1}{2}$H or $\frac{3}{4}$H temper aluminium.

Galvanized corrugated sheet

This low-cost roof covering is dealt with in CP 143 Part 2:1961 and the Steel Sheet Information and Development Association (SSIDA) provides information and advice.

Sheets should comply with BS 3083:1959 *Hot-dipped galvanized corrugated steel sheets for general purposes*. Accessories should comply with BS 1091:1963 *Pressed steel gutters, rainwater pipes, fittings and accessories*.

Type	Profile with nominal pitch	Gauge	Available sizes (max. and min.)	
			Width	Length
Corrugated sheet BS 2855	76mm 76mm / 19mm	18 to 24 swg. 1·22 mm to 0·56 mm	1118 to 508mm	Any length to 1·22 m
Trough sheet BS 3428 type A	127mm / 38mm	18 to 22 swg. 1·22 mm to 0·71 mm	1187 to 579mm	Any length to 7·62 m
Heavy trough sheet BS 3428 type B	130mm / 38 and 44mm	18 and 19 swg. 1·22 mm and 1·02 mm	1229 to 705mm	Any length to 7·62 m

295   Corrugated aluminium roofing sheet profiles

411

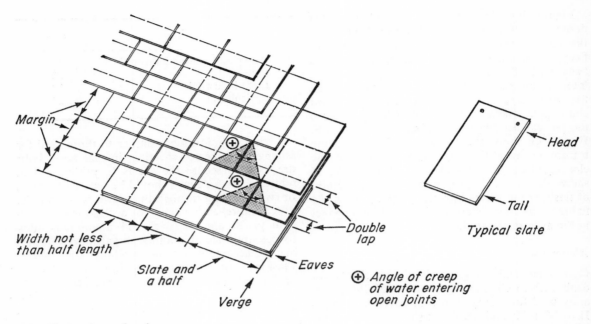

296   Slating in angle of creep

Corrugated sheets are normally 76 mm pitch but a 127 mm pitch is also available.

Standard lengths are 1220 to 3660 mm. Longer sheets can sometimes be used from ridge to eaves, thereby avoiding laps, which is particularly advantageous for low pitches.

Thickness gauges are from 30 swg—0·3 mm to 16 swg—1·6 mm.

Unprotected steel would have a very short life, but zinc coating (galvanizing) affords protection at a relatively low cost.

See *MBC: Materials*, chapter 9.

Protected metal roofing

Several proprietary profiled protected steel core sheets for roofing and vertical cladding are available. A well known example of this type of material (*Colour Galbestos*) uses a basic steel core, with a molten zinc coating incorporating a bonded protective layer of asbestos felt. The material is finally treated by a heavy coating of polyester resin to resist corrosion. The material is formed into 'box rib' profiles and is available in several muted colours.

The fixings for both galvanized corrugated sheet,

and protected metal roofing is similar to that for other corrugated sheet materials.

Slating

Natural slates

Roofing slates are obtained from Wales, North Lancashire, Westmorland and Cornwall. Slates should comply with BS 680:1944 *Roofing slates*. See *MBC: Materials*, chapter 4. There are more than 20 'standard' sizes of slate varying from the largest at 610 mm long by 355 mm wide and the smallest at 305 mm long to 205 mm wide.

When rainwater falls on to a pitched roof it will fan out and run over the surface at a given angle. This angle will depend upon the pitch of the roof and is commonly referred to as the angle of creep, see figure 296. The steeper the pitch the narrower the angle will be and this can be used as a guide to the minimum width of the slate that can be used. It follows that the shallower the pitch the wider the slates will have to be and as a general principle the more exposed the position of the roof the smaller the slate and the steeper the pitch must be. Thus the larger unit is laid on the shallower pitch.

The following list gives a range of the metric

412

equivalent sizes of slate most commonly used together with the recommended minimum rafter pitch.

Sizes of slates: length × width (mm) (metric equivalent dimensions)	Minimum pitch
305 × 205	45°
330 × 180	40°
405 × 205	35°
510 × 255	30°
610 × 305	25°
610 × 355	22½°

The thickness of slates varies according to the source, those from Westmorland and North Lancashire being relatively thick and coarser in surface texture. The thickest slates from any quarry are called *Bests* or *Firsts*, and the thinner slates, seconds and thirds. Thus, this description does not refer to quality, but is an indication of thickness. Where slates supplied vary in thickness the thinner slates should be used at the ridge and the thicker slates at lower courses.

Each row of slates is laid starting from the eaves, and is butt jointed at the side and overlapped at the head (see figure 296). Slates are laid double lap with special slates at the eaves and verge. This means that there are two thicknesses of slate *over* each nail hole as protection, making

in all, three thicknesses of material at the overlaps. The side joint should be left very slightly open so that water will drain quickly. Each slate is nailed twice. The slates should be holed so that the 'spoiling' will form a counter sinking for the nail heads. The slates are best holed by machine on the site so that the holes can be correctly positioned by the fixers. The nails should be of yellow metal, aluminium alloy, copper or zinc. They are 32 mm long for the lighter and smaller slates up to 63 mm long for the heavier slates. Galvanized nails are not recommended. The slates may be either centre nailed or head nailed. For centre nailing, the nail holes are positioned by reference to the gauge and lap so that the nails just clear the head of the slates in the course below. Centre nailed slates on battens and counter battens on felt are illustrated in figure 297. For head nailed slates the holes will be positioned about 25 mm from the upper edge of the slate. Head nailed slates on battens and counter battens on felt are illustrated in figure 298. The holes should not be nearer than 25 mm to the side of the slate. Centre nailing gives more protection against lifting in the wind or chattering. The technique of head nailing should therefore only be used on smaller sizes of slate. Because of the angle of creep the width of slate is chosen having in mind the pitch of the roof, the shallower the pitch the larger the unit required. The head-lap

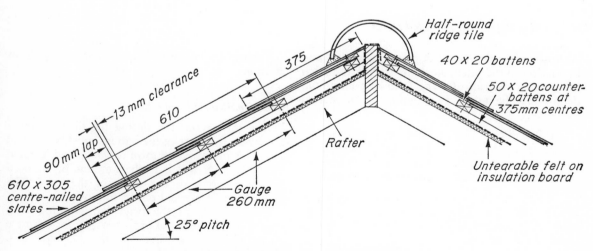

Section through ridge: centre nailed slates

297 Slating details: centre nailed slates

413

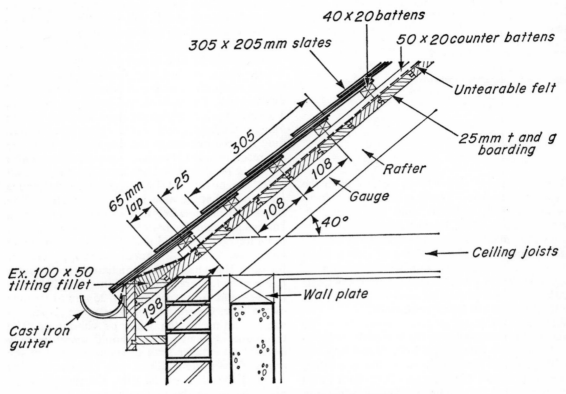

Section through eaves: head nailed slates

298   Slating details: head nailed slates

is chosen according to the degree of exposure, and in relation to the pitch, since the steeper the pitch the quicker the run off. The following minimum details can be taken as a guide for moderate exposure.

rafter pitch – 22½°.	head lap – 100 mm
rafter pitch – 25°.	head lap – 90 mm
rafter pitch – 30°.	head lap – 75 mm
rafter pitch – 40°.	head lap – 65 mm

For severe exposures, that is to say on sites which are elevated, and near the coast or where heavy snowfall is common the lap should be further increased as follows:

rafter pitch – 25°.	head lap – 100 mm
rafter pitch 30°– 40°.	head lap – 75 mm

(See CP 142 and BRS Digest 23.)

Vertical slating should have a minimum lap of 30 mm.

Centre nailed and head nailed

Before setting out the slating the distance from the centre to centre of the battens must be worked out. This distance is known as *gauge* and is equal to the *margin* which is the amount of exposed slate measured up the slope of the roof. The gauge may be worked out as follows:

First decide on the head lap required with regard to the degree of exposure, say for example 90 mm at 25° pitch, using 610 mm × 305 mm slates. Then for centre nailed slates:

$$\text{gauge} = \frac{\text{length of slate} - \text{lap}}{2}$$

$$= \frac{610 - 90}{2}$$

$$= 260 \text{ mm (see figure 297).}$$

If the slates are head nailed allowance must be made for the fact that the nail holes are positioned 25 mm from the top of the slates. For example, 65 mm lap for 305 mm × 205 mm slates at 40° pitch:

$$\text{Gauge} = \frac{\text{length of slate} - (\text{lap} + 25 \text{ mm})}{2}$$

$$= \frac{305 - (65 + 25)}{2}$$

$$= 108 \text{ mm (see figure 298).}$$

The battens upon which the slates are fixed should not be less than 40 mm wide and of sufficient thickness to prevent undue springing back as the slates are being nailed through them. Thus the thickness of the battens will depend upon the spacing of the rafters and for rafters at say 400 mm to 460 mm centres the battens should be 20 mm thick.

Eaves course of slates must always be head nailed and the length of the eaves slate is thus worked out as follows:

Length of slate at eaves = gauge + lap + 25 mm
Therefore for previous example

$$= 108 + 65 + 25 = 198 \text{ mm}$$

In order that the maximum width of lateral cover is maintained the slates are laid half bond so that the joints occur as near as possible over the centre of slates in the course below. This means that in each alternate course the slate at the verge will be 'slate and a half' in width. Slating can be laid so that the gauge diminishes towards the ridge and this is known as laying in 'diminishing courses'. This technique gives an attractive appearance, particularly where slates of differing width are used.

It requires skilled craftsmanship to ensure correct bonding, and minimum lap should be specified which can be increased by the slaters as required to maintain the diminishing margins. The technique is shown in figure 299, in which random width slates are illustrated. Slating should overhang slightly at the verge in order to protect the structure below. The average overhang of the slate is 50 mm and the edge of the slate is supported by using an undercloak of slate or plain asbestos sheeting bedded on the walling. The verge should have an inward tilt and the bedding mortar is usually 1 : 5 cement/sand by volume. The detail is shown in figure 300. The roof structure may also overhang the wall and be supported on sprockets built into the brickwork and finished off with a timber bargeboard. The verge slating will then project beyond the bargeboard, with a similar detail to figure 300.

Hips can be finished with lead rolls or with tiles but for the steeper pitches the neatest solution is to cut the slates and mitre them along the head using metal soakers lapped and bonded with each course and nailed at the top edges. Specially wide slates should be used so that the side bond is maintained when the slate is cut. Valleys are usually formed by having a dressed metal valley gutter and raking cut slates. As with hips specially wide slates are required so that they are sufficiently wide at their tails when cut. The slates are not bedded and do not have an undercloak. The traditional technique for the swept or laced valley formed by cutting slates to special shapes require skilled craftsmen and the specifier should make sure that adequate skilled labour is available for this work. Details are shown in figure 301. The flashing details where a chimney projects through a slated roof are illustrated in figure 305.

Asbestos cement slates

These should comply with BS 690 : 1968 *Asbestos cement slates and sheets*. Properties are discussed in *MBC: Materials*, chapter 10.

The loss of cement from the exposed surfaces slowly exposes the asbestos fibres. Fixing details, and typical details at eaves, verge, ridge and valley are shown in figure 302.

Tiling

Plain tiles

Plain tiles are available in clay or concrete. Like slates they are laid in bond with double laps and have no interlocking joints. Nearly all plain tiles are cambered from head to tail so that they do not lie flat on each other which prevents capillary movement of water between the tiles when they are laid on the roof. Some also have a camber in

415

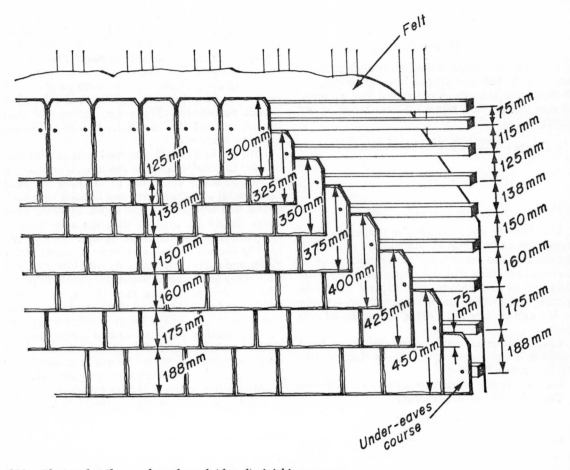

Felt

75 mm
115 mm
125 mm
138 mm
150 mm
160 mm
175 mm
188 mm

125 mm
300 mm
325 mm
350 mm
375 mm
400 mm
425 mm
450 mm

138 mm
150 mm
160 mm
175 mm
188 mm

75 mm

Under-eaves course

299   *Slating details: random slates laid to diminishing courses*

the width, but usually only on the upper surface. It should be noted that the camber in the length of the tile reduces the effective pitch, normally by about 9 degrees at 65 mm lap. Special tiles are available for use as ridges and to form hips and valleys; also 'tile and a half' for verges. Each plain tile has two holes for nailing and most are provided with nibs so that they may be hung on to the battens, see figure 300.

Clay plain tiles should comply with BS 402 : 1945 *Plain clay roofing tiles and fittings*. The equivalent metric sizes for standard clay plain tiles are 254 mm × 152 mm, 265 mm × 165 mm and 279 mm × 178 mm. The thickness is about 10 mm. There is a limited production in certain districts of hand-made tiles which are now only used for

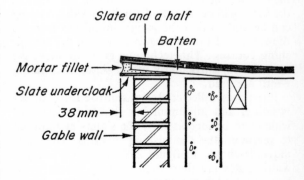

Slate and a half

Batten

Mortar fillet

Slate undercloak

38 mm

Gable wall

Section through verge

300   *Slating: verge detail*

416

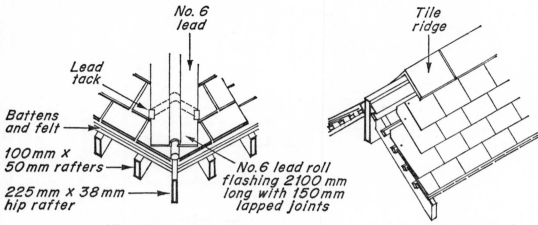

Lead
tack

No. 6
lead

Battens
and felt

100 mm x
50 mm rafters

225 mm x 38 mm
hip rafter

No.6 lead roll
flashing 2100 mm
long with 150mm
lapped joints

Hip with lead flashing

Tile
ridge

Typical ridge

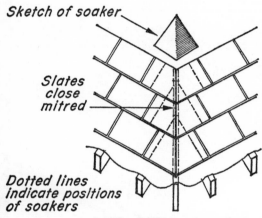

Sketch of soaker

Slates
close
mitred

Dotted lines
indicate positions
of soakers

Hip with lead soakers

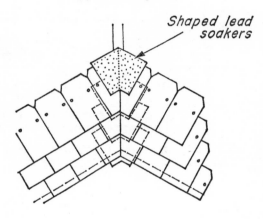

Shaped lead
soakers

Mitred valley

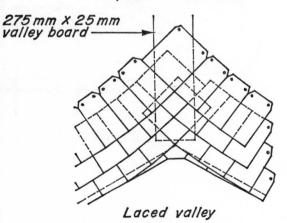

275 mm x 25 mm
valley board

Laced valley

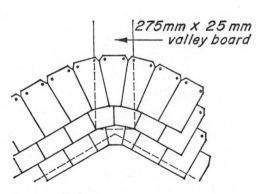

275mm x 25 mm
valley board

Circular swept valley

301   Slating details: hips, ridge, and valleys

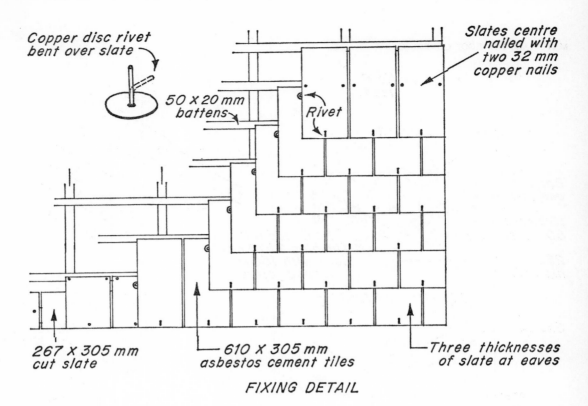

Copper disc rivet bent over slate

Slates centre nailed with two 32 mm copper nails

50 X 20 mm battens

Rivet

267 X 305 mm cut slate

610 X 305 mm asbestos cement tiles

Three thicknesses of slate at eaves

FIXING DETAIL

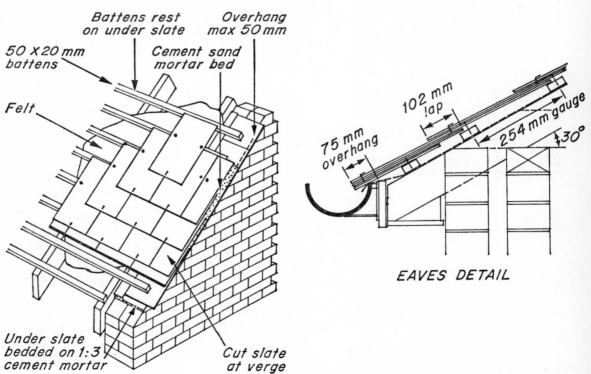

Battens rest on under slate

Overhang max 50 mm

50 X 20 mm battens

Cement sand mortar bed

Felt

Under slate bedded on 1:3 cement mortar

Cut slate at verge

VERGE DETAIL

102 mm lap

75 mm overhang

254 mm gauge

30°

EAVES DETAIL

302   Asbestos cement slates

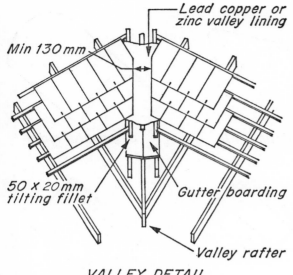

VALLEY DETAIL
(felt omitted)

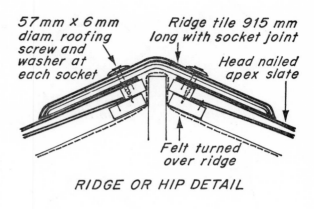

RIDGE OR HIP DETAIL

302   Asbestos cement slates (continued)

special work. These are slightly thicker than the machine-made tiles, varying between 13 mm and 16 mm. Special length tiles are required at eaves and at top courses.

Well burnt clay tiles are not affected by atmosphere and are resistant to frost. The minimum rafter pitch recommended in CP 142 : 1968 is 40 degrees.

Concrete plain tiles should comply with BS 473/550 (Combined) : 1967 *Concrete roofing tiles and fittings*. The fittings include half-round, segmental, hogsback and angular ridge and hip tiles, bonnet hip tiles and valley and angle tiles. The metric equivalent standard size for concrete plain tiles is 265 mm × 165 mm × approximately 10 mm thick. Concrete plain tiles usually cost less than clay tiles. They are usually faced with coloured granules which give a textured finish and are manufactured in a wide range of colours.

Concrete tiles as a result of their density and absence of any laminar structure when manufactured in accordance with the British Standard are not affected by frost. The minimum rafter pitch for these tiles recommended in CP 142 : 1968 in order to prevent rain and snow penetrating the joints is 35 degrees.

The lap for both clay and concrete plain tiling must not be less than 65 mm for moderate exposure.

Where exposure is severe this should be increased to 75 mm or 90 mm. It should be noted that increasing the lap decreases the pitch of individual tiles and for this reason the lap must never exceed one third of the length of the tile. The gauge – or spacing of the battens – on the roof slope is worked out as follows:

$$\text{Gauge} = \frac{\text{length of tile} - \text{lap}}{2}$$

For standard 265 mm × 165 mm tiles the

$$\text{gauge} = \frac{265 \text{ mm} - 65 \text{ mm}}{2} = 100 \text{ mm}$$

Plain tiles require nailing as follows:
1 Every fourth course and at the ends of each course adjacent to abutments and verges.
2 All cut tiles in swept valleys.
3 The tile and half and the adjacent tile in laced valleys.
4 Tiles adjacent to valley tiles, but not the valley tile itself.
5 In exposed positions every third course and in very exposed positions every course.
6 See CP 142 : 1968 for special recommendations for extra nailing at steep pitches of 50 degrees and over.

419

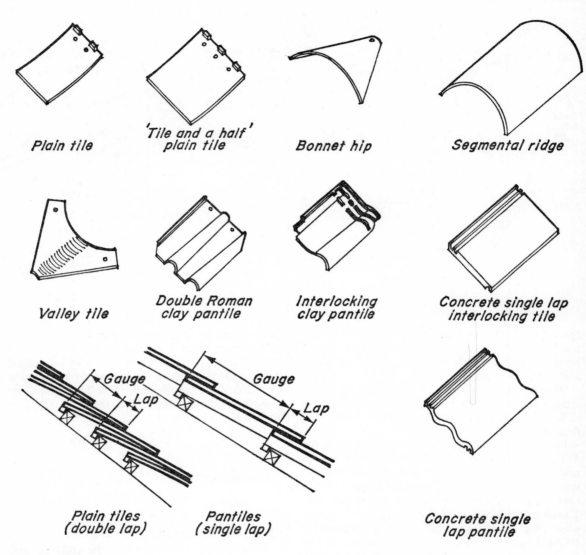

Plain tile

'Tile and a half' plain tile

Bonnet hip

Segmental ridge

Valley tile

Double Roman clay pantile

Interlocking clay pantile

Concrete single lap interlocking tile

Gauge

Lap

Gauge

Lap

Plain tiles (double lap)

Pantiles (single lap)

Concrete single lap pantile

303   Types of tile

Nails should be made from the following materials:
(a) Aluminium alloy complying with BS 1202 Part 3. These are extensively used and have excellent resistance to corrosion.
(b) Copper complying with BS 1202 Part 2. These have a high resistance to corrosion, but tend to be soft.
(c) Silicon-bronze of an alloy of 96% copper, 3% silicon and 1% manganese. These have

also a high resistance to corrosion, and are much harder than copper.

Figure 304 is a typical plain tiling detail sheet showing the construction at ridge, verge, valley and eaves. Note that an underlay of untearable felt must be provided under the battens. The type of felt (which must also be used in slating) is classified in BS 747 : 1961.

The felting is laid parallel to the ridge and each tier should be overlapped 150 mm at horizontal

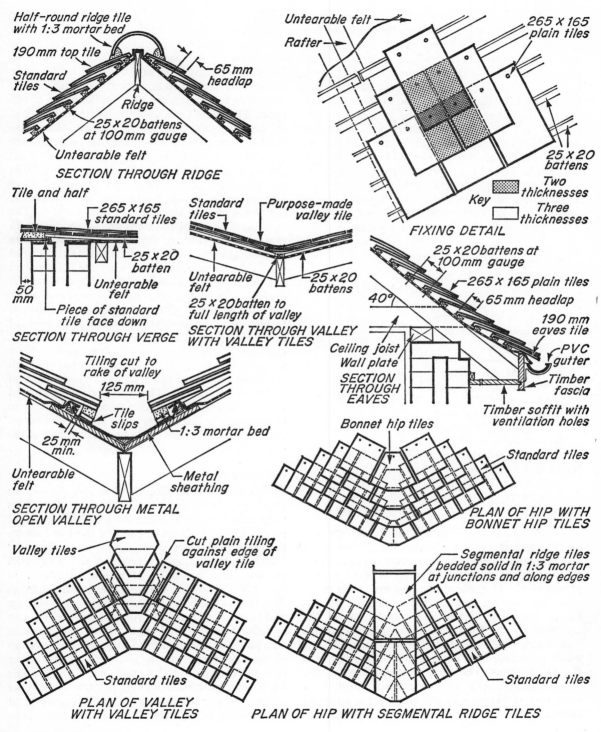

Half-round ridge tile with 1:3 mortar bed
190 mm top tile
Standard tiles
65 mm headlap
Ridge
25 x 20 battens at 100mm gauge
Untearable felt

SECTION THROUGH RIDGE

Untearable felt
Rafter
265 x 165 plain tiles
25 x 20 battens
Key
Two thicknesses
Three thicknesses

FIXING DETAIL

Tile and half
265 x 165 standard tiles
25 x 20 batten
50 mm
Untearable felt
Piece of standard tile face down

SECTION THROUGH VERGE

Standard tiles
Purpose-made valley tile
Untearable felt
25 x 20 battens
25 x 20 batten to full length of valley

SECTION THROUGH VALLEY WITH VALLEY TILES

25 x 20 battens at 100mm gauge
265 x 165 plain tiles
65 mm headlap
40°
190 mm eaves tile
PVC gutter
Ceiling joist
Wall plate
SECTION THROUGH EAVES
Timber fascia
Timber soffit with ventilation holes

Tiling cut to rake of valley
125 mm
Tile slips
1:3 mortar bed
25 mm min.
Untearable felt
Metal sheathing

SECTION THROUGH METAL OPEN VALLEY

Bonnet hip tiles
Standard tiles

PLAN OF HIP WITH BONNET HIP TILES

Valley tiles
Cut plain tiling against edge of valley tile
Standard tiles

PLAN OF VALLEY WITH VALLEY TILES

Segmental ridge tiles bedded solid in 1:3 mortar at junctions and along edges
Standard tiles

PLAN OF HIP WITH SEGMENTAL RIDGE TILES

joints. The felt will sag slightly between the rafters, which, providing the sag is not allowed to be too pronounced, will allow any moisture to find its way into the eaves gutter, where there should be ample turn down of the felt into the gutter. Note, however, that the Building Regulations 1965 require that the thermal insulation (U) of the roof and ceiling combined shall be not more than 1·42 W/m² °C. The U value of tiles over felt including the ceiling is 2·22 W/m² °C, and so further insulation will be required. Extra insulation can be placed over the ceiling or it is possible to use alternative groundwork (ie construction immediately below the tiling) to bring the U value into line with the requirements of the Regulations. The following figures will act as a guide:

(a) Tiles on battens over two layers of felt, counterbattens and 25 mm deal boarding $U = 1·36$ W/m² °C

(b) Tiles on battens over two layers of felt, counterbattens and 13 mm fibreboard $U = 1·31$ W/m² °C

(c) Tiles on battens over two layers of felt, counterbattens and 25 mm wood-wool slabs $U = 1·19$ W/m² °C

(d) Tiles on battens over two layers of felt, counterbattens and 13 mm expanded polystyrene $U = 1·08$ W/m² °C

(e) Tiles on battens over untearable felt with 25 mm thick glass fibre below $U = 0·98$ W/m² °C

The felt mentioned in (e) is a reinforced bitumen felt to which is bonded a 25 mm (or 50 mm) layer of fibreglass. Counterbattens are required whenever boarding or rigid sheeting is used in the groundwork. They should be laid over each rafter over the sheeting and the felt underlay. By this means the tiling battens are raised clear of the underlay by the thickness of the counterbattens (see figure 298) so allowing any wind-blown water penetration to drain away on the felt into the eaves gutter. The tiling battens, fixed to the correct gauge for the tiles concerned, should be a minimum of 25 mm × 20 mm when the supporting rafters are spaced at maximum 380 mm centres.

Where plain tiling abuts a chimney or other projection through a roof, the junction between the tiling and the brickwork must be made watertight by the use of metal flashings. Figure 305 shows the method of forming a back gutter and the use of stepped and apron flashings in lead. The same techniques are also applicable to slated roofs. The tiling (or slating) is weathered against the abutting wall by a series of lead soakers, one to each course, laid between the tiles or slates with an upstand against the wall. A lead flashing cut from a strip of lead sheet, the lower edge following the rake of the roof and the upper edge stepped to follow the coursing of the brickwork, is fixed over the upstands of the soakers. The horizontal edges of the steps are turned about 25 mm into the joints of the brickwork, secured by lead wedges and pointed in. The flashing is dressed round the front of the stack after the front apron has been fixed. The front of the chimney stack is flashed by a lead apron carried well down on to the tiles or slates. The top edge of the apron is turned into a horizontal brickwork joint, wedged and pointed in. The flashing to the back of the chimney is formed as a short valley gutter with a separate lead cover flashing, the top edge of which is turned, fixed into the brickwork joint with lead wedges and pointed. The lead should be carried over a tilting fillet well back under the eaves course of tiling above the chimney and should be dressed carefully over the tiles or slates at either end of the gutter as shown to ensure a close fit.

Single lap tiles

In this category of tiling there is a single overlap (double thickness) of one tile upon the other. This technique is known as pantiling and is of ancient origin. In this country it was first used in Eastern England, the influence probably coming from the Dutch craftsmen. Many types of single lap tiles are available, examples of which are shown in figure 303. The side lap in single lap tiling takes the place of the bond in plain tiling and in slating, and because of this the protection at the lap can be reduced to two thicknesses of material. The side lap, however, can be in the form of plain overlap or in the form of an interlock. The former are rarely made today and nearly all single lap tiles are of the interlocking pattern. Some types of interlocking tile have anti-capillary grooves at the head-lap of the tiles. This makes it possible to

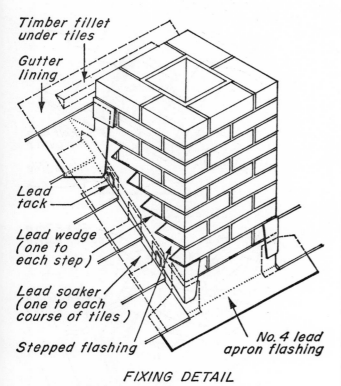

Timber fillet under tiles

Gutter lining

Lead tack

Lead wedge (one to each step)

Lead soaker (one to each course of tiles)

Stepped flashing

No. 4 lead apron flashing

FIXING DETAIL

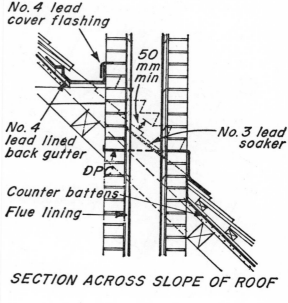

No. 4 lead cover flashing

50 mm min

No. 4 lead lined back gutter

DPC

Counter battens

Flue lining

No. 3 lead soaker

SECTION ACROSS SLOPE OF ROOF

DETAIL OF BACK GUTTER FLASHING

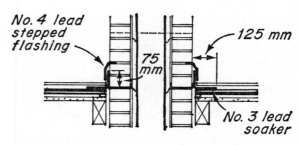

No. 4 lead stepped flashing

125 mm

75 mm

No. 3 lead soaker

SECTION ALONG SLOPE OF ROOF

305   Lead flashings to chimney: plain tile or slate roof coverings

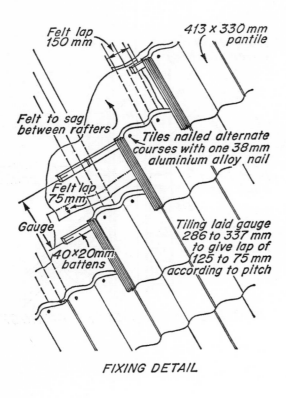

Felt lap 150 mm

413 × 330 mm pantile

Felt to sag between rafters

Tiles nailed alternate courses with one 38mm aluminium alloy nail

Felt lap 75mm

Gauge

40×20mm battens

Tiling laid gauge 286 to 337 mm to give lap of 125 to 75 mm according to pitch

FIXING DETAIL

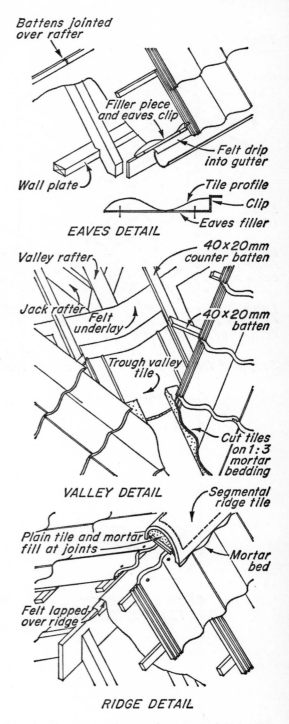

Battens jointed over rafter

Filler piece and eaves clip

Wall plate

Felt drip into gutter

Tile profile

Clip

Eaves filler

EAVES DETAIL

Valley rafter

40×20mm counter batten

Jack rafter

Felt underlay

40×20mm batten

Trough valley tile

Cut tiles on 1:3 mortar bedding

VALLEY DETAIL

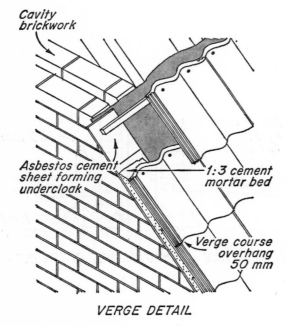

Cavity brickwork

Asbestos cement sheet forming undercloak

1:3 cement mortar bed

Verge course overhang 50 mm

VERGE DETAIL

Segmental ridge tile

Plain tile and mortar fill at joints

Mortar bed

Felt lapped over ridge

RIDGE DETAIL

306 Pantile details

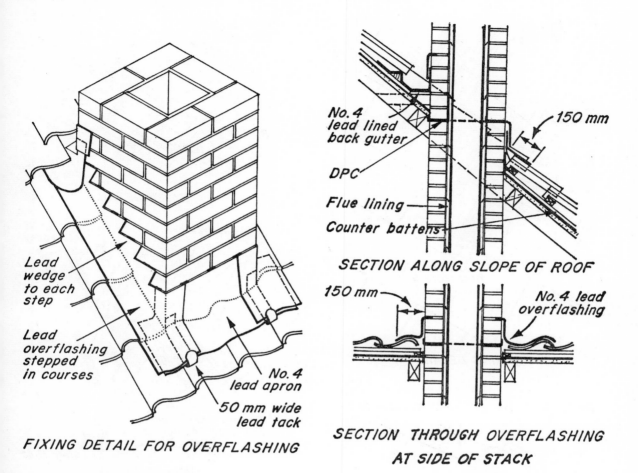

Lead
wedge
to each
step

Lead
overflashing
stepped
in courses

No. 4
lead apron

50 mm wide
lead tack

FIXING DETAIL FOR OVERFLASHING

No. 4
lead lined
back gutter

DPC

Flue lining

Counter battens

150 mm

SECTION ALONG SLOPE OF ROOF

150 mm

No. 4 lead
overflashing

*SECTION THROUGH OVERFLASHING
AT SIDE OF STACK*

307   *Lead flashings to chimney: pantile roof covering*

lay these tiles on roofs of comparatively flat pitch. The amount of side lap is determined by the shape of the tile. Head lap should never be less than 75 mm.

Certain patterns of single lap tiles can be laid at variable gauge. This should be used to avoid cutting tiles at top courses.

Figure 306 is a typical detail sheet showing the use of a concrete pantile with interlocking side lap. Each alternate course of tiles is shown nailed but, in certain severe exposure conditions, each tile in each course must be nailed. (See CP 3 Chapter 5: *Loading* 1970.) The eaves course of tiles projects about 50 mm over the edge of the fascia board and the felt underlay is drawn taut and

fixed in this case by a proprietary eave clip nailed to the top edge of the fascia board. Purpose made valley tiles on felt underlay form the valley detail. Alternatively, the valley could be lined with metal sheeting over valley boards. Verges should overhang about 50 mm and the undercloak can be formed from natural slate, asbestos-cement strip as shown, or plain tiles. The ridge is covered in the example by a segmental ridge tile bedded and pointed in 1:3 cement/sand mortar.

Figure 307 shows lead flashing details to a chimney in a roof covered with pantiles. The flashing at each side of the chimney is in one piece, the upper edge being stepped to follow the coursing of the brickwork. The horizontal edges of the

425

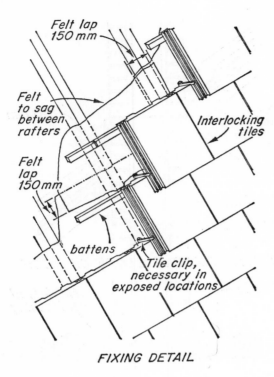

Felt lap
150 mm

Felt
to sag
between
rafters

Interlocking
tiles

Felt
lap
150 mm

battens

Tile clip,
necessary in
exposed locations

FIXING DETAIL

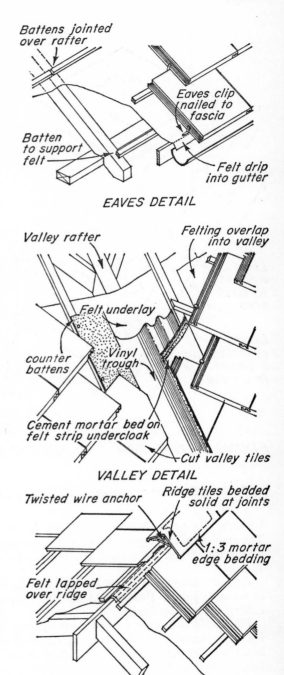

Battens jointed
over rafter

Eaves clip
nailed to
fascia

Batten
to support
felt

Felt drip
into gutter

EAVES DETAIL

Valley rafter

Felting overlap
into valley

Felt underlay

counter
battens

Vinyl
trough

Cement mortar bed on
felt strip undercloak

Cut valley tiles

VALLEY DETAIL

Twisted wire anchor

Ridge tiles bedded
solid at joints

Felt lapped
over ridge

1:3 mortar
edge bedding

RIDGE DETAIL

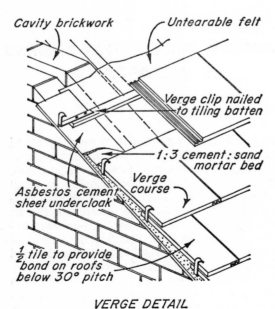

Cavity brickwork

Untearable felt

Verge clip nailed
to tiling batten

1:3 cement:sand
mortar bed

Verge
course

Asbestos cement
sheet undercloak

$\frac{1}{2}$ tile to provide
bond on roofs
below 30° pitch

VERGE DETAIL

308   *Interlocking concrete: tiling details*

steps are turned about 25 mm into joints of the brickwork and secured by lead wedges and pointed in. The free edge is dressed over the nearest tile roll and down into the pan of the tile beyond the roll. The front of the chimney stack is flashed with a lead apron which is carried down on to the tiles at least 125 mm and dressed to a close fit. Where the exposure is severe, the front edge should preferably be secured with lead tacks as shown. The top edge of the apron is turned into a brick-work joint, wedged and pointed in.

Figure 308 shows the details using a single lap interlocking tile of simple profile. The neat inter-locking detail at the side of the tile allows the adjacent units to lie in the same plane, giving an appearance of slating. Tiles of this and similar pattern on sites of moderate exposure can be laid on pitches down to between $22\frac{1}{2}$ degrees and $17\frac{1}{2}$ degrees. The tiles can be laid to a variable gauge, so that the head lap can be increased to avoid cut tiles at the ridge. The minimum headlap is 75 mm. The tiles are shown laid with broken joint and this is advisable on roofs of less than 30 degrees pitch. Where tiles are laid on roofs of lower pitch, the wind uplift increases. In consequence, the need for fixing becomes more important. On exposed sites, at lower pitches therefore, each tile is secured by a special clip nailed to the back of the batten carrying the course below. See CP 3 Chapter 5: *Loading* 1970. Under these conditions special verge clips are also used as shown on the detail. A special valley tile designed for use at low pitches is used in this example to form the valley gutter as an alternative to a metal open valley. The ridge tile is fixed by means of a special wire twisted around a nail driven into the ridge board. In addition, the ridge tiles are bedded solid at joints in 1 : 3 sand and cement mortar and edge bedded along both sides.

The following tables are based on the *Construction Indexing Manual* published by the RIBA (1968). References are given only to the chapters within which some aspect of the appropriate symbol will be found.

The following abbreviations are used:
    E & S: Environment and Services
       M: Materials
  S & F (1): Structure and Fabric
  S & F (2): Structure and Fabric
    C & F: Components and Finishes

Table 1 Elements

(1) Substructure

(10) *Site**
(11) Excavations, land drainage $S \& F (1)$ 4, 8, 11; $S \& F (2)$ 3, 11
(12)
(13) Floor beds $S \& F (1)$ 4, 8; $S \& F (2)$ 3
(14)
(15)
(16) Foundations, retaining structures $S \& F (1)$ 4; $S \& F (2)$ 3, 4
(17) Pile foundations $S \& F (1)$ 4; $S \& F (2)$ 3, 11
(18)
(19) *Building**

(2) Primary elements

(20) *Site**
(21) External walls, walls in general, and chimneys $S \& F (1)$ 1, 5, 9; $S \& F (2)$ 4, 5, 7, 10
(22) Internal walls, partitions $S \& F (1)$ 5; $S \& F (2)$ 4, 10; $C \& F$ 9
(23) Floors, galleries $S \& F (1)$ 8; $S \& F (2)$ 6, 10
(24) Stairs, ramps $S \& F (1)$ 10; $S \& F (2)$ 8, 10
(25)
(26)
(27) Roofs $S \& F (1)$ 1, 7; $S \& F (2)$ 9, 10
(28) Frames $S \& F (1)$ 1, 6; $S \& F (2)$ 5, 10
(29) *Building**

(3) Secondary elements if described separately from primary elements

(30) *Site**
(31) Secondary elements in external walls, external doors, windows $S \& F (1)$ 5; $S \& F (2)$ 10; $C \& F$ 3, 4, 5, 7
(32) Secondary elements in internal walls, doors in general $S \& F (2)$ 10; $C \& F$ 3, 7
(33) Secondary elements in or on floors $S \& F (2)$ 10

(34) Balustrades $C \& F$ 8
(35) Ceilings, suspended $C \& F$ 10
(36)
(37) Secondary elements in or on roof, roof lights, etc. $S \& F (2)$ 10; $C \& F$ 6
(28)
(39) *Building**

(4) Finishes if described separately

(40) *Site**
(41) External wall finishes $S \& F (2)$ 4, 10; $C \& F$ 14, 15, 16
(42) Internal wall finishes $C \& F$ 13, 15
(43) Floor finishes $C \& F$ 12
(44) Stair finishes $C \& F$ 12
(45) Ceiling finishes $C \& F$ 13
(46)
(47) Roof finishes $S \& F (2)$; $C \& F$ 18
(48)
(49) *Building**

(5) Services (mainly piped, ducted)

(50) *Site**
(51) Refuse disposal $E \& S$ 13
(52) Drainage $E \& S$ 11, 12
(53) Hot and cold water $E \& S$ 9, 10; $S \& F (1)$ 9; $S \& F (2)$ 6, 10
(54) Gas, compressed air
(55) Refrigeration
(56) Space heating $E \& S$ 7; $S \& F (1)$ 9; $S \& F (2)$ 6, 10
(57) Ventilation and air-conditioning $E \& S$ 7; $S \& F (2)$ 10
(58)
(59) *Building**

(6) Installations (mainly electrical, mechanical)

(60) *Site**
(61)
(62) Power $E \& S$ 14
(63) Lighting $E \& S$ 8
(64) Communications $E \& S$ 14

These classes are not used in general documentation but have special application in project documentation.

(65)

(66) Transport   *E & S* 15

(67)

(68) Security

(69) *Building**

(7) Fixtures

(70) *Site**

(71) Circulation fixtures

(72) General room fixtures

(73) Culinary fixtures   *C & F* 2

(74) Sanitary fixtures   *E & S* 10

(75) Cleaning fixtures

(76) Storage fixtures   *C & F* 2

(77)

(78)

(79) *Building**

---

* These classes are not used in general documentation but have special application in project documentation.

Tables 2/3   **Construction Form/Materials**
Table 2 is never used without Table 3

Table 2   **Construction form**

E   Cast in situ   *M* 8; *S & F (1)* 4, 7, 8;
     S & F (2) 3, 4, 5, 6, 8, 9
F   Bricks, blocks   *M* 2, 4, 6, 12; *S & F (1)*
     5, 9; *S & F (2)* 4, 6, 7
G   Structural units   *S & F (1)* 6, 7, 8, 10;
     S & F (2) 4, 5, 6, 8, 9
H   Section bars   *M* 2, *S & F (1)* 5, 6, 7, 8;
     S & F (2) 5, 6
I   Tubes, pipes   *S & F (1)* 9; *S & F (2)* 7
J   Wires, mesh
K   Quilts

L   Foils, papers (except finishing papers)
     M 9, 13
M   Foldable sheets   *M* 9
N   Overlap sheets, tiles   *S & F (2)* 4; *C & F* 18
P   Thick coatings   *M* 10, 11; *S & F (2)* 4;
     C & F 12, 13, 18
R   Rigid sheets, sheets in general   *M* 3, 12, 13;
     S & F (2) 4
S   Rigid tiles, tiles in general   *M* 4, 12, 13;
     C & F 12, 15
T   Flexible sheets, tiles   *M* 3, 9; *C & F* 17
U   Finishing papers, fabrics   *C & F* 17
V   Thin coatings   *C & F* 17
X   Components   *S & F (1)* 5, 6, 7, 8, 10;
     S & F (2) 4; *C & F* 2, 3, 4, 5, 6, 7, 8
Y   Products

Table 3   **Materials**
In formed products

e   Natural stone   *M* 4, *S & F (1)* 5, 10;
     S & F (2) 4
f   Formed (precast) concrete, asbestos based
     materials, gypsum, magnesium based
     materials   *M* 8; *S & F (1)* 5, 7, 8, 9, 10;
     S & F (2) 4, 5, 6, 7, 8, 9; *C & F* 13
g   Clay   *M* 5; *S & F (1)* 5, 9, 10; *S & F (2)*
     4, 6, 7
h   Metal   *M* 9; *S & F (1)* 6, 7; *S & F (2)*
     4, 5, 7
i   Wood   *M* 2, 3; *S & F (1)* 5, 6, 7, 8, 10;
     S & F (2) 4, 9; *C & F* 2
j   Natural fibres and chips, leather   *M* 3
m   Mineral fibres   *M* 10; *S & F (2)* 4, 7
n   Rubbers, plastics, asphalt (preformed),
     linoleum   *M* 11, 12, 13; *S & F (2)* 4, 9;
     C & F 12, 18
o   Glass   *M* 12, *S & F (1)* 5; *C & F* 5

In formless products

p   Loose fill, aggregates   *M* 8, 10, 15
q   Cement, mortar, concrete, asbestos based
     materials   *S & F (1)* 4, 7, 8; *S & F (2)* 3, 4,
     5, 6, 8, 9
r   Gypsum, special mortars, magnesium based
     materials   *M* 15; *S & F (2)* 4; *C & F* 13
s   Bituminous materials   *M* 11; *S & F (2)* 4

Agents, chemicals, etc.

t   Fixing, jointing agents, fastenings, iron-
     mongery   *M* 14; *C & F* 7
u   Protective materials, admixtures   *M* 1, 2, 8,
     9; *C & F* 17
v   Paint materials   *C & F* 17
w   Other chemicals

x   **Plants**
y   **Materials in general**   *M* 1

Table 4   **Activities Requirements**

Activities

(Af)	Administration, management in general
(Ag)	Communications in general
(Ah)	Preparation of documentation in general *C & F* 11
(Ai)	Public relations in general
(Aj)	Controls in general
(Ak)	Organizations in general
(Am)	Personnel, roles in general
(An)	Education in general
(Ao)	Research, development in general
(Ap)	Standardization, rationalization in general *C & F* 1, 11
(Aq)	Testing, evaluating in general *C & F* 1

(A1)	**Management** (offices, projects)
(A2)	Financing, accounting
(A3)	Design, physical planning *S & F (1)* 4; *S & F (2)* 3
(A4)	Cost planning, cost control, tenders, contracts
(A5)	Production planning, progress control *S & F (2)* 1, 2; *C & F* 1
(A6)	Buying, delivery
(A7)	Inspection, quality control *C & F* 1
(A8)	Handing over, feedback, appraisal
(A9)	Arbitration, insurance

(B)	**Construction plant** *S & F* 11; *S & F (2)* 2, 11

(C)	**Labour***

(D)	**Construction operations** *S & F (1)* 11; *S & F (2)* 2, 11

Requirements, properties

(E1)	**Construction requirements** *S & F (1)* 1, 2; *S & F (2)* 1; *C & F* 1
(E2)	**User requirements** *E & S* 1, 2, 3, 4, 5, 6; *C & F* 1
(E3)	Types of user
(E4)	**Physical features** *C & F* 1
(E6)	**Environment in general, amenities** *E & S* 1, 2, 3, 4, 5, 6
(E7)	External environment *E & S* 1, 2, 3, 4, 5, 6
(E8)	Internal environment *E & S* 1, 2, 3, 4, 5, 6
(F)	Layout, shape, dimensions, tolerances, metric *S & F (1)* 2; *C & F* 1
(G)	Appearance, aesthetics, art
(H)	**Physical, chemical, biological factors, technology** *C & F* 1
(I)	Air, water *E & S* 2, 3; *S & F (1)* 5
(J)	Heat, cold *E & S* 5
(K)	Strength, statics, stability *S & F (1)* 3
(L)	Mechanics, dynamics *S & F (1)* 4; *S & F (2)* 3
(M)	Sound, quiet *E & S* 6
(N)	Light, dark *E & S* 4, 8
(Q)	Radiation, electrical
(R)	Fire *M* 1; *S & F (2)* 10
(S)	Durability, weathering defects, failures, damage *M* 1, *S & F (1)* 4; *S & F (2)* 3, 4, 5
(U)	Special requirements, efficiency, working characteristics
(V)	**Effect on surroundings**
(W)	**Maintenance, alterations**
(Y)	**Economic, time requirements** *S & F (1)* 2; *S & F (2)* 3, 4, 5, 6, 9

* These classes are not used in general documentation but have special application in project documentation.

Index

Index